FLORIDA STATE
UNIVERSITY LIBRARIES

JUN 0 1 2001

TALLAHASSEE, FLORIDA

The Longman Companion to
Britain in the Eighteenth Century,
1688–1820

Longman Companions to History

General Editors: Chris Cook and John Stevenson

Now available

THE LONGMAN COMPANION TO THE EUROPEAN REFORMATION, *c.* 1500–1618
Mark Greengrass

THE LONGMAN COMPANION TO THE TUDOR AGE
Rosemary O'Day

THE LONGMAN COMPANION TO THE STUART AGE, 1603–1714
John Wroughton

THE LONGMAN COMPANION TO NAPOLEONIC EUROPE
Clive Emsley

THE LONGMAN COMPANION TO BRITAIN IN THE EIGHTEENTH CENTURY, 1688–1820
Jeremy Gregory and John Stevenson

THE LONGMAN COMPANION TO EUROPEAN NATIONALISM, 1789–1920
Raymond Pearson

THE LONGMAN COMPANION TO BRITAIN IN THE NINETEENTH CENTURY, 1815–1914
Chris Cook

THE LONGMAN COMPANION TO AMERICA IN THE ERA OF THE TWO WORLD WARS, 1914–1945
Patrick Renshaw

THE LONGMAN COMPANION TO THE MIDDLE EAST SINCE 1914 (Second Edition)
Ritchie Ovendale

THE LONGMAN COMPANION TO BRITAIN IN THE ERA OF THE TWO WORLD WARS, 1914–1945
Andrew Thorpe

THE LONGMAN COMPANION TO RUSSIA SINCE 1914
Martin McCauley

THE LONGMAN COMPANION TO AMERICA, RUSSIA AND THE COLD WAR, 1941–1998 (Second Edition)
John W. Young

THE LONGMAN COMPANION TO NAZI GERMANY
Tim Kirk

THE LONGMAN COMPANION TO THE LABOUR PARTY, 1900–1998
Harry Harmer

THE LONGMAN COMPANION TO BRITAIN SINCE 1945
Chris Cook and John Stevenson

THE LONGMAN COMPANION TO THE EUROPEAN UNION
Alisdair Blair

THE LONGMAN COMPANION TO EUROPEAN DECOLONISATION IN THE TWENTIETH CENTURY
Muriel Chamberlain

THE LONGMAN COMPANION TO GERMANY SINCE 1945
Adrian Webb

The Longman Companion to

Britain in the Eighteenth Century, 1688–1820

Jeremy Gregory and John Stevenson

LONGMAN
London and New York

Pearson Education Limited
Edinburgh Gate,
Harlow, Essex CM20 2JE,
United Kingdom
and Associated Companies throughout the world

DA
480
.G74
2000

© Jeremy Gregory and John Stevenson

The right of Jeremy Gregory and John Stevenson to be identified as authors of this Work has been asserted by them in accordance with the Copyright, Designs and Patents Act 1988.

All rights reserved; no part of the publication may be reproduced, stored in a retrieval system, or transmitted in any form or by any means, electronic, mechanical, photocopying, recording, or otherwise, without either the prior written permission of the Publishers or a licence permitting restricted copying issued by the Copyright Licensing Agency Ltd., 90 Tottenham Court Road, London W1P 9HE.

First published 2000 by Pearson Education Ltd

ISBN 0 582 279895 CSD
ISBN 0 582 279887 PPR

Visit us on the world wide web at
http://www.awl-he.com

British Library Cataloguing in Publication Data

A catalogue record for this book is available from the British Library

Library of Congress Cataloging-in-Publication Data

Gregory, Jeremy.
   The Longman companion to Britain in the eighteenth century, 1688–1820 / Jeremy Gregory and John Stevenson.
      p. cm. — (Longman companions to history)
   Includes bibliographical references (p.) and index.
   ISBN 0-582-27989-5 (hc.). — ISBN 0-582-27988-7 (pbk.)
   1. Great Britain—History—18th century Handbooks, manuals, etc.
I. Stevenson, John, 1946– . II. Title. III. Title: Companion to Britain in the eighteenth century, 1688–1820. IV. Series.
DA480.G74   1999
941.07—dc21   99–25136
                                                                                         CIP

Set in 9½/12pt New Baskerville by 35
Produced by Addison Wesley Longman Singapore (Pte) Ltd.,
Printed by Singapore

Contents

Preface	viii
Acknowledgements	x
Section One: Political chronologies	1
1.1 THE GLORIOUS REVOLUTION, 1685–89	3
1.2 POLITICAL CHRONOLOGY, 1689–1822	8
Section Two: The monarchy	31
2.1 BIOGRAPHICAL DETAILS OF MONARCHS AND THEIR ISSUE	33
2.2 THE JACOBITE LINE	36
2.3 THE STUART AND HANOVERIAN LINES	38
Section Three: Ministries and office-holders	39
3.1 MINISTRIES AND ADMINISTRATIONS	41
3.2 COMPOSITION OF ADMINISTRATIONS	43
3.3 MAJOR OFFICE-HOLDERS	66
Section Four: Parliament, elections and parliamentary reform	79
4.1 THE HOUSE OF COMMONS	81
4.2 THE HOUSE OF LORDS	95
4.3 THE IRISH PARLIAMENT	98
4.4 ELECTIONS	100
4.5 PARLIAMENTARY REFORM	111
Section Five: Foreign affairs and empire	119
5.1 PRINCIPAL TREATIES, 1689–1820	121
5.2 IRELAND, 1688–1823	154
5.3 BRITISH COLONIAL EXPANSION, 1688–1760	162
5.4 THE AMERICAN COLONIES	165
Section Six: Military and naval	173
6.1 OUTLINES OF BRITISH CAMPAIGNS	175
6.2 STRENGTH AND COST OF THE BRITISH ARMY, 1689–1815	195
6.3 STRENGTH AND COST OF THE BRITISH NAVY, 1689–1815	199
6.4 LOANS AND SUBSIDIES TO FOREIGN STATES DURING THE WARS OF 1793–1814	200

Section Seven: Law and order 205
7.1 MAJOR DEVELOPMENTS IN PUBLIC ORDER, 1688–1785 207
7.2 PUBLIC ORDER IN THE AGE OF REVOLUTION AND REFORM, 1789–1829 210
7.3 POPULAR DISTURBANCES IN BRITAIN (EXCLUDING IRELAND), 1688–1830 214
7.4 CRIMINAL STATISTICS 226
7.5 THE ABOLITION OF CAPITAL OFFENCES, 1808–30 228

Section Eight: Religion 231
8.1 THE CHURCH OF ENGLAND 233
8.2 PROTESTANT DISSENTERS 247
8.3 THE METHODIST MOVEMENT 250
8.4 ROMAN CATHOLICISM 253
8.5 SCOTLAND 256
8.6 WALES 259
8.7 IRELAND 262
8.8 MISSIONARY AND BENEVOLENT SOCIETIES 263

Section Nine: Financial and economic 265
9.1 PUBLIC FINANCE 267
9.2 COUNTRY BANKS IN ENGLAND AND WALES, 1784–1830 273
9.3 ENCLOSURE ACTS, 1760–1830 274
9.4 THE CORN LAWS 275
9.5 WHEAT PRICES 276
9.6 TRADE 277
9.7 PRODUCTION 278
9.8 TRANSPORT 281

Section Ten: Social and cultural 287
10.1 POPULATIONS, 1701–1821 289
10.2 PRINCIPAL URBAN POPULATIONS, 1650–1831 290
10.3 SOCIAL STRUCTURE OF THE POPULATION, 1696 291
10.4 DISTRIBUTION OF THE LABOUR FORCE, 1801–31 293
10.5 EDUCATION: NUMBER OF SCHOOLS AND CHILDREN ATTENDING, 1819 294
10.6 POOR RELIEF, 1783–1831 295
10.7 FRIENDLY SOCIETIES 296
10.8 CHARITIES AND PHILANTHROPIC SOCIETIES, 1698–1830 298
10.9 HOSPITAL FOUNDATIONS, 1720–1829 299
10.10 THE PRESS AND NEWSPAPERS 301
10.11 MAJOR SOCIAL LEGISLATION AND DEVELOPMENTS, 1691–1819 305

10.12	TRADE UNIONS	307
10.13	LOCAL GOVERNMENT	313
10.14	CULTURAL AND INTELLECTUAL CHRONOLOGY, 1688–1820	325

Section Eleven: Biographies — 365

Section Twelve: Glossary — 457

Section Thirteen: Select bibliography — 477

Section Fourteen: Maps — 537

Index — 545

Preface

During the past two decades, academic research has transformed historians' understanding of eighteenth-century Britain. Scholarly work on all aspects of history in this period (whether political, religious, social, economic, cultural or intellectual) has unearthed a much more complex and dynamic society than the traditional characterisation of this as the 'dull' century in British history implied. New topics, such as women's history and gender studies, have opened up additional areas for debate, while familiar topics, such as 'the agricultural revolution', 'the state of the Church of England' and the 'unreformed political system', have received fresh consideration which has significantly modified older interpretations. Moreover, some of the most exciting recent work on the period has been interdisciplinary in nature, crossing traditional boundaries between history, literature, the history of science and art history, as well as traversing conventional divides within the historical profession (such as the gulf between social and political historians). There is thus, we believe, a real need for an up-to-date one-volume guide which will not only give students an introduction to the broad parameters and structures of the age, but also absorb the fruits of this new research and convey it to a wider readership.

In writing this *Companion* to eighteenth-century Britain, we have been conscious of two issues which are central to the project. First, there is the problem of deciding precisely when the eighteenth century happened. The dates chosen for the volume, *c.* 1688–*c.* 1820, reflect historians' uncertainty about the exact dating of the eighteenth century. In political terms, many would agree that there is a great deal of sense in talking about a period between the Glorious Revolution of 1688 and the constitutional changes of 1828–32, although some social and economic historians would argue that the years after *c.* 1780 were very different from the ones before. Indeed, at the moment, historians of the eighteenth century are engaged in a debate about the nature of eighteenth-century society which reflects differing views over when it began and ended. Should it be seen as 'early modern', displaying continuities with the seventeenth century, or is it more appropriate to speak of it as 'modern', anticipating nineteenth-century developments? Because of this, historians have recently found the concept of the 'long eighteenth century' (see *Glossary*) useful to discuss a period which began in the late seventeenth century, and which stretched well into the nineteenth century. Such a wide chronological span allows consideration of those perennial tools of historical analysis: 'continuity' and 'change'.

Secondly, we have tried to take the word 'Britain' seriously. Books with 'Britain' in the title usually mean 'England'. This volume, however, attempts to provide basic information about Scotland, Ireland and Wales as well. This is partly because interesting new research has been done on these areas, and also because a major theme in recent historiography has been the concept of national identity. In some ways, this century has claims to being the time when, after the 1707 Act of Union between England and Scotland, and during the period of the 'Protestant ascendancy' in Ireland, 'British' identity was forged.

We are grateful to the many authors who are, in ever-increasing numbers it seems, continually researching and publishing on the long eighteenth century, and some of whose work is listed in the *Select Bibliography*. At times, we felt like the little boy with his finger in the dike in the Dutch folk tale – only just stopping short of being overwhelmed and submerged by the rapidly growing body of information and new interpretations concerned with the period. We have, no doubt, left out much which should have been included, and inevitably no volume of this type can ever hope to be definitive. In some areas, for instance, the data are unreliable or simply non-existent. But we hope that we have gathered together as many of the most useful facts and figures, and signalled as many of the historical debates, as can reasonably be included within the confines of a medium-sized reference work. And we appeal to those working in the field to point out any errors or omissions in this book, so that the volume may be corrected or enlarged in future editions.

Acknowledgements

In particular, Jeremy Gregory would like to thank Jeremy Black and Tony Claydon, as well as his colleagues in the Department of Historical and Critical Studies at the University of Northumbria for ideas and information; John Stevenson would like to thank Chris Cook for his cooperation and encouragement and Helen Stromme for assistance with the typing.

The publishers would like to thank the following for permission to reproduce copyright material:

Blackwell Publishers for a table from *British Industry, 1700–1950* by W.G. Hoffman (1955); Cambridge University Press for a table from *British Economic Growth, 1688–1959* by W.A. Cole and P. Deane (1969), a table from *Second Abstract of British Historical Statistics* by H.G. Jones and B.R. Mitchell (1971) and two tables from *The Turnpike Road System of England* by W. Albert (1972); and Macmillan Press Ltd for a table from *The Rise of the English Shipping Industry* by R. Davis (1962) and a table from *The Structure of Politics at the Accession of George III* by L.B. Namier (1929).

SECTION ONE

Political chronologies

1.1 The Glorious Revolution, 1685–89

1685
6 Feb. Accession of James II.
16 Feb. Lawrence Hyde, Earl of Rochester, appointed Lord Treasurer and Lord President of the Council (18 Feb.).
Apr. Meeting of Scottish Parliament expresses loyalty to James.
11 May. James orders Lord Treasurer to stop recovery of fines from specified 'loyal' recusants.
19 May. Parliament meets; James granted 'for life' the revenues conferred on Charles II. Earl of Danby released from the Tower.
26 May. House of Commons grand committee on religion passes two resolutions pledging them to defend the 'reformed religion' and calling for the enforcement of the laws against all dissenters. After the King displays his anger the Commons rejects the resolutions and accepts the royal pledge to defend the Church of England.
11 June. Outbreak of Monmouth rebellion. Parliament votes new duties on tobacco, sugar, French linen, brandies, calicoes and wrought silks, as well as restoring duties on wine and vinegar which had expired in 1681, against the security of which the King was empowered to raise £400,000.
30 June. Earl of Argyll executed for rising in support of Monmouth.
6 July. Defeat of Monmouth's army at Sedgemoor and capture of Monmouth.
15 July. Monmouth executed at Tower Hill.
Sept. Judge Jeffreys presides over 'Bloody Assizes' in the West Country.
28 Sept. Jeffreys appointed Lord Chancellor.
12–19 Nov. Parliament grants James a further £700,000 on the basis of new duties, but the King's request for Catholic officers to be permitted in the army provokes opposition. James prorogues Parliament (20 Nov.).
4 Dec. Earl of Sunderland appointed Lord President of the Council.

1686
Mar. Duke of Queensbury removed as Scottish Treasurer and office placed in commission.
June. In the collusive action of *Godden* v. *Hales* the Court of King's Bench ruled that James II had the right to dispense with the Test Act for particular cases. James proceeds to introduce further Roman Catholics into the army, and into the universities, Anglican Church and Privy Council.

14 June. Scottish Parliament prorogued after refusal to grant indulgence to Catholics.
July. James sets up a Court of Ecclesiastical Commission to control the church.
10 Dec. Earl of Rochester dismissed as Treasurer.

1687
12 Feb. Declaration of Indulgence issued to Roman Catholics and Quakers in Scotland.
4 Apr. James II granted extensive indulgence in England to Protestant dissenters and Roman Catholic recusants.
Apr. James orders Magdalen College, Oxford, to elect Anthony Farmer, a reputed Catholic. When the Fellows refused, the College was ordered to set aside their own choice and a visitation of ecclesiastical commissioners was sent to install him.
28 June. Second Declaration of Indulgence in Scotland.
2 July. Parliament, prorogued since 20 November 1685, dissolved.
3 July. D'Adda publicly received as papal nuncio.
July–Aug. James begins purge of office-holders, gathering pace in winter of 1687–88. Many Tory Anglicans dismissed from municipal corporations and replaced by nonconformists and Catholics. Many Lord and Deputy Lieutenants removed for showing unwillingness to repeal Test Acts. Scottish burghs ordered to cease elections and await royal nomination.
14 Nov. Official confirmation of Queen's pregnancy.

1688
3 May. Republication of the Declaration of Indulgence.
4 May. James II orders Anglican clergy to read the Declaration from the pulpit on two consecutive Sundays and bishops required to see to it that copies distributed.
18 May. Archbishop of Canterbury, Sancroft, and six other bishops personally petition the King to be excused from reading the Declaration, arousing the King's anger.
8 June. The 'Seven Bishops' are arrested on a charge of seditious libel and committed to the Tower.
10 June. Birth of son to James II and Mary of Modena, providing for a Catholic succession, and alleged by Protestants to be a child smuggled into the palace in a warming pan.
29–30 June. Trial and acquittal of the Seven Bishops.
30 June. Leading Whigs and Tories led by Danby, Shrewsbury, Devonshire, Compton, Sidney, Lumley and Russell invite William of Orange to invade England in defence of 'Liberties'.
30 Sept. William of Orange accepts invitation to invade England and issues a declaration denouncing the 'evil counsellors' who had subjected

the country 'in all things relating to their consciences, liberties and properties to arbitrary government' and calling for 'a free and lawful parliament' to be assembled 'as soon as possible'.

1 Nov. William and the Dutch invasion fleet successfully set sail for England.
5 Nov. William of Orange lands at Torbay with 15,000 Dutch troops.
14 Nov. Earl of Abingdon and Lord Cornbury join William's forces.
15 Nov. Risings in the North and Midlands in support of William.
19 Nov. James joins his army at Salisbury.
21 Nov. William begins march on London.
22 Nov. Northern and Midland 'rebels' issue a declaration from Nottingham setting forth their 'innumerable grievances' and calling on 'all good protestants and subjects' to support William.

After a Council of War, James decides to retreat with his forces to London. Churchill and Grafton leave James, followed by increasing elements of the royal army.

24 Nov. James's army begins retreat to London.
26 Nov. James reaches London and summons a Great Council to meet on the 27th.
27 Nov. At a Great Council in Whitehall attended by nine bishops and between thirty or forty peers, James is urged to dismiss Catholics from his service, issue a general pardon and call a new Parliament. Writs issued for a new Parliament on 15 January (28th), followed by a Proclamation promising free elections and immunity for all peers and members of the Commons.
29 Nov. James issues orders for his son to be sent to France.
30 Nov. *London Gazette* announces that Halifax, Nottingham and Godolphin were to treat with William on the King's behalf.
7–9 Dec. William meets royal commissioners at Hungerford and terms are arranged for an armistice while Parliament assembled.
10 Dec. James learns from the commissioners confirmation of William's terms. Meanwhile James secures the Great Seal, burns writs summoning Parliament and annuls those already sent out.

Mary of Modena and the royal heir flee to France.

11 Dec. James, having disposed of the Great Seal in the Thames, attempts to escape to France but is intercepted at Sheerness and forced to return to London (16th). Widespread anti-Catholic rioting in London and elsewhere. Meeting of peers and bishops at Guildhall issues Guildhall Declaration for a free Parliament to enact 'effectual securities for our religion and laws'. The City of London calls on William to enter London.
12 Dec. Commander of the fleet, Dartmouth, puts it under William's control. Provisional government under the presidency of Halifax established by the peers in London.

16 Dec. William summons the fleet to the Nore.
17 Dec. William summons a meeting of peers at Windsor to advise him on what to do about the King's return. It was decided that the King should go to Ham on the Thames.
18 Dec. James requests to go to Rochester, upon which William enters London.
20 Dec. William summons peers to meet him on the 21st to advise on calling 'a free parliament'.
23 Dec. James leaves for France.
26 Dec. William summons all those who had sat in Parliament in Charles II's time and a deputation from the City of London to advise him.
28 Dec. William accepts the invitation of both peers and Commons to take charge of the civil administration and to summon a convention.

1689
22 Jan. Meeting of Convention Parliament.
28 Jan. The Commons declares that James II had abdicated and that the throne was vacant and against a 'popish prince'.
8 Feb. Commons approve draft of Declaration of Rights, vesting the throne in William and Mary and the line of succession through Anne.
13 Feb. Parliament offers the crown to William and Mary, who are proclaimed King and Queen for their joint and separate lives, accompanying the offer with a Declaration of Rights. This asserted the 'true, ancient and indubitable rights of the people of this realm' and contained the following provisions: (i) that the making or suspending of law without consent of Parliament is illegal; (ii) that the exercise of the dispensing power is illegal; (iii) that the ecclesiastical commission court and other such like courts are illegal; (iv) that levying money without consent of Parliament is illegal; (v) that it is lawful to petition the sovereign; (vi) that the maintenance of a standing army without the consent of Parliament is illegal; (vii) that it is lawful to keep arms; (viii) that elections of members of Parliament must be free; (ix) that there must be freedom of debate in Parliament; (x) that excessive bail should never be demanded; (xi) that juries should be impanelled and returned in every trial; (xii) that grants of estates as forfeited before conviction of the offender are illegal; (xiii) that Parliament should be held frequently.

William and Mary were declared King and Queen for life, the chief administration resting with William; the crown was next settled on William's children by Mary; in default of such issue, on the Princess Anne of Denmark and her children; and in default of these, on the children of William by any other wife.

Parliamentary Committee begins preparation of Declaration into a draft Bill of Rights.

1 Mar. Oaths of allegiance and supremacy taken to William and Mary, some peers and members of the lower house, as well as six bishops and 400 clergymen, refuse, marking the beginning of the non-juror schism.
5 Mar. Earl of Nottingham made Secretary of State.
12 Mar. Landing of James II at Kinsale in Ireland opens his campaign to recapture the throne (*see* p. 154). Meeting of Scottish Convention.
11 Apr. Coronation of William and Mary.
11 May. William and Mary accept Claim of Right of Scottish Convention Parliament, asserting the constitutional liberties of the Kingdom.
24 May. Toleration Act exempts dissenters who had taken the oaths of allegiance and supremacy from penalties for non-attendance on the services of the established Church.

1.2 Political chronology, 1689–1822

1689
Jan. Meeting of Convention Parliament (22nd). Throne declared vacant (28th) by the Commons.
Feb. William and Mary proclaimed King and Queen for life (13th). Declaration of Rights drawn up, determining line of succession. Toleration Bill introduced in the Lords (28th).
Mar. Oaths of allegiance and supremacy (1st), refused by over 400 non-jurors. Earl of Nottingham made Secretary of State (5th). Bill of Comprehension introduced in Lords (11th). Landing of James II at Kinsale (12th).
Apr. Coronation of William and Mary (11th). Scottish Convention passes 'Articles of Grievance' (13th).
May. William and Mary accept crown of Scotland: Toleration Act passed by Parliament (24th); comprehension proposals dropped.
June. Scottish Convention meets as Parliament (5th).
Dec. Bill of Rights enacted, determining the line of succession and prohibiting a Catholic from succeeding to the throne, as well as reiterating the provisions of the Declaration of February (*see* p. 6).

1690
Feb. Convention Parliament dissolved (6th). Sancroft, five bishops and 400 clergy deprived of their living for refusing to take the oath to William and Mary.
Mar. Second Parliament of William and Mary meets (20th). Act of Recognition affirms the legality of the acts of the Convention Parliament.
May. Act of Grace gives indemnity to all supporters of James II, except those in treasonable correspondence with him (20th). Resignation of Shrewsbury and Halifax. Prorogation of Parliament and appointment of a council of nine to advise Mary during the King's absence (23rd). Lords of Articles abolished in Scotland (8th).
June. William leaves for Ireland (14th).
July. Battle of the Boyne (1st), defeat of James and his army.

1691
July. Defeat of French and Irish forces at Aughrim (12th).
Aug. William offers indemnity to all Highland clans still in rebellion if they will take oath of allegiance by end of year.

Oct. Treaty of Limerick effectively ends Irish war. Irish soldiers and officers offered free transportation to France; Irish Catholics to retain religious liberties as under Charles II (later repudiated by Irish Parliament).

1692
Jan. Earl of Marlborough (John Churchill) dismissed for communicating with James II (10th).
Feb. Massacre of Glencoe (13th).
Mar. Earl of Nottingham becomes sole Secretary of State.
May. Marlborough imprisoned in the Tower but released shortly afterwards.

1693
Mar. Lord Somers leads Whig 'Junto' as Lord Keeper.
Nov. Dismissal of Earl of Nottingham, Tory Secretary of State.

1694
Mar. Earl of Shrewsbury, member of Whig Junto, becomes Secretary of State.
May. Removal of leading Tories from government, apart from Danby and Godolphin, leaves power largely in the hands of the Whig Junto, consisting of Somers, Shrewsbury, Wharton, Russell and Montagu.
July. Charter of the Governor and Company of the Bank of England for the raising of a loan of £1,200,000 to finance the siege of Namur.
Dec. Triennial Act passed (3rd), providing for a new Parliament to be elected every three years; receives royal assent (22nd). Queen Mary dies of smallpox (28th). Expiration of the Licensing Act and effective end to press censorship.

1695
May. Duke of Leeds (formerly Earl of Danby) forced to resign as Lord President of Council (6th).
Oct. Dissolution of Parliament (11th).
Nov. Meeting of third Parliament of the reign, supported by a large Whig majority. Recoinage Act.

1696
Feb. Plot to kill the King uncovered led by Sir John Fenwick and Jacobites (14th); Oath of Association to defend William and Protestant succession promulgated throughout England and Wales.

1697
Jan. Execution of Sir John Fenwick (21st).
Apr. Lord Somers made Lord Chancellor (22nd); charter of Bank of England renewed.

May. Resignation of Godolphin as First Lord of the Treasury; appointment of Montagu (1st).
Sept. Treaty of Ryswick signed, ending War of the League of Augsburg.
Dec. Robert Harley's motion to disband all forces raised since 1680 approved by both houses of Parliament; resignation of Earl of Sunderland. Parliament established a civil list not exceeding £700,000 a year for the support of William himself and the civil administration. William III recognised by Louis XIV as King of England.

1698
Aug. William III commits England to Partition Treaty with Holland (19th), dividing Spanish possessions, without consulting ministers or Parliament.
Dec. Meeting of William's fourth Parliament (6th).

1699
Jan. Parliament forces William to reduce drastically the size of the English army and disband his Dutch guards.

Act for preventing growth of popery; all persons who refuse oaths of allegiance and supremacy to lose estates. Catholic school-teachers and priests liable to imprisonment for life.

1700
Mar. Second Partition Treaty with France and Holland ratified (14th). Scottish colonists forced to withdraw from Darien.
Apr. Parliament prorogued (11th). William forced to dismiss Somers as Lord Chancellor (17th).
July. Death of Duke of Gloucester, last of Anne's children.
Dec. Godolphin rejoins ministry as Treasurer.

1701
Feb. Parliament resumes sitting (6th); Harley elected Speaker of the Commons.
Apr. Commons begin impeachment proceedings against Whig ministers Somers, Orford and Montagu for failure to consult Parliament over Partition Treaties.
June. Act of Settlement passed determining that the Protestant succession should pass through the electress Sophia of Hanover, granddaughter of James I, next in line after Princess Anne (12th). The Act also declares that the sovereigns of Great Britain should be Protestant and not leave the kingdom without the consent of Parliament; that the country should not be involved in war for the defence of the foreign possessions of the sovereigns; that no foreigner should receive a grant from the Crown or hold office, civil or military; that ministers to be responsible for the acts of their sovereigns; that judges to hold office for life unless guilty of misconduct.

Sept. Death of James II (6th); James Edward proclaimed King of Great Britain and Ireland by Louis XIV.
Nov. Parliament dissolved (11th).
Dec. Sixth Parliament of William III (30th).

1702
Feb. Act for attainder against the Pretender, James Edward Stuart (20th); Act of Abjuration of Pretender, requiring oath of loyalty to King and heirs according to Act of Settlement (24th).
Mar. Death of William III; Queen Anne succeeds to the throne (8th). Marlborough made Captain-General of armed forces (24th).
Apr. Coronation of Queen Anne.
May. Declaration of war against France and Spain (4th). Godolphin appointed Lord Treasurer.
June. Scottish Parliament proclaims Anne Queen of Scotland and nominates commissioners to treat for Union with England.
Oct. Meeting of Anne's first Parliament (20th).

1703
Jan. Tory bill against occasional conformity defeated in the Lords.
Mar. Queen persuades the Earls of Nottingham and Rochester to dismiss several Whig Lord and Deputy Lieutenants, sheriffs and justices of the peace.
Aug. Scottish Parliament passes Act of Security claiming right to name Protestant successor to Queen Anne and safeguard Scottish Parliament, trade and religion from English domination. Refused royal assent.
Nov. Establishment of Queen Anne's Bounty.
Dec. Second bill against occasional conformity defeated in the Lords after Commons approval (7th).

1704
April. Henry St John becomes Secretary at War (20th).
May. Robert Harley made Secretary of State (18th).
Aug. Marlborough's victory at Blenheim (13th). Amended version of Scottish Act of Security given royal assent.
Dec. Further attempt to restrict occasional conformity defeated in Parliament (14th–15th).

1705
April. Dissolution of Anne's first Parliament (5th).
Sept. Scottish Parliament approves Act for appointment of commissioners to negotiate union with England.
Oct. Second Parliament of Anne's reign meets (25th).

1706

Apr. Scottish commissioners meet English commissioners at Westminster (16th).
May. Victory at Ramillies (23rd).
July. Articles of Union signed between English and Scottish Commissioners (22nd).
Dec. 3rd Earl of Sunderland appointed Secretary of State (3rd).

1707

Jan. Scottish Parliament ratifies Articles of Union (16th).
Mar. Act of Union joins kingdoms of England and Scotland under name of Great Britain (6th). The Act provides that the Princess Sophia of Hanover and her Protestant heirs should succeed to the Crown of the United Kingdom; that there would be one Parliament at Westminster to which Scotland should send 16 elective peers and 45 members of the Commons; that no more Scottish peers be created; that Scottish law and legal administration remain unchanged; that the Episcopal Church in England and Presbyterian in Scotland be unchanged; and for the adoption of a common flag – the Union Jack, a common coinage, and free Anglo-Scottish and colonial trade.
Apr. Final dissolution of Scottish Parliament (28th).
May. Union of England and Scotland comes into effect (1st).
Oct. Second Parliament of Anne reconvenes as first Parliament of Great Britain.

1708

Feb. Harley and St John dismissed from the Cabinet; Robert Walpole appointed Secretary at War (25th).
Mar. James Edward, the Old Pretender, lands in Scotland; but a French fleet sent to assist him was repulsed by Admiral Byng and he soon returned to France.
July. Battle of Oudenarde (11th).
Nov. The third Parliament of Queen Anne's reign meets (16th).

1709

Sept. Battle of Malplaquet (11th).
Oct. Townshend's Barrier treaty (29th). Copyright Act.
Nov. Dr Henry Sacheverell preaches a sermon at St Paul's Cathedral, condemning the toleration of nonconformists and praising divine right of monarchy (5th).
Dec. Dr Sacheverell impeached by House of Commons (13th).

1710

Feb.–Mar. Trial of Dr Sacheverell (27 Feb.–20 Mar.); Dr Sacheverell suspended from preaching for three years (23 Mar.); during trial

pro-Sacheverell riots occur in which London mobs sack several leading nonconformist meeting houses.
June. Sunderland dismissed as Secretary of State, South (14th).
Aug. Godolphin and Whig ministry dismissed by the Queen; Robert Harley, as Chancellor of Exchequer, and Henry St John, form Tory ministry (8th).
Sept. Dissolution of Parliament followed by election (21st).
Nov. Fourth Parliament of Anne meets with Tory majority (25th).

1711
Feb. Property Qualification Act passed, county MPs must own property worth £600 and borough MPs property worth £300 per annum.
Mar. Robert Harley made Lord Treasurer (29th).
May. Harley created Earl of Oxford (23rd).
Dec. Bill against occasional conformity introduced in the Lords by Nottingham (15th); Duke of Marlborough dismissed as Commander-in-Chief. Duke of Ormond becomes Commander-in-Chief.

1712
Jan. Anne creates 12 new Tory peers to ensure success of government peace initiative in Lords (1st); Robert Walpole imprisoned in Tower for alleged corruption as Secretary at War.
July. Henry St John created Viscount Bolingbroke.

1713
Apr. Peace of Utrecht (11th).
Aug. Anne's fourth Parliament dissolved, followed by elections. Earl of Mar appointed Secretary of State for Scotland (8th).

1714
Feb. Fifth Parliament of Queen Anne meets (16th).
May. Schism Act passed. No person allowed to keep a school unless a member of the Anglican Church.
July. Henry St John (Bolingbroke) secures dismissal of the Earl of Oxford and begins attempt to pack administration with Jacobite sympathisers. Severe illness of Queen Anne forces calling of Privy Council. Pro-Hanoverian Duke of Shrewsbury appointed Lord Treasurer in place of Oxford (30th).
Aug. Death of Queen Anne (1st); George I proclaimed King in London and leading cities. Bolingbroke dismissed from office.
Sept. George I arrives in England (18th). *Whig administration formed under Lord Stanhope.* Principal figures: Lord Stanhope (Secretary of State); Lord Halifax (First Lord of the Treasury); Lord Townshend (Secretary

of State); Earl of Nottingham (Lord President of the Council); Lord Sunderland (Lord Lieutenant of Ireland).
Oct. Coronation of George I (20th).

1715
Mar. Meeting of first Parliament of George I with large Whig majority (17th).
June. Bolingbroke, Ormond and Oxford impeached. Flight of Bolingbroke and Ormond; Oxford committed to the Tower. Widespread rioting followed by Riot Act strengthening power of magistrates by making many riots a capital offence.
Sept. Jacobite rising in Scotland under the Earl of Mar.
Oct. Robert Walpole appointed First Lord of the Treasury.
Nov. Jacobites defeated at Sheriffmuir and Preston.
Dec. Pretender (James III) arrives in Scotland (22nd).

1716
Feb. Pretender flees Scotland after failure of England to rise in support (10th). Impeachment of Jacobite leaders; execution of Derwentwater and Kenmure.
May. Septennial Act extends maximum duration of parliaments to seven years.
Dec. Lord Townshend dismissed as Secretary of State for opposing French alliance favoured by George I.

1717
Jan. Triple Alliance formed between England, France and Holland to uphold the Treaty of Utrecht (4th).
Feb. Convocation of the Church of England ceased to meet regularly.
Apr. Walpole resigns from administration, succeeded as First Lord by Stanhope. Addison and Sunderland become Secretaries of State.
July. Oxford released from the Tower (1st).

1718
Mar. Sunderland remodels ministry: Sunderland becomes First Lord of the Treasury, Stanhope Secretary of State, and Aislabie Chancellor of the Exchequer.
Aug. Quadruple Alliance formed between England, France, the Emperor and Holland.
Dec. War between England and Spain.

1719
Jan. Repeal of the Schism and Occasional Conformity Acts.

Apr. Peerage Bill to fix the number of peers in the House of Lords defeated.
Dec. Peerage Bill, reintroduced by the Duke of Buckingham, defeated in the Commons.

1720
Jan. Spain joins Quadruple Alliance, ending hostilities with England.
Feb. House of Commons accepts South Sea Company's scheme for taking over part of the national debt in return for exclusive trade in the South Seas.
Apr. Royal assent given to Act empowering South Seas Company to manage national debt (7th). Stocks begin a sharp rise.
June. Robert Walpole and Charles Townshend return to office as Paymaster-General and Lord President of the Council respectively.
Oct.–Nov. 'South Sea Bubble' begins to burst, with panic selling and the ruin of many investors.
Dec. Walpole begins restoration of public credit. Secret Committee appointed to investigate the affairs of the South Sea Company. The Company's directors are detained and those holding government posts dismissed and expelled from the House of Commons. Aislabie, Chancellor of the Exchequer, and Earl of Sunderland implicated.

1721
Feb. Death of Stanhope (5th); Townshend becomes Secretary of State in his place.
Mar. House of Commons votes Aislabie guilty of fraud, expels him from the House and commits him to the Tower. Sunderland acquitted on charges of corruption but eventually resigns.
Apr. *Walpole administration* formed. Principal figures: Robert Walpole (First Lord of the Treasury and Chancellor of the Exchequer); Lord Townshend (Secretary of State); Lord Carteret (Secretary of State).

1722
Apr. Death of Sunderland.
May. Atterbury plot by Jacobites uncovered. Leading Jacobite sympathisers arrested.
Oct. Meeting of George I's second Parliament (9th). Habeas Corpus suspended; penal taxes levied on Catholics and non-jurors; Francis Atterbury (Bishop of Rochester) exiled.

1723
May. Lord Bolingbroke pardoned and returns to England in June.
June. System of bonded warehouses established to prevent smuggling and increase revenues on tea and coffee.

1724
Apr. Carteret dismissed as Secretary of State and becomes Lord Lieutenant of Ireland; Thomas Pelham Holles, Duke of Newcastle, appointed Secretary of State and his brother, Henry Pelham, Secretary at War.

1725
Apr. City Elections Act regulating conduct of elections in London increases power of Court of Aldermen and leads to strong opposition to Walpole in the City.
July. Riots against malt tax in Scotland.
Sept. Treaty of Hanover between England, France and Prussia.

1726
Nov. Publication of *The Craftsman*, edited by Bolingbroke and Pulteney, attacking Walpole and his foreign policy.

1727
Feb. Hostilities break out between Britain and Spain.
June. Death of George I (11th); succession of George II. Walpole reappointed First Lord of the Treasury and Chancellor of the Exchequer. Civil List raised to £800,000 per annum.
July. George I's second Parliament formally dissolved.

1729
Nov. Treaty of Seville with Spain; confirmation of *assiento* treaty allowing limited trade with Spanish colonies; Gibraltar ceded to England.

1730
May. Lord Harrington replaces Townshend as Secretary of State.

1731
Mar. Treaty of Vienna; Austrian Emperor agrees to disband Ostend East India Company.

1733
Mar. Widespread opposition to Walpole's Excise Bill.
Apr. Walpole's majority in House of Commons reduced to 16 on Excise proposals; Walpole offers resignation to the King. Though remaining in office, Walpole postpones discussion of the Bill until June, effectively dropping the scheme.
May. Walpole narrowly staves off defeat in the House of Lords over handling of South Sea Company affairs.

1734
Mar. Motion to repeal Septennial Act defeated.
Apr. Dissolution of Parliament, followed by elections (16th).

1735
Jan. Second Parliament of George II meets (14th), the Walpole administration having lost seats but still commanding a substantial majority.

1736
Mar. Repeal of Test Act defeated 251 to 123 in Commons. Gin Act passed, taxing spirits and imposing licences for selling them, to come into force on 29 September.
July. Anti-Irish and Gin Act disturbances in London.
Sept. Porteous Riots in Edinburgh. Fine levied on the city.

1737
Sept. Frederick, Prince of Wales, quarrels with his father and sides openly with the opposition to Walpole.
Nov. Death of Queen Caroline (20th).

1738
Jan. Spanish attacks on British shipping denounced by the opposition in the Commons and the City of London.
Mar. Examination by Commons Committee of Captain Jenkins, who alleged ill-treatment at hands of Spanish Guardas Costas in 1731. Carteret succeeds in passing resolutions in House of Lords condemning Spanish right to search British ships in Spanish American waters.

1739
Jan. Convention of Pardo agreed between Britain and Spain over trade disputes.
Mar. Address approving Pardo Convention carried in the Commons by Walpole by only 28 votes against the opposition of William Pitt and the 'Patriots'.
Oct. Walpole forced to accede to demand for war with Spain – the 'War of Jenkins' Ear'.
Nov. Capture of Porto Bello by Admiral Vernon.

1740
Feb. Motion to investigate the Convention of Pardo rejected by 247 votes to 196.
Apr. Argyll dismissed from his military appointments because of increasing antipathy to Walpole. Hervey's replacement of Godolphin as Lord Privy Seal offends the Duke of Newcastle, who threatens resignation.
June. Death of Sir William Wyndham, chief leader of the Tories.
Oct. George Dodington loses his post as Commissioner of the Treasury and moves into opposition to Walpole.

1741

Feb. Motion for Walpole's dismissal defeated by 184 votes.
Apr. King's Speech invites Parliament to support the Pragmatic Sanction: £300,000 voted in subsidies for Queen Maria Theresa of Austria. Parliament dissolved (27th). In ensuing election Walpole's majority reduced to under 20 seats by defeats in Cornwall and Scotland.
Dec. Parliament reassembles and Walpole defeated in seven divisions.

1742

Feb. Walpole decides to resign after defeat over Chippenham election petition (11th). *Carteret administration* formed. Principal figures: John Carteret (Secretary of State); Earl of Wilmington (First Lord of the Treasury).

1743

Aug. Henry Pelham becomes First Lord of the Treasury in place of Earl of Wilmington.

1744

Mar. France declares war on Britain.
Nov. Carteret resigns after increasing disagreement in the Cabinet and Parliament about his foreign policy. *Pelham administration* formed. Principal figures: Henry Pelham (First Lord of the Treasury); Earl of Harrington (Secretary of State); Duke of Bedford (First Lord of the Admiralty).

1745

May. Battle of Fontenoy. Marshal Saxe defeats Duke of Cumberland.
July. Second Jacobite rebellion. The Young Pretender, Charles Edward Stuart, lands in Scotland and proclaims his father as James VIII of Scotland and James III of England (23rd). Highland clans rise in support.
Sept. The Pretender enters Edinburgh with 2,000 men (11th); Jacobite victory at Prestonpans (21st).
Dec. Pretender reaches Derby, but decides to retreat to Scotland because of lack of support in England (4th).

1746

Feb. Pelham, Newcastle, Hardwicke and Harrington resign after disagreements with the King over foreign policy. Bath and Granville attempt to form an administration. *Pelham administration* reformed. Principal figures: H. Pelham (First Lord of the Treasury); Earl of Harrington (Secretary of State); Duke of Newcastle (Secretary of State); William Pitt, the Elder (Vice-Treasurer of Ireland).
Apr. Defeat of Young Pretender and Jacobite forces at battle of Culloden (16th).
May. Pitt becomes Paymaster-General of the forces.

Aug. Disarming of the Highlands Act forbade the bearing of arms, wearing of the kilt and required the registration of all private schools.
Sept. Flight of the Young Pretender to France.

1748
Oct. Treaty of Aix-la-Chapelle ends War of Austrian Succession.

1751
May. Act passed for adoption of the reformed (Gregorian) calendar in England and the colonies. Year to begin from 1 Jan. instead of 25 Mar.; 11 days to be omitted from the calendar between 3 and 14 Sept. 1752.

1753
June. Jewish Naturalisation Act passed, but repealed the following year because of the popular opposition (Dec. 1754).

1754
Mar. Death of Pelham. *Newcastle administration* formed. Principal figures: Duke of Newcastle (First Lord of the Treasury); Earl of Holderness (Secretary of State); Henry Fox (Secretary at War); William Pitt (Paymaster).

1755
May. Admiral Boscawen fails to prevent French reinforcements reaching North America. Subsidy treaties agreed with Hesse-Cassel and Russia to provide troops in the event of war.
Nov. Henry Fox becomes Secretary of State; Pitt dismissed.

1756
Jan. Treaty between Britain and Prussia (16th).
May. Britain declares war on France (17th).
June. Loss of Minorca after failure of Admiral Byng to defeat French invasion fleet.
Oct. Henry Fox announces intention to resign after severe criticism of the conduct of the war in the House of Commons. Newcastle resigns; King asks Fox to form an administration, but refuses. Devonshire agrees to form an administration with Pitt (29th).
Nov. *Pitt–Devonshire administration* formed. Principal figures: Duke of Devonshire (First Lord of the Treasury); William Pitt (Secretary of State).

1757
Apr. King demands Pitt's resignation after failure to achieve success in the war. George Grenville (Treasurer of the Navy) and Legge (Chancellor of the Exchequer) resign with Pitt. Widespread popular support shown for Pitt.

July. After considerable negotiations *Pitt–Newcastle administration* formed. Principal figures: William Pitt (Secretary of State); Duke of Newcastle (First Lord of the Treasury); Henry Fox (Paymaster).

Militia Act remodels militia with members chosen by ballot; widespread rioting provoked (Aug.–Sept.).

Oct. Failure of Rochefort expedition; news of defeats in India and Canada leads to criticism of the conduct of the war in Europe.

Nov. Victory for Britain's ally, Frederick the Great, at Rossbach.

Dec. Victory of Frederick at Leuthen.

1758

Apr. At Second Treaty of Westminster, Prussia and Britain pledged themselves not to make a separate peace. Frederick granted an annual subsidy of £670,000.

July. Capture of Louisburg in North America (26th).

Nov. Occupation of Fort Duquesne by Colonel Forbes.

1759

May. Capture of Guadeloupe.

June. Capture of Fort Niagara in North America.

July. Bombardment of Le Havre thwarts French plans for invasion of Britain.

Aug. Boscawen's defeat of French fleet at Lagos (Cape St Vincent).

Sept. Wolfe's victory at Battle of the Plains of Abraham (13th) and capture of Quebec (18th).

Nov. Defeat of French fleet by Admiral Hawke at Quiberon Bay (20th).

1760

Sept. Surrender of Montreal to the British; virtual loss of Canada by the French.

Oct. Death of George II (25th); accession of George III.

1761

Oct. Resignation of Pitt the Elder because of disagreements with colleagues about his war policy. *Bute–Newcastle administration* formed. Principal figures: Duke of Newcastle (First Lord of the Treasury); Earl of Bute (Secretary of State).

1762

May. Duke of Newcastle resigns from government because of quarrel with Bute over foreign policy. *Bute administration* formed. Principal figures: Earl of Bute (First Lord of the Treasury); George Grenville (Secretary of State).

June. John Wilkes starts *The North Briton* to attack the Bute administration.

1763
Feb. First Treaty of Paris signed, ending Seven Years War (for provisions, *see* pp. 182–5).
Mar. Introduction of cider tax increases Bute's unpopularity.
Apr. Bute resigns in the face of increasing attacks in the press and Parliament. *Grenville administration* formed. Principal figures: George Grenville (First Lord of the Treasury and Chancellor of the Exchequer); Earl of Egremont (Secretary of State, later First Lord of the Admiralty); Earl of Halifax (Secretary of State). Wilkes arrested on a general warrant for an attack on the King in issue No. 45 of *The North Briton*.
Dec. Wilkes's arrest declared illegal by Chief Justice Pratt. Wilkes forced into exile after publication of *An Essay on Woman*.

1765
Mar. American Stamp Act passed to raise money for the defence of the American colonies by placing a charge on legal transactions. Six of the 13 colonies petitioned against the Act. (For American affairs, *see also* pp. 169–70.)
July. Grenville administration dismissed by the King. *First Rockingham administration* formed. Principal figures: Marquess of Rockingham (First Lord of the Treasury); Henry Seymour Conway (Secretary of State).

1766
Jan. Widespread petitioning movement against Stamp Act by English merchants.
Mar. Repeal of the Stamp Act with strong support of Pitt (now Earl of Chatham).
July. *Chatham administration* formed. Principal figures: Earl of Chatham (Lord Privy Seal); Duke of Grafton (First Lord of the Treasury); Charles Townshend (Chancellor of the Exchequer).

1767
June. Townshend's Revenue Act passed, imposing duties on tea and other articles imported into America to pay for defence and administration of the colonies.

1768
Mar. Wilkes elected MP for Middlesex.
May. Industrial and pro-Wilkes riots in London; 11 people killed by soldiers at the 'massacre' of St George's Fields.
Oct. Resignation of Earl of Chatham. *Grafton administration* formed. Principal figures: Duke of Grafton (First Lord of the Treasury); Lord North (Chancellor of the Exchequer).

1769
Feb. House of Commons votes that Wilkes was guilty of a seditious libel for letter criticising the government for the 'massacre' of St George's Fields; Wilkes expelled from the Commons; formation of the 'Supporters of the Bill of Rights' to support Wilkes and the cause of parliamentary reform.
May. Cabinet decides to retain duties on tea in spite of strong opposition from the American colonists.
June–July. Petitioning movement for reform of Parliament and reinstatement of Wilkes.

1770
Jan. Grafton resigns after securing a majority of 44 in the House of Commons after a motion on the administration's handling of the Middlesex election issue. *North administration* formed. Principal figure: Lord North (First Lord of the Treasury and Chancellor of the Exchequer).
Mar. Act repealing duties on paper, glass and paint, but retaining those on tea.
Apr. Edmund Burke publishes *Thoughts on the Causes of the Present Discontents*, accusing the King of dominating Parliament through 'influence' and calling for a revival of 'party'.

1771
Mar. Printers' Case. London printers reprimanded for publishing parliamentary debates and Lord Mayor and two aldermen of London imprisoned for a breach of the privileges of the House of Commons. But no serious attempts made to interfere with parliamentary reporting thereafter.

1773
Oct. Tea Act passed to aid finances of the East India Company by allowing direct export of tea to North America. American colonists resist imports and payment of duty.
Dec. Boston Tea Party. Protestors dump 340 chests of East India Company tea in Boston harbour.

1774
Apr. Motion in the House of Commons to repeal tea duty and pacify the colonists. Quebec Act passed granting toleration to Roman Catholics in Canada. Continental Congress meets at Philadelphia and agrees to defy coercive measures. Quebec Act passed for government of Canada.

1775
Jan. Chatham's motion proposing conciliation with the American colonies defeated.

Mar. Burke's conciliation proposals defeated.
Apr. British and American forces skirmish at Lexington (18th).
May. Second Continental Congress meets at Philadelphia (10th).
June. Battle of Bunker's Hill, Boston.
Aug. King's proclamation of rebellion in American colonies.

1776
July. American Declaration of Independence.

1777
Oct. Surrender of British forces at Saratoga.

1778
Feb. Treaty of Amity and Commerce signed between France and the American colonists. Charles James Fox's motion for virtual abandonment of the war against America defeated in the Commons.
Mar.–Apr. Motions criticising conduct of the war and urging reform of Parliament by reduction of Crown influence only narrowly defeated in Commons.

1779
June. Spain declares war on Britain. Siege of Gibraltar begins.
Dec. First meeting of Yorkshire reformers under Christopher Wyvill to concert plans for reform of Parliament. Widespread agitation in Ireland for removal of trade and constitutional restrictions.

1780
Feb. Yorkshire petition for parliamentary reform presented. Beginning of widespread petitioning movement for 'economical reform'. Burke presents proposals for reform.
Mar. Convention of reformers in London.
Apr. Dunning's resolution 'that the influence of the Crown has increased, is increasing, and ought to be diminished' carried by 233 votes to 215. Further attempts to attack the Crown's influence defeated by the administration and its supporters.
June. Protestant Association led by Lord George Gordon petitions Parliament for repeal of the Catholic Relief Act of 1778; followed by widespread rioting in London – the 'Gordon riots'.

1781
Nov. News of Cornwallis's surrender at Yorktown reaches England.

1782
Feb. Motion asserting the impracticability of the continued war with America passed in the House of Commons.

Mar. North only narrowly escapes defeat on two motions of no confidence. The King accepts North's resignation. *Second Rockingham administration* formed. Principal figures: Marquess of Rockingham (First Lord of the Treasury); Charles James Fox (Foreign Secretary).
May. Clerke's Act passed disqualifying government contractors from sitting in the Commons.
June. Crewe's Act passed disfranchising revenue officers of the Crown.
July. Burke's Civil Establishment Act passed controlling royal expenditure, pensions and offices. Paymaster's Office regulated. Death of Rockingham (1st) leads to formation of *Shelburne administration*. Principal figures: Earl of Shelburne (First Lord of the Treasury); William Pitt the Younger (Chancellor of the Exchequer); Thomas Townshend (Home Secretary).
Nov. Preliminaries of peace agreed with the American colonies.

1783
Jan. Preliminaries of peace signed with France and Spain.
Feb. Alliance of Fox and North and their supporters successfully challenges peace terms in the Commons; resignation of Shelburne.
Apr. *Fox–North administration* formed. Principal figures: Duke of Portland (First Lord of the Treasury); Lord North (Home Secretary); Charles James Fox (Foreign Secretary).
Apr. Pitt's proposals for parliamentary reform defeated in the Commons.
Sept. Treaty of Versailles signed between England, France and Spain (for details, *see* p. 189).
Dec. Fox's India Bill. Designed by Burke to transfer the authority of the East India Company to commissioners nominated by Parliament. Passes Commons but defeated in the Lords after pressure from the King. Ministers dismissed and *Pitt administration* formed. Principal figures: William Pitt (First Lord of the Treasury and Chancellor of the Exchequer); Lord Sydney (Home Secretary); H. Dundas (Treasurer of the Navy); Marquess of Carmarthen (Foreign Secretary); Duke of Rutland (Privy Seal).

1784
Mar. Parliament dissolved for general election. Pitt and his supporters gain a majority of over 100.
June. Pitt introduces first Budget. Begins to reorganise government debts and finances. Duties reduced to deter smuggling, and window tax introduced. New loans raised and a large number of indirect taxes levied. 'Board for Taxes' set up to administer collection.
July. Pitt's India Bill introduced, establishing a 'Board of Control' to administer the East India Company.

1785
Apr. Pitt's proposals for limited parliamentary reform defeated by 248 votes to 174. Pitt announces plans for a 'Sinking Fund' to liquidate the

national debt. Sets up five commissioners to investigate waste in government departments.

1786
May. Pitt's 'Sinking Fund' established.
Sept. Commercial treaty signed between Britain and France. Duties lowered on trade in manufactured goods and wine between the two countries.

1788
Nov. King's illness starts 'Regency Crisis'. Fox and the Whigs demand unfettered powers for the Prince of Wales.

1789
Feb. Recovery of the King ends crisis.
July. Storming of the Bastille in Paris (14th).
Nov. Meeting of the Revolution Society in London to celebrate the 'Glorious Revolution' of 1688–89; sermon preached by Dr Price welcoming the French Revolution.

1790
Nov. Burke publishes *Reflections on the Revolution in France*, bitterly attacking the revolution and its supporters.

1791
Mar. Publication of Thomas Paine's *Right of Man* Pt I (Pt II published in February 1792).
May. Burke and Fox quarrel publicly over the French Revolution.
July. 'Church and King' riots in Birmingham against dissenters.

1792
Jan. Formation of London Corresponding Society, first artisan-based political society.
May. Proclamation against seditious publications.
Nov. Formation of loyalist associations against 'Republicans and Levellers' begins.
Dec. Pitt fortifies the Tower, calls out the militia and begins preparations for war. Further proclamation against seditious writings and trial of Paine (in his absence) for seditious libel.

1793
Jan. Execution of Louis XVI of France.
Feb. France declares war on Britain and Holland.
May. Grey's motion for reform defeated by 282 votes to 41 in the Commons.
Oct. British Convention meets at Edinburgh.

Nov.–Dec. British Convention reassembles; dispersed by authorities and leaders tried and harshly sentenced (Jan.–Sept. 1794).

1794
May. Arrest of leaders of English reform societies on charge of high treason. Secret committees appointed to investigate radical societies. Habeas Corpus suspended.
July. Moderate Whigs under Portland join in the Pitt administration; Fox and his followers left in virtual isolation.
Oct.–Nov. Thomas Hardy and other radical leaders acquitted of high treason.

1795
July. Widespread food rioting in England; demonstrations against the war in London.
Oct. Mass meeting organised by London Corresponding Society in London. Attack on the King's coach by anti-war protestors at opening of Parliament.
Nov.–Dec. Government introduces 'Two Acts', extending the law of treason and prohibiting mass meetings unless approved by the magistracy.

1796
May. Failure of attempts to make peace with France.
Dec. Failure of French attempt to land at Bantry Bay, Ireland. Breakdown of further peace overtures to France.

1797
Feb. Bank crisis in Britain; temporary suspension of cash payments by the Bank of England. Defeat of Spanish fleet at Cape St Vincent. Failure of small French landing in Pembrokeshire.
Apr. Outbreak of naval mutiny at Spithead.
May. Mutiny at Spithead settled; outbreak of mutiny at the Nore.
June. Mutiny at the Nore suppressed and ringleaders hanged.
Sept. Negotiations for peace with France broken off.
Oct. Duncan defeats Dutch fleet at Camperdown.
Nov. Pitt's Finance Bill proposes new indirect taxes as well as an income tax.

1798
Jan. Pitt's Finance Bill approved by Parliament.
Apr. Remaining leaders of London Corresponding Society arrested.
May. Outbreak of rebellion in Ireland.
June. Defeat of Irish rebels at Vinegar Hill and suppression of rising in Ulster.

Aug. Landing of General Humbert and French troops in Ireland. Nelson defeats French fleet at the battle of the Nile.
Sept. Humbert's troops surrender.
Oct. Failure of French expedition to Lough Swilly and capture of Wolfe Tone.

1799
Apr. Pitt introduces income tax of 10 per cent.
July. Combination Act passed, prohibiting combinations of workmen to raise wages. Act passed prohibiting certain named political societies, including the London Corresponding Society and the United Irishmen.

1800
Jan. Peace overtures from Napoleon rejected by Pitt.
July. Second Combination Act passed, partly relaxing provisions of Act of 1799 (*see* pp. 309–10).
Aug. Act of Union. Ireland merged with Great Britain and Irish Parliament abolished.

1801
Feb. Resignation of Pitt because of the King's refusal to permit the introduction of Catholic Emancipation. *Addington administration* formed. Principal figures: Henry Addington (First Lord of the Treasury and Chancellor of the Exchequer); Duke of Portland (Home Secretary).
Apr. Danish fleet destroyed at Copenhagen.
Oct. Preliminary terms of peace agreed with France.

1802
Mar. Peace of Amiens signed with France.

1803
May. War resumed with France.

1804
May. Resignation of Addington. *Second Pitt administration* formed. Principal figures: William Pitt (First Lord of the Treasury and Chancellor of the Exchequer); Lord Hawkesbury (Home Secretary).
July. Napoleon's invasion army of 100,000 men and 2,000 transports assembled at Boulogne. Extensive anti-invasion preparations in England.

1805
Aug. Third Coalition formed with Britain, Austria and Russia. Napoleon begins movement of army of Boulogne to Central Europe.
Oct. Nelson defeats Franco-Spanish fleet at Trafalgar.

1806
Jan. Death of Pitt.
Feb. *Grenville administration* formed ('All the Talents'). Principal figures: Lord Grenville (First Lord of the Treasury); Charles James Fox (Foreign Secretary).
Sept. Death of Charles James Fox.
Nov. Napoleon's Berlin decrees close all European ports to British shipping.
Jan.–Nov. Orders in Council issued by Britain, in retaliation for Berlin decrees, ordering all neutral ships trading with Europe to proceed via Britain and pay duties.

1807
Mar. Resignation of 'All the Talents' ministry. *Portland administration* formed. Principal figures: Duke of Portland (First Lord of the Treasury); Spencer Perceval (Chancellor of the Exchequer).
May. Act abolishing the slave trade.
Sept. Bombardment of Copenhagen.
Nov. Napoleon issues Milan decrees for confiscation of all neutral shipping calling at British ports.

1808
Aug. Convention of Cintra signed in Lisbon, allowing French to evacuate Portugal on easy terms. Widespread protests in England.

1809
Jan. Committee appointed to investigate the Duke of York's involvement in the sale of army commissions.
June. Motion for parliamentary reform defeated in the Commons.
Sept.–Oct. Failure of Walcheren expedition. Resignation of Duke of Portland. *Perceval administration* formed. Principal figures: Spencer Perceval (First Lord of the Treasury and Chancellor of the Exchequer); Earl of Liverpool (Secretary for War and the Colonies).

1810
Feb. Government forced to appoint inquiry on the Walcheren expedition by vote in the House of Commons.
Mar. Government narrowly escapes defeat on motions of censure over Walcheren expedition.
Apr. Riots in London in support of radical MP Sir Francis Burdett.
Oct. George III suffers renewed bout of illness.

1811
Feb. Prince of Wales given virtually full powers as Prince Regent (confirmed 1812).
Mar. Beginning of Luddite disturbances in Midlands.

1812
Jan. Luddite disturbances spread to Yorkshire and Lancashire. Framebreaking made capital offence.
Mar. Widespread petitions against Orders in Council.
Apr. Height of Luddite disturbances; attack on Rawfolds Mill; assassination of William Horsfall by Luddite sympathisers.
May. Assassination of Spencer Perceval.
June. *Liverpool administration* formed. Principal figures: Earl of Liverpool (First Lord of the Treasury); Viscount Sidmouth (Home Secretary); Viscount Castlereagh (Foreign Secretary); Sir Robert Peel (Home Secretary). Orders in Council revoked.
July. Wellington defeats French at Salamanca.

1813
June. Wellington's victory at Vittoria.
Oct. Defeat of Napoleon at battle of Leipzig.

1814
Apr. Abdication of Napoleon.

1815
Mar. Napoleon returns from Elba, beginning of the 'Hundred Days'. Widespread petitioning movement and riots in London against passing of the Corn Laws, imposing a high protective tariff against imports of grain.
June. Defeat of Napoleon at Waterloo. Peace of Vienna signed.

1816
Apr. Income tax abolished after government defeat in the House of Commons. Beginning of widespread riots against distress in East Anglia and manufacturing districts.
Oct. First cheap edition of Cobbett's *Political Register* issued, the 'twopenny trash'.

1817
Jan. Attack on Prince Regent's coach leads to introduction of 'Gag Acts'; Habeas Corpus suspended, and restrictions placed on meetings.
Mar. March of the 'blanketeers' broken up by troops.
June. Pentrich 'rising' in Derbyshire led by Jeremiah Brandreth.

1819
Aug. Reform meeting at St Peter's Fields, Manchester, broken up by troops ('Peterloo'); followed by 'Six Acts' restricting meetings and the press, and allowing magistrates to seize arms and prevent drilling.

1820

Jan. Death of George III (29th); accession of George IV.
Feb. Cato Street Conspiracy uncovered.
June. George IV's estranged wife Caroline returns to claim her rights as Queen.
Nov. Government forced to abandon its attempt to deprive Queen Caroline of her title and dissolve her marriage to the King after widespread popular opposition.

1821

Aug. Riots in London at Queen Caroline's funeral.

1822

Jan. Peel becomes Home Secretary in place of Lord Sidmouth.
Aug. Castlereagh commits suicide; George Canning becomes Foreign Secretary.

SECTION TWO

The monarchy

2.1 Biographical details of monarchs and their issue

William III
Born 4 November 1650, the son of William II, Prince of Orange and Mary Stuart, daughter of Charles I. On 13 February 1689 William and Mary were made King and Queen for their joint and separate lives. William had married Mary, the daughter of James II, on 4 November 1677.

Anne
Born 6 February 1665, the daughter of James II and Anne Hyde. She acceded to the throne on 8 March 1702 and died 1 August 1714. On 28 July 1683 she married Prince George, the son of Frederick III of Denmark. The marriage produced:

William Born 24 July 1689. Created Duke of Gloucester, 27 July, he died on 30 July 1700.

Her other children were still-born or died in infancy.

George I
Born 28 May 1660, the son of Ernest Augustus, Elector of Hanover and Sophia, daughter of Frederick, the Elector Palatine. He acceded to the throne on 1 August 1714 and died 11 June 1727. On 21 November 1682 he married Sophia Dorothea, daughter of George William, Duke of Luneberg-Celle. The marriage produced the following children:

1. **George**   later George II (q.v.). Born 30 October 1683.
2. **Sophia Dorothea** Born 16 March 1687. Died 28 June 1757. On 17 November 1706 she married Frederick William, later King of Prussia.

George I's illegitimate children (by the Duchess of Kendal) were Petronille Melusine (born 1693) and Margaret Gertrude (born 1703).

George II
Born 30 October 1683, the son of George I and Sophia Dorothea. He acceded to the throne on 11 June 1727, and died 25 October 1760. On 22 August 1705 he married Caroline, the daughter of John Frederick, Margrave of Brandenburg-Anspach. The marriage produced the following children:

34   THE MONARCHY

1. **Frederick**	Born 20 January 1707. Died 20 March 1751. Created Prince of Wales 7 January 1729.
2. **Anne**	Born 22 October 1709. Died 12 January 1759. On 14 March 1734 she married Prince William IV of Orange.
3. **Amelia (Emily)**	Born 30 May 1711. Died 31 October 1786.
4. **Caroline Elizabeth**	Born 30 May 1713. Died 28 December 1757.
5. **George William**	Born 2 November 1717. Died in infancy.
6. **William Augustus**	Born 15 April 1721. Died 31 October 1765. Created Duke of Cumberland 27 July 1726.
7. **Mary**	Born 22 February 1723. Died 16 January 1772. On 8 May 1740 she married Frederick, later Landgrave of Hesse-Cassel.
8. **Louisa**	Born 7 December 1724. Died 8 December 1751. On 27 October 1743 she married Frederick, later King of Denmark.

George III

Born 24 May 1738, the son of Frederick, Prince of Wales, and Augusta, daughter of Frederick II, Duke of Saxe-Gotha. He acceded to the throne on 25 October 1760 and died on 29 January 1820. On 8 September 1761 he married Charlotte, daughter of Charles Louis, Duke of Mecklenburg-Strelitz. Because of the King's insanity, the Prince of Wales became regent on 5 February 1811.

George III's marriage produced the following children:

1. **George**	Later George IV. Born 12 August 1762. Died 26 June 1830.
2. **Frederick**	Born 16 August 1763. Created Duke of York 29 November 1784. Died 5 January 1827.
3. **William**	Later William IV. Born 21 August 1765. Died 20 June 1837.
4. **Charlotte**	Born 29 September 1766. Died 5 October 1828. Married, 18 May 1797, Frederick Charles, later King of Württemberg.
5. **Edward**	Born 2 November 1767. Created Duke of Kent 24 April 1799. Died 23 January 1820.
6. **Augusta**	Born 8 November 1768. Died 22 September 1840.
7. **Elizabeth**	Born 22 May 1770. Died 10 January 1840. Married, 7 April 1818, Frederick Joseph, Prince of Hesse-Homburg.
8. **Ernest Augustus**	Born 5 June 1771. Died 18 November 1851. Created Duke of Cumberland 24 April 1799. Succeeded as King of Hanover 20 June 1837.

BIOGRAPHICAL DETAILS OF MONARCHS

9. **Augustus** Born 27 January 1773. Died 21 April 1843. Created Duke of Sussex 27 November 1801.
10. **Adolphus** Born 24 February 1774. Died 8 July 1850. Created Duke of Cambridge 27 November 1801.
11. **Mary** Born 25 April 1776. Died 30 April 1857. Married, 22 July 1816, William, Duke of Gloucester.
12. **Sophia** Born 3 November 1777. Died 27 May 1848.
13. **Octavia** Born 23 February 1779. Died 3 May 1783.
14. **Alfred** Born 22 September 1780. Died 26 August 1782.
15. **Amelia** Born 7 August 1783. Died 2 November 1810.

2.2 The Jacobite line

James II
Born 14 October 1633, the son of Charles I and Henrietta Maria. He acceded to the throne on 6 February 1685, fled the kingdom on 23 December 1688 and died on 6 September 1701. He married twice: Anne Hyde, on 3 September 1660 (she died 31 March 1671), and Mary of Modena, on 30 September 1673. The children of James II were as follows:

1. **Mary** Born 30 April 1662, the daughter of Anne Hyde; married William, Prince of Orange. Proclaimed joint sovereign with her husband on 13 February 1689; died 28 December 1694.
2. **Anne** Born 6 February 1665, the daughter of Anne Hyde, acceded to the throne on 8 March 1702; died 1 August 1714.
3. **James Francis Edward** The 'Old Pretender' or James III; born on 10 June 1688, the son of Mary of Modena. Styled James III in 1701 by Louis XIV; attainted in 1702, he died in Rome on 1 January 1766.
4. **Louisa Maria Theresa** Born 28 June 1692, the daughter of Mary of Modena; died 18 August 1712.

Charles Edward Stuart
Also known as the 'Young Pretender' or 'Bonnie Prince Charlie', born 31 December 1720, the grandson of James II and son of James Francis Edward, the 'Old Pretender'. He landed in Scotland on 25 July 1745 to lead the Jacobite forces on behalf of the claims of his father to the throne of Great Britain. Following the decisive defeat of the Jacobite armies at Culloden on 16 April 1746, he spent several months as a fugitive in Scotland before escaping to France in September 1746. He died in exile in Rome on 31 January 1788.

Henry Benedict Maria Clement, Cardinal York
Born March 1725, the second son of James, the 'Old Pretender' or James III. He came to England to support his brother Charles Edward

in 1745, but on return to Italy became Bishop of Ostia and prefect of St Peter's Rome; Cardinal (1747), Archbishop of Corinth (1759), and Bishop of Tusculum (1761). Assumed title Henry IX of England, 1788, but accepted gift of money from George III after his residence sacked by the French in 1799. Died at Frascati, August 1807.

2.3 The Stuart and Hanoverian lines

Unless otherwise stated, the dates are those of accession.

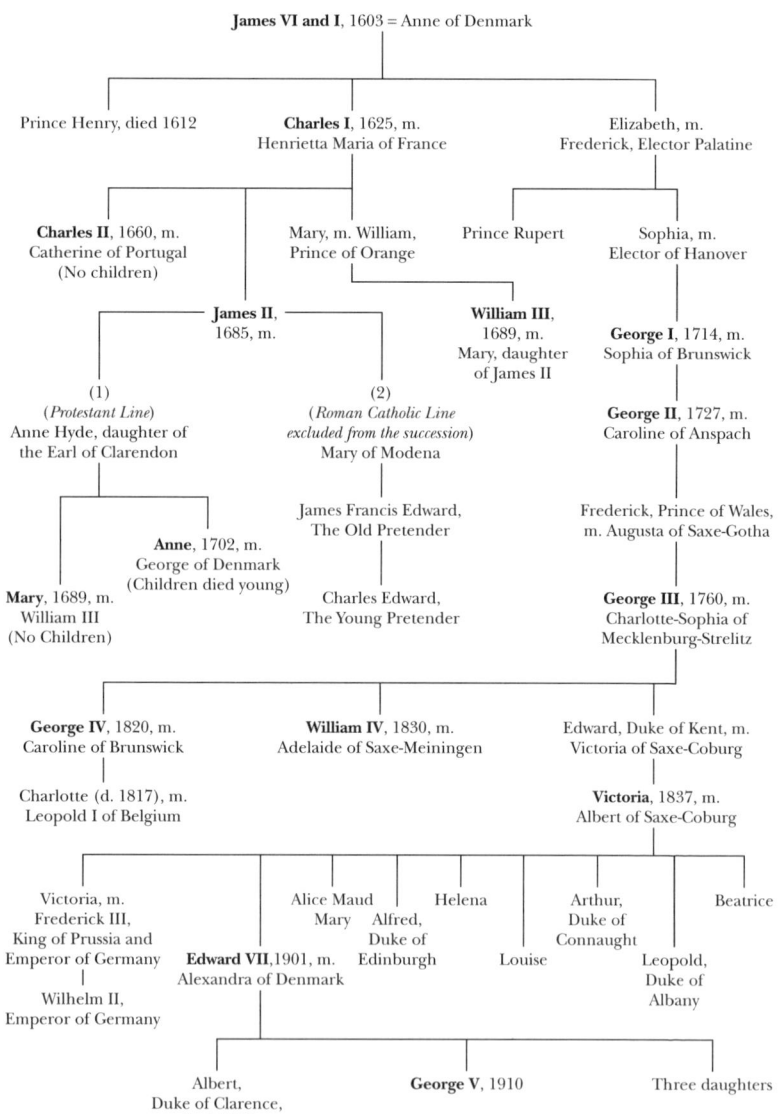

SECTION THREE

Ministries and office-holders

3.1 Ministries and administrations*

Chronological list

Date of formation	Name	Years covered
May 1702	Godolphin–Marlborough	1702–10
Aug. 1710	Harley	1710–14
Sept. 1714	Stanhope	1714–17
Apr. 1717	Stanhope–Sunderland (remodelled 1718)	1717–21
Apr. 1721	Walpole	1721–42
Feb. 1742	Carteret	1742–44
Nov. 1744	Pelham	1744–46
Feb. 1746	Bath	1746
Feb. 1746	Pelham	1746–54
Mar. 1754	Newcastle	1754–56
Nov. 1756	Pitt–Devonshire	1756–57
July 1757	Pitt–Newcastle	1757–61
Oct. 1761	Bute–Newcastle	1761–62
May 1762	Bute	1762–63
Apr. 1763	Grenville	1763–65
July 1765	1st Rockingham	1765–66
July 1766	Chatham	1766–68
Oct. 1768	Grafton	1768–70
Jan. 1770	North	1770–82
Mar. 1782	2nd Rockingham	1782
July 1782	Shelburne	1782–83
Apr. 1783	Fox–North	1783
Dec. 1783	Pitt	1783–1801

* The formation of administrations ultimately depended upon the power of appointment to major public offices and to the royal household by the Crown. Although such appointments were made throughout this period, and prior to it, it was only gradually with the development of parliamentary government as a regular feature of political life that wholesale changes in office-holders can be identified which relate to changes in royal favour or in the parliamentary situation. While it would be possible to suggest putative titles and dates of administrations prior to 1702, it was with the accession of Anne that the pattern of more readily identifiable ministries and administrations became more clearly evident.

Date of formation	Name	Years covered
Feb. 1801	Addington	1801–4
May 1804	2nd Pitt	1804–6
Feb. 1806	Ministry of All the Talents	1806–7
Mar. 1807	Portland	1807–9
Oct. 1809	Perceval	1809–12
June 1812	Liverpool	1812–27

3.2 Composition of administrations

Abbreviations for office-holders

Admir.	Lord High Admiral
Am. Cols	Secretary of State for the American Colonies
Bd Control	President of the Board of Control
BOT	President of the Board of Trade
Chanc. Exch.	Chancellor of the Exchequer
Comm.-in-Chief	Commander-in-Chief
D. Lanc.	Chancellor of the Duchy of Lancaster
1st Ld Treas.	First Lord of the Treasury
For. O.	Secretary of State for Foreign Affairs
Home O.	Secretary of State for the Home Department
Ld Chanc.	Lord Chancellor
Ld Keeper	Lord Keeper
Ld Lt of Ireland	Lord Lieutenant of Ireland
Ld Pres.	Lord President of the Council
Ld Steward	Lord Steward of the Household
Ld Treas.	Lord Treasurer
Master-Gen. of Ordnance	Master-General of Ordnance
Master of Mint	Master of the Royal Mint
Mins without portfolio	Minister without portfolio
Pay.-Gen.	Paymaster-General
PS	Lord Privy Seal
Sec. for Scotland	Secretary for Scotland
Sec. of State (North)	Secretary of State for the Northern Department
Sec. of State (South)	Secretary of State for the Southern Department
Sec. at War	Secretary at War
Treas. of the Navy	Treasurer of the Navy
War and Cols	Secretary of State for War and the Colonies

Administrations

Godolphin–Marlborough, 1702–10

Ld Treas.	Sidney Godolphin, Ld Godolphin	8 May 1702 (dism. 8 Aug. 1710)
Chanc. Exch.	Henry Boyle	29 Mar. 1701
	John Smith	11 Feb. 1708

Ld Pres.	Thomas Herbert, E. of Pembroke and E. of Montgomery	9 July 1702
	John Somers, Ld Somers	25 Nov. 1708
D. Lanc.	Sir John Leveson-Gower, Ld Gower	12 May 1702
	James Stanley, E. of Derby	1 June 1706
Master-Gen. of Ordnance	John Churchill, D. of Marlborough	1 July 1702
Sec. of State (South)	Daniel Finch, E. of Nottingham	2 May 1702 (vac. c. 22 Apr. 1704)
	Sir Charles Hedges	18 May 1704 (dism. Dec. 1706)
	Charles Spencer, E. of Sunderland	3 Dec. 1706 (dism. 13–14 June 1710)
	William Legge, Ld Dartmouth	15 June 1710 (vac. 6–13 Aug. 1713)
Sec. of State (North)	Sir Charles Hedges	2 May 1702
	Robert Harley	18 May 1704 (vac. 13 Feb. 1708)
	Henry Boyle	13 Feb. 1708 (vac. Sept. 1710)
PS	John Sheffield, M. of Normanby (D. of Buckinghamshire and of Normanby, 1703)	27 Apr. 1702
	John Holles, D. of Newcastle-Upon-Tyne (died 15 July 1711)	21 Mar. 1705
BOT	Thomas Thynne, Vt Weymouth	12 June 1702
	Thomas Grey, E. of Stamford	25 Apr. 1707
Admir.	Prince George of Denmark	20 May 1702
	Queen Anne (Lord High Admiral)	28 Oct. 1708
	Thomas Herbert, E. of Pembroke	29 Nov. 1708
	Edward Russell, E. of Oxford	8 Nov. 1709
Sec. at War	William Blathwayt	Aug. 1683
	Henry St John, Vt Bolingbroke	20 Apr. 1704
	Robert Walpole	25 Feb. 1708
Treas. of the Navy	Sir Thomas Littleton	29 May 1699
	Robert Walpole	21 Jan. 1710
Pay.-Gen.	John Howe	4 Jan. 1703
	Charles Fox	4 Jan. 1703
	James Brydges	1707

Harley, 1710–14 (formed Aug. 1710)

Ld Treas.	John Poulett, Earl Poulett	11 Aug. 1710
	Robert Harley, E. of Oxford	29 Mar. 1711
	Charles Talbot, D. of Shrewsbury (vac. Oct. 1714)	30 July 1714
Chanc. Exch.	Robert Harley	10 Aug. 1710
	Robert Benson	14 June 1711
	Sir William Wyndham	1 Nov. 1713
Ld Pres.	Laurence Hyde, E. of Rochester	21 Sept. 1710 (d. 21 May 1711)
	John Sheffield, D. of Buckinghamshire and of Normanby	14 June 1711
D. Lanc.	William Berkeley, Ld Berkeley	21 Sept. 1710
Master-Gen. of Ordnance	John Churchill, D. of Marlborough	1 July 1702
	Richard Savage, Earl Rivers	1 Jan. 1712
	James Douglas, D. of Hamilton and Brandon (d. 15 Nov. 1712)	1 July 1712
Sec. of State (South)	William Legge, Ld Dartmouth (E. of Dartmouth, 1711)	15 June 1710 (vac. 6–13 Aug. 1713)
	Henry St John, Vt Bolingbroke	17 Aug. 1713 (dism. 31 Aug. 1714)
Sec. of State (North)	Henry St John, Vt Bolingbroke	21 Sept. 1710
	William Bromley	17 Aug. 1713 (dism. Sept. 1714)
PS	John Holles, D. of Newcastle-Upon-Tyne (d. 15 July 1711)	21 Mar. 1705
	John Robinson, Bp of Bristol	31 Aug. 1711
	William Legge, E. of Dartmouth	21 Aug. 1713
BOT	Thomas Grey, E. of Stamford	25 Apr. 1707
	Charles Finch, E. of Winchilsea	12 June 1711
	Francis North, Ld Guildford	15 Sept. 1713
Admir.	Edward Russell, E. of Orford	8 Nov. 1709
	Sir John Leake	4 Oct. 1710
	Thomas Wentworth, E. of Strafford	30 Sept. 1712
Sec. at War	George Granville, Ld Lansdowne	28 Sept. 1710
	Sir William Wyndham	28 June 1712
	Francis Gwyn	21 Aug. 1713
Treas. of the Navy	Robert Walpole	21 Jan. 1710
	Charles Caesar	8 June 1711

MINISTRIES AND OFFICE-HOLDERS

Pay.-Gen.	James Brydges	1707
	Thomas Moore	1713
	Edward Nicholas	1713

Stanhope, 1714–17 (formed Sept. 1714)

1st Ld Treas.	Charles Montagu, E. of Halifax	11 Oct. 1714
	Charles Howard, E. of Carlisle	23 May 1715
	Robert Walpole	10 Oct. 1715
Chanc. Exch.	Richard Onslow	13 Oct. 1714
	Robert Walpole	12 Oct. 1715
Ld Pres.	Daniel Finch, E. of Nottingham	22 Sept. 1714
	William Cavendish, D. of Devonshire	6 July 1716
Ld Chanc.	William Cowper, Ld Cowper	21 Sept. 1714
PS	Thomas Wharton, Earl Wharton (Seal in Commission 30 Apr.– 2 Sept. 1715)	27 Sept. 1714
	Charles Spencer, E. of Sunderland	2 Sept. 1715
	Evelyn Pierrepoint, D. of Kingston-Upon-Hull	19 Dec. 1716
D. Lanc.	Heneage Finch, E. of Aylesford	4 Nov. 1714
	Richard Lumley, E. of Scarborough	12 Mar. 1716
Master-Gen. of Ordnance	John Churchill, D. of Marlborough	1 Oct. 1714
Sec. of State (South)	James Stanhope, Vt Stanhope	27 Sept. 1714
	Paul Methuen	22 June 1716
Sec. of State (North)	Charles Townshend, Vt Townshend	17 Sept. 1714
	James Stanhope, Vt Stanhope	12 Dec. 1716
Sec. for Scotland	James Graham, D. of Montrose	24 Sept. 1714
	John Ker, D. of Roxburghe	13 Dec. 1716
Pay.-Gen.	Robert Walpole	17 Sept. 1714
	E. of Lincoln	Oct. 1715
Admir.	Edward Russell, E. of Orford	14 Oct. 1714
Sec. at War	William Pulteney, E. of Bath	Sept. 1714
BOT	Francis North, Ld Guildford	15 Sept. 1713
	William Berkeley, Ld Berkeley	13 Dec. 1714
	Henry Howard, E. of Suffolk and Bindon	12 May 1715
Ld Lt of Ireland	Charles Spencer, E. of Sunderland	4 Oct. 1714
	Charles Townshend, Vt Townshend	13 Feb. 1717

Stanhope–Sunderland, 1717–18 (formed Apr. 1717)

1st Ld Treas.	James Stanhope, Vt Stanhope (Earl Stanhope, 1718)	12 Apr. 1717
Chanc. Exch.	James Stanhope, Vt Stanhope (Earl Stanhope, 1718)	15 Apr. 1717
Ld Pres.	Vacant from 30 Mar. 1717	
Ld Chanc.	William Cowper, Ld Cowper	21 Sept. 1714
Sec. of State (South)	Joseph Addison	15–16 Apr. 1717
Sec. of State (North)	Charles Spencer, E. of Sunderland	15–16 Apr. 1717
Sec. for Scotland	John Ker, D. of Roxburghe	13 Dec. 1716
PS	Evelyn Pierrepoint, D. of Kingston-Upon-Hull	19 Dec. 1716
D. Lanc.	Richard Lumley, E. of Scarborough	12 Mar. 1716
	Nicholas Lechmere, Ld Lechmere	19 June 1717
Pay.-Gen.	E. of Lincoln	Oct. 1715
Admir.	James Berkeley, E. of Berkeley	16 Apr. 1717
BOT	Henry Howard, E. of Suffolk and Bindon	12 May 1715
	Robert Darcy, E. of Holdernesse	31 Jan. 1718
Lt Lt of Ireland	Charles Powlett, D. of Bolton	27 Apr. 1717

Reconstructed Stanhope–Sunderland, 1718–21 (Mar. 1718)

1st Ld Treas.	Charles Spencer, E. of Sunderland	21 Mar. 1718
Ld Pres.	Charles Spencer, E. of Sunderland	16 Mar. 1718
	Evelyn Pierrepoint, D. of Kingston-Upon-Hull	6 Feb. 1719
	Charles Townshend, Vt Townshend	11 June 1720
Ld Chanc.	Thomas Parker, Ld Macclesfield	12 May 1718
Sec. of State (North)	James Stanhope, Earl Stanhope (d. 4 Feb. 1721)	18–21 Mar. 1718
	Charles Townshend, Vt Townshend	10 Feb. 1721
Sec. of State (South)	James Craggs (d. 16 Feb. 1721)	16 Mar. 1718
Chanc. Exch.	John Aislabie	20 Mar. 1718

PS	Evelyn Pierrepoint, D. of Kingston-Upon-Hull	19 Dec. 1716
	Henry Grey, D. of Kent	14 Feb. 1719
	Evelyn Pierrepoint, D. of Kingston-Upon-Hull	13 June 1720
Pay.-Gen.	E. of Lincoln	Oct. 1715
	Robert Walpole	11 June 1720
BOT	Robert Darcy, E. of Holdernesse	31 Jan. 1718
	Thomas Fane, E. of Westmorland	11 May 1719
Ld Lt of Ireland	Charles Powlett, D. of Bolton	27 Apr. 1717
	Charles, D. of Grafton	8 June 1720
Sec. for Scotland	John Ker, D. of Roxburghe	13 Dec. 1716
Admir.	James Berkeley, E. of Berkeley	16 Apr. 1717

Walpole 1721–42 (formed Apr. 1721)

1st Ld Treas.	Robert Walpole	4 Apr. 1721
Chanc. Exch.	Robert Walpole	3 Apr. 1721
Ld Chanc.	Thomas Parker, Ld Macclesfield (Seal in Commission Jan. 1725)	12 May 1718
	Peter King, Ld King	1 June 1725
	Charles Talbot, Ld Talbot of Hensol (d. 14 Feb. 1737)	29 Nov. 1733
	Philip Yorke, Ld Hardwicke	21 Feb. 1737
Ld Pres.	Charles Townshend, Vt Townshend	11 June 1720
	Henry Boyle, Ld Carleton	25 June 1721
	William Cavendish, D. of Devonshire (d. 4 June 1729)	27 Mar. 1725
	Thomas Trevor, Ld Trevor of Bromham (d. 19 June 1730)	8 May 1730
	Spencer Compton, E. of Wilmington	31 Dec. 1730
PS	Evelyn Pierrepoint, D. of Kingston-Upon-Hull (d. 5 Mar. 1726)	13 June 1720
	Thomas Trevor, Ld Trevor of Bromham	10 Mar. 1726
	Spencer Compton, E. of Wilmington (Seal in Commission 1 Jan. 1731)	8 May 1730
	William Cavendish, D. of Devonshire	12 June 1731

COMPOSITION OF ADMINISTRATIONS

	Henry Lowther, Vt Lonsdale	8 May 1733
	Francis Godolphin, E. of Godolphin	15 May 1735
	John Hervey, Ld Hervey of Ickworth	29 Apr. 1740
Admir.	James Berkeley, E. of Berkeley	16 Apr. 1717
	George Byng, Vt Torrington	29 July 1727
	Sir Charles Wager	25 Jan. 1733
D. Lanc.	Nicholas Lechmere (Ld Lechmere 1721)	19 June 1717
	John Manners, D. of Rutland	24 July 1727
	George Cholmondeley, E. of Cholmondeley	17 May 1736
Sec. of State (South)	John Carteret, Ld Carteret	4 Mar. 1721
	Thomas Pelham-Holles, D. of Newcastle-Upon-Tyne	6 Apr. 1724
Sec. of State (North)	Charles Townshend, Vt Townshend (vac. 16 May 1730)	10 Feb. 1721
	William Stanhope, Ld Harrington	19 June 1730
BOT	Thomas Fane, E. of Westmorland	11 May 1719
	Benjamin Mildmay, Earl Fitzwalter	14 May 1735
	John Monson, Ld Monson	27 June 1737
Ld Lt of Ireland	Charles, D. of Grafton	8 June 1720
	John Carteret, Ld Carteret	6 May 1724
	Lionel Cranfield, E. of Dorset	23 June 1730
	William Cavendish, D. of Devonshire	9 Apr. 1737

Carteret, 1742–44 (formed Feb. 1742)

1st Ld Treas.	Spencer Compton, E. of Wilmington	16 Feb. 1742
	Henry Pelham	27 Aug. 1743
Chanc. Exch.	Samuel Sandys, Ld Sandys	12 Feb. 1742
	Henry Pelham	12 Dec. 1743
Sec. of State (North)	John Carteret, Ld Carteret	12 Feb. 1742
Sec. of State (South)	Thomas Pelham-Holles, D. of Newcastle-Upon-Tyne	6 Apr. 1724
Ld Pres.	William Stanhope, E. of Harrington	13 Feb. 1742
Ld Chanc.	Philip Yorke, Ld Hardwicke	21 Feb. 1737

PS	John Hervey, Ld Hervey of Ickworth	29 Apr. 1740
	John Leveson-Gower, Ld Gower	13 July 1742
	George Cholmondeley, E. of Cholmondeley	12 Dec. 1743
D. Lanc.	George Cholmondeley, E. of Cholmondeley	17 May 1736
	Richard Edgcumbe, Ld Edgcumbe of Mount-Edgcumbe	22 Dec. 1743
BOT	John Monson, Ld Monson	27 June 1737
Admir.	Sir Charles Wager	25 Jan. 1733
	Daniel Finch, E. of Winchilsea and Nottingham	19 Mar. 1742
Ld Lt of Ireland	William Cavendish, D. of Devonshire	9 Apr. 1737

Pelham, 1744–46 (formed Nov. 1744)

1st Ld Treas.	Henry Pelham	27 Aug. 1743
Chanc. Exch.	Henry Pelham	12 Dec. 1743
Sec. of State (North)	William Stanhope, E. of Harrington	24 Nov. 1744
Sec. of State (South)	Thomas Pelham-Holles, D. of Newcastle-Upon-Tyne	6 Apr. 1724
Ld Pres.	William Stanhope, E. of Harrington	13 Feb. 1742
	Lionel Cranfield Sackville, D. of Dorset	3 Jan. 1745
Ld Chanc.	Philip Yorke, Ld Hardwicke	21 Feb. 1737
PS	George Cholmondeley, E. of Cholmondeley	12 Dec. 1743
	John Leveson-Gower, Ld Gower	26 Dec. 1744
D. Lanc.	Richard Edgcumbe, Ld Edgcumbe of Mount-Edgcumbe	22 Dec. 1743
BOT	John Monson, Ld Monson	27 June 1737
Admir.	Daniel Finch, E. of Winchilsea and Nottingham	19 Mar. 1742
	John Russell, D. of Bedford	27 Dec. 1744
Ld Lt of Ireland	William Cavendish, D. of Devonshire	9 Apr. 1737
	Philip Dormer Stanhope, E. of Chesterfield	8 Jan. 1745

COMPOSITION OF ADMINISTRATIONS

Bath, 1746 (Feb. 1746)
On 6 February 1746, George II asked the Earl of Bath (William Pulteney) and Earl Granville (John Carteret) to form a new administration, taking the offices of First Lord of the Treasury and Secretary of State (North) respectively. Henry Pelham, the Duke of Newcastle-Upon-Tyne, the Earl of Harrington and Lord Hardwicke resigned office. Although Bath and Granville took office for a few days, the King was forced to reappoint the previous administration.

Pelham, 1746–54 (formed Feb. 1746)

1st Ld Treas.	Henry Pelham	14 Feb. 1746
Chanc. Exch.	Henry Pelham	12 Dec. 1743
Sec. of State	William Stanhope, E. of Harrington	14 Feb. 1746
(North)	(vac. 28 Oct. 1746)	
	Philip Dormer Stanhope, E. of Chesterfield	29 Oct. 1746
	(vac. 6 Feb. 1748)	
	Thomas Pelham-Holles, D. of Newcastle-Upon-Tyne	6–12 Feb. 1748
Sec. of State (South)	Thomas Pelham-Holles, D. of Newcastle-Upon-Tyne	14 Feb. 1746
	John Russell, D. of Bedford	6–12 Feb. 1748
	(vac. 13 June 1751)	
	Robert Darcy, E. of Holdernesse	18 June 1751
Ld Pres.	Lionel Cranfield Sackville, D. of Dorset	3 Jan. 1751
	John Carteret, Earl Granville	17 June 1751
PS	John Leveson-Gower, Ld Gower	26 Dec. 1744
D. Lanc.	Richard Edgcumbe, Ld Edgcumbe of Mount-Edgcumbe	22 Dec. 1743
BOT	John Monson, Ld Monson	27 June 1737
	George Montagu, E. of Halifax	1 Nov. 1748
Admir.	John Russell, D. of Bedford	27 Dec. 1744
	John Montagu, E. of Sandwich	20 Feb. 1748
	George Anson, Ld Anson	22 June 1751
Ld Lieut. of Ireland	William Stanhope, E. of Harrington	Nov. 1746

Newcastle, 1754–56 (formed Mar. 1754)

1st Ld Treas.	Thomas Pelham-Holles, D. of Newcastle-Upon-Tyne	16 Mar. 1754
Chanc. Exch.	Sir William Lee	8 Mar. 1754
	Henry Bilson Legge	6 Apr. 1754
	Sir George Lyttelton	25 Nov. 1755

Ld Pres.	John Carteret, Earl Granville	17 June 1751
PS	John Leveson-Gower, Ld Gower (d. 25 Dec. 1754)	26 Dec. 1744
	Charles Spencer, D. of Marlborough	9 Jan. 1755
	Granville Leveson-Gower, Earl Gower	22 Dec. 1755
D. Lanc.	Richard Edgcumbe, Ld Edgcumbe of Mount-Edgcumbe	22 Dec. 1743
Sec. of State (North)	Robert Darcy, E. of Holdernesse	23 Mar. 1754
Sec. of State (South)	Sir Thomas Robinson (vac. Oct. 1755)	23 Mar. 1754
	Henry Fox (vac. 13 Nov. 1756)	14 Nov. 1755
BOT	George Montagu, E. of Halifax	1 Nov. 1748
Admir.	George Anson, Ld Anson	22 June 1751
Ld Lt of Ireland	Lionel Cranfield, D. of Dorset	15 Dec. 1750
	William Cavendish, D. of Devonshire	2 Apr. 1755

Pitt–Devonshire, 1756–57 (formed Nov. 1756)

1st Ld Treas.	William Cavendish, D. of Devonshire	16 Nov. 1756
Chanc. Exch.	Henry Bilson Legge	16 Nov. 1756
	William Murray, Ld Mansfield	13 Apr. 1757
PS	Granville Leveson-Gower, Earl Gower	22 Dec. 1755
D. Lanc.	Richard Edgcumbe, Ld Edgcumbe of Mount-Edgcumbe	22 Dec. 1743
Sec. of State (South)	William Pitt (dism. 6 Apr. 1757)	4 Dec. 1756
Sec. of State (North)	Robert Darcy, E. of Holdernesse (vac. 9 June 1757)	23 Mar. 1754
BOT	George Montagu, E. of Halifax	1 Nov. 1748
Admir.	Richard Grenville, Earl Temple	19 Nov. 1756
	Daniel Finch, E. of Winchilsea and Nottingham	6 Apr. 1757
Treas. of Navy	George Granville	25 Nov. 1756
Ld Lt of Ireland	William Cavendish, D. of Devonshire	2 Apr. 1755
	John Russell, D. of Bedford	3 Jan. 1757

COMPOSITION OF ADMINISTRATIONS 53

Pitt–Newcastle, 1757–61 (formed July 1757)

1st Ld Treas.	Thomas Pelham-Holles, D. of Newcastle-Upon-Tyne	29 June 1757
Chanc. Exch.	Henry Bilson Legge	2 July 1757
	William Wildman Barrington-Shute, Vt Barrington	19 Mar. 1761
Ld Pres.	John Carteret, Earl Granville	17 June 1751
PS	Richard Grenville-Temple, Earl Temple	5 July 1757
Ld Keeper	Sir Richard Henley	30 June 1757
D. Lanc.	Richard Edgcumbe, Ld Edgcumbe of Mount-Edgcumbe	22 Dec. 1743
	Thomas Hay, E. of Kinnoull and Ld Hay	24 Jan. 1758 (renewed 27 Feb. 1760)
Sec. of State (South)	William Pitt	27 June 1757
Sec. of State (North)	Robert Darcy, E. of Holdernesse	23 Mar. 1754
	John Stuart, E. of Bute	25 Mar. 1761
BOT	George Montagu, E. of Halifax	1 Nov. 1748
Admir.	George Anson, Ld Anson	2 July 1757
Treas. of Navy	George Grenville	25 Nov. 1756
Sec. at War	William Wildman Barrington-Shute, Vt Barrington	14 Nov. 1755
	Charles Townshend	18 Mar. 1761
Pay.-Gen.	Henry Fox	July 1757
Ld Lt of Ireland	John Russell, D. of Bedford	3 Jan. 1757

Bute–Newcastle, 1761–62 (formed Oct. 1761)

1st Ld Treas.	Thomas Pelham-Holles, D. of Newcastle-Upon-Tyne	29 June 1757
Chanc. Exch.	William Wildman Barrington-Shute, Vt Barrington	19 Mar. 1761
Ld Pres.	John Carteret, Earl Granville	17 June 1751
Ld Chanc.	Ld Henley	16 Jan. 1761
Sec. of State (South)	E. of Egremont	9 Oct. 1761
Sec. of State (North)	John Stuart, E. of Bute	25 Mar. 1761
BOT	Ld Sandys	21 Mar. 1761
Admir.	George Anson, Ld Anson	2 July 1757

PS	Richard Grenville-Temple, Earl Temple (Seal in Commission 16 Oct.– 25 Nov. 1761)	5 July 1757
	D. of Bedford	25 Nov. 1761
D. Lanc.	Thomas Hay, E. of Kinnoull and Ld Hay	24 Jan. 1758
Master-Gen. of Ordnance	Earl Ligonier	1 July 1759
Treas. of Navy	George Grenville	25 Nov. 1756
Sec. at War	Charles Townshend	18 Mar. 1761
Pay.-Gen.	Henry Fox	July 1757

Bute, 1762–63 (formed May 1762)

1st Ld Treas.	John Stuart, E. of Bute	26 May 1762
Chanc. Exch.	Sir F. Dashwood, Ld Le Despenser	29 May 1762
Ld Pres.	John Carteret, Earl Granville	17 June 1751
Ld Chanc.	Ld Henley	16 Jan. 1761
Sec. of State (South)	E. of Egremont	9 Oct. 1761
Sec. of State (North)	George Grenville	27 May 1762
	George Montagu, E. of Halifax	14 Oct. 1762
BOT	Ld Sandys	21 Mar. 1761
	Charles Townshend	1 Mar. 1763
Admir.	George Anson, Ld Anson	2 July 1757
	George Montagu, E. of Halifax	19 June 1762
	George Grenville	2 Jan. 1763
PS	D. of Bedford	25 Nov. 1761
D. Lanc.	Thomas Hay, E. of Kinnoull and Ld Hay	24 Jan. 1758
	Ld Strange	13 Dec. 1762
Master-Gen. of Ordnance	Earl Ligonier	1 July 1759
Treas. of Navy	William Wildman Barrington-Shute, Vt Barrington	8 May 1762
Sec. at War	Charles Townshend	18 Mar. 1761
	Welbore Ellis	Nov. 1762
	Ld Mendip	17 Dec. 1762
Pay.-Gen.	Henry Fox	July 1757

Grenville, 1763–65 (formed Apr. 1763)

1st Ld Treas	George Grenville	16 Apr. 1763
Chanc. Exch.	George Grenville	16 Apr. 1763

Ld Pres.	D. of Bedford	9 Sept. 1763
Ld Chanc.	Ld Henley	16 Jan. 1761
Sec. of State	E. of Egremont	9 Oct. 1761
(South)	George Montagu, E. of Halifax	9 Sept. 1763
Sec. of State	George Montagu, E. of Halifax	14 Oct. 1762
(North)	E. of Sandwich	9 Sept. 1763
BOT	Ld Wycombe	20 Apr. 1763
	E. of Hillsborough	9 Sept. 1763
Admir.	E. of Sandwich	23 Apr. 1763
	E. of Egmont	10 Sept. 1763
PS	D. of Marlborough	22 Apr. 1763
D. Lanc.	Ld Strange	13 Dec. 1762
Master-Gen. of Ordnance	M. of Granby	1 July 1763
Treas. of Navy	William Wildman Barrington-Shute, Vt Barrington	8 May 1762
Sec. at War	Ld Mendip	17 Dec. 1762
Pay.-Gen.	Henry Fox	July 1757

First Rockingham, 1765–66 (formed July 1765)

1st Ld Treas.	M. of Rockingham	13 July 1765
Chanc. Exch.	W. Dowdeswell	16 July 1765
Ld Pres.	E. of Winchilsea and Nottingham	12 July 1765
Ld Chanc.	Sir R. Henley	16 Jan. 1761
Sec. of State	H.S. Conway	12 July 1765
(South)	D. of Richmond	23 May 1766
Sec. of State	D. of Grafton	12 July 1765
(North)	H.S. Conway	23 May 1766
BOT	E. of Dartmouth	20 July 1765
Admir.	E. of Egmont	10 Sept. 1763
PS	D. of Newcastle-Upon-Tyne	15 July 1765
D. Lanc.	Ld Strange	13 Dec. 1762
Master-Gen. of Ordnance	M. of Granby	1 July 1763
Treas. of Navy	Vt Howe	9 Aug. 1765
Sec. at War	William Wildman Barrington-Shute, Vt Barrington	19 July 1765
Pay.-Gen.	Charles Townshend	May 1765

Chatham, 1766–68 (formed July 1766)

1st Ld Treas.	D. of Grafton	2 Aug. 1766
Chanc. Exch.	Charles Townshend	2 Aug. 1766
	Ld Mansfield	11 Sept. 1767
	Ld North	6 Oct. 1767

Ld Pres.	E. of Northington	30 July 1766
	Earl Gower	23 Dec. 1767
Ld Chanc.	Ld Camden	30 July 1766
Sec. of State (South)	E. of Shelburne	30 July 1766
Sec. of State (North)	H.S. Conway	23 May 1766
	Vt Weymouth	20 Jan. 1768
BOT	E. of Hillsborough	16 Aug. 1766
	Vt Clare	18 Dec. 1766
	E. of Hillsborough	20 Jan. 1768
Am. Cols	Ld Harwich	20 Jan. 1768
Admir.	Sir E. Hawke	10 Dec. 1766
PS	E. of Chatham (Seal in Commission Feb.–Mar. 1768. Chatham resumed office 21 Mar. 1768.)	30 July 1766
D. Lanc.	Ld Strange	13 Dec. 1762
Master-Gen. of Ordnance	M. of Granby	1 July 1763
Treas. of Navy	Vt Howe	9 Aug. 1765
Sec. at War	William Wildman Barrington-Shute, Vt Barrington	19 July 1765
Pay.-Gen.	Charles Townshend	May 1765
	Ld North and G. Cooke	10 Dec. 1766
	G. Cooke and T. Townshend	23 Dec. 1767

Grafton, 1768–70 (formed Oct. 1768)

1st Ld Treas.	D. of Grafton	2 Aug. 1766
Chanc. Exch.	Ld North	6 Oct. 1767
Ld Pres.	Earl Gower	23 Dec. 1767
Ld Chanc.	Ld Camden	30 July 1766
	C. Yorke	17 Jan. 1770
Sec. of State (South)	Vt Weymouth	21 Oct. 1768
Sec. of State (North)	E. of Rochford	21 Oct. 1768
BOT	E. of Hillsborough	20 Jan. 1768
Am. Cols	Ld Harwich	20 Jan. 1768
Admir.	Sir E. Hawke	10 Dec. 1766
PS	E. of Bristol	2 Nov. 1768
D. Lanc.	Ld Strange	13 Dec. 1762
Master-Gen. of Ordnance	M. of Granby	1 July 1763

Treas. of Navy	Vt Howe	9 Aug. 1765
Sec. at War	William Wildman Barrington-Shute, Vt Barrington	19 July 1765

North, 1770–82 (formed Jan. 1770)

1st Ld Treas.	Ld North	28 Jan. 1770
Chanc. Exch.	Ld North	6 Oct. 1767
Ld Pres.	Earl Gower	23 Dec. 1767
	Earl Bathurst	24 Nov. 1779
Ld Chanc.	(Seal in Commission 20 Jan. 1770–23 Jan. 1771)	
	Ld Apsley (Earl Bathurst 1775)	23 Jan. 1771
	Ld Thurlow	3 June 1778
Sec. of State	Vt Weymouth	21 Oct. 1768
(South)	E. of Rochford	19 Dec. 1770
	Vt Weymouth	9 Nov. 1775
	E. of Hillsborough	24 Nov. 1779
Sec. of State	E. of Rochford	21 Oct. 1768
(North)	E. of Sandwich	19 Dec. 1770
	E. of Halifax	22 Jan. 1771
	E. of Suffolk and Berkshire	12 June 1771
	Vt Weymouth (sole secretary)	7 Mar. 1779
	Vt Stormont (Secretariat reorganised Mar. 1782)	27 Oct. 1779
BOT	E. of Hillsborough	20 Jan. 1768
	E. of Dartmouth	31 Aug. 1772
	Ld Sackville-Germain	10 Nov. 1775
	E. of Carlisle	6 Nov. 1779
	Ld Grantham	9 Dec. 1780
Am. Cols	Ld Harwich	20 Jan. 1768
	E. of Dartmouth	14 Aug. 1772
	Ld Sackville-Germain	10 Nov. 1775
	W. Ellis (office abolished same year)	17 Feb. 1782
Admir.	Sir E. Hawke	10 Dec. 1766
	E. of Sandwich	12 Jan. 1771
PS	E. of Halifax	26 Feb. 1770
	E. of Suffolk and Berkshire	22 Jan. 1771
	D. of Grafton	12 June 1771
	E. of Dartmouth	10 Nov. 1775
D. Lanc.	Ld Strange	13 Dec. 1762
	Ld Hyde (E. of Clarendon 1776)	14 June 1771
Master-Gen.	M. of Granby	1 July 1763
of Ordnance	Vt Townshend	1 Oct. 1772

Treas. of Navy	Sir G. Elliot	19 Mar. 1770
	Ld Mendip	12 June 1777
Sec. at War	Vt Barrington	19 July 1765
	C. Jenkinson (later Ld Liverpool)	16 Dec. 1778

Second Rockingham, 1782 (formed Mar. 1782)

1st Ld Treas.	M. of Rockingham	27 Mar. 1782
Chanc. Exch.	Ld J. Cavendish	1 Apr. 1782
Ld Pres.	Ld Camden	27 Mar. 1782
Ld Chanc.	Ld Thurlow	3 June 1778
Home O.	E. of Shelburne	27 Mar. 1782
For. O.	C.J. Fox	27 Mar. 1782
BOT	Ld Grantham	9 Dec. 1780
Admir.	Vt Keppel	30 Mar. 1782
PS	D. of Grafton	27 Mar. 1782
D. Lanc.	Ld Ashburton	17 Apr. 1782
Master-Gen. of Ordnance	D. of Richmond	30 Mar. 1782
Treas. of Navy	I. Barré	10 Apr. 1782
Sec. at War	T. Townshend	27 Mar. 1782
Pay.-Gen.	E. Burke	27 Mar. 1782
Comm.-in-Chief	Gen. Conway	Mar. 1782

Shelburne 1782–83 (formed July 1782)

1st Ld Treas.	E. of Shelburne	14 July 1782
Chanc. Exch.	William Pitt	13 July 1782
Ld Pres.	Ld Camden	27 Mar. 1782
Ld Chanc.	Ld Thurlow	3 June 1778
Home O.	T. Townshend (Ld Sydney 1783)	10 July 1782
For. O.	Ld Grantham	17 July 1782
BOT	Ld Grantham	9 Dec. 1780
Admir.	Vt Keppel	30 Mar. 1782
	Vt Howe	28 Jan. 1783
PS	D. of Grafton	27 Mar. 1782
D. Lanc.	Ld Ashburton	17 Apr. 1782
Master-Gen. of Ordnance	D. of Richmond	30 Mar. 1782
Treas. of Navy	H. Dundas	19 Aug. 1782
Sec. at War	Sir G. Yonge	11 July 1782
Pay.-Gen.	I. Barré	17 July 1782

COMPOSITION OF ADMINISTRATIONS

Ld Steward	D. of Rutland	14 Feb. 1783
Comm.-in-Chief	Gen. Conway	Mar. 1782

Fox–North, 1783 (formed Apr. 1783)

1st Ld Treas.	D. of Portland	2 Apr. 1783
Chanc. Exch.	Ld J. Cavendish	5 Apr. 1783
Ld Pres.	Vt Stormont	2 Apr. 1783
Ld Chanc.	(Seal in commission 9 Apr–23 Dec. 1783)	
Home O.	Ld North	2 Apr. 1783
	Earl Temple	10 Dec. 1783
For. O.	C.J. Fox	2 Apr. 1783
BOT	Ld Grantham	9 Dec. 1780
Admir.	Vt Keppel	8 Apr. 1783
PS	E. of Carlisle	2 Apr. 1783
D. Lanc.	Ld Ashburton	17 Apr. 1782
	E. of Derby	29 Aug. 1783
Master-Gen. of Ordnance	D. of Richmond	30 Apr. 1782
	Vt Townshend	23 Dec. 1783
Treas. of Navy	Charles Townshend	11 Apr. 1783
Sec. at War	R. Fitzpatrick	11 Apr. 1783
Pay.-Gen.	E. Burke	8 Apr. 1783

Pitt, 1783–1801 (formed Dec. 1783)

1st Ld Treas.	William Pitt	19 Dec. 1783
Chanc. Exch.	William Pitt	27 Dec. 1783
Ld Pres.	Earl Gower	19 Dec. 1783
	Ld Camden	1 Dec. 1784
	Earl Fitzwilliam	11 July 1794
	E. of Mansfield	17 Dec. 1794
	E. of Chatham	21 Sept. 1796
Ld Chanc.	Ld Thurlow	23 Dec. 1783
	(Seal in commission June 1792–28 Jan. 1793)	
	Ld Loughborough	28 Jan. 1793
Home O.	Ld Sydney	23 Dec. 1783
	W. Grenville (Ld Grenville 1790)	5 June 1789
	H. Dundas	8 June 1791
	D. of Portland	11 July 1794
For. O.	Earl Temple	19 Dec. 1783
	M. of Carmarthen (D. of Leeds 1789)	23 Dec. 1783
	Ld Grenville	8 June 1791

BOT	Ld Grantham	9 Dec. 1780
	Ld Sydney	5 Mar. 1784
	Ld Hawkesbury	23 Aug. 1786
	(E. of Liverpool 1796)	
War and Cols (transferred from Home Office 1794)	H. Dundas	11 July 1794
Bd Control	Ld Sydney (Vt Sydney 1789)	3 Sept. 1784
	Ld Grenville	12 Mar. 1790
	H. Dundas	28 June 1793
Admir.	Earl Howe	30 Dec. 1783
	E. of Chatham	12 July 1788
	Earl Spencer	20 Dec. 1794
PS	D. of Rutland	23 Dec. 1783
	(Seal in commission 8 Mar–22 Nov. 1784)	
	Earl Gower (M. of Stafford 1786)	22 Nov. 1784
	D. of Marlborough	16 July 1794
	E. of Chatham	17 Dec. 1794
	E. of Westmorland	14 Feb. 1798
D. Lanc.	E. of Clarendon	31 Dec. 1783
	Ld Hawkesbury	6 Sept. 1786
	(E. of Liverpool 1796)	
Master-Gen. of Ordnance	D. of Richmond	13 Jan. 1784
	C.M. Cornwallis	13 Feb. 1795
Treas. of Navy	H. Dundas	5 Jan. 1784
	D. Ryder	2 June 1800
Sec. at War	Sir G. Yonge	24 Dec. 1783
	W. Windham	11 July 1794
Mins without portfolio	E. of Mansfield	June 1798–
	Earl Camden	Feb. 1801
Comm.-in-Chief	Ld Amherst	Jan. 1793

Addington, 1801–4 (formed Feb. 1801)

1st Ld Treas.	H. Addington	17 Mar. 1801
Chanc. Exch.	H. Addington	21 Mar. 1801
Ld Pres.	E. of Chatham	21 Sept. 1796
	D. of Portland	30 July 1801
Ld Chanc.	Ld Loughborough	28 Jan. 1793
	Ld Eldon	14 Apr. 1801

Home O.	D. of Portland	11 July 1794
	Ld Pelham	30 July 1801
	C.P. Yorke	17 Aug. 1803
For. O.	Ld Hawkesbury	20 Feb. 1801
	(2nd E. of Liverpool 1808)	
BOT	Ld Hawkesbury	23 Aug. 1786
	(E. of Liverpool 1796)	
War and Cols	Ld Hobart	17 Mar. 1801
Bd Control	H. Dundas	28 June 1793
	E. of Dartmouth	19 May 1801
	Vt Castlereagh	12 July 1802
Admir.	E. of St Vincent	19 Feb. 1801
PS	E. of Westmorland	14 Feb. 1798
D. Lanc.	E. of Liverpool	6 Sept. 1786
	Ld Pelham	11 Nov. 1803
Master-Gen.	C.M. Cornwallis	13 Feb. 1795
of Ordnance	E. of Chatham	16 June 1801
Treas.	D. Ryder	2 June 1800
of Navy	C. Bragge	21 Nov. 1801
	G. Tierney	3 June 1803
Sec. at War	C. Yorke	20 Feb. 1801
	C. Bragge	17 Aug. 1803
Master of	Ld Arden	18 Apr. 1801
Mint	J. Smyth	2 July 1802

Pitt, 1804–6 (formed May 1804)

1st Ld Treas.	William Pitt	10 May 1804
Chanc. Exch.	William Pitt	13 May 1804
Ld Pres.	D. of Portland	30 July 1801
	H. Addington	14 Jan. 1805
	(Vt Sidmouth 1805)	
	Earl Camden	10 July 1805
Ld Chanc.	Ld Eldon	14 Apr. 1801
Home O.	Ld Hawkesbury	12 May 1804
For. O.	Ld Harrowby	14 May 1804
	Ld Mulgrave	11 Jan. 1805
BOT	Ld Hawkesbury	23 Aug. 1786
	D. of Montrose	6 June 1804
War and	Earl Camden	12 May 1804
Cols	Vt Castlereagh	10 June 1805
Bd Control	Vt Castlereagh	12 July 1802
Admir.	Vt Melville	15 May 1804
	Ld Barham	30 Apr. 1805

PS	E. of Westmorland	14 Feb. 1798
D. Lanc.	Ld Mulgrave	6 June 1804
	E. of Buckinghamshire	14 Jan. 1805
	Ld Harrowby	10 July 1805
Master-Gen. of Ordnance	E. of Chatham	16 June 1801
Treas. of Navy	G. Canning	29 May 1804
Sec. at War	W. Dundas	15 May 1804
Master of Mint	Earl Bathurst	7 July 1804

All the Talents, 1806–7 (formed Feb. 1806)

1st Ld Treas.	Ld Grenville	11 Feb. 1806
Chanc. Exch.	Ld H. Petty	5 Feb. 1806
Ld Pres.	Earl Fitzwilliam	19 Feb. 1806
	Vt Sidmouth	8 Oct. 1806
Ld Chanc.	Ld Erskine	7 Feb. 1806
Home O.	Earl Spencer	5 Feb. 1806
For. O.	C.J. Fox	7 Feb. 1806
	Vt Howick	24 Sept. 1806
BOT	Ld Auckland	5 Feb. 1806
War and Cols	W. Windham	14 Feb. 1806
Bd Control	Ld Minto	12 Feb. 1806
	T. Grenville	16 July 1806
	G. Tierney	1 Oct. 1806
Admir.	C. Grey (Vt Howick, Apr. 1806)	11 Feb. 1806
	T. Grenville	29 Sept. 1806
PS	Vt Sidmouth	5 Feb. 1806
	Ld Holland	15 Oct. 1806
D. Lanc.	E. of Derby	12 Feb. 1806
Master-Gen. of Ordnance	E. of Moira	14 Feb. 1806
Treas. of Navy	R.B. Sheridan	22 Feb. 1806
Sec. at War	R. Fitzpatrick	7 Feb. 1806
Master of Mint	Ld Spencer	20 Feb. 1806
	C. Bathurst	27 Oct. 1806
Ld Chief Justice of the King's Bench	Ld Ellenborough	Feb. 1806
Min. without Portfolio	Earl Fitzwilliam	8 Oct. 1806

Portland, 1807–9 (formed Mar. 1807)

1st Ld Treas.	D. of Portland	31 Mar. 1807
Chanc. Exch.	S. Perceval	26 Mar. 1807
Ld Pres.	Earl Camden	26 Mar. 1807
Ld Chanc.	Ld Eldon	1 Apr. 1807
Home O.	Ld Hawkesbury	25 Mar. 1807
	(E. of Liverpool 1808)	
For. O.	G. Canning	25 Mar. 1807
BOT	Earl Bathurst	26 Mar. 1807
War and Cols	Vt Castlereagh	25 Mar. 1807
Bd Control	R. Dundas	6 Apr. 1807
	E. of Harrowby	17 July 1809
	R. Dundas	13 Nov. 1809
Admir.	Ld Mulgrave	4 Apr. 1807
PS	E. of Westmorland	25 Mar. 1807
D. Lanc.	S. Perceval	30 Mar. 1807
Master-Gen. of Ordnance	E. of Chatham	4 Apr. 1807
Treas. of Navy	G. Rose	15 Apr. 1807
Sec. at War	J.M. Pulteney	30 Mar. 1807
	Ld Gower	27 June 1809
Master of Mint	Earl Bathurst	25 Apr. 1807

Perceval, 1809–12 (formed Oct. 1809)

1st Ld Treas.	S. Perceval	4 Oct. 1809
Chanc. Exch.	S. Perceval	26 Mar. 1807
Ld Pres.	Earl Camden	26 Mar. 1807
	Vt Sidmouth	8 Apr. 1812
Ld Chanc.	Ld Eldon	1 Apr. 1807
Home O.	R. Ryder	1 Nov. 1809
For. O.	Earl Bathurst	11 Oct. 1809
	Ld Wellesley	6 Dec. 1809
	Vt Castlereagh	4 Mar. 1812
BOT	Earl Bathurst	26 Mar. 1807
War and Cols	E. of Liverpool	31 Oct. 1809
Bd Control	R. Dundas (Vt Melville 1811)	13 Nov. 1809
	E. of Buckinghamshire	7 Apr. 1812
Admir.	Ld Mulgrave	4 Apr. 1807
	C.P. Yorke	1 May 1810
	Vt Melville	24 Mar. 1812
PS	E. of Westmorland	25 Mar. 1807
D. Lanc.	S. Perceval	30 Mar. 1807

Master-Gen.	E. of Chatham	4 Apr. 1807
of Ordnance	E. of Mulgrave	5 May 1810
Treas.	G. Rose	15 Apr. 1807
of Navy		
Sec. at War	Vt Palmerston	27 Oct. 1809
Master of	Earl Bathurst	25 Apr. 1807
Mint		
Mins without	D. of Portland	Oct. 1809
portfolio	E. of Harrowby	Nov. 1809–June 1812
	Earl Camden	Apr.–June 1812

Liverpool, 1812–27 (formed June 1812)

1st Ld Treas.	E. of Liverpool	18 June 1812
Chanc. Exch.	N. Vansittart, Ld Bexley	9 June 1812
	F.J. Robinson	21 Jan. 1823
Ld Pres.	E. of Harrowby	11 June 1812
Ld Chanc.	Ld Eldon	1 Apr. 1807
Home O.	Vt Sidmouth	11 June 1812
	Robert Peel	17 Jan. 1822
For. O.	Vt Castlereagh	4 Mar. 1812
	G. Canning	16 Sept. 1822
BOT	Earl Bathurst	26 Mar. 1807
	E. of Clancarty	29 Sept. 1812
	F.J. Robinson	24 Jan. 1818
	W. Huskisson	31 Jan. 1823
War and	Earl Bathurst	11 June 1812
Cols		
Bd Control	E. of Buckinghamshire	7 Apr. 1812
	G. Canning	20 June 1816
	C. Bathurst	16 Jan. 1821
	C.W. Williams Wynn	8 Feb. 1822
Admir.	Vt Melville	24 Mar. 1812
PS	E. of Westmorland	25 Mar. 1807
D. Lanc.	C. Bathurst	23 June 1812
	E. of Buckinghamshire	23 Aug. 1812
	N. Vansittart	13 Feb. 1823
Master-Gen.	E. of Mulgrave	5 May 1810
of Ordnance	D. of Wellington	1 Jan. 1819
Treas.	G. Rose	15 Apr. 1807
of Navy	F.J. Robinson	12 Feb. 1818
	W. Huskisson	8 Feb. 1823
Sec. at War	Vt Palmerston	27 Oct. 1809

Master of	E. of Clancarty	30 Oct. 1812
Mint	W. Wellesley Pole	28 Sept. 1814
	T. Wallace	9 Oct. 1823
Mins without	Earl Camden	June–Dec. 1812
portfolio	E. of Mulgrave	Jan. 1819–May 1820

3.3 Major office-holders

First Lord of the Treasury

11 Oct. 1714	Charles Montagu, E. of Halifax
23 May 1715	Charles Howard, E. of Carlisle
10 Oct. 1715	Robert Walpole
12 Apr. 1717	Earl Stanhope
21 Mar. 1718	Charles Spencer, E. of Sunderland
4 Apr. 1721	Robert Walpole*
16 Feb. 1742	Spencer Compton, E. of Wilmington
27 Aug. 1743	Henry Pelham
6 Feb. 1746	E. of Bath†
14 Feb. 1746	Henry Pelham
16 Mar. 1754	Thomas Pelham-Holles, D. of Newcastle-Upon-Tyne
16 Nov. 1756	William Cavendish, D. of Devonshire
29 June 1757	Thomas Pelham-Holles, D. of Newcastle-Upon-Tyne
26 May 1762	John Stuart, E. of Bute
16 Apr. 1763	George Grenville
13 July 1765	M. of Rockingham
July 1766	E. of Chatham
Oct. 1768	D. of Grafton
28 Jan. 1770	Ld North
27 Mar. 1782	M. of Rockingham
14 July 1782	E. of Shelburne
2 Apr. 1783	D. of Portland
19 Dec. 1783	William Pitt
17 Mar. 1801	H. Addington
13 May 1804	William Pitt
11 Feb. 1806	Ld Grenville
31 Mar. 1807	D. of Portland
4 Oct. 1809	S. Perceval
18 June 1812	E. of Liverpool

* No office of Prime Minister existed in this period, but it is customary to regard Walpole as the first to wield Prime Ministerial authority. It was also to become common for such authority to be combined with the post of First Lord of the Treasury, but not in every case. See Section 3.2 for the offices held by the leading politicians in successive administrations.

† For the interruption of Henry Pelham's tenure of office in February 1746 *see* p. 18.

Lord Chancellor

1689–93	Seal in commission
23 Mar. 1693	Ld Somers
21 May 1700	Sir Nathan Wright (Ld Keeper)
11 Oct. 1705	William Cowper, Ld Cowper
29 Sept. 1708	Seal in commission
19 Oct. 1710	Ld Harcourt
21 Sept. 1714	William Cowper, Ld Cowper
12 May 1718	Thomas Parker, E. of Macclesfield
Jan. 1725	In commission
1 June 1725	Peter King, Ld King
29 Nov. 1733	Charles Talbot, Ld Talbot
21 Feb. 1737	Philip Yorke, E. of Hardwicke
20 Nov. 1756	Seal in commission
30 June 1757	Ld Henley (E. of Northington, 1764)
30 July 1766	Ld Camden
17 Jan. 1770	C. Yorke
20 Jan. 1770	Seal in commission
23 Jan. 1771	Earl Bathurst
3 June 1778	Ld Thurlow
9 Apr. 1783	Seal in commission
23 Dec. 1783	Ld Thurlow
June 1792	Seal in commission
28 Jan. 1793	Ld Loughborough (E. of Rosslyn, 1801)
14 Apr. 1801	Ld Eldon
7 Feb. 1806	Ld Erskine
1 Apr. 1807	Ld Eldon (E. of Eldon, 1821)
2 May 1827	Ld Lyndhurst

Lord President of the Council

14 Feb. 1689	Thomas Osborne, D. of Leeds
18 May 1699	Thomas Herbert, E. of Pembroke
29 Jan. 1702	Charles Seymour, D. of Somerset
9 July 1702	Thomas Herbert, E. of Pembroke
25 Nov. 1708	John Somers, Ld Somers
21 Sept. 1710	Laurence Hyde, E. of Rochester
14 June 1711	John Sheffield, D. of Buckinghamshire and of Normanby
22 Sept. 1714	Daniel Finch, E. of Nottingham
6 July 1716	William Cavendish, D. of Devonshire
16 Mar. 1718	Charles Spencer, E. of Sunderland
6 Feb. 1719	Evelyn Pierrepoint, D. of Kingston-Upon-Hull
11 June 1720	Charles Townshend, Vt Townshend
25 June 1721	Henry Boyle, Ld Carleton

27 Mar. 1725	William Cavendish, D. of Devonshire
8 May 1730	Thomas Trevor, Ld Trevor of Bromham
31 Dec. 1730	Spencer Compton, E. of Wilmington
13 Feb. 1742	William Stanhope, E. of Harrington
3 Jan. 1745	Lionel Cranfield Sackville, D. of Dorset
17 June 1751	John Carteret, E. Granville
9 Sept. 1763	D. of Bedford
12 July 1765	E. of Winchilsea and Nottingham
30 July 1766	E. of Northington
23 Dec. 1767	Earl Gower
24 Nov. 1779	Earl Bathurst
27 Mar. 1782	Ld Camden
2 Apr. 1783	Vt Stormont
19 Dec. 1783	Earl Gower
1 Dec. 1784	Earl Camden
11 July 1794	Earl Fitzwilliam
17 Dec. 1794	E. of Mansfield
21 Sept. 1796	E. of Chatham
30 July 1801	D. of Portland
14 Jan. 1805	Vt Sidmouth
10 July 1805	Earl Camden
19 Feb. 1806	Earl Fitzwilliam
8 Oct. 1806	Vt Sidmouth
26 Mar. 1807	Earl Camden
8 Apr. 1812	Vt Sidmouth
11 June 1812	E. of Harrowby

Lord Privy Seal

Mar. 1689	M. of Halifax
Feb. 1690	In commission
Mar. 1692	E. of Montgomery
May 1699	Vt Lonsdale
Nov. 1700	E. of Tankerville
June 1701	Seal in commission
27 Apr. 1702	John Sheffield, M. of Normanby (D. of Buckinghamshire and Normanby, 1703)
21 Mar. 1705	John Holles, D. of Newcastle-Upon-Tyne
31 Aug. 1711	John Robinson, Bp of Bristol
21 Aug. 1713	William Legge, E. of Dartmouth
27 Sept. 1714	Thomas Wharton, M. of Wharton
30 Apr. 1715	In commission
2 Sept. 1715	Charles Spencer, E. of Sunderland
19 Dec. 1716	Evelyn Pierrepoint, D. of Kingston-Upon-Hull
14 Feb. 1719	Henry Grey, D. of Kent

13 June 1720	Evelyn Pierrepoint, D. of Kingston-Upon-Hull
10 Mar. 1726	Thomas Trevor, Ld Trevor of Bromham
8 May 1730	Spencer Compton, E. of Wilmington
1 Jan. 1731	In commission
12 June 1731	William Cavendish, D. of Devonshire
8 May 1733	Henry Lowther, Vt Lonsdale
15 May 1735	Francis Godolphin, E. of Godolphin
29 Apr. 1740	John Hervey, Ld Hervey of Ickworth
13 July 1742	John Leveson-Gower, Ld Gower
12 Dec. 1743	George Cholmondeley, E. of Cholmondeley
26 Dec. 1744	John Leveson-Gower, Ld Gower
9 Jan. 1755	Charles Spencer, D. of Marlborough
22 Dec. 1755	Granville Leveson-Gower, Earl Gower
5 July 1757	Richard Grenville-Temple, Earl Temple
16 Oct. 1761	Seal in commission
25 Nov. 1761	D. of Bedford
22 Apr. 1763	D. of Marlborough
15 July 1765	D. of Newcastle-Upon-Tyne
30 July 1766	E. of Chatham
Feb. 1768	Seal in commission
21 Mar. 1768	E. of Chatham
2 Nov. 1768	E. of Bristol
26 Feb. 1770	E. of Halifax
22 Jan. 1771	E. of Suffolk and Berkshire
12 June 1771	D. of Grafton
10 Nov. 1775	E. of Dartmouth
27 Mar. 1782	D. of Grafton
2 Apr. 1783	E. of Carlisle
23 Dec. 1783	D. of Rutland
8 Mar. 1784	Seal in commission
22 Nov. 1784	Earl Gower (M. of Stafford, 1786)
16 July 1794	D. of Marlborough
17 Dec. 1794	E. of Chatham
14 Feb. 1798	E. of Westmorland
5 Feb. 1806	Vt Sidmouth
15 Oct. 1806	Ld Holland
25 Mar. 1807	E. of Westmorland

Secretary of State for the Northern Department

28 Oct. 1688	Richard Graham, Vt Preston
5 Mar. 1689	Daniel Finch, E. of Nottingham
26 Dec. 1690	Henry Sydney, Vt Sydney
3 Mar. 1693	Sir John Trenchard
23 Mar. 1694	Charles Talbot, D. of Shrewsbury

3 May 1695	Sir William Trumbull
2 Dec. 1697	James Vernon
5 Nov. 1700	Sir Charles Hedges
4 Jan. 1702	James Vernon
2 May 1702	Sir Charles Hedges
18 May 1704	Robert Harley
13 Feb. 1708	Henry Boyle
21 Sept. 1710	Henry St John (Vt Bolingbroke)
17 Aug. 1713	William Bromley
17 Sept. 1714	Charles Townshend, Vt Townshend
12 Dec. 1716	James Stanhope, Vt Stanhope
15–16 Apr. 1717	Charles Spencer, E. of Sunderland
18–21 Mar. 1718	James Stanhope, Earl Stanhope
10 Feb. 1721	Charles Townshend, Vt Townshend
19 June 1730	William Stanhope, E. of Harrington
12 Feb. 1742	John Carteret, Earl Granville
24 Nov. 1744	William Stanhope, E. of Harrington
6 Feb. 1746	John Carteret, Earl Granville
14 Feb. 1746	William Stanhope, E. of Harrington
29 Oct. 1746	Philip Dormer Stanhope, E. of Chesterfield
6–12 Feb. 1748	Thomas Pelham-Holles, D. of Newcastle-Upon-Tyne
23 Mar. 1754	Robert Darcy, E. of Holdernesse
25 Mar. 1761	John Stuart, E. of Bute
27 May 1762	George Grenville
14 Oct. 1762	E. of Halifax
9 Sept. 1763	E. of Sandwich
12 July 1765	D. of Grafton
23 May 1766	H.S. Conway
20 Jan. 1768	Vt Weymouth
21 Oct. 1768	E. of Rochford
19 Dec. 1770	E. of Sandwich
22 Jan. 1771	E. of Halifax
12 June 1771	E. of Suffolk and Berkshire
7 Mar. 1779	Vt Weymouth
27 Oct. 1779	Vt Stormont

Secretary of State for the Southern Department

14 Feb. 1689	Charles Talbot, E. of Shrewsbury
26 Dec. 1690	Daniel Finch, E. of Nottingham
3 Mar. 1693	Daniel Finch, E. of Nottingham (again)
2 Mar. 1694	Sir John Trenchard
30 Apr. 1695	Charles Talbot, D. of Shrewsbury
14 May 1699	Edward Villiers, E. of Jersey

5 Nov. 1700	James Vernon
4 Jan. 1702	Charles Montagu, E. of Manchester
2 May 1702	Daniel Finch, E. of Nottingham
18 May 1704	Sir Charles Hedges
3 Dec. 1706	Charles Spencer, E. of Sunderland
15 June 1710	William Legge, Ld (E. of) Dartmouth
17 Aug. 1713	Henry St John, Vt Bolingbroke
27 Sept. 1714	James Stanhope, Vt Stanhope
22 June 1716	Paul Methuen
15–16 Apr. 1717	Joseph Addison
16 Mar. 1718	James Craggs
4 Mar. 1721	John Carteret, Ld Carteret
6 Apr. 1724	Thomas Pelham-Holles, D. of Newcastle-Upon-Tyne
6–12 Feb. 1748	John Russell, D. of Bedford
18 June 1751	Robert Darcy, E. of Holdernesse
23 Mar. 1754	Sir Thomas Robinson
14 Nov. 1755	Henry Fox
4 Dec. 1756	William Pitt
6 Apr. 1757	Robert Darcy, E. of Holdernesse
27 June 1757	William Pitt
9 Oct. 1761	E. of Egremont
9 Sept. 1763	E. of Halifax
12 July 1765	H.S. Conway
23 May 1766	D. of Richmond
30 July 1766	E. of Shelburne
21 Oct. 1768	Vt Weymouth
19 Dec. 1770	E. of Rochford
9 Nov. 1775	Vt Weymouth
24 Nov. 1779	E. of Hillsborough

Chancellor of the Exchequer

9 Apr. 1689	Henry Booth, Ld Delamere
18 Mar. 1690	Richard Hampden
27 Apr. 1694	Charles Montagu
31 May 1699	John Smith
29 Mar. 1701	Henry Boyle
11 Feb. 1708	John Smith
10 Aug. 1710	Robert Harley
14 June 1711	R. Benson
1 Nov. 1713	Sir William Wyndham
13 Oct. 1714	Sir Richard Onslow
12 Oct. 1715	Robert Walpole
15 Apr. 1717	James Stanhope, Earl Stanhope

20 Mar. 1718	John Aislabie
21 Feb. 1721	Sir John Pratt
3 Apr. 1721	Sir Robert Walpole
12 Feb. 1742	Samuel Sandys, Ld Sandys
12 Dec. 1743	Henry Pelham
8 Mar. 1754	Sir William Lee
6 Apr. 1754	Henry Bilson Legge
25 Nov. 1755	Sir George Lyttelton
16 Nov. 1756	Henry Bilson Legge
13 Apr. 1757	William Murray, Ld Mansfield
2 July 1757	Henry Bilson Legge
19 Mar. 1761	William Wildman Barrington-Shute, Vt Barrington
29 May 1762	Sir Francis Dashwood, Ld Le Despenser
16 Apr. 1763	George Grenville
16 July 1765	W. Dowdeswell
2 Aug. 1766	Charles Townshend
11 Sept. 1767	Ld Mansfield
6 Oct. 1767	Ld North
1 Apr. 1782	Ld J. Cavendish
13 July 1782	William Pitt
5 Apr. 1783	Ld J. Cavendish
27 Dec. 1783	William Pitt
21 Mar. 1801	H. Addington
10 May 1804	William Pitt
5 Feb. 1806	Ld H. Petty
21 Mar. 1807	S. Perceval
9 June 1812	Nicholas Vansittart, Ld Bexley
21 Jan. 1823	F.J. Robinson

Secretary of State for the Home Department

27 Mar. 1782	E. of Shelburne
10 July 1782	T. Townshend (Ld Sydney, 1783)
2 Apr. 1783	Ld North
10 Dec. 1783	Earl Temple
23 Dec. 1783	Ld Sydney
5 June 1789	W. Grenville (Ld Grenville, 1790)
8 June 1791	H. Dundas
11 July 1794	D. of Portland
30 July 1801	Ld Pelham
17 Aug. 1803	C.P. Yorke
12 May 1804	Ld Hawkesbury
5 Feb. 1806	Earl Spencer
25 Mar. 1807	Ld Hawkesbury (E. of Liverpool, 1808)
1 Nov. 1809	R. Ryder

11 June 1812   Vt Sidmouth
17 Jan. 1822   Robert Peel

Secretary of State for Foreign Affairs
27 Mar. 1782   C.J. Fox
17 July 1782   Ld Grantham
 2 Apr. 1783   C.J. Fox
   Dec. 1783   Earl Temple
23 Dec. 1783   M. of Camarthen (D. of Leeds, 1789)
 8 June 1791   Ld Grenville
20 Feb. 1801   Ld Hawkesbury (2nd E. of Liverpool, 1808)
14 May 1804   Ld Harrowby
11 Jan. 1805   Ld Mulgrave
 7 Feb. 1806   C.J. Fox
24 Sept. 1806   Charles Grey, Vt Howick
25 Mar. 1807   G. Canning
11 Oct. 1809   Earl Bathurst
 6 Dec. 1809   Ld Wellesley
 4 Mar. 1812   Vt Castlereagh
16 Sep. 1822   George Canning

Secretary of State for the American Colonies
20 Jan. 1768   Ld Harwich
14 Aug. 1772   E. of Dartmouth
10 Nov. 1775   Ld Sackville-Germain
17 Feb. 1782   W. Ellis

Secretary of State for War and the Colonies
11 July 1794   H. Dundas
17 Mar. 1801   Ld Hobart
12 May 1804   Earl Camden
10 June 1805   Vt Castlereagh
14 Feb. 1806   W. Windham
25 Mar. 1807   Vt Castlereagh
31 Oct. 1809   E. of Liverpool
11 June 1812   Earl Bathurst

First Lord of the Admiralty
28 Feb. 1689   Arthur Herbert, E. of Torrington
20 Jan. 1690   Thomas Herbert, E. of Pembroke
10 Mar. 1692   Charles Cornwallis, Ld Cornwallis
15 Apr. 1693   Anthony Cary (Vt Falkland)
 2 May 1694   Edward Russell, E. of Orford
31 May 1699   John Egerton, E. of Bridgwater

4 Apr. 1701	Thomas Herbert, E. of Pembroke
20 May 1702	Prince George of Denmark
28 Oct. 1708	Queen Anne
29 Nov. 1708	Thomas Herbert, E. of Pembroke
8 Nov. 1709	Edward Russell, E. of Orford
4 Oct. 1710	Sir John Leake
30 Sept. 1712	Thomas Wentworth, E. of Strafford
14 Oct. 1714	Edward Russell, E. of Orford
16 Apr. 1717	James Berkeley, E. of Berkeley
29 July 1727	George Byng, Vt Torrington
25 Jan. 1733	Sir Charles Wager
19 Mar. 1742	Daniel Finch, E. of Winchilsea and Nottingham
27 Dec. 1744	John Russell, D. of Bedford
20 Feb. 1748	John Montagu, E. of Sandwich
22 June 1751	George Anson, Ld Anson
19 Nov. 1756	Richard Grenville, Earl Temple
6 Apr. 1757	Daniel Finch, E. of Winchilsea and Nottingham
2 July 1757	George Anson, Ld Anson
19 June 1762	E. of Halifax
2 Jan. 1763	George Grenville
23 Apr. 1763	E. of Sandwich
10 Sept. 1763	E. of Egmont
10 Sept. 1766	Sir Charles Saunders
10 Dec. 1766	Sir E. Hawke
12 Jan. 1771	E. of Sandwich
30 Mar. 1782	Vt Keppel
28 Jan. 1783	Vt Howe
8 Apr. 1783	Vt Keppel
30 Dec. 1783	Earl Howe
12 July 1788	E. of Chatham
20 Dec. 1794	Earl Spencer
19 Feb. 1801	E. of St Vincent
15 May 1804	Vt Melville
30 Apr. 1805	Ld Barham
11 Feb. 1806	Vt Howick
29 Sept. 1806	T. Grenville
4 Apr. 1807	Ld Mulgrave
1 May 1810	C.P. Yorke
24 Mar. 1812	Vt Melville
Apr. 1827	D. of Clarence

President of the Board of Trade (since 1696)

15 May 1696	John Egerton, E. of Bridgwater
9 June 1699	Thomas Grey, E. of Stamford

MAJOR OFFICE-HOLDERS 75

12 June 1702	Thomas Thynne, Vt Weymouth
25 Apr. 1707	Thomas Grey, E. of Stamford
12 June 1711	Charles Finch, E. of Winchilsea
15 Sept. 1713	Francis North, Ld Guildford
13 Dec. 1714	William Berkeley, Ld Berkeley
12 May 1715	Henry Howard, E. of Suffolk and Bindon
31 Jan. 1718	Robert Darcy, E. of Holdernesse
11 May 1719	Thomas Fane, E. of Westmorland
14 May 1735	Benjamin Mildmay, Earl Fitzwalter
27 June 1737	John Monson, Ld Monson
1 Nov. 1748	George Montagu, E. of Halifax
21 Mar. 1761	Ld Sandys
1 Mar. 1763	Charles Townshend
20 Apr. 1763	Ld Wycombe
9 Sep. 1763	E. of Hillsborough
20 July 1765	E. of Dartmouth
16 Aug. 1766	E. of Hillsborough
18 Dec. 1766	Vt Clare
20 Jan. 1768	E. of Hillsborough
31 Aug. 1772	E. of Dartmouth
10 Nov. 1775	Ld Sackville-Germain
6 Nov. 1779	E. of Carlisle
9 Dec. 1780	Ld Grantham
5 Mar. 1784	Ld Sydney
23 Aug. 1786	Ld Hawkesbury, E. of Liverpool (1796)
6 June 1804	D. of Montrose
5 Feb. 1806	Ld Auckland
26 Mar. 1807	Earl Bathurst
29 Sept. 1812	E. of Clancarty
24 Jan. 1818	Frederick John Robinson
31 Jan. 1823	William Huskisson

Chancellor of the Duchy of Lancaster

25 May 1687	Robert Phelipps
21 Mar. 1689	Thomas Bertie, D. of Ancaster and Kesteven
4 May 1697	Thomas Grey, E. of Stamford
12 May 1702	Sir John Leveson-Gower, Ld Gower
1 June 1706	James Stanley, E. of Derby
21 Sept. 1710	William Berkeley, Ld Berkeley
4 Nov. 1714	Heneage Finch, E. of Aylesford
12 Mar. 1716	Richard Lumley, E. of Scarborough
19 June 1717	Nicholas Lechmere, Ld Lechmere
24 July 1727	John Manners, D. of Rutland
17 May 1736	George Cholmondeley, E. of Cholmondeley

22 Dec. 1743	Richard Edgcumbe, Ld Edgcumbe of Mount Edgcumbe
24 Jan. 1758	Thomas Hay, E. of Kinnoull and Ld Hay
13 Dec. 1762	Ld Strange
14 June 1771	Ld Hyde, E. of Clarendon
17 Apr. 1782	Ld Ashburton
29 Aug. 1783	E. of Derby
31 Dec. 1783	E. of Clarendon
6 Sept. 1786	E. of Liverpool
11 Nov. 1803	Ld Pelham
6 June 1804	Ld Mulgrave
14 Jan. 1805	E. of Buckinghamshire
10 July 1805	Ld Harrowby
12 Feb. 1806	E. of Derby
30 Mar. 1807	S. Perceval
23 June 1812	C. Bathurst
23 Aug. 1812	E. of Buckinghamshire

Lord Lieutenant of Ireland (since 1700)

Dec. 1700	E. of Rochester
Feb. 1703	D. of Ormond
Apr. 1707	E. of Pembroke
Dec. 1708	E. of Wharton
Oct. 1710	D. of Ormond
Sept. 1713	D. of Shrewsbury
4 Oct. 1714	E. of Sunderland
13 Feb. 1717	Vt Townshend
27 Apr. 1717	D. of Bolton
8 June 1720	D. of Grafton
6 May 1724	Ld Carteret
23 June 1730	D. of Dorset
9 Apr. 1737	D. of Devonshire
8 Jan. 1745	E. of Chesterfield
Nov. 1746	E. of Harrington
15 Dec. 1750	D. of Dorset
2 Apr. 1755	D. of Devonshire
3 Jan. 1757	D. of Bedford
Apr. 1761	E. of Halifax
Apr. 1763	E. of Northumberland
June 1765	Vt Weymouth
Aug. 1765	E. of Hertford
Oct. 1766	E. of Bristol
Aug. 1767	Vt Townshend
Oct. 1772	E. of Harcourt

MAJOR OFFICE-HOLDERS 77

Dec. 1776	E. of Buckinghamshire
Nov. 1780	E. of Carlisle
Apr. 1782	D. of Portland
Aug. 1782	M. of Buckingham
May 1783	E. of Northington
Feb. 1784	D. of Rutland
Nov. 1787	M. of Buckingham
Oct. 1789	E. of Westmorland
Dec. 1794	Earl Fitzwilliam
Mar. 1795	Earl Camden
June 1798	M. Cornwallis
Apr. 1801	E. of Hardwicke
Mar. 1806	D. of Bedford
Apr. 1807	D. of Richmond
June 1813	Earl Whitworth
Oct. 1817	Earl Talbot

Secretary at War

Aug. 1683	William Blathwayt
20 Apr. 1704	Henry St John, Vt Bolingbroke
25 Feb. 1708	Robert Walpole
28 Sept. 1710	George Granville, Ld Lansdowne
28 June 1712	Sir William Wyndham
21 Aug. 1713	Francis Gwyn
Sept. 1714	William Pulteney, E. of Bath
Apr. 1717	James Craggs
Mar. 1718	Vt Castlecomer
May 1718	Robert Pringle
Dec. 1718	George Treby
Apr. 1724	Henry Pelham
May 1730	Sir William Strickland
May 1735	Sir William Yonge
July 1746	Henry Fox
14 Nov. 1755	William Wildman Barrington-Shute, Vt Barrington
18 Mar. 1761	Charles Townshend
Nov. 1762	Welbore Ellis
17 Dec. 1762	Ld Mendip
19 July 1765	William Wildman Barrington-Shute, Vt Barrington
16 Dec. 1778	Ld Hawkesbury
27 Mar. 1782	T. Townshend
11 July 1782	Sir G. Yonge
11 Apr. 1783	R. Fitzpatrick
24 Dec. 1783	Sir G. Yonge
11 July 1794	W. Windham

20 Feb. 1801	C. Yorke	
17 Aug. 1803	C. Bragge	
15 May 1804	W. Dundas	
7 Feb. 1806	R. Fitzpatrick	
30 Mar. 1807	J.M. Pulteney	
27 June 1809	Ld Gower	
27 Oct. 1809	Vt Palmerston	

Paymaster-General

1713	Thomas Moore and Edward Nicholas
17 Sept. 1714	Robert Walpole
Oct. 1715	E. of Lincoln
11 June 1720	Robert Walpole
Apr. 1721	Ld Cornwallis
1722	Spencer Compton
May 1730	Henry Pelham
1743	Sir Thomas Winnington
May 1746	William Pitt
Nov. 1755	{ E. of Darlington { Vt Dupplin
July 1757	Henry Fox
May 1765	Charles Townshend
10 Dec. 1766	Ld North and G. Cooke
23 Dec. 1767	G. Cooke and T. Townshend
Dec. 1768	R. Rigby
27 Mar. 1782	E. Burke
17 July 1782	I. Barré
8 Apr. 1783	E. Burke
Jan. 1784	W. Grenville
Apr. 1784	W. Grenville and Ld Mulgrave
Sept. 1789	Ld Mulgrave and M. of Graham
Mar. 1791	D. Ryder and T. Steele
July 1800	T. Steele and G. Canning
Mar. 1801	T. Steele and Ld Glenbervie
Jan. 1803	T. Steele and J.H. Addington
July 1804	G. Rose and Ld Somerset

SECTION FOUR

Parliament, elections and parliamentary reform

4.1 The House of Commons

Speakers of the House of Commons, 1688–1817

Date of election	Name	Constituency
19 May 1685	Sir John Trevor (1637–1717)	Denbigh
22 Jan. 1689	Henry Powle (1630–92)	Windsor
20 Mar. 1690	Sir John Trevor (1637–1717)	Yarmouth (I. of W.)
14 Mar. 1695	Paul Foley (1645–99)	Hereford
6 Dec. 1698	Sir Thomas Littleton (1647–1710)	Woodstock
10 Feb. 1701	Robert Harley (1661–1724)	New Radnor
25 Oct. 1705	John Smith (1655–1723)	Andover
16 Nov. 1708	Sir Richard Onslow (1654–1717)	Surrey
25 Nov. 1710	William Bromley (1664–1732)	Oxford University
16 Feb. 1714	Sir Thomas Hanmer (1677–1746)	Suffolk
17 Mar. 1715	Sir Spencer Compton (1673–1743)	Sussex
23 Jan. 1728	Arthur Onslow (1691–1768)	Surrey
3 Nov. 1761	Sir John Cust (1718–70)	Grantham
22 Jan. 1770	Sir Fletcher Norton (1716–89)	Guildford
31 Oct. 1780	Charles Wolfran Cornwall (1735–89)	Winchelsea
5 Jan. 1789	William Wyndham Grenville (1759–1834)	Buckinghamshire
8 June 1789	Henry Addington (1757–1844)	Truro
11 Feb. 1801	Sir John Mitford (1748–1830)	Northumberland
10 Feb. 1802	Charles Abbot (1757–1829)	Woodstock
2 June 1817	Charles Manners-Sutton (1780–1858)	Scarborough

Composition of the House

Period	England	Wales	Scotland	Ireland	County	Borough	Univ.	Total
1688–1707	489	24	—	—	92	417	4	513
1707–1800	489	24	45	—	122	432	4	558
1801–26	489	24	45	100	186	467	5	658

Prior to 1707, the House of Commons returned 513 members, 489 from England and 24 from Wales. The counties returned 92 members, the boroughs 417 and the ancient universities 4.

During the period 1707–00, after the addition of the Scottish members, the House of Commons returned 558 members, representing 314 constituencies. The detailed breakdown of these figures was as follows:

England, 489 members, 245 constituencies:
- 40 counties, returning 2 members each;
- 196 boroughs, returning 2 members each;
- 2 boroughs (London and the combined constituency of Weymouth and Melcombe Regis), returning 4 members each;
- 5 boroughs (Abingdon, Banbury, Bewdley, Higham Ferrers and Monmouth), returning 1 member each;
- 2 universities (Oxford and Cambridge) returning 2 members each.

Wales, 24 members, 24 constituencies:
- 12 12 counties, returning 1 member each;
- 12 boroughs, returning 1 member each.

Scotland, 45 members, 45 constituencies:
- 27 counties, returning 1 member each;
- 3 pairs of counties, 1 county in each pair alternating with the other in returning 1 member;
- 1 burgh (Edinburgh), returning 1 member;
- 14 groups of burghs, each returning 1 member.

This representation remained the same until 1800, when as a result of the Act of Union, total membership of the House of Commons increased to 658, with Ireland returning exactly 100 members, as follows:

	County	Borough	Univ.	Total
32 two-member counties	64			
2 two-member boroughs (Cork, Dublin)		4		
31 single-member boroughs		31		
Trinity College, Dublin			1	
Total, Ireland	64	35	1	100
Total, England, Scotland and Wales	122	432	4	558
Total, United Kingdom	186	467	5	658

Public petitions

A feature of the work of the House of Commons during the early part of the nineteenth century was the public petitions, which occupied a great part of the chamber's time. It was not until 1839 that these debates were discontinued, with their place gradually being taken by Questions to Ministers.

Session	No. of petitions presented
1785	298
1801	192
1812–13	1,699
1827	3,635
1833	10,394

The franchise

England and Wales

By a statute of 1430 (18 Hen. VI c.7), in the counties the voting qualification was the possession of freehold property valued for the land tax at 40 shillings per annum – the 40s. freeholder. In the boroughs various qualifications applied. The main types were:

Scot and Lot (SL) Right of voting vested in inhabitant householders paying poor rate.
Householder (H) Also known as 'potwalloper' franchise. Right of voting vested in all inhabitant householders not receiving alms or poor relief.
Burgage (B) Franchise attached to property in the borough.
Corporation (C) Right of voting confined to the corporation.
Freeman (FM) Right of voting belonged to the freemen of the borough (in the City of London in the livery, rather than in the freemen as a whole).
Freeholder (FH) Right of voting lay with the freeholders.

Scotland

In the Scottish counties the franchise belonged to freeholders possessing land valued at 40s. 'of old extent' or to owners of land rated at £400 Scots (*c.* £35 sterling). In Sutherland the vote also extended to tenants of the Earl of Sutherland. The Scottish boroughs, or burghs, were combined in groups for the purpose of electing MPs by a process of indirect election. Voting was vested in the small burgh councils.

Classification of English boroughs, 1760

Electors	SL	H	B	C	FM	FH	Total
5,000+	1	1	—	—	5	—	7
1,001–5,000	6	2	—	—	24	4	36
601–1,000	7	5	—	—	9	1	22
301–600	10	1	—	—	13	—	24
101–300	8	5	10	1	11	1	36
51–100	4	—	10	2	5	—	21
50–	2	—	15	26	13	—	56
Total	38	14	35	29	80	6	202

English counties

Constituency	MPs	Electors (est.)	Pop. 1831
Bedfordshire	2	2,000	95,483
Berkshire	2	3,000	145,389
Buckinghamshire	2	4,000	146,529
Cambridgeshire	2	3,000	143,955
Cheshire	2	5,000	334,391
Cornwall	2	2,500	302,440
Cumberland	2	4,000	169,681
Derbyshire	2	4,000	237,170
Devon	2	3,000	494,478
Dorset	2	3,000	159,252
Durham	2	3,000	253,910
Essex	2	6,000	317,507
Gloucestershire	2	6,000	387,019
Hampshire	2	5,000	314,280
Herefordshire	2	4,000	111,211
Hertfordshire	2	4,000	143,341
Huntingdonshire	2	2,000	53,192
Kent	2	8,000	479,155
Lancashire	2	8,000	1,336,854
Leicestershire	2	6,000	197,003
Lincolnshire	2	5,000	317,465
Middlesex	2	3,000	1,358,330
Monmouthshire	2	1,500	98,130
Norfolk	2	6,000	390,054
Northamptonshire	2	3,000	179,336
Northumberland	2	2,000	237,000
Nottinghamshire	2	3,000	225,000
Oxfordshire	2	4,000	152,156
Rutland	2	800	19,385
Shropshire	2	4,000	222,938
Somerset	2	8,000	404,200
Staffordshire	2	5,000	410,512
Suffolk	2	5,000	296,317
Surrey	2	4,000	486,326
Sussex	2	4,000	272,340
Warwickshire	2	4,000	336,610
Westmorland	2	2,000	55,041
Wiltshire	2	3,000	240,156
Worcestershire	2	4,000	211,563
Yorkshire	2	20,000	1,371,675

English boroughs, c. 1760

Constituency	Type of seat	MPs	Electors (est.)
Abingdon	SL	1	250
Aldborough	SL	2	50
Aldeburgh	FM	2	50
Amersham	SL	2	70
Andover	C	2	24
Appleby	B	2	250
Arundel	SL	2	200
Ashburton	B	2	250
Aylesbury	H	2	500
Banbury	C	1	18
Barnstaple	FM	2	350
Bath	C	2	30
Bedford	FM	2	1,000
Bere Alston	B	2	30–
Berwick-on-Tweed	FM	2	600
Beverley	FM	2	1,000
Bewdley	FM	1	50–
Bishop's Castle	FM	2	150
Bletchingley	B	2	90
Bodmin	C	2	36
Boroughbridge	B	2	64
Bossiney	FM	2	30–
Boston	FM	2	250
Brackley	C	2	33
Bramber	B	2	36
Bridgnorth	FM	2	1,000
Bridgwater	SL	2	250
Bridport	SL	2	200
Bristol	FM	2	5,000
Buckingham	C	2	13
Bury St Edmunds	C	2	37
Callington	SL	2	50
Calne	C	2	25
Cambridge	FM	2	150
Camelford	FM	2	20
Canterbury	FM	2	1,500
Carlisle	FM	2	1,000
Castle Rising	FM	2	50
Chester	FM	2	1,500
Chichester	SL	2	500

Constituency	Type of seat	MPs	Electors (est.)
Chippenham	B	2	129
Chipping Wycombe	FM	2	50
Christchurch	C	2	70
Cirencester	H	2	800
Clitheroe	B	2	102
Cockermouth	B	2	278
Colchester	FM	2	1,500
Corfe Castle	SL	2	100
Coventry	FM	2	2,500
Cricklade	FH	2	200–1,000
Dartmouth	FM	2	50–
Derby	FM	2	700
Devizes	C	2	30
Dorchester	SL	2	400
Dover	FM	2	1,000
Downton	B	2	100
Droitwich	C	2	14
Dunwich	FM	2	40–
Durham	FM	2	1,500
East Grinstead	B	2	36
East Looe	FM	2	50
East Retford	FM	2	150
Evesham	FM	2	1,000
Exeter	FM	2	1,500
Eye	SL	2	200
Fowey	SL	2	100
Gatton	SL	2	2
Gloucester	FM	2	2,000
Grampound	FM	2	50
Grantham	FM	2	400
Great Bedwyn	B	2	120
Great Grimsby	FM	2	200
Great Marlow	SL	2	250
Great Yarmouth	FM	2	800
Guildford	FM	2	200
Harwich	C	2	32
Haslemere	FH	2	100
Hastings	FM	2	50–
Hedon	FM	2	150
Helston	C	2	30–
Hereford	FM	2	1,000

Constituency	Type of seat	MPs	Electors (est.)
Hertford	FM	2	500
Heytesbury	B	2	26
Higham Ferrers	FM	1	80
Hindon	H	2	200
Honiton	H	2	700
Horsham	B	2	80
Huntingdon	FM	2	200–
Hythe	FM	2	100
Ilchester	H	2	200
Ipswich	FM	2	700
King's Lynn	FM	2	300
Kingston-Upon-Hull	FM	2	1,200
Knaresborough	B	2	100
Lancaster	FM	2	2,500
Launceston	FM	2	30–
Leicester	FM	2	2,500
Leominster	SL	2	500
Lewes	SL	2	200
Lichfield	FM	2	700
Lincoln	FM	2	1,000
Liskeard	FM	2	50
Liverpool	FM	2	2,000
London	FM	4	7,000
Lostwithiel	C	2	24
Ludgershall	FH	2	100
Ludlow	FM	2	500
Lyme Regis	FM	2	50
Lymington	FM	2	50–
Maidstone	FM	2	1,000
Maldon	FM	2	800–
Malmesbury	C	2	13
Malton	B	2	300
Marlborough	C	2	12–
Midhurst	B	2	200
Milborne Port	SL	2	120
Minehead	H	2	300
Mitchell	SL	2	50
Monmouth	FM	1	800
Morpeth	FM	2	250
Newark	SL	2	1,000

THE HOUSE OF COMMONS 89

Constituency	Type of seat	MPs	Electors (est.)
Newcastle-Under-Lyme	FM	2	600
Newcastle-Upon-Tyne	FM	2	2,500
Newport	B	2	200
Newport (I. of W.)	C	2	24
New Romney	C	2	40
New Shoreham	SL	2	100–800
Newton	C	2	36
Newtown (I. of W.)	B	2	40–
New Windsor	SL	2	300
Northallerton	B	2	200
Northampton	H	2	1,000
Norwich	FM	2	3,000
Nottingham	FM	2	2,000
Okehampton	FM	2	300
Old Sarum	B	2	7
Orford	FM	2	50–
Oxford	FM	2	1,000
Penryn	SL	2	200
Peterborough	SL	2	400
Petersfield	B	2	70
Plymouth	FM	2	200
Plympton Erle	FM	2	100
Pontefract	B	2	320–400
Poole	FM	2	100
Portsmouth	FM	2	100
Preston	H	2	800
Queenborough	FM	2	150
Reading	SL	2	600
Reigate	FH	2	200
Richmond	B	2	270
Ripon	B	2	150
Rochester	FM	2	600
Rye	FM	2	40–
St Albans	FM	2	500
St Germans	H	2	20
St Ives	SL	2	200
St Mawes	FM	2	25
Salisbury	C	2	54
Saltash	C	2	30–
Sandwich	FM	2	700

Constituency	Type of seat	MPs	Electors (est.)
Scarborough	C	2	50–
Seaford	SL	2	100–
Shaftesbury	SL	2	300
Southampton	FM	2	500
Southwark	SL	2	2,000
Stafford	FM	2	400
Stamford	SL	2	500
Steyning	SL	2	100
Stockbridge	SL	2	100
Sudbury	FM	2	800
Tamworth	SL	2	300
Taunton	H	2	500
Tavistock	FH	2	100
Tewkesbury	FM	2	500
Thetford	C	2	31
Thirsk	B	2	50
Tiverton	C	2	25
Totnes	FM	2	100
Tregony	H	2	150
Truro	C	2	24
Wareham	SL	2	500
Warwick	SL	2	500
Wells	FM	2	250
Weobley	B	2	100
Wendover	H	2	150
Wenlock	FM	2	500
Westbury	B	2	69
West Looe	FM	2	50
Westminster	SL	2	12,000
Weymouth and Melcombe Regis	FH	4	300
Whitchurch	B	2	70
Wigan	FM	2	100
Wilton	C	2	24
Winchelsea	FM	2	40–
Winchester	FM	2	70
Wootton Bassett	SL	2	250
Worcester	FM	2	2,000
Yarmouth (I. of W.)	C	2	50
York	FM	2	2,500

Universities

	MPs	Electors
Cambridge	2	500
Oxford	2	500

Welsh counties

Constituency	MPs	Electorate (approx.)	Pop. 1831
Anglesey	1	700	48,325
Breconshire	1	1,200	47,763
Cardiganshire	1	800	64,780
Carmarthenshire	1	1,000	100,740
Carnarvonshire	1	500	66,448
Denbighshire	1	2,000	83,629
Flintshire	1	1,000	60,012
Glamorganshire	1	1,500	126,612
Merionethshire	1	600	35,815
Montgomery	1	1,300	66,482
Pembrokeshire	1	2,000	81,425
Radnorshire	1	1,000	24,651

Welsh boroughs

Constituency	Type of seat	MPs	Electorate (approx.)	Pop. 1831
Beaumaris	C	1	24	10,817
Brecon	FM	1	100	5,026
Cardiff Boroughs	FM	1	500	14,034
Cardigan Boroughs	FM	1	4,000	8,230
Carmarthen	FM	1	100	17,641
Carnarvon Boroughs	FM	1	1,000	7,642
Denbigh Boroughs	FM	1	500	14,245
Flint Boroughs	SL	1	600	31,327
Haverfordwest	FM	1	500	10,832
Montgomery	FM	1	70	18,680
New Radnor Boroughs	FM	1	1,000	8,410
Pembroke Boroughs	FM	1	500	12,366

Scottish counties

Constituency	MPs	Electorate (approx.)	Pop. 1831
Aberdeenshire	1	180	177,657
Argyllshire	1	50	101,973
Ayrshire	1	200	145,055
Banffshire	1	120	48,604
Berwickshire	1	100	34,048
Dumfriesshire	1	50	73,770
Dunbartonshire	1	70	33,211
Edinburghshire	1	100	219,345
Elginshire	1	70	n.a. *c.* 34,000
Fife	1	150	128,839
Forfarshire	1	100	139,606
Haddingtonshire	1	70	36,145
Inverness-shire	1	100	94,797
Kincardineshire	1	50	31,431
Kirkcudbrightshire	1	100	40,590
Lanarkshire	1	100	316,819
Linlithgowshire	1	40	23,291
Orkney and Shetland	1	30	58,239
Peebleshire	1	30	10,578
Perthshire	1	100	142,894
Renfrewshire	1	100	133,443
Ross-shire	1	50	74,820[†]
Roxburghshire	1	100	43,663
Selkirkshire	1	50	6,833
Stirlingshire	1	70	72,621
Sutherland	1	30	25,518
Wigtownshire	1	50	36,258
Buteshire } *	1	12	14,151
Caithness	1	20	34,529
Clackmannanshire } *	1	25	23,801
Kinross-shire	1	25	*c.* 15,000
Nairnshire } *	1	20	*c.* 9,000
Cromartyshire	1	18	*c.* 9,000

* In alternate Parliaments one of each pair of counties was represented.
[†] This figure is the population for Ross and Cromarty.

Scottish burghs*

Constituency	MPs	Electorate (approx.)	Pop. 1831
Aberdeen Burghs	1	87	58,019
Anstruther Easter Burghs	1	92	—
Ayr Burghs	1	83	22,626
Dumfries Burghs	1	95	c. 20,000
Dysart Burghs	1	87	—
Edinburgh	1	33	162,156
Elgin Burghs	1	84	20,732
Glasgow Burghs	1	87	202,426
Haddington Burghs	1	99	17,755
Inverness Burghs	1	72	19,674
Linlithgow Burghs	1	94	—
Perth Burghs	1	125	25,571
Stirling Burghs	1	103	37,769
Tain Burghs	1	82	—
Wigtown Burghs	1	75	8,675

* An indirect system of election operated in all the Scottish burghs except Edinburgh, where the 33 members of the Town Council elected 1 MP directly. In the other burghs, the Town Councils nominated 1 delegate each, a majority of electors in each district electing 1 MP.

Patronage

Between 1794 and 1816, four lists of parliamentary patronage were compiled. The first was that drawn up by the Society of the Friends of the People and published in 1793 (*State of the Representation in England and Wales*). All the others were published by T.H.B. Oldfield – one in 1794 (*History of the Boroughs*, 2nd edn, II, pp. 477–84), compiled on the basis of the 1790 general election, another in 1797 (*History of the Original Constitution of Parliaments*, pp. 531–43), incorporating the results of the 1796 elections, and a final edition in 1816 (*Representative History of Great Britain and Ireland*, VI, pp. 285–96). There are numerous wide discrepancies in these figures. The totals below are thus only a rough guide.

England and Wales

	1793	1794	1797	1816
Number of members returned				
by peers: by nomination	92	92	93	115
by influence	72	103	124	103
by commoners: by nomination	80	102	74	85
by influence	57	54	70	52
by the Treasury etc.	7	8	9	16
Total (out of 513) for England and Wales	308	359	370	371

Scotland

	1793	1794	1797	1816
Returned by peers		30	20	31
commoners		9	13	14
the Treasury		—	12	—
Total (out of 558) for England, Wales and Scotland		398	415	416

Disbursement of secret service money, 1728–60

	£		£		£
1728	45,744	1739	74,250	1750	29,000
1729	57,880	1740	80,116	1751	32,000
1730	53,391	1741	80,977	1752	40,000
1731	63,918	1742	64,949	1753	35,000
1732	73,781	1743	54,300	1754	50,000
1733	87,470	1744	34,970	1755	40,000
1734	117,140	1745	24,000	1756	38,000
1735	66,630	1746	22,000	1757	50,000
1736	95,313	1747	41,000	1758	40,000
1737	61,999	1748	33,000	1759	30,000
1738	72,828	1749	38,000	1760	40,000

Source: L.B. Namier, *The Structure of Politics at the Accession of George III* (London, 1929) p. 242.

4.2 The House of Lords

Composition of the House

Sovereign and regnal year		Remarks	Dukes	Marquises	Earls
1714	1 George I	After the Union with Scotland in 1707	23	2	74
1727	1 George II		31	1	71
1760	1 George III		25	1	81
1820	1 George IV	After the Union with Ireland in 1801	25	17	100

	Viscounts	Barons	Representing Scotland	Representing Ireland	Archbishops and bishops	Total
1714	11	67	16		26	219
1727	15	62	16		26	222
1760	12	63	16		26	224
1820	22	134	16	28	30	372

Scottish representative peers

The provisions for electing the Scottish representative peers were contained in the Scottish Union with England Act 1707 (1706, c.7) and the Union with Scotland Act 1707 (6 Ann c.78). Later legislation, in 1847 and 1851, introduced certain changes.

There were 16 Scottish representative peers, elected for the period of each Parliament, with by-elections held when necessary to fill such vacancies as occurred. Elections were held in Edinburgh, with peers entitled to vote either in person, or by proxy, or by sending a signed list. The Lord Clerk Register (or the Clerks of Session) acted as Returning Officers.

The Lord Clerk Register

1705–8	Sir James Murray
1708–14	E. of Glasgow
1714–16	E. of Islay
1716	D. of Montrose
1716–33	Ld Polwarth (E. of Marchmont)
1733–9	E. of Selkirk
1739–56	M. of Lothian
1756–60	Alexander Hume Campbell
1768–1816	Ld Frederick Campbell
1816–21	Archibald Colquhoun

Irish representative peers

The provisions for the election of the Irish representative peers (before later modification in 1857 and 1882) were contained in an act of the Irish Parliament (40 Geo. III c.29) and the Union with Ireland Act 1800 (39 and 40 Geo. III c.67).

The original 28 peers (elected 2 Aug. 1800)

John Thomas	13th E. of Clanricarde
George Frederick	7th E. of Westmeath
Thomas	2nd E. of Bective
Robert	2nd E. of Roden
John Denis	3rd E. of Altamont
John	2nd E. of Glendore
Thomas	2nd E. of Longford
John	1st E. of Erne
Otway	1st E. of Desart
Robert	1st E. of Leitrim
Richard	2nd E. of Lucan
Robert	1st E. of Londonderry
Henry	1st Earl Conyngham
Francis	2nd E. of Llandaff
Robert	2nd Vt Wicklow
Thomas	1st Vt Northland
Laurence	Vt Oxmantown
Charles Henry	2nd Vt O'Neill
Francis	1st Vt Bandon
Richard Hely	1st Vt Donoughmore
Hugh	1st Vt Carleton
Richard	11th B. Calier
Edmund Henry	2nd B. Glentworth
George	1st B. Callen

Charles	Ld Somerton
Richard	1st Vt Longueville
Robert	1st B. Rossmore
James	B. Tyrawly

Elections on vacancy of Irish representative peers, 1800–30

Date	New peer	Replacing
15 Jan. 1805	2nd E. of Enniskillen	E. of Desart
15 Jan. 1805	2nd E. of Caleden	E. of Leitrim
17 Dec. 1806	2nd E. of Charlemont	E. of Llandaff
15 July 1807	3rd E. of Kingston	E. of Rosse
23 Jan. 1809	2nd E. of Clancarty	E. of Clanricarde
19 Apr. 1809	Vt Mountjoy	M. of Sligo
23 Jan. 1810	2nd E. of Rosse	E. of Normanton
7 Jan. 1812	2nd E. of Gosford	Vt Longueville
5 Apr. 1815	2nd E. of Mountcashel	E. of Westmeath

4.3 The Irish Parliament

MPs and size of county electorates for Irish House of Commons, *c.* 1783

	No. of MPs in 1783 (county and borough)	Size of county electorate (approx.)
Antrim	12	3,500
Derry	10	2,300
Down	14	6,000
Armagh	6	2,400
Tyrone	10	3,000
Fermanagh	4	2,537
Donegal	10	2,500
Leitrim	2	1,076
Monaghan	4	1,200
Louth	12	n.a.
Cavan	6	1,850
Longford	10	700
Roscommon	12	n.a.
Sligo	4	793
Mayo	4	1,000
Galway	8	700
Westmeath	10	1,120
Meath	14	1,200
Dublin	12	1,200
Wicklow	10	900
Kildare	10	n.a.
Queen's County	6	1,400
King's County	8	900
Kilkenny	16	1,050
Tipperary	8	1,600
Limerick	8	1,500
Clare	4	1,000
Cork	26	3,000
Kerry	8	1,000
Waterford	8	500
Wexford	18	n.a.
Carlow	6	n.a.

Representation in Ireland before and after the Act of Union

	MPs elected to Irish House of Commons, c. 1783	MPs elected to Westminster after the Act of Union, 1801
Antrim	12	5
Derry	10	4
Down	14	4
Armagh	6	3
Tyrone	10	3
Fermanagh	4	3
Donegal	10	2
Leitrim	2	2
Monaghan	4	2
Louth	12	4
Cavan	6	2
Longford	10	2
Roscommon	12	2
Sligo	4	3
Mayo	4	2
Galway	8	3
Westmeath	10	3
Meath	14	2
Dublin	12	5
Wicklow	10	2
Kildare	10	2
Queen's County	6	2
King's County	8	3
Kilkenny	16	3
Tipperary	8	4
Limerick	8	3
Clare	4	3
Cork	26	8
Kerry	8	3
Waterford	8	4
Wexford	18	4
Carlow	6	3

4.4 Elections

Elections and election results, 1689–1818

Introduction

An accurate return of election results in this period is fraught with difficulty. It must be noted at the outset that no general election in this period was in fact general, the number of contests ranging from high points such as 1710 and 1722 to the much lower numbers for elections such as 1747 and 1761 (*see* pp. 106–7). Even at the most heavily contested elections, a very large number of seats remained uncontested. Moreover, in spite of strong party feeling at some points in this period, notably in the reign of Queen Anne, the classification of MPs by party labels is a matter of some contention. Hence, unlike a modern election where almost all seats are contested by candidates standing under a clear party label, this period has both a fluctuating number of contests and uncertain party allegiances. None the less, scholars have attempted to estimate in general terms both the results of the contests that took place at elections and the resulting impact upon representation in the House of Commons. It should be noted that the result of an election was only one factor in determining the composition of the House of Commons: challenges on election petitions subsequent to an election, the allegiance of MPs returned from uncontested seats, and shifts in allegiance at, or shortly following, the sitting of a new parliament must also be taken into consideration. As a result, allegiance at the opening of a session did not necessarily reflect solely or even primarily the outcome of the last general election. Historians have therefore turned both to contemporary estimates of support and to division lists for estimates of groupings at the opening of a new parliament. Neither source, however, supplies completely reliable indications of allegiance and a degree of imprecision has to be accepted in any estimates so derived. Finally, the role and definition of political groupings and the importance of party allegiance remains a subject of much debate. 'Court and Country' divisions and Namierite analysis of political activity have considerably modified consideration of the importance of party labels for much of this period, although these views have also been subject to criticisms in their turn. The following summary of elections and their results must be viewed in the light of these qualifications.

1689
In the aftermath of the flight of James II, elections were called in January 1689 for the 'Convention Parliament'. Contests took place in nine counties and 41 boroughs. Although party divisions were not expressed strongly in the mood of national emergency and *de facto* interregnum, Parliament began to divide on partisan issues after the vesting of the throne in William and Mary. One hundred and fifty-one 'hard core' Tories have been identified from the vote against the throne being declared vacant on 5 February 1689, while the 174 members who voted in January 1690 for the Sacheverell clause have been identified as committed Whigs. Nearly 200 members, new and previously elected, can be considered as uncommitted in the Commons as a whole.

1690
The 'Convention Parliament' was prorogued on 27 January 1690 and dissolved ten days later because of William's dissatisfaction with the Whigs' attempt to monopolise office and the Tories' offer of a more favourable settlement of the Revenue. In the absence of division lists for the period 1690–96 a precise delineation of election results is not possible, but there were notable losses by the Whigs and early divisions saw substantial Tory majorities in the Commons, although these were to be eroded in the course of the Parliament with the rise of the Whig 'Junto'.

1695
William's decision to dissolve Parliament was taken before he left England to conduct the military campaigns on the Continent which concluded in the fall of Namur. The election results in the autumn saw significant Tory losses, including six in the City of London and in Westminster, although it was not until early 1696 that the various Whig factions were able to establish a clear majority in the House of Commons.

1698
An election was due in the summer of 1698 under the provisions of the Triennial Act. Parliament was prorogued on 5 July and dissolved two days later, elections taking place in July and August. Analysis of the election results suggests that the Whig 'Junto' lost its majority in the Commons with Tory candidates making significant gains in both county and borough seats.

1700
The instability of the existing Ministry following the election of 1698 led to a major reconstruction of the administration in the autumn of 1700,

creating a virtually Tory Ministry with only one Whig remaining in an important office. Dissolution of Parliament did not take place for a further six weeks, partly as a result of the news of the death of Charles II of Spain and its diplomatic repercussions. Eventually Parliament was dissolved on 19 December 1700. The resulting election led to substantial Tory gains with at least 30 former Whigs failing to be returned. Although not in itself sufficient to ensure a Tory majority in the Commons, subsequent divisions showed that the new Parliament contained a significant majority prepared to support the Tories.

1701

As early as September 1701 William III sought to go to the country to obtain a more favourable House of Commons, although the dissolution was not proclaimed until 11 November. In the subsequent election, although the Tories lost seats and some prominent members, the Whig gain was sufficiently small to leave both sides claiming a majority. The Whigs estimated a gain of 30 seats, but modern research has estimated that the new Parliament still contained a nominal Tory majority of 289 Tories to 224 Whigs. After Parliament met, however, the Tory majority was decreased by William's movement towards the Whigs and poor attendance on the part of Tory members. The first divisions were extremely close, the Speakership being carried for the Whigs by only four votes. By the end of February 1702, the Whigs were generally able to obtain a somewhat precarious majority in the divisions with uncommitted members taking the Whig side. Further clarification of the party situation was prevented by the death of William on 8 March 1702.

1702

The formation of a new administration containing many Tories, by Queen Anne, was followed by a general election in the summer, announced by a dissolution on 3 July. The election witnessed at least 87 contests in England and Wales. The election has been estimated at returning a Tory majority of over 130 seats in the new Parliament, reflected in Tory majorities of that order in the divisions of the autumn.

1705

Parliament was prorogued on 14 March 1705 and a dissolution followed shortly under the provisions of the Triennial Act. The election which followed was one of the most bitterly fought of the eighteenth century with over 100 contests in England alone, including 26 counties. According to modern calculations 267 Tories and 246 Whigs were returned, yielding a Whig gain of 60 seats over the previous administration.

1708

The election of 1708 marked the first election for the Parliament of Great Britain following the Act of Union with Scotland, signed the previous year, which entitled 45 Scottish MPs to sit at Westminster. Parliament was prorogued on 1 April and the elections took place in May. It has been suggested that the Whigs gained some 30 seats in England and Wales, producing 291 Whigs and 222 Tories returned. With most of the new Scottish MPs also voting in their favour, the Whigs were able to go on to win most of the votes on election petitions. Sunderland declared it 'the most Whig Parliament [there] has been since the Revolution'.

1710

Following a widespread replacement of the Whig administration in the spring and summer of 1710 with the filling of most of the important ministerial posts by Tories, and a strong tide of anti-Whig feeling in the country, the general election in the autumn produced widespread Tory gains, with contemporary estimates of at least two Tories elected for every Whig returned. Modern estimates suggest that 332 Tories and 181 Whigs were returned for England and Wales, with a Whig majority in Scotland somewhat mitigating the Tory landslide.

1713

The general election which took place in August and September 1713 occurred when both public opinion and the influence of the Court were still predisposed in favour of the Tories, resulting in a large Tory majority in England and Wales only somewhat diminished by a clear Whig majority in Scotland. *The History of Parliament* provides the following breakdown of results:

	Tories	*Whigs*
England	323	166
Wales	21	3
Scotland	14	31
Total	358	200

Decisions on election petitions, decided overwhelmingly in favour of the Tories, increased the nominal Tory majority to an estimated 372 Tories as opposed to 185 Whigs. This majority, however, proved less conclusive than it appeared as Parliament did not meet to conduct serious business until almost six months later on 2 March 1714, when parliamentary allegiance was beginning to be affected by the question of the Hanoverian succession, much reducing the effective Tory strength in divisions in the House of Commons.

1715

By the time of the death of Queen Anne on 1 August 1714, the Hanoverian succession had been largely secured by pro-Hanoverian appointments to the Privy Council. Parliament, which had been prorogued on 9 July 1714, met again on 5 August, but was prorogued once more on 25 August awaiting a fresh election, meeting again only to transact the formal business of further prorogation. The dismissal of Bolingbroke at the end of August and George I's arrival in the country on 19 September was followed by the construction of a Whig administration. When Parliament was formally dissolved in January 1715 the election took place in a climate which was flowing strongly against the Tories, who were being widely associated by Whig propaganda as opposing the Protestant succession and as betrayers of British policy interests in the Treaty of Utrecht. The election resulted in an almost complete reversal of party fortunes in 1713. *The History of Parliament* gives the following post-election returns:

	Tories	Whigs
England	195	294
Wales	15	9
Scotland	7	38
Total	217	341

Moreover, as was customary, election petitions were decided in favour of the majority party: of 46 Tory and 41 Whig petitions, no Tory petition was successful but 31 Tories were unseated. As a result, post-petition party strength altered to 372 Whigs to 186 Tories.

1722

Under the provisions of the Septennial Act passed in 1716, an election was due early in 1722 and Parliament was dissolved on 10 March. Against the background of the South Sea scandal and Walpole's increasing supremacy in the House of Commons, the Tories were eclipsed, making the election in some areas, like Scotland, more of a contest between rival groups of Whigs. In all there were more than 150 contests, a larger number than at any other election in the period 1688–1760 and at least 30 more than in 1715. Most of the returns for the English boroughs came in by the end of March, with the results for the English counties, Cornwall, Wales and Scotland coming in during April.

The results were 379 Whigs returned against 178 Tories, representing a Whig gain of almost 40 seats on the result in 1715. After election petitions had been heard the composition of the House of Commons has been estimated at 389 Whigs to 169 Tories.

1727

The general election which followed the death of George I witnessed 118 contests. Walpole, having secured the continuity of his administration after a brief period of uncertainty, was able to erode further the number of his opponents. Wales, which had produced a steady Tory majority hitherto, returned a Whig majority of 14 members, while the English boroughs moved ever more firmly under Whig control. The returns produced 427 Whigs and 131 Tories. Sixty-one petitions followed the elections, 24 of which were heard, resulting in three further Whig gains. The resulting House of Commons therefore consisted of 415 Whig ministerialists, an opposition Whig group of 15 led by Pulteney, and 128 Tories, a nominal majority of 272.

1734

The general election of 1734, called under the provisions of the Septennial Act, took place against the recent background of Walpole's controversial Excise Bill, which he had been forced to withdraw in April of the previous year in the face of bitter opposition and falling majorities. At the dissolution of Parliament in April 1734 the House of Commons has been estimated at containing 342 Whig supporters of the administration, 86 opposition Whigs and 130 Tories, representing a government majority of 126. The election witnessed 135 contests and was fiercely contested with some Tory successes in the English counties. The election returns were as follows:

Ministerial Whigs	326
Opposition Whigs	83
Tories	149

The government made a further four gains on election petitions, producing a House of Commons consisting of 330 ministerial supporters, 83 opposition Whigs and 145 Tories.

1741

Parliament was dissolved on 27 April 1741. Following the increasing difficulties of Walpole's administration, the government majority had fallen to around 50 seats, reflecting a considerable defection of ministerial supporters to the ranks of the opposition. The elections witnessed 94 contests but were not fought in a particularly excitable atmosphere. The administration lost seats in two areas of traditional support, Scotland, where the influence of the Duke of Argyll was committed against it, and in Cornwall, where the Prince of Wales lent his support to the opposition. As a result, the Ministry lost 21 seats in these two areas alone. The results produced were as follows:

Ministerial Whigs   286
Opposition Whigs   31
Tories   136

Five seats were left unfilled as a result of double returns, leaving a much reduced theoretical majority for the administration of 19.

However, when Parliament met on 1 December 1741, some 23 seats were vacant by death and double returns, reducing the nominal government majority still further to 16 (276 government supporters, 124 opposition Whigs and 135 Tories). In January and February 1742 the combined opposition sought further to reduce the government majority by contesting election returns. After several close votes, including a number of ministerial defeats, Walpole resigned after losing the determination of the election of Chippenham by 16 votes (241 to 225) on 2 February 1742.

1747

Parliament was dissolved on 18 June 1747. The re-establishment of the Pelham administration, following the unsuccessful attempt by Bath and Granville to form a new administration in February 1746, left a strong government majority of around 160. In a relatively quiet election with only 60 contests, the administration was able to exercise more of the customary influence in places such as Scotland and Cornwall than Walpole had been able to do in 1741. As a result the number of opposition MPs returned for Scotland was reduced from 26 to 10 (out of 45) and in Cornwall from 29 to 19 compared with 1741. Moreover, the seats in the metropolitan area which had often proved a centre of opposition support were largely taken by the ministry. The general election resulted in the following return:

Ministerial Whigs   338
Opposition Whigs   97
Tories   117

Election petitions resulted in the overturn of seven opposition MPs and the government was also successful in six double returns, giving a total when Parliament met of 351 ministerial supporters, 92 opposition Whigs and 115 Tories, a majority of 144.

1754

Henry Pelham died on 6 March 1754 while preparations were in train for a general election under the provisions of the Septennial Act. At least 62 constituencies went to the poll in 1754 with the influence of the Duke of Newcastle organising the government interest. According to a contemporary listing, the government was estimated to have gained a further 11 seats. The returns were as follows:

Government	368
Opposition Whigs	42
Tories	106
Doubtful	26

1761

Parliament was dissolved on 20 March 1761 and elections were held in circumstances which were somewhat unusual in the eighteenth century, in that there was no organised opposition in the House of Commons and, coming after the accession of George III, under his instructions that no government money should be used to assist the election of the administration's supporters. In the event, the election saw only 53 contests, the lowest number in the period 1688–1761. The election of 113 Tories, including 21 new members, scarcely diminished a substantial government majority.

1768

Parliament was dissolved on 11 March 1768 and the election held in the lull between the agitation over the Stamp Act and opposition aroused by the Townshend duties. In the absence of Chatham, who was ill, the Duke of Grafton as First Lord of the Treasury was effectively the leader of the administration, but made little effort to capitalise upon his position in the election. Although the election produced 30 more contests than 1761, the House was virtually unchanged, with some marginal increase in support for the Rockingham faction and Wilkes's success at Middlesex marking the first manifestation of urban radicalism.

1774

Parliament was dissolved on 22 June, nine months early. Lord North as First Lord of the Treasury was already dealing with the escalation of the American crisis and the need to take stronger action against the American colonists in New England. Accordingly he sought to do so with a fresh parliament. Heavy spending by the government ensured that in spite of some losses in popular constituencies, North estimated he had 321 certain supporters in the new parliament, while the main opposition grouping, the Rockinghams, were reduced by a dozen seats to 43.

1780

The Parliament elected in 1774 was dissolved on 1 September 1780, a year earlier than was necessary under the Septennial Act. Opposition successes in votes earlier in the year and concern about the conduct of the war were partly relieved by modest military success in July and the pro-government reaction in the wake of the Gordon Riots. North therefore seized the opportunity of a dissolution, but in spite of favourable expectations, the outcome was a closely balanced house in which government support was estimated at 260 seats to 254 opposition.

1784

The general election followed the destruction of the North administration and the failure of the three short-lived ones which succeeded it. The King's dismissal of Fox and North in December 1783 and his appointment of Pitt provided the immediate background to the dissolution. Having survived the early months of 1784, Pitt sought to strengthen his position through the dissolution on 25 March. According to modern estimates, the opposition are estimated to have lost between 70 and 100 seats. A closely balanced House prior to the election was converted into one with a Pittite majority of $c.$ 120 seats.

1790

Although preparations for an election had begun as early as 1788, the Regency Crisis delayed a dissolution until 11 June 1790, Pitt now seeking to rally support. With 92 contests, Pitt strengthened his position with an estimated 340 supporters to 183 opposition, and 35 'others'.

1796

The 1796 election followed the deep polarisation of parties which occurred in the aftermath of the French Revolution, symbolised by the division of the Whig Party and the fusion of the Portland Whigs with Pitt in June 1794. The Foxite opposition prior to the election was under 120 and often much lower and faced by a government phalanx of over 400 members. After the dissolution on 20 May 1796, one of the quietest elections of the period saw the opposition lose further ground. The estimates are that government supporters after the election numbered 424, with 95 opposition, 29 independents and 10 'doubtful'.

1802

The 1802 election took place in the somewhat uncertain situation brought about by Pitt's resignation in January 1801 and his replacement by Addington. It was also the first election to include the 100 new members brought into the Commons under the provisions of the Act of Union with Ireland, creating a House of 658 members. The immediate context of the dissolution on 29 June 1802 was the conclusion of the Peace of Amiens with France in March, thus Addington felt secure enough to test his support. There were 97 contests, but little change over the previous House. Estimates suggest 467 ministerial supporters, *c.* 150 opposition, 19 independents and 23 others.

1806

The 'Ministry of All the Talents' led by Grenville sought a dissolution on 25 October 1806 following the death of Fox, one of its leading figures in September, and the failure of peace negotiations with France. The factionalisation of politics and shifting allegiances during a period of short-lived administration make the calculation of results difficult, but the outcome has been estimated at 349 ministerial supporters, 92 opposition, 208 'neutral' and 9 independents.

1807

The formation of a new administration under the Duke of Portland prompted an early dissolution on 30 April 1807. The principal issue was Catholic Emancipation and the government received some vindication for its position. The number of pro-ministerial supporters has been estimated at 388, the opposition at 224, independents at 29 and 'others' also at 29.

1812

The dissolution occurred on 29 September 1812 with the First Lord of the Treasury, Lord Liverpool, seeking to confirm his position following his appointment in June. The result was favourable to the administration with a return of an estimated 400 ministerial supporters, 196 opposition and 62 others.

1818

The dissolution occurred on 10 June 1818, largely determined by the provisions of the Septennial Act. The largest number of English seats went to the poll since 1734, but Liverpool was returned with a safe majority in the polling, which occupied most of July.

Sources: The compilation of the above summary owes an enormous debt to the pioneering efforts of the *History of Parliament* project, notably the volumes edited by R. Sedgewick, *The History of Parliament: The House of Commons, 1715–1754* (Oxford, 1970), L. Namier and J. Brooke, *The History of Parliament: The House of Commons, 1754–1790* (London, 1964), and R.G. Thorne, *The History of Parliament: The House of Commons, 1790–1820* (London, 1986). Valuable additional information has been obtained from W.A. Speck, *Tory and Whig: The Struggle in the Constituencies, 1701–1715* (London, 1970), B.W. Hill, *The Growth of Parliamentary Parties, 1689–1742* (London, 1976) and *British Parliamentary Parties, 1742–1832* (London, 1985).

General elections, 1701–1818: number of contests

	England	Wales	Scotland	Ireland
1701	89 (18)	2		
1702	85 (18)	2		
1705	108 (26)	2		
1708	92 (14)	5	n.a.	
1710	127 (23)	4	n.a.	
1713	97 (12)	3	n.a.	
1715	111 (17)	8	9	
1722	127 (17)	9	20	
1727	96 (12)	13	9	
1734	107 (13)	8	20	
1741	65 (4)	11	18	
1747	51 (3)	2	7	
1754	60 (5)	4	2*	
1761	46 (4)	2	6	
1768	69 (8)	5	9	
1774	80 (11)	6	9	
1780	67 (2)	2	7	
1784	73 (7)	2	12	
1790	75 (8)	1	16	
1796	59 (4)	3	4	
1802	72 (6)	3	11	11
1806	62 (7)	1	12	12
1807	70 (11)	3	15	14
1812	57 (4)	7	14	18
1818	93 (11)	—	—	—

Notes: Figures in brackets denote county contests.
* Scottish counties only

Sources: In general, this list follows the standard authorities, primarily the volumes in the *History of Parliament*, supplemented by material in J. Cannon, *Parliamentary Reform, 1642–1832* (Cambridge, 1973), Appendix 3 and W.A. Speck, *Tory and Whig: The Struggle in the Constituencies* (London, 1970), Appendix E.

4.5 Parliamentary reform

The parliamentary reform movement: chronology

1763 Arrest of John Wilkes for issue No. 45 of the *North Briton*. General warrants declared illegal.

1768 Wilkes elected for Middlesex and refused seat in House of Commons.
Anti-bribery bill introduced in House Commons.

1769 Formation of Society of the Supporters of the Bill of Rights.

1770 Publication of Edmund Burke's *Thoughts on the Present Discontents* demanding limited reform and an end to corruption. William Dowdeswell introduces a bill for the disfranchisement of revenue officers.
Grenville's Election Act (10 Geo., III, c.16) allowed election petitions to be heard by select committee instead of in front of the whole house. Made perpetual in 1774.

1771 John Sawbridge's motion for leave to introduce a bill for shorter parliaments defeated by 105 votes to 54.
Printers' Case effectively left newspapers free to report debates in Parliament.
Franchise of borough of New Shoreham widened (11 Geo. III, c.55).

1774 Bill introduced to permit several polling places in each county.

1775 Beginning of American War of Independence.

1776 Publication of Major Cartwright's *Take Your Choice* outlines radical reform programme.
Wilkes seeks leave to bring bill before Parliament for 'a just and equal Representation of the People of England in Parliament'.

1778 Bill introduced to exclude government contractors from Parliament. Second bill introduced 1779. Both defeated by postponement.

1779   First meeting of Yorkshire reformers.

1780   Yorkshire petition presented to House of Commons.
Convention of county associations in London.
Bills for disfranchisement of revenue officers and exclusion of placemen from House of Commons defeated.
Dunning's resolution that the influence of the Crown 'has increased, is increasing and ought to be diminished' carried.
Burke's bills to reform civil establishment defeated.
Duke of Richmond's proposals for universal suffrage, annual election and equal electoral districts refused a hearing in House of Lords.
Society for Constitutional Information founded.

1782   Bill introduced by Lord Mahon to curtail election expenses.
Bill introduced for more effectual representation in Ireland.
Bills introduced to lower Scottish county franchise and abolish wadset voting.
Voting rights at Cricklade extended (22 Geo. III, c.31).
Revenue officers disfranchised (22 Geo. III, c.41); government contractors disqualified from sitting in House of Commons (22 Geo. III, c.45). Civil Establishment Act (22 Geo. III, c.82).
Rejection of Pitt's motion for a committee on parliamentary reform by 161 votes to 141.
Thatched House Tavern meeting in London proposes petitioning movement for 'a substantial Reform of the Commons' House of Parliament'.

1783   Pitt's proposals for the addition of at least 100 county members, gradual disfranchisement of corrupt boroughs, increased representation for London, and the prevention of bribery defeated by 293 votes to 149.
Debates on reform of Irish representation. Leave to introduce reform bill defeated by 158 votes to 49.

1784   Edinburgh convention for reform of Scottish representation.
Yorkshire Association ceases to meet after petitioning in January.

1785   Pitt's proposals to redistribute seats from 36 'decayed' boroughs to the counties and to enfranchise county copyholders defeated by 248 votes to 174.
Henry Flood's reform bill for Ireland defeated by 112 votes to 60.
Further convention of Scottish reformers in Edinburgh.

PARLIAMENTARY REFORM

1786   Attempt to raise issue of Scottish representation defeated in the Commons.

1787   Further move for inquiry into Scottish representation defeated.

1788   Scottish petitioning movement for reform (46 petitions).
Lord Mahon's Act for registration of country voters (28 Geo. III, c.36).
Meetings of Revolution Societies to celebrate the 'Glorious Revolution'.

1789   Lord Mahon's Act suspended and repealed before coming into operation (29 Geo. III, c.13 and 29 Geo. III, c.18).
Meeting of London Revolution Society addressed by Dr Richard Price, welcoming the French Revolution and calling for reform in the civil and religious establishment.

1790   Flood's motion to create 100 extra county members and remove seats from smaller boroughs withdrawn for lack of support.
Edmund Burke publishes *Reflections on the Revolution in France*.

1791   Publication of Thomas Paine's *Rights of Man, Part One*.
Formation of reform societies in Manchester and Sheffield.

1792   Formation of London Corresponding Society and the Society of the Friends of the People.
Publication of *Rights of Man, Part Two*.
Charles Grey states intention of raising reform motion in the Commons during the next session.
Motion for reform of the Scottish burghs defeated by 69 votes to 27.
Address of London Corresponding Society demanding annual elections and 'an equal Representation of the Whole Body of the People'.

1793   Charles Grey's motion to refer reform to committee defeated by 282 votes to 41.
British Convention meets in Edinburgh and dissolved by authorities.

1794   Mass meeting of London Corresponding Society at Chalk Farm, London, and preparations for a new Convention.

1795   Mass meetings of London Corresponding Society at St George's Fields and Copenhagen Fields.

1796 Missionary tours of London Corresponding Society members to Kent and Birmingham.

1797 Rejection of Charles Grey's motion for leave to bring a motion for reform by 256 votes to 91.

1800 Grey's motion to amend Act of Union by disfranchising 40 of the smallest English boroughs and reducing the number of proposed Irish MPs at Westminster defeated by 176 votes to 34.

1802 William Cobbett founds the *Political Register* and begins systematic criticism of government policy.

1804 Franchise at Aylesbury extended to three neighbouring hundreds (44 Geo. III, c.60).

1806 George Tierney's bill to prohibit conveyance of voters to poll by candidates defeated by 42 votes to 17.

1807 Election of Sir Francis Burdett and Lord Cochrane as radical candidates for Westminster.

1809 Anti-bribery act sponsored by John Christian Curwen passed preventing corrupt agreements to obtain seats (49 Geo. III, c.118).
Burdett's motion for limiting duration of parliaments and extending franchise to householders defeated by 74 votes to 54.

1810 Thomas Brand's proposals for extending county franchise to copyholders, borough franchise to householders paying parochial rates, triennial parliaments, redistribution of seats from decayed boroughs with compensation to patrons, and exclusion of placeholders defeated by 234 votes to 115.

1811 Formation of the Union for Parliamentary Reform.

1812 London Hampden Club constituted.
Defeat of Brand's motion to extend county vote to copyholders and abolish the right of nomination by 215 votes to 88.

1816 Widespread distress and agitation for reform.
Cobbett produces first cheap edition of the *Political Register*.
Spa Fields meetings in London.

1817 Convention of reformers at Crown and Anchor Tavern, London, to prepare reform campaign.
Burdett's motion for a select committee on reform defeated by 265 votes to 77.
March of the 'Blanketeers' and Pentrich 'Rising'.

1818 Sir Robert Heron's motion for triennial parliaments defeated by 117 votes to 42.
Burdett's motions for annual parliaments, manhood suffrage, secret ballot and equal electoral districts defeated by 106 votes to nil.

Major reform societies and clubs

The Society of the Supporters of the Bill of Rights
Formed in February 1769 under the aegis of the Rev. John Horne (Horne Tooke) to support Wilkes. It provided the organisation for the reform movement in the capital and was joined by several metropolitan MPs. Although weakened by a split when Horne Tooke set up the Constitutional Society in 1771, it provided the model for later political societies.

The Yorkshire Association
Grew out of a Yorkshire meeting of December 1779 when a committee was set up 'to prepare a Plan of Association on legal and constitutional grounds to support that laudable reform and such other measures as may conduce to restore the Freedom of Parliament'. It aimed at the shortening of parliaments and a more equal representation of the people, votes being withheld from any parliamentary candidate who declined to pledge himself to these reforms. Other counties formed similar associations, which met at a Convention of Representatives in March 1780.

The Association advocated the promotion of economical reform, the addition of 100 more county members, and triennial parliaments. It ceased activity after the failure of Pitt's plan of reform in April 1785.

The Society for Constitutional Information
Formed in April 1780 on the initiative of Major Cartwright to disseminate political information. Founder members included John Jebb, Thomas Brand Hollis and Richard Brinsley Sheridan. Members were elected by ballot with a subscription of not less than a guinea. Later members included Thomas Paine and John Horne Tooke. The Society was active in the reform campaigns of 1780–85 and also supported various philanthropic schemes. It was revived after 1789, sending a congratulatory address to the French National Convention in November 1792 and delegates to the British Convention at Edinburgh in October 1793. Papers of the

Society were seized and six members arrested on charges of high treason in May 1794.

London Revolution Society
The most important of several 'Revolution Societies' which met annually to celebrate the 'Glorious Revolution' of 1688. Organised with a committee and officers, the Society had no fixed constitution other than support of 'Whig' constitutional principles. Members included prominent London dissenters, such as Dr Richard Price, and leading Whig reformers. Its meeting on 4 November 1789 initiated the debate on the French Revolution when Price preached on the text of 'The Love of our Country', welcoming the French Revolution and urging repeal of the Test Acts and parliamentary reform in Britain. Price's sermon was the subject of bitter attack in Edmund Burke's *Reflections on the Revolution in France* (1790).

Manchester Constitutional Society
Set up on 5 October 1790 to obtain shorter parliaments and more equal representation. It was led by Manchester merchant Thomas Walker and organised on the basis of half-guinea subscriptions and monthly meetings. It corresponded with the Jacobin Club of Paris in 1792. It was followed by the formation of the Manchester Patriotic Reformation Societies. The Society ceased activity *c.* 1794.

Sheffield Society for Constitutional Information
The Society's first address was produced in December 1791. It was a society of 'tradesmen and artificers', claiming over two thousand members by 1792. Originally pledged to non-violence in pursuit of reform and equal representation, it produced cheap editions of Paine's *Rights of Man*. Its divisional organisation into 'tythings' provided the model for the London Corresponding Society. Evidence of arming was alleged in 1794. The Society was active in the anti-war campaign of 1794–95. It ceased open activity *c.* 1797.

London Corresponding Society
Formally constituted on 25 January 1792 on the initiative of Thomas Hardy, a master shoemaker. The Society was open to 'members unlimited' for a fee of one shilling and subscriptions of one penny per week. It adopted a programme of correspondence with other reform societies to promote universal suffrage and annual parliaments. It was organised in divisions of 30 members with a secretary, and delegates and sub-delegates were elected to a Central Committee. Delegates were sent to the British Convention in Edinburgh in October 1793. The Society organised a series of mass meetings in the capital, 1794–97. Its papers were

seized and Hardy was arrested in May 1794 on charge of high treason. By 1795 it had at least 70 divisions and 2,000 members in the capital. Committee members were seized and imprisoned on 19 April 1798. The Society was formally suppressed in July 1799 under provisions of 39 Geo. III, c.79.

The Friends of the People
An aristocratic Whig society, founded with the advice of Major Cartwright in April 1792. Subscription cost a guinea and a half. The object of the Society was 'To restore the freedom of election, and a more frequent exercise of their right of electing their representatives'. Members included Charles Grey, Richard Brinsley Sheridan, Thomas Erskine, George Lambton, George Tierney and Charles Whitbread. Satellite societies were formed in Southwark, Aldgate and Royston in Hertfordshire. Criticised by both radicals and conservatives for its moderation, it became defunct in 1796.

The Union for Parliamentary Reform
Grew out of 'friends to parliamentary reform' formed in 1811 by Major Cartwright. Supporters included Christopher Wyvill, Henry Hunt, Sir Francis Burdett, William Cobbett, Lord Cochrane and Thomas Coke. It declared for annual parliaments and taxpayer suffrage.

The Hampden Club
First projected by London reformers in May 1811 and formally constituted at the Thatched House Tavern on 20 April 1812. It was a dining society limited to those possessing or heir to £300 a year in land, with £2 a year subscription. It declared itself in favour of 'a reform in the representation of the people' and eventually adopted the same programme as the Union for Parliamentary Reform. Although the London Hampden Club was soon virtually defunct, Hampden and Union Clubs sprang up in the provinces on a more open basis, usually adopting a penny per week subscription. A conference of delegates to coordinate a national reform campaign held in January 1817 with Cartwright in the chair led to the adoption of a programme of manhood suffrage and secret ballot.

SECTION FIVE

Foreign affairs and empire

5.1 Principal treaties, 1689–1820

Date signed	Subject	Place signed
1689		
20 Apr.	Treaty with the Netherlands concerning the fitting out of a fleet	Whitehall
15 Aug.	Treaty with Denmark	Copenhagen
22 Aug.	Convention with the Netherlands concerning prohibition of commerce with France	London
24 Aug.	Treaty of friendship and alliance with the Netherlands	Whitehall
22 Oct.	Treaty with the Netherlands concerning ships taken from the enemy	Whitehall
9 Dec.	Accession of Great Britain to Grand Alliance between the Emperor and the Netherlands (12 May 1689)	—
1690		
16 May	Treaty of alliance with Elector of Brandenburg	Westminster
3 Nov.	Treaty of defensive alliance with Denmark and the Netherlands	Copenhagen
1691		
30 June	Convention with Denmark and the Netherlands touching the commerce in France	Copenhagen
22 Oct.	Treaty with the Netherlands concerning vessels captured and recaptured	Whitehall

Date signed	Subject	Place signed
1692		
31 Oct.	Convention with Spain and the Netherlands for the fleet in the Mediterranean	The Hague
22 Dec.	Subsidy treaty with the Netherlands and Elector of Hanover	The Hague
1693		
20 Feb.	Treaty of subsidy with Elector of Saxony	Dresden
2 Mar.	Instrument of England and the Netherlands for payment of 150,000 dollars to Elector of Saxony	Dresden
1694		
23 May	Treaty of subsidy with the Netherlands and Elector of Saxony	Dresden
11 Oct.	Additional articles with Tripoli	Tripoli
1695		
18 Mar.	Convention with the Emperor, the Netherlands and Bishop of Munster	The Hague
5 Apr.	Renewal of articles of peace with Algiers of 1686	Algiers
1696		
3 Dec.	Treaty with Denmark and the Netherlands	The Hague
1697		
20 Sept.	Articles of peace with France	Ryswick
1698		
14 May	Convention with Sweden and the Netherlands for entering into a defensive triple league	The Hague
28 June	Renewal of articles of peace with Algiers of 1686	Algiers

Date signed	Subject	Place signed
24 Sept./ 11 Oct.	Treaty with France and the Netherlands concerning settlement of succession of Spain on the Electoral Prince of Bavaria (First Partition Treaty)	Loo/The Hague
1699		
16 May	Articles of peace with Tunis	Tunis
1700		
16 Jan.	Treaty with Sweden	London
23–30 Jan.	Treaty of alliance with Sweden and the Netherlands	The Hague/London
3–25 Mar.	Treaty with France and the Netherlands for settling succession of Crown of Spain (Second Partition Treaty)	London/The Hague
17 Aug.	Treaty of peace and commerce with Algiers	Algiers
1701		
20 Jan.	Treaty of Alliance with Denmark and the Netherlands	Odensee
15 June	Treaty between Denmark and Britain, and the Netherlands	Copenhagen
10 Aug.	Additional articles with Algiers	Algiers
7 Sept.	Treaty with the Emperor and the Netherlands (accessions: Prussia, 18 Feb. 1702; Wolfenbuttel, 21 Apr. 1702; Treves, 22 June 1702; Elector of Mainz and Margrave of Brandenburg in the name of the Circle of Franconia, 24 June 1702; the Bishop of Constance and Duke of Württemburg in the name of the Circle of Swabia, 4 Aug. 1702; Elector of Mainz in his own name and that of the Circle of the Rhine, Sept. 1702; the Bishop of Munster, 18 Mar. 1703; Mecklemburg, 14 Sept. 1703; Savoy by Treaty with Britain, 4 Aug. 1704; the Bishop of Munster and Paderborn, 1 Mar. 1710)	The Hague

Date signed	Subject	Place signed
7 Oct.	Convention between Britain and the Netherlands, and Sweden confirming previous treaties	The Hague
11 Nov.	Particular and perpetual alliance with the Netherlands	The Hague
1702		
30 Dec. 1701–20 Jan. 1702	Treaty of alliance with Prussia and the Netherlands	The Hague/London
30 Dec. 1701–20 Jan. 1702	Treaty of subsidy between Britain and the Netherlands, and Prussia	The Hague/London
7/13 Feb.	Convention with the Netherlands and Landgrave of Hesse-Cassel	The Hague/London
12 Apr.	Articles with the Netherlands concerning the Pretender	The Hague
18 Apr.	Agreement with the Empire and the Netherlands for declaring war with France and Spain on the same day	The Hague
8 May	Convention with the Netherlands and Elector of Treves	The Hague
16–17 May	Convention with the Netherlands and Elector of Treves	The Hague/London
21 June	Convention with Brunswick-Lüneburg for a supply of 10,000 men	The Hague
16 Nov.	Convention with Brunswick-Lüneburg (with separate article, 12 Dec. 1702–2 Jan. 1703)	The Hague
1703		
13 Mar.	Convention with the Netherlands and Bishop of Munster	The Hague
15 Mar.	Convention with the Netherlands and Duke of Holstein	The Hague
15 Mar.	Convention with the Netherlands to employ 20,000 additional troops in 1703	The Hague

Date signed	Subject	Place signed
27 Mar.	Convention with the Netherlands and Duke of Saxe-Gotha	The Hague
31 Mar.	Convention with the Netherlands and Landgrave of Hesse-Cassel	The Hague
11 Apr.	Treaty with the Emperor and the Netherlands prohibiting commerce with France	The Hague
16 May	Treaty of defensive alliance between Britain, the Empire and the Netherlands, and Portugal	Lisbon
17 May	Convention with the Netherlands and Elector Palatine	The Hague
20 June	Treaty with the Netherlands for renewal of former treaties	Westminster
16 Aug.	Treaty of stricter alliance and for the tranquillity of Europe with Sweden and the Netherlands	The Hague
28 Oct.	Treaty of peace and commerce with Algiers	Algiers
20 Nov.–24 Dec.	Convention with Elector of Brunswick	London/The Hague
27 Dec.	Treaty of commerce with Portugal	Lisbon
1704		
4 Aug.	Treaty with Savoy (with separate article, 18 Nov.)	Turin
28 Nov.	Treaty with King of Prussia	Berlin
30 Dec.	Convention with Elector of Brunswick and Duke of Zell	London
1705		
20 Feb.	Treaty with Portugal concerning post office	London
20 June	Treaty of alliance with Principality of Catalonia	Genoa
3 Dec.	Treaty with Prussia renewing treaty of 1704	Berlin
8 Dec.	Convention with Elector of Hanover	Hanover

Date signed	Subject	Place signed
1706		
20 May	Convention with the Netherlands and Landgrave of Hesse-Cassel (further treaty, 25–27 Mar. 1701)	Cassel
26 May	Convention with the Netherlands and Elector Palatine	The Hague
22 Oct.	Treaty of commerce with Danzig	Danzig
18 Nov.	Convention with Elector of Brunswick-Lüneburg	The Hague
24 Nov.	Treaty with Prussia (further treaty, 19 Apr. 1708)	The Hague
24 Nov.	Treaty with the Netherlands for securing Protestant succession	
1707		
10 July	Treaty of peace and commerce with Spain	Barcelona
1708		
14 Apr.	Convention with the Emperor for 4,000 Imperialists to be sent from Italy to Catalonia	The Hague
14 Apr.	Convention with Elector of Hanover	The Hague
10 Mar.–17 Apr.	Convention with the Netherlands and Landgrave of Hesse-Cassel	Brussels/The Hague
1709		
14 Jan.	Convention with Elector of Brunswick	The Hague
22 Feb.	Convention with the Netherlands and Elector of Saxony (renewed 7 May 1710 and 24 Mar. 1711)	The Hague
31 Mar.	Treaty with the Netherlands and Prussia	The Hague
12 Apr.	Treaty with Prussia	The Hague
28 May	Articles preliminary to the treaties of a general peace (of 1713) between Britain, the Empire and the Netherlands, and France	The Hague

PRINCIPAL TREATIES, 1689–1820   127

Date signed	Subject	Place signed
29 Oct.	Treaty with the Netherlands for securing the succession to the Crown of Great Britain, and for settling a barrier for the Netherlands against France	The Hague
7 Nov.	Convention with Elector of Treves	The Hague
8 Nov.	Convention with Elector of Brunswick	The Hague
1710		
31 Mar.	Convention with the Netherlands and the Emperor concerning Imperial neutrality (renewed 4 Aug.)	
30 May	Treaty with Poland for two battalions	Camp before Douay
29 Oct.	Military convention between Marlborough and Prince Eugene	The Hague
15 Oct.	Convention with Elector of Brunswick	The Hague
30 Nov.	Convention with Elector of Treves	The Hague
7 Dec.	Military convention between Marlborough and Prince Eugene	The Hague
1711		
27 May	Military treaty between Marlborough and Prince Eugene	The camp at Warde
27 Sept.	Preliminary articles for a treaty of peace with France	London
22 Dec.	Confirmation of treaties with the Netherlands	London
28 Dec.	Convention with Elector of Brunswick	London
1712		
14 Jan.	Convention with Elector of Treves	The Hague
25 Jan.	Convention with the Netherlands and Elector of Brunswick	The Hague

Date signed	Subject	Place signed
24 Mar.	Convention with Elector of Saxony	The Hague
19 Aug.	Treaty of suspension of arms with France (prolonged 7–14 Dec.)	Paris
1713		
29–30 Jan.	Treaty with the Netherlands guaranteeing Protestant succession to Crown of Great Britain and the barrier of the Netherlands	Utrecht
8 Mar.	Declaration of commerce and navigation with the Two Sicilies	Utrecht
14 Mar.	Convention with the Emperor for evacuating Catalonia	Utrecht
14 Mar.	Convention with France for evacuating Catalonia	Utrecht
26 Mar.	The Assiento with Spain for supplying slaves to the Spanish West Indies	Madrid
27 Mar.	Preliminary treaty of peace with Spain	Madrid
11 Apr.	Treaty of peace and friendship with France	Utrecht
11 Apr.	Treaty of navigation and commerce with France (additional articles, 9 May)	Utrecht
13 July	Treaty of peace and friendship with Spain	Utrecht
26 July	Provisional regulation of trade in the Spanish Low Countries between Britain and the Netherlands	Utrecht
9 Dec.	Treaty of navigation and commerce with Spain	Utrecht
1714		
22 July	Treaty of peace, friendship and commerce with Morocco	Tehuan

Date signed	Subject	Place signed
1715		
26 July	Convention with Austrian Netherlands concerning import of British woollen cloths	London
15 Nov.	Treaty with United Provinces and Charles VI for restoration of Austrian Netherlands, to Charles, except for the barrier given to the United Provinces (Barrier Treaty)	Antwerp
14 Dec.	Treaty of commerce with Spain	Madrid
1716		
6 Feb.	Treaty with the Netherlands (with separate article, 3 Apr.)	London
25 May	Treaty of alliance with Emperor (additional article, 1 Sept. 1717)	London
26 May	Convention with Philip V of Spain for explaining the articles of the Assiento (1713)	Madrid
19 July	Treaty of peace with Tripoli	Tripoli
30 Aug.	Treaty of peace and commerce with Tunis	Tunis
29 Oct.	Treaty of peace and commerce with Algiers	Algiers
1717		
4 Jan.	Treaty of alliance with France and the Netherlands	The Hague
1718		
18 July	Convention with France for bringing about peace between the Emperor and the Kings of Spain and Sicily	Paris
18 July	Convention with France for settling separate and secret articles of Quadruple Alliance	Paris
2 Aug.	Quadruple Alliance with Charles VI, France and the Netherlands (accession: King of Sardinia, 8 Nov.)	London

Date signed	Subject	Place signed
22 Dec.	Convention with Charles VI and the Netherlands concerning the Barrier Treaty of 1715	The Hague
1719		
8 Feb.	Convention with Hamburg concerning the herring trade	Hamburg
14 Apr.	Capitulation for the Dutch troops	The Hague
4 Aug.	Treaty with Prussia	Berlin
29 Aug.	Preliminary convention with Sweden	Stockholm
27 Oct.	Convention between Sweden and Denmark (signed by Lord Carteret and the Swedish Minister)	Stockholm
30 Oct.	Convention with Denmark	Copenhagen
18 Nov.	Convention with Emperor and France, excluding sons of Philip of Spain and Elizabeth Farnese from succession to Tuscany, Parma and Piacenza	The Hague
1720		
21 Jan.	Treaty with Sweden	—
16 Feb.	Accession of Spain to convention between France and Britain of 18 July 1718	The Hague
17 Feb.	Accession of Spain to Treaty of London of 2 Aug. 1718	The Hague
29 Feb.	Convention for armistice by sea with France and Spain	The Hague
18 Mar.	Instrument of admission of King of Sardinia to Act of Accession of King of Spain to Treaty of London, signed by Britain, France, Spain, Sardinia and the Empire	The Hague
2 Apr.	Convention for suspension of arms by sea with France, Spain, Sardinia and the Empire	The Hague

Date signed	Subject	Place signed
1721		
23 Jan.	Treaty of peace and commerce with Morocco	Fez
13 June	Treaty with Spain	Madrid
13 June	Treaty of defensive alliance with France and Spain	Madrid
27 Sept.	Act of guarantee with France concerning the renunciations by the Emperor and the King of Spain	Paris
1722		
27 Aug.	Act of guarantee with France of the Kingdom of Sardinia	Versailles
1723		
10 Oct.	Treaty with Prussia	Charlottenbourg
1724		
24 Jan.	Act of guarantee with France	Cambrai
1725		
3 Sept.	Defensive treaty of alliance with France and Prussia	Hanover
1726		
9 Aug.	Act of accession of the Netherlands to Treaty of Hanover	The Hague
1727		
12 Mar.	Convention with Hesse-Cassel	London
14 Mar.	Accession of Sweden to Treaty of Hanover	Stockholm
16 Apr.	Treaty of alliance with France and Denmark	Copenhagen
31 May	Preliminary articles between the Emperor and the Allies of Hanover	Paris
25 Nov.	Treaty with Duke of Wolfenbuttel	London

Date signed	Subject	Place signed
1728		
14 Jan.	Articles of peace and commerce with Morocco (additional articles, July, 1729)	Mequinez
6 Mar.	Convention with the Emperor, Spain and the Netherlands concerning the execution of the Preliminaries of 31 May 1727	The Pardo
27 May	Renewal of former treaties with the Netherlands	London
1729		
18 Mar.	Treaty of peace with Algiers	Algiers
6/8 Sept.	Convention agreeing to mediation over differences with Prussia	Berlin
9 Nov.	Treaty of peace and friendship with France and Spain	Seville
21 Nov.	Accession of the Netherlands to treaty of 9 Nov.	Seville
1730		
31 Mar.	Articles of peace and commerce with Tripoli	Tripoli
1731		
16 Mar.	Treaty of peace and alliance with the Emperor, in which the Netherlands is included	Vienna
22 July	Treaty with Spain and the Emperor (accession: Tuscany 21 Sept.)	Vienna
17 Oct.	Convention with Bremen concerning the herring trade	Bremen
31 Oct.	Regulation signed by plenipotentiaries of Britain and Spain for introduction of Spanish garrisons into Tuscany	Leghorn
1732		
20 Feb.	Act of concurrence of the Netherlands to the Treaty of Vienna of 16 Mar. 1731	The Hague

Date signed	Subject	Place signed
20 Feb.	Article with the Netherlands concerning the East India Company at Ostend	The Hague
1734		
30 Sept.	Treaty and secret articles with Denmark	London
2 Dec.	Treaty of commerce with Russia	St Petersburg
15 Dec.	Treaty of peace with Morocco	—
1738		
9 Sept.	Convention with Spain	London
1739		
14 Jan.	Convention with Spain	The Pardo
14 Mar.	Treaty with Denmark	Copenhagen
1740		
9 May	Treaty with King of Sweden, as Landgrave of Hesse-Cassel	London
1741		
3 Apr.	Treaty with Russia	St Petersburg
24 June	Convention with Queen of Hungary	Hanover
1742		
23 Feb.	Cartel for exchange of prisoners with Spain	Paris
25 June	Convention with Queen of Hungary	London
18 Nov.	Treaty of defensive alliance with Prussia	London
11 Dec.	Treaty with Russia	Moscow
1743		
15 Feb.	Treaty with Austria-Hungary	London
13 Sept.	Definitive treaty of peace, union, friendship and mutual defence with Hungary and Sardinia	Worms

Date signed	Subject	Place signed
1744		
10 Feb.	Convention with Austria-Hungary	London
27 Apr.	Treaty of alliance with Elector of Cologne	London
May	Treaty of alliance with Elector of Mainz (prolonged June 1747)	—
4 July	Treaty with the Netherlands and the Elector of Cologne	The Hague
11 Aug.	Treaty with Queen of Austria-Hungary	London
18 Sept.	Convention with the Netherlands	London
1745		
8 Jan.	Treaty of alliance with Queen of Hungary, Poland and the Netherlands	Warsaw
2 Apr.	Treaty with Queen of Hungary	London
21 May	Treaty granting £60,000 to Sardinia	London
1 June	Convention with Queen of Hungary	At the quarters of General de Lapines
8 June	Convention with Queen of Hungary	Hanover
16 June	Treaty with King of Sweden, as Landgrave of Hesse-Cassel	Hanover
26 Aug.	Preliminary convention with Prussia (with further declaration signed in London, 12 Sept.)	Hanover
1746		
10 June	Convention with Queen of Hungary	London
10 June	Treaty with Sardinia	London
21 July	Subsidiary treaty with the Netherlands and Bavaria	Munich
30 Aug.	Provisional convention of subsidy between Britain and the Netherlands, and Queen of Hungary	The Hague

PRINCIPAL TREATIES, 1689–1820   135

Date signed	Subject	Place signed
1747		
12 Jan.	Convention for the campaign of 1747 with Austria-Hungary, the Netherlands and Sardinia	The Hague
12 June	Convention with Russia	St Petersburg
19 Nov.	Convention between Britain and the Netherlands, and Russia for passage of Russian troops across Germany	St Petersburg
27 Nov.	Convention with Russia	St Petersburg
1748		
26 Jan.	Convention for the campaign of 1748 with Austria-Hungary, the Netherlands and Sardinia (additional convention, 3 May)	The Hague
1 Feb.	Subsidiary convention with the Netherlands and Duke of Wolfenbuttel	The Hague
30 Apr.	Preliminary articles of peace with France and the Netherlands	Aix-la-Chapelle
18 Oct.	Treaty of Aix-la-Chapelle with France and the Netherlands (accessions: Spain, 20 Oct.; Austria-Hungary, 23 Oct.; Modena, 25 Oct.; Genoa, 28 Oct.; Sardinia, 7 Nov.)	Aix-la-Chapelle
1750		
15 Jan.	Treaty of peace with Morocco (additional articles, Feb. 1751)	Fez
22 Aug.	Alliance with Austria-Hungary and Bavaria	Hanover
22 Aug.	Alliance with the Netherlands and Bavaria	Hanover
5 Oct.	Treaty of commerce with Spain	Madrid
30 Oct.	Alliance with Russia and Austria-Hungary	St Petersburg

Date signed	Subject	Place signed
1751		
3 June	Additional article with Algiers	Algiers
13 Sept.	Alliance with the Netherlands and Poland	Dresden
19 Sept.	Treaty of peace and commerce with Tripoli	Tripoli
19 Oct.	Treaty of peace and commerce with Tunis	Bardo
1753		
11 May	Alliance with the Empire, Hungary and Modena	Vienna
1755		
18 June	Treaty with Landgrave of Hesse-Cassel	Hanover
30 Sept.	Treaty with Russia	St Petersburg
1756		
16 Jan.	Treaty with Prussia	London
1758		
11 Apr.	Treaty with Prussia	London
7 Dec.	Convention with Prussia	London
1759		
17 Jan.	Convention with Landgrave of Hesse-Cassel	London
9 Nov.	Convention with Prussia	—
1760		
14 Jan.	Treaty with Duke of Brunswick	Marburg
1 Apr.	Convention with Hesse-Cassel	London
28 July	Treaty of peace and commerce with Morocco	Fez
12 Dec.	Convention with Prussia	—
1761		
28 Jan.	Renewal of peace with Tripoli	Tripoli
3 Mar.	Protocol with Hesse	London

Date signed	Subject	Place signed
10 Aug.	Convention with Brunswick for troops	Brunswick
3 Nov.	Preliminary articles of peace with France and Spain (accession: Portugal, 22 Nov.)	Fontainebleau
1763		
10 Feb.	Definitive treaty of peace with France and Spain (accession: Portugal, 10 Feb.)	Paris
21 Sept.	Act of guarantee by Britain of treaty between France, Spain and Sardinia of 10 June 1763	London
1765		
27 Feb.	Convention with France	London
3 Aug.	Treaty of peace and commerce with Algiers	Algiers
1766		
5 Feb.	Treaty of commerce and alliance with Sweden	Stockholm
1 July	Treaty of amity and commerce with Russia	St Petersburg
1771		
22 Jan.	Spanish declaration and British counter-declaration concerning Falkland Islands	London
1776		
9 Jan.	Treaty of subsidy with Duke of Brunswick	Brunswick
15 Jan.	Treaty of subsidy with Landgrave of Hesse-Cassel	Cassel
5 Feb.	Treaty of subsidy with Hesse-Hanau	Hanau
20 Apr.	Subsidiary treaty with Prince of Waldeck	Arolsen
25 Apr.	Ulterior convention with Hereditary Prince of Hesse-Cassel, as Regent of Hesse-Hanau	Hanau

Date signed	Subject	Place signed
11 Dec.	Treaty with Landgrave of Hesse for corps of 1,067 men to serve in America	Cassel
11 Dec.	Convention with Hesse-Cassel	Cassel
1777		
1 Feb.	Treaty with Brandenburg-Anspach for corps of 1,200 infantry	Anspach
10 Feb.	Treaty with Hereditary Prince of Hesse, as Regent of Hesse-Hanau	Hanau
1778		
23 Apr.	Treaty of subsidy with Anhalt-Zerbst	Stade
1780		
12/28 Mar.	Cartel with France for general exchange of all prisoners taken at sea and brought to Europe (with additional article, 16/22 June)	London/Versailles
4 July	Explanatory article with Denmark concerning neutral trade	Copenhagen
1782		
30 Nov.	Provisional articles of peace with USA	Paris
1783		
20 Jan.	Preliminary articles of peace with France	Versailles
20 Jan.	Preliminary articles of peace with Spain	Versailles
24 May	Additional articles with Morocco	Sallee
2 Sept.	Preliminary articles of peace with the Netherlands	Paris
3 Sept.	Definitive treaty of peace with France	Versailles
3 Sept.	Definitive treaty of peace with Spain	Versailles
3 Sept.	Definitive treaty of peace and friendship with USA	Paris

Date signed	Subject	Place signed
1784		
20 May	Definitive treaty of peace and amity with the Netherlands	Paris
1786		
14 July	Convention with Spain concerning America	London
26 Sept.	Treaty of commerce and navigation with France	Versailles
1787		
15 Jan.	Explanatory convention with France	Versailles
30 Aug.	Reciprocal declaration with France to put in action six vessels of the line	Versailles
31 Aug.	Explanatory convention with France concerning French commercial establishments in India	Versailles
28 Sept.	Treaty of alliance with Landgrave of Hesse-Cassel	Cassel
2 Oct.	Convention with Prussia	Berlin
27 Oct.	Reciprocal declarations with France to stop the armament made on the occasion of the troubles in Holland	Versailles
1788		
15 Apr.	Treaty of defensive alliance with the Netherlands	The Hague
13 June	Provisional treaty of defensive alliance with Prussia	Loo-en-Gueldre
13 Aug.	Treaty of defensive alliance with Prussia	Berlin
1790		
9 Jan.	Alliance with Prussia and Holland	Berlin
24 July	Exchange of declaration and counter-declaration with Spain	Madrid

Date signed	Subject	Place signed
28 Oct.	Convention with Spain concerning America	Escurial
10 Dec.	Convention with the Netherlands, Empire and Prussia concerning the Austrian Netherlands	The Hague
1791		
8 Apr.	Treaty of peace with Morocco	Sallee
1793		
12 Feb.	Convention with Spain	London
4 Mar.	Articles with Elector of Brunswick-Lüneburg concerning body of troops entering British service	London
4 Mar.	Preliminary articles with Hanover concerning deployment of Hanoverian troops on the Continent in British pay	London
25 Mar.	Commercial convention with Russia	London
25 Mar.	Convention with Russia for concerted action against France	London
10 Apr.	Treaty of subsidy with Landgrave of Hesse-Cassel	—
25 Apr.	Treaty of alliance with Sardinia	London
25 May	Convention with Spain	Aranjuez
12 July	Convention with Sicily	Naples
14 July	Convention with Prussia	Mayence
23 Aug.	Second convention with Landgrave of Hesse-Cassel	Maykammer
30 Aug.	Convention with Emperor	London
21 Sept.	Treaty of subsidy with Margrave of Baden	Carlsruhe
26 Sept.	Treaty with Portugal	London
5 Oct.	Treaty of subsidy with Landgrave of Hesse-Darmstadt	Langen-Candel

Date signed	Subject	Place signed
1794		
7 Jan.	Article of agreement with Hanover for additional troops to be taken into British pay	London
11 Jan.	Agreement with Spain	Madrid
19 Apr.	Treaty of subsidy between Britain and the Netherlands, and Prussia	The Hague
19 Apr.	Separate convention with the Netherlands	The Hague
8 Nov.	Treaty of subsidy with Duke of Brunswick	Brunswick
19 Nov.	Treaty of amity, commerce and navigation with USA	London
1795		
18 Feb.	Treaty of defensive alliance with Russia	St Petersburg
4 May	Convention of loan with Emperor of Germany	Vienna
20 May	Treaty of defensive alliance with Emperor of Germany	Vienna
1796		
Jan.	Treaty with Algiers concerning Corsica	—
4 May	Explanatory article with USA concerning trade and intercourse with American Indians	Philadelphia
10 June	Treaty of subsidy with Hesse-Darmstadt	Frankfurt
1797		
21 Feb.	Treaty of commerce with Russia	St Petersburg
11 May	Declaration concerning treaty of 21 Feb.	Moscow
16 May	Convention of loan with Emperor of Germany	London

FOREIGN AFFAIRS AND EMPIRE

Date signed	Subject	Place signed
1798		
15 Mar.	Explanatory article with USA concerning the River St Croix	London
16 July	Article of peace and commerce with Tripoli	Tripoli
13 Sept.	Cartel for exchange of prisoners of war with France	London
25 Oct.	Declaration with American Commissioners concerning the River St Croix	Providence
1 Dec.	Treaty of alliance with King of the Two Sicilies	Naples
29 Dec.	Provisional treaty with Russia	St Petersburg
1799		
5 Jan.	Treaty of alliance with Turkey	Constantinople
22 June	Convention with Russia	St Petersburg
29 June	Declaration with Russia concerning treaty of Dec. 1798	St Petersburg
1800		
18 Jan.	Convention with Prince of Orange for receiving Dutch troops into British pay	—
11 Mar.	Convention with Prince of Orange concerning Dutch ships surrendered 30 Aug. 1799	—
16 Mar.	Treaty of subsidy with Bavaria	Munich
2 Apr.	First explanatory article of convention with Prince of Orange	—
20 Apr.	Treaty of subsidy with Duke of Württemberg	Louisbourg
30 Apr.	Treaty with Elector of Mayence	Pfora
10 June	Second explanatory article of convention with Prince of Orange	London
20 June	Convention with Emperor	Vienna

Date signed	Subject	Place signed
20 June	Secret convention granting Emperor an indemnity for his territorial losses	Vienna
15 July	Supplementary convention to Bavarian subsidy treaty of 16 Mar.	Amberg
29 Aug.	Preliminary convention with Denmark	Copenhagen
3 Sept.	Treaty of peace and commerce with Algiers	Algiers
1801		
Jan.	Treaty of commerce with Persia	—
Jan.	Political treaty with Persia	—
19 Mar.	Treaty with Algiers concerning Malta	Algiers
14 June	Treaty of peace with Morocco	Fez
17 June	Convention with Russia (accessions: Denmark, 23 Oct.; Sweden, 30 Mar. 1802)	St Petersburg
1 Oct.	Preliminary articles of peace with France	London
20 Oct.	Additional articles to convention of 17 June with Russia	Moscow
20 Oct.	Explanatory declaration with Russia	Moscow
23 Oct.	Convention with Denmark concerning neutral trade	Moscow
1802		
8 Jan.	Convention of claims with USA	London
27 Mar.	Definitive treaty of peace with France, Spain and Batavian Republic	Amiens
17 May	Postal convention with France	—
1803		
2 Jan.	Articles of agreement with Batavian authorities on evacuation of Cape of Good Hope	The Cape

Date signed	Subject	Place signed
25 July	Explanatory convention with Sweden concerning treaty of 1661	London
1804		
3 Dec.	Preliminary and secret convention with Sweden	Stockholm
1805		
11 Apr.	Treaty of concert with Russia (accession: Austria, 9 Aug.): additional articles, 10 May and 24 July	St Petersburg
9 Aug.	Declaration with Russia and Austria respecting future policy	St Petersburg
31 Aug.	Treaty with Sweden concerning convention of 1804	Helsingborg
3 Oct.	Treaty with Sweden	Beckascog
1807		
28 Jan.	Articles of treaty of peace and amity with Prussia	Memel
17 June	Convention with Sweden	London
23 June	Convention of subsidy with Sweden	Stralsund
27 June	Convention of subsidy with Prussia	London
7 July	Treaty between commanders of British and Spanish troops	Buenos Aires
22 Oct.	Convention of friendship and amity with Portugal	London
1808		
8 Feb.	Convention of subsidy with Sweden	Stockholm
30 Mar.	Treaty of alliance and subsidy with the Two Sicilies	Palermo
30 Aug.	Convention for evacuation of Portugal by French army	Lisbon
1809		
5 Jan.	Treaty of peace and commerce with Turkey	Dardanelles

PRINCIPAL TREATIES, 1689–1820   145

Date signed	Subject	Place signed
14 Jan.	Treaty of peace, friendship and alliance with Ferdinand VII of Spain (additional article, 21 Mar.)	London
1 Mar.	Convention with Sweden	Stockholm
12 Mar.	Preliminary treaty of friendship and alliance with Persia	Tehran
21 Apr.	Convention of loan with Prince Regent of Portugal	London
24 Apr.	Treaty of alliance with Austria	London
13 May	Treaty of alliance and subsidy with the Two Sicilies	Palermo
9 Sept.	Treaty with Algiers renewing existing treaties	
1810		
19 Feb.	Treaty of commerce and navigation with Portugal	Rio de Janeiro
19 Feb.	Treaty of friendship and alliance with Portugal	Rio de Janeiro
1812		
14 Mar.	Treaty of peace with Persia	Tehran
2 May	Treaty of commerce with Tunis	Bardo
10 May	Treaty of commerce with Tripoli	Tripoli
18 July	Treaty of peace, union and friendship with Russia	Orebro
18 July	Treaty of peace and friendship with Sweden	Orebro
12 Sept.	Supplementary treaty of alliance and subsidy with the Two Sicilies	Palermo
1813		
3 Mar.	Treaty of concert and subsidy with Sweden	Stockholm
12 May	Cartel for exchange of prisoners of war with USA	Washington
14 June	Convention with Prussia	Reichenbach

Date signed	Subject	Place signed
27 June	Convention with Russia	Reichenbach
6 July	Convention with Russia concerning holding German Legion in service of his Imperial Majesty	Peterswaldaw
30 Sept.	Supplementary convention of concert and subsidy with Prussia	London
30 Sept.	Supplementary convention of concert and subsidy with Russia	London
3 Oct.	Preliminary treaty of alliance with Austria	Toplitz
16 Oct.	Additional article with Tunis	Bardo
22 Oct.	Separate and additional article to treaty of concert and subsidy with Sweden of 3 Mar.	Leipzig
5 Dec.	Subsidiary agreement with Hanoverian government	London

1814

Date signed	Subject	Place signed
14 Jan.	Treaty of peace with Denmark (additional articles, 7 Apr.)	Kiel
3 Feb.	Armistice with Neapolitan forces	Naples
3 Feb.	Subsidiary agreement with Sardinia	London
5 Feb.	Convention with Spain for mutual restoration of vessels recaptured from the enemy	London
15 Feb.	Convention with Austria, Prussia and Russia concerning territorial arrangements of peace with France	Troyes
1 Mar.	Treaty of union, concert and subsidy with Austria	Chaumont
1 Mar.	Treaty of union, concert and subsidy with Prussia	Chaumont
1 Mar.	Treaty of union, concert and subsidy with Russia	Chaumont
18 Apr.	Convention with French armies for surrender of Genoa	St François d'Albaro
23 Apr.	Convention for suspension of hostilities with France	Paris

Date signed	Subject	Place signed
27 Apr.	Accession of Britain to treaty between Austria, Prussia, Russia and Napoleon of 11 Apr.	Paris
27 Apr.	Convention of armistice between British and Austrian armies in Italy and French army	Turin
28 May	Military convention between Britain, Austria, Prussia and Russia, and France	Paris
30 May	Definitive treaty of peace and amity with France	Paris
2 June	Convention with Prussia and Russia concerning Russo-German Legion	Paris
14 June	Protocol of conference with Austria, Russia and Prussia concerning union of Holland and Belgium	Vienna
29 June	Supplementary convention with Austria	London
29 June	Supplementary convention with Prussia	London
29 June	Supplementary convention with Russia	London
4 July	Convention with Post Office of Hamburg	London
5 July	Treaty of friendship and alliance with Spain (additional articles, 28 Aug.)	Madrid
13 Aug.	Convention with the Netherlands concerning trade and colonies	London
13 Aug.	Convention with Sweden concerning compensation for restoration of Guadeloupe to France	London
25 Nov.	Definitive treaty of friendship and alliance with Persia	Tehran
24 Dec.	Treaty of peace and amity with USA	Ghent

Date signed	Subject	Place signed
1815		
3 Jan.	Treaty of defensive alliance with Austria and France (accessions: Bavaria, 26 Jan.; the Netherlands, 31 Jan.)	Vienna
22 Jan.	Treaty with Portugal for restriction of slave trade	Vienna
8 Feb.	Declaration by Britain, Austria, France, Portugal, Prussia, Russia, Spain and Sweden concerning universal abolition of slave trade	Vienna
20 Mar.	Declaration of the Eight Powers (as above) on affairs of Swiss Confederation (accession: Swiss Confederation, 27 May)	Vienna
25 Mar.	Treaty of alliance with Austria, Prussia and Russia against Napoleon (accessions: France, 27 Mar.; Hanover, 7 Apr.; Portugal, 8 Apr.; Sardinia, 9 Apr.; Bavaria, 15 Apr.; Princes and Free Towns of Germany, 27 Apr.; the Netherlands, 28 Apr.; Baden, 13 May; Switzerland, 20 May; Hesse-Darmstadt, 23 May; Saxony, 27 May; Württemberg, 30 May; Denmark, 1 Sept.): supplemented by convention of 30 Apr.	Vienna
29 Mar.	Protocol of conferences between plenipotentiaries of the Eight Powers on the cessions of the King of Sardinia to the Canton of Geneva	Vienna
30 Apr.	Additional convention of alliance and subsidy with Austria, Prussia and Russia	Vienna
2 May	Treaty of subsidy with Sardinia	Brussels
13 May	Naval convention with Naples	Naples
19 May	Treaty of subsidy with Baden	Brussels

Date signed	Subject	Place signed
19 May	Treaty with Russia and the Netherlands concerning Russian–Dutch loan	London
20 May	Territorial treaty between King of Sardinia and Austria, Britain, France, Prussia and Russia (accession: Switzerland, 20 May)	Vienna
20 May	Convention with France concerning occupation of Martinique	Barbados
22 May	Convention with Sardinia for fortification of Genoa	Turin
31 May	Treaty between the Netherlands and Austria, Prussia, Britain and Russia concerning Kingdom of the Netherlands	Vienna
6 June	Treaty of subsidy with Württemberg	Brussels
7 June	Treaty of subsidy with Bavaria	Brussels

1816

Date signed	Subject	Place signed
17 Apr.	Declaration of Bey of Tunis concerning abolition of Christian slavery	Bardo
17 Apr.	Treaty with Tunis concerning Ionian Islands	Bardo
29 Apr.	Declaration of Bey of Tripoli concerning abolition of Christian slavery	Tripoli
29 Apr.	Treaty with Tripoli concerning Ionian Islands	Tripoli
20 May	Additional article with Algiers concerning Hanover	Algiers
30 June	Treaty with Hesse touching its renunciations and possessions	Frankfurt
28 Aug.	Declaration of Bey of Algiers concerning abolition of Christian slavery	Algiers
26 Sept.	Convention of commerce and navigation with King of the Two Sicilies	London

Date signed	Subject	Place signed
16 Nov.	Treaty with the Netherlands concerning Luxembourg, etc.	Frankfurt
1817		
28/9 Apr.	Arrangement with USA concerning naval forces on American Lakes	Washington
17 May	Convention with Turkish commissaries	Joannina
28 July	Additional convention with Portugal for prevention of slave trade (separate article, 11 Sept.; additional articles, 15 Mar. 1823)	London
23 Sept.	Treaty with Spain for abolition of slave trade (additional articles, 10 Dec. 1822)	Madrid
19 Oct.	Declaration of Bey of Tunis that Tunisian ships shall not cruise in English Channel (similar declaration by Bey of Tripoli, 8 Mar. 1818)	Bardo
1818		
25 Apr.	Convention between Britain, Austria, Prussia and Russia, and France for final liquidation of private claims upon French government (accessions: Hesse-Darmstadt, 5 May; Tuscany, 1 June; Saxony, 6 June; Bavaria, 12 June; Württemberg, 15 June; Sardinia, 30 June; Swiss Confederation, 2 July; Baden, 22 July; the Netherlands, 30 July; Parma, 3 Aug.; Hesse-Cassel, 26 Aug.; Denmark, 17 Sept.): additional articles, 4 July 1818	Paris
4 May	Treaty with Netherlands for preventing subjects engaging in slave trade (additional articles, 31 Dec. 1822 and 25 Jan. 1823)	The Hague
6 Oct.	Convention with Post Office of the Netherlands	The Hague

PRINCIPAL TREATIES, 1689–1820   151

Date signed	Subject	Place signed
9 Oct.	Convention with France for evacuation of French territory by Allied troops (accessions: Parma, 12 Nov.; Switzerland, 12 Nov.; Sardinia, 22 Mar. 1819; Baden, 28 Aug. 1819; Bavaria, 7 May 1820; Spain, 6 July 1820; Tuscany, 2 Dec. 1820)	Aix-la-Chapelle
20 Oct.	Convention of commerce with USA	London
1819		
2 Feb.	Definitive arrangement with France relative to liquidation of French indemnity, signed by Britain, Austria, Prussia, Russia and France	Paris
10 July	Treaty with Austria, Prussia, Russia and Baden	Frankfurt
20 July	General treaty of territorial commission assembled at Frankfurt, signed by Britain, Austria, Prussia, Russia (accessions: Baden, 4 Aug. 1820; Parma, 15 Aug. 1820; Tuscany, 10 Nov. 1820; Saxony, 18 Dec. 1820; Sardinia, 30 Dec. 1820)	Frankfurt
1820		
15 May	Final Act of ministerial conferences held at Vienna to complete and consolidate organisation of German Confederation	Vienna
9 June	Act of the Congress of Vienna, signed by Britain, Austria, France, Portugal, Prussia, Russia and Sweden (accessions: the Netherlands, 20 Oct.; Two Sicilies, 1 Feb. 1816; Sardinia, 15 Oct. 1816; Spain, 7 June 1817; Parma, 25 Jan. 1818; Hesse-Darmstadt, 1 Mar. 1818; Saxony, 10 Mar. 1818; Württemberg, 14 Apr. 1818; Denmark, 20 Apr. 1818; Tuscany, 22 Apr. 1818; Hesse-Cassel, 11 Jan. 1819; Bavaria, 7 May 1820)	Vienna

Date signed	Subject	Place signed
3 July	Convention between Prussian, English and French commanders for suspension of hostilities	St Cloud
3 July	Convention of commerce with USA	London
2 Aug.	Convention with Austria, Prussia and Russia concerning custody of Napoleon	Paris
10 Aug.	Capitulation of island of Guadeloupe, signed by Britain and France	Guadeloupe
12 Aug.	Convention with the Netherlands concerning colonies of Demerara, Essequibo and Berbice	London
18 Sept.	Accession of Britain to territorial treaty between Saxony and Prussia of 18 May	Paris
3 Nov.	Protocol of conference with Austria, Prussia and Russia to regulate disposition of territories ceded by France	Paris
5 Nov.	Treaty with Austria, Prussia and Russia concerning Ionian Islands (accessions: France, 27 Sept. 1816; Turkey, 24 Apr. 1819)	Paris
20 Nov.	Treaty of alliance and friendship with Austria, Prussia and Russia	Paris
20 Nov.	Definitive treaty with Austria, Prussia, Russia and France (accessions: Hesse-Cassel, 15 Oct. 1816; Spain, 8 June 1817; Bavaria, 20 Dec. 1817; Parma, 30 Jan 1818; Hesse-Darmstadt, 1 Mar. 1818; Saxony, 21 Mar. 1818; Sardinia, 9 Apr. 1818; Denmark, 21 Apr. 1818; Tuscany, 24 Apr. 1818; Württemberg, 14 Aug. 1818; the Netherlands, 8 Feb. 1822)	Paris

Date signed	Subject	Place signed
20 Nov.	Convention between Britain, Austria, Prussia and Russia, and France concerning French indemnity	Paris
20 Nov.	Convention with Austria, Prussia, Russia and France concerning occupation of a military line in France by an allied army	Paris
20 Nov.	Convention between Britain, Austria, Prussia and Russia, and France concerning claims of subjects of allied powers upon France	Paris
20 Nov.	Act signed with Austria, France, Prussia and Russia guaranteeing Swiss neutrality	Paris
20 Nov.	Protocol signed with Austria, Prussia and Russia respecting the 700 million francs France is to pay allied powers	Paris
20 Nov.	Convention with France concerning claims of British subjects	Paris

5.2 Ireland, 1688–1823

1688	Irish troops dispatched to England (Oct.). Londonderry refuses to accept Catholic garrison (Dec.).
1689	Landing of James II at Kinsale in Ireland (12 Mar.); joined by Tyrconnell and enters Dublin (24 Mar.). Siege of Protestants at Londonderry opens (20 Apr.). Irish Parliament issues an Attainder, confiscating the land of 2,000 of William's adherents (May). Siege of Londonderry lifted (28 July) by Kirke and defeat of Catholic forces at Newton Butler (28 July). William III sends Marshal Schomberg with 10,000 troops to Belfast (Aug.).
1690	Seven thousand French troops arrive at Kinsale to support James (Mar.). William lands in Ireland (14 June). William defeats James's forces at Battle of the Boyne (1 July) and James flees to France while his forces retreat to the west. First siege of Limerick repulsed (Aug.); Cork and Kinsale taken by William's forces.
1691	Fall of Athlone (30 June) and defeat of James's forces at Battle of Aughrim by Ginkel (12 July). Second siege of Limerick, which surrenders on 3 October. Treaty, or pacification, of Limerick offers free transportation to all Irish officers and soldiers desiring to go to France. Irish Catholics to have same religious liberties as enjoyed under Charles II and the right to carry arms and practise their professions. One million acres of 'rebel' estates confiscated.
1692	Meeting of Irish Parliament (Oct.). William and Mary recognised as rulers. Catholics prevented from sitting in Parliament and laws passed to limit their worship, ownership of property and education in defiance of Treaty of Limerick. Parliament prorogued for refusing to pass money bill (Nov.).

1693	Irish Parliament dissolved (June).
1695	Irish Parliament passes bills prohibiting Catholics from sending children abroad to be educated and preventing them bearing arms.
1697	Irish Parliament banishes all Roman Catholic bishops and monastic clergy. Treaty of Limerick ratified but modified to incorporate penal laws against Catholics.
1699	Irish export woollen trade restricted.
1703	Act passed determining conditions of Catholic worship; priests required to register name and parish in order to celebrate mass or face imprisonment or execution.
1704	Act prevents land being passed on to Catholics. Protestant dissenters excluded from office.
1709	Catholic clergy required to take Oath of Abjuration of Stuart pretender. Refused by 1,000 Catholic priests.
1710	Linen Board set up to supervise linen industry.
1713	Duke of Shrewsbury appointed Lord Lieutenant.
1714	Schism Act extended to Ireland.
1719	Law-suit of *Sherlock* v. *Annesley* leads to Act for better securing of the dependency of the Kingdom of Ireland upon the Crown of Great Britain, declaring that the British Parliament had full authority to make laws 'of sufficient force and validity to bind the kingdom and people of Ireland' and denying the status of the Irish House of Lords as a Court of Appeal. Act of Toleration granted religious freedom to Protestant dissenters, but Test Acts retained.
1720	Irish cotton industry restricted by British Parliament. Jonathan Swift publishes anonymously a pamphlet supporting Irish manufacturers against British. Duke of Grafton appointed Lord Lieutenant (June).
1722	Grant to William Wood, a Wolverhampton ironmaster, of a patent to coin money for Ireland (July) arouses controversy.

1723	Irish Parliament protests against 'Wood's halfpence' (Sept.) and refuses to transact further business.
1724	Lord Carteret replaces Grafton as Lord Lieutenant. Swift publishes first of *Drapier's Letters* (Feb.), attacking the new coinage and the constitutional relationship between Britain and Ireland.
1725	British government reduces amount of currency to be issued by Wood from £108,000 to £40,000. Attempt to prosecute printer of *Drapier's Letters* fails and government withdraws Wood's patent completely.
1727	Irish Catholics deprived of the vote.
1727–30	Series of poor harvests leads to widespread famine.
1730	Duke of Dorset becomes Lord Lieutenant (June). Dublin Society set up to encourage agriculture and the arts.
1740–1	Serious famine leads to between 80,000 and 400,000 deaths.
1745	Earl of Chesterfield becomes Lord Lieutenant and begins suspension of penal laws against Catholics.
1746	Irish forbidden to export glassware.
1747	Charles Lucas begins to publish the *Citizen's Journal*. John Wesley makes first of 42 visits to Ireland; first Methodist church established in Dublin.
1750	Roman Catholics admitted to lower grades of the army.
1753	Irish Parliament defeats money bill to dispose of Irish budget surplus to defray English national debt. Henry Boyle, Speaker of Irish Commons, dismissed as Chancellor of Exchequer. Widespread rejoicing in Dublin. Parliament prorogued.
1755	Duke of Devonshire appointed Lord Lieutenant to secure compromise on money bill. Boyle given earldom and other officials reinstated.
1759	Crowds invade Parliament on rumour of union with England. Henry Flood enters Parliament and leads 'patriots'. Restrictions on export of Irish cattle to England lifted.

1768	Octennial Act for Irish Parliaments.
1769	Defeat of government bills for augmentation of army, defeat of supply bill, attacks on pension list, and introduction of militia bill. Supply bill and army augmentation passed; Parliament prorogued until 1771.
1771	Act to extend leases to Roman Catholics reclaiming bogland.
1773	Defeat of measure to tax absentee proprietors.
1774	Act to provide form of oath of allegiance acceptable to Roman Catholics.
1755	Measures passed to open trade to Irish merchants and encouragement given to linen manufacture.
1775–76	Attacks on government policy towards American colonies and defeat of government money bills.
1776	First Volunteer companies formed in Wexford.
1777	New Irish Parliament meets for business and attacks state of trade and Financial administration. First Volunteer company in Belfast.
1778	Censure motion on state of Irish finances passed. Act passed to allow Catholics to take leases on land for life or up to 999 years; also to inherit or bequeath land on same terms as Protestants.
1778–79	Widespread Volunteer movement to repel French invasion and assert Irish rights.
1779	Demands for further easing of restrictions on Irish trade pressed in the English House of Commons. Widespread agitation for removal of trade restrictions. Demonstration of armed volunteers in Dublin (4 Nov.). Attack by English politicians in House of Commons over Irish trade issue. Acts forbidding the export of wool, woollen goods and glass from Ireland repealed.
1780	Irish permitted to trade with British settlements in Africa and America on same terms as rest of British Isles. Prohibitions on

import of gold and silver from Great Britain repealed. Irish allowed to import foreign hops and Turkey Company opened to Irish merchants.

Protestant dissenters released from having to take the Sacrament in the Church of Ireland.

Grattan's motion (19 Apr.) that 'the King's most excellent majesty, and the lords and commons of Ireland, are the only power competent to enact laws to bind Ireland' adjourned by 136 votes to 97.

Irish magistrates refuse to operate Mutiny Act and Mutiny Bill prepared in Irish Parliament passed. Perpetual Mutiny Act passed by British Parliament.

1782 Convention of Ulster Volunteers at Dungannon (15 Feb.) declare Poynings' Law 'unconstitutional and a grievance'; demand a measure of religious equality; control of the Mutiny Act; and same security of tenure for Irish as for English judges. Grattan's motion for Irish independence defeated by 137 votes to 68 (22 Feb.).

Resolution for independence passed unanimously (16 Apr.). 'The Constitution of 1782': repeal of legislative authority of British Parliament and passing of Yelverton's Act to end the power of the chief governor and council of Ireland to originate or alter bills; only bills enacted by Irish parliament to be transmitted to the King. Perpetual Mutiny Act replaced by biennial act and Irish judges granted same tenure as English.

Catholic relief acts passed concerning land, education, the residence of bishops and clergy, and registration of priests, but not granting full political rights.

1783 Renunciation Act (23 Geo. III, c.28) confirmed the complete legislative and judicial independence of Ireland.

National Volunteer Convention at Dublin chaired by Henry Flood agrees plan 'for the more equal representation of the people in parliament'. Irish Parliament refuses Flood leave to bring in reform bill by 157 votes to 77 (30 Nov.).

1783–84 Appeals for protective legislation for Irish manufactures raised in Irish Parliament but rejected.

1784 First power-driven machinery established in Ireland.

Bounties given to export of cotton. Foster's Corn Law providing bounties for export of grain.

1785	Proposals for commercial union between Ireland and England abandoned.
1790	Whig Club founded by Grattan and others to press for parliamentary reform.
1791	Society of United Irishmen founded in Belfast by Theobald Wolfe Tone and others for religious equality and radical reform of parliament. Similar societies set up in many other Irish towns and cities.
1792	Catholic relief bill removing disabilities attaching to marriages between Catholics and Protestants; Catholics admitted to the legal profession and restrictions on education removed. Provisions for granting political rights defeated. Catholic Convention in Dublin (3 Dec.) and petitions for further concessions.
1793	Catholic Relief Act. Roman Catholics admitted to parliamentary and municipal franchise on same terms as Protestants; granted right to bear arms; hold most civil and military offices; still to remain subject to exclusion from Parliament. Arms act passed to restrict imports of arms and ammunition. Convention Act prevents calling of further representative assemblies.
1794	Earl Fitzwilliam becomes Lord Lieutenant of Ireland (Aug.). Catholic Committee begins campaign for further relief measures.
1795	Fitzwilliam commits government to Catholic relief. Cabinet instructs him to oppose. Recalled (23 Feb.). Grattan's bill to admit Catholics to Parliament rejected (May). Wolfe Tone leaves for America. First 'Orange Society' founded after sectarian fighting in Armagh (Sept.). Outrages against Catholic peasantry.
1796	Insurrection Act passed, providing government with repressive powers to deal with disturbed areas. Suspension of Habeas Corpus. Creation of Protestant Yeomanry. Arming of United Irishmen. French expedition accompanied by Wolfe Tone fails to land at Bantry Bay (Dec.).

1797	Military repression of United Irish organisation in Ulster by General Lake (from Mar.). Followed by suppression of United Irishmen in other provinces. Grattan's reform bill fails to pass Parliament.
1798	Leaders of United Irishmen seized in Dublin (Mar.). Capture of Lord Edward Fitzgerald (19 May). Outbreak of rebellion (26 May). Attack on New Ross fails (5 June). Capture of Vinegar Hill (21 June) and defeat of Wexford rising. Ulster rising: attack on Antrim repulsed (7 June); defeat of Ulster rebels at Ballynahinch (13 June). Landing of General Humbert at Killala Bay (22 Aug.). Surrenders at Ballinamuch (8 Sept.). Recapture of Killala (23 Sept.) ends Connaught rising. Failure of Hardy's expedition to Lough Swilly and capture of Wolfe Tone (12 Oct.). Viscount Castlereagh becomes Chief Secretary of Ireland (Nov.).
1799	Defeat of government address to Irish Parliament requesting them to consider scheme of union with England by 111 votes to 106. Act establishing virtual martial law in Ireland.
1800	Motion pledging the continuing independence of the Irish Parliament defeated by 138 votes to 96 (16 Jan.). Proposals for legislative union between England and Ireland approved by 158 votes to 115 (6 Feb.). Terms of union accepted by both houses (28 Mar.). Act of Union receives royal assent (1 Aug.). By provisions of Act (39 and 40 Geo. III, c.67) Ireland merged with Great Britain in one Kingdom, to be known as 'The United Kingdom of Great Britain and Ireland'. Succession to the Crown to be governed by same provisions as the union between England and Scotland. Irish Parliament ceases to exist. Thirty-two Irish peers (28 temporal peers elected for life and 4 spiritual lords in rotation) to sit in the House of Lords. A hundred members (64 county, 35 borough and 1 university) to sit in the House of Commons. Church of England and Church of Ireland united. Commercial union (with some qualification) established. Financial systems to remain distinct, subject to review. Ireland to provide two-seventeenths of United Kingdom expenditure.

Separate act provides for £1,400,000 from Irish revenues to compensate Irish parliamentary officials and borough patrons. Last meeting of Irish parliament (2 Aug.).

1803   Emmett's 'rising' suppressed (23 July). Emmett and 21 others executed.

1808   Grattan's motion for Catholic Emancipation defeated in the Commons by 281 votes to 128.

1810   Catholic Committee set up to campaign for Catholic Emancipation. Reconstituted in 1811 as the Catholic Board.

1812   Motion to consider Catholic claims passed by 225 votes to 106.

1813   Emancipation bill defeated in committee.

1814   Catholic Board dissolved by government order.

1817   Irish and British exchequers united because of increase of Irish national debt.
Partial failure of potato crop.

1819   Catholic Emancipation bill defeated in the Commons.

1821   Catholic Emancipation defeated in the House of Lords.

1823   Catholic Association founded by O'Connell to campaign for political and other rights.

5.3 British colonial expansion, 1688–1760

1689 William and Mary recognise old Charters of colonies.

1690 East India Company makes peace with Mogul Empire; factory at Calcutta established.

1692 Revolution settlement of the New England colonies; new charter granted to Massachusetts; Governor and other officials to be appointed by the Crown.

1693 Carolina divided into North and South Carolina.

1695 Formation of Company of Scotland for trade with Africa and the Indies.

1696 Establishment of Board of Trade and Plantations.

1697 Under Treaty of Ryswick, Hudson's Bay company reduced to only one factory (Fort Albany).
Publication of Dampier's *New Voyage Round the World*.

1698 Major attack on old East India Company in new legislation with Act creating New East India Company.
Erection of Fort William to protect Calcutta.
First Darien expedition by Company of Scotland.

1699 Second Darien expedition also fails.

1702 Delaware becomes separate Crown Colony.
French portion of St Kitts captured at outbreak of the War of the Spanish Succession.
Merger agreed of rival East India Companies.

1703 Methuen Treaty with Portugal.

1704 English capture Gibraltar.

1708 Capture of Minorca.

BRITISH COLONIAL EXPANSION, 1688–1760   163

1709   Fusion of rival East India Companies completed. New body entitled United Company of Merchants of England trading to the East Indies.

1710   Capture of Nova Scotia.

1711   Formation of South Sea Company.

1713   Treaty of Utrecht signed. France ceded whole of Hudson's Bay, French St Kitts, the Newfoundland settlements and Nova Scotia (except for Cape Breton Island). Spain ceded Gibraltar and Minorca. The Assiento (the monopoly of supplying slaves to Spanish American colonies) also abandoned (granted to the South Sea Company).

1729   Dispute over government of Carolina resolved and divided into North and South Carolina by Act of Parliament.

1732   Proprietary grant to General James Oglethorpe of Georgia.

1733   New colony of Savannah founded by Oglethorpe.

1739   War of Jenkins' Ear.
       Capture of Porto Bello by Admiral Vernon.

1740   Expedition of Commodore George Anson to attack Spanish colonies on Pacific coast of South America. Oglethorpe from Georgia makes unsuccessful attack on Florida.

1741   Attack on Cartagena by Vernon and Wentworth.
       Dupleix appointed Governor of Pondicherry.

1742   Unsuccessful attack on Cuba.

1744   Capture of Annapolis (in Nova Scotia) by the French marks beginning of Anglo-French struggle over the colonies.

1745   British capture Louisburg; William Shirley (the Governor of Massachusetts) and William Pepperell, leader of the force, both received baronetcies.

1746   French capture of Madras by La Bourdonnais.

1747   Decisive naval victories by Anson at Cape Finisterre and Hawke at Belle Île. Unsuccessful French attacks on Fort St David (Cuddalore).

1748 Peace of Aix-la-Chapelle; mutual restoration of colonies. Four disputed islands (St Lucia, Dominica, St Vincent and Tobago) declared neutral.
Formation of the Ohio Company (followed by the Loyal Company and Greenbriar Company).

1749 Dupleix's unauthorised war in India; Chanda Sahib adopted by Dupleix as Nawab of the Carnatic; Chanda Sahib victorious at Battle of Ambur.
Marquis de Bussy power behind the throne in the Deccan.
Foundation of Halifax in Nova Scotia.

1750 British settlement begins on Gold Coast.

1751 British support for Mohammed Ali; Clive successfully attacked Arcot (capital of the Carnatic). Subsequent victory for Clive at Battle of Arni.

1752 Georgia becomes a Crown Colony.
Relief of siege of Trichinopoly: Mohammed Ali now the effective Nawab.

1753 Dupleix recalled (he received the order in 1754).
French in effective control of Ohio, establishment of Fort Duquesne.

1755 Defeat of General Edward Braddock's march to attack Fort Duquesne. Deportation of 6,000 French ('Arcadians') from Nova Scotia. Construction of Fort Edward on the east of the Hudson.

1756 Outbreak of Seven Years War. Initial French successes included fall of Minorca (Admiral Byng subsequently shot) and advances by Montcalm in Canada.
Nabob of Bengal imprsions British in 'Black Hole' of Calcutta.

1757 Further French successes in Canada; fall of Fort William Henry to Montcalm. British forced back to upper waters of the Hudson.
Battle of Plassey gives Clive mastery of Bengal.

1758 Repulse of Abercrombie before Ticonderoga; capture of Louisburg. Capture of Forts Duquesne and Frontenac.

1759 Capture of Forts Niagara and Ticonderoga. General Wolfe captures Quebec after battle of the Heights of Abraham.

1760 Surrender of Montreal and Canada to British.
Battle of Wandiwash breaks French power in India.

5.4 The American colonies

North America, 1689–1763

1689   On news of 'Glorious Revolution' in England, James II's appointee as president of New England, Sir Edmund Andros, seized and imprisoned in Boston (18 Apr.). Assembly of representatives meets at Boston. Proclamation of William and Mary.
King William's War sees operation of French with Indian support against the colonists.

1690   Sir William Phipps captures Port Royal (Apr.) but fails in attack on Quebec.

1692   New charter issued for Massachusetts and appointment of Sir William Phipps as governor. The charter of the colony included the provinces of Maine, Nova Scotia and all land north of the St Lawrence. The Crown to appoint the governor and vested in him the right of calling, proroguing and dissolving the general court, appointing military officers and law officers and of vetoing acts of the legislature and appointments made by it. The electoral franchise was extended to all freeholders with a yearly income of 40 shillings and all inhabitants having personal property to the amount of £40. Religious liberty granted to Roman Catholics.
Beginning of the Salem witch craze (Feb.). Twenty persons executed by October.
Construction of Fort William Henry in Maine.
College of William and Mary in Virginia.

1693   Penn dismissed from government of Pennsylvania.

1696   French capture fort at Pemaquid.

1697   At Peace of Ryswick both sides restore each other's conquests.

1699   French settle Louisiana.
First Scottish settlement at Darien.

1701	William Penn obtained a new charter for Pennsylvania. Yale College founded at New Haven, Connecticut.
1702	War of Spanish Succession leads to renewed fighting between France and Britain.
1703	Pennsylvania divided into the province and the territories with separate assemblies.
1704	French with Indian support defeat Deerfield, but Colonel Church leads expedition on the French settlements in New England.
1706	French and Spanish invade Carolina but repulsed.
1710	English fleet captures Port Royal and renamed Annapolis.
1711	Tuscaroras and other tribes attack colonists in Carolina, but eventually crushed by Barnwell.
1713	Treaty of Utrecht results in cession of Hudson Bay and Straits of Nova Scotia, Newfoundland and St Christopher to England. Treaty with eastern Indians at Portsmouth. Rectification of the boundary between Massachusetts and Connecticut.
1715	Yamassees and allied tribes attack Carolina, but repulsed.
1718	Captain Wood Rogers, governor of New Providence, suppresses the buccaneers in the West Indies and extirpates the pirates on the coast of Carolina.
1719	Beginning of discontent of colonists against the proprietary government in Carolina. The colonists' assembly refused to be dissolved and elected a new governor, resisting the old governor with arms.
1720	Prohibition of trade between Indians and French in New York.
1721	Royal Council declares Charter of Proprietors of Carolina forfeit and establishes a provisional royal government.
1722	In New York, governor Burnet opens negotiations with the Iroquois confederacy at Albany and establishes a trading-house at Oswego.

1724	Indian hostilities in New England with Abinakis.
1725	Yamassees assault English colonists in Carolina from Spanish Florida.
1726	Governor of Massachusetts, Shute, obtains from the Crown the power to suppress debate and limited power of adjournment by the representatives. In New York, a treaty brings new Indian tribes under English protection.
1728	Boundary between Virginia and North Carolina surveyed and settled.
1729	Agreement reached with proprietors of Carolina. Seven sold their titles and property, an eighth retained his property but lost his proprietary power. The Crown assumed the right of nominating governors and councils. The province was divided into North and South Carolina.
1731	Settlement of boundary between New York and Connecticut.
1733	Settlement of Georgia under James Oglethorpe and 20 other trustees for the Crown. Liberty of worship granted to all except Roman Catholics. First settlement established at Savannah.
1738	Foundation of Princeton College, New Jersey.
1739–48	War between Britain and Spain.
1740	Oglethorpe leads unsuccessful expedition against Florida. Expedition against Cartagena fails.
1741	Colonists attack Cuba.
1742	Spanish expedition against Georgia repulsed.
1744–48	War with France.
1745	Siege and capture of French fort of Louisburg on Cape Breton Island by colonial troops under William Pepperell.
1746	Projected attack on Canada by the colonists frustrated by the arrival of a French fleet, under D'Anville.

1747   Rioting in Boston against impressment of sailors.

1748   Treaty of Aix-la-Chapelle between England, France and Spain leads to reciprocal surrender of conquests in North America. Formation of the Ohio Company under a charter from the English Crown.

1750   Disputes between French and English over boundaries of Arcadia.

1751   Governor Clinton, of New York, in association with South Carolina, Massachusetts and Connecticut, concludes a peace with the 'Six Nations' Indian confederacy.

1752   Trustees of Georgia give up their Charter and Georgia is placed on the same footing as the other royal colonies. Introduction of Gregorian calendar in the colonies.

1753   George Washington despatched from Virginia to remonstrate with the French on the Allegheny and the Ohio for encroachments on Virginian territory.

1754   Virginia sends a force to the Ohio, part commanded by Washington, but he is captured and forced to withdraw. Conference of colonial delegates at Albany with the Six Nations. Benjamin Franklin draws up a plan for the union of all the colonies under a President appointed by the Crown, with an elected grand council of delegates, with a right of legislation subject to the veto of the President and the approval of the Crown. Connecticut, objecting to the veto power, refused to sign the proposal, which was later rejected both by the colonies and the Crown.

1756–63   War between England and France. Braddock sent from England to command forces in North America. Colonial governors and Braddock decide to mount three expeditions: against Fort Duquesne; against the fort at Niagara; and against Crown Point in New York. Meanwhile, 3,000 troops from Massachusetts captured forts Beausejour and Gaspereaux in Nova Scotia (June).
(For the further events of the Seven Years War in North America, *see* pp. 183–4.)

Events leading up to the American War of Independence

1763   Peace of Paris signed (10 Feb.). Britain gains Canada, Florida, Louisiana east of the Mississippi, Cape Breton and islands of the St Lawrence.
Proclamation establishing the Alleghenies as temporary boundary line beyond which colonies could not expand.

1765   Stamp Act passed (22 Mar.), imposing a stamp duty on legal transactions in America to pay for colonial defence.
Beginning of campaign in Britain and American colonies against the Act.

1766   Petitioning movement of British merchants against the Stamp Act. Appointment of parliamentary inquiry into merchant grievances. Passing of Declaratory Act, confirming sovereign right to tax the colonies. Stamp Act repealed.

1767   New York Assembly formally refuses to enforce the Mutiny Act. Massachusetts grants indemnity for all offences committed during Stamp Act disturbances.
Townshend introduces duties on paper, paint, glass, lead and tea imported into America (passed 2 June) to pay for colonial defence and establish a civil list within the colonies.
Boston enters a non-importation agreement against the duties.

1768   Massachusetts House of Representatives petitions against taxation without representation and circularises other colonies urging common action against the import duties.
Attacks upon customs officials and American Board of Customs forced to leave Boston.
Troops sent to New England.

1769   Cabinet decides to abolish all Townshend duties except those on tea (1 May).

1770   Townshend's Revenue Act amended leaving duties only on tea. Boston 'Massacre' (5 Mar.). British soldiers kill five people in a mob attacking a customs house.

1771   South Carolina assembly suspended for grant of £1,500 to the Society of the Supporters of the Bill of Rights in London.
Quarrels with assemblies of North Carolina and Georgia.

1772 Revenue cutter *Gaspee* boarded and burnt (10 June).
Committees of Correspondence formed to publicise grievances and coordinate colonial resistance.

1773 Tea Act passed. All duties on tea re-exported by East India Company to be remitted and direct export to America.
American resistance to landing of East India tea. In 'Boston Tea Party' (16 Dec.), three shiploads of tea dumped in Boston Harbour.

1774 Fuller's motion to repeal duty on tea defeated by 182 votes to 49. Coercive measures taken against American colonies. Boston Port Act closes Boston to shipping until compensation paid to East India Company and customs officers mistreated by the mob. Massachusetts Government Act deprives colony of the right to elect councillors and gives the Governor power to appoint and dismiss all civil officers except judges of the supreme court; also substitutes nominated jurors for elected ones and restricts town meetings. Administration of Justice Act provides for removal of trials to Britain or other colonies. Quartering Act provides for requisition of quarters for troops. Quebec Act provides for government of province of Quebec by an appointed Governor and Council. Toleration extended to Roman Catholics and provision made for payment of tithes by Roman Catholic communicants. French and English legal codes merged. Jurisdiction of Governor of Quebec extended along western edge of Pennsylvania to the Ohio and Mississippi. Continental Congress meets at Philadelphia. Considers and rejects a federal structure of government in North America controlling all aspects of administration but still subordinate to the British Parliament and Crown.
Congress decides on the 'Suffolk Resolves' for defiance of Coercive Acts, withholding of taxes until all privileges restored to Massachusetts, and defensive military preparations in the event of arrest of leaders.

1775 North's 'conciliatory propositions' put before the Commons. Chatham Conciliation Bill defeated.
Burke's conciliation proposals defeated (22 Mar.).
Governor Gage receives instruction to put down rebellion; British troops sent to seize rebel supplies at Concord, engage American forces at Lexington (18 Apr.).

1776 Second Continental Congress meets at Philadelphia (10 May).
Declaration of Independence (4 July).
(For events in the War of Independence, *see* pp. 187–9.)

The original 13 American colonies (in the order in which they ratified the American Constitution)

State	Date of ratification	First permanent settlement
Delaware	7 Dec. 1787	1683
Pennsylvania	12 Dec. 1787	1682
New Jersey	18 Dec. 1787	1664
Georgia	2 Jan. 1788	1733
Connecticut	9 Jan. 1788	1635
Massachusetts	6 Feb. 1788	1620
Maryland	28 Apr. 1788	1634
South Carolina	23 May 1788	1670
New Hampshire	21 June 1788	1623
Virginia	25 June 1788	1607
New York	26 July 1788	1614
North Carolina	21 Nov. 1789	1650
Rhode Island	29 May 1790	1636

SECTION SIX

Military and naval

6.1 Outlines of British campaigns*

War of the Grand Alliance, 1688–1697

1688
25 Sept. Louis XIV invades the Palatinate.

1689
12 May. Treaty between the Emperor and the Netherlands signed at Vienna; the accession of England (on 9 Dec.), Spain, Savoy, Brandenburg, Saxony, Hanover and Bavaria establishes the Grand Alliance.
25 Aug. Battle of Walcourt – Prince George Frederick of Waldeck, with an English contingent of 8,000 men under Marlborough, defeats the French.

1690
1 July. Battle of **Fleurus** – French under Duc de Luxembourg defeat the allies.
10 July. Battle of **Beachy Head** – Admiral de Tourville with 78 ships defeats Torrington's Anglo-Dutch fleet of 73.

1691
8 Apr. Mons falls to the French.
20 Sept. Waldeck defeated at the battle of Leuze.

1692
29 May–3 June. Battle of **La Hogue** – Admirals Russell and Rooke lead an Anglo-Dutch fleet of 96 ships to victory over de Tourville with 44.
3 Aug. Battle of Steenkerke – William III attacks Luxembourg's strong defensive position; he is repulsed, but the French are unable to pursue.

1693
27–8 June. Battle of **Lagos** – de Tourville attacks a Smyrna convoy, and, after beating off Rooke's escorting squadron, he destroys 100 ships.
29 July. William sends 20,000 men to relieve Liège, and stands with the rest of his army at **Neerwinden**, where he is attacked and defeated by Luxembourg.
11 Oct. French capture Charleroi.

* Names of major battles and engagements in bold within this subsection.

1695
Jan. Luxembourg dies, and is replaced by the Duc de Villeroi.
1 Sept. Namur surrenders to William.

1696
8 June. Assault on Brest a failure.

1697
20 Sept. Treaty of Ryswick – Louis XIV restores his conquests, and recognises William III as King of England.

Revolution of 1688 and the wars in Scotland and Ireland, 1688–91

1688
5 Nov. William of Orange lands at Torbay and advances on London; James II flees to France (*see* pp. 5–6).

1689
13 Feb. William and Mary proclaimed joint sovereigns of England.
22 Mar. James II lands in Ireland at Kinsale with 5,000 French soldiers. He marches with the Jacobite Earl of Tyrconnel to the north, where the Protestants have declared for William III.
29 Apr. Londonderry besieged. An English naval force under Capt. Leake raises the siege on 9–10 Aug. After local forces under Col. Wolseley defeat the Jacobites the siege of Enniskillen is lifted, and William's army overruns the whole of Ulster.
17 July. In Scotland a royalist army is routed at **Killiecrankie** by Jacobites led by Viscount Graham of Claverhouse and Dundee. He is killed in the battle, however, and the rising collapses.

1690
14 June. William lands in Ireland and advances on Dublin.
1 July. James is defeated at the battle of the **Boyne**, and flees to France.
Sept.–Oct. Marlborough takes Cork and Kinsale.

1691
12 July. Jacobites defeated at the battle of **Aughrim**.
13 Oct. Limerick surrenders on the signing of a treaty bringing the Irish war to a close.

War of the Spanish Succession, 1701–13

(a) Flanders

1700
Nov. Death of Charles II of Spain; Louis XIV's grandson becomes Philip V.

1701
7 Sept. Treaty between England, the Netherlands and the Emperor.

1702
8 Mar. Death of William III.
15 May. England declares war on France.
June–July. Marlborough advances into the Spanish Netherlands, but the Dutch deputies veto plans to bring the French to battle.
Sept.–Oct. Marlborough besieges the Meuse fortresses and captures Venlo, Roermond and Liège.

1703
May. Marlborough invades the electorate of Cologne and takes Bonn, but fails in his plan to seize Antwerp.

1704
Marlborough's intention is to concentrate the allied forces in the Danube Valley to save Vienna, drive the French out of Germany and eliminate Bavaria from the war.
May. Marlborough begins the march to the Danube.
June. Marlborough meets Prince Eugène and Louis of Baden at Mondelsheim, continuing with Louis to the Danube.
2 July. Marlborough captures **Donauwörth**, forcing the French to retreat southwards.
6 Aug. Marlborough and Eugène join forces, while Louis of Baden is sent to besiege Ingolstadt.
13 Aug. As the French and Bavarians advance, Marlborough and Eugène attack and decisively defeat them at **Blenheim**.

1705
Stalemate in the Low Countries. Marlborough pierces the French lines at Tirlemont on 18 July, but Dutch caution prevents him from exploiting this.

1706
23 May. Villeroi, marching towards Liège, is heavily defeated by Marlborough at **Ramillies**, and driven back to Courtrai.
June–Oct. Marlborough captures Antwerp, Dunkirk, Menin, Dendermonde and Ath, firmly establishing his hold on the Spanish Netherlands.

1707
Vendôme, who has replaced Villeroi, holds the Flanders front.

1708
4–5 July. French army take the offensive, and capture Ghent and Bruges.
11 July. Marlborough defeats Vendôme at **Oudenarde**.

12 July. Vendôme checks the pursuing Allies at Ghent.

Marlborough's plan for the invasion of France is not accepted. Instead Lille is besieged and falls on 22 Oct.

1709
Jan. Ghent and Bruges fall to the Allies.
29 July. Allies capture Tournai, and besiege Mons. Villars is ordered to defend Mons, so advances and entrenches at Malplaquet threatening the besiegers.
11 Sept. Marlborough and Eugène defeat the French at **Malplaquet**, but suffer very heavy casualties.
26 Oct. Mons surrenders.

1710
Marlborough captures Douai on 10 June and Béthune on 30 Aug.

1711
Marlborough succeeds in breaking the French 'ne plus ultra' defensive lines in Aug., but is dismissed from his command on 31 Dec.

1712
24 July. After the English contingent is withdrawn, Eugène is defeated by Villars at **Denain**.

1713
11 Apr. Treaty of Utrecht – the French cede Newfoundland, Nova Scotia, St Kitts and the Hudson Bay territory to England, and undertake to demolish the fortifications at Dunkirk. They also recognise the Protestant succession, and agree not to help the Stuarts.

(b) Spain and the Mediterranean

1702
Aug.–Sept. Anglo-Dutch force of 50 ships and 15,000 men under Admiral Rooke and the Duke of Ormonde repulsed at Cadiz.
12 Oct. Rooke destroys the Spanish treasure fleet in Vigo Bay.

1703
16 May. Portugal joins the alliance.

1704
Feb. Rooke lands the Archduke Charles with 2,000 English and Dutch troops at Lisbon.
4 Aug. Rooke captures Gibraltar.
24 Aug. French navy under the Count of Toulouse defeated by Rooke in battle of **Malaga**.

1705
10 Mar. Admiral Sir John Leake defeats a French squadron under Admiral de Pointis in battle of Marbella, and the siege of Gibraltar is lifted.
June. Allied troops under Admiral Sir Cloudesley Shovell and Lord Peterborough land in Catalonia.
3 Oct. Allies capture Barcelona, but are besieged by the French.

1706
30 Apr. French lift the siege of Barcelona when Lord Henry Galway leads an invasion of Spain from Portugal.
26 June. Galway captures Madrid, but the French retake it in Oct.
June–Sept. English fleet under Leake captures Cartagena, Alicante and the Balearic Islands of Mallorca and Ibiza.

1707
25 Apr. Galway's advance on Madrid is halted by the French under the Duke of Berwick at the battle of **Almanza**.
July–Aug. Prince Eugène besieges Toulon, with the support of the allied fleet under Shovell, but is unsuccessful, although the French had scuttled 50 ships in the harbour in case the city fell.

1708
Aug. Admiral Leake captures Sardinia.
Sept. General James Stanhope captures Minorca.

1710
May. Stanhope advances on Madrid, but has to retreat, pursued by Vendôme.
10 Dec. Stanhope is defeated and captured at **Brihuega**.

1714
11 Sept. French capture Barcelona.

1715
Feb. Spain and Portugal make peace by the Treaty of Madrid.

The Jacobite rebellions, 1715 and 1745 *See* p. 176 for Scotland in 1688–89

(a) 'The Fifteen'

1715
6 Sept. Earl of Mar raises Stuart standard at Braemar.
  A Jacobite army advances to Preston, but is forced to surrender there on 13 Nov. On the same day Mar fights an inconclusive battle with government troops led by the Duke of Argyll at **Sheriffmuir**.

22 Dec. James Edward, the Pretender, lands at Peterhead, but returns to France in Feb. 1716, as Jacobites disperse before advancing government forces. Attempts by the Duke of Ormond to land in Devon in Oct.–Dec. 1715 find no support.

(b) 'The Forty-Five'

1745

23 July. Charles Edward, the Young Pretender, lands in Scotland. His army of Highlanders enter Edinburgh on 17 Sept., and rout an English army under Sir John Cope at **Prestonpans** on 21 Sept.

4 Dec. Jacobite army reaches Derby, but then begin to retreat, pursued by the Duke of Cumberland. Jacobites win battles of Penrith, 18 Dec., and Falkirk, 17 Jan. 1746, but are decisively defeated at **Culloden** on 16 Apr.

1746

Sept. Charles Edward escapes to France.

War of the Quadruple Alliance, 1718–20

1717

4 Jan. England, France and Holland form the Triple Alliance to oppose Spanish ambitions in France and Italy. Spain occupies Sardinia in Nov. 1717 and Sicily in July 1718.

1718

2 Aug. Austria joins the Triple Alliance, and an English fleet lands Austrian troops near Messina, which surrenders in Oct. 1719.

11 Aug. Admiral Byng destroys Spanish fleet off **Cape Passaro**.

1719

Failure of Spanish expedition to Scotland. French army invades Spain, and British amphibious forces capture Vigo and Pontevedra.

5 Dec. Spanish Prime Minister, Alberoni, dismissed.

1720

17 Feb. Treaty of The Hague concludes the war. The succession to Tuscany, Parma and Piacenza is assured to Charles, eldest son of Philip of Spain and Elizabeth Farnese, while Philip renounces his claims in France and Italy. Sardinia is given to Victor Amadeus of Savoy in place of Sicily, which is made over to Austria.

A further conflict breaks out in 1727, when England and France seek to prevent Charles from taking over the Italian Duchies. After brief hostilities, negotiations are opened, and peace is made at the Treaty of Seville on 9 Nov. 1729, in which Charles's claims are recognised.

War of the Austrian Succession, 1739–48

1739
19 Oct. England declares war on Spain after prolonged commercial disputes (War of Jenkins' Ear).

Admiral Vernon captures Porto Bello Nov. 1739. But attacks on Cartagena, Cuba and Panama fail, and Vernon and General Wentworth are recalled in 1742.

In 1740–44 Anson carries out his circummavigation, raiding Spanish South American possessions.

1740
Oct. The death of Emperor Charles VI, the succession of Maria Theresa, and Frederick the Great's invasion of Silesia in December brings on the general European conflict, the War of the Austrian Succession.

1741
Sept. George II concludes a treaty with France neutralising Hanover.

1742
After Walpole's resignation in Feb., Carteret persuades George II to end Hanover's neutrality, and send an army of English, Hanoverians and Hessians (Pragmatic Army) under Lord Stair to the Low Countries.

1743
27 June. Joined by Dutch and Austrian troops, led by George II, the Pragmatic Army advances and defeats the French at **Dettingen**. Attempts to invade France are unsuccessful.

1744
Mar. France formally declares war on England, and a French army led by Marshal de Saxe invades the Low Countries.

A Franco-Spanish plan for an invasion of England comes to nothing. A drawn naval engagement takes place off Toulon in Feb.

1745
May. Saxe besieges Tournai, and defeats a relieving army at **Fontenoy** (11th). Tournai falls (22nd).
16 June. In North America an expedition captures Louisburg from the French.

1746
Saxe completes the conquest of the Austrian Netherlands, taking Brussels in Feb., Antwerp in June, and defeating the allies at **Roucoux** on 11 Oct.

1747
Saxe invades Holland, and defeats Cumberland at **Lauffeld** on 2 July.
  Admirals Anson and Hawke win decisive naval victories off **Cape Finisterre** in May and Oct.

1748
18 Oct. Treaty of Aix-la-Chapelle concludes the war. The main points are that Prussia retains Silesia and Glatz. Parma, Piacenza and Guastalla are ceded to Don Philip of Spain. France evacuates the Austrian Netherlands, restores the barrier fortresses to the Dutch and recognises the Hanoverian succession in England. Louisburg is exchanged for Madras, captured by the French in 1746.

The Seven Years war, 1756–63

(a) Europe

1756
29 Aug. Frederick the Great's invasion of Saxony begins the conflict in Europe (Britain and France had been at war since May 1756).

1757
July. A French army invades Hanover. Cumberland is defeated at **Hastenbeck**, and signs the Convention of Kloster-Seven on 8 Sept., disbanding his army.
5 Nov. Frederick the Great's victory at Rossbach. The Convention is repudiated, and Ferdinand of Brunswick is given command of the allied army.

1758
British subsidies to Frederick by the Treaty of London in April.
  Ferdinand launches an offensive against the French, pushing them across the Rhine on 27 Mar., and defeating them at Krefeld on 23 June. The French reply by invading Hesse.

1759
13 Apr. Ferdinand defeated by Broglie at **Bergen**.
1 Aug. Ferdinand defeats the French at **Minden**; they retreat from Hesse.

1760
Broglie is victorious at Korbach on 10 July, but this is offset by Ferdinand's victory at **Warburg** on 31 July. Hanover is saved, but a diversion on the lower Rhine is defeated by the French at **Kloster Kamp** on 16 Oct.

1761
Ferdinand's advance from Westphalia is defeated by Broglie near Grünberg on 21 Mar. A French counter-thrust is defeated at **Vellinghausen** on 15 July.
5 Oct. Pitt resigns, and Bute refuses to renew the subsidy treaty with Frederick.

1762
5 Jan. Death of Empress Elizabeth of Russia.
5 May. Treaty of St Petersburg – peace between Prussia and Russia.
22 May. Peace between Prussia and Sweden.

1763
15 Feb. Treaty of Hubertusburg signed by Prussia, Austria and Saxony, restoring the *status quo ante bellum.*

(b) North America

1754
3 July. A Virginian force led by George Washington is forced to surrender to the French at Fort Necessity.

1755
9 July. Braddock's expedition to attack Fort Duquesne is destroyed at the **Monongahela River.**

1756
Aug. Montcalm captures Forts Oswego and George, and builds Fort Ticonderoga.

1757
June–Sept. Failure of British expedition to attack Louisburg led by Lord Loudoun.

1758
A fourfold attack on the French planned.
July. Fort Duquesne and Louisburg captured by Amherst; but Abercromby's attack on Fort Ticonderoga fails.
Sept. Forts Frontenac, Oswego and Duquesne taken from the French.

1759
July. Fort Niagara falls to British expedition.
Aug. Ticonderoga and Champlain captured.

June–Sept. Attack on Quebec by Wolfe and Saunders. The French led by Montcalm are defeated in battle before **Quebec** 13 Sept., after Wolfe had scaled the Heights of Abraham. Quebec surrenders on 18 Sept.

1760
8 Sept. Marquis de Vaudreuil surrenders Montreal, and with it French Canada.

(c) Naval and minor operations

1755
8 June. Boscawen captures two French ships carrying reinforcements to Canada, although the rest escape. There is a general attack on French shipping.

1756
28 June. Minorca falls to the French. Admiral Byng, who had failed to relieve it after an inconclusive naval battle 20 May, is executed.

1757
Sept. Failure of a raid on Rochefort.

1758
Commodore Holmes captures Emden in Feb.
 Attacks on the French coast: Cherbourg taken in June, but expedition against St Malo repulsed in Sept.
 All French factories on the West African coast captured.

1759
May. Guadeloupe taken from the French.
18 Aug. Boscawen defeats the French Mediterranean fleet off Lagos.
20 Nov. Hawke destroys Brest squadron in battle of **Quiberon Bay**.

1760
Feb. French expedition to Ireland surrendered at Kinsale.

1761
June. Dominica and Belle Île captured from French.

1762
Jan. England declares war on Spain (4th), and seizes Havana in Aug., and Manila in Oct. A British army led by Lord Tyrawley helps the Portuguese to resist a Spanish invasion.
 Rodney forces the surrender of Martinique, Grenada, St Vincent and St Lucia.
 St John's, Newfoundland, is lost to the French.

(d) India

1746
Sept. Madras falls to the French, led by Dupleix and Admiral de la Bourdonnais, who had driven off Commodore Peyton in a naval engagement at Negapatam in July.
Nov. French begin unsuccessful siege of Fort St George; ended on arrival of Admiral Boscawen in Apr. 1748.

1748
Aug.–Oct. Dupleix successfully defends Pondicherry against Boscawen.
Oct. At the Treaty of Aix-la-Chapelle Madras is restored to Britain, in exchange for Louisburg.

1751
Chanda Sahib, Nawab of the Carnatic, besieges British garrison at Trichinopoly. As a diversion Robert Clive captures Chanda Sahib's capital, Arcot, and withstands a 50-day siege (Sept.–Nov.). Clive then defeats the French and their allies at Arni in Nov. 1751 and **Covrepauk** in Feb. 1752.

1754
Aug. Dupleix relieved of his post. His successor, Godeheu, makes peace with the British in the Carnatic.

1756
20 June. Surajah Dowlah, Nawab of Bengal, captures Calcutta, and imprisons 146 Europeans in the 'Black Hole', where 123 die.

1757
2 Jan. Robert Clive and Admiral Watson recapture Calcutta.
23 June. Clive routs Surajah Dowlah at **Plassey**.

1758
June. French force under Comte de Lally-Tollendal reach Pondicherry, and capture Fort St David.

Dec. 1758–Feb. 1759
Lally unsuccessfully besieges Madras.

1760
22 Jan. Eyre Coote defeats Lally at **Wandiwash**.

1761
15 Jan. Lally's surrender at Pondicherry marks the end of the French bid for power in India.

India, 1764–1814

1764
23 Oct. Mutiny in Bengal army crushed by Major Munro at **Buxar**.

1766–69
First Mysore War – ends when Hyder Ali concludes a defensive alliance with the East India Company.

1779–82
First Maratha War. Gwalior stormed by Captain Popham in 1780. Peace by the Treaty of Salbai.

1780–84
Second Mysore War.
1780. Hyder Ali invades the Carnatic, but is defeated by Coote at **Porto Novo** in June, Polliur in Aug., and Sholingarh in Sept.
Aug. 1782. French under Admiral de Suffren capture Trincomalee, and send aid to Hyder Ali.
1784. Ali's son, Tippoo Sahib, makes peace by the Treaty of Mangaloore.

1789–92
Third Mysore War. Tippoo Sahib attacks the ruler of Travancore, an ally of Britain. Cornwallis invades Mysore, storms the capital Bangaloore, and besieges Tippoo in Seringapatam. Tippoo makes peace in Mar. 1792.

1795–96
Ceylon captured from the Dutch.

1799
Fourth Mysore War. After a small French force land in Mysore, Lord Wellesley declares war, and Tippoo Sahib is killed when Seringapatam is stormed in May 1799.

1803–5
Second Maratha War.
1803. Arthur Wellesley defeats Sindhia of Gwalior at **Assaye** (23 Sept.) and **Argaum** (29 Nov.). General Lake storms Aligarh (4 Sept.); and defeats Marathas at Delhi (16 Sept.) and Laswari (1 Nov.). Sindhia submits (20 Dec.). Further uprisings by Marathas suppressed 1804–5.

1814
Nov. Britain invades Nepal. The Gurkhas are forced to make peace in 1816.

War of American Independence, 1775–83

1775
19 Apr. Detachment of 700 British troops sent from Boston by General Gage to destroy stores of the Massachusetts Militia at Concord. The force is opposed at Lexington, where the first shots of the war are fired, and harassed on the return march from Concord to Boston, suffering 273 casualties. Boston is besieged.
31 May. American troops before Boston adopted by the Second Continental Congress as the Continental Army, and George Washington appointed commander-in-chief on 15 June.
17 June. After receiving reinforcements, Gage attacks the American entrenchments on Breed's Hill (battle of **Bunker Hill**), suffering heavy losses in carrying them at the third attempt. Gage replaced by Howe.
Attack on Canada
May. Arnold and Ethan Allen seize Fort Ticonderoga and lesser posts on Lake Champlain. Montreal is taken in Nov., but an attack on Quebec fails in Dec. The following year Carleton, the British governor, retakes Montreal and forces the Americans back to Ticonderoga.

1776
4 Mar. Washington occupies Dorchester Heights commanding Boston Harbour. British forces evacuated to Halifax on 17 Mar.
4 July. Declaration of Independence.
July. Howe arrives off New York from Halifax with 30,000 men, and lands on Staten Island. He defeats Putnam in the battle of Long Island on 27 Aug., and occupies New York on 15 Sept.
  Washington, defeated in a skirmish at White Plains on 28 Oct., retreats across New Jersey, and crosses the Delaware into Pennsylvania on 8 Dec.
26 Dec. Washington crosses the Delaware by night, and attacks a force of Hessians at **Trenton**, taking 900 prisoners. As he withdraws he defeats the British at the battle of Princeton on 3 Jan. 1777.

1777
British plan to divide the rebel states by the line of the Hudson, with Burgoyne advancing from Canada, in cooperation with St Leger from Lake Ontario and Howe from New York. Burgoyne moves south with 8,200 men, and occupies Ticonderoga on 5 July.
16 Aug. Colonel Baum is sent to seize stores, but is defeated at **Bennington**.
19 Sept. Burgoyne suffers heavy losses in a battle at **Freeman's Farm**. He is now confronted by a greatly superior force under Gates.
  Meanwhile, St Leger has retreated after failing to take Fort Stanwix, and Clinton moves north from New York too late to influence the campaign.

7 Oct. Attempting to break out, Burgoyne is defeated at **Bemis Heights** and begins peace negotiations. He surrenders with 5,700 men at Saratoga on 17 Oct.

July. Howe sails from New York to Chesapeake Bay with 18,000 men, defeats the Americans at **Brandywine Creek** on 11 Sept., and occupies Philadelphia on 27 Sept.

4 Oct. Howe defeats Washington's attempt to mount a surprise attack on camp at **Germantown**. Washington's army spend a hard winter at Valley Forge.

1778

Treaties of commerce and alliance between France and the United States on 6 Feb. War between France and Britain on 17 June.

Clinton, who had succeeded Howe as commander-in-chief, begins the evacuation of Philadelphia, which is successfully carried out, despite a defeat by Washington at Monmouth on 28 June. Clinton now sends an army to overrun the southern states, hoping for loyalist assistance. Savannah is occupied on 29 Dec.

In the West Indies, the French capture Dominica on 8 Sept., but British forces take St Lucia on 13 Nov.

At sea an inconclusive engagement takes place between Keppel and D'Orvilliers off Ushant on 27 July. John Paul Jones successfully attacks British shipping in the Irish Sea.

1779

21 June. Spain enters the war. Gibraltar is besieged June 1779–Feb. 1783.
June–July. In the West Indies, D'Estaing takes St Vincent in June and Grenada on 4 July, and defeats Admiral Byron off Grenada on 6 July.
Aug. A Franco-Spanish fleet enters the Channel, but withdraws.
Sept.–Oct. Assaults on Savannah by French and American troops beaten off.

1780

8 Jan. Rodney defeats a Spanish fleet and relieves Gibraltar.
Feb.–Aug. Clinton lands with 12,000 men to attack Charleston, which falls on 12 May. Clinton returns to New York, leaving the pacification of South Carolina to Cornwallis, who defeats Gates at **Camden** on 16 Aug.
Aug. Armed neutrality formed by Russia, Sweden and Denmark to resist British seizure of enemy goods in neutral ships. Later joined by Prussia, Austria, Portugal, the Netherlands and the Kingdom of the Two Sicilies.
7 Oct. British raiding force under Colonel Ferguson defeated at King's Mountain.
20 Dec. Britain declars war on Holland. Warren Hastings seizes Dutch settlements of Negapatam and Trincomali, but an attempt on the Cape of Good Hope fails in 1781.

1781
17 Jan. British cavalry under Tarleton defeated by Morgan at **Cowpens**.
15 Mar. Cornwallis defeats Greene at Guilford, but suffers heavy losses.
July–Aug. Franco-Spanish occupation of Minorca. Port Mahan falls on 5 Feb. 1782.
Aug. Cornwallis establishes himself at Yorktown. He is besieged there by Washington and Rochambeau, and the French fleet under de Grasse, and forced to surrender on 19 Oct. Clinton's relieving force arrives too late on 24 Oct.

In the West Indies Rodney captures the Dutch islands of St Eustatius and St Martin in Feb. In June the French take Tobago, and in Oct. St Eustatius.

1782
Feb. French take St Kitts and Nevis.
12 Apr. Rodney's naval victory in the battle of **The Saints**.
30 Nov. Preliminary peace between Britain and the United States.

1783
3 Sept. Treaty of Versailles. Signed by Britain, France and the United States. Britain signs a separate treaty with Holland on 20 May 1784. Britain recognises the independence of the United States, and guarantees its fishing rights in the Newfoundland fisheries. France keeps St Lucia and Tobago. It returns Britain's other West Indian islands and Gambia, in return for its Indian stations, Senegal and Goree, and the right to a share in the Newfoundland fisheries. Spain retains Minorca and West Florida, and receives East Florida. Holland receives back its colonies apart from Negapatam.

Expeditions and naval operations, 1793–1814

1793
1 Feb. France, already at war with Austria, Prussia and Piedmont, declares war on Britain and Holland, and on Spain on 7 Mar.
Aug. Admiral Hood occupies Toulon after a royalist uprising. French successes on land force him to evacuate on 19 Dec.
Dec. Expedition of 12,000 men arrives too late to aid royalist rebels in La Vendée.

1793–95
Campaign in the Low Countries.
Duke of York sent to Low Countries at head of force of British, Dutch, Hanoverians and Hessians. He is defeated at Hondschoote in Sept. 1793, and Tourcoing in May 1794.

July 1794. French reoccupy Brussels. Austrians retreat towards the Rhine, and British fall back into Holland.
Apr. 1795. British army evacuated from Bremen after the French had overrun Holland.

1793–98
Campaign in the West Indies.
Nov. 1793. Seven thousand men under Grey sail with a squadron under Jervis to the West Indies. By 1796 military action, particularly involving slave revolts, and disease has resulted in 40,000 dead and 40,000 incapacitated.
1797. Trinidad captured.
Oct. 1798. Campaign ends with evacuation of San Domingo.

1794
1 June. Howe defeats French fleet off **Ushant**, but food convoy allowed to reach Brest safely.
Aug. British forces occupy Corsica.

1795
June. Emigrés landed from British ships at Quiberon Bay. They are defeated by Hoche on 16–20 July, and a small British force is evacuated on 20–21 July.
Nov. An expedition of 2,500 sails to La Vendée, but does not disembark.

1797
14 Feb. Jervis defeats Spanish fleet at **Cape St Vincent**.
11 Oct. Duncan defeats Dutch fleet at **Camperdown**.

1798
June. Irish rebels defeated at Vinegar Hill. A force of 1,200 French under General Humbert land in Killala Bay on 22 Aug., but Cornwallis forces their surrender on 8 Sept.
1 Aug. Nelson destroys French fleet at the battle of the **Nile**.
Nov. British capture Minorca.

1798–1800
British support uprising by Maltese against the French, who surrender on 5 Sept. 1800.

1799
Expedition to Den Helder.
27 Aug. British troops under Abercromby land in Holland; the Dutch navy in the Texel surrender. Russo-British force, now under the Duke of

York, plan to advance on Amsterdam, but is checked in battle of **Bergen-op-Zoom** on 19 Sept. Further attacks on 2 Oct. (battle of **Alkmaar**) and 6 Oct. make little progress.
18 Oct. By the Convention of Alkmaar the Allies agree to evacuate Holland.

1801
Campaign against the French in Egypt.
8 Mar. British troops under Abercromby land at Aboukir Bay. Attack on **Alexandria** fails on 13 Mar., but a French counterattack is beaten off on 21 Mar., though Abercromby is fatally wounded. His successor, Hutchinson, advances on Cairo, which the French agree to evacuate in June. French forces remaining in Alexandria surrender on 31 Aug.
2 Apr. Nelson, second-in-command to Sir Hyde Parker, defeats Danes in battle of **Copenhagen**.

1805
21 Oct. Nelson defeats Franco-Spanish fleet in the battle of **Trafalgar**.

1806
Jan. Expedition of 6,000 men under General Sir David Baird captures the Cape of Good Hope from the Dutch.

1806–7
Expeditions to South America.
June 1806. Home Popham, who had escorted Baird to Cape Town, takes 1,500 men under Beresford to attack Buenos Aires. Beresford forced to surrender in Aug. 1806. In 1807 General Whitelocke occupies Montevideo, and then moves against Buenos Aires, but has to withdraw.

1807
2–7 Sept. Danish fleet captured in second battle of Copenhagen.

1809
July. Walcheren Expedition – 40,000 men under Chatham sail for the Scheldt estuary to take Antwerp. They are delayed by resistance of Flushing, which surrenders on 16 Aug. There are heavy losses when fever breaks out. Half the force return to England in Sept.; the rest remain to garrison Walcheren, but are evacuated in Dec.

1810
Mauritius and Réunion captured.

1811
Java captured.

1813
Graham sent to Holland with 6,000 men to support an Orangeist revolt. But the Prussians fail to take part in an intended attack on Antwerp, and after an unsuccessful attack on Bergen-op-Zoom, Graham's force remain largely inactive until the end of the war.

Peninsular War, 1808–14

1807
Oct. French declare war on Portugal. Junot enters Lisbon on 30 Nov.

1808
Mar. French invasion of Spain. Joseph Bonaparte proclaimed King.
May. National rising in Spain. Dupont capitulates with 20,000 men to Spanish forces at Baylen on 19 July.
1 Aug. British army under Wellesley lands in Portugal. French defeated at **Roliça** on 17 Aug., and **Vimeiro** on 21 Aug.
30 Aug. Convention of Cintra signed, allowing Junot to evacuate Portugal. Sir John Moore given command of British army, which advances into Spain.
4 Dec. Napoleon enters Madrid. British retreat to the coast at Corunna.

1809
16 Jan. Battle of **Corunna** – Soult's attack is beaten off and the army evacuated, but Moore is killed.
22 Apr. Wellesley lands with British army at Lisbon, forces Soult to withdraw from Oporto, and defeats the French at **Talavera** on 28 July.

1810
10 July. French take Ciudad Rodrigo, and invade Portugal.
27 Sept. Wellington defeats Masséna at **Busaco Ridge**, then takes shelter behind fortified lines of the Torres Vedras.

1811
Mar. Masséna forced to retreat from Portugal. Wellington pursues him, besieges Almeida, and defeats a relieving army at **Fuentes de Oñoro** on 3–5 May. Almeida falls on 10 May.
16 May. As he moves to relieve Badajoz, Soult is defeated at **Albuera** by Beresford.

1812
Wellington takes the offensive, capturing **Ciudad Rodrigo** in Jan., and **Badajoz** in Apr. On 22 July, Wellington defeats Marmont at **Salamanca**. On 12 Aug. Wellington enters Madrid. However, he fails to take Burgos, and falls back to Ciudad Rodrigo.

1813
Wellington again advances, and defeats the French at **Vitoria** on 21 June. He drives Soult across the **Pyrenees** on 25 July–1 Aug., and invades France.

1814
Wellington defeats Soult at **Orthez** on 27 Feb., and **Toulouse** on 10 Apr.
18 Apr. Hostilities suspended after Napoleon's abdication.

Waterloo campaign, 1815

1815
1 Mar. Napoleon lands in France and enters Paris on 20 Mar.
25 Mar. Austria, England, Prussia and Russia conclude new alliance against Napoleon.
15 June. French army captures Charleroi.
16 June. Napoleon attacks Blücher's Prussians at **Ligny**, while Ney engages the Anglo-Dutch army at **Quatre Bras**. Ney recalls d'Erlon's army corps, which he had sent to help Napoleon, but it fails to return in time; both allied armies are able to conduct orderly retreats.
17 June. Grouchy sent to prevent Blücher joining Wellington, but Blücher has retreated towards Wavre and not Liège as Napoleon believed.
18 June. Battle of **Waterloo** – French attacks fail to drive Wellington from his defensive positions, and the arrival of Blücher in the later afternoon ensures the total defeat of the French.
22 June. Napoleon abdicates, and the Allies enter Paris on 7 July.

War of 1812

1812
19 June. Maritime grievances cause the United States to declare war on Britain. A plan for a three-fold attack on Canada fails, and British under General Brock force the surrender of Detroit on 16 Aug.

1813
24 Apr. American expedition captures and burns York (Toronto).
10 Sept. Americans under Commodore Perry win battle of Lake Erie. Americans advance, recapture Detroit on 29 Sept., and defeat General Proctor at the battle of the Thames on 5 Oct.
18 Dec. British take Fort Niagara.

1814
July. Americans advance across the Niagara River, take Fort Erie, and win battle of Chippewa on 5 July. But after battle of Lundy's Lane on 25 July they fall back on Fort Erie, which they later abandon in Nov.

Aug. British veterans under Ross land 40 miles from Washington, defeat the Americans at **Bladensburg** on 24 Aug, and capture and burn parts of the capital.
11 Sept. American naval force win battle of Plattsburg, halting a British invasion by way of Lake Champlain.
13 Sept. British attack on Baltimore repulsed.
24 Dec. War concluded by the Treaty of Ghent, largely restoring the pre-war situation.

1815
8 Jan. Before news of the peace reached him, Pakenham is killed leading an unsuccessful British attack on **New Orleans**.

Ships taken or destroyed by the naval and marine forces of Great Britain, 1793–1814

Force	In the French War, ending 1802				
	French	Dutch	Spanish	Other nations	Total
Of the line	45	25	11	2	83
Fifties	2	1	0	0	3
Frigates	133	31	20	7	191
Sloops, etc.	161	32	55	16	264
Total	341	89	86	25	541

Force	In the French War, ending 1814					
	French	Spanish	Danish	Russian	American	Total
Of the line	70	27	23	4	0	124
Fifties	7	0	1	0	1	9
Frigates	77	36	24	6	5	148
Sloops, etc.	188	64	16	7	13	288
Total	342	127	64	17	19	569

Source: J. Haydn, *Book of Dates* (London, 1857).

6.2 Strength and cost of the British army, 1689–1815

	Total supplies granted for the army (£)	Subsidies and pay of foreign troops (£)	No. of men voted	No. of officers and men in army according to Mutiny Act
1689	2,244,610			
1690	2,413,384			
1691	2,380,698		69,636	
1692	1,825,015		64,924	
1693	1,879,791	162,738	54,562	
1694	2,319,808		83,121	
1695	2,357,076	159,429	87,702	
1696	2,297,109		87,440	
1697	2,297,109		87,440	
1698	1,803,014		35,875	
1699	1,350,000		12,725	
1700	365,000		12,725	
1701	562,033		22,725	
1702	1,261,517	194,517	52,396	
1703	1,590,778	237,464	63,396	
1704	2,115,381	504,190	70,475	
1705	2,456,669	611,166	71,411	
1706	2,694,584	712,797	77,345	
1707	3,054,156	863,547	94,130	
1708	3,030,894	683,462	91,188	
1709	4,016,025	860,669	102,642	
1710	4,002,908	874,619	113,268	
1711	2,864,812	785,730	138,882	
1712	3,397,078	798,958	144,650	
1713	1,146,553	9,301	24,400	
1714	1,153,060		16,347	
1715	1,274,907		18,851	
1716	1,520,083		—	
1717	1,523,911	250,000	—	
1718	919,731		16,347	
1719	809,637		17,866	
1720	926,644		19,500	14,294 (home) 5,546 (abroad)

MILITARY AND NAVAL

	Total supplies granted for the army (£)	Subsidies and pay of foreign troops (£)	No. of men voted	No. of officers and men in army according to Mutiny Act
1721	904,174	72,000	19,840	12,434
1722	844,472		19,840	16,449
1723	941,990		23,840	16,449
1724	923,300		23,810	16,449
1725	912,968		23,810	16,087
1726	976,034	75,000	23,772	24,013
1727	1,391,730	270,000	32,058	22,950
1728	1,370,184	305,924	28,501	22,955
1729	1,352,099	316,259	28,882	17,709
1730	1,195,712	266,259	23,836	17,709
1731	1,196,060	247,509	23,756	17,709
1732	934,381	22,694	23,756	17,709
1733	907,593		23,756	17,704
1734	980,887		25,634	25,744
1735	1,149,228	56,250	34,354	17,704
1736	1,004,020	56,250	26,314	17,704
1737	1,039,199	42,187	26,314	17,704
1738	961,743		26,896	17,704
1739	1,021,494	70,583	26,896	35,963
1740	1,268,429	58,333	40,859	46,288
1741	1,703,195	295,752	53,395	46,284
1742	1,809,145	293,263	51,044	51,519
1743	2,546,487	265,195	51,696	51,936
1744	3,071,907	585,200	53,358	55,425
1745	3,028,535	933,219	53,128	74,187
1746	3,354,635	1,266,402	77,664	59,776
1747	3,191,432	1,364,707	61,471	61,489
1748	3,997,326	1,743,316	64,966	18,857
1749	1,730,477	213,991	28,399	18,857
1750	1,238,707	60,985	29,194	18,857
1751	1,077,345	30,000	29,132	18,857
1752	1,041,554	52,000	29,132	18,857
1753	1,069,235	52,000	29,132	18,857
1754	1,068,185	52,000	29,132	18,857
1755	1,139,548	52,000	31,422	34,263
1756	2,174,540	468,946	47,488	49,749
1757	2,516,119	355,639	68,791	53,777
1758	4,173,890	1,475,897	88,370	52,543
1759	4,882,444	1,968,178	91,446	57,294
1760	6,926,490	1,844,487	99,044	64,971
1761	8,615,293	2,091,659	105,221	67,776

STRENGTH AND COST OF THE BRITISH ARMY

		Total supplies granted for the army (£)	Subsidies and pay of foreign troops (£)	No. of men voted	No. of officers and men in army according to Mutiny Act
1762		7,810,539	1,023,583	120,633	17,536
1763		4,877,139	321,907	120,419	17,532
1764		2,781,652	422,995	31,773	17,421
1765		2,313,343	60,344	31,654	17,306
1766		2,060,414	50,000	31,752	16,754
1767		1,585,573	—	31,701	17,253
1768		1,472,484	—	31,700	17,142
1769		1,358,056	—	31,589	17,666
1770		1,547,931	45,565	30,949	23,432
1771		1,810,320	—	43,546	17,547
1772		1,514,656	—	30,641	17,070
1773		1,516,402	—	30,641	18,024
1774		1,534,721	—	30,641	18,024
1775		1,597,051	—	30,641	21,930
1776		3,500,367	560,455	50,234	20,752
1777		3,815,393	642,431	80,669	90,734
1778		4,833,667	624,157	82,995	20,057
1779		6,013,082	654,677	115,863	30,346
1780		6,796,502	2,418,806	122,677	35,005
1781		7,815,540	658,043	128,549	39,666
1782		7,817,767	724,120	131,989	49,455
1783		5,676,650	656,550	124,254	54,678
1784		4,158,073	182,772	30,680	17,483
1785		2,286,263	120,280	29,557	17,483
1786		2,042,730	—	33,544	18,053
1787		1,876,287	—	35,544	17,634
1788		2,081,905	—	32,117	17,634
1789		1,917,063	—	38,592	17,697
1790		1,874,075	—	38,784	17,448
1791	GB	1,961,326	36,094	39,377	17,448
	Ireland	512,093		15,502	
1792	GB	1,814,800	—	36,476	17,013
	Ireland	557,512		15,532	
1793	GB	3,968,559	455,852	131,181	17,013
	Ireland	919,616		20,232	
1794	GB	6,636,560	1,169,323	183,157	27,289
	Ireland	1,481,210		20,232	

		Total supplies granted for the army (£)	Subsidies and pay of foreign troops (£)	No. of men voted	No. of officers and men in army according to Mutiny Act
1795	GB	11,674,359	1,197,226	301,081	60,244
	Ireland	1,421,705		23,478	
1796	GB	11,907,399	200,000	217,575	119,380 (Mar.)
	Ireland	1,479,148		22,246	49,219 (Dec.)
1797	GB	15,988,089	500,000	207,447	60,765
	Ireland	2,701,839		40,901	
1798	GB	12,852,815	—	225,264	48,609
	Ireland	2,751,355		32,854	
1799	GB	12,600,609	825,000	225,343	52,051
	Ireland	4,174,583		35,515	
1800	GB	14,462,262	3,114,162	—	80,275
	Ireland	3,745,148			
1801		16,352,057	300,000	205,414	85,940
1802		12,871,338	—	279,855 (6 mths) 110,945 (6 mths)	84,445 (Mar.) 70,299 (June)
1803		12,786,619	—	197,827	66,574
1804		19,108,859	—	291,019	129,039
1805		18,581,127	—	284,305	135,121
1806		18,507,519	—	303,831	134,473
1807		20,055,947	180,000	309,065	121,529 (Mar.) 113,795 (June)
1808		20,839,189	1,400,000	331,777	124,063
1809		22,444,770	1,300,000	339,408	133,922
1810		21,717,080	1,380,000	340,835	98,780
1811		23,687,005	2,400,000	340,321	84,801
1812		27,574,757	2,400,000	342,273	245,996
1813		36,689,335	3,600,000	354,510	227,442
1814		37,276,850	4,300,000	362,125	236,497
1815		46,699,092	7,451,056	246,988	204,386 (Mar.) 190,767 (June)

6.3 Strength and cost of the British navy, 1689–1815

	No. of seamen and marines voted	No. borne (inc. marines on shore)	Total grant (£)
1689	21,695	22,322	1,198,648
1696	40,000	47,677	2,516,972
1700	7,000	7,754	956,342
1705	48,000	43,081	2,230,000
1712	48,000	38,106	2,260,000
1715	8,000*	13,475	1,146,748
1723	10,000*	8,078	736,389
1730	10,000*	9,686	863,787
1736	15,000*	17,010	1,037,436
1740	41,930	37,181	2,157,688
1744	51,550	53,754	2,521,085
1748	51,550	50,596	3,640,352
1751	8,000*	9,972	1,056,559
1757	66,419	63,259	3,503,939
1762	89,061	84,797	5,954,252
1767	20,287	15,755	1,869,321
1772	25,000	26,299	2,070,665
1776	28,000	31,084	3,227,056
1782	100,000	105,443	8,063,206
1787	18,000	19,444	2,286,000
1792	16,000	17,361	1,985,482
1798	120,000	119,592	13,449,389
1802	94,461	77,765	13,833,574
1807	130,000	130,917	17,400,337
1812	145,000	144,844	20,442,149
1815	85,384	78,891	19,032,700

* No marines voted in these years.
Source: Parliamentary Papers, 1868–9, vol. XXXV, pp. 693–5.

6.4 Loans and subsidies to foreign states during the wars of 1793–1814

	£	£
1793		
Hanover	492,650	
Hesse-Cassel	190,623	
Sardinia	150,000	
		833,273
1794		
Prussia	1,226,495	
Sardinia	200,000	
Hesse-Cassel	437,105	
Hesse-Darmstadt	102,073	
Baden	25,196	
Hanover	559,376	
		2,550,245
1795		
Germany, Imperial Loan (35 Geo. III, c.93)	4,600,000	
Baden	1,794	
Brunswick	97,722	
Hesse-Cassel	317,492	
Hesse-Darmstadt	79,605	
Hanover	478,348	
Sardinia	150,000	
		5,724,961
1796		
Hesse-Darmstadt	20,076	
Brunswick	12,794	
		32,870

LOANS AND SUBSIDIES TO FOREIGN STATES

	£	£
1797		
Hesse-Darmstadt	57,015	
Brunswick	7,571	
Germany, Imperial Loan (37 Geo. III, c.59)	1,620,000	
		1,684,586
1798		
Brunswick	7,000	
Portugal	120,013	
		127,013
1799		
Prince of Orange	20,000	
Hesse-Darmstadt	4,812	
Russia	825,000	
		849,812
1800		
Germany	1,066,666	
German Princes	500,000	
Bavaria	501,017	
Russia	545,494	
		2,613,177
1801		
Portugal	200,114	
Sardinia	40,000	
Hesse-Cassel	100,000	
Germany	150,000	
German Princes	200,000	
		690,114
1802		
Hesse-Cassel	33,451	
Sardinia	52,000	
Russia	200,000	
		285,451

	£	£
1803		
Hanover	117,628	
Russia	63,000	
Portugal	31,647	
		212,275
1804		
Sweden	20,119	
Hesse-Cassel	83,304	
		103,423
1805		
Hanover		35,341
1806		
Hanover	76,865	
Hesse-Cassel	18,982	
Germany	500,000	
		595,847
1807		
Hanover	19,899	
Russia	614,183	
Hesse-Cassel	45,000	
Prussia	180,000	
		859,082
1808		
Spain	1,497,873	
Sweden	1,100,000	
Sicily	300,000	
		2,897,873
1809		
Spain	529,039	
Portugal	600,000	
Sweden	300,000	
Sicily	300,000	
Austria	850,000	
		2,579,039

LOANS AND SUBSIDIES TO FOREIGN STATES

	£	£
1810		
Hesse-Cassel	45,150	
Spain	402,875	
Portugal	1,237,518	
Sicily	425,000	
		2,110,543
1811		
Spain	220,690	
Portugal	1,832,168	
Sicily	275,000	
Portuguese sufferers	39,555	
		2,367,413
1812		
Spain	1,000,000	
Portugal	2,167,832	
Portuguese sufferers	60,445	
Sicily	400,000	
Sweden	278,292	
Morocco	1,952	
		3,908,521
1813		
Spain	1,000,000	
Portugal	1,644,063	
Sicily	600,000	
Sweden	1,320,000	
Russia	657,500	
Russian sufferers	200,000	
Prussia	650,040	
Prince of Orange	200,000	
Austria	500,000	
Morocco	14,419	
		6,786,022
1814		
Spain	450,000	
Portugal	1,500,000	
Sicily	316,667	

	£	£
Sweden	800,000	
Russia	2,169,982	
Prussia	1,319,129	
Austria	1,064,882	
France (advanced to Louis XVIII to enable him to return to France)	200,000	
Hanover	500,000	
Denmark	121,918	
		8,442,578
		46,289,459

Source: G.R. Porter, *The Progress of the Nation*, vol. II (London, 1838), pp. 335–8.

SECTION SEVEN

Law and order

7.1 Major developments in public order, 1684–1785

The game laws (1684)
The taking of game by all except propertied landowners was forbidden by a succession of statutes at least from 1 James I, c.27, and the property qualification for taking game was further increased by 7 James I, c.11. Under 22 and 23 Car. II, c.25 only persons who possessed freehold estate of at least £100 per annum or a leasehold estate of at least £150 a year, or were the son or heir-apparent of an esquire or person of higher degree, were entitled to take game. The game laws also exposed crops to the damage of hunters and hounds during the hunting season. Further restrictions were introduced under 4 W. and M., c.23, while the 'Black Act' of 1723 made into felonies a large number of poaching and related offences which had hitherto been considered misdemeanours. The severity of the law was further increased by Acts subsequent to 1760, notably in 1770, 1800 and 1816.

The Riot Act (1715)
The Riot Act (1 Geo. I, st. 2, c.5) was passed in June 1715 in the wake of serious rioting following the accession of George I. The statute *supplemented* the existing common law offence of riot committed when three or more assembled together to achieve a common purpose by violence or tumult, by making more serious riots automatically a felony when previously they would normally be considered as misdemeanours. Earlier statutes such as I Mar. st. 2 c.12 (1553) and I Eliz. c.16 had taken steps in a similar direction, but only for the duration of the reign. The Act of 1715 made it a felony for 12 or more persons riotously to assemble and not to disperse within an hour after the proclamation requiring them to disperse; to oppose the making of such a proclamation and not to disperse within an hour after the making of the proclamation had been opposed; unlawfully to assemble to the disturbance of the public peace and when so assembled unlawfully and with force to demolish or pull down any church, chapel or other building for religious worship, or any dwelling-house, barn, stable or outhouse. It also empowered magistrates to call on the assistance of all able-bodied persons to put down riots and indemnified them for any injuries caused.

The Riot Act greatly strengthened the law against rioters by automatically making it a felony to remain assembled an hour after the reading of the Act, even if no further violent action was taken. By making such offences a felony, it provided for capital punishment in the case of serious riots, and permitted the use of lethal force to disperse them. However, there was a common misapprehension that an hour should be allowed to elapse before any action was taken against rioters whereas, in fact, reasonable force could be employed to disperse rioters at any time under the existing common law of riotous offences. The hesitancy of both magistrates and military to act was demonstrated on a number of occasions, notably in the case of the Gordon Riots of 1780.

The Transportation Act (1718)
The Transportation Act gave the courts the power to sentence those guilty of serious crimes and specified lesser offences to seven or fourteen years' transportation in the American colonies.

The 'Black Act' (1723)
The 'Black Act' following poaching affrays and other disturbances in Windsor Forest and Park made felonies (i.e. subject to capital punishment) a large number of aggravated poaching offences, adding substantially to the 'Bloody Code'.

Westminster Watch Act (1735)
An Act was passed enabling the householders of Westminster to pay for their own regular watchmen by means of a regular rate. Other metropolitan parishes adopted a similar system in subsequent years to provide a more reliable and responsible system of street patrols, often recruited from fit army veterans of good character.

The Bow Street Police Office (1739)
Sir Thomas De Veil, a former army colonel, was the first of a line of distinguished and active magistrates in Westminster. In 1739 he moved to a house in Bow Street from which he conducted business as a magistrate until 1746. In 1749 Henry Fielding took over this position, followed in 1754 by his blind half-brother John. These magistrates dispensed justice daily from the office and were noted for their lack of corruption. In 1753 Henry Fielding proposed, and had accepted by the Duke of Newcastle, a group of paid thief-takers to work under his direction. The 'Bow Street Constables' continued to be used throughout the century and were called in by provincial magistrates to assist with serious crimes.

London horse patrols (1752)
Henry Fielding organised a system of horse patrols to protect travellers on the roads surrounding the metropolis, but its expense led to it being discontinued by 1754. From 1756 a more limited system of patrol was

organised by John Fielding. It was later supplemented (c. 1763) by a Foot Patrol financed by £4,000 from the Civil List.

The Militia Act (1757)
The Elizabethan militia was a much decayed and little-used force by the mid-eighteenth century. The crisis of the Seven Years War and the need to counter a possible invasion threat and replace the regular forces of the Crown while they guarded the coasts or went abroad led, in 1757, to the creation of a militia for England and Wales (it did not apply to Scotland). The Militia Act envisaged a body of 60,000 men organised on a county basis, the bulk of whom were to be found by quotas levied on each county and filled by a ballot of all able-bodied men between 18 and 50 years of age. Militia service was for three years, although it was permitted to find a substitute or pay a fine of £10. The force was to train every Sunday between February and October and drill for a few days at Whitweek. When embodied it was to receive army pay and come under normal army discipline. Officers were selected according to property qualifications. Service overseas was not envisaged, although it could involve any part of the British Isles.

The introduction of the Act led to widespread rioting because of misplaced fears of service overseas and resentment that the rich could escape the ballot by paying the fine or buying a substitute. Although the full complement of militia took some time to embody, in the half century after 1757 it was to become, with supplementary legislation, an important domestic peacekeeping force.

1769
Attacks upon mills brought within the compass of the Riot Act of 1715 by 9 Geo. III, st. 2, c.5.

1785
Failure of Pitt's Police Bill for the Metropolitan district.

7.2 Public order in the Age of Revolution and Reform, 1789–1829

1789   Fall of the Bastille and outbreak of the French Revolution (July).

1790   Burke publishes *Reflections on the Revolution in France* (Nov.) warning of the dangers of the French Revolution.

1791   Thomas Paine produces *Rights of Man*, Part One in reply to Burke setting out radical agenda (Mar.; Part Two published in Feb. 1792).

1792   Proclamations against seditious publications (21 May and 1 Dec.). Formation of loyalist associations (first founded at London in Nov.).
Middlesex Justices Act (32 Geo. III, c.53) provides 21 professional magistrates and a force of constables for the Metropolitan district (excluding the City of London).
Thomas Paine tried and found guilty *in absentia* for seditious libel (Dec.).

1793   John Frost convicted of sedition (May).
Daniel Isaac Eaton tried for publishing seditious literature (June and July).
James Muir convicted of sedition (Aug.).
Thomas Fyshe Palmer convicted of sedition (Sept.).

1794   William Skirving convicted of sedition (Jan.).
Maurice Margarot convicted of sedition (Jan.).
Arrest of Thomas Hardy, Horne Tooke, John Thelwall and nine other reform leaders (May).
Suspension of Habeas Corpus (34 Geo. III, c.54) (May).
Appointment and first report of the Secret Committee of the House of Commons (May).
Second report of the Secret Committee of the House of Commons. First and second reports from the Committee of Secrecy appointed by the House of Lords (June).

Robert Watt and David Downie convicted of high treason (Aug.–Sept.).
Trial and acquittal of Hardy, Tooke and Thelwall on charges of high treason (Oct.–Nov.).

1795 The 'Two Acts': Treasonable and Seditious Practices Act (36 Geo. III, c.7), extending law of treason to spoken and written words; and Seditious Meetings Act (36 Geo. III, c.8), restricting public meetings and political lectures (Dec.).

1797 Unlawful Oaths Act (37 Geo. III, c.123). Oaths of secrecy and secret ceremonies made unlawful. Directed against political clubs but also used against trade unions.
Trials and executions of naval mutineers, including Richard Parker (June–Aug.).
Incitement to Mutiny Act makes seduction of the armed forces from their duty or incitement to mutiny a felony (37 Geo. III, c.70).

1798 Trials and conviction of United Scotsmen (Jan.–Sept.).
Seizure of United Englishmen and committee of the London Corresponding Society (Apr.).
Trials of John Binns, Arthur O'Connor and Rev. James O'Coigley for high treason; execution of O'Coigley (May–June).

1799 Reports of the Committees of Secrecy of the House of Commons and House of Lords (Mar.).
Act for the more effectual Suppression of Societies established for Seditious and Treasonable Purposes, and for better preventing Treasonable and Seditious Practices (39 Geo. III, c.79). Suppressed by name the United Irishmen, United Englishmen, United Scotsmen, United Britons, and London Corresponding Society (July).
Combination Act (39 Geo. III, c.81) *See* pp. 309–10.

1800 Combination Act (39 and 40 Geo. III, c.106). *See* pp. 309–10.
Thames Police Office permanently established at Wapping to police riverside districts of London.

1801 First Report of the Secret Committee of the House of Commons on treasonable and seditious practices in Great Britain and Ireland (Apr.).
Second Report of the Committee of the House of Lords (Apr.).
Second report of the Secret Committee of the House of Commons (May).

1802   William Lee and William Ronkesley of Sheffield tried and convicted for swearing illegal oaths (Dec.).

1803   Execution of Col. Marcus Despard for high treason (Feb.).

1810   Sir Francis Burdett imprisoned in the Tower of London for a libel of the House of Commons (Mar.–Apr.).

1812   Framebreaking Act (52 Geo. III, c.16) and Nottingham Peace Act (52 Geo. III, c.17) (Feb.). Unlawful Oaths Act (May). Preservation of Public Peace Act and Act of Indemnity (July). Committees of Secrecy appointed (June).

1813   Renewal of Nottingham Peace Act (remained in force until 1815).

1817   Reports of the Committees of Secrecy of the Houses of Commons and Lords (Feb.).
'Gag' Acts. Suspension of Habeas Corpus; Seditious Meetings Act; Act to prevent seduction of armed forces, and Act to make perpetual parts of the statute 36 Geo. III, c.7, respecting treasonable attempts on the Prince Regent (57 Geo. III, c.3, 55, 7, 19 and 6) (Feb.–Mar.). Trial and imprisonment of radical journalists T.J. Wooler and W. Hone for seditious libel.
Flight of Cobbett to America (Mar.).
Trial and acquittal of Spa Fields conspirators on charges of high treason (June).
Trial and execution of Jeremiah Brandreth at Derby for Pentrich 'rising' (Nov.).

1819   Peterloo 'Massacre'. Arrest of Henry Hunt and organisers.
'Six Acts': (i) Act to prevent delays in trials for misdemeanour (60 Geo. III and 1 Geo. IV, c.4); (ii) Act to authorise seizures of arms in disturbed districts (60 Geo. III and 1 Geo. IV, c.2); (iii) Act to prevent meetings for the training of persons in the use of arms (60 Geo. III and 1 Geo. IV, c.1); (iv) Act to prevent seditious assemblies of more than 50 persons except under specific circumstances (60 Geo. III and 1 Geo. IV, c.6); (v) Act to prevent blasphemous and seditious libels by permitting seizure of libellous material and banishment of authors on second offence (60 Geo. III and 1 Geo. IV, c.8); (vi) Newspaper Stamp Duties Act. Some pamphlets subjected to stamp duty and sureties to be given for payment of fines incurred as blasphemous or seditious libels (60 Geo. III and 1 Geo. IV, c.9).

1820 Seizure of Cato Street conspirators (Feb).
Trial and execution of Arthur Thistlewood and four other conspirators (Apr.–May).

1823 Peel's Gaol Act (4 Geo. IV, c.64). Laid down rules for the running of local gaols by Justices of the Peace; inmates to be classified and separated according to sex, age and type of offence.

1829 Metropolitan Police Act (10 Geo. IV, c.44). Established paid, uniformed police for the 'Metropolitan Police District', covering a radius of about 7 miles from the centre of London, excluding the City of London, controlled by two Justices (or 'Commissioners') under the authority of the Home Secretary.

7.3 Popular disturbances in Britain (excluding Ireland), 1688–1830

1688
Sept.–Nov. Attacks on Catholic property in London, York, Newcastle, Bristol, Norwich, Cambridge and Oxford.
Dec. Following the flight of James II from London further attacks on Catholic property in London and upon the embassies of Catholic powers. Similar attacks in the country and in Edinburgh a crowd sacks Holyrood Chapel.

1693–95
Food riots in the Severn Valley, Thames Valley, Northamptonshire, Essex and Suffolk.

1695
Election riots at Oxford, Exeter, Westminster and elsewhere.

1697
June. Anti-enclosure riots at Epworth, Lincolnshire.

1698
Election riots at Westminster.

1699
Drainage works destroyed by crowds at Deeping Fen, Lincolnshire.

1702
Attacks on dissenting meeting houses at Newcastle-Under-Lyme.

1703–4
Dec.–Feb. Anti-prelate and anti-government riots in Edinburgh.

1705
Election riots at Coventry, Chester, Salisbury and Honiton.

1707
Riots at Edinburgh and Dumfries against the Act of Union.

1709
Food disturbances at Kingswood, Tyneside, Essex and North Wales.

1710
Mar. Pro-Sacheverell disturbances at Oxford, Exeter, Hereford, Barnstaple, Gainsborough, Frome, Cirencester, Sherborne, Walsall, West Bromwich, Ely, Bridgnorth, York, Canterbury, Norwich, Nottingham, Northampton, Taunton, Liverpool, Chester, Northwich, Marlow, Whitchurch, Coventry, Chippenham, Newark and London. Framebreaking in London by Spitalfields weavers.

1713
Bristol election riot.

1714
Sept. Pro-Hanoverian disturbances in Bristol.

1715
June–Aug. Attacks upon dissenting meeting houses in over 30 towns, especially in Manchester and the Midlands.

1716
May. Political disturbances in Cambridge.
July. 'Mug-house' riots in London between Whigs and Tories. Five rioters hanged.

1717
Disturbances amongst the cloth workers in Taunton and Exeter during industrial dispute.

1719
May. Disturbances during keelmen's strike in Newcastle.
June. Weavers' disturbances in Norwich and Colchester. Attacks on women wearing calicoes in London by Spitalfields weavers.

1720
May. Further silk-weavers' disturbances in London. Riots in Tiverton against imported Irish worsteds.

1722
July. Pro-Jacobite disturbance at Leicester.

1723
Widespread poaching and other disturbances in Windsor Forest leads to the Black Act.

1725
Anti-malt tax riots in Edinburgh. Weavers' riots in Crediton.

1726
Riots in Lincoln because of work on the cathedral towers.
Nov. Riots in Wiltshire and Somerset by woollen workers.

1727
Anti-turnpike riots near Bristol.

1727–29
Food riots in Cornwall and North Wales.

1731
Anti-turnpike riots in Gloucestershire.

1732
Apr.–Oct. Riots at the Mayoral elections in Chester.

1734
Mar.–Apr. Widespread election riots.

1735
Anti-enclosure riots in Forest of Dean.

1736
July–Aug. Disturbances in London against the Gin Act and against Irish workmen.
Sept. Porteous riots in Edinburgh.

1737
Food riot in Penryn.

1738–40
Riots in West Country during dispute in woollen industry.

1740–41
Apr.–Jan. Extensive food riots in England and Wales; Newcastle Guildhall sacked.

1743
May and Oct. Attacks upon Methodists in Wednesbury.

1744
Apr. Attacks upon Methodists at St Ives, Cornwall.

1746
Apr.–May. Attacks on Catholic chapels in Liverpool. Also attacks on Catholic property in Bath and Sunderland.
Oct. Attacks on the houses of Jacobites in Manchester.

1749
July–Aug. Turnpikes demolished around Bristol.

1750
Mar.–May. Disturbances during keelmen's strike in the north-east.

1751
May. Two suspected witches killed by mob at Tring.

1754
Disturbances at the Oxford election. Election and anti-enclosure riots at Leicester.

1756–57
Aug.–Dec. Over 140 food riots in England and Wales.

1757
Aug.–Sept. Widespread riots against the operation of the Militia Act, especially in Yorkshire, Lincolnshire, Nottinghamshire, Bedfordshire, Hertfordshire, Cambridgeshire, Norfolk and Huntingdonshire.

1758
June. Anti-enclosure riots at Shaw Hill, Wiltshire.

1759
Anti-militia riots in Huntingdonshire.

1761
Mar. Disturbances at Gateshead, Morpeth, Whittingham and Hexham against Militia Act. Anti-enclosure riot at North Leigh Heath (Oxon).

1762
July. Food riot in Manchester.
Aug. Disturbances amongst Spitalfields weavers.
Nov.–Dec. Sailors' riots in Liverpool and Ormskirk.

1763
Oct. Machine-breaking by Spitalfields weavers.

1765
Jan. Houses attacked by mob in Devizes.
May. Attack on Duke of Bedford's house in London by Spitalfields weavers.
July. Anti-enclosure riot at West Haddon in Northamptonshire.
Aug. Anti-workhouse riots at Wickham Market, Bulcamp, Sibston, Yoxford and Nacton Heath in Suffolk.
Sept. Anti-enclosure riot at Walkworth near Banbury. Pit machinery broken during colliers' strike on Tyneside.

1766
Jan.–Nov. Widespread food rioting in England. Major centres of disturbance in the West Country, Thames Valley, Midlands and East Anglia.

1768
Mar.–May. Disturbances in London in support of John Wilkes.
Apr. Demonstrations by seamen of Newcastle, Sunderland and Shields in pursuit of a wage dispute.
Apr.–May. Disturbances during wage disputes of sailors and coal-heavers in London.
May. 'Massacre' of St George's Fields outside King's Bench Prison.
Aug. Disturbances amongst Spitalfields weavers during wage dispute.

1769
Feb.–Mar. Attacks on spinning and carding machines at Blackburn.
Mar. 'Battle of Temple Bar': pro-Wilkes demonstration in London.
Mar.–Sept. Widespread disturbances amongst Spitalfields weavers.

1771
Mar.–Apr. Pro-Wilkes riots in London.
Oct. Anti-enclosure disturbances at Swinehead, near Boston, Lincolnshire.

1772
Apr. Anti-enclosure disturbance at Redditch.
Apr.–June. Food riots, mainly centred in East Anglia and the West Country.
Dec.–Jan. Meal riots on Tayside.

1773
July–Aug. Renewed food rioting in England, especially in the Midlands and Cornwall.
Aug. Disturbances during strike of shipwrights' apprentices in Liverpool.

1775
June. Weavers' disturbances at Keighley during industrial dispute.
Aug. Rioting during sailors' wage dispute in Liverpool.

1776
Apr. Tinners' riots at Redruth and Falmouth over introduction of Staffordshire earthenware.
July. Riots in Shepton Mallet over the introduction of machinery in the woollen industry.
Oct. Riots at Wrexham over the employment of English colliers.

1778
Mar. Food riot at Flint.
May–Aug. Anti-militia riots at Henfield (Sussex) and Merionethshire.

1779
Jan.–Feb. Anti-Popery riots in Glasgow, Edinburgh and several other towns in Scotland.
June. Machine-breaking in Nottingham.
Oct. Cotton-spinning machinery broken at Chorley, Wigan, Bolton, Blackburn and Preston.

1780
June. Gordon riots in London.
Anti-Catholic riots in Bath.

1781
June. Machine-breaking at Frome.

1782
Oct. Food riots at Wolverhampton and Stourbridge.

1783
Mar.–July. Food riots, mainly in Staffordshire and Yorkshire.
July. Disturbances amongst stocking weavers in Nottingham.

1784
May. Election riots at Westminster, Liverpool, Coventry, Leicester and Buckingham.

1785
June. Disturbances amongst seamen, keelmen and labourers in Sunderland.

1787
Feb.–Mar. Riot at Bradford (Wilts) and Trowbridge over organisation of looms in single shops.

1788
July. Riots at Westminster election.
Nov. Disturbances at Stamford because of attempts to end bull-running.

1789
June. Food riots near Truro.

1790
June. Election riots at Carlisle, Leicester, Nottingham, York and Beverley.
Oct. Disturbances at Nottingham during framework knitters' dispute.

1791
July. Priestly riots in Birmingham by 'Church and King' mobs. Anti-enclosure riot in Sheffield.

1792
Mar. Destruction of power-loom factory in Manchester.
Apr. Attacks on dissenters in Nottingham.
May. Disturbance between soldiers and civilians in Sheffield. Machine-breaking at Woodchester, near Worcester. Disturbances over the price of meat at Nottingham. Riot over the price of provisions at Leicester.
June. Disturbance amongst the colliers at Leeds. 'Church and King' demonstrations in Manchester. Anti-government riots at Edinburgh. Riots in Gloucester against introduction of gig-mills.
June–Oct. Political disturbances at Aberdeen, Perth, Dundee, Peebles, Lanark and Duns.
July. Anti-clearance riot in Ross-shire.
Oct. Food riot at Great Yarmouth. Disturbances at Wigan during colliers' strike.
Oct.–Nov. Disturbances as a result of labour dispute amongst the seamen at Ipswich and South Shields.
Dec. Anti-Jacobin disturbances in Manchester.

1793
Feb. Food riots in Cornwall and South Wales.
Apr. Anti-enclosure disturbances in Flintshire.
June. Disturbances at Liverpool and Sheffield over the price of butter.
Aug. Political riots in Nottingham.
Sept. Riot against toll-gates in Bristol.
Oct. Disturbance in Birmingham against taxes levied for the Priestley riots. Disturbances during labour dispute amongst river-bank workers at Grantham.

1794
July. Political disorders in Nottingham between loyalists and reformers. Disturbances amongst Tyneside keelmen during labour dispute.
Aug. Anti-'crimp-house' disturbances in London. Several recruiting houses attacked.

1795
Feb.–Nov. Widespread food riots in England, Wales and Scotland. Disturbances against the use of the Winchester corn measure in South Wales.
Apr. Anti-recruiting riots in North Wales.
July. Food and anti-recruiting riots in London.
Oct. Mobbing of the King's coach in London.
Nov. Anti-recruiting disturbances in North Wales.

1796
Jan.–Apr. Renewed food riots in Wales, Cornwall, Midlands and Yorkshire.
July. Disturbances between recruiting parties and populace in Nottingham.
Nov.–Dec. Riots in Lincolnshire against operation of the Militia Act. Other disturbances in Norwich, Northampton, Wellingborough, Kettering, Wing, Oswestry, Barmouth, Ulverstone, Penrith, Bala, Machynlleth and Llanbrynmair.

1797
Apr.–May. Mutinies amongst sailors at Spithead and the Nore.
Nov. Cloth-mill destroyed at Beeston, Notts.
Dec. Machine-breaking at Frome in Somerset.

1798
Aug. Anti-enclosure riot at Gringly on the Hill, near Nottingham.

1799
June. Anti-enclosure riots at Wilbarston in Northampton.
Nov. Food riot at Huddersfield.

1800
Jan. Disturbances at St Clears, Carmarthenshire, over taxes.
Feb.–Nov. Widespread food rioting in England, Wales and Scotland.

1801
Jan.–Apr. Renewed food rioting in England and Wales.

1802
Apr.–Aug. Shearmen's riots in Wiltshire against the introduction of gig-mills.
July–Aug. Election riots at Coventry and Liverpool.
Aug. Disturbances amongst London shipwrights during an industrial dispute.

1803
Mar. Riots against press-gangs in Bristol.
Apr.–May. Disturbances against press-gangs in London.

1804
Aug. Riots in London during the Middlesex Election.

1806
Feb. Attack upon Excise officers at Llannon in Cardiganshire.

1807
May. Election riots in Liverpool.

1808
May–June. Disturbances following rejection of Minimum Wage Bill for weavers at several towns in Lancashire.

1809
Sept. Anti-enclosure disturbances in Carnarvonshire.
Oct.–Nov. 'Old Price' riots at Drury Lane Theatre, London.

1810
Apr. Disturbances in London at the arrest of Sir Francis Burdett.
July. Food riot in Wolverhampton market.
Sept. Riot at Dartmouth prison.
Oct. Riot in Porchester Castle prison. Disturbance amongst soldiers in Wakefield.
Nov. Theatre riot in Plymouth.

1811
Mar. Beginning of Luddite disturbances in Nottinghamshire. Extensive frame-breaking in the county until Nov. 1816.
Aug. Disturbances at Peterborough Theatre.
Nov. Disturbance at East India College, Hertford.
Dec. Theatre riots in Liverpool.

1812
Jan.–Sept. Luddite disturbances in Yorkshire.
Mar.–Apr. Machine-breaking in Lancashire and Cheshire.
Apr.–Nov. Widespread food riots in the industrial areas.
Apr. Riots in Manchester when crowd wrecks the Exchange newsroom.
May. Demonstrations in Nottingham to celebrate the assassination of Spencer Perceval.
Sept. Riot at Dartmoor prison.
Sept.–Oct. Anti-enclosure disturbances at Pistyll on the Lleyn peninsula.

1813
Feb. Anti-clearance riots at Kildonan in Sutherland.

Apr. Anti-enclosure riots in Carnarvonshire.
July. Riots against induction of a clergyman at Assynt, Sutherland.

1814
June. Labour disturbances amongst Leicester stocking weavers.

1815
Mar. Riots in London against passing of the Corn Laws. Disturbances amongst Tyneside keelmen during labour dispute. Farm machinery broken at Gosbeck, Suffolk.
July–Aug. Further machine-breaking disturbances in Suffolk.
Oct. Disturbances at Hull, Sunderland and South Shields during seamen's strike.
Nov. Disturbances amongst Bilston colliers following a wage cut.

1816
Feb. Machine-breaking at Huddersfield.
Apr.–June. Food riots, machine-breaking and arson in Norfolk, Suffolk, Cambridgeshire and Essex. Most serious disturbances at Bridport, Norwich, Downham Market, Littleport, Brandon and Ely.
July–Aug. Food riots at Frome, Stockport, Bolton, Coventry, Hinckley and Birmingham.
Oct. Disturbances in South Wales during strikes amongst colliers and ironworkers.
Nov.–Dec. Food riots at Carlisle, Huddersfield, Oldham, Sheffield and Dundee.
Dec. Spa Fields riots in London when the followers of Thomas Spence attempt to seize the Tower and the Bank of England.

1817
Jan. Attack upon the Prince Regent's coach on return from the state opening of Parliament. Disturbances amongst South Wales iron-workers.
Feb. Food riots at Amlwch and Tremadoc in Wales.
Mar. Food riot at Maryport. Strikes and food riots at Radstock. 'March of the Blanketeers' sets off from Manchester. Broken up near Stockport. Further disturbances in South Wales.
June. Pentrich 'Rising' in Derbyshire led by Jeremiah Brandreth. Huddersfield 'Rising'. Minor skirmishes.

1818
July–Aug. Disturbances during strike of Manchester cotton spinners.
Aug. Riots at Stockport during strike of power-loom weavers. Squatters' riots at Rhydoldog in Carnarvonshire.
Nov. Food riots amongst colliers at Whitehaven.

1819
July. Orange riots in Liverpool.
Aug. Peterloo 'Massacre' (16th). Reform disturbance at Macclesfield and Stockport.
Oct. Disturbances during keelmen's strike at North Shields.

1820
Feb. Cato Street conspiracy uncovered.
Mar. Election riot at Banbury. Disturbances at South Shields amongst seamen. Anti-clearance disturbances at Culrain, Gruids and Achness in Ross-shire and Sutherland.
Mar.–Apr. Disturbances amongst wool-croppers near Huddersfield and Barnsley 'Rising'.
Apr. 'Battle of Bonnymuir' near Glasgow between weavers and troops.
June. Demonstrations in London in support of Queen Caroline.
Nov. Widespread demonstrations in support of Queen Caroline.

1821
Jan. Disturbances in Shropshire during colliers' strike.
Mar. Anti-clearance disturbance at Gruids, Scotland.
Aug. Riots in London during funeral of Queen Caroline.

1822
May. Disturbances during colliers' strike in South Wales. Riots in Frome and Warminster over use of the guy-shuttle.
July. Disturbances amongst Norwich weavers over a wage reduction.
Oct.–Nov. Disturbances during keelmen's strike in the Tyne.

1824
Aug. Houses demolished by squatters at Fishguard.

1825
Aug. Disturbances during seamen's strike at Sunderland.

1826
Apr.–May. Power-looms broken at Accrington, Blackburn, Bury, Chaddeston, Rawtenstall, Long Holme, Edenfield, Summerseat and Manchester. Also attacks on power-looms by Bradford worsted weavers.

1829
May. Attacks on weaving factories and provision shops in Manchester.
June–July. Food disturbances in Bolton, Wigan and Preston.

1830
Apr. Beginning of 'Captain Swing' disturbances in southern counties of England.
Nov. Reform disturbances in London.
Dec. Disturbances in the Ruabon area as a result of a strike amongst the North Wales colliers.

Note: The list given above is not exhaustive. In general, incidents have been included which achieved contemporary notoriety or resulted in serious damage to persons or property.
Sources: R.F. Wearmouth, *Methodism and the Common People of the Eighteenth Century* (London, 1945), ch. 1; R. Quinault and J. Stevenson (eds), *Popular Protest and Public Order* (London, 1974); J.L. and B. Hammond, *The Skilled Labourer, 1760–1832* (London, 1919): G. Rudé, *The Crowd in History* (New York, 1964) and *Hanoverian London, 1714–1808* (London, 1971); D.J.V. Jones, *Before Rebecca* (London, 1973); T.C. Smout, *A History of the Scottish People, 1560–1830* (London, 1969); E.P. Thompson, *The Making of the English Working Class* (London, 1968); F.O. Darvall, *Popular Disturbances and Public Order in Regency England*, 2nd edn (Oxford, 1969); M. Thomis, *The Luddites* (Newton Abbot, 1970).

7.4 Criminal statistics

Commitals and convictions for indictable offences in England and Wales, 1805–30

	Total commitals, England and Wales	Convicted	Sentenced to death	Executed
1805	4,605	2,783	350	68
1806	4,346	2,515	325	57
1807	4,446	2,567	343	63
1808	4,735	2,723	338	39
1809	5,330	3,238	392	60
1810	5,146	3,158	476	67
1811	5,337	3,163	359	45
1812	6,576	3,913	450	82
1813	7,164	4,422	593	120
1814	6,390	4,025	488	70
1815	7,818	4,883	496	57
1816	9,091	5,797	795	95
1817	13,932	9,056	1,187	115
1818	13,567	8,958	1,157	97
1819	14,254	9,510	1,206	108
1820	13,710	9,318	1,129	107
1821	13,115	8,788	1,020	114
1822	12,241	8,209	921	95
1823	12,263	8,204	914	54
1824	13,698	9,425	1,017	49
1825	14,437	9,964	986	50
1826	16,164	11,007	1,146	57
1827	17,921	12,564	1,456	70
1828	16,564	11,723	1,086	79
1829	18,675	13,261	1,311	74
1830	18,107	12,805	1,351	46

Note: No national criminal statistics were collected before 1805.
Source: G.R. Porter, *The Progress of the Nation* (London, 1847), p. 642.

Capital convictions and executions in London and Middlesex, 1701–1820

	Capital convictions	Executions	Percentage of executions to capital convictions
1701–10	449	189	42
1711–20	1,084*	514*	47
1721–30	733*	450*	61
1731–40	526*	243*	46
1741–50	531*	338*	64
1751–60	411	281	68
1761–70	505	263	52
1771–80	779	357	46
1781–90	1,162	517	44
1791–1800	779	197	25
1801–10	836	104	12
1811–20	1,648	120	7

* Approximate figure.
Source: *Parliamentary Papers, 1818*, vol. XVI, pp. 184–5.

Capital punishment in London, 1701–1830

	Capital convictions	Executions	Percentage of executions to capital convictions
1701–50	3,323*	1,735*	52
1751–1800	3,636	1,615	44
1801–30	3,898	509	13

* Approximate figure.
Source: *Parliamentary Papers, 1818*, vol. XVI, pp. 184–5.

7.5 The abolition of capital offences, 1808–30

In 1800 there were about 200 capital offences on the statute book.

The Larceny Act, 1808 (48 Geo. 3, c.129) abolished the death sentence for larceny from the person, and broadened the definition of the offence. This was the first of the eighteenth-century capital statutes to be repealed, as a result of Romilly's campaign.

The Stealing from Bleaching Grounds Act, 1811 (51 Geo. 3, c.39), and the Stealing of Linen Act, 1811 (51 Geo. 3, c.41), two obsolete capital statutes, were also repealed by Romilly.

The Stealing in Shops Act, 1820 (1 Geo. 4, c.117), raised the minimum amount stolen in shops which would constitute a capital offence from 5s to £15.

The Judgement of Death Act, 1823 (4 Geo. 4, c.48), gave discretion to the judge to abstain from pronouncing the death sentence on a person convicted of any crime except murder, if the judge felt the offender was fit to be recommended for the King's mercy.

The Benefit to Clergy Act, 1823 (4 Geo. 4, c.53), abolished the death penalty for: (a) larceny of property to the value of 40s on ships on navigable rivers; (b) larceny of property to the value of 40s in shops.

'Peel's Acts' were essentially consolidating statutes, codifying the statute law on a number of offences:

1. The Criminal Statutes (Repeal) Act, 1827 (7 and 8 Geo. 4, c.27), consolidated about 90 statutes relating to larceny and allied offences, and repealed obsolete statutes on this subject.
2. The Indemnity Act, 1827 (7 and 8 Geo. 4, c.30), consolidated about 50 statutes relating to malicious injuries to property.
3. The Offences against the Person Act, 1828 (9 Geo. 4, c.31), consolidated 56 statutes relating to offences against the person.

The Criminal Justice Act, 1827 (7 and 8 Geo. 4, c.28), reversed the previous position on the punishment of felonies. Previously all felonies were automatically capital offences unless 'benefit of clergy' was allowed; by this Act, 'benefit of clergy' was abolished, and the death penalty restricted to those felonies from which 'benefit of clergy' had previously been excluded, or which new statutes would *expressly specify* should be capital. The punishment for non-capital felonies was to be transportation or imprisonment.

The Larceny Act, 1827 (7 and 8 Geo. 4, c.29), abolished the separate offence of grand larceny (theft of over 12*d*), which had carried the death sentence for a second offence. Simple larceny was now to constitute a single offence, punishable by imprisonment or transportation. The only larcenies which remained capital were: (a) larceny in a dwelling house of property worth £5 or more; (b) stealing horses, sheep or cattle.

The Forgery Act, 1830 (11 Geo. 4 and 1 Will. 4, c.66), consolidated the law relating to forgery. It abolished the death sentence for a number of offences, but retained it for 42 kinds of forgery. This Act was repealed by the Forgery Act, 1832 (2 and 3 Will. 4, c.123), which abolished the death sentence for all forgery offences, except forgery of wills and of powers of attorney for the transfer of government stock.

Sources: L. Radzinowicz, *A History of English Criminal Law and its Administration from 1750*, 4 vols (London, 1948–68), remains the best overall analysis of criminal law in this period. For popular disturbances see R.F. Wearmouth, *Methodism and the Common People of the Eighteenth Century* (London, 1945); E.P. Thompson, *The Making of the English Working Class*, 2nd edn (Harmondsworth, 1968); and J. Stevenson, *Popular Disturbances in England, 1700–1870* (2nd edn, London, 1992). For criminal statistics see *Parliamentary Papers, 1834*, vol. X, p. 299 and G.R. Porter, *The Progress of the Nation* (London, 1847), p. 642.

SECTION EIGHT

Religion

8.1 The Church of England

Chronology

1688 Archbishop Sancroft and six Bishops protest against James II's Delaration of Indulgence, suspending laws against Catholics and dissenters. Tried for seditious libel, but acquitted.

1689 Toleration Act allows dissenters to worship publicly on taking an oath and permits Quakers to affirm, but excludes Catholics and Unitarians. Attempt to alter the Prayer Book in order to attract the dissenters back to the Church of England fails owing to opposition of Convocation. Archbishop Sancroft, five Bishops and more than 400 clergy, the non-jurors, refuse to take oaths of supremacy and allegiance to William and Mary and are deprived of their livings.

1691 First Society for the Reformation of Manners founded.

1695 Locke's *Reasonableness of Christianity* published.

1698 The Society for Promoting Christian Knowledge is founded.

1701 Mission branch of the Society for Promoting Christian Knowledge is founded as the Society for the Propagation of the Gospel.

1703 Bill to prevent Occasional Conformity passes the House of Commons but is rejected by the Lords.

1704 Queen Anne's Bounty: Queen Anne surrenders the claim of the throne to first fruits and tenths to endow poorer clergy.

1707 Act of Security of Church of England excludes Presbyterians from holding office in England.

1709 Dr Sacheverell impeached after preaching against toleration of dissenters and denouncing the Whig Ministers as traitors to the Church.

1710	Trial of Dr Sacheverell at Westminster Hall leads to rioting in London and attacks on dissenting chapels. Lords order Sacheverell's sermon to be burnt and silence him for three years.
1711	Occasional Conformity Act passed against Protestant dissenters. Parliament votes £350,000 to build 50 churches in London.
1713	Bishop Gibson produces the *Codex Juris Ecclesiastici Anglicani*, a comprehensive study of the legal rights and duties of the English clergy and of the constitution of the Church.
1714	Schism Act introduced, forbidding nonconformists to teach.
1716	Negotiations between non-jurors and Greek Church for reunion.
1717	Convocation prorogued as a consequence of its censure of Hoadly, Bishop of Bangor, for his sermon declaring against tests of orthodoxy. Convocation does not reassemble again until 1852. Hoadly replies to the censure and 'Bangorian controversy' ensues.
1719	Repeal of Occasional Conformity and Schism Acts.
1723	Francis Atterbury, Bishop of Rochester, exiled for part in pro-Jacobite plot.
1727	First annual Indemnity Act introduced to cover breaches of the Test Act.
1729	John Wesley, junior Fellow of Lincoln College, Oxford, becomes leader of a strict religious society, dubbed Methodists.
1730	Tindal's *Christianity As Old As the Creation* declared that Christ merely confirmed the law revealed by the light of Nature.
1735	Hoadly's *Plain Account of the Lord's Supper*, describing the ceremony as purely memorial, attacked.
1736	Warburton's *Alliance of Church and State* argues for the necessity of an Established Church and a test on dissenters.
1739	George Whitefield starts open-air preaching near Bristol.
1745	Many of the non-jurors implicated in the Jacobite rebellion.

1746	SPCK produces Welsh Bible and Prayer Book.
1749	George Whitefield becomes chaplain to Lady Huntingdon. George Lavington's *The Enthusiasm of Methodists and Papists Compared* attacks Methodism.
1753	Lord Hardwicke's Marriage Act: clergy to be heavily punished for performing marriage ceremonies without previous publication of banns or production of licence.
1756	William Jones's *Catholic Doctrine of the Trinity* re-states High-Church opinions.
1757	Publication of Hume's *Natural History of Religion*.
1766	Francis Blackburne's *The Confessional* attacks the necessity for Church of England clergy to subscribe to the Thirty-Nine Articles.
1769	Archbishop Thomas Secker's *Lectures on the Church Catechism* and *Charges to the Clergy of the Dioceses of Oxford and Canterbury* provide manuals of pastoral care.
1771	Feathers' Tavern petition against subscription.
1774	Foundation of Theophilus Lindsey's Unitarian chapel.
1776	George Horne's *Commentary on the Book of Psalms*.
1780	'No Popery' riots led by Lord George Gordon.
1781	Countess of Huntingdon's Connexion separates from the Church of England.
1782	Charles Simeon begins the Evangelical Movement in Cambridge.
1790	Motions for repeal of the Test and Corporation Acts withdrawn from Parliament without a discussion.
1791	Priestley's house in Birmingham attacked by Church and King mob. Death of Wesley.
1793	*British Critic* founded to express High-Church views.
1794	Paley's *Evidences of Christianity* collects together the arguments against Deism.

236　RELIGION

1795　Methodist secession from the Church of England.

c. 1795　William Wilberforce, Henry Thornton, Sir James Stephen, Lord Teignmouth, Granville Sharp and John Venn form the evangelical Clapham Sect, and campaign for various philanthropic causes, including the end of the slave trade.

1798　Charles Daubeny's *A Guide to the Church* defends extreme High-Church views.

1799　Church Missionary Society founded.
Religious Tract Society founded.

1801　Pitt's proposals for Catholic relief blocked by opposition of the King.

1802　Paley's *Natural Theology* re-states the argument from design for the existence of God.

1804　British and Foreign Bible Society founded (along interdenominational lines).

c. 1810　Joshua Watson, William Stevens and Henry Handley Norris consolidate the Hackney Phalanx (or 'Clapton Sect') to promote High-Church views.

1811　National Society founded for educating the poor in the principles of the Church of England.

1817　Church Building Society founded.

1818　Church Building Act: Parliament grants £1,000,000.

1828　Repeal of the Test and Corporation Acts.
Second Church Building Act.

1829　Catholic Emancipation.

Archbishops and bishops
Province of Canterbury: England

Canterbury
1678　William Sancroft
1691　John Tillotson
1695　Thomas Tenison

1716	William Wake
1737	John Potter
1747	Thomas Herring
1757	Matthew Hutton
1758	Thomas Secker
1768	Hon. Frederick Cornwallis
1783	John Moore
1805	Charles Manners Sutton
1828	William Howley

London

1676	Henry Compton
1714	John Robinson
1723	Edmund Gibson
1748	Thomas Sherlock
1761	Thomas Hayter
1762	Richard Osbaldeston
1764	Richard Terrick
1777	Robert Lowth
1787	Beilby Porteus
1809	John Randolph
1813	William Howley
1828	Charles James Blomfield

Winchester

1684	Peter Mew(s)
1707	Jonathan Trelawney
1721	Charles Trimnell
1723	Richard Willis
1734	Benjamin Hoadly
1761	John Thomas
1781	Hon. Brownlow North
1820	Sir George Pretyman Tomline, Bt
1827	Charles Richard Sumner
1869	Samuel Wilberforce

Bath and Wells

1685	Thomas Ken(n)
1691	Richard Kidder
1704	George Hooper
1727	John Wayne
1743	Edward Willes
1774	Charles Moss

1802	Richard Beadon
1824	George Henry Law
1845	Hon. Richard Bagot

Bristol
1685	Jonathan Trelawney
1689	Gilbert Ironside
1691	John Hall
1710	John Robinson
1714	George Smalridge
1719	Hug Boulter
1724	William Bradshaw
1733	Charles Cecil
1735	Thomas Secker
1737	Thomas Gooch
1738	Joseph Butler
1750	John Conybeare
1756	John Hume
1758	Philip Yonge
1761	Thomas Newton
1782	Lewis Bagot
1783	Christopher Wilson
1792	Spencer Madan
1794	Henry Reginald Courtenay
1797	Folliott H.W. Cornewall
1803	Hon. George Pelham
1807	John Luxmore
1808	William Lort Mansel
1820	John Kaye
1828	Robert Gray

Chichester
1685	John Lake
1689	Simon Patrick
1691	Robert Grove
1696	John Williams
1709	Thomas Manningham
1722	Thomas Bowers
1724	Edward Waddington
1731	Francis Hare
1740	Matthias Mawson
1754	William Ashburnham
1798	John Buckner
1824	Robert James Carr

Ely

1684	Francis Turner
1691	Simon Patrick
1707	John Moore
1714	William Fleetwood
1723	Thomas Greene
1738	Robert Butts
1748	Thomas Gooch
1754	Matthias Mawson
1770	Edmund Keene
1781	James York
1808	Thomas Dampier
1812	Bowyer E. Sparke
1836	Joseph Allen

Exeter

1689	Jonathan Trelawney
1708	Offspring Blackall
1717	Lancelot Blackburn
1724	Stephen Weston
1742	Nicholas Claget
1747	George Lavington
1762	Frederick Keppel
1778	John Ross
1792	William Buller
1797	Henry Reginald Courtenay
1803	John Fisher
1807	Hon. George Pelham
1820	William Carey
1830	Christopher Bethell

Gloucester

1681	Robert Frampton
1691	Edward Fowler
1715	Richard Willis
1721	Joseph Wilcocks
1731	Elias Sydall
1735	Martin Benson
1752	James Johnson
1760	Williams Warburton
1779	James Yorke
1781	Samuel Halifax
1789	Richard Beadon
1802	George Isaac Huntingford

1815 Hon. Henry Ryder
1824 Christopher Bethell
1830 James Henry Monk (1836 united with Bristol)

Hereford
1662 Herbert Croft
1691 Gilbert Ironside
1701 Humphrey Humphries
1713 Philip Bisse
1721 Benjamin Hoadly
1724 Henry Egerton
1746 James Beauclerk
1787 Hon. John Harley
1788 John Butler
1803 Folliott H.W. Cornewall
1808 John Luxmoore
1815 George Isaac Huntingford
1832 Hon. Edward Grey

Lichfield
1671 Thomas Wood
1692 William Lloyd
1699 John Hough
1717 Edward Chandler
1731 Richard Smalbroke
1750 Frederick Cornwallis
1768 John Egerton
1771 Brownlow North
1774 Richard Hurd
1781 James Cornwallis
1824 Hon. Henry Ryder

Lincoln
1675 Thomas Barlow
1692 Thomas Tenison
1695 James Gardiner
1705 William Wake
1716 Edmund Gibson
1723 Richard Reynolds
1744 John Thomas
1761 John Green
1779 Thomas Thurlow
1787 George Pretyman

1820 Hon. George Pelham
1827 John Kaye

Norwich
1685 William Lloyd
1691 John Moore
1708 Charles Trimnell
1721 Thomas Green
1723 John Leng
1727 William Baker
1733 Robert Butts
1738 Thomas Gooch
1748 Samuel Lisle
1749 Thomas Hayter
1761 Philip Yonge
1783 Lewis Bagot
1790 George Horne
1792 Charles Manners Sutton
1805 Henry Bathurst
1837 Edward Stanley

Oxford
1688 Timothy Hall
1690 John Hough
1699 William Talbot
1715 John Potter
1737 Thomas Secker
1758 John Hume
1766 Robert Lowth
1777 John Butler
1788 Edward Smallwell
1799 John Randolph
1807 Charles Moss
1812 William Jackson
1815 Hon. Edward Legge
1827 Charles Lloyd

Peterborough
1685 Thomas White
1691 Richard Cumberland
1718 White Kennett
1729 Robert Clavering
1747 John Thomas
1757 Richard Terrick

1764   Robert Lambe
1769   John Hinchcliffe
1794   Spencer Madan
1813   John Parsons
1819   Herbert Marsh
1839   George Davys

Rochester
1684   Thomas Sprat
1713   Francis Atterbury
1723   Samuel Bradford
1731   Joseph Wilcocks
1756   Zachary Pearce
1774   John Thomas
1793   Samuel Horsley
1802   Thomas Dampier
1809   Walter King
1827   Hugh Percy
1827   George Murray

Salisbury
1667   Seth Ward
1689   Gilbert Burnet
1715   William Talbot
1721   Richard Willis
1723   Benjamin Hoadly
1734   Thomas Sherlock
1748   John Gilbert
1757   John Thomas
1761   Robert Hay Drummond
1761   John Thomas
1766   John Hume
1782   Hon. Shute Barrington
1791   John Douglas
1807   John Fisher
1825   Thomas Burgess

Worcester
1683   William Thomas
1689   Edward Stillingfleet
1699   William Lloyd
1717   John Hough
1743   Isaac Maddox

1759	James Johnson
1774	Brownlow North
1781	Richard Hurd
1808	F.H.W. Cornwall
1831	Robert James Carr

Province of York

York

1688	Thomas Lamplugh
1691	John Sharp
1714	William Dawes
1724	Lancelot Blackburn
1743	Thomas Herring
1747	Matthew Hutton
1757	John Gilbert
1761	Hon. R. Hay Drummond
1777	William Markham
1808	Hon. Edward V. Vernon Harcourt
1848	Thomas Musgrave

Durham

1674	Nathaniel Crew
1721	William Talbot
1730	Edward Chandler
1750	Joseph Butler
1752	Richard Trevor
1771	John Egerton
1787	Thomas Thurlow
1791	Hon. Shute Barrington
1826	William Van Mildert

Carlisle

1684	Thomas Smith
1702	William Nicolson
1718	Samuel Bradford
1723	John Waugh
1735	George Fleming
1747	Richard Osbaldeston
1762	Charles Lyttleton
1769	Edmund Law
1787	John Douglas
1791	Edward Venables Vernon

| 1808 | Samuel Goodenough |
| 1827 | Hugh Percy |

Chester
1686	Thomas Cartwright
1689	Nicholas Stratford
1708	William Dawes
1714	Francis Gastrell
1726	Samuel Peploe
1752	Edmund Keene
1771	William Markham
1776	Beilby Porteus
1788	William Cleaver
1800	Henry William Majendie
1810	Bowyer Edward Sparke
1812	George Henry Law
1824	Charles James Blomfield
1828	John Bird Sumner

Sodor and Man
1684	Baptist Levinz
1698	Thomas Wilson
1755	Mark Kildesley
1773	Richard Richmond
1780	George Mason
1784	Claudius Crigan
1813	George Murray
1828	William Ward

Churches, clergy and Easter Day communicants, 1801–31

	Churches and chapels	Clergy	Easter Day communicants ('000s)	Easter Day communicant density
1801	11,379	—	535	9.9
1811	11,444	14,531	550	8.9
1821	11,558	—	570	7.9
1831	11,883	14,933	605	7.2

Source: A. Gilbert, *Religion and Society in Industrial England* (London, 1976).

Regional variation in the average size of an Anglican parish in 1811

Region	Total no. of parishes	Area in acres	Average size of parish in acres
East	1,634	3,240,000	1,980
South-East	1,048	2,594,000	2,475
South Midlands	1,379	3,558,000	2,580
North Midlands	1,236	3,517,000	2,840
South-West	940	2,703,000	2,880
South	873	2,541,000	2,910
West Midlands	1,253	4,021,000	3,200
Cornwall	205	868,000	4,230
Yorkshire	630	3,898,000	6,190
North	290	3,419,000	11,790
North-West	156	1,852,000	11,860

Source: Ibid.

Plurality and non-residence

1704   Of 9,180 benefices paying first fruits and tenths, 5,082 were worth less than £80; 3,826 less than £50 and 1,200 less than £20 a year.

1802   2,500 benefices in patronage of bishops, deans and chapters
1,100 benefices in patronage of Crown
2,000 benefices in patronage of lay corporations, e.g. Oxford and Cambridge colleges
6,500 benefices in patronage of county families and individuals

1805   Clergy freed from ban under 21 Hen. VIII, c.13, now allowed to lease land for farming and to buy and sell for profit.

1807   4,412 resident incumbents for 11,164 parishes.

1810   About 1,500 resident incumbents had income under £150; 3,998 livings worth under £150, including 12 under £10 and 72 under £20. About 2,500 livings left to curates paid at £30–£40 a year.

1835   *The Extraordinary Black Book or Corruption Unmasked* gives the following distribution of Church revenues of £9,459,565 – 2 archbishops at £26,465 each; 24 bishops at £10,174; 28 deans at £1,580; 61 archdeacons at £739; 26 chancellors at £494; 844 prebendaries, canons, etc., at £338; 2,886 pluralist parsons holding 7,037 livings at £1,863; and 4,305 incumbents, half resident, at £764.

Revenues from bishoprics, 1760 (in order of revenue)

See	Revenue p.a. £	See	Revenue p.a. £
Canterbury	7,000	Lincoln	1,500
Durham	6,000	Rochester	600 (+ 900)
Winchester	5,000	Lichfield and	
York	4,500	Coventry	1,400
London	4,000	St Asaph	1,400
Ely	3,400	Bangor	1,400
Worcester	3,000	Chichester	1,400
Salisbury	3,000	Carlisle	1,300
Oxford	500 (+ 1,800)	Hereford	1,200
Norwich	2,000	Peterborough	1,000 +
Bath and Wells	2,000	Llandaff	500 (+ 450)
Bristol	450 (+ 1,150)	Gloucester	900 (+ rich Durham prebend)
Exeter	1,500		
Chester	900 (+ 600)	St David's	900 (+ two livings)

Note: Figures in parentheses indicate additional revenues.
Source: *A List of the Archbishops, Bishops, Deans, and Prebendaries in England and Wales, in His Majesty's Gift, with the reputed Yearly Value, of Their Respective Dignities* (London, 1762).

8.2 Protestant dissenters

Chronology

1688 James II orders a Declaration of Indulgence, suspending laws against Catholics and dissenters, to be read in all churches.

1689 Toleration Act allows dissenters to worship publicly on taking an oath, and permits Quakers to affirm, but excludes both Catholics and Unitarians. Protestant dissenters allowed to build chapels. Attempts to alter the Prayer Book to attract the dissenters back to the Church fails owing to opposition of Convocation.

1694 George Fox's *Journal* published.

1696 Toland's *Christianity not Mysterious* founding the Deist movement in England is burnt by the public hangman.

1697 Lord Mayor of London, a dissenter, openly practises Occasional Conformity.

1702 Defoe's *Shortest Way with Dissenters* satirises the sentiments of extreme High Churchmen.

1703 A bill to prevent Occasional Conformity passes the House of Commons but defeated in the Lords by the opposition of Whig peers.

1709 Dr Sacheverell preaches against toleration of dissenters.

1710 Trial of Dr Sacheverell leads to attacks on dissenting chapels in London.

1711 Occasional Conformity Act passed.

1714 Bolingbroke introduces the Schism Act, forbidding nonconformists to teach.

1715 Widespread attacks on dissenting meeting houses especially in London, the North-West and the Midlands.

1716   Dr Williams founds the Dr Williams Library, major centre of records of dissenters.

1718   Act of quieting and establishing corporations. Dissenters could retain seat without taking sacrament if not challenged within six months.

1719   Repeal of Schism and Occasional Conformity Acts. Meeting of Presbyterians at Salters Hall protests against the need to subscribe to a belief in the Trinity by the clergy, beginning a major shift towards Unitarianism.

1727   Walpole introduces the first annual bill of indemnity for neglect of the Test and Corporation Acts, enabling dissenters to take the sacrament after, not before, election.
Ministers of Presbyterian, Independent and Baptist congregations around London form General Body of Protestant Dissenting Ministers.

1728   Moravian mission established in England.

1729   Doddridge establishes a Presbyterian Academy at Market Harborough.

1732   Organisation of Protestant dissenting deputies to act as pressure group for dissenters.

1736   Attempt to relieve Quakers from tithes fails.

1767   Judgement by Lord Mansfield stopped City of London using dissenters to raise funds to build the Mansion House.

1770   Orthodox General Baptists form the separate General Baptist New Connexion. The old connexion gradually merges with the Unitarians. Bristol Education Society formed to enlarge Baptist college at Bristol; further colleges created in Nottingham (1797), Bradford (1804), Stepney (1810).

1787   Campaign for Repeal of Test and Corporation Acts presents petitions to Parliament. Bills for repeal defeated in 1787, 1789 and 1790.

1789   Leading Unitarian in London, Dr Richard Price, preaches to the London Revolution Society on the text 'On the Love of Our

Country', supporting reform of Church and State and offering congratulations to the French on their Revolution.

1790   Edmund Burke implicitly attacks Price and the dissenters in *Reflections on the Revolution in France* as opponents of the Church of England and enemies of the constitution.

1791   'Church and King' riots in Birmingham. House of leading dissenter, Joseph Priestley, destroyed by the crowd. Attacks on dissenters in other leading towns.

1792   Baptist Missionary Society formed.

1794   Joseph Priestley emigrates to United States.

1812   Formal repeal of Conventicle and Five Mile Act.

1813   Unitarian Relief Act.

Congregational, Particular Baptist and General Baptist New Connexion membership, 1750–1838

	Congregational members	Density	Particular Baptist		General Baptist New Connexion	
			Members	Density	Members	Density
1750	15,000		10,000		—	
1772	—		—		1,221	
1780	—		—		1,800	
1790	26,000		17,000		2,843	
1800	35,000	0.65	24,000	0.45	3,403	
1810	—		—		5,322	
1820	—		—		7,673	0.11
1830	—		—		10,869	0.13
1838	127,000	1.38	86,000	0.94	13,947	0.15

Source: A.D. Gilbert, *Religion and Society in Industrial England: Church, Chapel and Social Change, 1740–1914* (London, 1976), p. 34.

8.3 The Methodist movement

Chronology

1729 John Wesley, junior Fellow of Lincoln College, Oxford, becomes leader of a strict religious society formed by his brother Charles Wesley and dubbed 'Methodists'.

1738 John Wesley returns from America, falls under the influence of Peter Böhler, a Moravian, and is converted in Aldersgate on 24 May. George Whitefield undertakes missionary work in America.

1739 George Whitefield starts open-air preaching at Kingswood, Bristol. John Wesley follows Whitefield's example of preaching in the open air. Methodist Society meets in Old Foundry, Moorfields, London.

1740 Wesley severs his connection with the Moravians. He begins to employ lay preachers and build chapels. Wesley and Whitefield agree to differ over the doctrine of predestination.

1743 Methodists produce rules for 'classes'. Welsh Calvinistic Methodist body founded by Whitefield. Serious anti-Methodist rioting in Wednesbury.

1744 First Methodist Conference held at Foundry Chapel, London, consisting of John and Charles Wesley, four clergy and four lay preachers. Resolves that bishops are to be obeyed 'in all things indifferent', canons to be observed 'as far as can be done with a safe conscience' and 'societies to be formed where the preachers go'.

1747 Methodist societies grouped into circuits. First of John Wesley's visits to Ireland.

1749 Calvinists under Whitefield desert Wesley; Whitefield becomes chaplain to Lady Huntingdon.

1756 Wesley's *Twelve Reasons Against a Separation from the Church* attempts to restrain breakaway tendencies among his followers.

1760 Wesley's lay preachers take out licences as dissenting teachers; some begin to administer the sacraments.

1771 Francis Asbury (1745–1816) sails for America as Wesleyan missionary. First Methodist bishop in America.

1781 Lady Huntingdon's Connexion (Calvinist) separates from the Church of England.

1784 Deed of Declaration, beginning of modern Methodism (Arminian). Conference control over ministers and churches throughout Connexion.
Thomas Coke (1747–1814) ordained by John Wesley as 'superintendent' of Methodist Society in America. Bishops of Methodist Episcopal Church of America derive their orders from Coke.

1791 Death of Wesley.

1795 Separation of Methodists from Church of England.

1797 Methodist New Connexion.

1808 Expulsion by Wesleyan Methodist Conference of Hugh Bourne (1772–1852) for open-air preaching.

1812 Primitive Methodist Connexion formed by Hugh Bourne and William Clowes (1780–1851).

1818 Bryanites or Bible Christians separated from Methodists.

Methodist membership, 1767–1819

	Wesleyan membership	New Connexion	Combined total
1767	22,410		
1771	26,119		
1776	30,875		
1781	37,131		
1786	46,559		
1791	56,605		
1796	77,402		
1801	87,010	4,815	91,825
1806	103,549	5,586	109,135
1811	135,863	7,448	143,311
1816	181,631	8,146	189,777
1819	184,998	9,672	194,670

Total Methodist membership as a percentage of the adult English population, 1801–36

1801	1.6
1806	1.9
1811	2.3
1816	2.8
1821	2.9
1826	3.3
1831	3.4
1836	4.0

8.4 Roman Catholicism

Chronology

In 1685, England was divided into four districts by the Papacy – London, Midland, Western, Northern – in each of which a papal vicar exercised the authority normally possessed by the ordinary (bishop). In law Roman Catholic priests faced the penalties of high treason for saying Mass; unlicensed teachers could be fined 40s a day; laymen refusing to take an oath denying the spiritual authority of the Pope were guilty of recusancy. This meant they could not hold any office, keep arms, go to Italy, travel more than five miles without licence, or be executor, guardian, doctor or lawyer. They could not sit in Parliament nor on corporations. The nearest Protestant kin could claim lands from a Roman Catholic heir. Roman Catholics were also subject to double land tax.

In practice the treatment of Roman Catholics was not so severe as the laws allowed: few were punished for saying or hearing Mass and magistrates seldom tendered the recusancy oath except in times of national emergency.

1688 James II orders a Declaration of Indulgence to be read in all churches, suspending laws against both Catholics and dissenters. Widespread attacks on Catholic property in London, York, Norwich, Newcastle, Cambridge, Oxford, Bristol and elsewhere (continuing into January 1689), following on the birth of James II's heir. Flight of James II effectively ends his attempt to reimpose Catholicism in England.

1689 Roman Catholics excluded from terms of Toleration Act.

1695 Act passed 'for preventing growth of Popery'. Priests forbidden to exercise their functions and Catholics prevented from inheriting or buying land or sending their children abroad, unless they abjured their religion.

1714 Ultramontane Roman Catholics refuse to abandon claims of Pope Sixtus V to release subjects of a heretic monarch from oath of fealty.

1716 Recusancy laws enforced in many counties as a consequence of the Jacobite rising.

1717 Pope-burning processions held in London and Oxford to celebrate George I's return from Hanover.

1723 Levy of £100,000 placed on Roman Catholics as a result of Atterbury plot.

1746 Attacks on Catholic chapels in Liverpool and Sunderland following Jacobite rising.

1747 Duke of York, the brother of Charles Edward Stuart, created a cardinal (d. 1805).

1760 Pitt obtains from the Theological Faculties of the Sorbonne, Louvain and other universities, a declaration that the Pope has no civil authority in England, that he cannot absolve from the Oath of Allegiance, and that faith must be kept with heretics.

1778 Roman Catholic Relief Act permits Catholic worship. Purchase of land allowed and forfeiture of estates repealed. New oath of allegiance formulated for Catholics.

1780 Protestant Association presents petition to Parliament for repeal of the Roman Catholic Relief Act led by Lord George Gordon, provoking the 'Gordon riots' and widespread destruction of property in London. Attacks on houses of prominent supporters of Catholic Relief, Catholic embassies and chapels, but ordinary Catholics largely spared.

1788 English Catholics make 'Protestation' of loyalty which denied papal authority in temporal matters; signed by the four Vicars Apostolic, 240 priests and 1,500 laymen.

1791 Catholic Relief Act removes last of religious disabilities, but the Test Act continues to bar Catholics from Parliament and other civil offices.

1808 Roman Catholics given commissions in army and navy under stress of Napoleonic Wars.

1813 Catholic Emancipation defeated by Speaker's vote.

1817 Catholic Relief Bill again defeated.

Main centres of Roman Catholic refugees, 1794

Some 8,000 Roman Catholic priests and nuns, driven from the Continent by the French Revolution, were given sanctuary in Britain, e.g. 1,000 were welcomed at Winchester by Anglicans. Main centres were:

Priests

Benedictines	Acton Burnell, Salop; Downside, Som., 1814; Ampleforth, Yorks.
Cistercians	1794–1817 Lulworth, Dorset.
Dominicans	1794–1810 Carshalton, Surrey; novitiate Hinckley, Leics.
Franciscans	1794 Novitiate at Osmotherley, Yorks.
Jesuits	1794 Stonyhurst, Lancs.

Nuns

Benedictine	1794–1857 at Winchester; Preston, Lancs.; after 1811 Caverswall Castle, Staffs.
Canonesses	1794 Regular (Winderheim) English convent from Bruges at Hengrave Hall, Suffolk, till 1802, then back to Bruges. From Louvain to Hammersmith, then Amesbury, Wilts, 1799, and Spettisbury, Dorset.
Carmelites	1794 from Antwerp to Lanherne, Cornwall; St Helen's Auckland, Co. Durham. From Hoogstraet to Acton, Middlesex, then Canford House, Dorset, till 1825.
Cistercians	1794 Hammersmith till 1801, then Stapehill, Wimborne, Dorset.
Dominicans	1794–1839 from Spellekens Convent to Hartpury Court, nr Gloucester.
Franciscans (enclosed)	1794–1804 Abbey House, Winchester; then Taunton.
Mary, Institute of the Blessed Virgin	School at Hammersmith till 1796. Nuns moved to Bar Convent, York, oldest existing convent in England (1686).

Source: Anson, Peter F., *The Religious Orders and Congregations of Great Britain and Ireland* (Stanbrook Abbey, Worcester, 1949).

8.5 Scotland

1688 News of William III's landing leads to the beginning of restoration of Presbyterianism.

1689 Episcopal clergy ejected and Presbyterianism restored. All acts supporting episcopacy rescinded and episcopacy abolished, though some of the Scottish bishops perpetuate themselves and are still strongly supported in the East and North-East.

1690 Lay patronage abolished and Act of Supremacy rescinded. Ejected ministers restored and General Assembly meets.

1694 Roman Catholic vicariate established: two districts – Lowland and Highland; 1827 three districts – Eastern, Western, Northern.

1695 First Catholic bishop appointed for Scotland.

1698 Aikenhead executed for blasphemy at Edinburgh.

1700 Estimate that out of 900 parishes, ministers in 165 adhere to the Episcopal Church.

1707 Act of Union gives full rights to the Presbyterian Church of Scotland.

1711 Greenshields, an Episcopalian, is condemned by the Court of Session for using the English liturgy in Edinburgh, but the decision is reversed by the House of Lords.

1712 Toleration Act for Scotland. Right of nominating ministers restored to laymen, unless Roman Catholics, thereby depriving kirk sessions of the right of electing ministers. Strict Presbyterians refuse to recognise the Act restoring lay patronage.

1725 'Holy Bounty' granted to protestantise the Highlands.

1730 Glas attacks the civil establishment of the Church and forms the Glassite Sect, later developed by his son-in-law Sandeman.

1733 Secession from Church of Scotland led by Ebenezer Erskine in protest at lay patronage, the growth of toleration, and the threatened abolition of penal statutes against witchcraft.

1746 Following the Jacobite rebellion, the Scottish episcopal clergy are persecuted. Meetings of more than five are forbidden; public services are banned and made illegal to have churches or chapels. Some clergy resign their orders and others go into exile.

1747 Erskine's secession Church splits into Burghers, led by Erskine, and anti-Burghers.

1752 A compromise reached on lay patronage; presbytery could satisfy itself on life, learning and doctrine of patron's nominee.

1773 12 Jesuit fathers in Scotland when the Pope suppressed order.

1780 Bill to allow Roman Catholic priests to exercise office in Scotland withdrawn after riots in Edinburgh.

1784 Scottish Episcopal Church gave episcopate to American Church by consecration in Aberdeen of Samuel Seabury (1729–96), first Bishop of Connecticut.

1811 Congregational Union of Scotland.

Scottish bishops

(Although episcopal government in the Church of Scotland was abolished in 1689, some bishops continued to exercise their functions; dates of the death of bishops are given in parentheses.)

Aberdeen
1682*   George Haliburton (d. 1715)

Argyll
1688   Alexander Monro (not consecrated; d. 1698)

Brechin
1684   James Drummond (d. 1695)

---

* Dates given are those of consecration or, in the case of translation from another see, confirmation of new appointment.

Caithness
1680   Andrew Wood (d. 1695)

Dunblane
1684   Robert Douglas (d. 1716)

Dunkeld
1686   John Hamilton (d. 1689)

Edinburgh
1687   Alexander Rose (d. 1720)

Galloway
1688   John Gordon (d. 1726)

Glasgow
1687   John Paterson (d. 1708)

The Isles
1680   Archibald Graham (or MacIlvernock) (d. 1702)

Moray
1688   William Hay (d. 1707)

Orkney
1688   Andrew Bruce (d. 1699)

Ross
1696   James Ramsay (d. 1696)

St Andrews
1684   Arthur Rose (d. 1704)

8.6 Wales

1715   Thirty-five nonconformist chapels in Wales.

1730   Circulating schools started by Griffith Jones (1683–1761).

1735   'Conversion' of Howell Harris of Trevecca (1714–73), who leads movement to revitalise established church.

1746   SPCK Welsh Bible and Prayer Book.

1761   13,000 circulating schools open.

1767   Lady Huntingdon (1707–91) rents Trevecca House, North Wales, as training centre for her Connexion.

1770   First edition (Carmarthen) of Welsh family Bible published by Peter Williams (1722–96).

1784   Thomas Charles (1755–1814), Anglican curate, joins Methodists and organises his Sunday schools in Wales which have no age limit. 'Charles taught Wales to read.'

1800   Welsh Wesleyan Methodist Church (Arminian doctrines).
        One thousand chapels in Wales.

1811   First ordination of Welsh Methodists (Calvinist doctrines).

1818   Revival at Beddgelert, Carnarvonshire, led by Richard Williams.

1823   Confession of Faith of Welsh Methodists formulated.

1826   Constitutional deed gives Welsh Methodist Church legal existence but forbids any alteration in faith or doctrine.

Welsh bishops

Province of Canterbury: Wales

Bangor
1673	Humphrey Lloyd
1689	Humphrey Humphries
1702	John Evans
1716	Benjamin Hoadly
1722	Richard Reynolds
1723	William Baker
1728	Thomas Sherlock
1734	Charles Cecil
1738	Thomas Herring
1743	Matthew Hutton
1748	Zachary Pearce
1756	John Egerton
1769	John Ewer
1775	John Moore
1783	John Warren
1800	William Cleaver
1807	John Randolph
1809	Henry William Majendie
1830	James Colquhoun Campbell

Llandaff
1679	William Beaw
1706	John Tyler
1724	Robert Clavering
1729	John Harris
1739	Matthias Mawson
1740	John Gilbert
1749	Edward Cressett
1755	Richard Newcome
1761	John Ewer
1769	Jonathan Shipley
1769	Shute Barrington
1782	Richard Watson
1816	Herbert Marsh
1819	William van Mildert
1826	Charles Richard Sumner

St Asaph
1680	William Lloyd
1692	Edward Jones

1703	George Hooper
1704	William Beveridge
1708	William Fleetwood
1715	John Wynne
1727	Francis Hare
1732	Thomas Tanner
1736	Isaac Maddox
1743	John Thomas (elected December 1743 but translated before consecration)
1744	Samuel Lisle
1748	Robert Hay Drummond
1761	Richard Newcome
1769	Jonathan Shipley
1789	Samuel Halifax
1790	Lewis Bagot
1802	Samuel Horsley
1806	William Cleaver
1815	John Luxmore
1830	William Carey

St David's

1687	Thomas Watson (vacant 1699–1705)
1705	George Bull
1710	Philip Bisse
1713	Adam Ottley
1724	Richard Smallbrooke
1731	Elias Sydall
1732	Nicholas Claggett
1743	Edward Willes
1744	Richard Trevor
1753	Anthony Ellis
1761	Samuel Squire
1766	Robert Lowth
1766	Charles Moss
1774	James Yorke
1779	John Warren
1783	Edward Smallwell
1788	Samuel Horsley
1794	William Stewart (Stuart)
1801	George Murray
1803	Thomas Burgess
1825	John Banks Jenkinson

8.7 Ireland

(For events affecting Roman Catholics, including the Penal Laws and Catholic Emancipation, *see* pp. 253–4.)

Division of Population among Creeds

1800   Roman Catholic Irish   3,150,000
         Protestant Anglo-Irish   450,000
         Presbyterians   900,000
         Roman Catholics paid about £500,000 a year in tithes to Protestant clergy.

Dioceses of Church of Ireland, 1714–1830

Province of Armagh: Meath, Clogher, Kilmore or Tir Briuin, Ardagh (1692–1751 held by bishops of Kilmore; 1751–1839 held by archbishops of Tuam; then united to Kilmore), Down, Dromore, Derry, Raphoe, Tuam (archbishop till 1839), Killala, Elphin, Clonfert (united to Killaloe 1804) Kilmacduagh (1627–1836 held *in commendam* by bishops of Clonfert; united to Killaloe 1752).

Province of Dublin: Kildare, Ossory, Ferns, Cashel (archbishop until 1839) Waterford (united to Cashel 1832), Cork, Cloyne (united to Cork 1835), Limerick, Killaloe, Kilfenora (1661–1741 held by Archbishop of Tuam; 1742–52 held by Bishop of Clonfert; 1752 united to Killaloe).

8.8 Missionary and benevolent societies

1698	Society for the Promotion of Christian Knowledge.
1701	Society for the Propagation of the Gospel in Foreign Parts.
1740	Foundling Hospital, London (Capt. Thomas Coram, 1668–1751).
1758	Magdalen Hospital, London, for penitent prostitutes.
1780	Sunday Schools started by Robert Raikes of Gloucester.
1787	Quakers start Society for Abolition of Slave Trade.
	Proclamation Society against vice and immorality.
1793	Baptist Missionary Society (William Carey, 1761–1834).
1795	London Missionary Society, undenominational.
1796	Quakers' Retreat at York, first humane asylum with efforts to cure insane.
1799	Church Missionary Society for Africa and the East.
	Sunday School Union.
	Religious Tract Society.
1802	Society for Suppression of Vice.
1804	British and Foreign Bible Society.
1807	Abolition of Slave Trade.
	British and Foreign School Society.
1809	London Society for Promoting Christianity among the Jews.
1811	National Society to open Christian schools.
1813	Wesleyan Missionary Society.
1833	Emancipation of slaves.

SECTION NINE

Financial and economic

9.1 Public Finance

Income and expenditure: Great Britain, 1688–1801

	Total net income (£'000)	Total net expenditure (£'000)
1688–91*	8,613	11,543
1692†	4,111	4,255
1693	3,783	5,576
1694	4,004	5,602
1695	4,134	6,220
1696	4,823	7,998
1697	3,298	7,915
1698	4,578	4,127
1699	5,164	4,691
1700	4,344	3,201
1701	3,769	3,442
1702	4,869	5,010
1703	5,561	5,313
1704	5,394	5,527
1705	5,292	5,873
1706	5,284	6,692
1707	5,471	8,747
1708	5,208	7,742
1709	5,206	9,160
1710	5,248	9,772
1711	5,179	15,142‡
1712	5,748	7,864
1713	5,780	6,362
1714	5,361	6,185
1715	5,547	6,228
1716	5,582	7,076
1717	6,514	5,885
1718	6,090	6,534
1719	6,026	6,152
1720	6,323	6,002
1721	5,954	5,873
1722	6,150	6,978

	Total net income (£'000)	Total net expenditure (£'000)
1723	5,993	5,671
1724	5,773	5,438
1725	5,960	5,516
1726	5,518	5,543
1727	6,103	5,860
1728	6,741	6,504
1729	6,294	5,711
1730	6,265	5,574
1731	6,080	5,347
1732	5,803	4,974
1733	5,522	4,595
1734	5,448	6,360
1735	5,652	5,852
1736	5,762	5,793
1737	6,077	5,129
1738	5,716	4,725
1739	5,820	5,210
1740	5,745	6,161
1741	6,244	7,388
1742	6,416	8,533
1743	6,567	8,979
1744	6,576	9,398
1745	6,451	8,920
1746	6,249	9,804
1747	6,961	1,145‡
1748	7,199	1,194‡
1749	7,494	12,544‡
1750	7,467	7,185
1751	7,097	6,425
1752	6,992	7,037
1753	7,338	5,952
1754	6,827	6,030
1755	6,938	7,119
1756	7,006	9,589
1757	7,969	11,214
1758	7,946	13,200
1759	8,155	15,382
1760	9,207	17,993
1761	9,594	21,112
1762	9,459	20,040
1763	9,793	17,723
1764	10,221	10,686

	Total net income (£'000)	Total net expenditure (£'000)
1765	10,928	12,017
1766	10,276	10,314
1767	9,868	9,638
1768	10,131	9,146
1769	11,130	9,569
1770	11,373	10,524
1771	10,987	10,106
1772	11,033	10,726
1773	10,487	9,977
1774	10,613	9,566
1775	11,112	10,365
1776	10,576	14,045
1777	11,105	15,259
1778	11,436	17,940
1779	11,853	19,714
1780	12,524	22,605
1781	13,280	25,810
1782	13,765	29,234
1783	12,677	23,510
1784	13,214	24,245
1785	15,527	25,832
1786	15,246	16,678
1787	16,453	15,484
1788	16,779	16,338
1789	16,669	16,018
1790	17,014	16,798
1791	18,506	17,996
1792	18,607	16,953
1793	18,131	19,623
1794	18,732	28,706
1795	19,053	38,996
1796	19,391	42,372
1797	21,380	57,649
1798	26,946	47,422
1799	31,783	47,419
1800	9,674	12,383
1801	31,585	50,991

* 5 November 1688–29 September 1691.
† Years to 1752 ending 29 September, thereafter 10 October.
‡ Contains debt items consolidated from previous years.
Source: *State Papers*, 1868–69, XXXV.

Income and expenditure: United Kingdom, 1802–30

	Income (£ million)	Expenditure (£ million)
1802	39.1	65.6
1803	41.2	54.8
1804	42.4	53.0
1805	50.2	62.8
1806	55.0	71.4
1807	60.1	72.9
1808	64.8	73.3
1809	68.2	78.0
1810	69.2	81.5
1811	73.0	81.6
1812	71.0	87.3
1813	70.3	94.8
1814	74.7	111.1
1815	77.9	112.9
1816	69.2	99.5
1817	69.2	71.5
1818	57.6	58.7
1819	59.5	57.6
1820	58.1	57.5
1821	59.9	58.4
1822	61.6	58.4
1823	59.9	56.5
1824	58.5	54.3
1825	59.7	55.5
1826	57.7	54.1
1827	55.2	56.1
1828	54.7	55.9
1829	56.5	53.5
1830	55.3	53.7

Source: *State Papers*, 1868–69, XXXV.

National debt, 1691–1830 (£ million)

Year	Debt	Year	Debt
1691	3.1	1743	53.5
1692	3.3	1744	57.1
1693	5.9	1745	60.1
1694	6.1	1746	64.9
1695	8.4	1747	69.4
1696	10.6	1748	76.1
1697	16.7	1749	77.8
1700	14.2	1750	78.0
1701	14.1	1751	78.1
1702	14.1	1752	76.9
1703	13.6	1753	75.0
1704	13.4	1754	72.2
1705	13.0	1755	72.5
1706	13.0	1756	74.6
1707	14.5	1757	77.8
1708	15.2	1758	82.1
1709	19.1	1759	91.3
1710	21.4	1760	101.7
1711	22.4	1761	114.2
1712	34.9	1762	126.6
1713	34.7	1763	132.6
1714	36.2	1764	134.2
1715	37.4	1765	133.6
1716	37.9	1766	133.3
1717	39.3	1767	133.9
1718	39.7	1768	132.6
1719	41.6	1769	130.3
1720	54.0	1770	130.6
1721	54.9	1771	128.9
1722	52.7	1772	128.7
1723	53.6	1773	128.9
1724	53.8	1774	127.7
1725	52.7	1775	127.3
1726	52.9	1776	131.2
1729	52.1	1777	136.6
1730	51.4	1778	143.1
1731	51.7	1779	153.4
1732	50.1	1780	167.2
1733	50.0	1781	190.4
1734	49.1	1782	214.3
1735	49.3	1783	231.8
1736	49.7	1784	242.9
1737	48.5	1785	245.5
1738	47.5	1786	246.2
1739	46.9	1787	245.8
1740	47.4	1788	245.1
1741	48.8	1789	244.3
1742	51.3	1790	244.0

Year	Value	Year	Value
1791	243.2	1811	609.6
1792	241.6	1812	626.9
1793	242.9	1813	652.3
1794	249.6	1814	725.5
1795	267.4	1815	744.9
1796	310.4	1816	778.3
1797	359.2	1817	766.1
1798	391.2	1818	843.3
1799	426.6	1819	844.3
1800	n.a.	1820	840.1
1801	456.1	1821	838.3
1802	498.6	1822	831.1
1803	516.4	1823	836.1
1804	523.8	1824	828.6
1805	539.6	1825	820.2
1806	564.4	1826	811.0
1807	583.1	1827	810.0
1808	591.3	1828	806.4
1809	599.0	1829	801.3
1810	607.4	1830	798.2

Source: State Papers, 1898, LII, 1786–1890; State Papers, 1890–91, XLVIII.

Income tax: rates and yields, 1799–1816

	Net produce (£ million)	Standard rate in the £
1799	1.9	2s
1800	5.7	2s
1801	5.9	2s
1802	5.3	2s
1803	—	—
1804	4.9	1s
1805	3.9	1s
1806	5.0	1s 3d
1807	12.0	2s
1808	11.2	2s
1809	12.7	2s
1810	12.8	2s
1811	13.6	2s
1812	13.6	2s
1813	14.6	2s
1814	14.9	2s
1815	14.3	2s
1816	14.7	2s

9.2 Country banks in England and Wales, 1784–1830

Number of banks, excluding branches

1784	119	1813	660
1793	280	1814	657
1794	272	1815	626
1796	301	1816	575
1797	230	1817	577
1798	312	1818	596
1800	370	1819	595
1801	383	1820	606
1802	397	1821	609
1803	410	1822	623
1804	414	1823	641
1805	438	1824	660
1806	478	1825	684
1807	515	1826	597
1808	573	1827	600
1809	631	1828	615
1810	654	1829	640
1811	656	1830	628
1812	646		

Source: *English Historical Documents, 1783–1832*, vol. XI (London, 1959), p. 596.

9.3 Enclosure Acts, 1760–1830

1760–69	385	1800–9	847
1770–79	660	1810–19	853
1780–89	246	1820–29	205
1790–99	469		

Source: G.R. Porter, *The Progress of the Nation* (London, 1836), pp. 155–6.

9.4 The Corn Laws

13 Geo. III, c.43 (1773)
Export prohibited at or above average of 44s per quarter; 5s bounty when price under 44s. Imports at or above 48s subject to 6d duty; over 44s and under 48s, duty of 17s; duty of 22s on imports when average price under 44s.

31 Geo. III, c.30 (1791)
Export prohibited at or above 46s; average 44s to 46s, export allowed without bounty; export with 5s bounty when average prices under 44s. Imports, when average price at or above 54s, subject to 6d duty; between 50s and 54s, import duty of 2s 6d; at average of under 50s, duty of 24s 3d.

44 Geo. III, c.109 (1804)
Export, when average price above 54s, prohibited; export permitted but without bounty when average price of wheat over 48s and under 54s; 5s bounty on exports when prices at or under 48s $7\frac{1}{2}d$; duty on imports when prices at or above 66s; duty of 3s $1\frac{1}{2}d$ when prices between 63s and under 66s; duty of 30s $3\frac{3}{4}d$ when prices under 63s.

55 Geo. III, c.26 (1815)
Full freedom of import without duty when price of wheat at or above 80s per quarter. All imports prohibited when price below 80s.

9 Geo. IV, c.60 (1828)
Introduction of sliding scale of duties with steep fall in the duty on imported corn after the price of corn rose above 66s; at 66s the duty payable was 20s 8d, at 73s only 1s.

Sources: C.R. Fay, *The Corn Laws and Social England* (Cambridge, 1932); D.G. Barnes, *The History of the English Corn Laws from 1660–1846* (London, 1930).

9.5 Wheat prices

Average price of wheat in England and Wales, 1771–1830 (per imperial quarter)

	s	d		s	d
1771	48	7	1801	119	6
1772	52	3	1802	69	10
1773	52	7	1803	58	10
1774	54	3	1804	62	3
1775	49	10	1805	89	9
1776	39	4	1806	79	1
1777	46	11	1807	75	4
1778	43	3	1808	81	4
1779	34	8	1809	97	4
1780	36	9	1810	106	5
1781	46	0	1811	95	3
1782	49	3	1812	126	6
1783	54	3	1813	109	9
1784	50	4	1814	74	4
1785	43	1	1815	65	7
1786	40	0	1816	78	6
1787	42	5	1817	96	11
1788	46	4	1818	86	3
1789	52	9	1819	74	6
1790	54	9	1820	67	10
1791	48	7	1821	56	1
1792	43	0	1822	44	7
1793	49	3	1823	53	4
1794	52	3	1824	63	11
1795	75	2	1825	68	6
1796	78	7	1826	58	8
1797	53	9	1827	58	6
1798	51	10	1828	60	5
1799	69	0	1829	66	3
1800	113	10	1830	64	3

Source: B.R. Mitchell and P. Deane, *Abstract of British Historical Statistics*, 2nd edn (Cambridge, 1971), p. 488.

9.6 Trade

Overseas trade, 1700–1819* (annual average in £000 per decade)

	Exports	Imports
1700–9	4,400	4,800
1710–19	4,900	5,600
1720–29	5,000	6,800
1730–39	5,900	7,700
1740–49	6,500	7,300
1750–59	8,700	8,300
1760–69	10,000	10,700
1770–79	9,300	12,100
1780–89	10,200	13,800
1790–99	17,500	21,800
1800–9	25,400	28,700
1810–19	35,000	31,640

* Figures up to 1772 are for England and Wales only; from 1772 to 1804 for Great Britain; after 1804 for the United Kingdom, including Ireland.

The coal trade, 1685–1820 (selected dates)

	Shipped coastwise from Newcastle (000s of Newcastle chaldrons; 1 chaldron = 53 cwt)	Shipped coastwise from Sunderland (000s of Newcastle chaldrons)	Imported into London (000s of London chaldrons; 1 chaldron = $25\frac{1}{2}$ cwt)
1685	235	62	—
1700	205	—	335
1725	266	—	471
1750	288	162	458
1780	366	225	657
1800	585	322	1011
1820	757	416	1321

Source: B.R. Mitchell and P. Deane, *Abstract of British Historical Statistics*, 2nd edn (Cambridge, 1971), pp. 108–10, 122.

9.7 Production

Output of cloth milled in the West Riding, 1727–1815: selected dates

	Broad cloth		Narrow cloth	
	000 pieces	000 yards	000 pieces	000 yards
1727	29.0	—	—	—
1740	41.4	—	58.6	—
1750	60.4	—	78.1	—
1760	49.4	—	69.6	—
1770	93.1	2,772	85.4	2,256
1784	138.0	4,094	116.0	3,357
1795	251.0	7,760	155.1	5,173
1805	300.2	10,079	165.8	6,193
1815	330.3	10,394	162.4	6,650

Source: *Report of the Select Committee on the Woollen Manufacture* (*State Papers*, 1806, III; *State Papers*, 1806–20, XII).

Exports of cotton textiles, 1740–1829

	Annual average value (£000s)	Percentage of total exports in value
1740–49	11	Neg.
1750–59	88	1
1760–69	227	2
1770–79	248	3
1780–89	756	7
1790–99	2,631	15
1800–9	9,995	39
1810–19	18,712	53
1820–29	28,000	62

Neg. = negligible

Pig iron production, 1720–1830: selected dates (000 tons)

1720	25.0
1788	68.3
1796	125.0
1806	243.9
1823	455.2
1830	677.4

Source: R. Meade, *The Coal and Iron Industries of the United Kingdom* (London, 1882), pp. 829 ff.; T.S. Ashton, *Iron and Steel in the Industrial Revolution* (Manchester, 1924), p. 235.

Output of tin and copper, 1726–1830: selected dates (000 tons)

	Tin	Copper
1726	1.5	5.0
1740	1.7	5.0
1750	2.9	9.4
1760	2.7	15.8
1770	3.0	30.8
1780	3.0	36.6*
1790	3.2	33.3
1800	2.5	56.0
1810	2.0	66.0
1820	3.0	91.5
1830	4.4	135.7

* 1784.
Source: R. Hunt, *British Mining* (London, 1884), pp. 887, 889.

Industrial production, 1801–30 (1913 = 100):
The Hoffman Index (including building)

1801	6.64	1816	9.24
1802	6.85	1817	9.51
1803	7.06	1818	9.81
1804	7.27	1819	10.13
1805	7.42	1820	10.46
1806	7.64	1821	10.83
1807	7.80	1822	11.25
1808	7.94	1823	11.66
1809	8.08	1824	12.08
1810	8.22	1825	12.50
1811	8.36	1826	12.89
1812	8.49	1827	13.30
1813	8.63	1828	13.71
1814	8.80	1829	14.14
1815	8.99	1830	14.60

Source: W.G. Hoffman, *British Industry, 1700–1950* (Oxford, 1955).

9.8 Transport

Canals

1698	Acts: Colchester obtains Act to improve river Colne from Colchester to sea at Wivenhoe.
1699	Acts: Act for improvement of Dee navigation.
1701	Construction: Exeter Canal enlarged from Topsham to Exeter.
1703	Construction: Grimsby improves channel by diversion of river Freshney.
1733	Acts: Dee Navigation Act passed.
1737	Construction: Completion of 10-mile cut from Chester to Flint on Dee estuary.
1757	Construction: Completion of Sankey navigation from Newton le Willows to the Mersey.
1759	Acts: First Bridgewater Act passed.
1760	Acts: Amended Bridgewater (including provision for the aqueduct at Barton).
1761	Construction: Bridgewater completed.
1762	Acts: Bridgewater extension to Runcorn.
1766	Acts: Trent and Mersey; Staffordshire and Worcestershire.
1768	Acts: Coventry; Droitwich, Birmingham (Birmingham to Autherley); Forth and Clyde; Borrowstowness.
1769	Acts: Oxford. Construction: Birmingham canal completed from Wednesbury to Birmingham.

282 FINANCIAL AND ECONOMIC

1770   Acts: Leeds and Liverpool; Monkland.

1771   Acts: Chesterfield; Bradford.

1772   Acts: Chester; Market Weighton.
       Construction: Staffordshire and Worcestershire completed; Bridgewater joined to Mersey.

1774   Acts: Huddersfield Broad (Sir John Ramsden's); Bude.
       Construction: Bradford completed.

1775   Acts: Gresley.

1776   Acts: Stourbridge; Dudley.
       Construction: Chesterfield completed.

1777   Acts: Erewash.
       Construction: Trent and Mersey completed; work stopped on Leeds and Liverpool (Leeds and Liverpool ends were both open).

1778   Acts: Basingstoke.
       Construction: work stopped on Oxford (open to Banbury).

1779   Construction: Stroudwater open.

1780   Acts: Thames and Severn.

1783   Acts: Birmingham and Fazeley.

1786   Construction: work restarted on Oxford.

1788   Acts: Shropshire (Tub Boat) Canal.
       Construction: First canal inclined plane built by William Reynolds on Ketley Canal.

1789   Acts: Andover; Cromford.
       Construction: Thames and Severn completed.

1790   Acts: Glamorganshire.
       Construction: Oxford; Birmingham and Fazeley; Forth and Clyde completed; work restarted on Leeds and Liverpool.

1791   Acts: Royal Military; Worcester and Birmingham; Hereford and Gloucester; Manchester, Bolton and Bury; Kington and Leominster; Neath.

TRANSPORT   283

1792   Acts: Nottingham; Ashton; Lancaster; Wryley and Essington; Coombe Hill; Monmouthshire.
Construction: Shropshire completed.

1793   Acts: Oakham; Grantham; Ulverston; Nutbrook; Derby; Grand Junction; Caistor; Shrewsbury; Stainforth and Keadby; Dearne and Dove; Stratford-Upon-Avon; Brecknock and Abergavenny; Ellesmere; Warwick and Birmingham; Old Union; Gloucester and Berkeley; Aberdare; Barnsley; Crinan.

1794   Acts: Montgomeryshire; Somersetshire Coal Canal; Wisbech; Peak Forest; Huddersfield Narrow; Swansea; Grand Junction (branches to Buckingham, Aylesbury and Wendover); Warwick and Braunston; Rochdale; Kennet and Avon; Ashby.
Construction: Glamorganshire Canal opened from Merthyr Tydfil to Cardiff.

1795   Acts: Bridgewater (extension to Leigh); Grand Junction (Paddington branch) Wiltshire and Berkshire; Newcastle-Under-Lyme; Ivelchester and Langport.

1796   Acts: Salisbury and Southampton: Grand Western; Warwick and Napton; Aberdeenshire.
Construction: Lune aqueduct completed.

1797   Acts: Polbrock.
Construction: Ashton; Shrewsbury completed.

1798   Construction: Swansea completed; Huddersfield Narrow (Huddersfield to Marsden and Ashton to Stalybridge opened; Hereford and Gloucester (Gloucester to Ledbury) opened.

1799   Construction: Warwick and Birmingham; Warwick and Napton; Barnsley completed.

1800   Acts: Thames and Medway.
Construction: Peak Forest completed.

1801   Acts: Croydon; Grand Surrey; Leven.
Construction; Grand Junction (Buckingham and Paddington branches) completed.

1802   Construction: Nottingham completed.

1803   Acts: Tavistock; Caledonian.
Construction: Pontcysyllte aqueduct completed.

1804 Construction: Dearne and Dove: Rochdale completed.

1805 Construction: Grand Junction (main line from Brentford to Braunston) completed.

1806 Acts: Glasgow, Paisley and Johnstone.

1807 Acts: Isle of Dogs.

1808 —

1809 Construction: Perpendicular lift invented by John Woodhouse, erected at Tardebigge on Worcester and Birmingham.

1810 Acts: Grand Union.
Construction: Kennet and Avon completed.

1811 Acts: Bridgewater and Taunton.

1812 Acts: Regent's; North Walsham and Dilham; London and Cambridge Junction.

1813 Acts: Wey and Arun Junction; North Wilts.
Construction: Grand Junction (Aylesbury branch) completed.

1814 Acts: Newport Pagnell.
Construction: Grand Western (Loudwell to Tiverton) completed.

1815 Acts: Pocklington; Sheffield.
Construction: Grand Junction (Northampton branch) completed.

1816 Construction: Leeds and Liverpool completed.

1817 Acts: Portsmouth and Arundel; Edinburgh and Glasgow Union.

1819 Acts: Bude; Carlisle.
Construction: North Wiltshire completed.

1820 Construction: Regent's completed.

1821 Act passed for Stockton and Darlington Railway.

1822 Construction: Caledonian; Edinburgh and Glasgow Union completed.

1823   Acts: Harecastle New Tunnel.

1824   Acts: Kensington; Hertford Union.

1825   Acts: Baybridge; Liskeard; English and Bristol Channels Ship Canal.

1826   Acts: Birmingham and Liverpool Junction; Macclesfield; Alford. Construction: Lancaster completed.

Turnpike Acts

Turnpike Acts by period, 1663–1839 (England)

	No. of Acts passed		No. of Acts passed
1663–1719	37	1761–72	205
1720–29	46	1773–91	65
1730–39	24	1792–1815	173
1740–50	39	1816–39	139
1751–60	184		

Source: W. Albert, *The Turnpike Road System of England, 1663–1844* (Cambridge, 1972).

Turnpike Acts by area, 1663–1839

	No. of Acts passed
Home counties	73
Southern counties	134
East Anglia	61
Western counties	102
Far West	68
Northants, Cambs., Hunts. and Beds.	45
South Midlands	58
North Midlands	84
East Midlands	75
Yorkshire and Lancashire	148
Far North	64

Source: W. Albert, *The Turnpike Road System of England, 1663–1844* (Cambridge, 1972).

Shipping registered in English ports in the eighteenth century (000 tons)

	1702	1788
London	140.0	315.3
Newcastle	11.0	106.1
Liverpool	8.6	76.1
Sunderland	3.9	53.6
Whitehaven	7.2	52.3
Hull	7.6	52.1
Whitby	8.3	47.9
Bristol	17.3	37.8
Yarmouth	9.9	36.3

Source: R. Davis, *The Rise of the English Shipping Industry* (London, 1962), p. 35.

SECTION TEN

Social and cultural

10.1 Populations, 1701–1821 (millions)

	England and Wales	Scotland	Ireland
1701	5.8	1.0	—
1711	6.0	—	2.8
1721	6.0	1.1	2.9
1731	6.1	—	3.0
1741	6.2	—	—
1751	6.5	1.3	3.2*
1761	6.7	—	3.5†
1771	7.1	1.4‡	—
1781	7.5	—	4.1
1791	8.3	1.5	4.8
1801	9.2	1.6	5.2
1811	10.3	1.8	5.9
1821	12.1	2.1	6.8

* 1754.
† 1767.
‡ 1775.

Sources: N.L. Tranter, *Population since the Industrial Revolution: The case of England and Wales* (London 1973), p. 41; B.R. Mitchell and P. Deane, *Abstract of British Historical Statistics* (Cambridge, 1962), p. 8; K.H. Connell, *The Population of Ireland, 1750–1845* (Oxford, 1950), p. 25.

10.2 Principal urban populations, 1650–1831

	1650	1700	1750	1801	1831
Aberdeen	—	—	—	27,000	57,000
Bath	1,000	2,500	6,500	33,000	51,000
Birmingham	3,500	7,000	23,500	71,000	144,000
Bristol	15,000	20,000	40,000	61,000	104,000
Cambridge	8,500	9,000	9,500	10,000	21,000
Chester	7,500	9,000	11,000	15,000	21,000
Colchester	9,500	10,000	9,500	12,000	16,000
Coventry	7,000	7,000	12,000	16,000	27,000
Edinburgh	25,000	35,000	57,000*	83,000	162,000
Exeter	12,000	14,000	15,000	17,000	28,000
Glasgow	—	12,000	25,000	77,000	202,000
Hull	3,500	6,000	11,000	30,000	52,000
Leeds	4,000	6,000	11,000	53,000	123,000
Leicester	3,500	5,500	9,000	17,000	41,000
Liverpool	1,500	5,500	22,000	82,000	202,000
London	400,000	550,000	675,000	959,000†	1,656,000†
Manchester	4,500	8,000	18,000	89,000	223,000
Newcastle	12,000	15,000	25,000	33,000	54,000
Norwich	20,000	30,000	36,000	36,000	61,000
Nottingham	5,000	7,000	12,000	29,000	50,000
Oxford	8,500	9,000	10,000	12,000	21,000
Plymouth	5,000	7,000	14,000	40,000	66,000
Portsmouth	3,000	5,000	10,000	33,000	50,000
Sheffield	2,500	3,500	12,000	46,000	92,000
Sunderland	3,000	5,000	9,000	24,000	39,000
Worcester	8,000	8,500	9,500	11,000	19,000
Yarmouth	10,000	11,000	12,000	17,000	25,000
York	10,000	10,500	12,000	17,000	26,000

* 1755.
† London Metropolitan Police distinct.
Note: Prior to 1801 most figures are approximate.

10.3 Social structure of the population, 1696

Gregory King's estimate of the population and wealth of England and Wales, Calculated for 1696

Rank	No. of families	Persons	Yearly income per family (£)	Yearly expenditure per family (£)	Total income of group (£)
Temporal Lords	160	6,400	2,800	2,400	448,000
Spiritual Lords	26	520	1,300	1,100	33,800
Baronets	800	12,800	880	816	704,000
Knights	600	7,800	650	498	39,000
Esquires	3,000	30,000	450	420	1,350,000
Gentlemen	12,000	96,000	280	268	3,360,000
Clergy, superior	2,000	12,000	60	54	120,000
Clergy, inferior	8,000	40,000	45	40	360,000
Persons in the law	10,000	70,000	140	119	1,400,000
Sciences and liberal arts	16,000	80,000	60	57.10s	960,000
Persons in offices (higher)	5,000	40,000	240	216	1,200,000
Persons in offices (lower)	5,000	30,000	120	108	600,000
Naval officers	5,000	20,000	80	72	400,000
Military officers	4,000	16,000	60	56	240,000
Common soldiers	35,000	70,000	14	15	490,000
Freeholders (better sort)	40,000	280,000	84	77	3,360,000
Freeholders (lesser)	140,000	700,000	50	45.10s	7,000,000
Farmers	150,000	750,000	44	42.15s	6,600,000
Labouring people and servants	364,000	1,275,000	15	15.5s	5,460,000

Rank	No. of families	Persons	Yearly income per family (£)	Yearly expenditure per family (£)	Total income of group (£)
Cottagers and paupers	400,000	1,300,000	6.10s	7.6.3d	2,600,000
Artisans, handicrafts	60,000	240,000	40	38	2,400,000
Merchants by sea	2,000	16,000	400	320	800,000
Merchants by land	8,000	48,000	200	170	1,600,000
Shopkeepers, tradesmen	40,000	180,000	45	42.15s	1,800,000
Common seamen	50,000	150,000	20	21.10s	1,000,000
Vagrants		30,000	2	3	60,000

10.4 Distribution of the labour force, 1801–31 (estimated percentage of the total occupied population)

	Agriculture, forestry, fishing	Manufacture, mining, industry	Trade and transport	Domestic and personal	Public, professional and other
1801	35.9	29.7	11.2	11.5	11.8
1811	33.0	30.2	11.6	11.8	13.3
1821	28.4	38.4	12.1	12.7	8.5
1831	24.6	40.8	12.4	12.6	9.5

Source: W.A. Cole and P. Deane, *British Economic Growth, 1688–1959* (Cambridge, 1969), p. 142.

10.5 Education: number of schools and children attending, 1819

	England	Wales	Scotland
Parochial schools			
No.	—	—	942
Children	—	—	54,161
Endowed schools			
No.	4,167	209	212
Children	165,433	7,625	10,177
Unendowed schools			
No.	14,282	572	2,479
Children	478,849	22,976	112,187
Sunday schools			
No.	5,162	301	807
Children	452,817	24,408	53,449

Source: Parliamentary Papers, 1820, XII, pp. 342–55.

10.6 Poor relief, 1783–1831

	£		£
Average of 1783–85	1,912,241	Average of 1821–22	6,358,703
1803	4,077,891	1822–23	5,773,096
1812–13	6,656,105	1823–24	5,736,898
1813–14	6,294,584	1824–25	5,786,989
1814–15	5,418,845	1825–26	5,928,501
1815–16	5,724,506	1826–27	6,441,088
1816–17	6,918,217	1827–28	6,298,000
1817–18	7,890,148	1828–29	6,332,410
1818–19	7,531,650	1829–30	6,829,042
1819–20	7,329,594	1830–31	6,798,889
1820–21	6,958,445		

Source: G.R. Porter, *The Progress of the Nation* (London, 1851), p. 517.

10.7 Friendly societies

Counties	Total population in 1801	Members of Friendly Societies	
		1803	1815
Middlesex	818,129	72,741	60,579
Lancaster	682,731	104,776	137,655
Yorks, West Riding	563,953	59,558	74,005
Devon	343,001	31,792	48,607
Kent	307,624	12,633	15,640
Somerset	273,750	19,848	23,883
Norfolk	273,371	14,821	13,587
Surrey	269,049	19,199	21,805
Gloucester	250,803	19,606	24,567
Stafford	239,152	32,852	41,213
Essex	226,437	14,890	34,425
Southampton	219,656	4,733	11,013
Suffolk	210,431	11,448	13,335
Lincoln	208,557	7,530	8,658
Warwick	208,190	17,000	26,330
Chester	191,751	14,828	19,626
Cornwall	188,269	16,736	21,390
Wiltshire	185,107	11,330	15,302
Salop	177,639	19,144	23,638
Derby	161,142	22,681	22,412
Durham	160,861	11,556	13,115
Sussex	159,311	4,419	4,790
Northumberland	157,101	11,606	12,193
Yorks., North Riding	155,506	9,718	8,885
Nottingham	140,350	15,202	19,149
Yorks., East Riding	139,433	11,248	11,371
Worcester	139,333	12,845	13,458
Northampton	131,757	8,062	10,150
Leicester	130,081	10,889	15,425
Cumberland	117,230	7,788	9,807
Dorset	115,319	3,795	5,952

Counties	Total population in 1801	Members of Friendly Societies	
		1803	1815
Oxford	109,620	5,010	5,922
Berkshire	109,215	2,843	3,558
Buckingham	107,444	4,079	5,917
Hertford	97,577	8,622	10,477
Cambridge	89,346	3,173	4,524
Hereford	89,191	2,811	2,854
Bedford	63,393	2,730	3,647
Monmouth	45,582	3,799	7,923
Westmorland	41,617	2,435	1,278
Huntingdon	37,568	1,740	2,470
Rutland	16,356	1,704	1,398
Wales	541,546	30,130	45,097
Total	8,872,980	704,350	861,657

10.8 Charities and philanthropic societies, 1698–1830

1698	Society for the Promotion of Christian Knowledge
1701	Society for the Propagation of the Gospel in Foreign Parts
1756	Marine Society
1769	Relief of the Infant Poor (London)
1773	Thatched House Society (for aid to those in debtors' prisons)
1785	Sunday School Society
1788	Philanthropic Society (for Children)
1790	Liverpool School for the Indigent Blind
1793	Baptist Missionary Society
1795	London Missionary Society
1800	St Giles in the Fields School for the Indigent Blind; Society for Bettering the Condition of the Poor
c. 1800	Church Missionary Society
1804	British and Foreign Bible Society
1811	National Society for Promoting Education; Association for the Relief of the Manufacturing and Labouring Poor
1814	British and Foreign School Society
1818	Church Building Society
1823	Anti-Slavery Society
1824	Royal National Life-boat Institution
	Royal Society for the Prevention of Cruelty to Animals
1830	Liverpool Night Asylum for the Houseless

10.9 Hospital foundations, 1720–1829

1720	Westminster
1726	Guy's
1734	St George's London
1738	Bath General
1739	Foundling
	Queen Charlotte's
1740	London Hospital
	York County
1745	Durham, Newcastle-Upon-Tyne and Northumberland Infirmary
	Gloucester Infirmary
	Liverpool Royal Infirmary
	Middlesex
	Shrewsbury Infirmary
1746	Middlesex County
	Worcester Royal Infirmary
	London Lock
1750	City of London Maternity
1751	St Luke's London
1752	Manchester Royal Infirmary
1753	Devon and Exeter
1758	Magdalen
1763	Newcastle Lunatic Asylum
1765	Westminster Lying-in
1766	Manchester Royal Lunatic Asylum
1767	Leeds Infirmary
	Addenbrooke's, Cambridge
1769	Lincoln County
1770	Radcliffe Infirmary, Oxford
1771	Leicester Infirmary
1776	Hereford General Infirmary
1777	York Lunatic Asylum
1782	Nottingham General
1784	Hull Royal Infirmary
1787	Wakefield
1791	Kent and Canterbury

1792	Liverpool Royal Lunatic Asylum
1796	Manchester Fever
	Royal Sea Bathing Hospital (Margate)
1802	House of Recovery (Gray's Inn Road)
	London Fever
1805	Moorfields
1806	Exeter Eye
1810	Taunton and Somerset
1814	Royal Hospital for Diseases of the Chest
1816	Royal Ear
	Royal Westminster Ophthalmic
	Royal Waterloo Hospital for Children and Women
1818	West London Infirmary (Charing Cross Hospital)
1828	Royal Free
1829	Manchester Hospital for Children

10.10 The press and newspapers

Newspaper legislation, taxes and prices

Until the middle of the nineteenth century, newspaper proprietors were obliged to pay stamp, advertisement and paper duties. Together they comprised what Radicals criticised as 'taxes on knowledge', resulting in small circulations of expensive newspapers. Their complete abolition by 1861 made possible the cheap daily provincial newspaper.

	Stamp duty per sheet	Advertisement duty	Pamphlet duty per sheet	Postal rate for 55 miles	Cost of a newspaper in London
1712	$1d$	$1s$	$2s$	$3d$	$2d$
1757	$1d$ minimum	$2s$	"	"	"
1776	$1\frac{1}{2}d$	"	"	"	$3d$
1780	"	$2s\,6d$	"	"	"
1784	"	"	"	$4d$	"
1789	$2d$	$3s$	"	"	$4d$
1796	"	"	"	$5d$	"
1797	$3\frac{1}{2}d$	"	"	"	$4\frac{1}{2}d$–$6d$
1801	"	"	"	$6d$	"
1805	"	"	"	$7d$	"
1812	"	"	"	$8d$	$5d$–$7d$
1815	$4d$	$3s\,6d$	$3s$	"	$7d$
1833	"	$1s\,6d$	"	"	"

Development of newspapers and periodicals, 1685–1821

1685   *Dublin Newsletter* founded.

1690   *Worcester Journal* founded.

1695   Licensing Act suspended, permitting publication of books outside London, Oxford and Cambridge. *Stamford Mercury* founded.

1702	*Daily Courant*, first daily newspaper published; *Bristol Post Boy* founded.
1708	*Norwich Postman* founded.
1711	*The Spectator* launched; *Nottingham Guardian (Journal)* founded; *North Mail* and *Newcastle Journal* founded.
1712	Stamp Act passed imposing 1*d* duty per sheet. *Norwich Gazette* and *Liverpool Courant* founded.
1714	*Exeter Mercury* founded.
1720	*Northampton Mercury* founded.
1726	Weekly *Lloyd's List* established; *Reading Mercury* founded.
1728	*Faulkner's Journal* set up in Dublin.
1731	*Gentleman's Magazine* established; *The Scots Magazine* founded.
1734	Daily *Lloyd's List* established.
1737	*Belfast Newsletter* established.
1741	*Coventry Standard* and *Birmingham Gazette* founded.
1748	*Aberdeen Press and Journal* established.
1754	*Yorkshire Post* and *Jackson's Oxford Journal* established.
1758	*Annual Register* founded.
1759	The *Public Ledger* founded.
1762	Wilkes founds the *North Briton*.
1763	Arrest of Wilkes on a general warrant and seizure of printers and publishers over issue No. 45 of the *North Briton*. Wilkes released from prison but No. 45 burnt at Cheapside as 'a scandalous and seditious libel'. *Freeman's Journal* founded in Dublin.
1769	*Morning Chronicle* founded.

1771	'Printers' Case' makes reporting of parliamentary debates effectively legal.
1772	*Morning Post* founded.
1780	*British Gazette and Sunday Monitor* is Britain's first Sunday newspaper; *Morning Herald* founded, originally a radical paper.
1785	*Daily Universal Register* begun (became *The Times* in 1788).
1791	*The Observer* first appeared – a Sunday newspaper.
1792	*The Courier* founded, with John Parry as proprietor and John Thelwell as editor. *The Sun* first appears with William Pitt and friends as proprietors and George Rose as editor. A government organ to 1815.
1794	*Morning Advertiser* founded, the organ of the Incorporated Society of Licensed Victuallers.
1795	Peter and Daniel Stuart become proprietors of the *Morning Post*.
1798	Newspaper Publication Act puts publishers under close supervision of magistrates.
1799	Coleridge appointed literary editor of the *Morning Post*.
1800	*Bell's Weekly Dispatch* (later the *Sunday Dispatch*) founded, with Robert Bell as proprietor/editor. Liberal/radical in politics.
1802	*The Political Register* (weekly) first published by William Cobbett.
1803	Nicholas Byrne becomes editor/proprietor of the *Morning Post*.
1808	*The Examiner*, a Sunday newspaper, founded, with John and Leigh Hunt as manager and editor.
1812	Dr (Sir) John Stoddart becomes editor of *The Times*.
1814	New steam presses used for printing *The Times*.
1815	Newspaper stamp duty becomes 4*d* per copy.
1816	Cobbett's 2*d Political Register* ('Tuppenny Trash') published.

1817 John Black becomes editor of the *Morning Chronicle*. *Reformist Register* published.

1820 Imprisonment of Richard Carlile of *The Republican*. Thwaites Wright becomes editor of the *Morning Herald*.

1821 *Manchester Guardian* first published: John Edward Taylor proprietor, Jeremiah Garnett editor.

Many newspapers were founded in this period which had only a temporary existence; only some of the more prominent are listed here.

10.11 Major social legislation and developments, 1691–1819

1691	Register of parishioners in receipt of poor relief to be kept.
1694	Wartime tax on births, marriages, and deaths, at 2*s*, 2*s* 6*d* and 4*s* respectively. Higher duties for the wealthy.
1697	Settlement Act. Strangers were allowed to enter a parish provided that they possessed a settlement certificate showing that they would be taken by their old parish if they required poor relief. Paupers and their families were to wear a capital 'P' on their clothing. Punishment for disobeying the instruction could be loss of relief, imprisonment, hard labour and whipping.
1722–23	Parishes encouraged to build or rent workhouses and allowed to contract out their maintenance and supervision. Parishes allowed to form unions to set up viable workhouses.
1736	Gin Act. Required retailers to take out a licence of £50 and pay a duty of £1 on every gallon sold.
1747	Master and servant Act. Disputes between master and servant might be referred to the Justices. Apprentices' indentures could be cancelled in cases of ill-treatment.
1752	Gregorian Calendar introduced. Eleven days, 3–13 September, were removed from the calendar in order to bring the existing calendar into conformity with the Gregorian. Year to start from 1 January instead of from March.
1753	Hardwicke's Marriage Act. This declared that marriages could only be solemnised after the publication of banns, which were to be recorded in the marriage register or in a separate book.
1773	Spitalfields Weavers Act (13 Geo. III, c.68). Act empowering magistrates to regulate wages of persons employed in silk manufacture.

1782 Gilbert's Act (22 Geo. III, c.83). Parishes permitted to combine for more effective administration; able-bodied and infirm to be separated and only latter to be sent to the workhouse; work to be provided for able-bodied poor with wages supplemented from poor rate if necessary; 'Guardians' of the poor to be appointed to administer relief.

1793 Friendly Societies Act (33 Geo. III, c.54). An Act which gave legal protection to contributory clubs which provided pensions and insurance against sickness and unemployment amongst workmen and others. Especially common amongst the skilled workers of London from the end of the seventeenth century, the Act gave the Societies legal protection for their funds if registered with a magistrate. Although sometimes used as a cover for trade union activity, Friendly Societies were explicitly excluded from the ban upon combinations of workmen.

1795 The 'Speenhamland system'. Adopted by the Berkshire justices at Speenhamland (6 May 1795) to supplement wages on a sliding scale dictated by the price of bread. Elements of this system had been operated by individual parishes as early as the 1780s under the provisions of Gilbert's Act.

1802 The Health and Morals of Apprentices Act (42 Geo. III, c.87). Applied to cotton mills only. Male and female apprentices to have separate accommodation; all to have two suits of clothes a year and daily instruction. All night working of children to stop and daywork limited to 12 hours, exclusive of meals. A local magistrate and clergyman (not mill-owners) appointed by magistrates at Quarter Sessions to act as visitors and enforce the Act.

1819 Cotton Factory Act (59 Geo. III, c.66). No children to be employed in spinning cotton or its preparation under age of 9. Hours for children and youths between 9 and 18 limited to 12 hours per day exclusive of meals.

10.12 Trade unions

Chronology of trade union developments, 1762–1825

1762   Liverpool seamen's strike.

1765   Colliers' strike in the North-East over the yearly 'bond'. Successful campaign of Spitalfields weavers against import of French silks (5 Geo. III, c.48).

1767–68 Series of industrial disputes amongst the London trades, including Spitalfields weavers, coal-heavers, seamen, hatters, tailors, watermen, sawyers and coopers.

1768   Seamen's strike in the North-East.

1773   Spitalfields Weavers Act (13 Geo. III, c.68) obtained to regulate wages of Spitalfields weavers.

1775   Liverpool sailors' strike.

1778–79 Framework knitters' campaign for a minimum wage act rejected by Parliament. Some machine-breaking in Lancashire.

1792–93 Widespread strikes reported in both London and the provinces, especially amongst East Coast seamen, Lancashire miners and Liverpool shipyard workers.

1793   Friendly Societies Act (33 Geo. III, c.54) gives societies legal status and protection for their funds.

1797   Unlawful Oaths Act (37 Geo. III, c.123) makes secret oath-taking illegal. Used to restrict trade union organisation.

1799   Combination Act (39 Geo. III, c.86). *See* pp. 309–10. Association of Lancashire weavers formed.

1800   Combination Act (39 and 40 Geo. III, c.106). *See* p. 310.

1801	Extensive strike of shipwrights in government dockyards.
1802	Shipwrights' strike in Thames civilian yards organised by John Gast. Petition of South-Western clothiers against gig-mills. Stoppage of work and machine-breaking.
1803	First annual suspension of woollen statutes. Strike of Tyne keelmen.
1805	Woollen workers petition for regulation of wool trade.
1807	Cotton weavers petition for minimum wage bill.
1808	Manchester cotton weavers' strike.
1809	Repeal of protective legislation in the woollen industry. Tyne keelmen's strike.
1810	London printers prosecuted for conspiracy. Lancashire spinners' strike.
1811	Beginning of Luddite campaign in Nottinghamshire.
1812	Scottish weavers' strike. Framework-knitters bill to regulate the trade rejected in the House of Lords.
1813	Wage clauses of 5 Eliz. c.4 empowering judges to fix wage rates repealed by 53 Geo. III, c.40. Robert Owen publishes *A New View of Society*.
1814	Apprenticeship regulations of 5 Eliz. c.4 abolished by 54 Geo. III, c.96.
1815	Seamen's strike in North-East England.
1816	New Lanark mill opened. Strikes in several districts, especially amongst iron-workers and colliers.
1818	Weavers' and spinners' strikes in Lancashire. Attempts to form a 'General Union of Trades'.
1819	Keelmen's strike on Tyneside.

1820   Scottish weavers' strike.

1821   Robert Owen's *Report to the County of Lanark*.
            The London Co-operative and Economical Society formed.

1824   Act to repeal the Laws relative to the Combination of Workmen (5 Geo. IV, c.95). *See* pp. 310–11.

1825   Act revising the Law affecting Combinations (6 Geo. III, c.129).
            Widespread strikes in England and Scotland.
            John Gast and others establish *Trades Newspaper*.

The Combination Acts

Combinations of workmen were already illegal under both common law and statute law by the 1790s, but required the cumbersome procedures of trial by jury before the, usually, twice-annual Assizes in the major county town, imposing both delay and expense. In order to facilitate speedier prosecution at a lower level, Combination Acts covering more than 40 specific trades had been passed by the late 1790s, permitting offences to be dealt with by magistrates and lesser punishments to be meted out than at the Assizes. The general Combination Act grew out of the government's readiness to turn a petition in a specific trade into a wider prohibition of workmen's organisations.

Combination Act 1799

Unintended result of petition of master millwrights of London for a bill to outlaw combination of journeymen millwrights and regulate their wages. Suggested by Wilberforce, promoted by Pitt.

Provisions Summary prosecution before a single magistrate on credible evidence of one or more witnesses.
   Maximum sentence three months in gaol or two months in House of Correction with hard labour.
   Illegal to:

1. combine with another to improve conditions or raise wages;
2. try to induce another to leave his work (e.g. strike);
3. refuse to work with another (e.g. boycott a non-member of a combination);
4. attend a meeting with purpose of improving wages and conditions, persuade another to attend one, raise money for one;
5. contribute to expenses of a person tried under the Act; and
6. hold money for a combination and refuse to answer questions about it.

Petitions against 1799 Act Objected to:

1. vagueness of language used to describe offences under Act;
2. summary jurisdiction: held to deprive citizens of right to trial by jury;
3. bias in favour of employers, many of whom were magistrates;
4. possibility of trial before a man's own employer;
5. compulsion to answer questions about money possibly held for a combination: incriminate oneself or face automatic sentence under Act; and
6. difficulties placed in way of man sentenced under Act to raise money for appeal: if appeal successful, financial supporters not liable under Act; but if appeal unsuccessful, supporters automatically offenders against it.

Combination Act 1800

Playwright Sheridan put workers' case in House of Commons. 1799 Act repealed, replaced by 1800 Act.

Changes

1. Two magistrates instead of one to try cases.
2. Employer-magistrates prohibited from trying cases of men in their own trade.
3. Arbitration provision to deal with disputes (rarely invoked).
4. Masters prohibited from combining to reduce wages, increase hours or worsen conditions (no reported cases).

Offences otherwise as in 1799 Act. Thus, the Combination Acts of 1799 and 1800 contained no new legal principle. The Acts were intended to provide a general speedy remedy against combinations, which were already illegal on numerous grounds.

The repeal of the Combination Acts

Movement for reform headed by Francis Place, master tailor of Charing Cross, former journeyman breeches-maker. Joseph Hume, radical MP, led the movement within Parliament. On 12 February 1824, Hume moved resolutions in House of Commons for committee to consider laws on: (1) emigration of artisans; (2) exportation of machiners; and (3) combinations of workmen.

Combination Act 1824

Provisions

1. Previous statutes relating to combinations, including Act of 1800, almost entirely repealed.

2. Combinations – (a) to get increase or fix wages; (b) to lessen or alter hours; (c) to reduce amount of work; (d) to induce another to depart from employment before end of time for which hired, or (e) to quit or return his work before end of time for which hired, or (f) to refuse to enter into employment; or (g) to regulate production or management methods – not to be liable to indictment or prosecution for conspiracy or other crime under common or statute law.

   A similar provision applied to combinations of masters.
3. Violence to persons or property, or threats or intimidation, which achieved purposes 2(a) to (g), made an offence, whether committed by an individual or by a combination; penalty was imprisonment and being 'kept to hard labour' for up to two months.
4. Administration by summary trial before two magistrates; master, or fathers or sons of masters, engaged in any trade or manufacture being excluded from administering this law.

Purpose of Act was to make peaceful negotiation lawful, but to outlaw the use of violence, etc., to coerce an agreement (not particularly well drafted for this).

Large strikes of 1825, accompanied by violence, rioting and even murder, made Parliament reconsider, leading to the Combination Act of 1825.

Combination Act 1825

Parliamentary Committee set up to inquire into working of 1824 Act. Chaired by Wallace, Master of Mint; Hume also on Committee, and he with Place managed to reduce the severity of the 1825 Act. Trade union committees set up all over country to agitate against re-enactment of Combination Laws.

Provisions

1. Combination Act of 1824 repealed.
2. Act exempted from prosecution only those combinations of workmen or masters which met together solely to agree what wages or hours of employment to require or demand. Combinations for any other objects unlawful. The effect of this provision was to allow collective bargaining only over wages and hours; strikes or lock-outs to alter *these* terms not in practice regarded as unlawful, though the Act did not confer a *right* to strike or lock-out (no such provision being known to English law until the Industrial Relations Act of 1971).
3. A series of offences introduced, each punishable by imprisonment with or without hard labour for up to three months: the use of:

(a) *violence*, construed by judges to mean the infliction of bodily harm or any act of injury to property, with the intention to coerce another;
(b) *threats*, construed as creating fear in a person's mind that some evil might befall him, with a coercive result;
(c) *intimidation*, i.e. fear created by actions rather than words (as in (b)) with the effect of coercing another;
(d) *molestation*, vaguely meaning interference with another – e.g. as by picketing; and
(e) *obstruction*, e.g. of right of free passage into or out of work, along a highway, etc. Also applied to picketing, in order to force someone to:
    (i) leave his employment;
    (ii) refuse to take employment;
    (iii) join a club or association;
    (iv) contribute to a fund;
    (v) obey rules, for example, of a combination;
    (vi) change his method of manufacture; or
    (vii) limit the number of his apprentices, and so on.

The overall effect of the statute was to enforce a narrow definition of the lawful activities of a trade union, confining these to peaceful collective bargaining over wages and hours only. Combination to negotiate outside these limits was liable at law not only as contravening the terms of the statute, but as criminal conspiracy at common law 'in restraint of trade'. In addition, many of the methods which a union might employ in furtherance of its objectives were liable to prosecution as intimidation, etc., crimes which were exceedingly ill defined.

10.13 Local government

The county

Administrative divisions

County For the purposes of administration England and Wales were divided into 52 counties (40 and 12 respectively), two of which, Lincolnshire and Yorkshire, were subdivided into 'parts' or 'ridings'. Scotland was divided into 33 counties.

County corporate By 1689 there were 19 cities and boroughs styled 'counties in themselves' by royal charter (viz. Bristol, Canterbury, Carmarthen, Chester, Coventry, Exeter, Gloucester, Haverford West, Hull, Lichfield, Lincoln, London, Newcastle, Norwich, Nottingham, Poole, Southampton, Worcester, York). These were exempt from control by the county sheriff, but most remained within the military jurisdiction of the Lord Lieutenant.

County palatine By 1689, those counties in which the prerogatives exercised by the Crown had been claimed by a great earl or a Bishop (Lancashire, Cheshire, Durham and the Isle of Ely) largely conformed to the more general county organisation of England and Wales. Elements of palatinate prerogative, largely formal in character, were to remain until the nineteenth century in Durham and Lancashire.

Hundred (or wapentake, ward, lathe, rape) An administrative subdivision of the county under a group of justices and a High Constable for matters of law, order and rate collection.

Parish (*see also* pp. 318–20) Smallest administrative unit, into which hundreds were subdivided; under a Petty Constable for matters of law, order and rate collection.

County administration

Function Designed to enable central government to extract from the county its service to the State – not to encourage establishment of local self-government; but a large proportion of adult males, all unpaid, were involved in the structure of local government as jurymen or officials at parish level.

Controls exercised by central government

1. All major officers (except coroners) appointed and dismissed by the monarch.
2. The Court of King's Bench could overrule the justices of the peace by taking cases out of their hands or quashing their verdicts if a mistake had been made.
3. All civil officers required to present themselves at the Assizes before the King's judges to give an account of the maintenance of law and order within the county.
4. The Privy Council could issue orders at any time for immediate implementation of statutes and common law.

Services demanded by central government and executed by county officials

1. Military service: either the *posse comitatus* (against internal rebellion) or the *militia* (for national defence).
2. Taxes: aids, subsidies, land tax, ship money, etc.
3. Maintenance of the peace.
4. Upkeep of main bridges and gaols.

County officers

Lord Lieutenant Office dated from mid-sixteenth century; its holder was normally chosen from among the greatest noblemen and appointed for life; he presided over the whole county. One man could hold office for more than one county. From 1689 the office was often combined with that of Custos Rotulorum (Keeper of the Rolls of the Peace). Responsible for organising the county militia and nominating justices of the peace; frequently a member of Privy Council.

Deputy Lieutenants Controlled the militia during absences of the Lord Lieutenant; normally nominated by the latter (subject to royal approval) from amongst the ranks of the lesser nobility or greater gentry.

Custos Rotulorum A civil officer, keeper of the county rolls; from the sixteenth century the office was increasingly combined with that of Lord Lieutenant.

High Sheriff Appointed for one year, normally from amongst the minor nobility; service was obligatory. The office had declined in importance since the Middle Ages. Responsible for the County Court, control of parliamentary elections, nomination of jurymen and ceremonial duties for judges of Assize.

Under Sheriff A professional appointed for one year by the High Sheriff to undertake all but his ceremonial duties; responsible for execution of all writs and processes of law, for suppression of riots and rebellions, and for holding the County Court.

High Bailiff Appointed by the High Sheriff to execute his instructions in the hundred.

Foot Bailiff (or Bound Bailiff) Appointed by the High Sheriff or Under Sheriff to carry messages or search out individuals for the execution of justice.

Clerk of the Peace A professional officer receiving fees for his services to individuals; appointed for life by the Custos Rotulorum. *Duties*: to draft formal resolutions of the justices at Quarter Sessions and to advise them on matters of law. Duties often performed by a Deputy Clerk (a leading solicitor in the county town).

Coroner A professional officer earning fees from his service; between two and 12 elected for life by freeholders of the county from amongst their own number (in certain liberties the traditional right of appointment held by an individual or group – e.g. the Dean of York in the Liberty of St Peter, York; holders of office then known as **franchise coroners**). *Duties*: to hold inquests on (1) suspicious deaths, committing to trial anyone whom the Coroner's Jury find guilty of murder; (2) treasure trove, pronouncing on rightful ownership.

High Constable Appointed normally for one year by Quarter Sessions; service was obligatory; assisted by petty constables in each parish. *Duties*: to execute instructions of the justices in the hundred; towards the end of the seventeenth century also responsible for collecting the county rate assessed at Quarter Sessions and for repair of bridges and gaols.

Justices of the Peace Gradually, under the Tudors and Stuarts, took over from the great officers the government of the county, both judicial and administrative, executing statutes issued from central government. *Qualifications for office*: had to be a £20 freeholder resident in the county; to receive the sacraments in accordance with the Anglican rite; to have sworn the oaths of allegiance and supremacy; and to have (in theory) some knowledge of law and administration. The Justices Qualification Act of 1744 laid down that each justice had to have an estate or freehold, copyhold or customary tenure of the value of £100. Nominated by the Lord Lieutenant and appointed by the monarch, normally for life, from amongst the noblemen and gentry. *Duties*: 'to keep and cause to be kept all ordinance and statutes for the good of our peace' and 'to chastise and punish all persons that offend' against such statutes. Commission revised in 1590 to enable justices to act in three ways: individually; jointly, with colleagues in a division; collectively, as a General Sessions of the County.

Court of Quarter Sessions A General Sessions of the Peace for the whole county to be held four times a year; all justices of the peace summoned to attend under the theoretical chairmanship of the Custos Rotulorum; also summoned were the Sheriff, high bailiffs, high constables, coroners and petty constables, who were required to report offences from within their areas. *Juries in attendance*: one Jury of Inquiry from each hundred; a Grand Jury and petty juries from the county at large. *Functions*:

1. to try private individuals for breaches of the law;
2. to hear presentments against parishes or hundreds (or against individual officers) for failure to carry out their duties;
3. to carry out routine administration – e.g. licensing of traders, maintenance of gaols and bridges, regulation of wages and prices, supervision of houses of correction, etc; and
4. to hear appeals against decisions by local justices.

Private or Special Sessions Divisional Sessions, usually based on the hundred and meeting in many cases at monthly intervals. *Summoned to attend*: justices from the division; local parish and hundred officials. Empowered by Privy Council Order (1605) to deal with all matters not requiring juries (e.g. vagrancy, poor relief, etc.).

Petty Sessions Various legislation empowered any two justices sitting together to appoint local overseers of the poor and surveyors of the highways, to supervise accounts of parochial officials, to make rates, to license alehouses, to make orders for maintenance of illegitimate children and removal of paupers, to try and punish certain categories of offenders (e.g. poachers, unlicensed ale-keepers, rioters, etc.) and to hear and commit to Quarter Session more serious cases (e.g. larceny, assault, etc.).

The Quorum Clause The Commission required that, where only two justices were sitting, one should be a justice who had been 'named' in the Commission (i.e. who possessed real knowledge of the law). By the end of the seventeenth century, this clause was scarcely valid, because all justices were named as the quorum.

Justices acting individually Each justice had the power:

1. to commit suspects to the county gaol to await trial;
2. to require a person by summons to appear at the next Quarter Sessions;

3. to punish by fine or stocks those guilty of profane oaths, drunkenness, non-attendance at church, breaking the Sabbath, rick-burning or vagrancy; and
4. to present at Quarter Sessions any parishes or parish officers failing in their responsibilities for highway maintenance and poor relief.

County Court   Although by the seventeenth century most of its dealings had been taken over by Quarter Sessions etc., it still met under the High Sheriff (or, in practice, the Under Sheriff). *Functions*:

1. to recover civil debts under 40s;
2. to witness the High Sheriff's return of the writs requiring election of a Coroner and of two knights of the shire to represent the county in Parliament; and
3. to assess, with the help of a jury, matters of compensation (for road-widening etc.).

Grand Jury (or Grand Inquest)   Composed of between 12 and 24 men, usually drawn from landowners, merchants, manufacturers, clergy and other professional people. An Act of 1692 laid down that a juror should possess freehold, copyhold or life tenure land worth at least £10 per year. An Act of 1730 added leaseholders of £20 a year. An Act of 1696 provided for lists of jurors to be compiled by constables and presented to Quarter Sessions. Summoned by the High Sheriff to attend for one or two days at Quarter Sessions or Assizes; verdicts and presentments valid if at least 12 members agreed. *Functions*:

1. to consider criminal bills of indictment; then as 'true bills' (if a *prima facie* case had been established) or to reject them with the endorsement 'ignoramus';
2. to consider presentments of parishes and hundreds (or individual officers) for neglect of their duty, and to return a 'true bill' (as above) if case established;
3. to make a formal presentment for repair of the county gaol, county hall, bridges or houses of correction before county funds were released for these purposes by the justices; and
4. to express county opinion on matters of common concern in petitions to Parliament or presentments at Quarter Sessions or Assizes (e.g. over unlawful assemblies, vagrancy, etc.).

Hundred Jury (or Petty Jury or Inquiry)   Each hundred and borough would have its own Petty Jury, composed of between 12 and 24 men and summoned by the High Sheriff through the high bailiffs. Unanimity not required in verdicts or presentments if at least 12 members agreed. *Functions*: to make a presentment at Quarter Sessions of any public nuisances (especially concerning rivers, bridges, roads) or any local officials neglectful of duties. By the end of the seventeenth century these juries were falling into disuse: tasks taken over by high constables and petty constables.

Traverse or Felons' Juries Formed from a panel of petty jurymen summoned by the High Sheriff from the county as a whole; used to decide issues of fact in criminal trials.

The parish
Administrative function

By the seventeenth century the parish was both the ecclesiastical division (in which a priest performed his duties to the inhabitants) and a unit of local government within the larger area of a hundred. By employing unpaid amateurs as parish officers, supervised by justices of the peace, the central government succeeded in collecting its dues and enforcing its statutes even at the remotest local level.

Nature of parish office

Terms of office Service unpaid, compulsory, one year's duration (or until a replacement appointed).

Qualification for office No property of religious qualification: in some parishes all males serviced in rotation, in others holders of certain units of land served in rotation.

Exemptions from office Peers, clergy, members of Parliament, barristers, justices of the peace, revenue officers, members of the Royal College of Physicians, aldermen of the City of London; exemption could also be gained by paying a fine or finding a substitute.

Responsibilities Officer personally responsible to the justices or to the Bishop (in the case of churchwardens), not to the parish, duties were arduous, time-consuming and often unpopular.

Parish officers

Churchwardens Usually between two and four appointed annually. Method of appointment varied considerably: by methods described above, by election at an open or closed meeting of the Vestry, by nomination of retiring churchwardens, by appointment by the incumbent – or by a combination of these. Sworn in by the Archdeacon. Responsible for:

1. maintenance and repair of church fabric;
2. provision of materials required for services;
3. allocation of seats in church;
4. maintenance of churchyard;
5. annual report to the Bishop on the progress of the incumbent, condition of the fabric and moral state of the parish;
6. assistance to the Constable and surveyors of highways in civil duties within the parish;
7. assistance to overseers of the poor in relief of poverty, lodging of the impotent poor, apprenticing of children; and
8. levying a church rate on all parishioners when required for poor-law purposes, and maintaining proper accounts.

Constable Established in office by two justices (or, occasionally, by surviving manorial Court Leet): responsible to justices of the peace, working under High Constable for the hundred; expenses paid by a 'constable's rate' on the parish or by fees for specific duties. Duties:

1. to deal with grants according to the law;
2. to supervise alehouses;
3. to call parish meetings as required;
4. to apprehend felons;
5. to place minor trouble-makers in the stocks;
6. to attend the justices in Petty and Quarter Sessions, making presentments on law-breakers, etc.; and
7. to levy the county rate in the parish.

Surveyor of the Highways Established by statute in 1555; formally appointed by the Constable and churchwardens after consultation with other parishioners; responsible to the justices of the peace for giving a regular report on state of the roads, for receiving instructions on work to be done and for rendering his accounts. *Duties:*

1. to direct 'statute labour' as required on local roads (wealthier inhabitants to send men, oxen and horses; ordinary parishioners to offer six days' personal labour);
2. to collect fines from defaulters and commutation fees from those who bought exemption;
3. to order the removal of obstructions from the highways (e.g. overgrown hedges and trees, undrained ditches, etc.); and
4. to collect a highway rate, if authorised at Quarter Sessions, and any fines imposed on the parish for failure to maintain its highways.

In 1691 the law was altered whereby the justices chose a surveyor from a list of those eligible provided by the inhabitants. The surveyor was obliged to survey the highways three times a year and organise the statute labour provided by landowners to repair the roads or collect money in lieu.

Overseers of the Poor Established by statute in 1597; between two and four appointed for each parish by the justices to whom they were responsible. *Duties* (in cooperation with churchwardens):

1. to relieve destitute people;
2. to remove paupers without settlement rights to their former parish;
3. to make provision for illegitimate children;
4. to apprentice destitute children;
5. to assess and collect the poor rate;
6. to prepare accounts for the justices.

Minor paid offices Parish Clerk, Sexton, Bellringer, Scavenger, Town Crier (or Bellman), Hayward, Hogwarden, Pinder, Beadle, Dog Whipper, Vestry Clerk.

Parish Vestry

A parish meeting held in church at Easter, and at other times if necessary. *Functions*:

1. to elect usually one churchwarden;
2. to decide on a church rate to defray the churchwarden's expenses and to cover repairs to the fabric;
3. to make any new by-laws for the parish; and
4. to administer the pound and common pasture.

Municipal corporations

By 1689 there were approximately 200 boroughs in England and Wales which had received the privilege of incorporation through royal charter and possessed some or all of the powers listed below.

Powers of the Corporation

1. To own, administer and sell property and land.
2. To administer the common meadow and wasteland.
3. To control trade; to hold markets and fairs.
4. To return burgesses to sit in Parliament.
5. To create a magistracy for the purpose of holding borough Petty Sessions and borough Quarter Sessions.
6. To formulate by-laws.
7. To levy local taxes and tolls.

Obligations of the Corporation

1. To collect the King's revenue and to execute his writs.
2. To maintain the King's peace; to enforce his laws; to organise the nightly watch.
3. To support financially the borough's burgesses in Parliament.
4. To repair walls, bridges and streets.
5. To administer charitable trusts for schools, hospitals, poor people, etc.

Membership of the Corporation

Method of gaining membership, seldom stipulated in the Charter, varied considerably. Qualifications required for gaining 'freedom' included at least one of the following:

1. ownership of freehold within the borough (in some cases only the owners of certain specified burgages would qualify);
2. working an apprenticeship under a freeman of the borough (usually for seven years);
3. birth (i.e. sons of freeman) or marriage (i.e. husbands of freeman's widow or daughter);
4. membership of local guilds or trade companies;
5. co-option by gift, redemption or purchase;
6. membership of the Governing Council (i.e. no freemen outside). Freemen were normally admitted to membership by formal presentment of a local jury. Freemen could also be disfranchised for breach of duty, misdemeanour, etc.

Minor officials of the Corporation

Responsible to the chief officers; often salaried or collecting fees; possessing uniform or staff of office.

Agricultural officials Haymakers, pound-keepers, woodwards, pasture-masters, common-keepers, mole-catchers, swineherds, etc.

Market officials Bread-weighers, butter-searchers, ale-tasters, searchers and scalers of leather, searchers of the market, fish and flesh searchers, coalmeters, cornprizers, etc.

Order and maintenance officials Water bailiffs, bridge-keepers, Serjeant-at-Mace or Beadle, Town Crier or Bellman, Scavenger or Street Warden, Cleaner of the Castle Walks, Cleaner of the Water Grates, Sweeper of Streets, Weeder of Footpaths, etc.

Chief officers of the Corporation

Mayor (or Bailiff, Portreeve, Alderman, Warden) Named in the Charter as head of the Corporation; with wide powers. Presided at all meetings of the Council; responsible for the management of Corporate estates; always a justice of the peace, presided at the borough Quarter Sessions; responsible for courts under the Corporation's jurisdictions; usually acted as Coroner and Clerk of Market; sometimes acted as Keeper of Borough Gaol and Examiner of Weights and Measures; appointed minor officials.

Bailiffs Status varied considerably – in 40 boroughs they were heads of the Corporation, in about 100 they were minor officials, in about 30 they were chief officers. Normally two bailiffs. As chief officers, responsible for summoning juries, accounting for fines, collection of rents, etc.; sometimes acted also as Treasurer, Coroner, Keeper of Borough Gaol, Clerk of Market; often, as justices of the peace, sat as judges on borough courts; occasionally undertook duties of Sheriff within the borough. Usually elected by the Council.

Recorder A lawyer; legal adviser to the Corporation. President at some of the borough courts, administered oath of office to Mayor; as a justice of the peace, sat at the Borough Court of Quarter Sessions; usually received an attendance fee or nominal stipend.

Chamberlain (or Treasurer, Receiver) The treasurer of the Corporation, usually appointed by the Council.

Town Clerk Usually appointed by the Council, but not a member of it. Responsible for a wide range of administration; often Clerk of the Peace, Clerk of the Magistrates and clerk of all the borough courts; sometimes Coroner, Keeper of the Records, Deputy Recorder, president of the borough court.

Aldermen Known usually as the Mayor's Brethren, sometimes responsible for ensuring that by-laws were enforced in a particular ward of the borough; but principally a permanent and select consultative council (always part of the Common Council). Also collectively performed some judicial functions (licensing alehouses, making rates, appointing constables, etc.); tenure was normally for life.

Councillors Usually 12, 24 or 48 in number; had no specific functions other than to form the Court of Common Council (together with the aldermen and chief officers).

Courts of the Corporation

Court of Record (or Three Weeks' Court, of Pleas Court or Mayor's Court) A court of civil jurisdiction consisting of one or more of the specified judges (usually, Mayor, Bailiff, Recorder, Town Clerk, aldermen, etc.); often met every three weeks. Jurisdiction limited to suits arising within the borough; usually personal actions for debt or concerning land.

Court Leet Right to hold court normally granted in the Charter; responsible for minor criminal jurisdiction, making of by-laws, control of commons and wastes, appointment of officers and admission of new tenants and freeholders. Administrative functions gradually taken over by the administrative courts during the latter part of the seventeenth century.

Borough Court of Quarter Sessions Gradually took over criminal jurisdiction from the Court Leet; normally only six justices of the peace, all of whom held particular positions (e.g. Mayor, Recorder, High Steward, Common Clerk, Coroner, etc.); often sat monthly or even weekly to hear a great variety of offences and complaints and to pass administrative orders.

Court of Pie Powder Held by Mayor or deputy to deal summarily with offenders at the market or fair.

Court of Orphans Held by Mayor or deputy to administer estates of minors.

Court of Conservancy Held by Mayor or deputy to enforce rules concerning the river.

Court of Admiralty Held by Mayor or deputy to deal with matters concerning harbours, fishing or shipping.

Court of Common Council An administrative court consisting of aldermen, councillors and chief officers; members fined for absence, sworn to secrecy and obliged to wear their gowns of office; committees appointed to deal with particular functions; by the seventeenth century had acquired wide powers of administration.

10.14 Cultural and intellectual chronology, 1688–1820

	Key political and historical events	Literature	Science and philosophy
1688	Glorious Revolution; flight of James II	Aphra Benn, *Oroonoko*	
1689	Convention Parliament; accession of William III and Mary II; Bill of Rights; Toleration Act; Battle of Killiecrankie; Nine Years War (to 1697)		Locke, *Two Treatises of Government*; *First Letter on Toleration*
1690	Battle of the Boyne General election		Locke, *An Essay Concerning Human Understanding*; *Second Letter on Toleration*
1691			
1692	Glencoe Massacre National debt founded Salem witch-craze	Temple, *Essay upon Ancient and Modern Learning*	
1693	White's Club in London established		Locke, *Some Thoughts Concerning Education*
1694	Death of Mary II Founding of Bank of England Triennial Act	Mary Astell, *A Serious Proposal to Ladies* Wotton, *Reflections upon Ancient and Modern Learning*	
1695	Expiry of Licensing Act General election	John Bellers, *Proposals for Raising a Colledge of Industry* Congreve, *Love for Love* Gibson's edition of Camden's *Britannia*	

CULTURAL AND INTELLECTUAL CHRONOLOGY

Religion and the Churches	Music	Art and architecture
Trial of the Seven Bishops		
	Purcell, *Dido and Aeneas*	Wren works at Hampton Court (–1694)
Episcopal Church in Scotland disestablished		Talman, Uppark House, Sussex Sir Godfrey Kneller begins series of 'Hampton Court Beauties' portaits
Hickes, *Apology for the New Separation* Ray, *The Wisdom of God in the Works of Creation* First Society for the Reformation of Manners founded	Dryden–Purcell, *King Arthur*	Wren completes Royal Hospital, Chelsea (begun in 1682)
First Boyle lectures 'for proving the Christian religion against notorious infidels' given by Bentley	Purcell, *The Fairy Queen*	Sir William Bruce, Drumlanrig Castle
Leslie, *Short and Easy Way with the Deists*		J. Tijou, *New Book of Drawings*
	Purcell, *Te Deum* and *Jubilate*	
Locke, *The Reasonableness of Christianity* George Stanhope, *A Paraphrase and Comment upon the Epistles and Gospels* Tillotson, *Sermons* (14 vols –1704)	Purcell, *Funeral Sentences for Queen Mary*	Wren begins Royal Hospital for Seamen, Greenwich (–1716)

	Key political and historical events	Literature	Science and philosophy
1696	Jacobite plot to assassinate William III	Vanbrugh, *The Relapse*	Gregory King, *Natural and Political Observations upon the State and condition of England* (not published until the nineteenth century)
1697	Treaty of Ryswick	Dryden, *Alexander's Feast* Vanbrugh, *The Provoked Wife*	William Dampier, *A New Voyage Round the World*
1698	First Partition Treaty General election	Collier, *Short View of the Immorality and Prophaness of the English Stage* Molyneux, *Case of Ireland* Ward, *London Spy* (–1709)	
1699		Bentley, *Dissertation on the Letters of Phalaris*	
1700	Second Partition Treaty	Astell, *Some Reflections on Marriage* Congreve, *The Way of the World*	
1701	Act of Settlement General election (Tory success); 2nd election (Whig success) Invention of seed-drill by Jethro Tull	Defoe, *True-Born Englishman* Dennis, *Advancement and Reformation of Modern Poetry*	Norris, *Ideal and Intelligible World*
1702	Death of William III; accession of Queen Anne; War of Spanish Succession (–1713)	Clarendon, *The True Historical Narrative of the Rebellion and Civil Wars in England* (–1704) Defoe, *The Shortest Way with the Dissenters* Rowe, *Tamerlane* The *Daily Courant* published	
1703	Great Storm		

Religion and the Churches	Music	Art and architecture
Atterbury, *Letter to a Convocation Man* Tate and Brady, *New Version of the Psalms* Toland, *Christianity Not Mysterious*		
		Formal opening of rebuilt St Paul's
Society for the Promotion of Christian Knowledge founded		
Atterbury, *The Rights, Powers and Privileges of an English Convocation* Wake, *Principles of the Christian Religion*		Vanbrugh begins Castle Howard (–1726)
Steele, *The Christian Hero* Society for the Propagation of the Gospel in Foreign Parts founded		
Edmund Calamy, *Account of the Ministers . . . ejected by the Act of Uniformity* William King, *Origin of Evil* Convocation Controversy (–1717)		Kneller begins series of 'Kit Cat Club' portraits (–1717)

	Key political and historical events	Literature	Science and philosophy
1704	Battle of Blenheim	Defoe, *Review* (–1714) Dennis, *Grounds of Criticism in Poetry* Rymer, *Foedra* (–1717) Swift, *Tale of a Tub; Battle of the Books*	Newton, *Opticks*
1705	General election Haymarket Theatre opens	Dunton, *Life and Errors* *Edinburgh Courant* founded	Halley, *Astronomiae Cometicae*
1706	Battle of Ramillies	Defoe, *Apparition of Mrs Veal* Farquhar, *The Recruiting Officer*	
1707	Act of Union with Scotland	Eachard, *History of England* Farquhar, *The Beaux' Stratagem*	
1708	Death of Prince George (Queen Anne's husband); General election Battle of Oudenarde		Shaftesbury, *Letter concerning Enthusiasm*
1709	Battle of Malplaquet	Rowe publishes the first critical edition of Shakespeare Steele et al., *The Tatler* (–1711)	Berkeley, *Essay towards a New Theory of Vision* Shaftesbury, *Essay on Humour and Wit; The Moralists*
1710	General election (Tory gains) Trial of Dr Sacheverell Riot of keelmen, Newcastle	Swift et al., *The Examiner* (–1711)	Berkeley, *Treatise Concerning the Principles of Human Knowledge*
1711		Addison, Steele et al., *The Spectator* Pope, *Essay on Criticism* Swift, *The Conduct of the Allies*	Shaftesbury, *Characteristics*

Religion and the Churches	Music	Art and architecture
Queen Anne's Bounty returns first fruit and tenths to the Church Robert Nelson, *Companion for the Festivals and Fasts of the Church of England*		Talman, Dyrham Park Hawksmoor, The Orangery, Kensington Palace
Astell, *The Christian Religion as Profess'd by a Daughter of the Church of England* George Stanhope, *Paraphrase and Comment on the Epistles and Gospels*		Blenheim Palace begun (Vanbrugh and Hawksmoor) (−1725)
Watts, *Hymns and Spiritual Songs* French Prophets arrive in England Bingham, *Antiquities of the Christian Church*		Society of Antiquaries founded (given Royal Charter in 1751) Thornhill paintings for Great Hall, Greenwich Hospital (−1712)
Sacheverell, *The Perils of False Brethren in Church and State* Strype, *Annals of the Reformation*		
		Exterior of St Paul's completed (begun 1675)
Whiston, *Primitive Christianity Revived* Act for building 50 new churches in London Occasional Conformity Act		Thomas Archer, St John's Smith Square (−1728)

	Key political and historical events	Literature	Science and philosophy
1712	Thomas Newcomen invents steam engine	Arbuthnot, *History of John Bull*	
1713	General election Treaty of Utrecht	Addison, *Cato* Anne Finch, Countess of Winchilsea, *Miscellaneous Poems* Pope, *Windsor Forest* Smith, *History of the Lives and Robberies of the Most Notorious Highwaymen* Steele, *Guardian* (–1714)	
1714	Death of Queen Anne Schism Act	Pope, *Rape of the Lock* Mandeville, *Fable of the Bees*	
1715	General election (Whig success) Jacobite rebellion Riot Act	Elizabeth Elstob, *Rudiments of Grammar for the English Tongue* Pope, *The Iliad* (–1720)	Eclipse of the sun predicted by Halley
1716	Septennial Act	Addison, *Freeholder*	
1717			
1718	Quadruple Alliance		
1719	Repeal of Schism and Occasional Conformity Acts Peerage Bill Declaratory Act: Ireland	Defoe, *Robinson Crusoe* Trenchard and Gordon, *Cato's Letters*	
1720	South Sea Bubble		

Religion and the Churches	Music	Art and architecture
Clarke, *Scripture Doctrine of the Trinity* William Derham, *Physico-Theology* Gibson, *Codex Juris Ecclesiastici Anglicani*	Handel settles in London	Gibbs, St Mary Le Strand (–1717)
Schism Act Gilbert Burnet completes *History of the Reformation* (first vol. 1679) John Johnson, *The Unbloody Sacrifice* John Walker, *Account of the Sufferings of the Clergy during the Commonwealth period*		Bridgeman begins working at Stowe gardens Hawksmoor begins Christ Church, Spitalfields (–1729)
Derham, *Astro-Theology* Watts, *Divine Songs for the Use of Children*		Stephen Switzer, *Nobleman, Gentleman and Gardener's Recreation*
	Three Choirs festival begins	Hawksmoor additions to All Souls College, Oxford (–1735)
Bangorian Controversy (–1720)	Handel, *Water Music*; *Chandos Anthems*	Sir James Thornhill, Scenes from the Life of St Paul (St Paul's)
		Campbell, *Vitruvius Britannicus* (–1725)
Meeting of Presbyterians at Salters Hall to protest against subscription of belief in the Trinity		Alexander Pope begins his garden at Twickenham
Mandeville, *Free Thoughts on Religion*		Colen Campbell begins Stourhead Vanbrugh begins Seaton Delaval (–1728)

	Key political and historical events	Literature	Science and philosophy
1721			
1722	General election; Atterbury plot	Defoe, *Journal of the Plague Year*; *Moll Flanders*	
1723	Waltham Black Act; Wood's Half-pence		
1724		Burnet, *A History of My Own Time* (–1734); Defoe, *Roxana*; *Tour thro' the Whole Island of Great Britain* (–1726); Swift, *Drapier's Letters*	
1725	Allan Ramsay founds Britain's first circulating library	Allan Ramsay, *The Gentle Shepherd*	Francis Hutcheson, *Inquiry into the Origin of our Ideas of Beauty and Virtue*
1726	Guy's Hospital founded	Bolingbroke et al., *The Craftsman* (–1750); Swift, *Gulliver's Travels*; Thomson, *The Seasons* (–1730)	
1727	Death of George I; accession of George II; general election	Dyer, *Grongar Hill*; Thomson, *To the memory of Newton*	Newton, *Principia* (1687) trans. into English; Stephen Hales, *Vegetable Staticks*
1728		Chambers, *Cyclopaedia*; J.T. Desaguliers, *The Newtonian System of the World, the Best Model of Government. An Allegorical Poem*; Gay, *The Beggar's Opera*; Pope, *The Dunciad* (–1743)	Hutcheson, *Nature and Conduct of the Passions and Affections*
1729	Treaty of Seville	Swift, *Modest Proposal*; Thomson, *Britannia*	

Religion and the Churches	Music	Art and architecture
Wollaston, *Religion of Nature delineated* Cotton Mather, *The Christian Philosopher*		Vanbrugh begins Grimsthorpe, Lincs (−1726) Gibbs, St Martin-in-the-Fields (−1726)
John Hutchinson's *Moses' Principia* attacks Newton		
		Boyle and Kent, Chiswick House (−1729)
Butler, *Fifteen Sermons preached at the Rolls Chapel* Law, *Christian Perfection*		John Wood the elder begins Queen Square, Bath (−1736)
Thomas Woolston, *Six Discourses on Miracles* (−1730) Moravians in London	Handel, *Zadok the Priest*	William Adam, Hopetoun House, near Edinburgh, façade Kent, *Designs of Inigo Jones*
Law, *A Serious Call to a Devout and Holy Life* Shuckford, *Sacred and Profane History of the World*	Edinburgh music society founded	Batty Langley, *New Principles of Gardening*
Methodist society formed at Oxford		William Adam, *Vitruvius Scoticus* (not published until 1811)

	Key political and historical events	Literature	Science and philosophy
1730		Duck, *Poems* Fielding, *Tom Thumb*	
1731	Dublin Agricultural Society founded	George Lillo, *The London Merchant, or the History of George Barnwell* Pope, *Epistle to Burlington* *The Gentleman's Magazine* (–1907)	
1732		Benjamin Franklin, *Poor Richard's Almanack* Pope, *Epistle to Bathurst*	Berkeley, *Alciphron*
1733	Excise Bill Crisis John Kay's first flying shuttle War of Polish Succession begins	Pope, *Essay on Man* Voltaire, *Letters on the English Nation*	Cheyne, *English Malady* Tull, *Horse-Hoeing Husbandry*
1734	General election		
1735	Westminster Watch Act	Pope, *Epistle to Dr Arbuthnot* Thomson, *Liberty*	
1736	Gin Act Porteous riots in Edinburgh Repeal of statutes against witchcraft	Duck, *Poems on Several Occasions*	

CULTURAL AND INTELLECTUAL CHRONOLOGY 337

Religion and the Churches	Music	Art and architecture
Strickland Gough, *Enquiry into the Causes of the Decay of the Dissenting Interest* Sherlock, *Trial of the Witnesses of the Resurrection of Jesus* Tindal, *Christianity as Old as Creation*		
		Royal Dublin Society founded Rysbrack, monument to Sir Isaac Newton, Westminter Abbey
Waterland, *Nature, Obligation and Efficacy of the Christian Sacraments* Protestant Dissenting Deputies founded	Handel, *Esther* (first oratorio in English) Academy of Ancient Music founded	Hogarth, *A Harlot's Progress*
George Thomson begins evangelical ministry in Cornwall Secession from Church of Scotland led by Ebenezer Erskine		Society of Dilettanti founded to encourage art
Great Awakening in America begins		William Kent works at Stowe Gardens Hawksmoor, gothic towers, Westminster Abbey
Hoadly, *Plain Account of the Nature and End of the Lord's Supper* Wesley, *Journal* (–1790) Conversion of Howell Harris		Hogarth, *The Rake's Progress* Burlington and Kent, Holkham Hall, Norfolk Wood the elder begins Prior Park, Bath (–1748)
Butler, *Analogy of Religion* Cruden, *Concordance to the Bible* Warburton, *The Alliance Between Church and State*; *Divine Legation of Moses* (–1741)		

338 SOCIAL AND CULTURAL

	Key political and historical events	Literature	Science and philosophy
1737	Death of Queen Caroline Stage Licensing Act		
1738	Invention of fly-shuttle by John Kay	Johnson, *London*	
1739	Convention of the Pardo War of Jenkins' Ear Execution of Turpin Coram establishes Foundling Hospital Bow Street Police Office founded		Hume, *Treatise of Human Nature*
1740	General election War of the Austrian Succession (–1748) Anson begins voyage round the world	Richardson, *Pamela* (–1741) Thomson and Mallet, *Alfred*	Production of crucible steel by Benjamin Huntsman of Sheffield
1741		Fielding, *Apology for the Life of Mrs Shamela Andrews*	Hume, *Essays: Moral and Political*
1742	Resignation of Walpole	Fielding, *Joseph Andrews* Young, *Night Thoughts* (–1745)	
1743	Battle of Dettingen Gin Act	Fielding, *Jonathan Wild*	
1744	Keelmen riots, Newcastle Deptford and Woolwich shipyards disputes	Akenside, *Pleasures of the Imagination* Sarah Fielding, *Adventures of David Simple* Garrick, *Essay on Acting* Johnson, *Life of Savage* Warton, *The Enthusiast*	Berkeley, *Siris, or Reflections on Tar-Water*
1745	Jacobite Rebellion		

Religion and the Churches	Music	Art and architecture
Wesley (ed.), *Psalms and Hymns* David Wilkins, *Concilia Magnae Britanniae et Hiberniae*		James Gibbs, Radcliffe Camera, Oxford (–1748)
Edmund Gibson (ed.), *A Preservative against Popery*	Founding of the Royal Society of Musicians of Great Britain	Ware's edition of *Palladio*
Whitfield and Wesley begin open-air preaching in Bristol Wesley, *Hymns and Sacred Poems* (–1749)	Handel, *Saul* and *Israel in Egypt*	
Richard Challoner, *The Garden of the Soul* Whitefield, *Short account of God's dealings with George Whitefield*	Arne, *Rule Britannia* Grassineau, *A Musical Dictionary*	Hogarth, portrait of *Captain Coram*
	Founding of the Madrigal Society in London	Scheemaker, statue of Shakespeare, Westminster Abbey
Wesley, *Character of a Methodist* Welsh Calvinistic Methodist body founded	Handel, *The Messiah* first performed in Dublin	Langley, *Gothic Architecture Improved*
First Methodist Conference	Handel, *Dettingen Te Deum*	Roger Morris begins Inverary Castle, Scotland Establishment of porcelain factories at Chelsea, Bow, Derby and Lowestoft
		Hogarth, *Marriage à la Mode*

340 SOCIAL AND CULTURAL

	Key political and historical events	Literature	Science and philosophy
1746	Battle of Culloden Disarming of the Highlands Act Lock Hospital for venereal diseases founded		
1747	General election	Thomas Carte, *History of England* (–1755) Hannah Glasse, *The Art of Cookery* Kippis et al., *Biographia Britannica* (–1766) Richardson, *Clarissa* (–1748)	Needham, *Observations Microscopiques*
1748	Treaty of Aix-la-Chapelle	Smollett, *Roderick Random* Thomson, *The Castle of Indolence*	Hume, *Philosophical Essays concerning Human Understanding*
1749		Bolingbroke, *Idea of a Patriot King* (written in 1738) John Cleland, *Fanny Hill; or memoirs of a Woman of Pleasure* Fielding, *Tom Jones* Sarah Fielding, *The Governess* Johnson, *The Vanity of Human Wishes*	Hartley, *Observations on Man*
1750	Earthquake in London 'Blue-stocking' group begins Lunar Society founded in Birmingham (first formal meeting 1775)	Fielding, *Enquiry into the Causes of the Late Increase of Robbers* Johnson, *The Rambler* (–1752)	Richard Russell, *A Dissertation on the Use of Sea Water in the Diseases of the Glands*
1751	Frederick, Prince of Wales died Clive captures Arcot	Gray, *Elegy written in a Country Churchyard* Fielding, *Amelia* Smollett, *The Adventures of Peregrine Pickle*	Hume, *Enquiry Concerning Principles of Morals* Kames, *Essays on the Principles of Morality and Natural Religion*

Religion and the Churches	Music	Art and architecture
Hervey, *Meditations and Contemplations* SPCK Welsh Bible and prayer book	Handel, *Judas Maccabaeus*	Copland, *A New Book of Ornaments* (promoting the rococo) Hogarth, *The March to Finchley*
		Hogarth, *Industry and Idleness* Garrick joins management at Drury Lane Rebuilding of Strawberry Hill, Twickenham, by Horace Walpole
		'Capability' Brown executes first independent design at Warwick Castle Hogarth, *O the Roast Beef of Old England*
Lavington, *The Enthusiasm of Methodists and Papists Compar'd* (–1751) Law, *Spirit of Prayer* Middleton, *A Free Inquiry into the Miraculous Powers* Wesley, *A Plain Account of the People called Methodists* Whitefield deserts Wesley	Handel, *Solomon*; *Music for the Royal Fireworks*	Gainsborough, *Mr and Mrs Robert Andrews*
		William Shenstone, *Unconnected Thoughts on Gardens*
Robert Clayton, *Essay on Spirit*		Hogarth, *Beer Street* and *Gin Lane* Arthur Devis, *The James Family* Worcester Porcelain Company founded

	Key political and historical events	Literature	Science and philosophy
1752	Gregorian calendar adopted in Britain	Smart, *Poems* Charlotte Lennox, *The Female Quixote*	Bolingbroke, *Study and Use of History*
1753	Jewish Naturalisation Act Hardwicke's Marriage Act British Museum founded	Lowth, *De Sacra Poesi Hebraeorum* Richardson, *Sir Charles Grandison* (–1754) Smollett, *Ferdinand Count Fathom*	Hogarth, *The Analysis of Beauty*
1754	General election Society of Arts founded	Hume, *History of England* (–1762)	
1755	Lisbon earthquake	Johnson, *A Dictionary of the English Language*	Hutcheson, *System of Moral Philosophy*
1756	Fall of Minorca Seven Years War (–1763)	John Home, *Douglas*	
1757	Battle of Plassey Admiral Byng shot	Brown, *Estimate of the Manners and Principles of the Times* Dyer, *The Fleece* Smollett, *History of England*	Burke, *A Philosophical Enquiry into the Origin of our Ideas of the Sublime and Beautiful* Richard Price, *A Review of the Principal Question in Morals*
1758	Magdalen Hospital for penitent prostitutes founded Threshing machine invented	Johnson, *The Idler* (–1760)	Comet predicted by Halley in 1705
1759	Capture of Guadeloupe Battle of Minden Capture of Quebec British Museum opened	Johnson, *Rasselas* William Robertson, *History of Scotland*	Adam Smith, *The Theory of Moral Sentiments*

Religion and the Churches	Music	Art and architecture
	Avison, *Essay on Musical Expression*	
		Battersea enamel factory develops printed decoration for porcelain
Jonathan Edwards, *Free Will*		Wood, The Circus, Bath (–1766) Thomas Chippendale, *The Gentleman and Cabinet-maker's Director*
Doddridge, *Hymns*		Gainsborough, *Milkmaid and Woodcutter*
Jones, *Catholic Doctrine of the Trinity*		
Hume, *Natural History of Religion* Jenyns, *Free Inquiry into the Nature and Origin of Evil*		Chambers, *Designs of Chinese Buildings*
		Carr, Harewood House Paine and Adam, Kedleston Hall

	Key political and historical events	Literature	Science and philosophy
1760	George II died; accession of George III Capture of Montreal James Stuart ('Old Pretender') died; Pope refused to recognise 'Young Pretender' as Charles III	Mauduit, *Considerations on the present German War* Ossian (Macpherson), *Fragments of Ancient Poetry collected in the Highlands* Sterne, *Tristram Shandy* (–1767)	
1761	General election Bridgewater Canal opened	Goldsmith, *Citizen of the World*	
1762	War with Spain Whiteboys attack tithes in Ireland	Richard Hurd, *Letters on Chivalry and Romance* Ossian (Macpherson), *Fingal*	
1763	Treaty of Paris John Wilkes arrested for his attack on King's speech in the *North Briton*, No. 45 Newcastle Lunatic Asylum founded	Blair, *On the Poems of Ossian* Catherine Macaulay, *History of England* (–1783) Christopher Smart, *Song to David*	
1764	Hargreaves' spinning jenny	Evan Evans, *Some Specimens of the Poetry of the Antient Welsh Bards* Walpole, *Castle of Otranto*	Reid, *Inquiry into the Human Mind on the Principles of Common Sense*
1765	Stamp Act	Johnson's edition of Shakespeare Percy, *Reliques of Ancient English Poetry*	Blackstone, *Commentaries on the Laws of England* (–1769)
1766		Henry Brooke, *The Fool of Quality* Goldsmith, *The Vicar of Wakefield* Smollett, *Travels through France and Italy*	Cavendish discovered hydrogen Pennant, *British Zoology* (–1770)

Religion and the Churches	Music	Art and architecture
	Boyce, collection of cathedral music	
	Noblemen's and Gentlemen's catch club, London	Boulton's metalware factory Adam, Osterley Park (–80)
	Royal Artillery band formed	Allan Ramsay, *George III* James Stuart and Nicholas Revett, *The Antiquities of Athens*
Henry Venn, *Compleat Duty of Man*		Horace Walpole, *Anecdotes of Painting* (–1771) Benjamin West settles in London
	Dibdin, *The Shepherd's Artifice*	Adam, *Ruins of the Palace of the Emperor Diocletian at Spalatro* Adam, Kenwood House (–1779) 'Capability' Brown appointed royal gardener
Fordyce, *Sermons to Young Women*		Wedgwood produces Queen's ware pottery
Francis Blackburne, *The Confessional*		George Stubbs, *The Anatomy of the Horse* Collection of Etruscian, Greek and Roman Antiquities from the Cabinet of the Honourable William Hamilton* (–1776)

	Key political and historical events	Literature	Science and philosophy
1767	Addenbrooke's Hospital, Cambridge	Ferguson, *Essay on the History of Civil Society*	Priestley, *The History and Present State of Electricity;*
1768	General election Cook's first voyage	*Encyclopaedia Britannica* (–1771) Gough, *British Topography* Sterne, *A Sentimental Journey through France and Italy* Arthur Young's *Tours* begin (–1771)	Priestley, *Essay on the First Principles of Government*
1769	Wilkesite petitioning movement Arkwright, spinning machine Steelboy disturbances in Ulster (–1770)	Shakespeare Jubilee *Letters of Junius* (–1772)	Burke, *Observations on the Present State of the Nation*
1770	Cook at Botany Bay Falkland Islands crisis Suicide of Chatterton	Goldsmith, *The Deserted Village*	Beattie, *Essay on Truth* Burke, *Thoughts on the Causes of the Present Discontents*
1771	Arkwright's first spinning-mill	Mackenzie, *The Man of Feeling* Richard Price, *Appeal to the Public on the Subject of the National Debt* Smollett, *The Expedition of Humphry Clinker*	
1772	Royal Marriages Act Warren Hastings governor of Bengal Coke begins to farm at Holkham Somersett Case	*The Morning Post* founded	

CULTURAL AND INTELLECTUAL CHRONOLOGY 347

Religion and the Churches	Music	Art and architecture
Wesley, *Hymns for the Use of Families*		Royal Crescent, Bath, begun
Countess of Huntingdon founds seminary at Trefecca Expulsion of six Methodists from Oxford University	Birmingham Music Festival founded	Royal Academy founded Edinburgh New Town begun Adam brothers, The Adelphi, London (–1775) Wright, *Experiment on a Bird in an Air Pump*
Secker, *Lectures on the Church Catechism; Charges to the Clergy of the Dioceses of Oxford and Canterbury*		Wedgwood founds potteries at Etruria Reynolds, *Discourses on Art* (–1790)
Foundation of General Baptist New Connexion		John Carr, Constable Burton, Yorkshire Adam, Mellestairs Gainsborough, *Blue Boy* Stubbs, *White Horse Frightened by a Lion* Wilson, *Snowdon from Llyn Nantil*
Wesley, *Collected Prose Works* (–1774) Francis Asbury first Methodist missionary in America Wesleys split with Calvinstic Methodists Feathers' Tavern petition against subscription		S. and N. Buck, *Antiquities . . . with Views* (begun in 1711) Vertue, *Anecdotes of Painting in England* Walpole, *Modern Gardening* West, *Death of General Wolfe*
	First Chester Music Festival	Chambers, *Dissertation on Oriental Gardening* Zoffany, *The Academicians of the Royal Academy* Sir James Clerk, Rossdhu, Strathclyde

	Key political and historical events	Literature	Science and philosophy
1773	Boston Tea Party Cook in Antarctic East India Regulating Act Newcastle Assembly Rooms	Hester Chapone, *Letters on the Improvement of the Mind* Goldsmith, *She Stoops to Conquer* Hawkesworth, *Voyages in the Southern Hemisphere*	
1774	General election Omai in London Hansard first printed	Earl of Chesterfield, *Letters to his Son* William Hutchinson, *An Excursion to the Lakes in Westmorland and Cumberland* Thomas Warton, *History of English Poetry* (–1781)	Priestley discovers oxygen
1775	War of American Independence (–1783)	Burke, *Speech on Conciliation with America* Johnson, *Journey to the Western Isles of Scotland*; *Taxation No Tyranny* Sheridan, *The Rivals* Spence, *Real Rights of Man* Wesley, *Calm Address to the American Colonies* John Whitaker, *History of Manchester*	Watt perfects the steam engine
1776	American Declaration of Independence	Bentham, *Fragment on Government* Cartwright, *Take Your Choice* Gibbon, *History of the Decline and Fall of the Roman Empire* (–1788) Paine, *Common Sense* Price, *Observations on the Nature of Civil Liberty* Smith, *The Wealth of Nations*	

Religion and the Churches	Music	Art and architecture
		Adam, *Works in Architecture* John Carr, Assize Court, York
Foundation of Lindsey's unitarian chapel		Walpole, *Description of Strawberry Hill* Wedgwood produces Jasper ware
		Bath, Royal Crescent completed Agmordisham Vesey, Lucan House, Dublin Gainsborough, *Portrait of the Hon. Mrs Graham* Reynolds, *Miss Jane Bowles* Wyatt rebuilds Sheffield Park, Sussex, in Gothic style
George Horne, *Commentary on the Book of Psalms* Toplady, *Psalms and Hymns* Soame Jenyns, *View of the Internal Evidence of the Christian Religion*	Burney, *History of Music* (–1789) Hawkins, *General History of the Science and Practice of Music* Concert of Antient Music founded	Chambers, Somerset House (–1796) Wyatt, Radcliffe Observatory

350 SOCIAL AND CULTURAL

	Key political and historical events	Literature	Science and philosophy
1777	Battle of Saratoga Bath and West of England Agricultural Society founded	John Brand, *Observations on Popular Antiquities* Chatterton, 'Rowley' poems James Cook, *A Voyage towards the South Pole and Round the World* Howard, *State of the Prisons* Sheridan, *The School for Scandal*	Priestley, *Disquistions concerning Matter and Spirit*; *Doctrine of Philosophic Necessity*
1778	War with France Brooks' Club founded	Fanny Burney, *Evelina* Malone, *Attempt to Ascertain Order in which the Plays of Shakespeare were Written* Thomas West, *A Guide to the Lakes*	
1779	Iron bridge built at Coalbrookdale, Shropshire Crompton's mule developed Siege of Gibraltar Association Movement for Parliamentary Reform founded	Johnson, *Lives of the Poets* (–1781) Sheridan, *The Critic*	
1780	General election 'No Popery' riots led by Lord George Gordon Yorkshire petitions for parliamentary reform Grattan and Irish Volunteers demand Home Rule		Bentham, *Introduction to the Principles of Morals and Legislation*
1781	Surrender at Yorktown Literary and Philosophical Society founded in Manchester		Watson, *Chemical Essays* (–1787) Uranus discovered by Herschel
1782	Battle of the Saints Gilbert's Act enables parishes to nominate guardians to find work	Gilpin, *Observations on the River Wye*	

Religion and the Churches	Music	Art and architecture
Arminian Magazine begins Relief obtained for Catholics regarding land and education		Joseph Wright first exhibition at Royal Academy Nollekens, *Venus Chiding Cupid*
Cowper and Newton, *Olney Hymns* Hume, *Dialogues Concerning Natural Religion* Dissenting ministers and schoolmasters relieved from subscription to 39 Articles		Mason, *The English Garden* Gillray and Rowlandson caricature Carr, Royal Crescent, Buxton
Sunday schools started by Robert Raikes of Gloucester		John S. Copley, *Death of Chatham*
Countess of Huntingdon's Connexion separates from Church of England Priestley, *History of the Corruptions of Christianity* Charles Simeon begins Evangelical movement in Cambridge		Wright of Derby, *Sir Brooke Boothby* Henry Fuseli, *The Nightmare*

	Key political and historical events	Literature	Science and philosophy
1783	Treaty of Versailles	George Crabbe, *The Village*	
1784	General election India Act Roya Mail coach services started	Richard Price, *Observations on the Importance of the American Revolution; and the means of rendering it a benefit to the world* Arthur Young, *Annals of Agriculture* (–1809)	Ordnance Survey of England established
1785	Cartwright's power loom	Boswell, *Tour to the Hebrides* Cowper, *The Task* *The Times* founded (initially *Daily Universal Register*)	Paley, *Principles of Moral and Political Philosophy*
1786		Beckford, *Vathek* Burns, *Poems Chiefly in the Scottish Dialect* Gilpin, *Observations on Cumberland and Westmorland*	
1787	Impeachment of Warren Hastings		William Marshall, *General Survey of the Rural Economy*
1788	Convict settlement at Botany Bay	First edition of *The Times*	
1789	Fall of the Bastille Mutiny on the *Bounty* Revolution Society meets in London	Blake, *Songs of Innocence* Price, *Discourse on the Love of Our Country* Ann Radcliffe, *Castles of Athlin and Dunbayne*	Gilbert White, *Natural History and Antiquities of Selborne*
1790	General election	Blake, *The Marriage of Heaven and Hell* Burke, *Reflections on the Revolution in France*	

Religion and the Churches	Music	Art and architecture
Consecration in Aberdeen of Samuel Seabury, first bishop of Connecticut	Handel Commemoration (repeated in 1785–87; 1790–91)	Bewick, engravings for *Select Fables* Reynolds, *Mrs Siddons as Tragic Muse*
Johnson, *Prayers and Meditations*		John Soane, Chillington Hall, Staffs. Gainsborough, *Mrs Siddons; The Morning Walk* George Stubbs, *The Haymakers*
		Thomas Baldwin and John Palmer, The Pump Room and Colonnade, Bath
Hannah More, *Thoughts on the Manners of the Great*		James Barry, *King Lear weeping over the body of Cordelia*
		Hepplewhite, *The Cabinet Maker and Upholsterer's Guide* Soane, Bank of England (–1833)
		Adam, Edinburgh University T. Lawrence, Portrait of Queen Charlotte
		Wyatt, Castle Coole, Northern Ireland Bewick, *A General History of Quadrupeds*

	Key political and historical events	Literature	Science and philosophy
1791	Priestley's house in Birmingham attacked *Observer* founded Bentham presents his Panopticon prison Society of United Irishmen started by Theobald Wolfe Tone	Boswell, *The Life of Samuel Johnson* Burke, *Appeal from the New to the Old Whigs* Mackintosh, *Vindiciae Gallicae* Paine, *Rights of Man*	
1792	London Corresponding Society founded for the circulation of radical literature	Bage, *Man as he Is* Hannah More, *Village Politics* Mary Wollstonecraft, *Vindication of the Rights of Woman* Arthur Young, *Travels in France*	
1793	War between Britain and France Board of Agriculture founded (Arthur Young as secretary) Foundation of the Literary and Philosophical Society of Newcastle-Upon-Tyne	William Godwin, *Enquiry Concerning Political Justice* Spence, *Pig's Meat* Thelwall, *Politics for the People*	
1794	Habeas Corpus Act suspended	William Blake, *Songs of Experience* Patrick Colquhoun, *Observations and Facts relative to Public Houses* Godwin, *Caleb Williams* Paine, *Age of Reason* Ann Radcliffe, *The Mysteries of Udolpho*	Erasmus Darwin, *Zoonomia; or the Laws of Organic Life*
1795	Speenhamland decision for poor relief Treasonable Practices and Seditious Meetings Act Catholic seminary founded at Maynooth with government grant	Blake, *The Song of Los*	James Hutton, *Theory of the Earth*

CULTURAL AND INTELLECTUAL CHRONOLOGY   355

Religion and the Churches	Music	Art and architecture
Death of Wesley Tone, *Argument on Behalf of the Catholics of Ireland*	Hayden composes six Grand Symphonies for concerts in London	Adam, Charlotte Square, Edinburgh (–1807) George Morland, *Inside a Stable* Nollekens, portrait bust of Charles James Fox Sheraton, *Cabinet-Maker and Upholsterer's Drawing Book* (–1794) Francis Wheatley, *Cries of London*
Foundation of the Baptist Missionary Society		George Morland, *Outside the Ale House Door*
British Critic founded		
Paley, *Evidences of Christianity*		James Wyatt, Plas Newydd, Anglesey Payne Knight, *The Landscape. A Didactic Poem* Humphry Repton, *Sketches and Hints on Landscape Gardening* Uvedale Price, *Essay on the Picturesque*
Methodist secession from Church of England		John Flaxman, Mansfield monument, Westminster Abbey

	Key political and historical events	Literature	Science and philosophy
1796	General election Jenner begins vaccination against smallpox	Edward Gibbon, *Autobiography* Lewis, *The Monk* Edmund Burke, *Letter to a Noble Lord*	
1797	Defeat of Dutch fleet at Camperdown Naval mutiny at Nore and Spithead		Eden, *The State of the Poor*
1798	Battle of the Nile Irish rebellion Smithfield Club, London, founded	Wordsworth and Coleridge, *Lyrical Ballads* (including *Rime of Ancient Mariner* and *Tintern Abbey*)	Jenner, *Enquiry into the Cause and Effect of Cow-pox* Malthus, *Essay on the Principle of Population* (2nd edn 1803)
1799	Combination Act	Wordsworth, *The Prelude*	
1800	Combination Act Act of Union with Ireland Owen's 'model' factory at New Lanark founded	Maria Edgeworth, *Castle Rackrent*	
1801	General election Pitt proposes Catholic relief, but resigns First census of England and Wales	Bloomfield, *Farmer's Boy* James Hogg, *Scottish Pastorals*	
1802	General election Peace of Amiens First Factory Act	Cobbett, *Political Register* *Edinburgh Review* founded Scott, *Minstrelsy of the Scottish Border*	Dalton's Table of Atomic Weights
1803	War with France Building of Caledonian canal begun	Lancaster, *Improvements in Education*	

CULTURAL AND INTELLECTUAL CHRONOLOGY 357

Religion and the Churches	Music	Art and architecture
		Rowland Burdon, Sunderland Bridge Wyatt begins Fonthill (–1812)
Methodist New Connexion formed Wilberforce, *A Practical View of the Prevailing Religious System of Professed Christians in the Higher and Middle Classes . . . contrasted with Real Christianity*		Bewick, *A History of British Birds* (–1804)
Charles Daubeney, *A Guide to the Church* Hannah More, *Cheap Repository Tracts*		Sawrey Gilpin, *Horses frightened by a Thunderbolt*
Church Missionary Society founded Religious Tract Society founded		
		Wyatt remodels Windsor Castle (–1813)
Southcott, *The Strange Effects of Faith*		Wyatt, Belvoir Castle (1801–13)
Paley, *Natural Theology* Society for the Suppression of Vice founded Joanna Southcott's revelations		William Atkinson, Scone Palace, Perthshire
		Norwich Society of Artists formed

	Key political and historical events	Literature	Science and philosophy
1804		Blake, *Jerusalem; Milton*	
1805	Battle of Trafalgar Battle of Austerlitz		
1806	Ministry of All the Talents formed General election		Davy isolates sodium and potassium by electrolysis
1807	General election Abolition of slave trade Cardinal Henry of York, last male Stuart, dies	Crabbe, *The Parish Register* Lamb, *Tales from Shakespeare* Wordsworth, *Ode on Intimations of Immortality*	
1808	Convention of Cintra	Scott, *Marmion*	Dalton, *A New System of Chemical Philosophy*
1809	*Quarterly Review* founded	Hannah More, *Coelebs in Search of a Wife*	
1810	George III suffers mental illness		
1811	Prince of Wales becomes Regent Luddite attacks in Nottinghamshire	Jane Austen, *Sense and Sensibility*	
1812	General election Spencer Perceval assassinated	Byron, *Childe Harold's Pilgrimage*	Central London streets lit by gas

CULTURAL AND INTELLECTUAL CHRONOLOGY   359

Religion and the Churches	Music	Art and architecture
British and Foreign Bible Society founded		Horticultural Society of London founded
		Telford, iron bridge over Ellesmere Canal
		John Sell Cotman, *Greta Bridge*
		J.M.W. Turner, *The Shipwreck*
		Repton, *Inquiry into the Changes of Taste in Landscape Gardening*
Clapham Sect founded		J.M.W. Turner, *Sun rising through the Vapour*
		Wyatt, Ashridge Park (–1813)
		William Porden, The Dome, Brighton Pavilion
Anne and Jane Taylor, *Hymns for Infant Minds*		J. Bond, Waterloo Bridge
Primitive Methodist Connexion formed		Nash begins Regent Street, London
National Society for Educating the Poor in the Principles of the Established Church founded		
Act of William III against Unitarians repealed	Crotch, *Palestine*	William Combe, *The Tours of Dr Syntax in Search of the Picturesque* (illustrated by Rowlandson)
Formation of Baptist Union of Great Britain		J.M.W. Turner, *Snowstorm: Hannibal and his army crossing the Alps*
		John Loudon, *Hints on the Formation of Gardens and Pleasure Grounds*

	Key political and historical events	Literature	Science and philosophy
1813	Elizabeth Fry visits prisons	Jane Austen, *Pride and Prejudice* Shelley, *Queen Mab*	Owen, *A New View of Society* Hedley's 'Puffing Billy' steam locomotive
1814		Jane Austen, *Mansfield Park* Patrick Colquhoun, *Treatise on the Population, Wealth, Power and Resources of the British Empire in Every Quarter of the World* Scott, *Waverley*	Stephenson builds steam locomotive
1815	Battle of Waterloo Congress of Vienna Corn Law prohibits import of foreign corn unless domestic price exceed 80*s*		Davy invents miners' safety lamp
1816	Spa Fields riot 'Bread or Blood' riots in East Anglia	Jane Austen, *Emma* Cobbett, *Political Register* Coleridge, *Christabel*; *Kubla Khan* Peacock, *Headlong Hall* Scott, *Old Mortality*	Davy, *Practical Hints on the Application of Wire-Gauze to Lamps for Preventing explosions in coal mines*
1817	*Blackwood's Magazine* founded	Coleridge, *Biographia Literaria* Mill, *History of British India* Scott, *Rob Roy*	Ricardo, *Principles of Political Economy and Taxation*
1818	General election	Jane Austen, *Northanger Abbey*; *Persuasion* Byron, *Don Juan* Susan Ferrier, *Marriage* Mary Shelley, *Frankenstein*	

CULTURAL AND INTELLECTUAL CHRONOLOGY 361

Religion and the Churches	Music	Art and architecture
Methodist Missionary Society founded	The Philharmonic Society founded in London	
Joanna Southcott dies		John Constable, *Old Sarum*
Foundation of the Methodist Bible Christian Society		Nash begins Brighton Pavilion J.M.W. Turner, *Dido building Carthage; or the Rise of the Carthiginian Empire* James Ward, *Gordale Scar*
		Flaxman, the Nelson monument, St Paul's Blore and Atkinson, Abbotsford John Martin, *Joshua Commanding the Sun to Stand still* Henry Raeburn, *Master Henry Raeburn*
		Constable, *Flatford Mill* John Martin, *The Bard* Thomas Rickman, *An Attempt to Discriminate the Styles of English Architecture*
Church Building Society founded Bible Christians separate from Methodists		Bewick, *Fables of Aesop*

	Key political and historical events	Literature	Science and philosophy
1819	Peterloo Massacre; 'Six Acts'	Keats' Odes To a Nightingale and On a Grecian Urn Scott, *Ivanhoe*	Telford begins Menai Straits suspension bridge
1820	Death of George III; accession of George IV; general election; trial of Queen Caroline; Cato Street and Grange Moor conspiracies	Blake, *Jerusalem* Clare, *Poems, Descriptive of Rural Life* Mill, *Essay on Government* Owen, *Report to the County of New Lanark* Shelley, *Prometheus Unbound*	First iron steamship launched

Religion and the Churches	Music	Art and architecture
		John Constable, *A Scene on the River Stour*
John Wade, *The Black Book; or Corruption Unmasked!*		Samuel Brown, Union Bridge, Berwick on Tweed

SECTION ELEVEN

Biographies

Selecting who are the most important people of the eighteenth century is a totally arbitrary and necessarily biased judgement. We will, inevitably, have missed out some individuals who deserve a mention. But we hope we have included the most common names who will crop up during your reading.

Adam, Robert (1728–92), Scottish architect. He trained in his father's Edinburgh office. After travelling to Greece and Italy, he set up an architectural practice in London in 1758. The 'Adam style', which was inspired by his travels, was associated with light, graceful and highly decorative interiors, and was best shown in town and country houses such as Kedleston Hall, Derbyshire (1760–61), Syon House (1760–69), Osterley Park (1761–80) and Home House (1773–77), near London. His most impressive civic work was Charlotte Square, Edinburgh. His Edinburgh Bridewell (1791), which was developed in correspondence with Jeremy Bentham, showed his abilities as an institutional architect. His most influential publication was an archaeological description of the *Ruins of the Palace of the Emperor Diocletian at Spalatro* (1764). Adam was architect to George III, 1761–69.

Addington, Henry, 1st Viscount Sidmouth (1757–1844), Prime Minister. He was the son of a country doctor and was educated at Winchester and Oxford. He became MP for Devizes in 1783 and was made speaker in 1789. George III approved of his opposition to Catholic emancipation, and he was appointed Prime Minister in 1801. He was instrumental in negotiations for the Peace of Amiens of 1802. In 1805 he became a peer, and served in various ministries. Addington was Home Secretary from 1812 to 1821 and was known for his conservative policies, backing the Suspension of the Habeas Corpus Act of 1817 and the Six Acts of 1819. After leaving office in 1824 he continued to vote against Catholic emancipation and parliamentary reform.

Addison, Joseph (1672–1719), essayist and politician. Born at Milston, Wiltshire, he was the son of a Church of England cleric and was educated at Charterhouse and Oxford. His 'The Campaign' (1705), a poem which praised Marlborough's victory at Blenheim, made him popular with the Whigs, and he was elected MP for Lostwithiel in 1708, and for Malmesbury in 1710. He defended the Whigs in the *Whig Examiner* (1710). Addison contributed to Steele's *The Tatler* in 1709 and edited *The Spectator* with Steele from 1711–12 and, on his own, in 1714. He also wrote the anti-Jacobite periodical *The Freeholder* (1715–16). His tragedy *Cato* (1713) was well received.

Anne, Queen (1665–1714), the second daughter of James, Duke of York and Anne Hyde, his first wife. She married Prince George of Denmark in 1683, and in 1688 supported William of Orange and her elder sister Mary against their father, although relations with them were soon difficult. She became Queen in 1702. Although much influenced by the Marlboroughs (calling them 'Mr and Mrs Freeman', and they her 'Mrs Morley') until she rowed with them in 1710, modern scholarship has rehabilitated her reputation and now recognises that she was a formidable political figure in her own right. A devout (and High-Church) supporter of the Church of England, she established Queen Anne's Bounty, which helped augment the stipends of poor clergy. She had 17 pregnancies; only five children were born, four died in infancy, and her last remaining child, the Duke of Gloucester, died in 1700 aged 10. Under Anne, the parliaments of England and Scotland were united in 1707.

Anson, George (1697–1762), English naval commander and circumnavigator of the world. He joined the navy in 1712 and commanded a Pacific expedition in 1739. After capturing a Spanish treasure ship in 1743, he became a wealthy man. The account of his journey was a best-seller. He served as First Lord of the Admiralty for periods between 1751 to 1762, where he carried out reforms which contributed to the navy's success in the Seven Years War.

Arbuthnot, John (1667–1735), physician and man of letters. He was born in Scotland and studied medicine at St Andrews University. He came to London and became physician to Queen Anne. Arbuthnot was a friend of Swift, Pope and Gay, and with them he founded the Scriblerus Club. Alongside medical, scientific and other literary works, he published his *History of John Bull* (1712), which introduced the figure of John Bull, the archetypal Englishman.

Archer, Thomas (1668–1743), architect. He was the younger son of a Warwickshire gentleman, and educated at Oxford. He travelled on the Continent from 1691 to 1695. Archer held the office of groom porter at court and was a member of the 1711 church-building commission. He is best known for designing houses, churches and monuments in the baroque style.

Arkwright, Richard (1732–92), industrialist and inventor. He was born in Preston and set up a business in Bolton. With John Kay he produced the horse-driven water frame, patented in 1769, where mechanically driven rollers, rotating at different speeds, drew out the cotton fibres and a flyer inserted twist into the yarn. The patent was challenged with success by Lancashire cotton masters in 1781 and 1785. Arkwright set up a horse-driven factory in Nottingham in 1769. He played a significant part in the foundation of the cotton industry.

Arne, Thomas (1710–78), composer and violinist, produced operas, masques and incidental music for the London stage. His opera *Artaxerxes* (1761) was arguably the most popular full-length English opera written before the twentieth century, and his most famous composition was 'Rule Britannia', written for the masque *Alfred* (1740). In 1738 he wrote a score for Milton's *Comus* and was given an honorary doctorate in music from Oxford in 1759. For the Shakespeare Jubilee in 1769 Arne collaborated with Garrick in an *Ode upon Dedicating a Building to Shakespeare*.

Astell, Mary (1666–1731), polemicist and champion of women's rights. She was born into a coal merchant's family in Newcastle-Upon-Tyne, where her uncle was curate of St Nicholas's church. Astell went to London in 1688 and was given financial support by Archbishop Sancroft. She lived in Chelsea, and published in 1694 *A Serious Proposal to the Ladies*. This urged wealthy women to establish Protestant nunneries. Her *Some Reflections on Marriage* (1700) noted that marriage was a potentially tyrannical relationship for women. In 1705 her *The Christian Religion as Profess'd by a Daughter of the Church of England* was an attack on materialism, and she opposed Locke's views on education.

Atterbury, Francis (1662–1732), Church of England cleric and High-Church Tory. He was educated at Westminster and Oxford, and opposed James II's attempts to impose Catholicism on the university. His *Letter to a Convocation Man* (1696) was a rallying cry for High-Church views. Atterbury became Bishop of Rochester in 1713, and the Whig supremacy after 1716 drove him into Jacobitism. He was detected and forced into exile in 1723.

Austen, Jane (1775–1817), novelist. She was born in Hampshire, the daughter of a Church of England clergyman. Although substantially written during the 1790s, she published *Sense and Sensibility* in 1811 and *Pride and Prejudice* in 1813, while *Northanger Abbey* appeared after her death, in 1818. *Mansfield Park* was begun in 1811 and was published to some acclaim in 1814, *Emma* was published in 1816, and *Persuasion* in 1818. Austen left an unfinished novel, *Sanditon*. She died of Addison's Disease in Winchester.

Avison, Charles (1709–70), organist and composer. In 1736 he was appointed organist at St Nicholas's church, Newcastle-Upon-Tyne, where he organised subscription concerts, which were among the first in Britain. He wrote over sixty concertos and published his *Essay on Musical Expression* (1752), which was a landmark in musical criticism.

Bakewell, Robert (1725–95), farmer. He became interested in the selective breeding of sheep and cattle, and his model farm at Dishley,

Leicestershire, was a tourist site. He developed the Leicestershire longhorn cattle, and he was the first to carry on the trade of ram-letting on a large scale.

Banks, Joseph (1743–1820), explorer, botanist and President of the Royal Society. He was educated at Eton and Oxford and in 1763 sailed to Newfoundland and Labrador on HMS *Niger*. He accompanied Captain Cook on HMS *Endeavour* to view Venus from Tahiti and to search for the southern continent (1768–71). In 1778 he was elected President of the Royal Society and encouraged the Royal Institution, Kew Gardens, and the colonisation of Australia.

Barbauld, Anna Laetitia (1743–1825), writer. She was born in Leicestershire, the daughter of John Aikin, a nonconformist minister, and was educated by him and later at the Warrington Dissenting Academy. In 1774 she married Rochemont Barbauld, who was from a Huguenot family, and they moved to Suffolk to run a boys' school. She published *Poems* (1773), and wrote devotional works for children as well as more political pieces, including *Address to the Opposers of the Repeal of the Corporation and Test Acts* (1790); *Epistle to William Wilberforce* (1791); and *Remarks on Mr Gilbert Wakefield's Enquiry* (1791). She edited *The British Novelists* (1810) in 50 volumes.

Beckford, William (1709–70), politician. His wealth was based on his estates in Jamaica. He was educated at Westminster and Oxford and became MP for Shaftesbury in 1747, and then for London in 1754. He supported parliamentary reform and was Lord Mayor of London, 1762–63 and 1769–70. Beckford was a supporter of John Wilkes.

Beckford, William, the younger (1759–1844), author and eccentric. He inherited a large fortune from his father. After travelling in Europe he wrote *Vathek*, which was published in 1787. Beckford was MP for Hindon, 1784–94 and 1806–20. In 1796 he commissioned James Wyatt to create an inhabitable ruined monastery at Fonthill. The huge 276-feet-high tower collapsed in 1825.

Behn, Aphra (1640–89), credited with being the first English female novelist, was born in Wye, Kent. As a child, she lived for some years in Surinam and on her return to England in 1658 she married a Dutchman. Behn operated as a spy in the Netherlands, and wrote plays and novels, the most famous being *Oroonoko* (1688).

Bell, Andrew (1753–1832) founded the 'Madras' system of education, where much of the teaching was done by the cleverer pupils. He was educated at St Andrews, spent some time in Virginia, and in 1787 went to India. He became superintendent of the Madras Male Orphan Asylum, where, because of a shortage of teachers, he devised his new method of teaching. The system was adopted by the National Society for Promoting the Education of the Poor in the Principles of the Established Church (founded in 1811, with Bell as superintendent), and by the time of Bell's death 12,000 schools had been established.

Bellers, John (1654–1725), Quaker and philanthropist, whose *Proposals for Raising a Colledge of Industry* (1695) attempted to look after the sick and educate children. He also argued for the creation of a European state, with a supreme court which would solve international disputes.

Bentham, Jeremy (1748–1832), utilitarian and philosophical radical. He was educated at Westminster and Oxford and qualified as a barrister. He endeavoured to reform the legal system on the grounds of utility. He published *A Fragment on Government* in 1776, which rejected the natural law system and ridiculed notions of an original contract. Bentham's *Introduction to the Principles of Morals and Legislation* was privately printed in 1780, but not published until 1789. In this work he put forward his theory of utility in terms of the greatest happiness of the greatest number, which established utilitarianism as a systematic theory of moral and political decision making. His 'felicific calculus' showed which action was the most pleasurable and thus the most rational. Bentham visited Russia in 1785 and developed the idea of 'The Panopticon', for the total surveillance of prisoners.

Bentinck, William, 1st Earl of Portland (1649–1709), adviser to William III. A member of a Dutch noble family, Bentinck was an intimate of William's from the early 1670s, and came over with him in 1688. He fought at the Boyne and at Loudon, and was instrumental in negotiations for the Treaty of Ryswick and the partition treaties.

Bentley, Richard (1662–1742), classical scholar. He was born in Oulton, Yorkshire, and educated at Wakefield and Cambridge. He participated in the controversy about the merits of ancient and modern learning, and his *Dissertation on the Letters of Phalaris* (1699) was a triumph of modern scholarship. Bentley gave the first Boyle lecture in 1692: *A Confutation of Atheism from the Origin and Frame of the World*, which applied Newtonian principles to theology. In 1700 Bentley was appointed master of St John's College, Cambridge, where he was involved in lengthy rows with the fellows.

Berkeley, George (1685–1753), bishop and philosopher, was born in Kilkenny, of English extraction. He was a fellow of Trinity College, Dublin, and between 1713 and 1720 was in London and travelled in Europe. He was made Dean of Derry in 1724, and procured funds for a college in Bermuda, with the intention of converting the natives to Christianity. He was in America from 1728 to 1732. In 1734 Berkeley was appointed Bishop of Cloyne. His *Treatise Concerning the Principles of Human Knowledge* (1710) and his *Three Dialogues* (1713) propounded an idealist philosophy against the materialism of Locke and Newton. His *Siris* (1744) advocated tar-water as a panacea.

Bewick, Thomas (1755–1828), animal artist and engraver, and regarded as the father of modern wood engraving. He was born at Cherryburn, near Newcastle-Upon-Tyne. Bewick was the apprentice and then the partner of Ralph Beilby. He was best known for his illustrations of natural history, shown in his *A General History of Quadrupeds* (1790), *A History of British Birds* (1797–1804) and *Fables of Aesop* (1818).

Blackmore, Sir Richard (1655–1729), poet and physician. He was educated at Westminster and Oxford and, after medical training, was appointed physician to William III, and knighted, in 1697. He was also physician to Queen Anne. Blackmore wrote a number of religious and medical works, including a poem *The Creation* (1712).

Blackstone, Sir William (1723–80), English jurist. He was called to the Bar in 1746 and in 1758 he was appointed as the first Vinerian Professor of Law at the University of Oxford. His *Commentaries on the Laws of England* (1765–69), based on the lectures he had delivered at Oxford, was an attempt to view the law as an ordered body of knowledge. He was MP for Hindon, Wiltshire, from 1761 to 1770.

Blair, Hugh (1718–80), clergyman. He was educated at Edinburgh, where he became Professor of Rhetoric and Regius Professor of Rhetoric and Belles Lettres (1762–63). Blair was part of the Edinburgh Enlightenment and encouraged Macpherson to publish *Fragments of Ancient Poetry* (1760).

Blake, William (1757–1827), artist, poet and engraver. He began as a book-engraver, developing a method for illustrating and printing his own poems. His *Songs of Innocence*, which attempted to merge image and text, was published in 1789, followed by *Songs of Experience* in 1794. His *Jerusalem* was published between 1804 and 1820 and his *Milton* in 1804 to 1808. Blake wrote several prophetic works, notably *The French Revolution* (1791), *America* (1793) and *Europe* (1794). His interest in the apocalypse was influenced by the Swedish philosopher and mystic Emanuel Swedenborg (1688–1772), who inspired Blake's *Marriage of Heaven and Hell* (1790–93).

Blathwayt, William (1649–1717), career civil servant who managed to work for a number of governments, despite the political vicissitudes of the time. He was Secretary to the Lords of Trade and Plantations, 1675, Chief Clerk in the office of Secretary of State, 1681–83, Secretary at War, 1683–1704, where he accompanied William III to Flanders each summer, Clerk of Privy Council, 1696–1706. He was MP for Bath, 1693–1710. He built the fine house at Dyrham Park, Gloucestershire, with its remarkable collection of Delftware, and retired there in 1710.

Bligh, William (1754–1817), vice-admiral. He was born in Plymouth, and after entering the navy, accompanied James Cook on his second world voyage, 1772–74, and discovered bread-fruit in Tahiti. In 1787 Bligh commanded HMS *Bounty* to Tahiti to bring bread-fruit plants back to England, but was cast adrift in an open boat by his mutinous crew. He landed at Timor in 1789, and returned to England in 1790. He was made captain-general and Governor of New South Wales in 1805, but was deposed in 1808, and imprisoned until 1810. Bligh returned to England in 1811.

Bolingbroke, Henry St John, 1st Viscount (1678–1751), Tory politician and author. He was the son of a Whig. Elected MP for Wootton Bassett in 1701, he became leader of the extreme Tories and was Secretary at War, 1704–8. Bolingbroke was instrumental in securing the Treaty of Utrecht, 1713, which lost him Hanoverian support. Dismissed by George I, Bolingbroke went to France and served the Old Pretender. He was allowed to return to England in 1723, but could not take his seat in the Lords. He became leader of opposition to Walpole, writing for *The Craftsman* from 1726. Bolingbroke retired to France in 1735 and wrote *The Idea of a Patriot King* (1738). In his *Letters on the Study and Use of History* (privately printed 1735, published 1752) he observed that 'history is philosophy teaching by examples'.

Bosanquet, Mary (1739–1815), Methodist preacher. She was the wife of John Fletcher, the vicar of Madeley, Shropshire, and helped him in his parish work. After his death in 1785 she continued to live in the parsonage house and directed the work of the curate. She also preached in local Methodist meeting houses. She was involved in a correspondence with John Wesley concerning the propriety of female preaching.

Boswell, James (1748–95), writer. He was the son of Lord Auchinleck, and educated at Edinburgh and Glasgow universities. He went on the Grand Tour, where he was introduced to Voltaire and Rousseau. Boswell came to London in 1763, where he met Samuel Johnson. He wrote his *The Life of Samuel Johnson* (1791), *Journal of a Tour to the Hebrides* (1785) and an *Account of Corsica* (1768).

Boulton, Matthew (1728–1809), engineer and entrepreneur. Born in Birmingham, he expanded the family's button and stamping business, and established his Soho Works in 1760. In 1773 he purchased a two-thirds share in James Watt's patent for the steam engine. Boulton argued for the reform of copper currency, and patented improved machinery for minting currency in 1790.

Boyce, William (1711–79), organist and composer. He was a chorister at St Paul's, and was appointed composer at the Chapel Royal in 1736 and organist in 1738. He conducted the Three Choirs Festival in 1737 and was made Master of the King's Musick in 1755. Although he composed operas and symphonies, Boyce is best known as a composer of church music. His *Cathedral Music* (1760–73) played a crucial role in preserving the English choral tradition.

Boyle, Richard, 3rd Earl of Burlington and 4th Earl of Cork (1694–1753), architect and patron. He made a visit to Italy, 1714–19, and returned to England with the aim of reviving Palladian architecture. With William Kent he was responsible for the Palladian revival. Burlington had Kent's *The Designs of Inigo Jones* (1727) published. Burlington's own architectural designs included Westminster School, and the Assembly Rooms in York. His collaborations with Kent are shown at Holkham Hall, Norfolk, and at his own Palladian villa, Chiswick House.

Boyle, Robert (1627–91), scientist. The youngest son of the 1st Earl of Cork, he was educated at Eton, and went on the Grand Tour from 1639 to 1644. He was part of the scientific group which met at Wadham College, Oxford, in the 1650s and which was to be a basis for the Royal Society. He collaborated with Robert Hooke in making and conducting experiments with an air pump. He published *The Sceptical Chemist* in 1661 and he formulated Boyle's law, which stated that the volume of a given mass of gas varies inversely with the pressure when the temperature is constant. He was a devout and pious man, and in his will he founded the Boyle Lectures.

Bridgeman, Charles (16?–1738), royal gardener to George I. From 1709 he worked at Blenheim with Vanbrugh, Wise and Switzer, and by 1716 he was employed at Stowe, collaborating with Vanbrugh, as well as at Eastbury and Claremont. During the 1720s he worked at Down Hall, Houghton, Wimpole and Kedleston. Bridgeman was employed in the royal gardens from 1726 and was made royal gardener in 1728. His designs represented a transition between the formal geometric plans of the late seventeenth and early eighteenth centuries and the 'natural' layouts of Brown, using traditional features alongside ha-has and asymmetrical lawns.

Bridgewater, Francis Egerton, 3rd Duke of (1736–1803). Inheriting the title from his brother in 1748 at the age of 11, he became famous for exploiting the coal assets of his Lancashire estates. In 1761 he had a 6-mile canal constructed from Worsley to Salford, and followed this with the 28-mile Manchester to Liverpool canal along which he ran a passenger service.

Brown, John (1715–66), clergyman and writer. He was educated at Wigton and Cambridge, and was a minor canon of Carlisle, rector of Great Horkesley, Essex from 1756, and of St Nicholas's, Newcastle-Upon-Tyne from 1761. His *Estimate of the Manners and Principles of the Times* (1757) was an attack on luxury and 'effeminacy'. He committed suicide when doctors forbade him to go to St Petersburg, where he had hoped for a top post in education.

Brown, Lancelot (1716–83), landscape designer, nick-named 'Capability' on account of his allusions to the 'capabilities' of a property. He was born in Kirkharle, Northumberland, of a farming family. He worked for Sir William Loraine at Kirkharle, then under Lord Cobham at Stowe, where he developed his characteristic style with its clumps and belts of trees, serpentine lakes, and grassland stretching up to the house. After 1749 he set up as a freelance designer; among his many commissions were Blenheim, Bowood, Chatsworth, Harewood, Nuneham Courtenay, Petworth and Sheffield Park. He was appointed master gardener at Hampton Court in 1764. He was also an architect, working on houses, orangeries, garden buildings and bridges.

Brummell, George Bryan 'Beau' (1778–1840), dandy. The son of Lord North's private secretary, he acquired a reputation for his exquisite clothes and manners while at Eton, and on moving to London became a judge of style, promoting personal cleanliness and refinement in dress. He was a friend of George, Prince of Wales, until he fell from favour in 1811. He retired to Calais in 1816 having accumulated gaming debts.

Burgoyne, John (1722–92), soldier and dramatist. He was educated at Westminster and entered the army in 1740. After eloping with the daughter of the Earl of Derby in 1743, he lived for nine years in France. He distinguished himself during the Seven Years War in the Iberian Peninsula by the capture of Valenia de Alcantara (1762). Burgoyne entered Parliament a Tory in 1761. In 1774 he was sent to America, and fought at Bunker's Hill. He was forced to surrender at Saratoga in 1777. Returning to England, his allegiances were now Whig, and he was appointed Commander-in-Chief in Ireland, 1782–83. His plays included *The Maid of the Oaks* (1775) and *The Heiress* (1786).

Burke, Edmund (1729–97), politician and political thinker. He was born in Dublin, the son of a Catholic mother and Protestant father. He was educated at a Quaker school and Trinity College, Dublin. He studied law in London, and in 1757 published his *Philosophical Inquiry into the Origin of our Ideas of the Sublime and Beautiful*. He became MP for Wendover in 1766, and represented Bristol from 1774 to 1780 and Malton from 1780 to 1794. He showed sympathy for the Americans' rejection of the imposition of taxes by the British government, and wrote *Reflections on the Revolution in France* (1790), which was critical of the French Revolution.

Burnet, Gilbert (1643–1715), bishop and historian. He was born in Edinburgh, educated at Aberdeen and became professor of divinity at Glasgow. He settled in London in the 1670s and became associated with the opposition Whigs. Burnet went to Holland, became an intimate of William of Orange, and came over with him in 1688. He was made Bishop of Salisbury and became the leading apologist for the new regime. Burnet's works included *The History of the Reformation* (1679), *A Discourse of the Pastoral Care* (1692) and *A History of my Own Time* (published after his death, 1724–34).

Burney, Charles (1726–1814), musical historian, composer and organist. He was born in Shrewsbury, and went to London in 1744 as Arne's apprentice. He travelled widely in Europe where he located material for his *History of Music*, which was published between 1776 and 1789.

Burney, Fanny [Frances] (1752–1840), novelist and dramatist, the daughter of the above. Her first novel, *Evelina*, was published anonymously in 1778. Her *Cecilia* (1782) was well received and she was made second keeper of the robes at Queen Charlotte's court in 1786. She married General d'Arblay, a French refugee, in 1791. They lived in France from 1802 to 1812. She published *Camilla* in 1796 and *The Wanderer* in 1814.

Burns, Robert (1759–96), poet, the son of an Ayrshire tenant farmer. Educated by the parish schoolteacher. His *Poems Chiefly in the Scottish Dialect*, which included 'To a mouse', and 'Holy Willie's prayer', appeared in 1786, and he contributed to James Johnson's *The Scots' Musical Museum* (1789 onwards). Politically he was a radical, who initially supported the French Revolution, but in 1795 he joined the Dumfries Volunteers.

Bute, John Stuart, 3rd Earl of (1713–1792), Prime Minister. He was tutor to the Prince of Wales from 1755, and after George III's accession, he became Secretary of State, and First Lord of the Treasury from May 1762 to April 1763. He played a significant part in the diplomatic manoeuvrings which led to the Peace of Paris in 1763. Bute aroused anti-Scottish sentiment, especially since it was believed that he remained a 'minister behind the curtain' after his resignation.

Butler, Lady Elizabeth (1739–1829), one of the ladies of Llangollen. The daughter of an Irish aristocrat, she eloped in 1778 with Sarah Ponsonby, and, to the displeasure of their families, settled in Llangollen, Wales. Their unorthodox relationship, their cult of rural retirement, and their literary friendships made them celebrities of their day.

Butler, James, 2nd Duke of Ormond (1665–1745). He was born in Dublin and was educated in France (from 1675) and Oxford. He was a supporter of the Prince of Orange, defending his cause in Ireland at the battle of the Boyne. In 1702 he was appointed commander of the English and Dutch land forces which accompanied Sir George Rooke's fleet against Cadiz. In 1703 he was made Lord Lieutenant of Ireland. He succeeded Marlborough in the post of captain-general of the army, but was deprived of the post at the accession of George I in 1714. He became a Jacobite sympathiser, and played a prominent part in the 1715 uprising. He lived on the Continent after 1715, and never returned to England.

Butler, Joseph (1692–1752) bishop and theologian. The son of a Presbyterian linen-draper, he was educated in a dissenting academy. He conformed to the Church of England and went to Oxford. A protégé of Lord Chancellor Talbot and Queen Caroline, Butler was appointed Bishop of Bristol in 1738, Dean of St Paul's in 1740, and Bishop of Durham in 1750. He published *Fifteen Sermons preached at the Rolls Chapel* (1726), which argued that morality consisted of living in accordance with the principles of self-love, benevolence and conscience, and *The Analogy of Religion* (1736), which was widely believed to have vanquished Deism.

Byng, John (1704–57), English naval commander. The younger son of Viscount Torrington, he joined the navy at the age of 14, becoming rear admiral in 1745. In 1751 Byng was elected MP for Rochester. In 1756, at the start of the Seven Years War, he was sent to protect Minorca from the French. He retreated from battle, was court-martialled and shot. Voltaire satirised the episode in *Candide* (1759), observing that the English sometimes shot an admiral 'to encourage the others'.

Byrom, John (1692–1763), poet and teacher of short-hand. He was educated at Merchant Taylors' School and Cambridge. He studied medicine at Montpellier in 1716, and taught short-hand in Manchester, and also at London and Cambridge. His system of short-hand was copyrighted in 1742. He was a Jacobite sympathiser and wrote hymns, notably 'Christians awake!'

Byron, George Gordon, 6th Baron (1788–1824), Romantic poet. Educated at Harrow and Cambridge, he toured Europe and published, to great acclaim in 1812, the first two cantos of *Childe Harold's Pilgrimage*. In the same year he made his maiden speech in the Lords, which was an attack on the Frame-Breaking Bill, where he took the workers' side. After separating from his wife, he left England in 1816, never to return. In 1824, he fought in the Greek War for Independence, and died of fever. *Don Juan*, often considered his masterpiece, was unfinished. Byron encapsulated the romantic hero.

Cameron, Donald of Lochiel (1695–1748), leading Jacobite. His father had participated in 1715 uprising. Cameron advised Prince Charles Edward in 1745, and his clan made up the majority of Charles's troops. Cameron was involved in the march to Derby, and was wounded at Culloden. He escaped to France in 1746.

Campbell, Colen (1676–1729), architect. He was a Scottish lawyer, who qualified in Edinburgh in 1702. After travelling abroad, he had settled in England by 1710. He was chief clerk and surveyor at the Office of Works, 1718–19, architect to the Prince of Wales from 1719, and surveyor of Greenwich Hospital, 1726. He designed the Rolls House, Chancery Lane (1717), and Mereworth Castle (1720). He published *Vitruvius Britannicus* (1717–25).

Canning, George (1770–1827), politician. He was educated at Eton and Oxford and became MP for Newport in 1794, censuring the Revolution in France. He was appointed Foreign Secretary in 1807. He fought a duel with Castlereagh after the failure of the 1812 Walcheren expedition. In 1818 Canning was made President of the Board of Control, returning to the foreign secretaryship in 1822. He was asked to form a government in 1827, but died after three months in office.

Carlile, Richard (1790–1843), publisher and republican. He was born in Devon and moved to London in 1813, where he sold radical newspapers. He supported the views of Thomas Paine and was imprisoned for libel in 1817 and 1819–25. He was the editor of *The Republican* from 1819 to 1826.

Caroline, Queen (1683–1737), wife of George II. The daughter of John Frederick, the margrave of Brandenburg-Anspach, she married George in 1705. She was a gifted linguist who read widely and enjoyed controversy. Caroline had a penchant for interesting clergymen such as Samuel Clarke, Joseph Butler, George Berkeley and Benjamin Hoadly. She backed inoculation against smallpox, and supported Robert Walpole's ministry.

Caroline of Brunswick, Queen (1768–1821), wife of George IV. She married George in 1795, but had separated from him by early 1796. She lived on the Continent and was accused of adultery in 1806, although she was cleared of the charge. On George's accession to the throne in 1820, Caroline returned to England demanding to be acknowledged as Queen. Her case was supported by the government's opponents, and she became something of a national celebrity. She appeared at Westminster Abbey at George's coronation in 1821, dying shortly after.

Carter, Elizabeth (1717–1806), poet, translator and essayist. She was born in Deal, where her father was the perpetual curate. She was the eldest daughter in a large family and after her mother's death ran the household. Taught by her father, she acquired an excellent knowledge of languages, astronomy and history. She published her *Poems* (1738) and her translation of *Sir Isaac Newton's Philosophy Explained for the use of Ladies* (1739) from Alagarotti's *Newtonism per le dame*. Her claim to fame was her translation of the *Works of Epictetus* (1758). Many of her letters to a wide number of blue-stockings were published after her death.

Carteret, Lord John, Earl Granville (1690–1763), politician and diplomat. He was promoted for his diplomatic skills in negotiating with the Baltic, 1717–20, becoming Secretary of State for the Southern Department in 1721. Walpole made him Lord Lieutenant of Ireland in 1724, to minimise Carteret's potential as a political rival, and dismissed him from office altogether in 1730. Carteret became a leader of opposition to Walpole, taking the post of Secretary of State for the Northern Department when Walpole fell from office in 1742. His policy there was to aid Austria in the War of the Austrian Succession. This led to an outcry in Parliament, and he resigned in 1744. He become Lord President in 1751.

Cartwright, Major John (1740–1824), radical political reformer. He was a Lincolnshire farmer who urged for an overhaul of the political system. He championed the case of the American colonists, and in *Take your Choice* (1776) for universal male suffrage, annual elections and a reorganisation of the electoral system. The Society for Constitutional Information was founded by him in 1780. Cartwright was active in radical politics in the borough of Westminster after 1805, and founded the Hampden clubs, 1812–17, which aimed to enfranchise all tax-payers and abolish income tax.

Castlereagh, Robert Stewart, Viscount, 2nd Marquis of Londonderry (1769–1822), statesman. From Ireland, he was elected to the Irish House of Commons in 1790, entering Westminster in 1794. Although favourable to political reform, he was a defender of the Irish connection with Britain, helping to put down the Irish Rebellion of 1798, and backing the Act of Union of 1800. He was a firm supporter of Catholic emancipation, which meant that he resigned when George III vetoed it in 1801. Castlereagh was War Secretary from 1805. He quarrelled with Canning in 1812, which led to them both resigning their positions. He was Foreign Secretary from 1812 to 1822, where he established and maintained the anti-Napoleonic coalition. He represented Britain at the Congress of Vienna in 1814–15. He supported the abolition of the slave trade. He committed suicide in 1822.

Centlivre, Susanna (?–1723), playwright. She is believed to have been born in Holbeach. Almost nothing is known of her early years, but by 1700 she was moving within a wide circle of literary figures, and was writing verse. She married Joseph Centlivre in 1707. She wrote sixteen full-length plays and three shorter farces. Her first success was *Love's Contrivance* (1703). *The Gamester* (1705) was a hit, as was *The Busy Body* (1709), *The Wonder: a Woman keeps a Secret* (1714) and *A Bold Stroke for a Wife* (1718).

Challoner, Richard (1691–1781), Catholic divine and author. He was born at Lewes, the son of Presbyterian parents, and converted to Catholicism as a boy. He was trained at Douai for the priesthood. He became vice-president of the college, returning to England in 1730. Challoner was consecrated Bishop of Debra in 1741 and became Vicar Apostolic in 1748. He wrote a large number of devotional and controversial works, notably *The Garden of the Soul* (1740), which long remained a popular work.

Chambers, Sir William (1723–76), architect. He was born in Sweden, of Scottish parents. Chambers was educated in England and travelled in Europe and the Far East, publishing his *Designs of Chinese Buildings* (1757) and his *Treatise of Civil Architecture* (1759). He was tutor to the Prince of Wales, and designed George III's coronation coach. He played a central part in the development of the architectural profession. Chambers designed Somerset House (1775) and the Orangery at Kew.

Chapone, Hester Mulso (1727–1801), poet and essayist. She was born at Twywell, Northamptonshire, the daughter of a gentleman farmer. She read widely and knew a large number of literary figures, most notably Samuel Richardson. She married John Chapone in 1760; he died the following year. She wrote for Johnson's *The Rambler*, but her major work was the popular *Letters on the Improvement of the Mind* (1773).

Chatterton, Thomas (1752–70), poet. He was born in Bristol and was publishing his poetry by the age of 12. He based a series of fake-medieval poems on originals he claimed to have found among the archives of the church of St Mary Redcliffe, Bristol, writing them in the guise of a fictitious fifteenth-century monk, 'Thomas Rowley'. He lived in London from 1770, in poverty. He died in the same year, probably of self-administered arsenic poisoning.

Chippendale, Thomas (1718–79), furniture designer and maker. He was born in Otley, Yorkshire, the son of a joiner. He moved to London in 1748. His *The Gentleman and Cabinet-Maker's Director*, a pattern book for a complete set of furniture, appeared in 1754, and was a great commercial success. This enabled him to open a shop in St Martin's Lane, where he produced a wide variety of goods. He worked with Robert Adam from 1770.

Churchill, Charles (1731–64), poet and satirist. He was born in Westminster, the son of a curate. He was educated at Westminster School, and was ordained, serving as a curate in Somerset, 1754, in Essex, 1756, and succeeding his father as curate of St John's, Westminster, 1758–63. He was best known for his 'Rosciad' and his 'Apology'. He was a supporter of John Wilkes. He died in Boulogne.

Churchill, John, Duke of Marlborough (1650–1722), general and statesman. He was the son of a royalist squire, and was a courtier and soldier to James II. He helped to defeat Monmouth's rebellion in 1685, and from 1683 was an intimate of the future Queen Anne. He played a crucial role in the Glorious Revolution, leading those army officers who went over to William. He became Duke of Marlborough, but then lost monarchical backing because he supported the claims of Anne. In 1700 Marlborough was given the role of leading British troops in the Low Countries. He led the great victory over the French at Blenheim in 1705, and in 1706 at Ramillies. His victories at Oudenarde, in 1708, and especially that at Malplaquet, 1709, were seen as unduly expensive. He was dismissed in 1711, but George I reinstated him, and Marlborough helped to put down the Jacobite uprising of 1715. He was given Blenheim Palace, as a gift from the nation.

Churchill, Sarah, Duchess of Marlborough (1660–1744). She was the daughter of a Hertfordshire landowner and married the above in 1678. She became a lady of the bedchamber to the then Princess Anne in 1683. She was a fervent Whig, and had a large amount of influence over the Princess. When Anne became Queen, Sarah became Mistress of the Robes, Groom of the Stole and Keeper of the Privy Purse. After several years of bickering, the two fell out in 1710, and the Marlboroughs were effectively exiled from court. Sarah was an opponent of the baroque-style Blenheim palace, and quarrelled with Vanbrugh over its design. In 1742 she published an apologia for her behaviour at court.

Cibber, Colley (1671–1757), actor and dramatist. He was in the Earl of Devonshire's levy for the Prince of Orange in 1688, became known as a comedy actor, and acquired a reputation for playing eccentric characters. From 1711 he had a share in the management of the Drury Lane Theatre, London. His own plays included *Love's Last Shift* (1696) and the anti-Jacobite *The Nonjuror* (1717). He was made Poet Laureate in 1730.

Clare, John (1793–1864), poet. He was born in Helpstone, Northamptonshire, the son of a labourer. He published *Poems Descriptive of Rural Life and Scenery* (1820), *The Village Minstrel* (1821), *The Shepherd's Calendar* (1827) and *The Rural Muse* (1835). He entered an asylum in Epping in 1837, and after escaping from there was confined in the Northampton Asylum from 1841 until his death.

Clarke, Samuel (1675–1729), theologian. He was educated at Cambridge, and became a follower of Isaac Newton. He gave the Boyle Lectures in 1704–5: *On the Being and Attributes of God*. His *Scripture-Doctrine of the Trinity* (1712) was a significant contribution to the debates about the Trinity, and he was accused of Arianism. He edited Homer's *Iliad* in 1729. He held several posts in the Church, becoming rector of St James's, Westminster in 1709.

Clive, Robert (1725–74), English colonial administrator and soldier. He was born in Shropshire and joined the East India Company in Madras in 1744. During the Anglo-French conflict he became a hero, seizing the city of Arcot in 1751. He moved to Bengal in 1756, and defeated the French at the battle of Plassey in 1757. In 1760 he came back to England and was promoted to the Irish peerage. In 1765 he was made Governor of Bengal and he established the East India Company as the main political force of the region. He returned to England in 1767, and was politically active. He was acquitted of corruption in India before parliamentary committees in 1772. He committed suicide.

Cobbett, William (1762–1835), radical journalist and writer. He was born in Surrey, joined the army in 1784, and was active in Nova Scotia. When he came back to England in 1791 Cobbett tried to expose the financial corruption in the army, and was forced to flee. He settled in America, defending the British cause in the French wars. He returned to England in 1800 as a Tory. But his suspicion of 'the system' led him to agitate for political reform. His *Political Register* (begun in 1802) was a vehicle for his radical ideas. Cobbett's *Rural Rides*, accounts of his tours through England, where he savaged the landowning classes, was published in 1830. He was elected MP for Oldham in 1833.

Coke, Thomas William, 1st Earl of Leicester 'Coke of Norfolk' (1754–1842), agricultural improver. He was educated at Eton, went on the Grand Tour and inherited in 1776. Coke was MP for Norfolk from 1776 to 1806 and between 1807 and 1832, and he supported parliamentary reform. His agricultural improvements included pioneering the 'Norfolk rotation', which encouraged a more intensive land-use by abandoning the fallow period, and he was the first to grow wheat instead of rye in the region. His interest in agricultural reform was, however, anticipated by his predecessors.

Coleridge, Samuel Taylor (1772–1834), Romantic poet and philosopher. He was born at Ottery St Mary, Devon, the son of a clergyman. He was educated at Christ's Hospital and Cambridge. The *Lyrical Ballads* (1798) which he wrote with Wordsworth, included his 'Rime of the Ancient Mariner'. He also wrote political journalism (*The Friend*, 1809–1810). Coleridge became interested in radical literary and political criticism, influenced by German philosophy, publishing *Biographia Literaria* (1817), *Aids to Reflection* (1825) and *On the Constitution of Church and State* (1829).

Collier, Jeremy (1650–1726), non-juring clergyman. He was educated at Ipswich and Cambridge, was lecturer at Gray's Inn, London from 1685, and published pamphlets against William III between 1688 and 1693. He publicly absolved on the scaffold two of those executed for the assassination plot on William in 1696. His *A Short View of the Immorality and Prophaness of the English Stage* appeared in 1698. He became a minister to a non-juring congregation in London, was consecrated a non-juring bishop in 1713, and he himself ordained bishops after 1716. His office for communion produced a schism within the non-jurors from 1718.

Collier, Mary (flourished 1740–60), poet. She described herself as a 'washer woman' in her *The Woman's Labour* (1739), which was a reply to Stephen Duck's *The Thresher's Labour*. Her *Poems on Several Occasions* was published in 1762.

Collingwood, Cuthbert, 1st Baron (1750–1810). He was born in Newcastle-Upon-Tyne, and entered the navy in 1761. He was a close friend of Nelson. He was present at the naval battles of 'The Glorious First of June', 1794, Cape St Vincent, 1797, and at Trafalgar, 1805, when he took command after Nelson's death.

Collins, William (1721–1759), poet. He was the son of a prosperous Chichester hatter, and was educated at Winchester and Oxford. He wrote his *Persian Eclogues*, which he later published in 1742, while he was at school. After leaving Oxford in 1743 he moved in London literary circles. His *Odes on Several Descriptive and Allegorical Subjects* appeared in 1746. He left London in the early 1750s in a state of ill-health and depression. He died in Chichester.

Colquhoun, Patrick (1745–1820), magistrate and business man. He was born in Dundee, and was city magistrate in London from 1792 to 1818. He was interested in poor relief and social policy. His *New and Appropriate System of Education for the Labouring People* (1806) aimed at eradicating poverty. His *Wealth, Power and Resources of the British Empire* (1814) gave estimates of the national income.

Combe, William (1741–1823), satirical poet. He was educated at Eton, travelled in France and Italy, and on his return to London compiled and translated travels and histories for the booksellers from 1774 to 1821. He had a hit with *The Diaboliad* (1776), but was best known for his *Tours of Dr Syntax* (1812, 1820 and 1821), which satirised the contemporary vogue for the picturesque.

Congreve, William (1670–1729), dramatist and poet. Born in Ireland, he was educated at Kilkenny school and Trinity College, Dublin. His best known plays were the comedies *The Old Batchelour* (1695), *The Double Dealer* (1693), *Love for Love* (1695) and *The Way of the World* (1700).

Constable, John (1776–1837), English landscape painter. He was born at East Bergholt, Suffolk, the son of a miller. He studied at the Royal Academy schools in London and began to paint portraits, but after 1802 devoted himself to painting landscape and nature. He also painted two altar-pieces, *Christ Blessing Little Children* (for Brantham church, 1804) and *Christ Blessing the Bread and Wine* (Nayland church, 1809). In 1819 he was elected an associate of the Royal Academy and exhibited his *A Scene on the River Stour*. His *The Hay Wain* (1821) was very well received in France, where it was exhibited in 1824.

Cook, James 'Captain Cook' (1728–1779), explorer. He was born in Yorkshire, the son of an agricultural labourer, and, after an apprenticeship where he was taught navigation, he entered the navy in 1746. In 1763 he was the surveyor of HMS *Newfoundland*, and in 1768 he was the leader of the expedition in the *Endeavour*, taking scientists to observe the transit of Venus on Tahiti. He then circumnavigated and charted New Zealand, and discovered the eastern coast of Australia. His second voyage, 1772–75, disproved the myth of the Southern Continent, and he discovered Tonga and the New Hebrides. His final voyage, from 1776, was to search for the north-west passage to the Pacific. He discovered the Hawaiian Islands, and was killed by natives there.

Coram, Thomas (1668–1751) sea-captain and philanthropist. He helped to found the colony of Georgia. His major achievement was the establishment in 1739 of the Foundling Hospital, London, for abandoned children.

Cornwallis, Charles, 2nd Earl of (1738–1805), soldier. He was active in the American War of Independence, leading the British forces in South Carolina. His troops were forced to surrender at Yorktown in 1781, signalling the loss of the colonies. From 1786 to 1793 he was Governor-General of Bengal. In 1798 Cornwallis became Lord Lieutenant of Ireland, helping to put down the 1798 rebellion. He died in India.

Cotman, John Sell (1782–1842), landscape painter. He was born in Norwich, going to London in 1798 to study. In 1807 he settled in Norwich, and became President of the Norwich society of artists in 1811. Cotman visited Normandy to make architectural studies in 1817–19, and in 1834 became Professor of Drawing at King's College, London. His best known work was probably *Greta Bridge* (1805).

Cowper, William (1731–1800), poet. He was born in Berkhampsted and was educated at Westminster and the Middle Temple. In 1754 he was called to the Bar. He suffered from depression and attempted suicide. He spent some time in a mental hospital, and in 1765 went to live with the Unwin family at Huntingdon. In 1767 Cowper moved to Olney with Mrs Unwin. With John Newton (1725–1807), an evangelical, he wrote the *Olney Hymns* (1779). His most famous poem was *The Task* (1785).

Crabbe, George (1754–1832), poet and clergyman. He was born in Aldburgh, Suffolk, the son of a customs warehouse keeper. After some initial medical training, he went to London, where he was acquainted with some of the leading literary figures of the day. Crabbe took holy orders in 1781, and became the domestic chaplain to the Duke of Rutland before receiving further preferment. His *The Village* (1783) was a grim portrayal of rural poverty. He published *The Borough* in 1807. He was rector of Trowbridge from 1814.

Crompton, Samuel (1753–1827), inventor of the 'mule', which was a spinning-machine used in the cotton industry. He was born in Bolton, the son of a farmer. He perfected his design in 1779.

Crowley, Sir Ambrose (1658–1713), industrialist. He was born in Worcestershire, the son of Quaker parents. After settling in London he set up an iron foundry in Sunderland. He moved his business to Winlaton, just outside Newcastle-Upon-Tyne in 1691. His business expanded greatly during the wars between 1689 and 1713. He was knighted in 1707.

Cumberland, William Augustus, 1st Duke of (1721–65). He was the second son of the future George II. He fought at the battle of Dettingen, and was made captain-general of the British army in 1745. He suppressed the Jacobite rebellion of 1745–46, with the victory at Culloden. He was nicknamed 'the Butcher' for his savage treatment of the Highlanders.

Dalton, John (1766–1844), chemist. He was born in Manchester. He ran a Quaker school from 1778, and from 1794 he was employed by the Manchester Literary and Philosophical Society. He gave lectures at the Royal Institution, London, 1803–4. Dalton pioneered the atomic table, and his *A New System of Chemical Philosophy* was published in 1808.

Dampier, William (1651–1715), seaman, pirate and writer. He participated in the Anglo-Dutch war of 1674, and from 1679 pillaged Spain's interests in South America. The return voyage in 1683 took in Australia. His *A New Voyage Round the World* (1697) revitalised interest in the Pacific, and stimulated his second voyage to Western Australia and New Guinea in 1699.

Darby, Abraham (1698–1717), industrialist. The son of a Quaker farming family from Worcestershire, he entered the malt-mill making trade. In 1709 he leased a furnace in Coalbrookdale, Shropshire, establishing the iron industry in the region. The Iron Bridge at Broseley was made by the family business in 1779.

Darwin, Erasmus (1731–1802), scientist and poet. He was educated at Cambridge and Edinburgh universities, and practised as a physician in the West Midlands. His major work *Zoonomia* (1794–96) classified diseases in terms of their physiological functions. His poem *The Botanic Garden* (1789–91) attempted to combine science and art. He was one of the founders of the Birmingham Lunar Society (1775), and of the Derby Philosophical Society (1783).

Dashwood, Francis (1708–81), dilettante. He had a notorious life on the Continent, and on his return he was a leading figure in the Society of Dilettanti, founded in 1736, and in the Hell-Fire club ('Medenham Monks'), which he established in 1755.

Davy, Sir Humphry (1778–1829), chemist. He was born in Cornwall, and spent some time in Bristol, where he met others interested in science. In 1801 he took up an appointment at the Royal Institution. He invented the 'Davy Lamp' in 1815 and in 1820 he became President of the Royal Society.

De Quincey, Thomas (1785–1859), author. He was educated at schools in Bath and Manchester before going to Oxford. There he began taking opium. His *Confessions of an English Opium Eater* was published in 1822. He knew the leading Romantic poets and published his 'Recollections of the Lake Poets' in *Tait's Magazine* in 1834. He was interested in German metaphysics. His *The Logic of Political Economy* was published in 1844.

Defoe, Daniel (*c*. 1660–1731), writer. He was born in London, although the precise date of his birth is unclear. Defoe was educated at a dissenting academy, and was an apologist for William III's regime with *The True-Born Englishman* (1701). His *The Shortest Way with the Dissenters* (1702), which satirised extreme High-Church views, landed him in gaol. He wrote government propaganda for Robert Harley, notably *The Review*. His *Robinson Crusoe* (1719), *A Journal of the Plague Year* (1722), *Moll Flanders* (1722) and *Roxana* (1724) have been seen as significant precursors of the novel. His *A Tour thro' the Whole Island of Great Britain* (1724–26) was a land-mark in British travel writing.

Delany, Mary (1700–88), letter writer. She was the daughter of a prominent West Country Tory family. She was sent to Court at an early age, but the death of Queen Anne dashed the family's hopes. Her first marriage in 1718 was to a wealthy landowner who was nearly 60. After his death in 1725 she settled in London and travelled to Ireland, where she met Swift. In 1743 she married Dr Patrick Delany, Dean of Down. When he died in 1768, she settled in London, becoming a member of the Blue-Stocking Circle. She knew the royal family.

Dennis, John (1657–1734), literary critic. He was educated at Cambridge, and in 1705 was made royal waiter in the port of London. Dennis wrote several tragedies, including *Appius and Virginia* (1709). He defended the theatre against the criticisms of Jeremy Collier and William Law. His critical works included *The Advancement and Reformation of Modern Poetry* (1701), *Three Letters on Shakespeare* (1711) and *Remarks on the Fable of the Bees* (1724).

Derham, William (1667–1735), clergyman and scientist. He was educated at Oxford, took holy orders, and became Vicar of Wargrave in 1682 and of Upminster in 1689. He gave the Boyle lectures in 1713 which were published as *Physico-Theology*, and his *Astro-Theology* (1715) championed the argument from design.

Desaguliers, John Theophilus (1683–1744), scientist and pioneer of popular science lectures. He was born in La Rochelle, and came to England with his father, who was a Huguenot refugee. Desaguliers was educated at Cambridge and became a follower of Newton, whose ideas he popularised with a series of public experiments. He invented the planetarium and published works on physics, astronomy and mechanics.

Devonshire, Georgiana, Duchess of (1757–1806). She was the eldest daughter of the 1st Earl Spencer. She was well travelled, and in 1774 married the 5th Duke of Devonshire. She was committed to the Whig cause, and campaigned on behalf of Charles James Fox in the 1784 election. She was a heavy gambler, and wrote poetry and letters, which were later published.

Dodd, William (1729–77), clergyman. He was educated at Cambridge, and became chaplain at the Magdalen House 'for penitent prostitutes' in 1758. He wrote the popular *The Beauties of Shakespeare* in 1752 and was the editor of *The Christian Magazine* from 1760 to 1767. He became a royal chaplain. In 1777 he forged a bond for £4,200 in the name of Lord Chesterfield, his former pupil. He was hanged, despite petitions written on his behalf, including one from Samuel Johnson.

Doddridge, Philip (1702–51), nonconformist minister and hymn writer. He was the twentieth child of a prosperous London merchant. He resisted offers to become ordained with the Church of England and became a nonconformist minister. He ran a dissenting academy at Market Harborough between 1725 and 1729, and in 1729 opened one at Northampton. Doddridge attempted to break down divisions within nonconformity and between nonconformity and the Established Church. His publications included *Free Thoughts on the Most Probable Means of Reviving the Dissenting Interest* (1730) and *On The Rise and Progress of Religion in the Soul* (1745). He wrote hymns, including 'Hark the Glad Sound, thy Saviour comes' and 'O God of Bethel, by whose Hand!' He died in Lisbon.

Dodington, George Bubb, Lord Melcombe (1691–1762), politician. He was born George Bubb, the son of an MP. Educated at Winchester and Oxford, he was elected MP for Winchelsea in 1715. In 1720 he inherited a fortune and Eastbury Park (a Vanbrugh mansion) from his uncle, and took his name. He was MP for Bridgewater between 1722 and 1754. From 1722 to 1740 he was a Lord of the Treasury, but joined the Prince of Wales in opposition in 1740. He was appointed Treasurer of the Navy by Pelham in 1744, again siding with the Prince in 1749. In 1754 he became MP for Weymouth. He was given a peerage in 1761. He was a friend of Voltaire.

Dryden, John (1631–1700), poet. From a moderately wealthy landowning family, he was educated at Westminster and Cambridge. He wrote on Cromwell's death in *Heroic Stanzas* (1658), and extolled the Restoration regime in *Astrea Redux* (1660), *To his Sacred Majesty* (1661) and *Annus Mirabilis* (1667). He was made Poet Laureate in 1668 and Historiographer Royal in 1670. His *Absalom and Achitophel* (1681) supported the monarchy during the Exclusion Crisis. His religious writings included *Religio Laici* (1681), in defence of the Church of England, and his *The Hind and the Panther* (1687), written after he had converted to Catholicism. In 1688 he was dismissed from his court posts, but wrote plays and translations from classical writers.

Duck, Stephen (1705–56), 'the thresher poet'. He was a Wiltshire labourer, whose attempts at poetry caught the attention of Queen Caroline. She made him Yeoman of the Guard in 1733. His *Poems on Several Occasions*, which included his 'The Thresher's Labour', was published in 1736. He became ordained and was made Rector of Byfleet in 1753. He drowned himself.

Dundas, Henry, 1st Viscount Melville (1742–1811), politician. The son of Lord Arniston, he was educated at Edinburgh, becoming Solicitor-General for Scotland in 1766 and MP for Midlothian from 1774 to 1790. He carried the resolution that Warren Hastings should be recalled from India. He was MP for Edinburgh from 1790 to 1802, and was Home Secretary from 1791 to 1794. In 1806 he was impeached for corruption in office, was found guilty of negligence, but acquitted.

Dunning, John, 1st Baron Ashburton (1731–83), lawyer and politician. He defended the East India Company against the Dutch in 1762, was Solicitor-General from 1768 to 1770 and MP for Calne in 1768 and from 1770 to 1782. He is famous for his resolution of 1780 that 'the influence of the Crown has increased, is increasing, and ought to be diminished'. His *Inquiry into the Doctrines lately promulgated concerning Juries, Libels etc* was published in 1764.

Edgeworth, Maria (1768–1849), novelist and educational writer. She was born at Black Bourton, Oxfordshire, the daughter of a politically liberal and enlightened man, who had helped found the Lunar Society. She moved with her family to Ireland in 1782, where she settled. She was her father's amanuensis and helped him run his estate. She defended female education in her *Letters for Literary Ladies* (1795) and, with her father, published in 1798 *Practical Education*, which was heavily reliant on the theories of Rousseau. Her novels, which were generally great successes, included *Castle Rackrent* (1800), *Belinda* (1801), *Patronage* (1814), which was arguably the most commercially successful novel of the day, and *Helen* (1834). Also with her father, she published *Irish Bulls* (1802), which was a defence of the Irish dialect.

Edwards, Jonathan (1703–58), American theologian and philosopher. He was born in East Windsor, Connecticut, and educated at Yale. In 1727 he succeeded his grandfather as minister of the congregationalist church at Northampton, Mass., where his preaching of hard-line Calvinism helped to inspire the 'Great Awakening'. In 1750 Edwards was dismissed from his post for expousing too rigid a doctrine, and he became a missionary to the Housatonnuck Indians at Stockbridge, Mass. He was made president of the College of New Jersey (Princeton) in 1757. His principal work was *Careful and Strict Enquiry into the Modern Prevailing Notions of the Freedom of the Will* (1754).

Elstob, Elizabeth (1683–1756), Anglo-Saxon scholar. She was born in Newcastle-Upon-Tyne, the daughter of a merchant. Her father died in 1688, and after being brought up by her uncle, she went to live in London with her brother William, a clergyman and scholar. She began to publish her own studies. After William's death in 1715 she retired in debt to Evesham. She was eventually supported by a number of subscribers, including Queen Caroline and the Duchess of Portland, who made her governess to her children in 1738. Her publications included Aelfric's *An Anglo-Saxon Homily* (1709) and *Rudiments of Grammar for the English Tongue* (1715).

Erskine, John, 11th Earl of Mar (1675–1732), Jacobite leader. He inherited his estates in 1688, and became a supporter of William III's court in 1696. He backed the Union of England and Scotland of 1707, and was made Secretary of State for Scotland and Keeper of the Signet. In 1713, however, he endorsed a motion in the House of Lords for the repeal of the Union. He proclaimed his allegiance to George I in 1714, but went to Scotland and raised James III's standard at Braemar, marching on Perth. He had a large following, but lack of resolution meant that the rebellion was a failure. He went with James to France. But he soon began intriguing against James, and betrayed Atterbury to the British government in 1722. Mar was known as 'Bobbing John' for so frequently changing sides. He lived out his life in France, trusted by no one.

Erskine, Thomas (1750–1823), lawyer. He was the son of the Earl of Buchan, and after serving in the navy and army, he went up to Cambridge and was called to the Bar in 1778. He rose to eminence as counsel for the defence in the trials of Baillie, Stockdale and Paine's *The Rights of Man*. Erskine was MP for Portsmouth, 1783 and 1790–1806, and Lord Chancellor, 1806–7. He defended Queen Caroline in 1820, protested against the Corn Law Bill of 1822, and worked for the cause of Greek Independence, 1822–23.

Fell, Margaret (1614–1702), Quaker polemicist. She was born in Lancashire and married Thomas Fell, a lawyer, in 1632, who died in 1658. They lived at Swarthmore Hall. She met George Fox in 1652 and converted to Quakerism. She was imprisoned for her beliefs from 1664 to 1668 and married Fox in 1669. Her writings include *A Declaration . . . to the King* (1660), *Women's Speaking Justified . . . by the Scriptures* (1666) and *An Epistle against uniform Quaker Costume* (1700).

Fenwick, Sir John (1645–97), Jacobite conspirator. From a Northumberland family, he rose though the army and was elected MP for Northumberland from 1677 until 1685. He put forward the bill of attainder against Monmouth in 1685. After 1688 he plotted against William and Mary. He insulted Queen Mary in 1691 and was involved in plots to kill William III in 1695 and 1696. He was examined by the House of Commons, attainted and beheaded.

Ferguson, Adam (1723–1816), Scottish social philosopher. He was born in Perthshire, and educated at St Andrews. He became deputy chaplain of the Black Watch regiment and fought at the battle of Fontenoy. He left the Church in 1754 and became librarian to the Edinburgh faculty of advocates. He was professor of natural philosophy at Edinburgh from 1759, and in 1764 took the chair in moral philosophy. His works included *An Essay on the History of Civil Society* (1767), *A History of the Progress and Termination of the Roman Republic* (1783) and *Principles of Moral and Political Science* (1792).

Fielding, Henry (1707–54), writer and magistrate. He was born in Somerset, into a gentry family, and educated at Eton and Leyden, where he studied law. He settled in London and made a reputation as the author of comic plays. His play *Love in Several Masques* (1728) was a success, as was *Tom Thumb* (1730). His anti-Walpole satires provoked the Licensing Act of 1737, after which plays had to be censored by the Lord Chamberlain. Fielding returned to the law, and was called to the Bar in 1740. He now combined the roles of lawyer, magistrate and writer. He was JP for Bow Street from 1748, where he attempted to reduce crime and disorder. His novels included *Shamela* (1741), which was a skit on Richardson's *Pamela*, *Joseph Andrews* (1742), *Tom Jones* (1749) and *Amelia* (1751). His *Journal of a Voyage to Lisbon*, published posthumously in 1755, charted his last trip to Lisbon, where he died, in pursuit of health.

Fielding, Sir John (d. 1780), magistrate. He was the half-brother of Henry and Sarah Fielding. Fielding was blind from birth and carried on the plans of Henry Fielding to break up robber-gangs in London. He proposed a scheme for sending 'distressed boys' into the navy (1755), and published pamphlets with plans for rescuing deserted girls (1758). Fielding was lampooned for asking David Garrick to suppress performances of *The Beggar's Opera* in 1773.

Fielding, Sarah (1710–68), novelist. She was born in East Stour, Dorset, the daughter of a landed family and the sister of Henry. She attended boarding school in Salisbury and later learned Latin and Greek. In the 1740s she lived in London. She wrote her first novel, *David Simple* (1744), because of financial difficulties. Her other novels include *The Governess* (1749) a book for children, *Cleopatra and Octavia* (1757), *The Countess of Dellwyn* (1759) and *Ophelia* (1760). Her *Memoirs of Socrates* (1762) was a translation from Xenophon.

Fiennes, Celia (1662–1741), travel writer. She was born near Salisbury, the daughter of Puritan parents. Her grandfather was Viscount Say and Sele, who had opposed Charles I. She visited Bath *c.* 1687 and settled in London about 1691. Her travel writings date from 1685 to 1703. She toured the North and Kent in 1697, and most of the rest of the country in 1702–3. The accounts of her travels were first published as *Through England on a Side Saddle in the time of William and Mary* (1888).

Finch, Daniel, 2nd Earl of Nottingham (1647–1730), politician. He was educated at Westminster and Oxford. He opposed the 'Exclusion' and was Commissioner of the Admiralty from 1681 to 1684. He was regarded as a leader of the High-Church Tories, and although he distrusted James II's romanising tendencies, he only aligned with William when James deserted. He became Secretary of State and was largely responsible for the Toleration Act. Losing office in 1693, he was Secretary again 1702–4, where he promoted a bill against occasional conformity. He was made Lord President in 1714, but dismissed in 1716.

Flaxman, John (1755–1826), sculptor, illustrator and designer. He was the son of a plasterer and studied at the Royal Society schools. He worked for Wedgwood before travelling to Italy between 1787 and 1794, where he produced his illustrations for the *Iliad* and the *Odyssey*. His monuments commemorating Lord Mansfield in Westminster Abbey and Nelson in St Paul's are his most famous works. He was appointed the Royal Academy's first Professor of Sculpture in 1810.

Fox, Charles James (1749–1806), politician. The third son of Henry Fox, he was educated at Eton and Oxford, and became MP for Midhurst in 1768, when still technically under-age. He represented the constituency until 1774 and was MP for Malmesbury, 1774–80, and for Westminster, 1780–1806. After holding a minor government office, he sided with the opposition and was a critic of British policy towards America and a supporter of parliamentary reform. He became Foreign Secretary under Rockingham in 1782 but resigned during the peace proposals with America of 1783. He sided now with North, whom he had previously attacked. They tried to reform the East India Company, but when the India bill was defeated, they were replaced by Pitt. During George III's illness in 1788, Fox hoped that the Prince of Wales would back him. When the King recovered, Fox was widely blamed for meddling. He was delighted with the outbreak of the French Revolution in 1789 but his constant opposition of war lost him many of his supporters. In 1804 George III vetoed Fox becoming Foreign Secretary. He was finally given the post in 1806. He was a heavy gambler and notorious womaniser.

Fox, Henry (1705-74), politician. He joined Parliament in 1735 as MP for Hindon, and he represented Windsor from 1741 to 1761. He was backed by Walpole and by Pelham, becoming Secretary at War in 1746. He was not trusted by the Duke of Newcastle, and he made an unimpressive Secretary of State in 1755-56. After the coalition between Newcastle and the elder Pitt in 1757, Fox was granted the highly financially advantageous but politically marginal post of Paymaster-General. In 1762-63 he was given the task of steering the 1763 Peace of Paris through the Commons, which he did by sacking from office most of Newcastle's supporters. He was made Lord Holland in 1763. His secret marriage to Lady Georgiana Lennox in 1744 was the social scandal of the day.

Francis, Philip (1740-1818), probable author of the 'Junius Letters'. He was a clerk in the war office when 69 anonymous letters were written to the *Public Advertiser* between 1769 and 1772. These attacked some of the leading ministers of the day, and even the king.

Franklin, Benjamin (1706-90), American statesman and scientist. Born in Boston, Mass., he was early on involved in the management of his brother's newspaper, the *New England Courant*. Franklin then worked as a printer in Philadelphia, and was in London from 1724-1726. In 1732 he began publishing *Poor Richard's Almanac*, which reached unprecedented circulation. In 1746 Franklin started his researches into electricity, proving that lightning and electricity are identical, and advocating the use of lightning-conductors to safeguard buildings. He was sent to England in 1757 to insist upon the right of the province to tax the proprietors of land held under the Penn charter for the cost of defending it from the French and Indians. During this visit, Franklin was awarded honorary degrees from Oxford and Edinburgh universities. In 1764 he visited England again to contest Parliament's right to tax the American colonies without representation. He returned to America in 1775, and participated in debates leading up to the Declaration of Independence. He was in Paris from 1776 enlisting French aid for the American cause, and was the United States' minister in Paris until 1785. Franklin was President of the State of Pennsylvania, and a delegate to the convention which framed the constitution of the USA.

Fraser, Simon, 12th Baron Lovat (?1667–1747), Jacobite. He was educated at Aberdeen. After family intrigues, whereby he sought to obtain the estates of his cousin Lord Lovat by making Lovat's dowager marry him, he succeeded to the title in 1699. He had been outlawed for treason in 1698, but was pardoned by William in 1700. In the same year he had visited James III in France, and had settled there by 1702, having again been outlawed because of his behaviour to Lady Lovat. He pretended to have converted to Roman Catholicism, promising Louis XIV support in an invasion on Scotland. He rallied his clan in 1715, but was pardoned. He was made sheriff of Inverness, but was deprived of the office in 1737 because of his links with Prince Charles. In 1745 he was arrested, despite not giving the Prince much support. He was beheaded.

Frederick Lewis, Prince of Wales (1707–51). He was the eldest son of George II and was born and brought up in Hanover, only coming to England in 1728. He spent much of his time rowing with his parents and during the 1730s became involved with the opposition politicians. He married Augusta of Saxe-Coburg in 1736, and when George II denied him a fixed income he fell out with his father and was effectively exiled from court. He set up a rival centre of influence at Leicester House, which was a major meeting-place for the opponents of Walpole. He played a part in Walpole's downfall in 1742, and from then until 1747, when the Prince became associated with the Tories, relations with his father were less strained. The 'Leicester House' group in Parliament collapsed when he died.

Fry, Elizabeth (1780–1845), reformer. She was born near Norwich, the daughter of the banking and Quaker Gurney family. She married Joseph Fry, a Quaker banker, in 1800 and went to live in London. Her sister's husband, Thomas Fowell Buxton, was an advocate of prison reform, and by 1813 she had begun visiting Newgate prison. In 1817 she established an association to relieve women prisoners. She spoke before the 1818 parliamentary committee inquiry into London's prisons, urging that useful work be found for prisoners. She showed compassion for female convicts transported to Australia. By 1828 she had become interested in hospitals and the insane. She visited France in 1838, reporting on the state of the prisons, and made similar visits to Switzerland, Southern Germany, the Netherlands and Denmark.

Fuseli, Henry [Johann Heinrich Fussli] (1741–1825), painter and writer. He was born in Zurich, was ordained and went to Berlin. In 1763 he was brought to England by Sir Andrew Mitchell, where he helped create an interest in the German *Sturm und Drang* movement. His translation of Winckelmann's *The Painting and Sculpture of the Greeks* was published in 1765. He developed his interest in painting, and was in Rome between 1770 and 1778. His paintings include *The Nightmare* (1782) and several works, including *Titania and Bottom*, for Boydell's Shakespeare Gallery. He was Professor of Painting at the Royal Academy from 1799 to 1825.

Gainsborough, Thomas (1727–1788), landscape and portrait painter. He was born in Sudbury, Suffolk, and studied in London from 1740 to 1748, where he was taught by Hogarth, Hayman and others. He worked as a portrait painter in Ipswich during the 1750s and in Bath from 1760 until 1764. The works he produced in this period, such as the *Blue Boy*, were influenced by the paintings of Van Dyck (1559–1641). He was elected a founder member of the Royal Academy in 1768, and moved permanently to London in 1774. He won the patronage of the royal family, of aristocrats, and of leading politicians. His early *Mr and Mrs Andrews* (1749) is significant in that the landscape of their estate is given as much attention as the sitters.

Garrick, David (1717–79), actor, manager and dramatist. He was born in Hereford and studied at Samuel Johnson's school near Lichfield. He went to London with Johnson in 1737 and in 1741 made a name for his performance as Richard III. In 1747 he became co-manager of the Drury Lane Theatre and he was concerned to reform both the plays and their audiences. He visited France and Italy from 1763 to 1765. In 1769 he organised the Shakespeare Jubilee at Stratford. He retired in 1776. Garrick published *An Essay on Acting* in 1744.

Gay, John (1685–1732), dramatist and poet. He was born at Barnstaple, of a dissenting family, and was apprenticed to a London silk-mercer. His earliest poems included *Rural Sports* (1713) and *The Shepherd's Week* (1714). He formed the Scriblerus Club with Pope, Arbuthnot and Swift. His *Trivia* (1715) was a skit on life in London. He was given the post of commissioner of the English state lottery. His *The Beggar's Opera* (1728), a musical drama which blended political satire and popular songs, was a sensation. It was produced at Lincoln's Inn Fields by John Rich, allegedly making 'Gay rich and Rich gay'. The sequel *Polly* (1729) was banned by the Lord Chamberlain.

George I (1660–1727). The eldest son of Ernest Augustus, Elector of Hanover, and Sophia, granddaughter of James I, he succeeded to the

British throne in August 1714. He was already known to the Whigs on account of their joint antagonism to the Tory peace with France at Utrecht in 1713. On his accession, he backed a majority of Whig MPs, which has been seen as crucial in establishing five decades of 'Whig supremacy', and the few Tories he supported were dismissed after the 1715 Jacobite rebellion. He was particularly interested in foreign affairs, actively participating in the Quadruple Alliance of 1718, and in maintaining control over the army. He favoured his German advisers, largely because of his limited use of English, but he was more active in politics than traditional interpretations of his reign have implied. As was to become the norm in the eighteenth-century royal family, George's relations with his eldest son (the future George II) were tense, and in 1717 the Prince was banned from court, and established a rival one at Leicester House. For a time this attracted opposition politicians such as Walpole and Townshend who had quarrelled with Stanhope and Sunderland. The 'South Sea Bubble' of 1720 could have been an enormous ministerial crisis, but was averted by Walpole, who salvaged the potential disaster, and who, after 1722 became leading minister despite his previous flirtation with the opposition. Although the King went back to Hanover only seven times, his supposed prioritisation of the electorate over British interests was frequently commented upon. He was generally sympathetic to Enlightenment thought, promoting toleration in religion, encouraging inoculation against small-pox, and endowing regius professorships at Oxford and Cambridge to encourage the study of modern history, diplomacy and languages. George died at Osnabruck.

George II (1683–1760). He was born in Herrenhausen. He acquired a reputation as a courageous soldier, and in 1708 he fought as a British ally in the War of the Spanish Succession. On his accession in 1727, his favoured minister, Spencer Compton, was unable to obtain an adequate civil list, which made it possible for Walpole to become the King's chief minister. George was persuaded by Walpole to refrain from becoming involved in the War of the Polish Succession (1733–37). The King's visits to Hanover (twelve times during his reign) aroused criticisms that he subordinated British interests to that of the electorate. During the War of the Austrian Succession in 1741 he broke with his allies and declared Hanover neutral, without consulting his ministers in Britain. George led the troops, the last British monarch so to do, at the battle of Dettingen (1743). Modern scholarship has demonstrated that the king was more in control over politics than has usually been allowed, and in major decisions he had the ultimate say. Although devoted to his wife, Queen Caroline, he took a number of mistresses, and after Caroline's death in 1737, Lady Dartmouth was the chief object of his affections. His relations with his elder son, Prince Frederick, were severely strained, leading the Prince to be effectively exiled from the court for much of the 1730s and parts of the 1740s. George got on better with his younger son, the Duke of Cumberland, who shared his love of the military.

George III (1738–1820). The son of Frederick Lewis, Prince of Wales, he was the first Hanoverian monarch to be born in England, becoming Prince of Wales in 1751, on his father's death. From 1755 George's tutor was Lord Bute. Historians have debated how far Bute influenced the young Prince with ideas of monarchical superiority and with attempting to increase the royal prerogative over the politicians. What is certain is that when George became King in 1760, Bute was quickly advanced to political office, and became Prime Minister from 1762 to 1763. From 1763 until 1770, when Lord North became the leading minister, there were four premiers, the instability being created in part by the suspicion that Bute was the effective power behind the throne. During North's term of office, ministerial stability was achieved, and the real crisis was relations with America. The Declaration of Independence of 1776 was an attack on the monarch, and George refused to acknowledge that the colonies were lost, even after the defeat at Yorktown in 1781. North was dismissed and the King hoped to achieve more of his wishes, but to no avail, while the North–Fox coalition frustrated the political agenda. The younger Pitt was able to destroy the overthrow of the coalition by defeating, with the King's backing, the India bill of 1783. In 1788 George became ill, and the regency crisis arose because of his apparent madness. Modern research has suggested that the king's illness was due to porphyria, an hereditary metabolic illness. He became almost permanently incapacitated after 1810, and in 1811 a regency was established. George was a sincere Anglican and abided by his coronation oath to support the Protestant religion by opposing Catholic emancipation in 1801, leading to the resignation of Pitt.

George IV (1762–1830), Prince Regent, 1811–20, King, 1820–30. He was the eldest son of George III. On reaching his majority in 1783 he became associated with the Foxite opposition, and although he fell out with them over his secret marriage, they joined forces over the regency crisis of 1788 during George III's illness, where they expected to lead the government once the Prince became regent. During the French Revolution, George hoped to be given a military command, but was thwarted by his father. He broke with the Whigs on Fox's death in 1806, and once he became regent in 1811, the existing Tory ministers were confirmed in office. George became King in 1820 and his magnificent coronation in 1821 helped to boost his popularity, and his visits to Scotland in 1822 and Ireland were well-received public relations exercises. Towards the end of his reign, he was forced to accept the repeal of the

Test and Corporation Acts in 1828 and the granting of emancipation to Catholics in 1829. George's personal life was a farce. In 1785 he secretly married the Catholic widow Maria Fitzherbert, in contravention of the Act of Settlement and the Royal Marriages Act. His marriage in 1795 to Caroline of Brunswick was unhappy, and they separated almost at once. He tried to have her convicted on the grounds of adultery. George was a keen promoter of the arts, and spent large sums building and furnishing Carlton House and Brighton Pavilion.

George, Prince, of Denmark (1653–1708), husband of Queen Anne. He was the younger son of Frederick III of Denmark and, after a military and scientific training, he fought against Sweden in the 1670s. He married Anne in 1683, as part of diplomatic union between England and Denmark against the Dutch. When Anne came to the throne in 1702 he was appointed Lord High Admiral. He was a devoted supporter of his wife, although contemporaries found him a bore. Famously, Charles II observed of him: 'I have tried him drunk and I have tried him sober and there is nothing in him.'

Gibbon, Edward (1737–94), historian. He was the son of a country gentleman and, after 14 months at Oxford, he converted to Catholicism. He was sent by his father to Lausanne in Switzerland, and returned to the Protestant faith. From 1760 to 1762 he was a captain of the Hampshire militia. Having visited Rome in 1764, he began work in 1773 on his *Decline and Fall of the Roman Empire*, published between 1776 and 1788, and which was a triumph of historical scholarship. Gibbon was sympathetic to the *philosophes* and attempted to write secular history. His view that the rise of the Christian religion had destroyed the Roman Empire aroused controversy. In 1774 he was elected to parliament and was given a minor post by Lord North. Gibbon spent most of his last years in Lausanne writing his autobiography, which was published posthumously in 1796 as his *Memoirs*.

Gibbons, Grinling (1648–1721), woodcarver and sculptor. He was born in Rotterdam, the son of a London citizen. Gibbons was in London by 1668 and was taken up by John Evelyn, who introduced him to Christopher Wren and Charles II. He was appointed master carver in wood to Charles II and worked at Windsor Castle, 1677–82, Trinity College Library, Cambridge, 1689–90, Trinity Chapel, Oxford, 1691, St Paul's Cathedral, 1694–97, and Hampton Court, 1701–10. His wood carvings of flowers, fruit, small animals and cherubs were particularly admired.

Gibbs, James (1682–1754), architect. He was born in Aberdeen and was raised as a Roman Catholic. He travelled to Rome in 1703 and spent six years studying under Carlo Fontana. After his return to England, he became surveyor to the 1711 Act for the building of 50 new churches. He held the post of architect of the ordinance from 1727. He designed St Mary le Strand (1714) and St Martin-in-the-Fields (1722–26). He was the architect of the Radcliffe Camera, Oxford, which was finished in 1748. He also designed the Senate House at Cambridge.

Gibson, Edmund (1689–1748), clergyman. He was educated at Oxford, and translated Camden's *Britannia* into English in 1695. During the Convocation controversy, he defended the rights of the Archbishop, and was appointed to the rectory of Lambeth in 1703. His scholarly research into ecclesiastical history and law was published as *Codex Juris Ecclesiae Anglicanae: or the Statutes, Constitutions, Canons, Rubrics, and Articles of the Church of England* (1713). He was made Bishop of Lincoln in 1716, and was moved to London in 1723. He was a 'High-Church Whig' and advised Walpole on Church matters, being nicknamed 'Walpole's Pope'. Their relationship broke down in 1736 after Walpole had supported the Quakers' Tithe bill. In 1737 Gibson was not appointed Archbishop of Canterbury, although many expected him to be so.

Gilbert, Thomas (1720–98), Poor Law reformer. He was the son of a Staffordshire gentleman, and was called to the Bar in 1744. He worked for some time as land agent for Lord Gower. He was elected MP for Newcastle-Under-Lyme from 1763 to 1768 and for Lichfield between 1768 and 1795. Gilbert promoted the 1782 Act which allowed two or more parishes to unite to form poor law unions, and the 1793 Act which permitted clergy to borrow money from Queen Anne's Bounty to build houses which would ensure that they resided in their parishes. Another Act of 1793 encouraged the creation of Friendly Societies.

Gillray, James (1756–1815), caricaturist. He studied at the Royal Academy schools and began his political and social satires in the 1780s. His attacks on leading politicians, the royal family and Napoleon were marked by their detailed and often cruel exaggeration of an individual's dominant features. He became insane in 1810.

Gilpin, William (1724–1804), clergyman and writer on the picturesque. He was born near Carlisle, and educated at Oxford. He kept a school at Cheam and was made Vicar of Boldre in Hampshire from 1777. He wrote lives of various Protestant reformers, and his *Lectures on the Church Catechism* were published in 1779. He was best known, however, for his 'Observations on Picturesque Beauty', which were accounts of his summer tours taken while he was a schoolmaster, and published some years later, notably his *Observations on the river Wye* (1782), his *Observations* on . . . *Cumberland* (1786) and *Observations on the Western parts of England* (1786). His theoretical principles were set out in his *Three Essays: On Picturesque Beauty; On Picturesque Travel; and on Sketching Landscape* (1792).

Godolphin, Sidney Godolphin, 1st Earl of (1645–1712), politician. He was MP for Helston from 1668 to 1679 and for St Mawes from 1679 to 1681. He was made a baron in 1684 and given the earldom in 1706. Although he was a Tory, Godolphin held offices under administrations of a range of political complexions. He was a Lord of the Treasury (1679), Secretary of State for the Northern Department and First Lord of the Treasury (1684–85, 1690–96 and 1700–1). After Queen Anne came to the throne he led the administration with Marlborough (the 'duumvirate') and they were joined from 1704 to 1708 by Robert Harley (the 'triumvirate'). Godolphin was especially successful in raising money to fight wars. He was dismissed from office in 1710.

Godwin, William (1756–1836), novelist and radical political thinker. He was educated at Hoxton dissenting academy and became a dissenting minister. He became an atheist, and argued for the need to act rationally and benevolently without the need of human institutions. In 1797 Godwin married Mary Wollstonecraft; she died at the birth of their daughter Mary (who married Shelley). His second wife was Mrs Clairmont. His *Enquiry Concerning Political Justice*, which argued for the perfectibility of mankind, was published in 1793. Godwin published the novel *The Adventures of Caleb Williams* in 1794, and in the same year wrote *Cursory Strictures*, which defended 12 members of the London Corresponding Society against the charge of high treason. He wrote a life of Mary Wollstonecraft, *Memoirs of the author of a Vindication of the Rights of Woman* (1798), and a novel, *St Leon* (1799), which idealised her. Other novels included *Fleetwood* (1805), *Mandeville* (1817) *Cludesley* (1830) and *Deloraine* (1833).

Goldsmith, Oliver (1730–74), Irish poet, essayist, dramatist and novelist. He was born in Ireland, the son of a clergyman, and educated at Trinity College, Dublin. He studied medicine at Edinburgh and Leyden, and spent 1755–56 in Europe. Goldsmith settled in England and began earning a living as a writer for the periodical press, initially for *The Monthly Review* and *The Critical Review*. He produced his own periodical, *The Bee*, in 1759. *The Citizen of the World* (1760–62), a collection of essays, was highly successful, as were his poems *The Traveller* (1764) and *The Deserted Village* (1770). His popular novel, *The Vicar of Wakefield*, appeared in 1766, and his most successful play was *She Stoops to Conquer* (1773). Goldsmith also wrote histories of Rome (1769), England (1771) and Greece (1773).

Gordon, Lord George (1751–93), politician. He was the third son of the 3rd Duke of Gordon, and was elected to Parliament in 1774. Gordon was President of the Protestant Association and in 1780 he presented a petition attacking concessions to Catholics. After a six-day riot, Gordon was tried, and then acquitted for treason. He later converted to Judaism and, having been convicted of libel, ended his life in Newgate prison.

Grafton, Augustus Henry Fitzroy, 3rd Duke of (1735–1811), politician. He was MP for Bury St Edmunds in 1756, and succeeded to the dukedom in 1757. He was Secretary of State for the Northern Department, 1765–66, and nominal head of the 1766 Chatham administration. After Chatham's resignation in 1768, Grafton became Prime Minister until 1770. He was Lord Privy Seal, 1771–75, and again in 1782–83.

Granby, John Manners, Marquis of (1721–70), soldier. He entered Parliament in 1742. Granby was a distinguished soldier who became a popular hero after his role at the battles of Minden (1759) and Warburg (1760). He was Master-General of the Ordnance from 1763, and Commander-in-Chief from 1766.

Grattan, Henry (1746–1820), Irish politician. The son of a recorder of Dublin, he was educated at Trinity College, Dublin, and was called to the Irish Bar in 1772. In 1775 he was elected MP for Charlemont in the Irish House of Commons. He became leader of the patriot group and helped secure Irish legislative independence in 1782. Grattan established the Irish Whig Club in 1790, becoming MP for Dublin. He advocated parliamentary reform and wanted concessions for Catholics. In 1800 he protested against the Act of Union. In 1805 he sat as MP for Malton in the Westminster Parliament, representing Dublin from 1806 to 1820. He was buried in Westminster Abbey.

Gray, Thomas (1716–71), poet. He was born in Cornhill, the son of a scrivener. He was educated at Eton and Cambridge. Having intended to read for the Bar, he travelled to France and Italy with Horace Walpole, from 1739 to 1741. Falling out with Walpole, Gray returned to Cambridge in 1741, where he lived for the rest of his life. His poems include 'Ode on a distant prospect of Eton College', published in 1747. His *Odes* (1757) were not well received. In 1768 he was appointed Professor of History at Cambridge. His 'Elegy Written in a Country Churchyard' (1751) was his most influential poem. He was buried in Stoke Poges.

Grenville, George (1712–70), Prime Minister. The son of Richard Grenville of Wootton Hall, Buckinghamshire, he trained as a lawyer, entering Parliament in 1741 as MP for Buckingham, which he represented for the rest of his life. He was a member of the 'Boy Patriot' group associated with Pitt the elder. He was Treasurer of the Navy from 1756 to 1762. In 1761 he was offered the secretaryship of state, but declined. Grenville became leader of the house, and in 1762 was appointed Secretary of State for the Northern Department, and then First Lord of the Admiralty. In 1763 he was made First Lord of the Treasury. During his term in office, the Stamp Act was passed in 1765, which resulted in hostilities with America, and early proceedings were initiated against John Wilkes.

Grenville, William Wyndham, 1st Baron (1759–1834). The third son of the above. He was educated at Eton and Oxford. He was MP for Buckingham, 1782–84, and for Buckinghamshire, 1784–90. In 1790 he was created 1st Baron Grenville. He was Chief Secretary for Ireland, 1782–83, Paymaster, 1783–89, Vice-President of the Board of Trade, 1786–89, Speaker, 1789, Home Secretary, 1789–90, President of the Board of Control, 1790–93, Foreign Secretary, 1791–1801, and Prime Minister, 1806–7. His time in office saw the abolition of the slave trade. He was also a distinguished classical scholar.

Grey, Charles, 2nd Earl (1764–1845), Prime Minister. He was the son of General Sir Charles Grey of Fallodon, Northumberland and was educated at Eton and Cambridge. Grey was elected MP for Northumberland in 1786. He was a committed Whig, and was instrumental in founding the Association of the Friends of the People in 1792. This helped to split the Whigs in 1794; some siding with Pitt, leaving Grey and Fox to lead the bulk of the party in opposition. In 1798 Grey and others seceded from Parliament on account of Pitt's repressive policies. In 1806, Grey was appointed First Lord of the Admiralty, and became Foreign Secretary at the end of the year. On Fox's death, Grey took over the leadership of the party. In 1807 he succeeded to the peerage, and sat in the Lords. He stood for Catholic emancipation and parliamentary reform. In 1830 Wellington's refusal to countenance reform meant that Grey was asked to form a ministry. The Great Reform Act was Grey's greatest achievement. In 1834 his cabinet split over the Irish Church question and he resigned. He retired to Howick, Northumberland. Grey had a scandalous affair with Georgiana, Duchess of Devonshire, and she had a daughter by him in 1792. He married Mary Ponsonby in 1794.

Halley, Edmond (1656–1742), astronomer. He was educated at St Paul's and Oxford. He travelled to Italy in 1681 and was made Assistant Secretary to the Royal Society and editor of its *Transactions* from 1685 to 1693. He was Deputy Controller of the Mint at Chester from 1696 to 1698, and was appointed Savilian Professor of Geometry at Oxford in 1710 and Astronomer Royal in 1721. He accurately predicted the return in 1758 of the comet of 1456, 1531, 1607 and 1682.

Hamilton, Emma (1765–1815), society figure. She was born Amy Lyon. As a society beauty, she was frequently painted by George Romney. She was first mistress of Sir Harry Fetherstonhaugh, and then from 1782 of Charles Greville. In 1791 she married Sir William Hamilton (1730–1803), the British representative in Naples and Sicily. She was famous for her 'attitudes'. She entertained Nelson's sailors before the battle of the Nile in 1798, and became his mistress. She died in Calais.

Handel, George Frederick (1685–1759), composer. He was born in Halle, Germany, where he became cathedral organist. He travelled in Italy between 1706 and 1710, and composed his 'Dixit Dominus' (1710). He was made Kapellmeister to the Elector of Hanover (the future George I), and came to London in 1710. His opera *Rinaldo* (1711) was a great success, and by 1712 he had settled permanently in England. He composed the *Te Deum* and the *Jubilate* to celebrate the Treaty of Utrecht, and was granted a £200 pension by Queen Anne. George I increased this, and Handel wrote the *Water Music* for him in 1717. He was resident composer to the Duke of Chandos at his country house at Canons, for whom he wrote the *Chandos Anthems* (1717–18). He composed 'Zadok the Priest' for the coronation of George II in 1727, which has been sung at every coronation since. He was appointed music director of the Royal Academy of Music. He composed some operas in the Italian style, notably *Giulio Cesare* (1724) and *Tamerlano* (1724). He developed the English oratorio, beginning with *Esther* in 1732. His *Messiah* was first performed in 1742 and *Judas Maccabaeus* in 1746. His physical condition deteriorated after 1745, but he was able to write the *Music for the Royal Fireworks* (1749) and the oratorios *Theodora* (1750) and *Jephtha* (1751). Handel took English nationality in 1727. He went blind in 1752, but continued to direct concerts until his death.

Hanway, Jonas (1712–86), philanthropist. He was born in Portsmouth, and became apprenticed to a merchant at Lisbon. He lived there for 12 years, and moved to Russia between 1743 and 1750 before returning to England. He supported the Foundling Hospital from 1756, and in the same year founded the Marine Society which helped boys to get a naval career. In 1758 he was involved in setting up the Magdalen hospital for penitent prostitutes. He also promoted Sunday schools and argued against the drinking of tea.

Hargreaves, James (1720–78), inventor. From Lancashire, he was a weaver who invented the spinning jenny in 1764 and patented it in 1770. His house was mobbed in 1768 and he was involved in expensive litigation to protect the patent.

Harley, Robert, 1st Earl of Oxford and Earl Mortimer (1661–1724), politician and bibliophile. He was born in Herefordshire and was elected MP for Tregony, 1689–90, and for New Radnor Boroughs, 1690–1711. He was the leader of the Country Party. In 1702 he was chosen Speaker of the Commons for the third time, and in 1704 took up his appointment as Secretary of State for the Northern Department. He was dismissed in 1708, partly for his growing attachment to the Tory party. Harley exacted revenge on his opponents by gaining Queen Anne's confidence and master-minding the fall of the Marlborough–Godolphin Ministry in 1710. In that year, he took over as Chancellor of the Exchequer, and in 1711 became First Lord of the Treasury. Harley's attempt to create a non-party ministry failed, and he was dismissed from office in 1714. He was impeached by George I in 1715, and imprisoned in the Tower until 1717. Harley's vast collection of manuscripts and printed books formed the core of the British Museum library.

Harris, Howell (1714–73), Welsh Methodist leader. He was born at Trefecca, near Brecon. He went into teaching from 1730, having intended to be ordained in the Church of England. He had a conversion experience in 1735 and after beginning studies at Oxford, returned to Wales. In 1737 he started open-air preaching. He established a Protestant monastery at Trefecca in 1752. He joined the militia in an attempt to combat French Catholicism.

Hartley, David (1705–57), philosopher. He was educated at Cambridge and practised as a physician in Newark, Bury St Edmunds and London. His *Observations on Man* (1749) developed the theory of associationism.

Hastings, Selina, Countess of Huntingdon (1707–91), founder of the Countess of Huntingdon's Connexion and Methodist leader. She was the daughter of Earl Ferrers, marrying in 1728 the Earl of Huntingdon. The lived at Donington Hall, Leicestershire. She was converted to Methodism, becoming a member of the first Methodist society formed in Fetter Lane in 1739. She appointed George Whitefield her chaplain in 1748. When Wesley and Whitefield split in 1749, she sided with Whitefield's more Calvinistic doctrines. She used her position as a peeress to promote Methodist chaplains, building chapels in places such as Brighton (1761), Bath (1765), Tunbridge Wells (1769) and Worcester (1773), which formed her 'connexion'. In 1768 she established Trefecca House to train ministers. She tried to remain loyal to the Church of England, but in 1779 she was forced to have her chapels registered as dissenting places of worship. She left the Church of England in 1781.

Hastings, Warren (1732–1818), Governor-General of India. He entered the East India Company in 1750, and became a member of the Bengal council. He returned to England in 1764, having made a large fortune. In 1769 he went back to India and was appointed Governor of Bengal in 1772. The next year he was made the first Governor-General of India. During his time in office, he reformed much of the East India Company's systems. He established a parliamentary Board of Control for east India matters, and retired again to England. The Board later impeached him for murder and extortion. Hastings' trial lasted from 1788 to 1795. He was eventually acquitted. Hastings also had a scholarly interest in Orientalism.

Hawksmoor, Nicholas (1661–1736), architect. He was born in Nottinghamshire. He was a pupil of Christopher Wren's from 1679 and was Vanbrugh's assistant from 1700, helping him at Blenheim and Castle Howard. He was a surveyor to the 1711 Act for building 50 new churches. His best known works were St Anne's, Limehouse, St George-in-the-East, Christ Church, Spitalfields, the western towers of Westminster Abbey, the Clarendon Building, Oxford, the north quadrangle at All Souls College and the mausoleum at Castle Howard.

Hazlitt, William (1778–1830), essayist and social reformer. He was born in Maidstone, the son of an Irish unitarian minister, and was brought up in Shropshire. After dabbling as a painter, he turned to writing. He was theatre critic of *The Times* from 1816. His *Characters of Shakespeare's Plays* (1817), *Lectures on the English Poets* (1818) and *English Comic Writers* (1819) became classics in their field. His *The Spirit of the Age* (1825) was a comprehensive survey of English literature. His *Political Essays* (1819) engaged with a range of topics. In 1828–30 he published his largely hagiographical biography of Napoleon. His two marriages were unhappy and short-lived.

Hepplewhite, George (?–1786), cabinet-maker. He started his business in London in about 1760, having been an apprentice to the firm of Gillows in Lancaster. Although not much is known about his life, his importance lies in his *The Cabinet Maker and Upholsterer's Guide*, published posthumously in 1788, which provided designs for a wide range of household furniture.

Herring, Thomas (1693–1757), Archbishop of Canterbury. He was educated at Cambridge, and was appointed royal chaplain in 1726, Dean of Rochester, 1732, Bishop of Bangor from 1737 to 1743, and Archbishop of York from 1743 to 1747, where he played a crucial role in forming an association to defend the Hanoverian regime and to raise money for the government during the 1745 Jacobite Rebellion. He was made Archbishop of Canterbury in 1747.

Herschel, William (1738–1822), astronomer. He was born in Hanover where he had a musical upbringing, and was secretly sent to England by his parents in 1757. He was an organist in Halifax, 1765, and then in Bath from 1766. From 1773 he began to construct optical instruments and to observe the stars from 1774 with his own reflecting telescope. He discovered Uranus in 1781 (which he named *Georgius Sidus*, after George III), and was appointed court astronomer in 1782. He moved to Slough in 1785 and the King financed a design for a 40-foot telescope. His other observations led him to deduce that the Sun was moving with respect to the fixed stars, and, with his sister Caroline, he estimated the form of the Milky Way.

Hervey, Frederick Augustus, 4th Earl of Bristol (1730–1803), clergyman and traveller. He was the third son of John, Baron Hervey of Ickworth, and was educated at Westminster and Cambridge. He travelled in Italy and Dalmatia, and was made Bishop of Cloyne in 1767 and Bishop of Derry in 1768. He spent a great deal of money on the see, and favoured the relaxation of penal laws against the Catholics and the abolition of the tithe. Hervey played a major part in the Volunteers' Convention of 1783, and supported parliamentary reform and the admission of Catholics into the House of Commons. He died at Albano.

Hervey, James (1714–58), clergyman and devotional writer. He was educated at Lincoln College, Oxford, while John Wesley was a fellow there. Hervey was incumbent of Weston Favell and Collingtree from 1752. His evangelical *Meditations and Contemplations* were published in 1746–47. He also wrote *Dialogues between Theron and Aspasio* (1755), which was attacked by Wesley.

Hickes, George (1642–1715), clergyman and nonjuror. He was educated at Oxford, and became chaplain to the Duke of Lauderdale in 1676. After holding several posts in the Church he was appointed Rector of Alvechurch in 1686. He was deprived in 1690 for refusing to take the oaths of allegiance to William and Mary. He went to St Germains in 1693, and was given the title 'Bishop of Thetford'. In 1713 he consecrated three nonjurors as bishops. His publications included *Case of Infant Baptism* (1683), *Anglo-Saxon Grammar* (1690), *An Apology for the New Separation* (1691) and editions of the *Imitatio Christi*.

Highmore, Susanna (1725–1812), poet. She was born in Effingham, Surrey, the daughter of a moderately wealthy yeoman farmer. In 1716 she married Joseph Highmore, a portrait painter. Together, they moved in London literary circles. She wrote a number of poems, including 'On Seeing a Gate Carried by Two Men through Lincoln's Inn Fields, 1743', a spoof on Pope's 'On an Old Gate erected in Chiswick Gardens'.

Hoadly, Benjamin (1676–1761), clergyman and polemicist. He was born in Kent and educated at Cambridge. After holding livings in London, he was made Bishop of Bangor, 1716, Hereford, 1721, Salisbury, 1723, and Winchester, 1734. He attacked Atterbury and the High-Church clergy from 1705, and his sermon of 1717, which advocated private judgement and sincerity over ecclesiastical authority, provoked the 'Bangorian controversy', leading to the suspension of Convocation. Hoadly has been seen as representing the worst aspects of the Hanoverian Church, although modern research indicates that he was more conscientious and spiritually concerned than his detractors have thought.

Hogarth, William (1697–1764), painter and engraver. He was born in London and established himself as an illustrator, before engraving scenes of contemporary society and painting portraits. He attempted to initiate a native school of English art, and founded the St Martin's Lane Academy in 1735. His engravings of 'modern moral subjects' – notably *A Harlot's Progress* (1732), *A Rake's Progress* (1735), *Marriage à la Mode* (1745), *Gin Lane* (1751) and *Industry and Idleness* (1747) – were widely distributed. He wrote *The Analysis of Beauty* (1753), which expounded his theories of the 'line of beauty' and the 'line of grace'. Among his portraits is *Captain Thomas Coram* (1740). Hogarth was a philanthropist, helping to establish the Foundling Hospital. In 1757 he was appointed Sergeant-Painter to the King. His last years were dominated by his sense of being marginalised from the artistic scene.

Hogg, James (1770–1835), poet and novelist. He was born in Etterick forest, and earned a living as a shepherd. He was largely self-taught, and when he began publishing his poetry he was known as 'the Etterick Shepherd'. He was discovered by Sir Walter Scott. Hogg published *The Mountain Bard* (1807), and moved to Edinburgh in 1810. *The Queen's Wake* (1813) established his reputation as a poet. From 1816 he moved to a farm in Yarrow, and combined farming with writing. *The Memoirs and Confessions of a Justified Sinner* (1824) is a psychological novel. In his articles for the Tory *Blackwood's Magazine* Hogg adopted the persona of the archetypal Scotsman.

Home, John (1722–1806), Scottish dramatist. He was born in Leith, educated for the kirk, and fought against the Jacobites in Edinburgh in 1745. Within the kirk, he was known for his moderate views. He was the author of *Douglas: A Tragedy* (1756), one of the most successful plays of the time, and which led a Scottish admirer to shout out 'Whaur's yer Wullie Shakespeare noo?' at the first London performance. He was one of Bute's advisers, and was given a royal pension. His *The History of the Rebellion in the Year of 1745* (1802) is an interesting account by a contemporary participant.

Hooke, Robert (1635–1703), scientist. He worked with Robert Boyle on the air pump and was appointed curator to the Royal Society in 1662, with one of his roles being to perform experiments at meetings. His *Micrographia* (1665), with its immensely detailed depiction of 'The Flee', helped to publicise the microscope.

Horne, George (1730–92), clergyman. He was born in Kent, educated at Oxford, and became President of Magdalen College from 1768 to 1790. Horne was Dean of Canterbury from 1781 and was made Bishop of Norwich in 1790. He was the leader of the High-Church Hutchinsonian clergy, but was admired by John Wesley. His *Commentary on the Book of Psalms* was published in 1776.

Howard, John (?1726–1790), prison reformer. He was born in London, and lived at Cardington, Bedfordshire, from the 1760s. He was made Sheriff of Bedfordshire in 1773 and his experiences in that post led him to undertake a number of prison visits throughout Britain and Europe. His *The State of the Prisons in England and Wales* (1777) revealed the atrocious condition of prisons and the need for reform. Howard died during a visit to Russia. A statue was placed in St Paul's in his memory.

Hume, David (1711–76), philosopher and historian. He was the son of a Presbyterian laird, and was educated at Edinburgh, where he became an atheist. His *Treatise of Human Nature* (1739–40) attempted to show that all human belief and action was rooted in certain principles of human psychology. But the book 'fell dead-born from the press'. His *Enquiry Concerning Human Understanding* (1748) argued that reason could undermine religion, and his *Enquiry Concerning the Principles of Morals* (1751) showed that morality could be established on a secular basis. His *History of England* (1754–62) was immensely popular. He was a leading player in the Scottish Enlightenment.

Hume, Joseph (1777–1855), parliamentary radical. He started as a surgeon in India and was elected MP for Weymouth in 1812. He entered Parliament as a Tory, but by 1818 had become a radical and sat for a series of Scottish boroughs. He supported a range of liberal causes, from Catholic emancipation, Poor Law reform and free trade to the widening of the franchise and the repeal of the Combination Acts.

Hunt, Henry (1773–1835), radical reformer. He was a Wiltshire gentleman farmer. Hunt was imprisoned in 1800 after insulting a colonel, and this hastened his radical beliefs. He wanted a wholesale reform of the political system, and advocated the need for universal suffrage, annual parliaments and the ballot box. In the winter of 1816–17 he led three anti-government demonstrations in Spa Fields, London, which earned him the epithet 'Orator' Hunt. He presided at the meeting at St Peter's Fields, Manchester, which culminated in the Peterloo massacre of 1819, and was imprisoned in 1820. He was elected MP for Preston in 1830, but voted against the 1832 Reform Act because it did not address fundamental issues of working-class representation.

Hunter, John (1728–93) and William (1718–83), Scottish anatomists. William was educated at Edinburgh and London and in 1746 set up an anatomy school in Covent Garden. He was appointed physician to Queen Charlotte, and delivered her children. John joined his brother in the capital in 1748. He undertook military service as an army surgeon in Portugal, and on his return made a number of important anatomical discoveries. He received royal backing in 1776. He assembled a large collection of pathological and physiological specimens.

Huskisson, William (1770–1830), politician. The son of an impoverished Warwickshire gentleman, he was educated in Paris, being looked after by a wealthy relative. He became secretary to the British ambassador there. He returned to England and was MP for Morpeth, 1796–1802, Liskeard, 1804–7, Harwich, 1807–12, Chichester, 1812–23, and for Liverpool, 1823–30. He was Secretary to the Treasury, 1804–5, and 1807–9. He was President of the Board of Trade, 1823–27, and Secretary for War and the Colonies, 1827–28, but resigned over the question of the redistribution of the disfranchised seats at East Retford and Penryn. He supported Catholic emancipation and the additional representation of Leeds, Liverpool and Manchester. He died by being run over by a train at the opening of the Manchester–Liverpool railway.

Hutcheson, Francis (1694–1746), philosopher. He was born in Ireland, of a Scottish Presbyterian family. He was educated at Glasgow University. He became a Presbyterian minister and ran a private school in Dublin during the 1720s. His *Inquiry into the Origin of our Ideas of Beauty and Virtue* (1725) was a defence of a moral theory of aesthetics and behaviour. His *Essay in the Nature and Conduct of the Passions and Affections* was published in 1728. In 1729 he was made Professor of Moral Philosophy at Glasgow.

Hutchinson, John (1674–1737), religious and scientific thinker. He was steward and land surveyor to the Duke of Somerset, and became interested in fossils and geology. His scientific and religious writings, notably *Moses' Principia* (1724), was an attack on Newtonian science, and was taken up by the 'Hutchinsonians'. He also invented an improved timepiece for determining longitude.

Hutton, James (1726–97), geologist. He was the son of an Edinburgh merchant, and studied chemistry and medicine at Edinburgh, Paris and Leyden universities. He began farming in 1754, but continued his scientific researches, publishing his *The Theory of the Earth* (1795), which was a significant contribution to the uniformitarian theory of geology.

Hyde, Henry, 2nd Earl of Clarendon (1638–1709), politician. He was the son of Lord Chancellor Clarendon, and his sister, Anne Hyde, was the first wife of the future James II. He was an MP from 1661, and inherited the earldom in 1664. He acted as Private Secretary, then Lord Chamberlain, and finally Treasurer to Queen Catherine of Braganza, wife of Charles II. He was Lord Privy Seal and Lord Lieutenant of Ireland from 1685 to 1687. He was opposed to James's romanising policies and was dismissed from office in 1687. He did not take the oaths of allegiance to William and Mary, and was suspected of Jacobitism, being imprisoned in 1690 and 1691.

Hyde, Laurence, 1st Earl of Rochester (1642–1711), politician and younger brother of the above. He was MP from 1660 to 1681, and First Lord of the Treasury from 1679 to 1691. He was made a viscount in 1681 and then earl in 1682. He was appointed Lord President of the Council, 1684–85, and then Lord Treasurer, 1685–86. He was dismissed from office for not converting to Catholicism. He was a high Tory, but supported William and Mary after 1688, and was made Lord Lieutenant of Ireland from 1700 to 1703, and Lord President of the Council, 1710–11.

Inchbald, Elizabeth (1753–1821), playwright, novelist and critic. She was born at Stanningfield, near Bury St Edmunds, the daughter of a farmer. She was brought up a Catholic. In 1772 she ran away to London, and attempted to become an actress. In the same year she married Joseph Inchbald, an actor and portrait painter. The couple acted in theatres in provincial England, Scotland and France. Inchbald died in 1779, and Elizabeth made her London debut in 1780. She retired from the stage in 1789, and concentrated on her writing. She died in Kensington House, an establishment for Catholic women. Her work for the theatre included adaptations from continental works. Her first novel, *A Simple Story* was published in 1791. This was followed by *Nature and Art* (1796).

James II (1633–1701). The younger son of Charles I, he spent his youth in exile. At the Restoration, as Duke of York, he established for himself a naval career as Lord Admiral. From 1667 he attempted to secure an alliance with France, and converted to Catholicism in 1672. Because of the 1673 Test Act, he was forced to relinquish his naval post. He married, as his second wife, the Catholic Mary of Modena in 1673. In

1678, the 'Popish Plot', whereby Charles would be murdered and James placed on the throne, led to moves to exclude James from the line of succession. James succeeded to the throne in 1685, but his seemingly absolutist and pro-Catholic policies aroused suspicion and disaffection. The birth of a son in June 1688 led some to invite William of Orange to intervene. James fled to France in December 1688. He was present at the battle of the Boyne, 1690, and lived at St Germains, protected by Louis XIV.

James Frances Edward Stuart (1688–1766), 'the Old Pretender'. He was the son of James II, and it was his birth in June 1688 which led to the Glorious Revolution. Louis XIV recognised him as the heir to the British throne in 1701 and this hastened the War of the Spanish Succession. James was active in a variety of plots to restore him to the throne. He participated in the 1715 uprising in Scotland, and fled to France in 1716. He married Clementina Sobieska in 1719, and lived in Rome for much of the rest of his life.

Jenner, Edward (1749–1823), discoverer of vaccination. He was an associate of John Hunter's and practised medicine in Berkeley, Gloucestershire. His *An Inquiry into the Cause and Effect of Cow-pox* (1798) was crucial in disseminating the idea of vaccination, although it initially aroused much controversy. He was given a parliamentary grant of £10,000 in 1802 and another was voted in 1806. The National Vaccine Establishment was founded in 1808.

Johnson, Samuel (1709–84), lexicographer, critic, biographer, writer. He was born in Lichfield, the son of a bookseller. He was educated locally, and had a year at Pembroke College, Oxford, between 1728 and 1729, but left because of poverty. He tried to make a career as a teacher in Lichfield, but from 1737 he worked as a writer in London for various periodicals, including *The Gentleman's Magazine* from 1738. His *London* came out in 1738, and in 1744 he published the life of his friend Richard Savage. From 1746 to 1755 he worked on his *Dictionary of the English Language*. He wrote *The Vanity of Human Wishes* in 1749, edited the twice-weekly newspaper *The Rambler* from 1750 to 1752, *The Idler* (a weekly paper) from 1758 to 1760, and published his novel *Rasselas* in 1759. He was given a pension from 1762. He produced an edition of Shakespeare's *Works* in 1765, *A Journey to the Western Isles of Scotland* in 1775, and his *Lives of the Poets* appeared between 1779 and 1781. He was introduced to James Boswell in 1763, whose *Life of Johnson* (1791) records Johnson's opinions and conversations with members of the Literary Club which Johnson helped to found in 1764. He married Elizabeth Porter in 1735. She died in 1752.

Jones, William, 'of Nayland' (1726–1800), clergyman. He was born in Northamptonshire, the descendant of Colonel Jones, the regicide, and educated at Charterhouse and University College, Oxford. He was a close friend of George Horne. He was vicar of Bethersden, 1763–5, rector of Pluckley, 1765–77, and perpetual curate of Nayland, 1777–1800. His publications included *The Catholic Doctrine of the Trinity* (1756), and *Physiological Disquisitions* (1781).

Jones, Sir William (1746–94), orientalist. He was educated at Harrow and Oxford. He had an immense aptitude for languages and became fluent in 13, with a working knowledge of 28 others. He was called to the Bar in 1774, received his knighthood in 1774 and was made a judge in the High Court of Calcutta from 1783. In India, he founded the Bengal Asiatic Society (1784). His publications included *A Dissertation on the Orthography of Asiatick Words in Roman Letters* (1784), *On the Origin and Families of Nations* (1792) and extracts from the Vedas. He died in India.

Kauffman, Angelika (1741–1807), painter. She was born in Switzerland, and became well known as a portrait painter in Milan. She came to London in 1766. In 1767 she painted Queen Charlotte and decorated the flower room at Frogmore. She was one of the original Academicians and exhibited 82 pictures at the Royal Academy between 1769 and 1797. She left England in 1781 and settled in Rome, where she painted many important European potentates.

Kay, John (1704–79), inventor of the flying shuttle. He was born near Bury, Lancashire, the son of a yeoman farmer. He patented the flying shuttle in 1733. This was originally designed to lessen the work needed in broad-loom weaving, but was most useful in the Lancashire cotton industry. After experiencing difficulties in safeguarding his patent, Kay settled in France in 1747, where he was given a government grant to educate French weavers in using the shuttle.

Kean, Edmund (1787–1833), actor. Having been a child star in London, he spent his youth in the provincial theatre. In 1814 he made his London come-back at Drury Lane, playing the part of Shylock to great acclaim. He was one of the most distinguished tragic actors of the early nineteenth-century. He made two acting tours to America in the 1820s.

Keats, John (1795–1821), poet. He was born in London, the son of a livery stableman. He trained as a surgeon's assistant, but by 1816 had begun to publish poetry. His *Endymion* was published in 1818 and his *Odes* in 1819. He died in Rome.

Keith, George, 10th Earl of Marischal (1693–1778), Jacobite leader. He succeeded to the earldom in 1712, and led the cavalry at the battle of Sheriffmuir in 1715. He commanded the Spanish–Jacobite expedition of 1719, and escaped to Spain. He became a favourite of Frederick the Great of Prussia, being appointed Prussian ambassador in Paris in 1751. He was pardoned by George II in 1759, but returned to Prussia in 1764.

Ken, Thomas (1637–1711), clergyman. He was educated at Winchester and Oxford, and became chaplain to the future Queen Mary at The Hague, 1679–80. In 1684, he became Bishop of Bath and Wells. Ken attended the Duke of Monmouth at his execution in 1685. He was one of the seven bishops who refused to comply with James II's Declaration of Indulgence. He did not swear allegiance to William and Mary and was deprived in 1691. He was a poet and wrote hymns.

Kent, William (1685–1748), architect, landscape designer and painter. He was born in Bridlington, Yorkshire. He lived in Italy from 1709 to 1719, where he trained as a painter, acted as an art dealer, and met Lord Burlington. On his return to London, he developed an interest in architecture under Burlington's patronage. In 1727 Kent published *The Designs of Inigo Jones*. He was employed by the Office of Works, and designed the Horse Guards (built after his death) and the Royal Mews. His architectural commissions included Holkham Hall (from 1734), and his landscape designs included Chiswick, Stowe and Rousham.

King, Gregory (1648–1712), genealogist and herald. The son of a Lichfield surveyor, he was educated at the grammar school there, and at the age of 14 left school to help his father make maps. He became clerk to Sir William Dugdale in 1662 and was appointed Rouge Dragon Pursuivant in 1677, and Registrar of the College of Arms from 1684 to 1694. His *Natural and Political Observations and Conclusions upon the State and Condition of England* (compiled in 1696) was a pioneering piece of social and economic analysis.

Kneller, Sir Godfrey (1646–1723), portrait painter. He was born in Lubeck and, having studied with Rembrandt, settled in England in around 1676. During 1684–85, he was in France, painting Louis XIV. He was appointed principal painter to the court by William III in 1688, and he was knighted in 1691. His works included the 'Hampton Court beauties', commissioned by Queen Mary, and the 'Kit Cat Club' portraits, which were pictures of many of the leading Whig politicians and society figures, and the equestrian portrait of William III (1697).

Lamb, Charles (1775–1834), writer. He was born in London, was educated at Christ's Hospital, and worked in East India House as a clerk. He suffered from a mental illness in 1795–96, and his sister Mary, in a fit, killed their mother in 1796. Charles wrote with Mary *Tales from Shakespear* [*sic*] (1807), written to make Shakespeare's stories accessible to children. He attempted to do the same for the *Odyssey* in *The Adventures of Ulysses* (1809). The *Essays of Elia* appeared in 1823.

Lancaster, Joseph (1778–1838), educationalist. He was from a nonconformist family, and established a school in London in 1798, giving free education to those unable to pay. His system of education was based on non-denominational Christian principles, and relied on the monitor system and mechanical methods of instruction, so that 1,000 boys could be taught at once, as laid out in his *Improvements in Education* (1803). The British and Foreign School Society, based on Lancaster's model, was started in 1804. Lancaster emigrated to America in 1818.

Langley, Batty (1696–1751), architectural writer and designer. He was born in Twickenham, the son of a gardener. He published several works on landscape gardening, but became best known for his efforts to popularise latest developments in architectural fashions for the master-builder. His *Gothic Architecture Improved* (1st edn, 1742) was an early defence of Gothic architecture.

Lavington, George (1684–1762), clergyman. He was educated at Winchester and Oxford, and was Bishop of Exeter from 1747 to 1762. He was a formidable opponent of early Methodism. His *The Enthusiasm of Methodists and Papists Compar'd* was published between 1749 and 1751.

Law, William (1686–1761), religious writer. He was born in King's Cliffe, near Stanford, and was educated at Cambridge. In 1714 he declined to take the oaths of allegiance to George I, and established a school for 14 girls at King's Cliffe. He joined the family of Edward Gibbon's grandfather as tutor. His *Christian Perfection* was published in 1726 and his *A Serious Call to a Devout and Holy Life* appeared in 1728. His *The Case of Reason* (1732) was an attack on Deism and scepticism. By 1737 he had become a follower of the mystical writings of the seventeenth-century German author Jakob Boeheme. He retired to King's Cliffe in 1740, and was joined in 1744 by the historian's aunt Hester, who wanted to put the precepts of the *Serious Call* into practice.

Lawrence, Thomas (1769–1830), painter. He was born in Bristol, to an inn-keeping family. His portrait of Queen Charlotte (exhibited 1790) was much admired and he was given the post of painter to the King in 1792. In 1818 he was commissioned to paint the portraits of all those who played leading roles in the wars with Napoleon, and these were hung in the Waterloo Chamber, Windsor Castle. He was made an academician in 1794, and was elected President in 1820. He was knighted in 1815.

Lennox, Charlotte (1720–1804), writer. She was probably born in Gibraltar, and grew up in New York, where her father was a soldier. After her father died in 1743, Charlotte was sent to England, and received the patronage of the Countess of Rockingham and Lady Isabella Finch. She dedicated her first volume of poems to them in 1747. She married the impecunious Alexander Lennox in the same year. After failing to make a living as an actress, she maintained the family by writing and translating. By the mid-1750s she was one of the most widely read authors of her day. She died, however, in poverty. Her novels included *The Life of Harriot Stuart* (1750), *The Female Quixote* (1752), *Sophia* (1762) and *Euphemia* (1790). Her translations included Voltaire's *The Age of Louis XIV* (1752).

Leslie, Charles (1650–1722), clergyman and non-juror. He was born in Ireland, the son of the Bishop of Clogher, and educated at Trinity College, Dublin. He became ordained and was made Chancellor of Connor in 1686. He refused to take the oaths in 1689, and published several controversial works, including *The State of the Protestants in Ireland under the late king James' Government* (1692), works attacking the Whig clergy, and pamphlets in defence of the sacrament. His newspaper, *The Rehearsal* (1704–9) was a counter-blast to Defoe's *Review*. A warrant was issued for his arrest in 1710, and he escaped to St Germains in 1711. He returned to England for a short time, but in 1713 took up a place in the Pretender's household at Bar-le-Duc.

Liverpool, Charles Jenkinson, 1st Earl of (1727–1808), politician. Educated at Charterhouse and Oxford, he was Private Secretary and Under-Secretary of State, 1761–62, MP for Cockermouth, 1761–67, Appleby, 1767–72, Harwich, 1772–74, Hastings, 1774–80, Saltash, 1781–86, and held various minor posts until the fall of Lord North in 1782. Jenkinson was offered governmental office in 1784 and became President of the Board of Trade, 1786–1803. He was made Lord Hawkesbury in 1786 and Earl of Liverpool in 1796.

Liverpool, Robert Banks Jenkinson, 2nd Earl of (1770–1828), politician. The son of the above, he was educated at Charterhouse and Oxford. He was in Paris at the storming of the Bastille, and he joined the Commons in 1790 as MP for Appleby. He was MP for Rye, 1796–1803, and was Foreign Secretary, 1801–3, Home Secretary, 1804–6 and 1807–9, and War Secretary, 1809–12. He was made Prime Minister in 1812 and made an effective war-time leader. He opposed parliamentary reform but wanted to do something for the Catholics without giving them full emancipation. The repressive legislation embodied in the Six Acts (1819–20) was an attempt to maintain law and order. He retired in 1827.

Locke, John (1632–1704), philosopher. He was born in Somerset into a Puritan family. He was educated at Westminster and Oxford, and became interested in the new science and medicine. He moved to London in 1667 to become secretary and physician to the Earl of Shaftesbury, and began to move in radical political circles. He was in exile in France from 1675 to 1679 and in Holland, 1683–89. His *Two Treatises of Government* were written in the early 1680s, although not published until 1689. In that year Locke returned to England and also published his *Letter Concerning Toleration* and his *An Essay concerning Human Understanding* appeared in 1690, which was a vindication of empiricism. He advised the Whig governments of the 1690s, and wrote *Some Thoughts concerning Education* (1693) and *The Reasonableness of Christianity* (1695). He worked at the Board of Trade from 1696 to 1700.

Lyttelton, George, 1st Baron (1709–73), politician. He was educated at Eton and Oxford and was MP for Okehampton from 1735 to 1756. He opposed Walpole, and became a Lord of the Treasury, 1744–54. He was a member of the 'Cobhamite party' and became Chancellor of the Exchequer in 1755. He opposed the repeal of the Stamp Act in 1766. He was a friend of Pope's and a patron of a number of literary figures including James Thomson who praised him in *The Seasons*.

McAdam, John Loudon (1756–1836), road-builder. He was born in Scotland and fought in the British army during the War of American Independence. He returned to Ayrshire in 1783 and ran the British Tar Company. Having got into debt he sold up and moved to Falmouth in 1798 as agent for revictualling the navy. During his many travels he perfected his system of improving roads by placing layers of small stone chips on to the subsoil so that the roads were made impermeable to water. He was made surveyor to the British Turnpike Trust in 1815 and began rebuilding roads. In 1820 Parliament voted him a grant of £2,000. He was made Surveyor-General of Metropolitan Roads in 1827.

Macaulay, Catherine (1731–91), historian. She was the daughter of John Sawbridge, a radical Kent politician. She married George Macaulay in 1760, who died in 1760, leaving her comfortably off. She published her *History of England from the Accession of James I to that of the Brunswick Line* (1763–83), which was a staunch defence of a radical Whig interpretation of events. She wrote against Burke's *Present Discontents* in her *Observations on a Pamphlet, entitled Thoughts on the Present Discontents* (1770), in which she proposed frequent elections and extension of the suffrage. In 1774 she moved to Bath and began a *History of England from the Revolution to the Present* (1778), which was critical of William III and Walpole. She married William Graham in 1778, 26 years her junior. In 1784 they went to America, and then France. They returned to England, and her last work was a reply to Burke's *Reflections*.

Macdonald, Flora (1722–90), Jacobite heroine. She was the daughter of a farmer from the Hebrides and met Prince Charles Edward in 1746 during his flight from Culloden. She helped him reach Skye, and was imprisoned after the Prince's escape. She was released by the 1747 Act of Indemnity, and with her husband emigrated to North Carolina in 1774 and returned to Scotland in 1779.

Mackenzie, Henry (1745–1831), author. He was educated in Edinburgh and became Comptroller of the Taxes for Scotland. His *The Man of Feeling* (1771) was a landmark in the history of the sentimental novel. He also wrote *The Man of the World* (1773), where the main character was a villain, and *Julia de Roubigné* (1777). Mackenzie was chairman of the committee which investigated Macpherson's 'Ossian'.

Macpherson, James (1736–96), author. The son of a farmer, he was born near Kingussie. He was educated at Aberdeen and Edinburgh universities. He produced *Fragments of Ancient Poetry, Collected in the Highlands of Scotland, and Translated from the Galic or Erse Language* in 1760. He collected material for *Fingal, an Ancient Epic Poem, in Six Books* (1762), which was followed by *Temora* (1763). These created a sensation, purporting to be translations of epics written by Ossian in an early part of Scottish history. Many Scots were convinced of their authenticity; but Samuel Johnson and others doubted their provenance. Henry Mackenzie's investigating committee, reporting in 1805, viewed the poems as largely fakes. Macpherson also wrote a *History of the House of Great Britain from the Restoration to the Accession of the House of Hanover* (1775) and published a translation of the *Iliad* (1773).

Malthus, Thomas Robert (1766–1834), political economist. He was born near Guildford, the son of Daniel Malthus, a wealthy gentleman. He was educated at the Warrington dissenting academy and in 1784 went to Cambridge. He became ordained and was appointed curate of Okewood, Surrey. In 1798 he published anonymously *An Essay on the Principle of Population as it affects the future Improvement of Society, with Remarks on the Speculations of Mr Godwin, M. Condorcet, and other writers*. He toured Scandinavia in 1799, and France and Switzerland in 1802 before producing a second edition of the *Essay* in 1803. He was appointed rector of Walesby,

Lincolnshire in 1803. He was given the post of Professor of History and Political Economy at the East India Company's College in Hailebury, Hertfordshire, in 1805.

Mandeville, Bernard (1670–1733), author. He was born in Dort, Holland, and studied medicine at Leyden. He settled in England, and published a poem 'The Grumbling Hive, or Knaves turn'd Honest' in 1705. His *The Fable of the Bees, or Private Vices and Public Benefits* (1714), with its essentially pessimistic view of human nature, was highly controversial. Other publications included *A Modest Defence of Public Stews* (1724), which advocated government regulation of bawdy-houses, an *Essay on Charity and Charity Schools* and *A Search into the Nature of Society* (both 1723).

Manley, [Mary] Delarivière (1663–1724), author. She was born in Jersey, the daughter of the governor of the island. She had a bigamous relationship with her cousin John Manley, and bore him a son. She lived in Exeter from 1694 to 1696 and wrote two plays: *The Lost Lover, or the Jealous Husband* (1696) and *The Royal Mischief* (1696). Her novels included *The New Atlantis* (1709), which was an attack on leading Whig politicians, and *The Adventures of Rivella* (1714), which was largely autobiographical. She took over from Swift as editor of *The Examiner* in 1711. She had several affairs, including being mistress for some years of John Tilly, warden of the Fleet prison.

Mansfield, William Murrary, 1st Earl of (1705–93), judge. He entered Parliament in 1742 as MP for Boroughbridge, and was appointed Chief Justice in 1756. Mansfield was a legal reformer who insisted on the superiority of the courts over parliaments as instruments for developing legal rules. Tolerant in religious matters, his house was burnt down in the Gordon Riots of 1780.

Marshall, William (1745–1818), agricultural writer. He traded in the West Indies and in 1774 took a farm near Croydon. In 1780 he became land agent in Norfolk to Sir Harbord Harbord. He published his *Minutes of Agriculture* (1780) and his *A General Survey of the Rural Economy of England* (1787–98). He was instrumental in establishing the Board of Agriculture in 1793. He also wrote a vocabulary of Yorkshire dialect.

Martin, John (1789–1854), painter. He was born at Haydon Bridge, near Hexham. He moved to London in 1806 and was apprenticed to a coach painter and then to a china painter. He exhibited at the Royal Academy in 1812. His works included *Joshua Commanding the Sun to Stand still* (1816), *The Bard* (1817), *The Fall of Babylon* (1819), and *Belshazzar's Feast* (1821). He also engraved illustrations of Milton's works and the Bible. Martin's *The Fall of Nineveh* was exhibited in Brussels in 1833.

Mary II (1662–94). She was the elder daughter of James, Duke of York (later James II) and Anne Hyde, his first wife. She married William of Orange, her cousin, in 1677. After 1688 they became joint monarchs, and Mary acted as regent during William's long absences on the Continent in the early 1690s. Relations with her sister Anne, who was opposed to the idea of William being a joint ruler, were strained after 1689. Historians are only now recognising her importance in creating loyalty to the Crown in the years after 1688, and her staunch Anglicanism was crucial in keeping the support of the Church of England. Her funeral in 1695 was a scene of national mourning.

Mary of Modena (1658–1718), wife of James II. She was an Italian princess, who, as a devout Catholic, had intentions of becoming a nun. She became James II's second wife in 1673. None of her first five children survived. But she gave birth to a son (the Old Pretender) in June 1688, thereby hastening the Glorious Revolution. The child was widely believed to have been someone else's and smuggled in in a warming pan. Mary left England in December 1688 and lived at St Germains to the end of her life. She had a daughter in 1692.

Masham, Abigail (d. 1734), intimate of Queen Anne. She was a distant relative of Sarah, Duchess of Marlborough, and, through her, Abigail was appointed Woman of the Bedchamber to the Queen. She married Samuel Masham, Groom of the Bedchamber to Prince George, in 1707. She was instrumental in breaking the power of the Marlboroughs at court in 1710. Again, in 1711, she supported St John against Harley. She was able to obtain military posts for her brother, Jack Hill, who led the unsuccessful expedition to Quebec in 1711, and in 1712 her husband was made Lord Masham.

Mason, William (1724–97), poet. He was born in Hull, the son of a clergyman. He was educated at Cambridge where he became a friend of Thomas Gray. After being ordained, Mason was appointed Rector of Aston, near Rotherham, in 1754, where he was noted as a diligent clergyman, and in 1756 he was made a prebendary of York. He wrote poems on various subjects, as well as a *Life* of Gray (1774), and composed music.

Metcalf, John (1717–1810), road-builder. After being infected by smallpox at the age of 6, he became blind (thereafter known as 'Blind Jack of Knaresbrough'). He made a living as a travelling fiddler and dealt in horses. He established a stage wagon to York from Aberdeen in 1754 and in 1765 obtained a contract to build roads. He built over 180 miles of road in the north of England.

Mill, James (1773–1836), philosopher. He was born in Scotland, the son of a shoemaker. He was educated at Edinburgh University and spent some time as a Presbyterian preacher. In 1802 he settled in London and earned a living as a journalist and writer. He was influenced by Bentham and made an important contribution to utilitarian philosophy, writing on a range of issues from education, politics, law, and economy to history and psychology. In 1806 he began work on his *History of British India* (published 1817) and he was made assistant examiner by the directors of the East India Company in 1819 and chief examiner in 1832. His *Essay on Government* (1820) was a bid for democracy against monarchy. His influential *Elements of Political Economy* appeared in 1821. He was instrumental in the founding of University College, London in 1828. He was the father of John Stuart Mill.

Molyneux, William (1656–98), political philosopher. He was born in Ireland, educated at Trinity College, Dublin, and entered the Middle Temple. He was appointed Surveyor-General of the King's Buildings, 1684–88, and Commissioner for the Army Accounts in 1690. He was MP for Dublin University in 1692 and 1695, and was author of *The Case of Ireland's being bound by Acts of Parliament in England Stated* (1698).

Montagu, Elizabeth (1720–1800), essayist and member of Blue-Stocking Circle. She was brought up with her sister Sarah Scott in Kent and Cambridgeshire, and they were given a good education. In 1742 she married the wealthy Edward Montagu, who was a doctor and owner of estates and coalmines. After his death in 1775 she supervised his estates. She lived in London and became a literary hostess, modelling her evening soirées on the French salons. She contributed to the *Dialogues of the Dead* (1760) and *An Essay on the Writings and Genius of Shakespear* [sic] (1769). Four volumes of her letters were published by her nephew in 1809 and 1813.

Montagu, Lady Mary Wortley (1689–1762), essayist. She was born in London, the daughter of the future Duke of Kingston. She eloped with Edward Wortley in 1712. She moved in Whig literary circles, and in 1712 accompanied her husband, the ambassador to Turkey, to Constantinople. She contracted smallpox in 1715, and in 1718 she had her son vaccinated against the virus. They returned to England. After developing a crush on Francesco Algorotti, an Italian bisexual, she went to live in Florence in 1739, hoping he would join her. Their relationship came to nothing, but she remained abroad for the next 20 years, writing and gardening. Her accounts of her time at Constantinople, *Embassy Letters*, were published posthumously in 1763.

More, Hannah (1745–1833), dramatist and religious writer. She was born in Stapleton, Bristol, the daughter of a school-master. From 1773 she began her visits to London and became known to some of the leading literary figures of the day, in particular David Garrick. In this period she wrote a number of successful plays, including *The Inflexible Captive* (1774), *Percy* (1777) and *The Fatal Falsehood* (1779). From the mid-1780s she became more involved in humanitarian issues and became associated with the evangelical Clapham Sect. In 1789 she established a school at Cheddar. More wrote *Village Politics* in 1793, aimed at the poor and designed to put forward reactionary political views. Her Cheap Repository tracts were a series of moral tales, including *The Shepherd of Salisbury Plain* (1795). Her novel *Coelebs in Search of a Wife* (1809) set out her vision of the ideal wife.

Morland, George (1763–1804), artist. He was born in London, the son and grandson of painters. Morland first exhibited at the Royal Academy at the age of 10. He was particularly influenced by Flemish and Dutch genre scenes and he painted views of English rural life and pictures of animals. His *The Angler's Repast* was engraved in 1780 and his *The Inside of a Stable* (1790) was very popular. He drank heavily; his own epitaph on himself was 'here lies a drunken dog'.

Murray, Lord George (?1700–60), Jacobite leader. He was the son of the 1st Duke of Atholl, and he participated in the 1715 rebellion and in the 1719 expedition. He fought in the Sardinian army and joined Prince Charles Edward in 1745. He was a commander at the siege of Carlisle, was at Derby, and continued to harass Hanoverian troops. He warned against making a stand at Culloden, but led the right wing at the battle. In 1746 he retired to France and, after travelling on the Continent, died in Holland.

Nash, John (1752–1835), architect. He was born in London, the son of a millwright. After getting into debt, he made a living by designing houses for the Welsh gentry. He was also the architect of Carmarthen county gaol. He came back to London, and after a time collaborating with Humphry Repton, he worked for a number of patrons, including the Prince Regent. His works included All Souls', Langham Place, Marble Arch and the Brighton Pavilion.

Nash, Richard (1674–1762), 'Beau Nash'. He was born in Swansea, the son of a glass-maker. He trained as a lawyer, but he became involved in gambling, and moved to Bath by 1705. He became master of ceremonies there where he set and maintained standards of behaviour. He died in poverty, but was buried in Bath Abbey.

Nelson, Horatio (1758–1805), admiral. He was born at Burnham Thorpe, East Anglia, the son of the rector. He entered the navy in 1770, and in 1779 was made a post-captain, and saw service in the Arctic, and in the East and West Indies. He was unemployed between 1787 and 1793. He first met Emma Hamilton, who later became his mistress, in 1793. In the same year he was sent to the Mediterranean, where he lost an eye during the 1794 occupation of Corsica, but in July of that year lost his right arm at the battle of Santa Cruz. He rose to be an admiral in 1797, after his part in the battle of Cape St Vincent. In 1798 he destroyed the French fleet near Alexandria and was created Baron Nelson of the Nile. In 1801 he crushed the Danish fleet in Copenhagen harbour, putting his telescope to his blind eye to avoid seeing his superior's order to disengage. Nelson was appointed to the Mediterranean command in 1803. The French admiral, Villeneuve, eluded his blockade of Toulon in the spring of 1805, but after a pursuit, Nelson defeated the Franco-Spanish fleet at Trafalgar. He died just three hours before victory.

Nelson, Robert (1665–1715), religious writer. He was born in London, the son of a merchant, and was educated at St Paul's, beginning studies at Cambridge, which he never completed. Nelson lived on the Continent during the 1680s, and after his return to England became a non-juror before 1694. Though an opponent of Archbishop Tillotson, the Archbishop died in his arms in 1694. Nelson was a supporter of the religious societies, the societies for the reformation of manners, the SPCK and the SPG. In 1710 he was appointed one of the commissioners to build 50 new London churches. His *A Companion for the Festivals and Fasts of the Church of England* (1704) was a popular manual of Anglican piety.

Newcomen, Thomas (1663–1729), inventor of the steam-engine. He was born in Dartmouth. His invention of the atmospheric steam-engine was an improvement of the 'fire engine' patented in 1698 by Thomas Savery. Newcomen's 1705 engine was designed to drive pumps for draining mines.

Newton, Isaac (1642–1727), scientist. He was born near Grantham, Lincolnshire, and educated at Cambridge. He was appointed to the Lucasian chair of mathematics at Cambridge in 1669, and pursued his interests in mathematics, alchemy and biblical study. He submitted his first paper to the Royal Society in 1672, which proved that white is a mixture of all the colours. His *Opticks*, based on this paper, was not published until 1704. His greatest work, the *Philosophiae Naturalis Principia Mathematica* (*The Mathematical Principles of Natural Philosophy*), which demonstrated the theory of gravity, appeared in 1687. Newton was MP for Cambridge University, 1698 and 1701–2, and in 1696 was appointed Warden, and then Master, of the Mint. He was President of the Royal Society from 1703. He was an Arian.

North, Frederick, 2nd Earl of Guildford (1732–92), politician. He was the eldest son of the 1st Earl, and entered Parliament in 1754 as MP for Banbury. He was appointed to the Treasury Board in 1759 by the Duke of Newcastle, who was his cousin. He left office in 1765, but returned in 1766. He was made Chancellor of the Exchequer in 1767, and became First Lord of the Treasury in 1770. The Quebec Act of 1774, which he championed, was notable for its tolerance towards Catholics. The biggest issue of his Ministry was the war against America. He was on excellent terms with George III, who refused his repeated attempts to resign. He was eventually released from office after the British surrender at Yorktown in 1781. In 1783 he was made Home Secretary in his coalition with Charles James Fox, but was dismissed at the end of the year. He went blind in 1786, but continued to sit in the House of Commons. He succeeded to the title in 1790.

O'Connell, Daniel (1775–1847), Irish politician, known as 'the Liberator'. He was born into an aristocratic Irish Catholic family and was called to the Irish Bar in 1798. He was the leader of the movement for Catholic emancipation. He founded the Catholic Association in 1823, which aimed at emancipation, the end of the Union and the abolition of tithes. He was elected MP for County Clare in 1828 but, as a Catholic, was unable to take up his seat. After the granting of emancipation in 1829 he was elected MP for County Clare, and for Waterford in 1832. He established the National Repeal Association in 1841 to secure the repeal of the 1800 Act of Union. The Irish Famine from 1845 caused him much distress, and he died in Italy.

Oglethorpe, James Edward (1696–1785), colonist of Georgia. He was educated at Oxford and entered the army in 1710. He served with Prince Eugene in eastern Europe. Oglethorpe was appointed chairman of the parliamentary committee on debtors' prisons in 1729, and in 1732 he obtained the charter for the settlement of Georgia as a refuge for paupers and as a barrier against Spanish aggression in America. In administering the colony, he aroused much opposition, both from his ban of negro slaves, and from the Wesleys. He failed to repulse the Spanish attack on St Augustine in 1740. He returned to England in 1743 and acted against the Jacobites in Lancashire in 1745. He was MP for Haslemere from 1722 until 1754.

Owen, Robert (1771–1858), factory manager and utopian socialist. He was born in Welshpool, Montgomeryshire, and owned cotton mills in Lancashire and New Lanark (Strathclyde). From 1800 to 1825 he was known as a kind and successful man of business, attempting to create a model factory by employing no young children, limiting adult hours and providing educational facilities. His *A New View of Society* (1813–18) was an important socialist manifesto. In his *Report to the County of Lanark* (1820), he argued for factory reform, national education, and for cooperative socialism.

Paine, James (1725–1789), architect. He was born in Hampshire, probably the son of a carpenter. He was a student at the St Martin's Lane Academy, and his first commission was as clerk of works at Nostell Priory, Yorkshire. In 1750 he took over the north country practice of Daniel Garrett, and between 1745 and 1770 designed or altered some 30 country houses in the North, including Alnwick, Chatsworth and Kedleston. He joined the Office of the King's Works in 1745, and took a trip to Italy in 1755. He was made President of the Society of Artists of Great Britain in 1770, and was also JP for Middlesex and Surrey.

Paine, Thomas (1737–1809), radical writer. He was born in Thetford, Norfolk, the son of a Quaker stay-maker, and earned a livelihood as a stay-maker and exciseman, until he was dismissed for agitating for more pay. In 1774 he went to Philadelphia, at the suggestion of Benjamin Franklin, and was active in the fight for American independence. His *Common Sense* (1776) was a trenchant plea for complete independence for the colonies. He returned to England in 1787 (via France), and published his *The Rights of Man* (1791–2), which was a reply to Burke's *Reflections*. In fear of being arrested, he moved to France and was made a French citizen in 1792. He was opposed to the execution of Louis XIV and his *Age of Reason* (1794) was a critique of the atheism of the revolution, as well as an attack on conventional Christianity. In 1802 he returned to America, where he died. In 1819 Cobbett exhumed his bones, and brought them back to England, planning a memorial. The bones were lost.

Paley, William (1743–1805), clergyman and writer. He was educated at Cambridge and was made archdeacon of Carlisle in 1782. His *Evidences of Christianity* (1794) was a best-selling collection of the arguments against Deism and his *Natural Theology* (1802) was a powerful statement of the argument from design, with its celebrated analogy of an abandoned watch, from which he argued the existence of God as designer, for as 'the watch must have had a maker', so must the natural world. He also published, in 1785, *Principles of Morals and Political Philosophy*, which was a defence of theological utilitarianism.

Payne Knight, Richard (1750–1824), writer on the picturesque. He was the son of a clergyman from Herefordshire. He travelled in Italy in 1767, 1777 and 1785, where he began collecting bronzes. In 1780 he entered Parliament as MP for Leominster and from 1784 to 1806 was MP for Ludlow. He was a supporter of Fox. He wrote on a range of classical and antiquarian topics, but was best known for his poem *The Landscape* (1794), which attacked the aesthetic theories of 'Capability' Brown and advocated the picturesque.

Pelham, Henry (1695–1754), politician. The youngest son of a baron, Pelham entered Parliament in 1717 as MP for Sleaford. He was MP for Sussex, 1722–54, and was made Secretary at War, 1724, and Paymaster-General in 1730. In 1743 Pelham was given the post of First Lord of the Treasury, which ensured that by 1744, with his brother, he was in effective control of government. In 1746 he and his brother forced George II to accept them on their own terms, and together with Newcastle and Hardwicke, Pelham directed a 'broad-bottomed' ministry.

Pelham-Holles, Thomas, 1st Duke of Newcastle (1693–1768), politician. He was educated at Westminster and Cambridge. In 1714 he was created Earl of Clare and Duke of Newcastle in 1715 after he had helped to raise an army against the Pretender. In 1717 he was made Lord Chamberlain of the Household and was a member of the regency council during George I's periodic visits to Hanover. Newcastle was appointed Secretary of State for the Southern Department in 1724. After Walpole's fall in 1742, Newcastle had control over foreign affairs, and was able to direct much Crown and ecclesiastical patronage. When Pelham died in 1754, Newcastle became First Lord of the Treasury; he was forced to resign in 1756 after suffering serious defeats in the war with France. In 1757 he joined with Pitt, and was reinstated as First Lord. He resigned in 1762. He was Lord Privy Seal, 1765–66.

Penn, William (1644–1718), Quaker leader. He was the son of an admiral and educated at Oxford and Lincoln's Inn. He became a Quaker in 1667 and in publications such as *The Great Case of Liberty of Conscience* (1671) pleaded their cause. In 1680 he petitioned Charles II for a grant of land in America, and in 1681 he founded Pennsylvania, drawing up its liberal and religiously tolerant constitution. Penn was its governor, and in 1683 was responsible for the peace treaty with the Delaware Indians. He was a supporter of James II's policy of religious toleration for dissenters, although he probably misjudged James's intentions. He lost favour after 1688, and was suspected because of his links with James.

Perceval, Spencer (1762–1812), politician. He was a son of the Earl of Egmont. Educated at Cambridge, he was involved with the evangelicals there. He became a barrister, and was appointed a commissioner of bankrupts in 1790. Perceval was elected MP for Northampton in 1796.

He became Solicitor-General in 1801 and Attorney-General in 1802. He was a committed and devout Anglican, which made him a firm opponent of Catholic Emancipation. He was Chancellor of the Exchequer, 1807–12, and after the Canning/Castlereagh duel was given the post of Prime Minister. In 1812 he was assassinated by John Bellingham, who mistook him for Castlereagh.

Percy, Thomas (1729–1811), clergyman and antiquarian. He was born in Bridgnorth, Shropshire, the son of a grocer. He was educated at Oxford and was Rector of Easton Maudit, 1757–82, Dean of Carlisle, 1778–82, and then Bishop of Dromore from 1782, where he was a model diocesan. Percy amassed a collection of ancient ballads, and published *The Reliques of Ancient Poetry* in 1765.

Petty, William, 2nd Earl of Shelburne (1737–1805), politician. He trained in the army and entered Parliament as MP for Wycombe in 1760, succeeding to the title in 1761. He was Secretary for the Southern Department from 1766 to 1768. In 1782 he was Home Secretary, being promoted to the post of the First Lord of the Treasury in 1782–83, when he was involved in the negotiations leading to the Peace of Paris, 1783. His house at Bowood was a centre for intellectuals such as Priestley, Price and Bentham. He was created Marquis of Landsdowne in 1784.

Piozzi, Hester Thrale (1741–1821), diarist and travel writer. She was born near Pwlheli, Wales, the daughter of a landed gentleman. She was brought up in London and received a good education. She was married to Henry Thrale in 1763, much against her will. She moved in London literary circles. After Thrale's death in 1781 she married in 1784 the Catholic Italian musician Gabriel Piozzi, which caused a scandal. With him, she travelled though France, Italy and Germany and wrote *Anecdotes of the Late Samuel Johnson* (1786), and found materials for her *Observations and Reflections in . . . France, Italy and Germany* (1789). In 1795 she settled near Denbigh, Wales. She died in Clifton.

Pitt, William 'the Elder', 1st Earl of Chatham (1708–78), politician. He was MP for Old Sarum, 1735–47, for Seaford, 1747–54, for Aldborough, 1754–56, and for Okehampton, 1757–66. He became Vice-Treasurer of Ireland in 1746, Paymaster-General, 1746–55, and Secretary of State, 1756–57 and 1757–61. He was Lord Privy Seal from 1766, acting as Prime Minister, 1766–68. He was created Earl of Chatham in 1766. He made his reputation as an opponent of Walpole's, and for much of the early 1750s was a vociferous critic of the administration. He was an effective war leader in the Seven Years War. He supported some of the colonists' claims, although he stopped short of advocating independence. He collapsed and died during a debate in the Lords.

Pitt, William 'the Younger' (1759–1806), politician. He was the second son of the above. He became MP for Appleby, 1781–84, and for Cambridge University, 1784–1806. He was Chancellor of the Exchequer, 1782–83, and Prime Minister and Chancellor, 1783–1801 and 1804–6. He was the youngest ever Prime Minister. Pitt was chosen by George III as an alternative to the Fox–North coalition, and emerged as a powerful leader in the House of Commons. He carried out sweeping administrative reforms in the 1780s and was sympathetic to parliamentary reform. From 1793 he led Britain in the war against Revolutionary France, repressing radicalism at home and initiating new financial increases, such as the income tax. He resigned when the King refused to allow Catholic Emancipation in 1801, but returned to office in 1804.

Pope, Alexander (1688–1744), poet and translator. He was born in London, the son of Roman Catholic parents. He suffered from an illness as a child which left him permanently stunted. He was brought up in Windsor Forest. He published his *Pastorals* in 1709, and in 1711 his *Essay on Criticism*. *Windsor-Forest* (1713) has been seen as a pro-Jacobite poem, and brought him into contact with the Scriblerus Club. He produced his *Rape of the Lock* (1714) and began his translation of the *Iliad*. He moved to Twickenham in 1718, where he created a garden in the 'English style'. His translation of the *Odyssey* appeared in 1725, as did his edition of Shakespeare's *Works*. Versions of *The Dunciad* came out in 1728–29, with additions and revision in 1742–43. His *Moral Essays* were published in 1731–35, his *Essay on Man*, 1733–34, and his *Imitations of Horace*, 1733–38. He was increasingly associated with the opposition to Walpole.

Porteus, Beilby (1731–1808), clergyman. He was educated at Cambridge, where he won the Seatonian poetry prize, and after serving as chaplain to Archbishop Secker, became Bishop of Chester, 1776–87, and of London, 1787–1808. He was a supporter of the evangelical movement, was an early patron of the Church Missionary Society, and joined the British and Foreign Bible Society. He encouraged Hannah More.

Potter, John (?1674–1747), clergyman. He was born in Wakefield, the son of a linen-draper. Potter was educated at Oxford, and became Regius Professor of Divinity there in 1707. He was made Bishop of Oxford in 1715, and was moved to Canterbury in 1737. Potter's publications included *Archaeologia Graeca; or the Antiquities of Greece* (1697) and *Discourses on Church Government* (1707).

Price, Richard (1723–91), radical thinker. Born in Wales, he was educated at Moorfields Academy. From 1758 he was Minister of Newington Green. He published *A Review of the Principal Questions in Morals* (1757) and *Observations on the Nature of Civil Liberty* (1776), which supported the cause of the colonists in the American War of Independence. In 1789 Price showed his sympathy for the French Revolution in his sermon delivered on 4 November 1789, later published as *A Discourse on the Love of our Country*, which provoked Burke to write his *Reflections*.

Price, Uvedale (1747–1829), writer on the picturesque. He was born in Yazor, Herefordshire, and inherited a large fortune on the death of his father in 1761. He was educated at Eton and Christ Church, where he became a friend of Charles James Fox. He travelled with Fox to Italy. Price spent considerable sums of money improving his estates, where he put into practice his theory of picturesque beauty, against the theories of Brown and Repton. His views were outlined in his *An Essay on the Picturesque* (1794).

Priestley, Joseph (1733–1804), scientist and radical political thinker. He was born in Yorkshire, the son of a cloth-dresser, and became a Presbyterian minister at Nantwich. He was one of the original members of the Unitarian Society, founded in 1791. His house in Birmingham was mobbed and his laboratory burnt down in July 1791 by an anti-French revolutionary 'Church and King' mob. In 1794 he emigrated to America. His publications included *An Essay on the First Principles of Government* (1768), which was an important contribution to the development of utilitarianism, and *A History of the Corruptions of Christianity* (1782). He was the discoverer of oxygen and researched into the nature of electricity.

Prior, Matthew (1664–1721), poet. He was born in Wimborne, Dorset, the son of a joiner. He was educated at Westminster and Cambridge. He was made secretary to the ambassador at The Hague and was involved in negotiations for the Treaty of Ryswick. He became affiliated to the Tories and was a secret agent in Paris at the negotiations leading to the Treaty of Utrecht. He was imprisoned in 1714. His poems included *The Hind and the Panther Tranvers'd to the Story of the Country Mouse and the City Mouse* (1687), which was a skit on Dryden's poem, and occasional verses such as *Carmen Seculare* (1700), which was an ode in honour of William III.

Pulteney, William, 1st Earl of Bath (1684–1764), politician. He was MP for Hedon, 1705–34, and Middlesex, 1734–42. He became Secretary of State at War in 1714. He was originally a supporter of Walpole from 1717 to 1720, but became disaffected when he was not given a role in the government after 1722. By 1725 he had joined the opposition organised by Bolingbroke. His venom was fuelled when not given the chance to take over from Walpole in 1727. He helped to defeat Walpole during the 1733 Excise Crisis and was instrumental in pressing for war with Spain, which led to Walpole's fall in 1742. He was created Earl of Bath in 1742. Apart from a brief attempt in 1746 to replace Henry Pelham, he was henceforth marginalised from politics.

Radcliffe, Ann (1764–1832), novelist. She was the daughter of a London tradesman, and she married William Radcliffe, the manager of *The English Chronicle*, in 1786. She wrote 'gothic novels' and published *The Castles of Athlin and Dunbayne* (1789), *A Sicilian Romance* (1790), *The Romance of the Forest* (1791), *The Mysteries of Udolpho* (1794), for which she received an unprecedented £500 advance, and *The Italian* (1797).

Radcliffe, John (1652–1714), physician and benefactor. He was born in Yorkshire, the son of an attorney, was educated at Oxford, and practised as a physician first in Oxford and from 1684 in London. At the height of his career he earned £7,000 a year. He was appointed physician to Princess Anne in 1686, who dismissed him in 1694 when he suggested that her distemper was 'nothing but the vapours', and to William III after 1688. He was elected a Tory MP for Buckingham in 1713. In his will he left £140,000, most of which went to Oxford University to build the Radcliffe Camera and the Radcliffe Infirmary.

Raeburn, Henry (1756–1823), portrait painter. He was born in Edinburgh, the son of a manufacturer, and had started to paint pictures of his friends at the age of 16. After marrying a rich widow in 1778, he studied in Rome, and returned to Edinburgh in 1787, where he became a fashionable portrait painter for Scottish society. He was knighted in 1822, during George IV's visit to Edinburgh.

Ramsay, Allan (1713–84), portrait painter. He was born in Edinburgh, the son of a poet. He studied in London under the Swedish artist Hysing in 1734, and toured Italy from 1736 to 1738. He settled in London in 1739 and was appointed principal portrait painter to George III in 1767. An accident to his right arm in 1773 ended his painting career, and he devoted himself to travel and to writing.

Ray, John (1627–1703), naturalist. He was born in Essex, the son of a blacksmith, and was educated at Cambridge. He was ordained in 1660 but did not subscribe to the 1662 Act of Uniformity. He concentrated on his career as a naturalist and attempted to describe all living things. His *Historia Plantarum* (1686–1704) was a systematic classification of plant life, and has led him to be called the father of natural history. *The Wisdom of God in the Works of the Creation* (1691) discussed the adaptation of organisms to the environment as witness to God's design.

Repton, Humphry (1752–1818), landscape gardener. He was born in Bury St Edmunds, and spent some of his youth in Holland. He became a professional landscape gardener to support his growing family. Repton's major stylistic contribution was to add formal parterres and terraces. His technique was to use his 'red books' to show his clients the 'before' and 'after' effects. His *An Inquiry into the Changes of Taste in Landscape Gardening* was published in 1806.

Reynolds, Sir Joshua (1723–92), portrait and history painter. He was born in Plympton, Devon, the son of a clergyman, and after working under Thomas Hudson, went to Italy between 1749 and 1752, where he studied the Old Masters. He was a founder member and first President of the Royal Academy, 1768, and was knighted in 1769. The *Discourses* which he delivered to the students at the Royal Academy between 1769 and 1790 were influential statements on the theory of art.

Ricardo, David (1772–1823), economic theorist. He was born in London, of Dutch parents, and entered his father's firm as a stockjobber in 1793. He made a great deal of money on the Stock Exchange and bought Gatcombe Park in 1814. He was elected MP for the Irish borough of Portarlington in 1819. His *On the Principles of Political Economy and Taxation* (1817) became an influential statement of political economy.

Richardson, Jonathan, the Elder (1665–1745), portrait painter. He was born in London. He painted many of the most influential figures of the day, including Steele and Pope. His *Theory of Painting* (1715) became the standard work on aesthetics. His son Jonathan (1664–1771) also attempted to make a living as an artist, but suffered because he was short-sighted.

Richardson, Samuel (1689–1761), novelist. He was born near Derby, the son of a joiner, and in 1706 was apprenticed to a London printer. He established his own business in 1721, and wrote *The Apprentice's Vade Mecum* in 1733, which was a rule-book for the novice tradesman. His epistolary novels, *Pamela, or Virtue rewarded* (1740–41), *Clarissa* (1747–48), and *Sir Charles Grandison* (1753–54) were best-sellers.

Robertson, William (1721–92), historian. He was educated at Edinburgh University, and, having been a Presbyterian parish minister, became Principal of the university in 1762. His *History of Scotland during the reigns of Queen Mary and King James VI* (1759) was followed by his *History of the Reign of Charles V* (1769), *The History of America* (1777) and a *Disquisition concerning the knowledge which the Ancients had of India* (1791). He was leader of the group of moderate Presbyterians who dominated the Kirk in the second half the eighteenth century.

Rockingham, Charles Watson Wentworth, 2nd Marquis of (1730–82), politician. He was educated at Westminster and Cambridge and was appointed Lord of the Bedchamber in 1751 but resigned in 1762 to participate in the opposition to Bute. In 1765 he was appointed First Lord of the Treasury, organising the repeal of the Stamp Act, 1766. He resigned again in 1766 and became a trenchant supporter of 'economical reform'. He returned to power in 1782, but died after a few weeks in office.

Romilly, Samuel (1757–1818), legal reformer. He was born in London, the son of a Huguenot. He was appointed a King's Council in 1800 and in 1806 Solicitor-General. He was MP for Queenborough (1806), Wareham (1808), Arundel (1812), and Westminster (1818). He opposed the 1815 Corn Law and the suspension of Habeas Corpus in 1817. He supported Catholic Emancipation and abolition of slavery. After the death of his wife, he committed suicide.

Romney, George (1734–1802), painter. He was born in Beckside, near Dalton-in-Furness, the son of a builder and cabinet-maker. Romney developed an early talent for portrait painting. He married in 1756 and, leaving his wife and family, settled in London in 1762. He visited Italy, 1773–75. He became infatuated with Emma Hamilton, painting numerous portraits of her.

Roubilliac, Louis-François (?1702–62), sculptor. He was born in Lyons, and had settled in London by 1735. The statue of Handel (1738) for Vauxhall Gardens made his name, and he was commissioned to undertake seven major monuments for Westminster Abbey, including the monument to Lady Elizabeth Nightingale (1761). He taught sculpture at the St Martin's Lane Academy from 1745.

Rowe, Elizabeth (1674–1737), poet and religious writer. She was born in Ilchester, Somerset, the daughter of a dissenting Presbyterian preacher. She received patronage from the Thynne family at Longleat, and from Thomas Ken, the non-juror who had settled there. She married Thomas Rowe in 1713, and they moved to London. On his death in 1715, she retired to Frome. Her early poems were published by the Athenian Society. Her religious works include *Friendship in Death, or Letters from the Dead to the Living* (1728), *Letters Moral and Entertaining* (1728–32) and *Devout Exercises of the Heart* (1738).

Rowe, Nicholas (1674–1718), poet and dramatist. Rowe was educated at Westminster School, and, having studied at the Middle Temple, pursued a career as a playwright. His tragedies included *The Ambitious Step-Mother*

(1700), *Tamerlane* (1702) and *The Fair Penitent* (1703). In 1709 he published an edition of Shakespeare's *Works* and was appointed Poet Laureate in 1715.

Rowlandson, Thomas (1756–1827), artist and caricaturist. He was born in London, and after studying at the Royal Academy schools in 1772, visited France. He was noted for his political satires in the 1780s, but was best known for his satire of social fashions and foibles. His 'Dr Syntax' series (1809–21), notably the *Tour of Dr Syntax in Search of the Picturesque* (1812), satirised contemporary vogues.

Rysbrack, John Michael (1694–1770), sculptor. He was born in Antwerp, where he studied under Michel van der Voort. He had moved to England by 1720, and set the vogue for the classical style. Examples of his work included Robert Walpole in the garb of a Roman senator and the equestrian statue of William III in Bristol. He was responsible for more than eighty monuments, including that to Newton in Westminster Abbey and Marlborough's tomb at Blenheim.

Sacheverell, Henry (1674–1724), clergyman. He was the grandson of a nonconformist minister who had been ejected in 1662. Sacheverell was educated at Magdalen College, Oxford, and became a spokesman for 'high-flying' High-Church views. Following his outspoken sermon preached on 5 November 1709, taking as his text 'In perils amongst false brethren', which attacked the Whig government for allegedly putting the Church of England in danger by favouring the dissenters, Sacheverell was impeached in February 1710 for seditious libel. Riots broke out in London on the night of 1/2 March, and dissenting meeting houses were burnt. The election of October 1710 resulted in a strong Tory victory on the back of 'the Church in danger' slogan. Sacheverell was made rector of St Andrew's, Holborn in 1713. He died after slipping on a frost-covered stone step outside his house.

Sancroft, William (1617–1693), clergyman. He was born at Fressingfield, Suffolk, the son of a yeoman farmer. He was educated at Cambridge, but was deprived of his fellowship at Emmanuel College in 1651. From 1657 he was on the Continent, but returned at the Restoration and became Master of Emmanuel in 1662 and Dean of St Paul's in 1664. He was promoted to the archbishopric of Canterbury in 1678. He attempted, unsuccessfully, to reconvert James, Duke of York to the Protestant faith, and crowned him King in 1685. He did much to revitalise the Church, by improving the standards of the clergy and by using the Church courts to impose Anglicanism on the parishes. He declined to sit on the Court of Ecclesiastical Commission and in 1688 was one of the seven bishops who refused to read James's declaration of indulgence, for which he was imprisoned, but then acquitted. Although he did not condemn William's declaration of November 1688, Sancroft refused to swear loyalty to him as King. He was deprived of his office in 1690 and in 1691 was evicted from Lambeth Palace, after which he retired to Fressingfield.

Sandwich, John Montagu, 4th Earl of (1718–92), politician. He served three terms in office as First Lord of the Admiralty (1748–51, 1763, 1771–82), and did much to promote administrative reforms there. He was a promoter of the arts, and in particular music. He is remembered as the creator of the sandwich.

Scott, Sarah (1774–88), novelist and historian. She was the younger sister of Elizabeth Montagu. She received a good education, and in 1752 married George Scott, the sub-preceptor to the Prince of Wales. They separated in 1753, and she lived with her friend Lady Barbara Montagu, devoting themselves to charitable works. Her writings were published anonymously or pseudonymously. Her novels were *The History of Cordelia* (1750), *Agreeable Ugliness* (1754), *A Journal through every stage of Life* (1754), *A Description of Millennium Hall* (1762), *The History of Sir George Ellison* (1766) and *A Test of Filial Duty* (1772). The histories were *The History of Gustavus Ericson, king of Sweden* (1761), *The History of Mecklenburgh* (1762), occasioned by the marriage of George III and Charlotte of Mecklenburgh, and *The Life of Theodore Agrippa Daubigné* (1772).

Scott, Sir Walter (1771–1832), poet and novelist. He was born in Edinburgh, the son of a lawyer. He was educated at Edinburgh University and called to the Bar in 1792. He was appointed Sheriff-Depute of Selkirkshire in 1799. In 1809 Scott became a partner with John Ballantyne in the bookselling business and built a house at Abbotsford in 1811. His interest in the Border tales and ballads was stimulated by Percy's *Reliques*, and he produced *Minstrelsy of the Scottish Border* (1802–3), and his romantic poem *The Lay of the Last Minstrel* in 1805. His other poems were *Marmion* (1808), *The Lady of the Lake* (1810), *Rokeby* and *The Bridal of Triermain* (1813), *The Lord of the Isles* (1815) and *Harold the Dauntless* (1817). His historical novels were published anonymously: *Waverley* (1814), *Guy Mannering* (1815), *The Antiquary* (1816), *The Black Dwarf and Old Mortality* (1816), *Rob Roy* (1817), *The Heart of Midlothian* (1818), *The Bride of Lammermoor* and *A Legend of Montrose* (1819), *Ivanhoe* (1819), *The Monastery* (1820), *The Abbot* (1820), *Kenilworth* (1821), *The Pirate* (1821), *The Fortunes of Nigel* (1822), *Peveril of the Peak* (1823), *Quentin Durward* (1823), *St Ronan's Well* (1823), *Redgauntlet* (1824), *The Betrothed* and *The Talisman* (1825), *Woodstock* (1826), *Chronicles of Canongate* (1827), *St Valentine's Day*, or *The Fair Maid of Perth* (1828), *Anne of Geierstein* (1829), *Count Robert of Paris* and *Castle Dangerous* (1831). He also wrote plays and works of historical scholarship. He became involved in a bankruptcy case after 1825, which hastened his death.

Secker, Thomas (1693–1768), clergyman. He was born in Sibthorpe, Nottinghamshire, the son of a dissenter. He was educated at Attercliffe dissenting academy, with the intention of becoming a dissenting minister. In 1716 Secker went to London to study medicine, and furthered his studies at Leyden. He was persuaded to take orders within the Church of England, and was made Rector of Houghton-le-Spring, 1724, of Ryton, 1727, of St James's, Piccadilly, 1733, Bishop of Bristol, 1735, Bishop of Oxford, 1737, Dean of St Paul's, 1750, and Archbishop of Canterbury, 1758. His *Charges* to the clergy of his dioceses were much used manuals of pastoral care, and his *Lectures on the Church Catechism* (1769) were popular until the nineteenth century. He was a conscientious and able diocesan, and attempted to improve the pastoral oversight of the Church.

Seward, Anna, 'the swan of Lichfield' (1747–1809), poet and letter writer. She was born in Derbyshire and lived in Lichfield from 1754 when her father became a canon of the cathedral. She remained there until her death, apart from visits to London and Bath. The family knew Samuel Johnson and she had a wide circle of correspondents; six volumes of her letters were published in 1811. She wrote a large number of poems commemorating events, and in 1810 Sir Walter Scott edited her *Poetical Works* in three volumes.

Shaftesbury, Anthony Ashley Cooper, 3rd Earl of (1671–1713), philosopher and essayist. His ill health after 1702 excluded him from leading an active political life, and he concentrated on moral and intellectual philosophy. His writings were collected in *The Characteristics of Men, Manners, Opinions, and Times* (1711). He was best known for his attack on the selfish theory of Thomas Hobbes, advocating in its place benevolence. He also saw a close correlation between art and morality.

Sharp, Granville (1735–1813), anti-slavery campaigner. He was born in Durham, the son of the Archdeacon of Northumberland, and the grandson of an Archbishop of York. He was a government clerk in London and in 1765 became acquainted with Jonathan Strong, a destitute slave. He chaired the Committee for the Abolition of the Slave Trade from 1787 and established the African Institution to end the trade completely after its suppression in the British Empire. He founded the Society for the Conversion of the Jews in 1808 and the Protestant Union against Catholic Emancipation in 1813.

Shelley, Mary Wollstonecraft (1797–1851), author. She was the daughter of William Godwin and Mary Wollstonecraft, who died shortly after Mary's birth. She eloped with Shelley in 1814 and they lived in Europe, marrying when his wife committed suicide in 1816. Her best-known novel, *Frankenstein, or the Modern Prometheus*, was published in 1818. Shelley died in 1822, and Mary came back to England, and maintained herself by writing, including *Valperga* (1823), *The Last Man* (1826) and *Lodore* (1835).

Shelley, Percy Bysshe (1792–1822), Romantic poet. He was born in Sussex, the son of an MP, and educated at Eton and Oxford, from where he was sent down for writing the pamphlet 'The Necessity of Atheism'. After an unfortunate first marriage, Shelley eloped with the above in 1814, and they lived on the Continent. He mixed in radical circles, being a friend of Godwin and Byron. He published *Queen Mab* in 1813 and *Prometheus Unbound* in 1820. On hearing of the Peterloo Massacre in 1819, he wrote *The Masque of Anarchy*, which was published after his death.

Shenstone, William (1714–1763), poet and landscape gardener. He was born in Worcestershire and educated at Oxford, where he published his *Poems on Various Occasions* (1737). His best-known works included *The Judgement of Hercules* (1737) and *The Schoolmistress* (1742). He transformed his farm at the Leasowes, Halesowen, into a landscape garden.

Sheraton, Thomas (1751–1806), furniture designer. He was born in Stockton-on-Tees, and moved to London in 1790. His popular *The Cabinet-Maker and Upholster's Drawing Book* (1791–94) was a wide-ranging manual on furniture design. He was deeply religious.

Sheridan, Richard Brinsley (1751–1819), politician and playwright. He was the son of an Irish actor-manager. *The Rivals* was performed at Covent Garden in 1775 and was immensely successful, and this was followed by other plays, including *The School for Scandal* (1777) and *The Critic* (1779). He entered Parliament in 1780 as MP for Stafford, and was an ally of Charles James Fox. He was offered the post of Under-Secretary for Foreign Affairs in 1782, and became Secretary to the Treasury in 1783. His speech, lasting over five hours, at the impeachment of Warren Hastings in 1787 brought him fame as an orator. He held the post of Treasurer to the Navy, 1806–7. He lost his seat in 1811 and he died in near poverty.

Sherlock, Thomas (1678–1761), clergyman. He was educated at Cambridge, where his rivalry began with Benjamin Hoadly, who was two years his senior. Sherlock was appointed Master of the Temple, and he held the post until 1752. He was one of Hoadly's leading opponents in the Bangorian controversy, being chairman of the committee appointed to report on Hoadly's 'nature of the kingdom or Church of Christ'. Sherlock was made Bishop of Bangor in 1728, of Salisbury in 1734, and of London in 1748. His *A Trial of the Witnesses of the Resurrection of Jesus* (1729) was a defence of the historical occurrence of miracles.

Shipley, Jonathan (1714–88), clergyman. He was educated at Oxford, and became Rector of Silchester, 1743, Dean of Windsor, 1760, Bishop of Llandaff, 1769, and Bishop of St Asaph, 1769–88. Shipley was a friend of Benjamin Franklin, and was an opponent of British policy towards the American colonies. He advocated repeal of the Test and Corporation Acts and wanted parliamentary reform.

Shippen, William (1673–1743), Jacobite. He was the son of a clergyman and, having trained to be a barrister, entered Parliament in 1707 as Tory MP for Bramber, which he also represented between 1710 and 1713. He represented Saltash, 1713–15, and Newton, Lancashire, 1715–43. Shippen was a constant critic of the Hanoverian dynasty, but did not get involved with any of the plots to place the Pretender on the throne.

Siddons, Sarah (1755–1831), actress. She was the eldest child of Roger Kemble, an actor-manager, and travelled throughout England as part of the family's theatrical company. She had a season in London (1775–56) which was not a success, but her second attempt in 1782 saw her regarded as the greatest tragic actress of her day. She excelled in Shakespearean roles, and in particular as Lady Macbeth. Reynolds painted a portrait of her as 'the Tragic Muse' in 1783, which is often considered to be his masterpiece. She retired in 1812, making a brief, unsuccessful, come-back in 1819.

Simeon, Charles (1759–1836), evangelical leader. He was born in Reading and while at Eton underwent a religious conversion in 1776. He went up to King's College, Cambridge, and became ordained. He was made Vicar of Holy Trinity, Cambridge, 1786–1836, and became a leading force in the evangelical revival. He was a founder member of the Church Missionary Society in 1797, and was active in the British and Foreign Bible Society.

Sloane, Sir Hans (1660–1753), physician and scientist. He was physician to the Governor of Jamaica, 1687–89, and published a catalogue of the plants of Jamaica in 1696. He was Secretary of the Royal Society, 1693–1712, and President of the Royal College of Physicians, 1719–35. His collection of books and manuscripts was bought by the nation and placed in Montague House, later the British Museum.

Smart, Christopher (1722–71), poet. He was born near Tonbridge, Kent, and educated at Durham School and Cambridge, where he was noted as a classical scholar. He moved to London in 1749, and earned his living as a journalist. In 1756 he became ill, and between 1759 and 1763 was installed in a private madhouse in Bethnal Green, having shown signs of religious mania. He published his *A Song to David* in 1763, but declined into poverty and debt, dying within the rules of the King's Bench prison. During his time at Bethnal Green he composed *Jubilate Agno* (which was not published until 1939).

Smith, Adam (1723–90), economic theorist. He was born at Kircaldy, Fife, and educated at Glasgow University, and Balliol College, Oxford. In 1748 he was appointed Lecturer in Edinburgh, and became Professor of Logic at Glasgow in 1751, moving to the chair of Moral Philosophy in 1752. In 1759 he published *The Theory of Moral Sentiments*, which brought him recognition. He resigned his professorship in 1764 to be tutor to the Duke of Buccleuch, travelling with him to France. On his return to Kircaldy he concentrated on his major work, *An Inquiry into the Nature and Causes of the Wealth of Nations*, published in 1776, and which advocated free trade and competition.

Smith, Sidney (1771–1845), clergyman and writer. He was educated at Winchester and Oxford, and moved to Edinburgh, helping to found the *Edinburgh Review* in 1802 as a counter-blast to the Tory *Quarterly Review*. He wrote for the journal for over 25 years, contributing articles on Catholic Emancipation, Church reform, slavery, etc. He moved to London in 1803, and became known as a witty supporter of the Whigs. He published *The Letters of Peter Plymley* in 1807, which advocated Catholic Emancipation. Smith was Rector of Foston, Yorkshire, from 1806, and in 1829 was given the living of Combe Florey, Somerset. He was appointed a canon of St Paul's in 1831.

Smollett, Tobias (1721–71), novelist and surgeon. He was born near Dunbarton, the son of a wealthy laird. He was educated at Glasgow University and became apprenticed to a surgeon. He settled in London, and after serving as a surgeon in the navy during war in the West Indies, 1741–43, he established a practice in London. His novels included *Roderick Random* (1748), *Peregrine Pickle* (1751) and *Humphry Clinker* (1771), which, ranging from London to the provinces of England and to Scotland and Wales, can be regarded as a 'British' novel. In 1756 he was the founder-editor of the *Critical Review*, a literary journal, and he published a continuation of Hume's *History of England* (1757–58). He was the editor of the pro-government newspaper *The Briton*, which was attacked by John Wilkes in *The North Briton*. Ill health led him to take a continental tour, and he published his *Travels through France and Italy* in 1766. He died at Leghorn.

Soane, Sir John (1753–1837), architect. He was of humble origins, and changed his name from 'Swan' to 'Soane'. He was a Royal Academy medallist in 1772 and 1776 and travelled to Italy between 1777 and 1780, where he was influenced by Greek and Italian classical styles. In 1788 he was invited to design the new Bank of England. Other commissions included the Westminster Law Courts and Dulwich Art Gallery. He was knighted in 1831.

Somerset, Charles Seymour, 6th Duke of (1662–1748), 'the proud duke'. He was Gentleman of the Bedchamber to Charles II and James II, but James discharged him in 1687 for not publicly greeting the papal nuncio. He supported William in 1688, but sided with the Princess Anne. In 1702 he was given the post of Master of the Horse, but lost it when the Marlborough–Godolphin faction fell from power in 1712. At the Hanoverian succession he resumed his office.

Southcott, Joanna (1750–1814), religious fanatic. She was born in Devon and began life as a dairy-maid before entering domestic service. She joined the Methodists in 1791, and started having religious experiences. In 1793 she announced that she was the woman in the Book of Revelations, chapter 12 who would give birth to the second Christ in 1814, and began to 'seal' the 144,000 elect, at a charge, although she abandoned this when one of her elect was hanged for murder in 1809. She published *The Strange Effects of Faith* in 1801. She came to London in 1802. Her *Prophecies announcing the Prince of Peace* appeared in 1814. She died of a brain disease. On her death she left a box which was said to contain prophecies, and which was to be opened after a century. It was opened in 1927, and was found to contain, among other pieces of trivia, a nightcap and a lottery ticket.

Southey, Robert (1774–1843), writer. He was born in Bristol, the son of a linen-draper. He was expelled from Eton for starting a magazine, *The Flagellant*, and went up to Oxford, where he planned the ideal settlement, the Pantisocracy, with Coleridge. He was a supporter of the French Revolution and travelled to Portugal in 1795, marrying Edith Fricker in the same year (Coleridge married her sister). After visiting Spain in 1800, he settled in the Lake District. He became increasingly conservative, receiving a government pension in 1807, and writing for the Tory *Quarterly Review* from 1809. In 1813 he was made poet laureate, and published his *Life of Nelson*. He wrote a *History of Brazil* (1810–19) and a *Life of Wesley* (1820). In 1821 appeared his *A Vision of Judgement*, which was written to commemorate the death of George III. Other works included his *History of the Peninsular War* (1823–32), *The Book of the Church* (1824) and *A Tale of Paraguay* (1825). Peel granted him a government pension of £300 p.a. in 1835. He became insane.

Spence, Thomas (1750–1814), radical reformer. He was born in Newcastle-Upon-Tyne and earned a living as a bookseller. His 'Plan', first aired in 1775, argued for the public ownership of land. He settled in London in 1787 and became a member of the London Corresponding Society in 1792. He produced a periodical, *Pig's Meat*, from 1793 to 1796, and was imprisoned several times.

Spencer, Charles, 3rd Earl of Sunderland (1674–1722), politician. He was the son of the 2nd Earl and became MP for Tiverton in 1695, where he was a noted Whig spokesman and publicist. In 1700 he married a daughter of the Duke and Duchess of Marlborough and in 1706 was appointed Secretary of State for the Southern Department. He urged for the impeachment of Sacheverell in 1710, thereby losing royal favour. After the Hanoverian succession he was not given the high office he wanted, and worked for the downfall of Walpole and Townshend, whom he ousted in 1717, taking over from Townshend as Secretary of State for the Northern Department. He was promoted to the First Lordship of the Treasury in 1718, becoming co-leader of the government with Stanhope. The South Sea Bubble of 1720 forced him to resign leadership to Walpole, and although he was able to maintain influence with George I, he died unexpectedly in 1722.

Spencer, Robert, 2nd Earl of Sunderland (1641–1702), politician. He had experience as an ambassador, and in 1678 was appointed Secretary of State, but was dismissed in 1681 for supporting the exclusion of James, Duke of York from the throne. By 1682 he had returned to favour, becoming the chief figure of government, and a proponent of pro-French foreign policy. He was made Lord President of the Council in 1685, and managed the Crown's patronage. He was responsible for the implementation of James's pro-Catholic policies, and announced his own conversion to the Catholic faith in June 1688. When William invaded, Sunderland urged James to reverse his policies, but was dismissed. Sunderland fled to Holland, and returned in 1690, when he reconverted. He began to advise William III, and was made Lord Chamberlain in 1697, which a hostile House of Commons forced him to give up in 1698. He remained a confidant of the King.

Stanhope, James Stanhope, 1st Earl (1673–1721), politician, soldier and diplomat. Militarily, Stanhope received recognition for his role in the

War of the Spanish Succession. He was MP for Newport in 1701, and for Cockermouth, 1702–13 and 1714–17. At the accession of George I, Stanhope was appointed Secretary of State for the Southern Department, 1714–16, for the Northern Department, 1716–17, 1718–21, and First Lord of the Treasury and Chancellor of the Exchequer, 1717–18. With Sunderland, he was in control of the ministry from 1717 until 1720. His diplomatic skills were demonstrated at the Triple and Quadruple Alliances of 1717 and 1718.

Stanhope, Philip Dormer, 4th Earl of Chesterfield (1694–1773), politician, diplomat and writer. He became an MP in 1715 and served in the future George II's household. He was Ambassador to The Hague, 1728–32, and on his return became involved with the opposition to Walpole. In 1745 he allied himself with Pelham, and took the post of Lord Lieutenant of Ireland. In 1746 he was made Secretary of State for the Northern Department, but resigned in 1748. His *Letters to his Son* were published posthumously in 1774.

Stanhope, William, 1st Earl of Harrington (1690–1756), soldier and politician. He was active in the English army in Spain, and became a general. In 1715 he was elected MP for Derby and was made Ambassador to Spain. Walpole appointed him Secretary of State in 1730, and after Walpole's fall he continued in office, being made Lord President of the Council, 1742–45. He was reinstated as Secretary of State in 1744, and from 1746 to 1750 was Lord Lieutenant of Ireland.

Steele, Sir Richard (1672–1729), writer and politician. He was born in Dublin, educated at Charterhouse and Oxford, and joined the army. He published *The Christian Hero* in 1701. From 1717 he was employed as a government information officer. He edited *The Tatler*, 1709–11, and, with Addison, *The Spectator*, 1711–13, and *The Guardian*, 1713. In that year he took a seat in Parliament as MP for Stockbridge, but was expelled in 1714 for his attack on the Harley Ministry. He was knighted in 1715. By 1718 he had fallen out with Addison, and after writing a successful play, *The Conscious Lovers* (1722), lived the rest of his life in Wales.

Sterne, Laurence (1713–68), clergyman and novelist. He was born in Ireland, the son of a soldier. He was educated at Cambridge and became ordained in 1737. He was made Vicar of Suttton-in-the-Forest, York, 1738, Prebendary of York, 1741, and Vicar of Coxwold, 1760. He published *Tristram Shandy* in five instalments between 1759 and 1767. Suffering from consumption, he travelled to France and Italy, 1762–64. His *A Sentimental Journey* was published in 1768. He died in debt.

Stuart, Prince Charles Edward (1720–88), 'the Young Pretender'. He was the elder son of the 'Old Pretender' and grandson of the exiled James II. He was born in Rome. In 1744 he went to France to prepare for the proposed invasion of England. He sailed for Scotland in July 1745 with the object of raising a rebellion in the Highlands to activate French help. He was able to take most of Scotland and reached as far as Derby. The rebellion was crushed at Culloden, after which 'Bonnie Prince Charlie' had to go into hiding. He was later expelled from France, and died in Rome.

Stubbs, George (1724–1806), painter and engraver. He was born in Liverpool and studied anatomy in York in 1750. He visited Rome in 1754. In 1766 he brought out a series of engraved plates, *The Anatomy of the Horse*, which were based on ten years' intensive study and dissections.

Swift, Jonathan (1667–1745), clergyman and writer. He was born in Dublin and was educated at Kilkenny School and Trinity College, Dublin. In 1689 he was made Secretary to Sir William Temple, and was ordained in 1694. By 1699 he had returned to Ireland as Vicar of Laracor, and made frequent trips to England, where he moved in literary circles. In 1704 he published *A Tale of a Tub* and in 1710 wrote for *The Examiner*. In 1711 his *The Conduct of the Allies* attacked the war with France. He was appointed Dean of St Patrick's Cathedral, Dublin, in 1713 and represented Irish interests against the English government. His *Drapier's Letters* (1724) attacked the introduction of 'Wood's halfpence' to Ireland. Swift published *Gulliver's Travels* in 1726 and his *A Modest Proposal for Preventing the Children of the Poor from being a Burden to their Parents or Country* in 1729.

Talbot, Catherine (1721–70), poet, essayist and letter writer. She came from a clerical family, and her father, who was the son of a Bishop of Durham, died before she was born. Catherine and her mother lived in the household of Thomas Secker, who later became Bishop of Oxford and then Archbishop of Canterbury. Catherine moved in literary and social circles. She wrote poems and some works of piety, which were published after her death. She was best known for her letters to Elizabeth Carter.

Tate, Nahum (1652–1715), writer. He was born in Ireland and educated at Trinity College, Dublin. His reworkings of Shakespeare's plays were frequently performed. Tate was appointed Poet Laureate in 1692 and Historiographer-Royal in 1702. With Nicholas Brady (1659–1726), Tate published the popular *New Version of the Psalms* (1696) in metre. His major original poem was *Panacea – a Poem on Tea* (1700).

Telford, Thomas (1757–1834), civil engineer and road-builder. He was born in Dumfries, the son of a shepherd. From 1780 he was employed as a stonemason in building houses in Edinburgh's New Town. He moved to London in 1782. Amongst a variety of projects, he managed road- and bridge-building in the Scottish Highlands, developed the Shrewsbury to Holyhead road (from 1802), and built suspension bridges at Menai (1820) and Conwy (1822).

Tenison, Thomas (1636–1715), clergyman. He was born at Cottenham, the son of a clergyman. He was educated at Cambridge and was Rector of St Martin-in-the-Fields, 1680–92, St James's, Piccadilly, 1686–92, Archdeacon of London, 1689–92, Bishop of Lincoln, 1692–95, and Archbishop of Canterbury from 1695. Tenison was a firm supporter of William III and backed the foundation of the Society for the Promotion of Christian Knowledge, the Society for the Propagation of the Gospel, charity schools and the societies for the reformation of manners.

Thelwall, John (1764–1834), political reformer. He was the son of a London silk mercer, and after some legal training, began to earn his living as a writer. His *Politics for the People, or Hogwash* (1793) led to Thelwall being charged for treason. Apart from political writings, from 1800 Thelwall developed speech therapy.

Thistlewood, Arthur (1770–1820), political radical. He imbibed revolutionary ideas while serving in the army during the American and French wars. Thistlewood organised the Spa Fields meeting in 1816, and led the group of London extremists arrested for conspiring to murder Liverpool and the Cabinet in 1820. He was a convicted of high treason for the Cato Street Conspiracy and hanged.

Thomson, James (1700–48), poet and dramatist. He was born at Ednham, on the Scottish borders, the son of a clergyman. After being educated at Edinburgh University, he settled in London in 1725. He was taken up by Lord Lyttelton, and in 1731 was tutor to Charles Talbot, accompanying him on the Grand Tour. His poems included *The Seasons* (1726–30), *Liberty* (1735–36) and *The Castle of Indolence* (1748). His masque *Alfred* (1740) contained 'Rule Britannia', which was set to music by Thomas Arne. He also wrote tragedies: *Sophonisba* (1730), *Agamemnon* (1738), *Edward and Eleanora* (1739) and *Tancred and Sigismunda* (1745).

Thornhill, James (1675–1734), painter. He was born in Dorset, and became the leading British-born Baroque painter. His works included the Painted Hall at Greenwich (1708–27), the dome of St Paul's Cathedral (1714–19) and the ceiling of the Hall at Blenheim (1716). He was knighted in 1720.

Tillotson, John (1630–94), clergyman. He was educated at Cambridge. Tillotson was ordained into the Church of England in 1661, and was appointed lecturer at St Lawrence Jewry, were he became noted for his 'plain preaching style'. He became a royal chaplain and was made Dean of Canterbury in 1672. He advocated comprehension of nonconformists. He was made Dean of St Paul's in 1689 and became Archbishop in 1691. His *Sermons* (14 vols, 1695–1704) were held up as models of lucid prose and 'the plain style'.

Tindal, Matthew (1657–1733), Deist. He was born in Devon, and educated at Oxford, where he became a fellow of All Souls. His *The Rights of the Christian Church Asserted* (1706) was a defence of the Low-Church position, and his *A Defence of the Rights of the Christian Church* (1709) was burnt by order of the House of Commons in 1710. His *Christianity as Old as Creation* (1730) was an attack on revealed religion.

Toland, John (1670–1722), Deist. He was born in Ireland, to a Roman Catholic family, but he converted to Protestantism in 1686. He went to Glasgow University in 1687, and studied divinity at Leyden. He went to Oxford in 1694, publishing *Christianity Not Mysterious* in 1696. This was burnt by the Irish House of Commons in 1697. He published a *Life of Milton* in 1697. He defended the Act of Succession of 1701 in his *Anglia Libera* (1701), which brought him the favour of the Electress Sophia. He spent some time in Hanover and Berlin, and returned to England in 1710, writing against High-Churchmen and Jacobites. His *Pantheisticon* (1720) expounded a pagan creed. He died in poverty, ruined by the South Sea Bubble.

Tone, Wolfe (1763–98), Irish patriot. He was born in Dublin, the son of wealthy Protestant parents. He was a supporter of Catholic Emancipation, publishing *An Argument on behalf of the Catholics of Ireland* (1791). He played a major role in founding the United Irish Society in 1791. Having been implicated in a treason trial, Tone spent a short time in America and from 1796 to 1798 was the United Irish Emissary in France, where he tried to secure French help for the Irish republican movement. In 1796 and 1798 he participated in the French invasions, and, after being captured in 1798, committed suicide.

Tooke, John Horne (1736–1812), political radical. He was the son of a poulterer named Horne, and later adopted the name of a friend Tooke. He was educated at Cambridge, and after becoming ordained became the incumbent of a chapel at ease at Brentwood in 1760. He was a supporter of Wilkes in the 1768 Middlesex election and in 1769 helped to found the Society of the Supporters of the Bill of Rights. He formed the Constitutional Society in 1771, and in 1774 had to account before the House of Commons for his attack on the Speaker, and was imprisoned in 1778 for his support of the American colonists. Tooke joined the Society for Constitutional Information in 1780, and was member of the London Corresponding Society from 1792. In 1794 Tooke was arrested for high treason, but was acquitted. He made several attempts to enter Parliament, and in 1801 became member for Old Sarum. In the same year an act was passed making clergymen ineligible for parliament.

Townshend, Charles, 2nd Viscount (1674–1738), politician and agriculturalist. He succeeded to the peerage in 1687, and became a leading Whig politician after 1688. He married Robert Walpole's sister in 1713 and was appointed Secretary of State for the Northern Department in 1714. He was made Lord Lieutenant of Ireland in 1717, and with Walpole resigned from government in that year. In 1720 he was made Lord President of the Council and again Secretary of State in 1721. He and Walpole ran the government for most of the 1720s, but he resigned in 1730, largely because of disagreements over foreign policy. He spent the remaining years of his life concentrating on improving his estates, and was nicknamed 'Turnip Townshend' for the crop rotation system he devised.

Townshend, Charles (1725–67), politician. A grandson of the above, he entered Parliament in 1747 as MP for Great Yarmouth. Townshend was made Lord of the Admiralty, 1754, Secretary at War, 1761–62, President of the Board of Trade, 1763, and was appointed Chancellor of the Exchequer in 1766. In 1767 his 'Townshend duties' was an attempt to raise money by imposing taxes on a range of goods imported from America, which contributed to the revolt of the colonists. He died of a fever in late 1767.

Trenchard, John (1662–1723), political writer. A Whig, a supporter of reform in Britain, and a bitter critic of William III's policies, he wrote, with Walter Moyle, *An Argument showing . . . a Standing Army . . . inconsistent with a Free Constitution* (1697). He cooperated with Thomas Gordon in a London weekly, *The Independent Whig* (1720–21), and in weekly letters signed 'Cato' (1720–23) published in the *London Journal*. Trenchard was a fierce critic of the failure to punish those involved in the South Sea Company and he was MP for Taunton from 1722.

Trimmer, Sarah (1741–1810), author. She was born in Ipswich, the daughter of an architectural draughtsman, who later taught drawing to the future George III. Sarah married James Trimmer in 1762, and they lived at Brentford. She was a devout Anglican evangelical and published a number of works for children, including *An Easy Introduction to the*

Knowledge of Nature and reading the Holy Scriptures, adapted to the capacities of children (1780), *Sacred History* (1782), *Abridgements of the Old and New Testaments* (1793), as well as commentaries on the catechism and prayer book. She was a keen supporter of the Sunday school movement, publishing *The Oeconomy of Charity* (1787) on behalf of the cause. Her *Fabulous Histories, designed for the Instruction of Children, respecting their treatment of animals,* appeared in 1786, of which the section entitled 'The History of the Robins' remained very popular.

Trotter, Catherine (1679–1749), dramatist, poet and philosopher. She was born in London, the daughter of a naval captain who became a Jacobite. After her father's death, Catherine was forced to become a writer, and her *Agnes de Castro* was performed in 1695. Her first real success was with *Fatal Friendship* (1698). She met John Locke, and in 1702 published *A Defence of Mr Locke's Essay on Human Understanding* and in 1727 *A Vindication of Mr Locke's Christian Principles.*

Tull, Jethro (1674–1741), advocate of the seed-drill. He came from a minor gentry family and began farming at the end of the seventeenth century in Oxfordshire and Berkshire. His publication of 1733, *The Horse-Hoeing Husbandry,* popularised the use of the seed-drill.

Turner, John Mallord William (1775–1851), artist. He was born in London, the son of a barber. He was educated at the Royal Academy schools, and first exhibited at the Academy in 1790. From 1792 he began his sketching tours of Britain and Europe. Works include *Frosty Morning* (1813), *The Fighting Téméraire* (1839) and *Rain, Steam and Speed – the Great Western Railway* (1844).

Vanbrugh, Sir John (1664–1726), dramatist and architect. He was born in London, of a Dutch family, who moved to Chester after 1665. He was a soldier from 1686, and was imprisoned in France from 1688 to 1692. Vanbrugh had great success with his plays: *The Relapse, or Virtue in Danger* (1696), *The Provok'd Wife* (1697) and *The Confederacy* (1705). In *c.* 1700 he was commissioned to design Castle Howard, and he was made Comptroller of the Board of Works in 1702. He worked on Blenheim Palace from 1705. His other works included King's Weston, near Bristol (1705–25), Grimsthorpe (1715–30) and Seaton Delaval (1718–29).

Vernon, Edward (1684–1757), admiral and politician. He was the son of a Secretary of State to William III and joined the navy in 1699. He entered Parliament in 1722 as MP for Penryn, but lost his seat in 1734. After war was declared on Spain in 1739 he was given the post of vice-admiral and went to the West Indies. He became a national hero after defeating the Spanish forces at Porto Bello. He returned to Parliament in 1742 as MP for Ipswich, and although he became an admiral in 1745, Vernon was dismissed after publishing letters critical of the government.

Wade, George (1673–1748), soldier. In 1715 he entered Parliament as MP for Hindon, and became MP for Bath in 1722. He was in Scotland between 1724 and 1740, where he oversaw military road-building. He was made a field marshal in 1743 and he fought in Flanders in 1744. In 1745 he was appointed leader of the army in Newcastle during the Jacobite rebellion.

Wade, John (1788–1845), radical author. He was the leader-writer of *The Spectator*, 1828–58. His *The Black Book* (1820–23) exposed corruption and sinecures in the political and ecclesiastical worlds.

Wake, William (1657–1737), clergyman. He was educated at Oxford, and became chaplain to the English Ambassador in Paris, where he developed a continuing interest in the French Church, later attempting to create a union between the French Gallican and Anglican Churches. He was made a canon of Christ Church, Oxford, 1689–1702, Dean of Exeter, 1703–5, Bishop of Lincoln, 1705, and Archbishop in 1716. He lost influence after 1723 to Edmund Gibson. His writings included *The State of the Church and Clergy of England* (1703), which was a reply to Francis Atterbury's writings on Convocation. His *The Principles of the Christian Religion* (1700), a commentary on the catechism, was much used in the eighteenth century.

Walpole, Horace, 4th Earl of Orford (1717–97), letter writer and artistic connoisseur. He was the fourth son of Robert Walpole, and was educated at Eton, where he formed a friendship with Thomas Gray. He travelled to Italy with Gray from 1739 to 1741. He became an MP in 1741, representing Callington, Castle Rising and Lynn successively until 1768. He bought a villa at Strawberry Hill, Twickenham, in 1747, which he Gothicised. He wrote the Gothick novel *The Castle of Otranto* (1764), and his *Historic Doubts on Richard III*, which attempted to acquit Richard of the crimes of which he was accused, was published in 1768. Walpole's *Memoirs* were published in the nineteenth century.

Walpole, Robert (1676–1745), politician, often styled the first Prime Minister. He was born into a Norfolk gentry family and entered Parliament as MP for Castle Rising, 1701–2, and sat for King's Lynn, 1702–12, 1713–42. In 1701 he served on the Committee for Privileges and Elections, and in 1705 became a member of the council to Prince George of

Denmark. Walpole was given the offices of Secretary at War, 1708, and Treasurer of the Navy, 1710. Because of his involvement in the War of the Spanish Succession and his role in the trial of Dr Sacheverell, Walpole was impeached for corruption, sent to the Tower in 1711, and expelled from Parliament in 1712. In 1714 he was promoted to the post of Paymaster-General, becoming First Lord of the Treasury and Chancellor of the Exchequer in 1715. He was charged with the conduct of Bolingbroke's impeachment. In 1717 Walpole entered the opposition and re-entered the government in 1720. He helped save the government and the Hanoverian dynasty in 1720–21 during the aftermath of the South Sea Bubble. Walpole's rise to power was greatly helped by the fortuitous deaths and removal from office of his major rivals, and by his management of the Atterbury plot which allowed him to use the Jacobite threat to consolidate his power base, and enabled him to accuse his opponents of being Jacobites. His control of the patronage system and his use of the House of Commons as the centre of political power, marked by his refusal to accept a peerage in 1723, contributed to his maintenance of office. In the Excise Crisis of 1733 Walpole was made to withdraw unpopular policy, and he lost support in Scotland for his repressive treatment of the Porteous riots in 1736. For much of his time in office he favoured a pacific foreign policy which enabled him to keep taxation low. Walpole was forced in 1739 to declare war on Spain, and in 1742 he fell from power, becoming Earl of Orford.

Warburton, William (1698–1779), clergyman and writer. He was apprenticed to an attorney for five years, until he was ordained in 1727. He held several posts in the Church, becoming Dean of Bristol in 1757 and Bishop of Gloucester in 1759. He was much involved in religious controversy, and his *The Alliance of Church and State* (1736) was a defence of the inter-dependence of Church and State. *The Divine Legation of Moses* (1737–41) contended for the divine origin of the Mosaic law, and was an attack on Deism. His *The Doctrine of Grace* (1762) was a denunciation of Methodism. Warburton also moved in literary circles and published an edition of Shakespeare's *Works* in 1741 and an edition of Pope's *Works* in 1751.

Waterland, Daniel (1683–1740), clergyman and theologian. He was educated at Cambridge, and held various posts in the Church, becoming Archdeacon of Middlesex in 1730. He was active in many of the theological debates of the day, particularly those concerning the Trinity, Deism and the nature of the Eucharist. His major writings were *A Vindication of Christ's Divinity* (1719), *Eight Sermons in Defence of the Divinity of our Lord Jesus Christ* (1720) and *The Nature, Obligation and Efficacy of the Christian Sacraments* (1732).

Watson, Richard (1737–1816), clergyman. He was educated at Cambridge, and in 1764 was elected Professor of Chemistry, and in 1771 Regius Professor of Divinity. He was made Archdeacon of Ely in 1779, and became Bishop of Llandaff in 1782. Watson advocated reforms within the Church, particularly concerning the redistribution of ecclesiastical revenues, and was a critic of the war against America. In 1796 he published *An Apology for the Bible*, against the writings of Thomas Paine.

Watt, James (1736–1819), steam engineer. He was instrument-maker to Glasgow University, and in partnership with Boulton patented a number of developments, including reciprocation (1782) and parallel motion (1784).

Watts, Isaac (1678–1748), nonconformist hymn writer. He was born in Southampton, and entered the Stoke Newington Dissenting Academy in 1690. In 1699 he was appointed assistant, and in 1702 pastor of the Mark Lane independent congregation in London. Ill health forced him to retire in 1712. His hymns included 'When I survey the wondrous Cross' and 'O God, our help in ages past'. Collections of his hymns were brought out as *Hymns and Spiritual Songs* (1707) and *The Psalms of David Imitated* (1719). His *Divine Songs for the Use of Children* (1715) was the first hymn book written especially for children. He also wrote educational manuals and poetry.

Wedgwood, Josiah (1730–95), potter and manufacturer. He was born into a family of potters from Staffordshire, and by 1758 had established his own firm, setting up the factory at Etruria in 1769. He was an effective advertiser, and called his new creamware Queen's Ware after Queen Charlotte. In politics he was liberal, supporting both the American and French Revolutions and advocating the abolition of slavery. He was a founder member of the Lunar Society of Birmingham.

Wellesley, Arthur, 1st Duke of Wellington (1769–1852), soldier and Prime Minister. He was the son of an Irish peer. Having been educated at Eton, he entered the army and served in the Low Countries during the wars with France. In India he showed his skills, leading the victories at Assaye and Argaum in 1803. He was sent to Portugal in 1808, which he successfully defended from the French. In 1815 he commanded the British troops at the Battle of Waterloo. He was MP for Trim, 1790–95, for Rye, 1806, for Mitchel in 1807, and for Newport, 1807–9. He acted as Chief Secretary for Ireland between 1807 and 1809, and from 1819 to 1827 he was Master-General of the Ordnance. In 1828 he became Prime Minister, but resigned in 1830 over his refusal to countenance franchise reform. Wellington was Foreign Secretary, 1834–35, and Minister Without Portofolio from 1841 to 1846.

Wesley, Charles (1707–88), Methodist leader and hymn writer. He was educated at Oxford, and after being ordained became a leading Methodist preacher. His hymns (over 7,000) included 'Hark! The Herald Angels Sing' and 'Jesu, Lover of my Soul'. He remained closer to the Church of England than his brother John, disapproving in particular of the latter's ordinations.

Wesley, John (1703–91), the founder of Methodism. His father was a Church of England cleric and his mother was the daughter of a Presbyterian minister. Wesley was educated at Oxford, and became a fellow of Lincoln College. In 1729 he was the founder of a group of devout Christians who were called Methodists because of their strict methods of study and practice. He was a missionary to Georgia, and became influenced by the Moravians. He himself was converted in 1738 and set about evangelising England. Wesley travelled all over Britain, and began field preaching. In 1784 he began to ordain clergy for America. He remained, however, within the Church of England.

Wesley, Samuel (1662–1735), clergyman and poet. He was educated in London for the Independent ministry, 1678–83, when he entered Oxford. He published a volume of verse, *Maggots*, in 1685, and became a naval chaplain in 1689. He was made Rector of South Ormsby in 1690 and was the joint-editor of the *Athenian Gazette* from 1691 to 1697. He was Rector of Epworth from 1695 to 1735 and published against nonconformist academies in 1703. He was the father of John and Charles Wesley.

Wesley, Samuel (1766–1837), musician. He was the son of Charles Wesley and gave subscription concerts in London from 1779. He converted to Roman Catholicism in 1784 and was responsible for introducing J.S. Bach's organ music to London after 1800. Wesley became a lecturer in music in London after 1811 and in 1824 was appointed organist in Camden Town. He was a prolific composer.

Wesley, Susannah (1669–1742), mother of John and Charles Wesley. She was the youngest daughter of Samuel Annesley, a leading London dissenter. Her reading of theology convinced her to conform to the Church of England at the age of 13. She married Samuel Wesley, who became the Rector of Epworth. She quarrelled with her husband over William III's right to rule, and this prompted a marital dispute between 1701 and 1702, during which time they did not sleep together. After a house-fire, they were reconciled, and John Wesley was born in 1703. Another fire in 1709, from which John was rescued, convinced her of his special status. Susannah was responsible for the education of her children (she had 19, of whom only nine survived infancy) and submitted them to a rigorous regime. In 1712, while Samuel was in London as proctor in Convocation, Susannah began to hold religious services in her kitchen.

West, Benjamin (1738–1820), historical painter. He was born in Pennsylvania, the son of Quaker parents. He painted portraits in Philadelphia and New York, and after studying and painting portraits in Italy from 1760 to 1763, he settled in London. He was a member of the Incorporated Society of Artists from 1765. West was a favourite of George III from 1767 until 1811, when the King became almost completely insane, and was appointed historical painter to the King in 1772 and Surveyor of the Royal Pictures in 1790. He was also employed to decorate St George's Hall and Chapel at Windsor. West was a founder member of the Royal Academy, and President in 1792. His *Death of Wolfe* was exhibited in 1771. West introduced modern costume into historical painting.

Whiston, William (1667–1752), theologian and mathematician. He was educated at Cambridge, and was made Vicar of Lowestoft in 1698. He succeeded Newton in 1703 as Lucasian Professor of Mathematics at Cambridge. He was expelled from the university in 1710 because of his Arian views, and in 1747 joined the General Baptists. His writings included *A New Theory of the Earth* (1696), *Accomplishment of Scripture Prophecies* (1708) and *Primitive Christianity Revived* (1711).

White, Gilbert (1720–93), naturalist. He was born in Selbourne, Hampshire, where his grandfather was vicar. He was educated at Oxford, and after being ordained became curate at Selbourne. From 1751 he kept a 'Garden Kalendar' and later a 'Naturalist's Journal'. He corresponded with Thomas Pennant and Daines Barrington, two naturalists, after 1767, and his correspondence formed the basis of his *Natural History and Antiquities of Selborne* (1789).

Whitefield, George (1714–70), Methodist leader. He was born at Gloucester, where his parents ran the Bell Inn, and was educated at Oxford, where he met the Wesleys. He accompanied them to Georgia in 1738 and founded an orphanage there. When he returned to England in 1739 he began to preach in the open air to the Kingswood colliers. He established a chapel in Bristol in 1741 and opened the Tabernacle in Tottenham Court Road, London. In the 1740s his Calvinist views clashed with the Wesleys' Arminian theology, and split the Methodist movement. He visited Ireland, Scotland and America, where he died.

Wilberforce, William (1759–1833), evangelical leader and anti-slavery campaigner. He was born in Hull, the son of a merchant, and educated at Cambridge. He entered Parliament in 1780 as MP for Hull, and represented Yorkshire, 1784–1812, and Bramber, 1812–25. He was converted in 1784/85 and became a leading force in the evangelical movement, helping to found the Proclamation Society (1787), the Society for Bettering the Condition of the Poor (1796), the Church Missionary Society (1799), and the Bible Society (1804). He was associated with the Clapham Sect. His publications included *A Practical View of the Prevailing Religious System of Professed Christians* (1797). From 1787 he was instrumental in promoting the anti-slavery cause in Parliament, and a law was passed in 1807 which abolished the slave trade. He also supported the movement for the complete emancipation of slavery within the British Empire, which was effected in 1833.

Wilkes, John (1727–97), radical politician. He was the son of a Clerkenwell distiller, and studied at Leyden. Wilkes was elected MP for Aylesbury in 1757, and became a stern critic of the government, and especially of the influence of Bute. He was arrested in 1763 for seditious libel after the publication of No. 45 of his paper *The North Briton*. He was able to challenge the use of general warrants in his arrest, but was condemned by Parliament for obscene publications for his *Essay on Woman*, and went to the Continent in 1764. Wilkes was returned in 1768 (and in the next three elections) as MP for Middlesex, but was expelled from the House. In 1774 he became Lord Mayor of London and was able to take up his seat. He was a supporter of the American cause and advocated religious freedom. The slogan 'Wilkes and Liberty' was the battle-cry of popular radicalism. His supporters formed the Bill of Rights Society in 1769 to further his cause. As he grew older Wilkes became more conservative, and helped to put down the Gordon riots of 1780 and was opposed to the French Revolution.

William III (1650–1702). He was the posthumous son of William II of Orange and Mary Stuart, the daughter of Charles I. During his youth, the Orangeists were effectively removed from power, but in 1660 their fortunes revived. He visited England in 1670, and was suspicious of Charles II's relations with Louis XIV. The 1672 Anglo-French attack saw William being seen as the Dutch national hero. In 1677 he married Mary, daughter of James II. In 1688 he was invited to rescue English liberties. His reign was marked by two principal developments: the involvement of Britain in wars against France, which helped make Britain into a major European force; and the increase in parliamentary power. He died after falling from a horse which he had confiscated from the Jacobite conspirator Sir John Fenwick.

Winchilsea, Anne Finch, Countess of (1661–1720), poet and dramatist. She was born near Southampton, the daughter of a distinguished Hampshire family. Her parents died when she was young, and Anne became maid-in-waiting to Mary of Modena. She married Captain Heneage Finch, son of the Earl of Winchilsea, in 1684. In 1688 they could not take the oaths of loyalty to William and Mary, and by 1690 had retired to Eastwell Park in Kent. Anne developed female friendships, notably with Elizabeth Rowe, and circulated her poems in manuscript. Her poems ranged from nature and love poems to reworkings of Scripture and translations. In 1713 she published *Miscellany Poems on Several Occasions, Written by a Lady* (1713).

Windham, William (1750–1810), politician. He was educated at Eton and Oxford, and was an intimate of Burke and Johnson. He became MP for Norwich in 1784 and was instrumental in the impeachment of Warren Hastings. From 1794 until 1801, he was Secretary at War. He was opposed to the 1802 peace, and this lost him his seat. He helped William Cobbett to found the *Political Register* in 1802, and was a member of the government in 1809–10, serving in the War and Colonial Office. He died of a tumour.

Wolfe, James (1727–59), soldier. He was born in Westerham, Kent, and entered the army in 1724. He fought at Dettingen in 1743 and was active at Falkirk and Culloden in 1745–46. Wolfe was a member of the Rochefort expeditionary force. He fought at Louisburg in 1758, and led the attack on Quebec in 1759, during which he died in victory at the battle of the Heights of Abraham.

Wollstonecraft, Mary (1759–1797), author. She was born in London, and her father became a gentleman farmer. She was employed by a publisher in London and went to Paris in 1792 to witness the French Revolution. She became part of a radical group, associating with Godwin, Paine, Blake and Wordsworth. She married Godwin in 1796, and died in childbirth. Her writings included *Mary, A Fiction* (1788), a novel, and the polemical *Vindication of the Rights of Woman* (1792).

Wood, John, the Elder (1705–54), architect. He was born in Bath and was educated at the Blue Coat school there. He did some work in London as a speculative builder, but saw possibilities in the development of Bath, and returned there in 1727. He was responsible for starting the Georgian redevelopment of the town, designing houses for the Duke of Chandos, Queen Square, the Circus, and North and South Parade. He also designed Prior Park.

Wood, John, the Younger (1732–82), architect. Son of the above, he completed the Circus in Bath. He was responsible for designing the Royal Crescent, Brock Street and the Assembly Rooms.

Wordsworth, William (1770–1850), poet and writer. He was born in Cockermouth, the son of an attorney. He was educated at Cambridge. In 1790 he toured France, the Alps and Italy, and returned to France in 1791, where he was inspired by the ideals of the French Revolution. On his return to England, he published a number of poems, and, with Coleridge, produced the *Lyrical Ballads* (1798), which was central to the development of Romantic poetry. In 1799 he settled in Grasmere with his sister Dorothy. In 1813 he was appointed stamp distributor for Westmorland, and moved to Rydall Mount. Wordsworth gradually abandoned his early radical political stance to become more conservative. In 1843 he was made Poet Laureate. He published *The Excursion* in 1814, *The White Doe of Rylstone* in 1815, and *The Prelude* posthumously in 1850. His prose works included *A Description of the Scenery of the Lakes in the North of England* (1810).

Wren, Christopher (1632–1723), architect and scientist. He was born in Wiltshire, the son of a clergyman. He was educated at Oxford, and made a reputation as a scientist. He was appointed Professor of Astronomy at Gresham College in 1657, and at Oxford, 1661–73. Wren designed the Sheldonian Theatre, Oxford (1664–69), and was responsible for designing the new city churches built after the Great Fire, including St Paul's Cathedral. He was made Surveyor-General of the King's Works in 1669, Comptroller at Windsor 1684, and at Greenwich Hospital, 1696. He was President of the Royal Society, 1681–83, MP for Plympton, 1685, for Windsor in the Convention Parliament and for Weymouth in 1701. He was dismissed from the Works in 1718, but continued as Surveyor of St Paul's and Westminster Abbey.

Wright, Joseph (1734–97) 'of Derby', painter. He was born in Derby and studied under Hudson from 1751 to 1753 and 1756 to 1757. He worked in Liverpool from 1769 to 1771 and in Bath from 1775 to 1776 as a portrait painter. He visited Italy in 1774–75, and witnessed an eruption of Vesuvius. During the 1760s he exhibited scenes of scientific subjects at the Society of Artists, notably *A Philosopher Lecturing on the Orrery* (1766) and *An Experiment on a Bird in the Air Pump* (1768). During the 1780s he painted a number of portraits. He was elected a member of the Royal Academy in 1784, but declined.

Wright, Thomas (1711–86), scientist. He was born near Durham and was trained as a maker of philosophical instruments. He taught mathematics locally, and his reputation was such that he was offered, but declined, the Professorship of Mathematics at the Imperial Academy of St Petersburg. In the *Original Theory of the Universe* (1750), Wright anticipated the modern physico-philosophical theory of the material universe. He also published *Louthiana, or an Introduction to the Antiquities of Ireland* (1748).

Wyatt, James (1746–1813), architect. He was born in Staffordshire, the son of a builder. Wyatt was taken by Lord Bagot to Rome and Venice, where he studied architecture. He adapted the Old Pantheon in Oxford Street, London, for theatrical performances, 1770–72, and was appointed Surveyor of Westminster Abbey in 1776. He was responsible for carrying out restorations at Lincoln, Hereford, Durham, Salisbury and Lichfield cathedrals. He built the Royal Military College at Woolwich, 1796, and was made Surveyor-General to the Board of Works, 1796, and Architect to the Board of Ordnance, 1806. He participated in the Gothic revival, designing Fonthill Abbey for William Beckford.

Wyndham, Sir William (1687–1740), politician. He became MP for Somerset in 1710, and was given the posts of Master of the Buckhounds, 1711–12, Secretary at War, 1712–13, and Chancellor of the Exchequer, 1713. In 1714 he was dismissed by George I, and planned a Jacobite uprising. He was arrested, but was released, and professed himself to be a Hanoverian Tory. He was the effective leader of the Tory party in the 1720s and 1730s

Wyvill, Christopher (1740–1822), clergyman and advocate of parliamentary reform and religious toleration. He was educated at Cambridge, and was Rector of Black Notley, Essex. In 1779 he was instrumental in forming the Yorkshire Association, which advocated cuts in government expenditure, annual parliaments and an increase in the number of independent MPs. He organised a range of mass meetings, petitions to Parliament and letters to the press.

Yearsley, Ann (1752–1806), poet and novelist, known as 'Lactilla'. She was born in Clifton, near Bristol, of labouring parents. She delivered milk, and in 1784 was taken up by Hannah More, who encouraged Yearsley in her poetry writing. Her *Poems on Several Occasions* was published in 1784, and the money she earnt was invested by Hannah More and Elizabeth Montagu. More and Yearsley fell out, and eventually she won the right to control her own money. Other publications included *Poems on Various Subjects* (1787) and *The Rural Lyre* (1796).

York, Frederick Augustus, Duke of (1763–1827). He was the second son of George III, and at the age of six months was made Bishop of Osnabruck, which he gave up in 1803. He entered the army, and studied his profession in Germany. He commanded English troops against the French in Flanders in 1793. He was made field marshal in 1795, and commander-in-chief in 1798–1809, when he was removed from office because of the behaviour of his mistress, Mary Anne Clarke. He was reinstated in 1811.

York, Henry Benedict (1725–1807). He was the younger son of James, the Old Pretender, and was born in Rome. He went to France in 1745 to support his brother. In 1747 he was made cardinal of York. When his brother died in 1788, Henry called himself 'Henry IX'. During the French Revolutionary invasion of Italy in 1799, his property at Frascati was confiscated, but George III gave him a pension. The monument to his memory erected in St Peter's Rome was paid for by the Prince Regent, the future George IV. He left the crown jewels taken by James II to George IV.

Yorke, Philip, 1st Earl of Hardwicke (1690–1764), Lord Chancellor. He rose from a fairly humble background to become Solicitor-General in 1719 and Lord Chancellor in 1737. He was MP for Lewes, 1719, and for Seaford, 1722–34. He presided over the trials of the Jacobite peers and advocated the harsh measures after the 1745 Jacobite uprising. Hardwicke was responsible for seeing through the Marriage Act of 1753, which bears his name.

Young, Arthur (1741–1820), agricultural writer and farmer. He was the son of a clergyman, and after being apprenticed to a merchant, took on a farm at Bradfield, Berkshire, 1763–66, and then at North Minns, Hertfordshire, 1768. He published widely on agricultural topics, including *Observations on the Present State of the Waste Lands of Great Britain* (1773), and became agent to Lord Kingsborough in Ireland, publishing *Tour in Ireland* in 1780. In 1784 he began the 47-volume *Annals of Agriculture*. He visited the Pyrenees in 1787, and was again in France in 1788, and in Italy in 1789. His *Travels in France* appeared in 1792. He was made Secretary to the Board of Agriculture in 1793.

Young, Edward (1683–1765), clergyman, poet and dramatist. He was born near Winchester and educated at Oxford. Early works included the tragedies *Busiris* (1719) and *The Revenge* (1721). He published a series of satires, *The Universal Passion*, between 1725 and 1728. He became ordained and was made Rector of Welwyn in 1730. His most popular poem was *The Complaint, or Night Thoughts on Life, Death and Immortality* (1742–45).

Zoffany, John (1733–1810), painter. He was born in Germany and, after travelling in Italy, settled in England in 1758. His first work was to paint clock-faces, but he began to paint actors in theatrical scenes, particularly Garrick. He was favoured by the royal family. Zoffany worked in Italy from 1772 to 1779, and went to India, where he made a successful career painting the English colonials and Indian princes. He returned to England in 1789.

SECTION TWELVE

Glossary

Advowson The right to appoint a clergyman to an ecclesiastical benefice. Treated under English law as a piece of property which could be transferred by sale or grant.

Affective family Used by late twentieth-century historians to describe the family unit bound together by sentiment, which is thought by some (notably Lawrence Stone) not to have fully developed until the eighteenth century.

***Ancien Régime* (the old order)** Term used by some French and European historians to denote the period from the late seventeenth century to the era of the French Revolution. More controversially, applied by J.C.D. Clark to describe England from 1688 to 1828/29, or from 1660 to 1832.

Ancients and moderns The late seventeenth- and early eighteenth-century debate over the 'battle of the books' was a wide-ranging fight over the ranking of contemporary learning versus ancient and Renaissance scholarship. Amongst others, William Temple's (1628–99) *Essay upon the Ancient and Modern Learning* (1692) championed the case of the 'ancients', and William Wotton's (1666–1727) *Reflections Upon Ancient and Modern Learning* (1694) argued the case for contemporary superiority.

Anticlericalism Antipathy to the Church, and especially to the clergy, which could take various forms. Resentment and suspicion of the clergy's political, intellectual, social and economic position all found expression in this period. Perhaps the most common form was economic, where resentment of paying tithes (*q.v.*) created tensions between clergy and their parishioners.

Arianism Derived from the views of Arius (*c.* 250–*c.* 336 AD). Arians believed that although created by God, Christ had not in fact co-existed with God from eternity. In the eighteenth century, Presbyterianism split over the suggestion that it had been infiltrated by Arianism (Salters' Hall, 1719), and Arianism also established itself within Scottish universities. (*See also* Socinianism *and* Unitarianism.)

Aristocracy By some historians used to describe titled members of society with their families (that is, the nobility), and by others to include both the peerage and gentry, whether titled or not.

Arminianism The rejection of predestination and Calvinism. Its followers maintained that all in principle could be saved. In practice, the dominant theological position of the Church of England for most of the period, it was also held by John Wesley against George Whitefield's championship of Calvinism.

Augustan   Term derived from the period of literary eminence under the Roman emperor Augustus (27 BC–AD 17) during which Virgil, Horace, and Ovid flourished. Generally taken to refer to the early to mid-eighteenth century, with writers such as Addison, Pope, Steele and Swift greatly admiring their Roman counterparts and imitating their works, although modern literary historians have found the term problematic for imposing a false homogeneity on the period. (*See also* Classicism.)

Balance of power   Doctrine of maintaining a European system in which no single power was dominant. Britain was traditionally concerned to support coalitions opposing one power gaining hegemony over the rest of Europe.

Baroque   Artistic style often associated with absolutist and Catholic rulers in seventeenth- and eighteenth-century Europe, it found its expression in England in the late seventeenth and early eighteenth centuries in architectural masterpieces such as St Paul's Cathedral, Castle Howard and Blenheim Palace. Characterised by grandeur and magnificence, it had stylistically given way to more classically inspired and restrained forms by the 1720s.

Bill of Rights   Passed by Parliament in December 1689, this confirmed the Declaration of Rights. It highlighted James II's abuses of the royal prerogative, and laid down the order of succession, which was the heirs of Mary followed by the heirs of Anne. Catholics, or those married to Catholics, could not succeed to the throne. The Bill received statutory recognition in the Act of Settlement, 1701.

Bloody Code   Phrase used to describe the English system of capital statutes, which numbered over 200 by the end of the eighteenth century (*see* p. 228).

Blue-water strategy   Phrase used to describe policy of maritime and colonial warfare in preference to the high-cost continental strategy associated with defence of Hanoverian interests.

Book of Common Prayer   In 1548 Edward VI established a commission of 12 bishops and clergy to oversee the passage of a uniform order of service. This was established by the 1549 Act of Uniformity, and contained morning and evening services and forms for the administration of the sacrament, baptism and the eucharist. The Prayer Book was revised in 1552, 1559 and 1662. It remained the norm for worship in the Church of England until the twentieth century.

'Bread or blood riots' Disturbances in East Anglia in the spring and summer of 1816 when agricultural labourers protested against their poor pay and conditions. The protest took the form of arson, cattle-maiming and sheep-stealing. The worst disturbances occurred at Littleport in May, after which two were killed and over a hundred arrested. Five were hanged and nine transported.

'Broad-bottomed administration' Name given to the coalition formed in December 1744, and including Henry Pelham, Newcastle, Hardwicke, Chesterfield, Lyttleton, Gower, Bedford, Hinde and Doddington. It was instrumental in unifying the Whigs and in rehabilitating the Tories.

Burgage borough Franchise limited to owners or tenants of buildings or plots of land called 'burgages'.

Calendar reform During the eighteenth century, Europe moved from the Julian Calendar (Old Style; OS), to the Gregorian Calendar (New Style; NS). Britain changed in 1752, during which 11 days in September were 'lost'.

Calvinism Derived from the theological system of the French reformer John Calvin (1509–64), its followers believed in predestination. Although found in the Thirty-Nine Articles (*q.v.*) of the Church of England, it was more central to nonconformity in the late seventeenth and eighteenth centuries. Calvinism was dominant in Scotland, and was central to the evangelical revivals in England and Wales.

Catechism A manual of Christian doctrine, adopting a dialogue form of question and answer.

Catholic Emancipation (or Relief) Issue of freeing Roman Catholics from disabilities which prevented them holding offices, voting and serving in Parliament. Not finally secured until 1829.

Clapham Sect Formed from leading evangelicals (*q.v.*) within the Church of England, who lived in the village of Clapham in South London. Believing in personal salvation through good works, they campaigned on behalf of the abolition of the slave trade and were involved in a number of humanitarian causes, including Sunday schools, penal reform and promoting a high standard of public morality. Leading members included William Wilberforce (1759–1833), Hannah More (1743–1833), Henry Thornton (1760–1815), James Stephen (1758–1832) and Zachary Macaulay (1768–1838).

Classicism The deliberate imitation of the works of antiquity which can be found in all the arts during the late seventeenth and eighteenth centuries (neo-classicism). The Romantic movement saw itself in part as a revolt against classicism.

Collective bargaining by riot Term used by E.J. Hobsbawm to describe the actions of workmen in breaking machines and damaging the property of masters in pursuit of industrial disputes, most notably seen in Luddism (*q.v.*).

Combination Acts Laws against 'combinations' – organisations of workmen – enacted in 1799 and 1800 and repealed in 1824 and 1825 (*see* pp. 309–12).

Confessional state Term used by European historians to describe the interplay of religion and state building in Europe from the sixteenth to the eighteenth centuries, where a state had a single confession of faith, established by law, to which the whole population conformed. Used by J.C.D. Clark, more controversially, as a label for England in the long eighteenth century (*q.v.*), and which, according to him, came to an end in 1828–29 with the repeal of the Test Acts and with the advent of Catholic Emancipation (*q.v.*).

Convocation Assemblies of clergy, originally dating from the seventh century. By the fifteenth century the bishops and lower clergy had split into the upper and lower houses. Disputes arose between the Whiggishly inclined upper house and the more Tory lower house in 1689 and between 1700 and 1717, after which Convocation was suspended. For the rest of the period, Convocation had a purely formal function, and only met again as a discussion body after 1850.

Corn Laws Used to describe the Corn Law of 1815, which prevented the import of foreign grain until the domestic price reached 80*s* per quarter, and its successor of 1828, which introduced a sliding scale of tariffs.

Countess of Huntingdon's Connexion Methodist grouping, of Calvinistic leanings, founded by Selina Countess of Huntingdon. George Whitefield, the prominent Methodist, was appointed her chaplain in 1751 and she established a number of chapels which helped to spread evangelical and Methodist views.

County movement Late eighteenth-century movement for moderate parliamentary reform led by prominent county gentlemen such as Christopher Wyvill. Led to the formation of the Yorkshire Association in 1779, and petitioning movement for reform. (*See also* Economical reform.)

Court and Treasury Party Group of office-holders or placemen who could generally be relied upon to support an eighteenth-century administration. Perhaps numbering as many as 100–120 MPs by 1760, their numbers were reduced by economical reform (*q.v.*) and administrative reorganisation from the 1780s onwards.

Deism Belief in one supreme being. Its exponents championed natural religion, and emphasised reason over faith. Its classic expression was John Toland's *Christianity Not Mysterious* (1696), which attacked revelation and the supernatural.

Diocese Administrative unit of the Church of England, under the jurisdiction of a bishop.

Dissenter General term for those who separated themselves from the communion of the Church of England. Technically included Roman Catholics, but often taken to mean just Protestant dissenters.

East India Company Despite earlier foundations, to compete against the Dutch, it was only in 1709 that the English East India Company was properly consolidated for the trade of the spice islands and for trade with China. The company began to acquire a territorial empire in India after the battle of Plassey in 1757. The Regulation Act of 1773 and the India Act of 1784 brought more parliamentary control over the company.

Economical reform Late eighteenth-century movement led by Edmund Burke, among others, aiming to reduce the number of sinecurists and place-holders in Parliament. Economical reform legislation was passed in 1782. (*See also* County movement.)

Emancipation, *see* Catholic Emancipation.

Empiricism Philosophical movement whose starting point was John Locke's *Essay Concerning Human Understanding* (1690), which rejected claims to innate ideas and rested understanding on experience instead. Other 'British empiricists' included David Hume.

Enclosure Areas of land separated by boundaries and usually owned by individuals. They often replaced open fields and commonly owned ground. Although much of Britain had been enclosed in previous centuries, the period after 1750 saw an intensification of the movement with over a thousand enclosure acts passed between 1760 and 1800, and over eight hundred acts passed between 1800 and 1815. The effects of this on British agriculture and on the agricultural workforce have been much debated.

Enlightenment European-wide movement of the eighteenth century, most commonly connected with French *philosophes* such as Voltaire, and associated with the championing of modern science and reason against religion. French intellectuals often claimed to be have been inspired by English writers like Isaac Newton and John Locke, and in the mid-eighteenth century the 'Scottish Enlightenment' included figures such as David Hume and Adam Smith.

Enthusiast Term of abuse applied to those perceived to be religiously misguided, notably the Methodists.

Evangelicals Group within Church of England who in the late eighteenth century sought to combat what they perceived to be clerical apathy, while accepting Anglican discipline. Emphasised importance of moral earnestness and proclaimed salvation by faith. They gave rise to important philanthropic movements in the nineteenth century. (*See also* Clapham Sect.)

Excise Tax or duty charged on goods before sale to the consumer. Walpole's attempt to increase the range of goods on which excise could be charged led to the Excise Crisis of 1733.

Financial Revolution Term used to describe the establishment under William III, Anne and the early Hanoverians of an effective system of public credit seen in the creation of the Bank of England and the national debt.

Fiscal-military state Term used to describe Britain (and by implication other European states) by John Brewer in *The Sinews of Power* (1989) expressing the primary requirement of the State to maintain an extensive fiscal and credit regime in order to compete militarily in international politics.

Free-thinker Those, according to Anthony Collins in his *Discourse of Free Thinking* (1713), who judged for themselves using evidence and reason, particularly with regard to religious matters. These included Deists such as Anthony Collins and the Earl of Shaftesbury. Often used by orthodox churchmen as a term of abuse to castigate their opponents.

Gothic Originated in the mid-eighteenth century interest in the medieval period, and affected various art forms, including architecture (Walpole's

Strawberry Hill and Beckford's Fonthill) and literature (Walpole's novel *The Castle of Otranto*, 1764). By the late eighteenth century the medieval emphasis in the literary form had given way to an interest in the macabre and the supernatural (Gothick novel).

Grand Tour Practice of sending young gentlemen to complete their education by travelling in Europe, learning modern languages, studying art and meeting major figures. Although it had precedents in previous centuries, it came into its own in the hundred years after 1688.

Greek Revival Architectural and artistic movement which in the late eighteenth and early nineteenth centuries challenged the near-monopoly of the Roman-dominated classical models. Much influenced by J.J. Wincklemann's *On the Imitation of Greek Art* (1755) and James Stuart and Nicholas Revett's *The Antiquities of Athens* (1762), those architects who worked in the style included Sir Robert Smirke (1780–1867), who designed the British Museum, 1815–16, and William Wilkins (1778–1839), who was responsible for East India College, Hertfordshire, 1806–9, and Downing College, Cambridge, 1807–20. The style was also used, to a lesser and more diffused extent, by Soane and Nash.

Grub Street An actual street in London, not far from the unpleasant Moorfields and the lunatic hospital, Bedlam. Term came to refer to hack writers generally, and, as a concept, 'Grub Street' was explored by Alexander Pope in later versions of *The Dunciad* (1743).

Habeas Corpus Short-hand for the writ which could obtain the release of those imprisoned without charge or not brought to trial.

Hampden Clubs Founded between 1812 and 1817 by Major John Cartwright to further the cause of parliamentary reform, they were named after the seventeenth-century parliamentarian John Hampden (1594–1643).

High Church Section within the Church of England upholding belief in sacraments and ritual, the authority of the Church hierarchy, and the close relationship between Church and State. In the seventeenth and eighteenth centuries associated with political support for the monarch as head of Church and State, and later with opposition to the removal of disabilities on dissenters and Roman Catholics.

Holland House Holland House in Kensington, London, became a fashionable salon during the early nineteenth century, patronised by leading Whig politicians, as well as writers, painters and actors. Hence, sometimes used as a term to describe Whig opinion generally.

Hutchinsonians Clerical followers of John Hutchinson who attacked not only the Newtonian influence in science, but Enlightenment (*q.v.*) thought more generally. Maintained High-Church (*q.v.*) principles, and in some respects anticipated the Oxford Movement of the 1830s.

Independents Backbench MPs not directly dependent upon the administration or opposition, regarded as the 'floating vote' in the eighteenth- and early nineteenth-century House of Commons before party discipline became more effective. Variously estimated at no more than 80 members (L. Namier) and up to 300–350 (J. Owen), the independents could usually be counted upon to support an administration unless its credibility was seriously undermined by the opposition.

Jacobins Radical faction of the French revolutionaries of 1789 led by Robespierre. In Britain, a derogatory term applied by loyalists to French sympathisers and reformers in general. Used by historians to denote British radicals with similar aims and ideology as their French counterparts.

Jacobites Supporters of the hereditary succession of the House of Stuart following the dethronement of James II in 1688–89. Jacobite risings took place after the death of Queen Anne in 1715, and again in 1745–46. Sympathy was strongest on the Scottish Highlands, but it was often suspected that many Tories supported the Jacobite cause in England. It was crushed as a political force after 1746.

Justice of the Peace (JP) A magistrate appointed to preserve the peace in a county or town.

King's Friends, *see* Court and Treasury Party.

Kit Cat Club A London dining club of the early eighteenth century, named after Christopher Cat who owned the tavern where it met, and popular with some of the leading Whig political figures and prominent artists and intellectuals of the day. Members included Congreve, Addison, Pope, Vanbrugh and Kneller. Portraits of the members were painted by Kneller.

Latitudinarian A term of abuse used from the late seventeenth century to characterise those clergy who, while conforming to the Church of England, attached relatively little importance to dogmatic truth, ecclesiastical organisation and liturgical practice.

Leicester House, *see* Reversionary interest.

Liberal Toryism Reforming Toryism associated with the later years of Lord Liverpool's administration and his leading ministers, Canning, Peel and Huskisson.

Long eighteenth century A term favoured by some modern historians in their attempt to see a coherent period of history from the late seventeenth to the early nineteenth centuries. At its widest, the terms covers the period from 1660 to 1832, but it is more usually taken to be from 1688.

Low Church Church of England clergy who gave a relatively low place to the claims of the episcopate, and who frequently sympathised with dissenters, in contrast to the High Churchmen. Originally used of the latitudinarians (*q.v.*).

Luddism Phase of widespread machine-breaking in the North and Midland counties of England between 1811 and 1817. Machine-breaking was said to be carried out on the orders of a mythical 'Ned Ludd' or 'General Ludd'. Machine-breaking began in Nottinghamshire as part of the campaign of the framework-knitters for greater regulation of their trade and higher wages for work in a period of high prices and unemployment. Disturbances spread to Yorkshire, where shearing-frames were destroyed by the wool-croppers, and to Lancashire, where power looms were attacked. The main disturbances were over by the end of 1812 when some 10,000 troops were deployed in the manufacturing districts.

Marriage Act, 1753 Known as 'Hardwicke's Act', after the Lord Chancellor, this act reformed marriage law in England. Before 1753 a marriage could consist of a free exchange of vows between a couple, which led to couples being married secretly, and was therefore prone to abuse. The act established that only weddings in a church, according to the rites set out in the Book of Common Prayer, and with the banns read, would be lawful. Only Jews and Quakers were exempt, and it was not until 1836 that dissenters were allowed to marry within their own churches.

Moral economy Phrase used by E.P. Thompson to describe the underlying sense of legitimacy displayed in many eighteenth-century crowd actions and a traditional value system often at odds with commercial and capitalist development.

Namierite Method of analysing political action and membership of political parties which stresses the role of individuals and their interests rather than their beliefs and ideologies; after Sir Lewis Namier, author of *The Structure of Politics at the Accession of George III* (1929).

National debt System of long-term and effectively perpetual credit for the government, inaugurated in 1692 and greatly expanded with the creation of the Bank of England (1694) and in loans raised to fight the War of Spanish Succession. An essential part of the Financial Revolution (*q.v.*) and a crucial underpinning of the fiscal-military state (*q.v.*).

Newtonian Derived from the writings of Isaac Newton, the dominant philosophy of the Enlightenment, influencing all fields of science.

Nonconformist, *see* Dissenter.

Non-jurors Those members of the Church of England unable to take oaths of allegiance and supremacy to William and Mary for fear of breaking their oaths to James II. Included Archbishop Sancroft, eight bishops (three of whom died before they were deprived), about 400 parish clergy and some laymen, as well as virtually all the Scottish Episcopalian clergy and one Irish bishop.

Occasional Conformity Act, 1711 Barred nonconformists from taking communion in an Anglican church to qualify for national or municipal office in accordance with the Test and Corporation Acts. There had been earlier attempts to pass a bill in 1702–4. Repealed in 1719.

Old Corruption Term used to describe the unreformed political and ecclesiastical system before the 1832 Reform Act and the beginning of reform in the Church of England, characterised by patronage and influence. A term favoured by contemporary radicals, and later historians; recent research has, however, greatly modified our understanding of the eighteenth century as the 'age of corruption'.

Palladian Term derived from Andrea Palladio (1508–80), whose *Four Books of Architecture* (1570) was based on the works of Vitruvius, architect of Augustus' time who taught the correct use of the classical orders. Taken up by Inigo Jones (1573–1652) in England, Palladio's principles were championed by Colen Campbell and Lord Burlington as a counterblast to the Baroque (*q.v.*).

Papist Derogatory name for Roman Catholics.

Peerage Bill Bill introduced in 1719 to maintain the peerage's position by limiting the number of peerage creations and to settle the unsatisfactory Scottish representation in the House of Lords. It was also designed to protect Sunderland and Stanhope in the Commons should the Prince of Wales (who opposed them) succeed to the throne. The bill advocated that the King could make only 6 more peerages and the 16 elected

Scottish peers in the Lords were to be replaced by 25 hereditary ones. The bill was defeated.

Peterloo 'Massacre' Name for the break-up of a peaceful reform demonstration in St Peter's Fields, Manchester, on 16 August 1819, when the local magistrates sent in troops to arrest the radical orator Henry Hunt. Eleven people were killed and over 400 injured. 'Peterloo' was a pun on Waterloo.

Pluralism Practice of holding more than one benefice. Usually used within an ecclesiastical context.

Pocket boroughs *See* 'Rotten' boroughs.

Polite society View of the eighteenth century as a period of the growth of sensibility (*q.v.*) and refinement in contrast with the earlier period. See, for example, P. Langford, *A Polite and Commercial People: England, 1727–1783* (1989).

Poor Laws Eighteenth-century laws regarding the poor, and the help they could receive, were framed by the 1601 Elizabethan Poor Law, which established that each parish was responsible for the maintenance of its own poor. Impotent poor were to be provided for, and work was to be found for the able-bodied. These were to be distinguished from the undeserving and idle. Most eighteenth-century legislation operated within this framework. Pressure was placed on the system after 1750 by the rising population and growing unemployment. In the 1790s, *ad hoc* arrangements, such as the Speenhamland system (*q.v.*), were introduced. The framework was overhauled by the New Poor Law of 1834, which formalised the workhouse system.

Potwalloper Franchise qualification prior to Reform Act of 1832. In some boroughs, every man who had a family and boiled a pot there qualified for the franchise, if resident for six months, and not in receipt of poor rates. Such voters were considered susceptible to bribery and instructions from borough patrons.

Pretender, Old James Edward Stuart (1688–1766), son of dethroned King James II. Known as 'Old Pretender' to the throne of England and backed by Jacobite (*q.v.*) support in Britain. He was unsuccessful in his attempt to prevent the succession of the Elector of Hanover in 1714, and in the rising of the following year.

Pretender, Young Charles Edward Stuart (1720–1788), known as 'Bonny Prince Charlie'. Son of the above, he led the rising in Scotland in

1745–46; aimed to place his father on the throne. Defeat at the battle of Culloden in 1746 effectively ended the danger of a Stuart restoration.

Protestant ascendancy Term for the political and religious dominance by the Protestant minority in Ireland from the seventeenth to the nineteenth centuries.

'Pudding-time' Phrase used to describe the period of relative political quiescence between the 'rage of party' (*q.v.*) and the mid-eighteenth century, associated with the era of Walpolean dominance and the rise of the Pelhams.

Queen Anne's Bounty Established in 1704 to augment the livings of the poorer clergy. Originally made up from the return of first fruits and tenths, it later attracted individual bequests.

Radical First used to describe the supporters of universal suffrage, annual parliaments and secret ballot. Major Cartwright contrasted 'radical' and 'moderate' parliamentary reform as early as 1776 in *Take Your Choice*, and in 1792 the London Corresponding Society promulgated a 'Plan of Radical Reform'. Proposals for 'radical' reform were taken up by writers and speakers such as William Cobbett and Henry Hunt. The campaign for 'radical' reform continued after 1832 in the Chartist movement.

Rage of party Phrase used to describe the period of intense party strife especially between *c.* 1702 and *c.* 1715 occasioned by conflicts over politics, religion and foreign policy, and which encouraged the growth of the electorate, frequent general elections and the growth of the press.

Rector An incumbent who received both great and small tithes. Where the great tithes had been impropriated to a lay rector, the incumbent was a vicar.

Recusant A Roman Catholic who refused to attend church. From the late sixteenth century this was punishable by fines, imprisonment, and for a priest, death. Although the position of recusants was temporarily helped by the Declarations of Indulgence of 1672, 1687 and 1688, they were not included in the 1689 Toleration Act (*q.v.*). Nevertheless, for much of the eighteenth century the full force of the law was rarely applied against them.

Regency Politically the period between 1811, when the Prince of Wales (later George IV) ruled during his father's illness, and 1820, when he succeeded to the throne after his father's death. Stylistically, the term is often associated with a rather more nebulous period stretching back into the 1790s (when the Prince became a leading patron of the arts) and lasting until his death in 1830. Although hard to define with precision, hall-marks of the style include a stress on strict neo-classicism, as well as on Egyptian, Etruscan, Gothic and French motifs. The period was also one of social unrest, witnessing the tensions of the war with France, agricultural unemployment and growing political agitation. The **Regency Crisis** occurred between late 1788 and early 1789, when George III suffered from a mental breakdown. It was expected that the Prince of Wales would become regent and dismiss Pitt and call on Fox and Portland to form a ministry. The King recovered, however.

Reversionary interest   Name given to politicians who clustered about the Prince of Wales in the eighteenth and early nineteenth centuries. In 1718 the then Prince of Wales (later George II) bought Leicester House in London, hence sometimes called the Leicester House interest.

Riot Act, 1715   Passed by the Whigs to deal with the threat of a Jacobite insurrection. The act established that if 12 or more people tumultuously assembled, and refused to disperse within one hour of a magistrate reading a proclamation, they could face the death penalty. The procedure became known as 'reading the Riot Act'.

'Robinocracy'   Collective name for supporters of Sir Robert Walpole.

Romanticism   A shift in artistic taste in Britain and Europe from the late eighteenth century which rejected much of the Enlightenment and the fashion for neo-classicism. It has been linked politically to the French Revolution and to the popular wars of independence in Poland, Spain and Greece. It highlighted emotion, individualism and the imagination and is associated in particular with the Romantic poets Wordsworth, Coleridge and Byron.

'Rotten' boroughs   Boroughs where, prior to the 1832 Reform Act, the electorate had shrunk almost to nothing. Among the most notorious were Gatton and Old Sarum. They were a source of influence for borough owners. Sometimes called 'Pocket' boroughs.

Schism Act, 1714   Tory measure designed to stamp out dissent by preventing nonconformists and Catholics from educating their children in their own schools. Queen Anne died on the day that the act was to take effect, and George I did not enforce it. It was repealed in 1719.

Scot and Lot   Franchise based on ability to pay the poor rate.

Sensibility Movement of the second half of the eighteenth century which sought to emphasise the virtues of feeling, benevolence and people's natural capacity to be moved by the sight of sorrow. It found its most noted literary expression in Henry Mackenzie's novel *The Man of Feeling* (1771), but was much parodied, notably by Jane Austen in *Northanger Abbey* (1818) and *Sense and Sensibility* (1811).

Settlement, Act of, 1701 After the death of Queen Anne's son, the Duke of Gloucester, in 1700, this laid down the line of succession to the throne by putting aside more than 50 Catholic claimants and giving it to Sophia, Electress of Hanover, a grand-daughter of James I. In 1714, Anne was succeeded by Sophia's son, George I.

Settlements and Removals Act, 1662 Remained in force until 1834. Those likely to be chargeable on the parish for poor relief could be evacuated to their native parish.

Six Acts Repressive legislation passed by Lord Sidmouth in 1819 in the aftermath of Peterloo (*q.v.*), prohibiting meetings of more than 50 people, preventing military drilling, increasing newspaper duties, permitting magistrates to search for arms and seditious writings, and speeding up judicial proceedings.

Society for Constitutional Information Founded in 1780 by Major John Cartwright to promote parliamentary reform. Ceased to meet after 1794.

Society for the Promotion of Christian Knowledge (SPCK) Founded in 1698 by Thomas Bray to provide and publish religious literature.

Society for the Propagation of the Gospel in Foreign Parts (SPG) Founded in 1701 to spread Christianity to the colonies. In 1716 the SPG founded a college in Barbados.

Socinianism More extreme than Arianism (*q.v.*), it denied the pre-existence of Christ, and asserted that Jesus was merely a good man. (*See also* Arianism *and* Unitarianism.)

South Sea Bubble Financial crisis of 1720, resulting from the collapse of the South Sea Company.

Speenhamland system Method of outdoor relief (i.e. given to people who remained outside the workhouse) announced by the Berkshire JPs at Speenhamland in Berkshire in May 1795 by which parochial rates were used to supplement wages on a sliding scale according to the price of bread.

Storming the closet Eighteenth-century term for seizure of major positions in government by winning the support of the monarch and forcing expulsion of the existing administration.

Subscription Controversy Issue over subscription to the Thirty Nine Articles (*q.v.*) which was demanded of all clergy and those matriculating at Oxford and graduating from Cambridge universities. Reached a head in 1771 with the Feathers' Tavern petition, after which a small group of clergy left the Church of England and became Unitarians (*q.v.*).

Take-off Phrase used to describe a distinctive phase of a sudden spurt in economic growth led by a few 'leading sectors', associated with the work of the American economic historian W.W. Rostow. More recently, economic historians have adopted a broader, longer term view of industrialisation.

Talents, Ministry of all the Coalition formed between 1806 and 1807 after Pitt's death. It comprised the followers of Fox, Grenville and Addington, but collapsed after George forbade the discussion of Catholic Emancipation. The coalition was responsible for the abolition of the slave trade in 1807.

Test Acts Refers to Act of 1673 which required all office-holders to receive the sacrament of the Church of England, and Act of 1678 which made the same requirement of MPs. In force until 1828 for Protestant dissenters, and 1829 for Catholics.

Thirty-Nine Articles A set of doctrinal statements to define the position of the Church of England. Written in the sixteenth century, these were appended to the 1662 edition of the Book of Common Prayer.

Tithes Originally a tenth of all produce given by members of the parish to support clergy; by the eighteenth century this had frequently been 'commuted' into cash payments. Tithe disputes arose in the period between clergy and those who were not members of the Church of England, and from parishioners who resented clergy gaining from improvements in agricultural production. The Tithe Commutation Act of 1836 was designed to alleviate these tensions.

Toleration Act, 1689 Commonly known as the 'Toleration Act' by contemporaries and by later historians, it was originally entitled an 'act for exempting their majesties' Protestant subjects dissenting from the Church of England from the penalties of certain laws', which suggests that it was less 'tolerant' than has sometimes been suggested. Protestant dissenters could worship in unlocked meeting houses, providing they had been licensed, and their minister subscribed to the Thirty-Nine Articles (*q.v.*) except those concerning baptism and Church government.

Tory Originally a term of abuse to label Roman Catholic bandits (Toraighe) in Ireland in the 1640s, the name became current in the Exclusion Crisis (1678–1682) for a supporter of hereditary succession, the royal prerogative, divine right and loyalty to the Church of England. After the deposition of James II many became Jacobites (*q.v.*), and the taint of Jacobitism excluded them from office for 30 years after 1715. By the end of the eighteenth century, the term was being applied to those who upheld the prerogatives of George III, resisted the removal of disabilities from dissenters and Roman Catholics, and opposed parliamentary reform. The name 'Tory' was revived by Canning in the early nineteenth century for the natural party of government which was opposed to the Whigs (*q.v.*).

Union, Act of (Ireland) United the parliaments of Great Britain and Ireland, and abolished the Irish Parliament in Dublin. It came into force on 1 January 1801. Ireland was given 100 MPs and 28 Irish peers, and 4 bishops of the Church of Ireland could sit in the Lords. It lasted until 1920.

Union, Act of (Scotland) Union of England and Scotland to form the kingdom of Great Britain. Scottish representation at Westminister consisted of 45 MPs and 16 peers. Free trade was established, but the Scots kept their own legal system and the Presbyterian religious establishment.

Unitarian Rejected the Trinity and the divinity of Christ in favour of the single personality of the Godhead. Theophilus Lindsey (1723–1808) formed the first Unitarian denomination, opening in 1774 Essex Chapel, London. (*See also* Arianism *and* Socinianism.)

United Irishmen Society established in Belfast in 1791 by Wolfe Tone to seek removal of religious and political grievances. After the outbreak of war with France, many United Irishmen looked to French aid and adopted republicanism. From 1796 repression of its activities drove the movement underground, but its members conspired with the French to mount an invasion of Ireland and formed links with radicals in England. The movement was largely destroyed by the abortive 1798 rebellion, the break-up of the Despard conspiracy in 1802 and the defeat of Robert Emmet's rising in 1803.

Utilitarianism Philosophical and political belief that the greatest happiness of the greatest number should be the goal of all activity. Although it had a long pedigree, its fully fledged form was that given by Jeremy Bentham, who attempted to apply the principle of utility to law and punishment.

Vicar   Incumbent entitled only to the small tithes of the parish.

Whig   Derived from the label 'Whiggamore', which was given to Scottish covenanter rebels in the late 1640s, the term came to be associated with the parliamentary party which emerged in the late seventeenth century, and dominated British politics in the first half of the eighteenth century. Whigs were defenders of parliamentary government, ministerial responsibility and Protestantism. The 'Glorious Revolution' of 1688–89 was regarded as a triumph of Whig principles and the Whigs monopolised power following the Hanoverian succession in 1714, but in the later eighteenth century fell from favour under George III and became associated with religious toleration, economical reform (*q.v.*) and opposition to the revival of monarchical authority. Divided by the French Revolution, they became supporters of moderate parliamentary reform in the 1820s and passed the Reform Act of 1832.

Whiteboys   Association of Irish peasants, first formed in about 1761 in County Tipperary to redress grievances. They wore white shirts and committed agrarian outrages at night.

SECTION THIRTEEN

Select bibliography

Abbreviations

A.	Albion
Ag.H.	Agricultural History
Am.H.R.	American Historical Review
B.I.H.R.	Bulletin of the Institute of Historical Research
B.J.E.S.	British Journal for Eighteenth-Century Studies
B.S.S.L.H.	Bulletin of the Society for the Study of Labour History
C.H.J.	Cambridge Historical Journal
D.U.J.	Durham University Journal
E.	Economica
Econ.H.R.	Economic History Review
E.E.H.	Explorations in Economic History
E.H.R.	English Historical Review
E.L.	Eighteenth-Century Life
H.	History
Hist.	The Historian
H.J.	Historical Journal
H.L.Q.	Huntingdon Library Quarterly
H.S.	History of Science
H.T.	History Today
H.W.J.	History Workshop Journal
J.B.S.	Journal of British Studies
J.Eccl.H.	Journal of Ecclesiastical History
J.Econ.H.	Journal of Economic History
J.F.H.	Journal of Family History
J.H.I.	Journal of the History of Ideas
J.M.H.	Journal of Modern History
J.S.H.	Journal of Social History
J.U.H.	Journal of Urban History
L.H.	Literature and History
L.J.	The London Journal
N.H.	Northern History
P.B.A.	Proceedings of the British Academy
P.H.	Parliamentary History
P.P.	Past and Present
Proc.Wesley Hist.Soc.	Proceedings of the Wesley Historical Society
S.C.H.	Studies in Church History
S.H.	Social History
T.H.A.S.	Transactions of the Hunter Archaelogical Society
T.R.H.S.	Transactions of the Royal Historical Society
W.H.R.	Welsh History Review
W.M.Q.	William and Mary Quarterly

General

In the past twenty years an enormous amount has been published on every aspect of eighteenth-century Britain which has transformed our understanding of the period. The days are long gone when 'keeping up with the reading' was easier for historians of the eighteenth century than for most of their colleagues, and new titles are appearing almost daily. But, despite the myriad views, nuances and rival interpretations now on offer, much of this burgeoning literature can be seen as contributing to a wide-ranging debate about the nature of the eighteenth-century State and eighteenth-century society more generally. At heart, the controversy hinges on those perennially fascinating topics for historians, the issues of continuity and change. As Bill Speck, in a useful review article has asked, 'will the real eighteenth century stand up?' ('Will the real eighteenth century stand up?', *H.J.* [1991]). Was the eighteenth century distinguished more by the impulses of change and modernity, or did it represent a period of continuity with the past? Is the century and a half after 1688 better seen as a continuation of the seventeenth century, or as anticipating the nineteenth? Put simply, is the eighteenth century more reliably characterised as part of the early modern period, or as part of the modern?

In a sense, of course, the answer is both. The dates covered by this volume, 1688–1820, indicate the problems involved in using century divides as the proper way to parcel up the past. Nevertheless, a great deal of the scholarship on the period can be seen as a contribution to this overall debate of defining the central features of the eighteenth century. In some ways the recent controversy can usefully be seen to have started with the work of J.C.D. Clark, who in his *English Society, 1688–1832: Ideology, Social Structure and Political Practice During the Ancien Régime* (1985) argued that eighteenth-century society was dominated by the Church, the monarchy and the aristocracy. His analysis self-consciously went against the grain of earlier studies which had tended to stress the diminution in the role of the Church and religion, the triumph of Parliament, and the growth of the middle class. The significance of Clark's work is that he related many of the concerns of the eighteenth century to the previous one, and thereby challenged the assumptions of those who had stressed that the eighteenth century was characterised by modernity. His points were further developed in *Revolution and Rebellion: State and Society in England in the Seventeenth and Eighteenth Centuries* (1986) and in *The Language of Liberty, 1660–1832: Political Discourse and Social Dynamics in the Anglo-American World* (1994). Although it would be true to say that much of what Clark had to say had been implicit in the work of other historians (notably John Cannon, *Aristocratic Century* [1984], Ian Christie, *Stress and Stability in late Eighteenth-Century Britain* [1984] and

J.A.W. Gunn, *Beyond Liberty and Property: The Process of Self-Recognition in Eighteenth-Century Political Thought* [1983]), his interpretation had an immense impact, leading one reviewer to remark that the eighteenth century was now the most exciting period to study. In 1989 Paul Langford published his volume in the New Oxford History of England which he entitled *A Polite and Commercial People: England, 1727–1783,* and which covertly attacked Clark's analysis by highlighting the modernity of the period, and the pivotal role played by the emerging middle class. Critiques of Clark's position were also made by J. Innes, 'Jonathan Clark, Social History and England's "Ancien régime"', *P.P.* (1987) (and the reply by Clark), R. Porter, 'English Society in the eighteenth century revisited', in J. Black (ed.), *British Politics and Society from Walpole to Pitt* (1990), the articles by Clark, Porter and Black in *B.J.E.S.* (1992), Black, 'England's *Ancien Régime*', *H.T.* 38 (1988), G.S. Rousseau, 'Revisionist polemics: J.C.D. Clark and the collapse of modernity in the age of Johnson', in P.J. Korshin (ed.), *The Age of Johnson* (1989), and the special number of *Albion* (1989).

Many of the issues raised by Clark's works, and the points made by his critics, are dealt with in a clear and judicious way by F. O'Gorman in his *The Long Eighteenth Century: British Political and Social History, 1688–1832* (1997), which sums up a great deal of the recent research and addresses head-on the issue of the nature of State and society in the eighteenth century. Also clear and authoritative, and particularly good at presenting succinct overviews of individual topics, are G. Holmes, *The Making of a Great Power: Later Stuart and Early Georgian Britain, 1660–1722* (1993) and G. Holmes and D. Szechi, *The Age of Oligarchy: Pre-Industrial Britain, 1722–1783* (1993). Both these are up-to-date surveys of political, social, economic and cultural history. The later chapters of B. Coward, *The Stuart Age: England, 1603–1714* (2nd edn, 1994) and D.L. Smith, *A History of the Modern British Isles: The Double Crown, 1603–1707* (1998) are also excellent introductions to the period, as are the early chapters of G. Williams and J. Ramsden, *Ruling Britannia: A Political History of Britain, 1688–1988* (1990).

There are a number of general surveys of the end of the seventeenth and early eighteenth centuries, of which J.R. Jones, *County and Court, England 1658–1714* (1978) and J.P. Kenyon, *Stuart England* (1976) are the most helpful. For eighteenth-century England, W.A. Speck, *Stability and Strife: England 1714–1760* (1977) and I.R. Christie, *Wars and Revolutions: Britain 1760–1815* (1982) are essential guides. B.W. Hill, *The Growth of Parliamentary Parties, 1689–1742* (1976) and *British Parliamentary Parties, 1742–1832* (1985) are two excellent political narratives at parliamentary level. J.B. Owen, *The Eighteenth Century, 1714–1815* (1974) is still a useful political history, and the older studies by D. Marshall, *Eighteenth-Century England, 1714–1815* (2nd edn, 1975), J. Steven Watson, *The Reign of George III, 1760–1815* (1960) and C. Wilson, *England's Apprenticeship, 1603–1763* (2nd edn, 1984) remain serviceable. C. Jones (ed.), *Britain in the First Age of Party, 1680–1750: Essays Presented to Geoffrey Holmes* (1987) covers political, religious, social and cultural topics. For the transition through to the nineteenth century, see A. Briggs, *The Age of Improvement, 1783–1867* (1959) and E.J. Evans, *The Forging of the Modern State, 1783–1870* (2nd edn, 1995).

There are several good overviews of social and economic history. In particular, J. Rule, *Albion's People: English Society, 1714–1815* (1992), his *The Vital Century: England's Developing Economy, 1714–1815* (1992) and M. Daunton, *Progress and Poverty: An Economic and Social History of Britain, 1700–1850* (1995) are clear summaries of recent research. Also useful are J. Sharpe, *Early Modern England: A Social History, 1550–1760* (1987), R.W. Malcolmson, *Life and Labour in England, 1700–1780* (1981), M. Reed, *The Georgian Triumph* (1983), D. Hay and N. Rogers, *Eighteenth-Century English Society: Shuttles and Swords* (1997) and R. Porter, *English Society in the Eighteenth Century* (2nd edn, 1990), which is an especially lively and stimulating read.

Several works span the period at a more interpretative level. In J. Cannon (ed.), *The Whig Ascendancy: Colloquies on Hanoverian England* (1981), a number of distinguished historians set out their views on the period from 1680 through to 1830, attached to which are the 'colloquies' or comments by other contributors to the volume; and L. Colley, *Britons: Forging the Nation, 1707–1837* (1993) makes a powerful case for the ways in which a British national identity emerged. Her views can also be found in 'Britishness and Otherness: an argument' *J.B.S.* (1992), and 'Whose nation? Class and national consciousness in Britain, 1750–1830', *P.P.* (1986). J. Brewer, *Sinews of Power: War, Money and the English State, 1688–1783* (1989) argues for the rise of the 'fiscal-military state', and J.R. Jones, *Britain and the World, 1649–1815* (1980) places the subject in a larger context.

In recent years a number of scholars have pointed to the need to study 'British history', and to recognise the ways in which Scotland and Ireland impinged on the English scene, rather than seeing the history of England as the history of Britain, or treating Scottish and Irish history in isolation. See, in particular, H. Kearney, *The British Isles: A History of Four Nations* (1989), A. Murdoch, *British History, 1660–1832* (1998), M. Pittock, *Inventing and Resisting Britain: Cultural Identities in Britain and Ireland, 1685–1789* (1997) and the growing number of essay collections: B. Bradshaw and J. Morrill (eds), *The British Problem, c. 1534–1707: State Formation in the Atlantic Archipelago* (1996), A. Grant and K. Stringer (eds), *Uniting the Kingdom: The Making of British History* (1995), S. Ellis and S. Barber (eds), *Conquest and Union: Fashioning a British State, 1585–1725* (1995), L. Brockliss and D. Eastwood (eds), *A Union of Multiple*

Identities: The British Isles, 1750–1850 (1997) and A.M. Claydon and I. McBride (eds), *Protestantism and National Identity: Britain and Ireland, 1650–1850* (1998). T.M. Devine and D. Dickson (eds), *Ireland and Scotland, 1660–1850: Parallels and Contrasts in Economic and Social Development* (1983) and M. Hechter, *Internal Colonisation: The Celtic Fringe in British National Development, 1536–1966* (1975) are stimulating forays into comparative history. It is also worth looking at J.C.D. Clark, 'English history's forgotten context: Scotland, Ireland, Wales', *H.J.* (1989) and the essays by D. Hayton, 'John Bull's other kingdoms: Ireland' and D. Szechi, 'John Bull's other kingdoms: Scotland' in C. Jones (ed.), *Britain in the First Age of Party* (1987).

For Scotland, see B.P. Levak, *The Formation of the British State: England, Scotland and the Union, 1603–1707* (1987), W. Ferguson, *Scotland 1689 to the Present* (1968), T.C. Smout, *A History of the Scottish People, 1560–1830* (1969) and D. Whyte, *Scotland's Society and Economy in Transition, c. 1500–c. 1760* (1997). Good introductions are offered too by the volumes of the Arnold New History of Scotland: R. Mitchison, *Lordship to Patronage: Scotland, 1603–1745* (1983) and B. Lenman, *Integration, Enlightenment and Industrialization: Scotland, 1746–1832* (1981). See also D. Szechi, *The English Ministers and Scotland, 1707* (1994), Lenman's essay 'A client society: Scotland between the '15 and the '45', in J. Black (ed.), *Britain in the Age of Walpole* (1984) and C. Harvie, *Scotland and Nationalism: Scottish Society and Politics, 1707–1994* (1994). T. Devine, *Clanship to Crofters' War: The Social Transformation of the Scottish Highlands* (1994) is an interesting reappraisal of a crucial topic. M. Pittock, *The Invention of Scotland: The Stuart Myth and Scottish Identity* (1991) and C. Kidd, *Subverting Scotland's Past: Scottish Whig Historians and the Creation of an Anglo-British Identity, 1689–1830* (1993) are provocative. R. Houston, *Scottish Literacy and Scottish Identity: Literacy and Society in Scotland and Northern England, c. 1600–1800* (1988), his *Social Change in the Age of Enlightenment: Edinburgh, 1660–1760* (1994), J. Robertson, *The Scottish Enlightenment and the Militia Issue* (1985) and M. Fray, *The Dundas Despotism* (1992) illuminate aspects of Scottish history.

Ireland is also well covered by general texts: R.F. Foster, *Modern Ireland, 1600–1972* (1988) is a readable 'revisionist' account, while J.C. Beckett, *The Making of Modern Ireland, 1603–1923* (1969) is admirably straightforward. T.W. Moody and W.E. Vaughan, *A New History of Ireland: IV, Eighteenth-Century Ireland, 1691–1800* (1986) and D. Dickson, *New Foundations: Ireland, 1660–1800* (1987) are recommended overviews. J. Simms, *Jacobite Ireland, 1685–91* (1969), his *The Williamite Confiscation in Ireland, 1690–1703* (1956), N. Curtis, *The United Irishmen* (1994), T. Bartlett, *The Fall and Rise of the Irish Nation: The Catholic Question, 1690–1830* (1992), I. McBride, *Scripture Politics: Ulster Presbyterians and Irish Radicalism in the Late Eighteenth Century* (1998), J. Smyth, *Men of No*

Property: Irish Radicals and Popular Politics in the Late Eighteenth Century (1992), M. Elliott, *Partners in Revolution* (1982), A.P. Malcolmson, *John Foster: The Politics of the Anglo-Irish Ascendancy* (1992), G. O'Brien, *Anglo-Irish Politics in the Age of Grattan and Pitt* (1987) and R.B. McDowell, *Ireland in the Age of Imperialism and Revolution, 1760–1801* (1979) are more detailed analyses of particular issues. S.J. Connolly, *Religion, Law and Power: The Making of Protestant Ireland, 1660–1760* (1992) and N. Canny, *Kingdom and Colony: Ireland in the Atlantic World, 1500–1800* (1988) are challenging interpretations.

Wales has been well served by G.A. Williams, *When Was Wales? A History of the Welsh* (1985), G.H. Jenkins, *The Foundation of Modern Wales: Wales, 1642–1789* (1987), his *Literature, Religion and Society in Wales, 1660–1730* (1978) and T. Herbert and G.E. Jones (eds), *The Remaking of Wales in the Eighteenth Century* (1988). P. Jenkins, *The Making of a Ruling Class: The Glamorgan Gentry, 1640–1790* (1983) is broader than the title might imply.

Selected topics

1. The Revolution of 1688–89

Beware of taking an oversimplified view of James II and the Revolution settlement. Recent work has considerably modified the nineteenth-century interpretation of a villainous James opposed by a united and moderate opposition. Make sure you pay particular attention to the period from James's flight to the accession of William and Mary. The divisions within the political nation, the difficulties of removing a king without lapsing into civil war, and the problems of achieving a settlement in a hurry were all factors which conditioned events. Recent work on figures such as Locke and the Tories suggests many cracks papered over and more agreement on what people were against than what they were for. The tercentenary provided some opportunity to reappraise, notably R. Beddard (ed.), *The Revolutions of 1688* (1991), J. Israel (ed.), *The Anglo-Dutch Moment: Essays on the Glorious Revolution and Its World Impact* (1991), L. Schwoerer (ed.), *The Revolution of 1688/9: Changing Perspectives* (1991), J.R. Jones (ed.), *Liberty Secured? Britain before and after 1688* (1992) and D. Hoak and M. Feingold (eds), *The World of William and Mary: Anglo-Dutch Perspectives on the Revolution of 1688–9* (1996).

Sources and documents *English Historical Documents, 1660–1714*, vol. VIII (ed. A. Browning, 1953) and J.P. Kenyon (ed.), *The Stuart Constitution, 1603–1688*, part III (1966), J. Kenyon (ed.), *Halifax, Complete Works* and John Locke, *Two Treatises of Government* (ed. P. Laslett, 1960), with a good introduction.

Secondary works   J. Miller, *The Glorious Revolution* (1983, 2nd edn, 1997) sums up the issues. W.A. Speck, *Reluctant Revolutionaries: Englishmen and the Revolution of 1688* (1988) and J. Miller (ed.), *The Seeds of Liberty: 1688 and the Shaping of Modern Britain* (1988) are two modern reappraisals. Also valuable are J.R. Jones, *The Revolution of 1688 in England* (1972), L. Pinkham, *William III and the Respectable Revolution* (1962) and the later chapters of H. Nenner, *The Right to be King: The Succession to the Crown of England, 1603–1714* (1995). The events leading up to the 1688 Revolution are discussed in J.R. Western, *Monarchy and Revolution: The English State in the 1680s* (1972) and J. Childs, *The Army, James II and the Glorious Revolution* (1980), and the underlying role of anti-Catholicism is explored in J. Miller, *Popery and Politics in England, 1660–1688* (1976). The European dimension is examined in J. Carswell, *The Descent on England* (1969). The constitutional position is clearly set out in B. Kemp, *King and Commons, 1660–1832*, chs 2 and 3; an alternative is D. Lindsey Keir, *The Constitutional History of Modern Britain since 1485* (new edn, 1969). L.G. Schwoerer, *The Declaration of Rights, 1689* (1981) and R. Ashcraft, *Revolutionary Politics and Locke's Two Treatises of Government* (1986) examine radical Whig views of the settlement (see also the Laslett introduction under *Sources*). Broader analyses of the settlement are C. Roberts, *The Growth of Responsible Government in Stuart England* (1966) and J.H. Plumb, *The Growth of Political Stability in England* (1969). For a review of Plumb's argument, see G. Holmes, 'The achievement of stability', in J. Cannon (ed.), *The Whig Ascendancy* (1980). The important financial settlement is definitively dealt with in P.G.M. Dickson, *The Financial Revolution in England: A Study in the Development of Public Credit, 1688–1756* (1967).

Post-Revolution developments are discussed in G. Holmes (ed.), *Britain after the Glorious Revolution, 1689–1714* (1969), especially in J. Carter's essay, and in J. Miller (ed.), *The Seeds of Liberty: 1688 and the Shaping of Modern Britain* (1988). William's role is explored in S. Baxter, *William III* (1966), while B.W. Hill, *The Growth of Parliamentary Parties, 1689–1742* (1976) narrates the course of political events. More interpretative are H. Horwitz, *Parliament, Policy and Politics in the Reign of William III* (1973) and D. Rubini, *Court and Country, 1688–1702* (1976), while stress on ideology can be found in the early parts of J.P. Kenyon, *Revolution Principles: The Politics of Party, 1689–1720* (1977), H.T. Dickinson, *Liberty and Property: Political Ideology in Eighteenth-Century Britain* (1977) and T. Claydon, *William III and the Godly Revolution* (1996). For the operation of politics in London, see G.S. De Krey, *A Fractured Society: The Politics of London in the First Age of Party, 1688–1715* (1985), and for the rise of the 'Country interest', D. Hayton, 'The "Country" interest and the party system, 1689–c. 1720', in C. Jones (ed.), *Party and Management in Parliament, 1660–1784* (1984).

Articles On the revolution itself, see J. Childs, '1688', *H.* 73 (1988), H.T. Dickinson, 'How revolutionary was the Glorious Revolution of 1688?', *B.J.E.S.* (1988), J.P. Kenyon, 'The Earl of Sunderland and the Revolution of 1688', *C.H.J.*, xi (1955), J.H. Plumb, 'The elections to the Convention Parliament, 1688-9', *C.H.J.* (1935-37), R. Frankle, 'The formulation of the Declaration of Rights', *H.J.* (1974), H. Horwitz, 'Parliament and the Glorious Revolution', *B.I.H.R.* (1974), his '1689 (and all that)', *P.H.* (1988) and D. Szechi, 'The Jacobite revolution settlement, 1689-1696', *E.H.R.* (1993). G. Straka, 'The final phase of divine right theory in England', *E.H.R.* (1962) is also important. Popular involvement is discussed in W.L. Sachse, 'The mob and the Revolution of 1688', *J.B.S.* (1964-65). Significant articles on the financial settlement are E.A. Reitan, 'From revenue to civil list, 1689-1702', *H.J.* (1970), C. Roberts, 'The constitutional significance of the financial settlement of 1690', *H.J.* (1977), C. Brooks, 'Public finance and political stability: the administration of the Land Tax, 1688-1720', *H.J.* (1974) and D. Rubini, 'The battle of the banks', *E.H.R.* (1976). For political developments in the 1690s, see H. Horwitz, 'Parties, connections and parliamentary politics, 1689-1714', *J.B.S.* (1966) and J.A. Downie, 'The commission of public accounts and the formation of the Country Party', *E.H.R.* (1976). A bold interpretation of the wider significance of 1688 is J.C.D. Clark, 'A general theory of party, opposition and government, 1688-1832', *H.J.* (1980).

2. The reign of Queen Anne and the Hanoverian succession

The reign of Queen Anne and the rage of party has been reinterpreted in recent years. The relevance and meaning of 'party' have been subjected to examination, and studies of constituency politics, particularly elections and the electorate, have added a new dimension to our study of politics, carrying the discussion of political attitudes beyond the confines of Westminster. The place of religious strife requires consideration and the bitter conflict over foreign policy it involved. The 'inevitability' of the Hanoverian succession also demands critical scrutiny.

Sources and documents G.S. Holmes and W.A. Speck (eds), *The Divided Society, 1694-1716* (1967) is a short, lively collection of documents. A. Browning (ed.), *English Historical Documents, 1660-1714* (1953) has the usual wide selection of documents for the series. Jonathan Swift, *The Conduct of the Allies* (1711) is a lively tract on foreign policy, reprinted in A. Ross and D. Woolley, *Jonathan Swift* (Oxford Authors Series, 1984). Equally interesting is Gregory King, 'Natural and political observations ... upon the state of England', reprinted in G.E. Barnett (ed.), *Two Tracts by Gregory King* (1936).

Secondary works A useful and thought-provoking guide is T. Harris, *Politics under the Later Stuarts: Party Conflict in a Divided Society, 1660–1715* (1993). The standard modern interpretation is G.S. Holmes, *British Politics in the Age of Anne* (1967, revised edn, 1987), while *Religion and Party in Late Stuart England* (Historical Association pamphlet, 1975) is a briefer version of some of his views. J.H. Plumb, *The Growth of Political Stability in England 1675–1725* (1967) remains an important analysis of the issues, while B.W. Hill, *The Growth of Parliamentary Parties, 1689–1742* (1976) offers a detailed account of proceedings at parliamentary level. These studies implicitly refute the analysis of politics based upon family groupings in R. Walcott, *English Politics in the Early Eighteenth Century* (1956). The development of political activity in the localities is discussed in W.A. Speck, *Tory and Whig: The Struggle in the Constituencies, 1701–1715* (1970) and G.S. Holmes, *The Electorate and the National Will in the First Age of Party* (1976). W.A. Speck, *The Birth of Britain: A New Nation, 1700–1710* (1994) is a year-by-year account of the first decade of the eighteenth century. There is a wholesale assault on received opinions in J.C.D. Clark, *English Society, 1688–1832* (1985), especially ch.1 (pts i–iv), and the emphasis on ideological factors is reiterated in J.P. Kenyon, *Revolution Principles: The Politics of Party, 1689–1720* (1977) and H.T. Dickinson, *Liberty and Property: Political Ideology in Eighteenth-Century Britain* (1977). The role of the Country interest is discussed in D. Hayton, 'The "Country" interest and the party system, 1689–c. 1720', in C. Jones (ed.), *Party and Management in Parliament, 1660–1784* (1984).

The broader social stability underpinning the changes of ruler in 1689 and 1714 is examined by G.S. Holmes, 'The achievement of stability: the social context of politics from the 1680s to the age of Walpole', in J. Cannon (ed.), *The Whig Ascendancy* (1981). A number of essays on the character of British politics after 1689 are also included in G.S. Holmes (ed.), *Britain after the Glorious Revolution 1689–1714* (1969). B. Kemp, *King and Commons 1660–1832* (1957) has an admirably clear view of the constitutional position, whilst for financial affairs see P.G.M. Dickson, *The Financial Revolution in England: A Study in the Development of Public Credit, 1688–1756* (1967), especially chs 1–3. The background of foreign policy as a source of conflict is considered in P. Langford, *Modern British Foreign Policy: The Eighteenth Century, 1688–1815* (1976) and J.R. Jones, *Britain and the World, 1649–1815* (1980). Two areas of foreign policy are discussed in D.B. Horn, *Great Britain and Europe in the Eighteenth Century* (1967) and J. McLachlan, *Trade and Peace with Old Spain, 1667–1739* (1940).

For religious issues, see G.V. Bennett, 'Conflict in the Church', in G. Holmes (ed.), *Britain after the Glorious Revolution*. The growing party and religious bitterness towards the end of Anne's reign is explored in G.S. Holmes, *The Trial of Dr Sacheverell* (1973), G.V. Bennett, *The Tory*

Crisis in Church and State: The Career of Francis Atterbury, Bishop of Rochester (1975) and G.V. Every *The High Church Party* (1956). Of the principal figures, see B. Hill, *Robert Harley: Speaker, Secretary of State and Premier Minister* (1988), J.A. Downie, *Robert Harley and the Press: Popularity and Public Opinion in the Age of Swift and Defoe* (1979), H.T. Dickinson, *Bolingbroke* (1970), H. Horwitz, *Revolution Politiks: The Career of Daniel Finch, 2nd Earl of Nottingham, 1647–1730* (1961) and R.A. Sundstrom, *Sidney Godolphin: Servant of State* (1993). E. Gregg, *Queen Anne* (1980) rescues the Queen from the caricature role often ascribed to her, and R. Bucholz, *The Augustan Court: Queen Anne and the Decline of Court Culture* (1993) is a masterly study of the role of the Court in the early eighteenth century. For the manoeuvres prior to 1714, see G. Holmes, 'Harley, St. John and the Death of the Tory Party' in his *Britain after the Glorious Revolution, 1689–1714* (1969) and D. Szechi, *Jacobitism and Tory Politics, 1710–14* (1984). For the Scots, the crucial issue of these years was the Act of Union, for which see P.W.J. Riley, *The Union of England and Scotland: A Study in Anglo-Scottish Politics of the 18th Century* (1979), D. Szechi and D. Hayton, 'John Bull's other kingdoms: the English government of Scotland and Ireland', in C. Jones (ed.), *Britain in the First Age of Party* (1987), T.C. Smout, 'The road to Union', in G. Holmes (ed.) *Britain after the Glorious Revolution*, M. Goldie, 'Divergence and Union: Scotland and England, 1660–1707', in B. Bradshaw and J. Morrill (eds), *The British Problem* (1996) and J. Robertson (ed.), *A Union for Empire: Political Thought and the Union of 1707* (1995).

Articles Two views on party affiliation are expressed in H. Horwitz, 'Parties, connections, and parliamentary politics, 1689–1714: review and revision', *J.B.S.* (1966) and D.A. Rubini, 'Party and the Augustan constitution: politics and the power of the executive', *A.*, (1978). The seminal article on the growth of the electorate is J.H. Plumb, 'The growth of the electorate in England from 1600 to 1715', *P.P.* (1969). C. Brooks, 'Public finance and political stability: the administration of the Land Tax, 1688–1720', *H.J.* (1974) links finance and politics. For religious tensions, J. Spurr, 'The Church of England, comprehension and the Toleration Act of 1689', *E.H.R.* (1989) is a detailed account of an important piece of legislation, and J. Flaningham, 'The occasional conformity controversy: ideology and party politics, 1697–1711', *J.B.S.* (1977) is an examination of a vexed issue. The controversy surrounding Sacheverell is considered in M. Ransome, 'Church and dissent in the election of 1710', *E.H.R.* (1941). The struggle over the Hanoverian succession is explored in H.N. Fieldhouse, 'Bolingbroke's share in the Jacobite intrigue of 1710–14', *E.H.R.* (1937), M.A. Thomson, 'The safeguarding of the Protestant succession', *H.* (1954), E. Gregg, 'Was Queen Anne a Jacobite?', *H.* (1972) and E. Cruikshanks, 'The Tories and the succession in the 1714

Parliament', *B.I.H.R.* (1973). Two case studies of electoral behaviour at the time of the Hanoverian succession are W.A. Speck, 'The general election of 1715', *E.H.R.* (1975) and N. Landau, 'Independence, deference and voter participation: the behaviour of the electorate in early-eighteenth-century Kent', *H.J.* (1979). 'Country' politics are discussed in D. Hayton, 'Moral reform and Country politics in the late seventeenth-century House of Commons', *P.P.* (1990) and J.A. Downie, 'The commission of public accounts and the formation of the Country Party', *E.H.R.* (1976). For divisions over foreign policy, see R. McJimsey, 'A country divided? English politics and the Nine Years War', *A.* (1991).

3. Walpole and the consolidation of the Whig supremacy

Walpole's period of office has dominated historians' discussion of the period from 1715 to 1745. The nature of his power and its significance for the conduct of politics in the period have provided a major theme. The relationship between Crown and Parliament and the position of Walpole as *de facto* Prime Minister shed light on the working out of the constitutional implications of the Revolution Settlement. The weakening of party feeling from the 1720s provided an opportunity for a different style of politics in which patronage and 'influence' played a more crucial part than 'party'. As a result, much of the writing on this topic concerns the 'structure' of politics. Much recent work, however, has attempted to re-ideologise the first half of the eighteenth century: Clark, Hill, Colley and others stress the fissures as much as the 'stability'. Surprisingly little attention has been paid to Walpole's policies themselves, though there has been a revival of interest in the ideological basis of the 'Whig oligarchy' and the role of public opinion.

Sources and documents E.N. Williams (ed.), *The Eighteenth-Century Constitution* (1960) has a good selection of contemporary documents, as has D.B. Horn and M. Ransome, *English Historical Documents, vol. X: 1714–83* (1957). Lord Hervey, *Memoirs* (3 vols, ed. R. Sedgwick, 1931) provides a fascinating account of court politics under Walpole. There is a vast amount of material on the structure of local politics in R. Sedgwick, *The House of Commons 1715–1754* (2 vols, 1970).

Secondary works The ghost of Namier's interpretation of eighteenth-century politics still stalks the scene, especially his view of 'patronage politics'; see L.S. Namier, *The Structure of Politics at the Accession of George III* (1929), especially the section on why people entered politics. Two modern overviews are W.A. Speck, *Stability and Strife: England 1714–1760* (1977) and P. Langford, *A Polite and Commercial People* (1989). J. Black, *Sir Robert Walpole and the Structure of Politics in Early Eighteenth-Century*

Britain (1990) is an up-to-date appraisal, as is F. O'Gorman, *Voters, Patrons and Parties: The Unreformed Electorate of Hanoverian England, 1734–1832* (1989), see especially chs 1, 3 and 5. J.H. Plumb, *The Growth of Political Stability in England, 1675–1725* (1967) is a classic account now under some attack. H.T. Dickinson, *Walpole and the Whig Supremacy* (1973) and B. Kemp, *Sir Robert Walpole* (1976) are both useful shorter works. A good collection of essays is J. Black (ed.), *The Age of Walpole* (1984). See also G.S. Holmes, 'Sir Robert Walpole', in H. Van Thal (ed.), *The Prime Ministers*, vol. 1 (1974). On the older view of the pattern of politics in this period, see J. Owen, *The Eighteenth Century, 1714–1815* (1974), ch 5; his views are also stated in J. Owen, *The Pattern of Politics in Eighteenth-Century England* (Historical Association pamphlet, 1962). Owen's views and those of other writers on the Whig oligarchy have come under scrutiny in J.C.D. Clark, *English Society, 1688–1832* (1985), see especially ch. 1. The structural interpretations of Namier and Owen are also implicitly challenged in the introduction to R. Sedgwick (ed.), *The House of Commons, 1715–1754* (1970) and in the pro-party analysis of B.W. Hill, *The Growth of Parliamentary Parties, 1689–1742* (1977). Discussion of the issues can be found in J. Cannon (ed.), *The Whig Ascendancy* (1981), chs 2 and 3. For a different perspective on some of these see R. Hatton, *George I: Elector and King* (1978), J. Beattie, *The English Court in the Reign of George I* (1967) and B. Williams, *Stanhope: A Study in Eighteenth-Century War and Diplomacy* (1932). For the survival of Tory/Jacobite support, see topic 4. One of the most important episodes of Walpole's career is discussed in J. Carswell, *The South Sea Bubble* (1960, revised edn, 1993), but see also P.G.M. Dickson, *The Financial Revolution* (1967). On other issues, see P. Langford, *The Excise Crisis: Society and Politics in the Age of Walpole* (1975), and Walpole's concern with Jacobitism is brought out in G.V. Bennett, 'Jacobitism and the Rise of Walpole', in N. McKendrick (ed.), *Historical Perspectives* (1974) and P.S. Fritz, *The English Ministers and Jacobitism between the Rebellions of 1715 and 1745* (1975). The foreign policy background is discussed in P. Langford, *Modern British Foreign Policy: The Eighteenth Century, 1688–1815* (1976), J. Black, *British Foreign Policy in the Age of Walpole* (1986), and the more detailed D.B. Horn, *Great Britain and Europe in the Eighteenth Century* (1967) and J. McLachlan, *Trade and Peace with Old Spain, 1667–1739* (1940). S. Targett, 'A pro-government newspaper during the Whig ascendancy: Walpole's *London Journal*, 1722–1738', in K. Shweizer and J. Black (eds), *Politics and the Press in Hanoverian England* (1989) is a rare discussion of pro-Walpolean propaganda.

The opposition to Walpole is considered in A.S. Foord, *His Majesty's Opposition, 1714–1830* (1964), L. Colley, *In Defiance of Oligarchy: The Tory Party, 1714–1760* (1981), H.T. Dickinson, *Bolingbroke* (1970), I. Kramnick, *Bolingbroke and his Circle: The Politics of Nostalgia in the Age of Walpole* (1968), N. Rogers, *Whigs and Cities* (1990), Q. Skinner, 'The principles and practice of opposition: the case of Bolingbroke versus Walpole', in N. McKendrick (ed.), *Historical Perspectives: Studies in English Thought and Society in Honour of J.H. Plumb* (1974), and B.A. Goldgar, *Walpole and the Wits: The Relation of Politics to Literature, 1722–44* (1977). The important role of London is considered in L.S. Sutherland, 'The city of London in eighteenth-century politics', in R. Pares and A.J.P. Taylor (eds), *Essays Presented to Sir Lewis Namier* (1956), N. Rogers, 'Resistance to oligarchy', in J. Stevenson (ed.), *London in the Age of Reform* (1977), A.J. Henderson, *London and the National Government, 1721–1742: A Study of City Politics and the Walpole Administration* (1945). Popular protest is considered in E.P. Thompson, *Whigs and Hunters: The Origin of the Black Act* (1975), adding another dimension to the study of the Whig oligarchy.

The political scene after the fall of Walpole is best studied in J.B. Owen, *The Rise of the Pelhams* (1956), R. Browning, *The Duke of Newcastle* (1975), T.W. Perry, *Public Opinion, Propaganda and Politics in Eighteenth-Century England* (1962) and in the somewhat hard-going J.C.D. Clark, *The Dynamics of Change: The Crisis of the 1750s and the English Party Systems* (1982).

Articles See M. Ransome, 'Division lists in the House of Commons, 1715–1760', *B.I.H.R.* (1942), E.A. Reitan, 'The civil list in eighteenth-century British politics', *H.J.* (1966), B. Williams, 'The Duke of Newcastle and the general election of 1734', *E.H.R.* (1897), T.F.J. Kendrick, 'Sir Robert Walpole, the old Whigs and the bishops, 1733–1736', *H.J.* (1968), E.R. Turner, 'The excise scheme of 1733', *E.H.R.* (1927) and W. Speck, 'Whigs and Tories dim their glories: English political parties under the first two Georges', in J. Cannon (ed.), *The Whig Ascendancy*. On the opposition to Walpole, see L. Colley, 'Eighteenth-century English radicalism before Wilkes', *T.R.H.S.* (1981) and J.C.D. Clark, 'The politics of the excluded: Tories, Jacobites and Whig patriots, 1715–1760', *P.H.* (1983). On foreign policy, see G. Gibbs, 'Parliament and foreign policy in the age of Stanhope and Walpole', *E.H.R.* (1962) and D. McKay, 'The struggle for control of George I's northern policy', *J.M.H.* (1973). On financial matters, see J.V. Beckett, 'Land Tax or excise: the levying of taxation in seventeenth- and eighteenth-century England', *E.H.R.* (1985). On the war of 1739, see K. Wilson, 'Admiral Vernon and popular politics in mid-Hanoverian Britain', *P.P.* (1988). On the Church, see S. Taylor, 'Sir Robert Walpole, the Church of England and the Quakers' Tithe Bill of 1736', *H.J.* (1985). A useful corrective to the received opinions about George II is J.B. Owen, 'George II reconsidered', in A. Whiteman, J.S. Bromley and P.G.M. Dickson (eds), *Statesmen, Scholars and Merchants: Essays in Eighteenth-Century History Presented to Dame Lucy Sutherland* (1973). The post-Walpole period is examined in J.C.D. Clark, 'The decline of party, 1740–60', *E.H.R.* (1978).

4. Jacobitism

Jacobitism is gradually being reclaimed from the realms of romantic fiction to reflect increasingly upon the insecurity of the Hanoverian succession and the many opportunities for division within the political nation which still existed after 1714. The role of Jacobitism as an ideology of opposition is worth considering, especially for the way in which it shaded off into Toryism and the opposition to Walpole. The manipulation of the Jacobite issue by Walpole has also received attention. The topic also provides an opportunity to discuss the 'Scottish dimension' of eighteenth-century British power politics.

Sources and documents Sources for this difficult subject are notoriously difficult to handle. By their very nature, Jacobite conspirators were unlikely to produce material which has survived in an easily manageable form. Nevertheless, some inkling of the range of sources can be found in A. Browning (ed.) *English Historical Documents, 1660–1714* (1953) and D.B. Horn and M. Ransome (eds), *English Historical Documents, 1714–1783* (1957), W.B. Coley (ed.), *The Jacobites' Journal and Related Writings* (1974), L.G. Wickham-Legg, 'Extracts from Jacobite Correspondence, 1712–1714', *E.H.R.* (1915).

Secondary works E. Gregg, *Jacobitism* (Historical Association Pamphlet, 1988), M. Pittock, *Jacobitism* (1998) and G.H. Jones, *The Mainstream of Jacobitism* (1954) are good places to start. E. Cruikshanks and J. Black (eds), *The Jacobite Challenge* (1988), F. McLynn, *The Jacobites* (1985), E. Cruikshanks (ed.), *Ideology and Conspiracy: Aspects of Jacobitism, 1689–1759* (1982) and P. Monod, *Jacobitism and the English People, 1688–1788* (1989) offer a fresh assessment of Jacobite activity; see also L. Gooch, *The Desperate Faction? The Jacobites of North-East England, 1688–1745* (1995) and J.C.D. Clark, *English Society, 1688–1832* (1985), especially ch. 3. Holmes' essay in G.S. Holmes (ed.), *Britain after the Glorious Revolution* (1969) discusses the political struggle preceding Anne's death, but see also D. Szechi, *Jacobitism and Tory Politics, 1710–14* (1984). For the survival of Bolingbroke's influence, see I. Krammick, *Bolingbroke and his Circle: The Politics of Nostalgia in the Age of Walpole* (1968) and H.T. Dickinson, *Bolingbroke* (1970). A.S. Foord, *His Majesty's Opposition 1714–1830* (1964) discusses the place of the Jacobites in the other factions aiming for the overthrow of Walpole, as does C.B. Realey, *The Early Opposition to Sir Robert Walpole* (1931). One centre of popular Jacobitism was London, for which see G.S. De Krey, *A Fractured Society: The Politics of London in the First Age of Party* (1985). For support for the extent of influence on the Tory opposition to Walpole, see ch. v of the introductory survey of R. Sedgwick (ed.), *The House of Commons, 1715–1754* (1970) and

E. Cruikshanks, *Political Untouchables: The Tories and the '45* (1979). These views are considered critically in W. Speck, 'Whigs and Tories dim their glories', in J. Cannon (ed.), *The Whig Ascendancy* (1981) and by L. Colley, *In Defiance of Oligarchy: The Tory Party, 1714–60* (1981). The effects of Jacobitism on Walpole are considered by G.V. Bennett in 'Jacobitism and the rise of Walpole', in N. McKendrick (ed.), *Historical Perspectives* (1974). P.S. Fritz, *The English Ministers and Jacobitism between the Rebellions of 1715 and 1745* (1975) is a valuable study of the exploitation of the Jacobite 'threat' by Walpole, while for the risings themselves, see B. Lenman, *The Jacobite Risings in Britain, 1689–1746* (1980), his essay on Scotland in J. Black (ed.), *Britain in the Age of Walpole* (1985) and W.A. Speck, *The Butcher: The Duke of Cumberland and the Suppression of the '45* (1981). The plot of 1722 is well analysed in G.V. Bennett, *The Tory Crisis in Church and State* (1975). Good biographical studies include D. Daiches, *Charles Edward Stuart* (1973) and F. McLynn, *Charles Edward Stuart* (1988). The broader cultural resonances of Jacobitism are studied in M. Pittock, *Poetry and Jacobite Politics in Eighteenth-Century Britain and Ireland* (1994).

For the Scottish dimension, see the volumes in the Arnold History by Mitchison and Lenman, B. Lenman's essay (above) in Black. See also D. Szechi and D. Hayton, 'John Bull's other kingdoms: the English government of Scotland and Ireland', in C. Jones (ed.), *Britain in the First Age of Party* (1987) and D. Szechi *The Jacobites and Europe, 1688–1788* (1994). The European dimension is considered in P. Langford, *Modern British Foreign Policy: The Eighteenth Century, 1688–1815* (1976) and J.R. Jones, *Britain and the World, 1649–1815* (1980), J. Black, *A System of Ambition? British Foreign Policy 1660–1793* (1991), J. Black, *British Foreign Policy in the Age of Walpole* (1985), and for the long-running Anglo-French conflict, J. Black, *Natural and Necessary Enemies* (1986). Spain is considered in J. McLachlan, *Trade and Peace with Old Spain, 1667–1739* (1940).

Articles D. Szechi, 'The Jacobite revolution settlement, 1689–1696', *E.H.R.* (1993) is crucial. N. Rogers, 'Popular disturbances in early Hanoverian London', *P.P.* (1978) gives a good account of pro-Tory and crypto-Jacobite feeling in London. Also see E. Cruikshanks and H. Erskine-Hill, 'The Waltham Black Act and Jacobitism', *J.B.S.* (1985). P.D.G. Thomas, 'Jacobitism in Wales', *W.H.R.* (1963) is good on an often neglected area of British politics. H.N. Fieldhouse, 'Bolingbroke and the idea of non-party government', *E.H.R.* (1937), E. Gregg, 'Was Queen Anne a Jacobite?', *H.* (1972), and M.A. Thomson, 'The safe-guarding of the Protestant succession', *H.* (1954) are all relevant. See also J.C.D. Clark, 'The politics of the excluded: Tories, Jacobites and Whig patriots, 1715–1760', *P.H.* (1983), and B. Lenman, 'The Jacobite diaspora, 1688–1746', *H.J.* (1980). On government measures, see P.S. Fritz, 'The anti-Jacobite intelligence system of the English ministers 1715–45', *H.J.* (1973)

and G.V. Bennett, 'English Jacobitism, 1710–1715: myth and reality', *T.R.H.S.* (1982). On the '45, see N. Rogers, 'Popular disaffection in London during the forty-five', *L.J.* (1975) and I.R. Christie, 'The Tory Party and the '45', *H.J.* (1987).

5. The machinery of the British State: national and local government

How Britain was governed in the eighteenth century has been the subject of some debate. Traditionally the period has been seen as one of weak central government (at least in comparison to the eras which preceded and succeeded it) and where government was very much in the hands of local élites. Recent research has tended to challenge the notion of a weak central administration, and John Brewer, for example, in *The Sinews of Power: War, Money and the English State, 1688–1783* (1989), has argued forcefully for the State's capacity to intervene in the localities in the creation of the 'fiscal-military state'. So too, at both national and local level, eighteenth-century government has been charged with 'corruption'. Again recent research has tended to modify some of the most vehement denunciations of would-be reformers, and has begun to appreciate the strength, efficiency and flexibility of government at all levels.

Sources and documents   E.N. Williams, *The Eighteenth-Century Constitution* (1970), A. Browning (ed.), *English Historical Documents, 1660–1714* (1953), D.B. Horn and M. Ransome (eds), *English Historical Documents, 1714–1783* (1957), and A. Aspinall and E.A Smith (eds), *English Historical Documents, 1783–1832* (1959) contain much material relvant to the formal relationship between the centre and the localities.

Secondary works   D. Eastwood, *Government and Community in the Provinces, 1700–1870* (1997) provides a succinct overview of recent debates and highlights the relationship between local and national government. See also his *Governing Rural England: Tradition and Transformation in Local Government, 1780–1840* (1994). The massive investigation by S. and B. Webb, *English Local Government from the Revolution to the Municipal Corporations Act* (11 vols, 1903–29) remains a mine of information, although some of their assumptions about the paralysis of local government have been challenged by more recent writers. For various aspects of the State's machinery, see P. Langford, *The Excise Crisis: Society and Politics in the Age of Walpole* (1975), P.G.M. Dickson, *The Financial Revolution in England: A Study in the Development of Public Credit, 1688–1756* (1967), R.R. Nelson, *The Home Office, 1782–1801* (1969), J.V. Beckett, *Local Taxation: National Legislation and the Problem of Enforcement* (1980), I.R. Christie, *Stress and Stability in Late Eighteenth-Century Britain* (1984), W.R. Ward, *The English*

Land Tax in the Eighteenth Century (1953), C. Emsley, *Policing and Its Context* (1983) and D. Dean and C. Jones (eds), *Parliament and Locality, 1660–1939* (1998). Aspects of local government are explored in A. Fletcher, *Reform in the Provinces: The Government of Stuart England* (1986), L.K. Glassey, *Politics and the Appointments of the Justices of the Peace, 1675–1725*, N. Landau, *The Justices of the Peace, 1679–1760* (1984), B. Keith-Lucas, *The Unreformed Local Government System* (1980) and J.R. Western, *The English Militia in the Eighteenth Century, 1660–1802* (1965). On the law, as an agent of State, see E.P. Thompson, *Whigs and Hunters: The Origin of the Black Act* (1975), D.P. Hay, P. Linenbaugh and E.P. Thompson (eds), *Albion's Fatal Tree* (1975) and the critique by J.H. Langbein, 'Albion's fatal flaws', *P.P.* (1983), and P.B. Munsche, *Gentlemen and Poachers: The English Game Laws, 1671–1834* (1981). The Church's role as an agent of State should not be ignored, in particular see: D. McClatchey, *The Oxfordshire Clergy, 1777–1869* (1960), P. Horn, *A Georgian Parson and his Village: The Story of David Davies, 1742–1819* (1984) and P. Virgin, *The Church in an Age of Negligence: Ecclesiastical Structure and the Problems of Church Reform* (1989).

Particular regions are dealt with in E. Moir, *Local Government in Gloucestershire, 1775–1800* (publications of the Bristol and Gloucestershire Archaeological Society, 1969), J.D. Chambers, *Nottinghamshire in the Eighteenth Century* (1966), M. de Lacy, *Prison Reform in Lancashire, 1700–1850: A Study in Local Administration* (1986), B. Keith-Lucas, *Parish Affairs: The Government of Kent under George III* (1986) and R.W. Davis, *Political Change and Continuity, 1760–1885: A Buckinghamshire Study* (1972). Government in Wales is studied in D.W. Howell, *Patriarchs and Parasites: The Gentry of South-West Wales in the Eighteenth Century* (1986) and P. Jenkins, *The Making of a Ruling Class: The Glamorgan Gentry, 1640–1790* (1983). Government in Ireland is discussed in S. Connolly, *Religion, Law and Power: The Making of Protestant Ireland, 1660–1760* (1992), and for Scotland see B. Lenman, *Integration, Enlightenment and Industrialisation: Scotland, 1746–1832* (1981). The relationship between the centre and the localities in the formulation of government policy is examined in L. Davison, T. Hitchcock, T. Kiern and R.B. Shoemaker (eds), *Stilling the Grumbling Hive: The Response to Social and Economic Problems in England, 1688–1750* (1992). For the administration of the poor laws, as a particularly pressing problem for local government, see P. Slack, *The English Poor Law, 1531–1782* (1990), G.W. Oxley, *Poor Relief in England and Wales, 1601–1834* (1974) and J.D. Marshall, *The Old Poor Law, 1795–1834* (1985). The issue of 'corruption' is dealt with by P. Harling, *The Waning of Old Corruption: The Politics of Economical Reform in Britain, 1779–1846* (1996).

Articles See in particular, G. Aylmer, 'From office holding to civil service: the genesis of the modern bureaucracy', *T.R.H.S.* (1980), D. Eastwood,

'"Amplifying the province of the legislature": the flow of information and the English State in the early nineteenth century', *Historical Research*, 62 (1989), his 'Patriotism and the English State in the 1790s', in M. Philp (ed.), *The French Revolution and British Popular Politics* (1991), G.C.F. Forster, 'Government in provincial England under the later Stuarts', *T.R.H.S.* 33 (1983), J. Kent, 'The centre and the localities: state formation and parish government in England, c. 1640–1740', *H.J.* (1995), J. Hoppitt, 'Reforming Britain's weights and measures, 1660–1824', *E.H.R.* 108 (1993), J. Innes, 'Parliament and the shaping of eighteenth-century English social policy', *T.R.H.S.* 40 (1990), P. Langford, 'Property and "virtual representation" in eighteenth-century England', *H.J.* (1988), P. Harling, 'Rethinking "old corruption"', *P.P.* (1995) and W. Rubinstein, 'The end of "old corruption" in Britain, 1780–1860', *P.P* (1982).

6. The creation of a class society

Reflecting the transitional quality of the period, the nature of English society (its social structure and social relations) in the eighteenth century has always been a matter of dispute. Was it a traditional society, based on estates and orders, or can we date the origins of social classes from this period? Historians first focused on relations between the landed class and the lower class, but recently more attention has been given to the middle class. Class can be defined in different ways; it is important to consider not only socio-economic characteristics based on occupations and types of income but also contemporary perceptions. Class implies the possibility of class conflict: in a hierarchical society, were relations between social groups based on deference and paternalism or conflict and insubordination?

Sources and documents James Woodforde, *The Diary of a Country Parson* (ed. J. Beresford, 1949) evokes social relations in the rural world. Daniel Defoe, *The Complete English Tradesman* (1735; Penguin edn, 1987) examines the new commercial classes. James Boswell, *London Journal, 1762–3* (ed. F.A. Pottle, 1950 and 1966) is an account of London life. Thomas Turner, *The Diary of Thomas Turner, 1754–65* (ed. D. Vaisey, 1985) deals with Sussex life in the mid-century. Contemporary (eighteenth-century) descriptions of the social structure are discussed in G. Holmes, 'Gregory King and the social structure of pre-industrial England', *T.R.H.S.* (1977), P. Laslett, *The World We Have Lost Further Explored* (1983), ch. 2 and P. Mathias, *The Transformation of England* (1979), ch. 9.

Secondary works and articles The case for an understanding of eighteenth-century society in terms of class was made by E.P. Thompson,

'Eighteenth-century English society: class struggle without class?', *S.H.* (1978); see also his 'Patrician society, plebeian culture', *J.S.H.* (1974), the early chapters of *The Making of the English Working Class* (1968) and his *Customs in Common* (1991). For an alternative point of view, see P. Laslett, *The World We Have Lost* (3rd edn, 1983), ch. 2 and H. Perkin, *The Origins of Modern English Society* (1969). For the birth of the language of class, see P. Corfield, 'Class by name and number in eighteenth-century Britain', *H.* (1987). For social mobility, see D. Rapp, 'Social mobility in the eighteenth century: the Whitbreads of Bedfordshire, 1720–1815', *Econ.H.R.* (1974). A summary of some of the debates can be found in R. Porter, 'English society in the eighteenth century revisited', in J. Black (ed.), *British Politics and Society from Walpole to Pitt* (1990).

On the lower classes, see R.W. Malcolmson, *Life and Labour in England 1700–1780* (1979), J. Rule, *The Experience of Labour in Eighteenth-Century England* (1981) and M. Reed and R. Wells (eds), *Class Conflict and Protest in the English Countryside, 1700–1880* (1990). On urban and industrial workers, see C.R. Dobson, *Masters and Journeymen* (1980). On rural labour, see K.V. Snell, *Annals of the Labouring Poor: Social Change in Agrarian England 1660–1900* (1985) and A. Kussmaul, *Servants in Husbandry in Early Modern England* (1981). G.E. Mingay, *English Landed Society in the Eighteenth Century* (1956) and *The Gentry: The Rise and Fall of a Ruling Class* (1976), especially chs. 3–5, examine the landed classes. For the nobility, see J. Cannon, *Aristocratic Century: The Peerage of Eighteenth-Century England* (1984), his 'The isthmus repaired: the resurgence of the English aristocracy, 1660–1716', *P.B.A.* (1982) and J.V. Beckett, *The Aristocracy in England 1660–1914* (1986). L. Stone and J.C.F. Stone, *An Open Elite? England, 1540–1880* (1984) is a major reassessment of the possibility of entry into the landed classes. See also ch. 2 of H. Perkin's *The Origins of Modern English Society* (1969) and L.B. Namier, 'The social foundations' in his *England in the Age of the American Revolution* (2nd edn, 1961). On the ownership of property, see P. Langford, *Public Life and the Propertied Englishman, 1689–1789* (1991), H.J. Habbukuk, 'English land-ownership, 1680–1740', *Econ.H.R.* (1940), his *Marriage, Debt and the Estates System: English Landownership, 1650–1950* (1994), C. Clay, 'Marriage inheritance and the rise of large estates in England, 1660–1815', *Econ.H.R.* (1968), B. Holderness, 'The English land market in the eighteenth century', *Econ.H.R.* (1974) and E. Spring, *Law, Land, and Family: Aristocratic Inheritance in England, 1300–1800* (1993). J. Brewer and S. Staves (eds), *Changing Conceptions of Property in the Seventeenth and Eighteenth Centuries* (1994) is a wide-ranging collection.

Recently, the middle classes have received much more attention. On the 'rise of the middle classes' generally, see P. Earle's ambitiously titled book, *The Making of the English Middle Class* (1989), J. Barry and

C. Brooks (eds), *The Middling Sort of People: Culture, Society and Politics in England 1550–1800* (1992), D. Wahrman, *Taming the Middle Class: The Political Representation of Class* (1995), and the issue of *J.B.S.* 32 (1993) which was devoted to the theme of 'Making the English middle class, c. 1700–1850'. The development of the professional classes is considered in G.S. Holmes, *Augustan England: Professions, State and Society, 1680–1730* (1982), P.J. Corfield, *Power and the Professions in Britain, 1700–1850* (1995), E. Hughes, 'The professions in the Eighteenth Century', *D.U.J.* (1951) and N. Rogers, 'Land and lineage: the big bourgeoisie of Hanoverian London', *S.H.* (1979). Since the middling sort generally lived in towns, the growing literature on urban areas will be relevant: see especially P. Corfield, *The Impact of English Towns* (1982), P. Borsay, *The English Urban Renaissance: Culture and Society in the Provincial Town, 1660–1770* (1989), P. Clark (ed.), *The Transformation of English Provincial Towns, 1600–1800* (1984), C.W. Chalklin, *The Provincial Towns of Georgian England: A Study of the Building Process, 1740–1820* (1974), and the collection of articles in P. Borsay (ed.), *The Eighteenth-Century Town* (1990). On London, see D. George, *London Life in the Eighteenth Century* (1925; reprint edn, 1966), G. Rudé, *Hanoverian London* (1971), M. Byrd, *London Transformed: Images of the City in the Eighteenth Century* (1978), J. Summerson, *Georgian London* (1962 edn), and the relevant chapters of R. Porter, *London: A Social History* (1995). Studies of other urban areas include J. Money, *Experience and Identity, Birmingham, 1770–1800* (1978), G. Jackson, *Hull in the Eighteenth Century: A Study in Economic and Social History* (1972), R.S. Neale, *Bath, 1680–1850: A Social History* (1981), P.M. Horsley, *Eighteenth-Century Newcastle* (1971), R. Houston, *Social Change in the Age of Enlightenment: Edinburgh, 1660–1760* (1994), R. Newton, *Eighteenth-Century Exeter* (1984) and R. Wilson, *Gentlemen Merchants: The Merchant Community in Leeds, 1700–1830* (1971). Also see P. Corfield, 'Walking the city street: the urban odyssey in eighteenth-century England', *J.U.H.* (1990), P. Borsay, 'The English urban renaissance: the development of provincial culture, c. 1680–c. 1760', *S.H.* (1976–77), P. Borsay and A. McInnes, 'The emergence of a leisure town: or an urban renaissance', *P.P.* 126 (1990), Borsay's 'The rise of the promenade: the social and cultural use of space in the English provincial town, c. 1660–1800', *B.J.E.S.* (1986), J. Ellis, ' "On the town": women in Augustan England', *H.T.* 45 (1995) and E.A. Wrigley, 'A simple model of London's importance in changing England's society and economy, 1650–1750', *P.P.* (1967). Much of the literature pertaining to the consumer revolution (under topic 9) is pertinent to a discussion of the middling sorts.

One way of studying the relationship between the élite and the non-élite is to look at philanthropy and charity. On this, see B.K. Gray, *A History of English Philanthropy* (1905), B. Rodgers, *Cloak of Charity: Studies in Eighteenth-Century Philanthropy* (1949), D. Owen, *English Philanthropy,*

1660–1960 (1965) and D. Andrew, *Philanthropy and Police: London Charity in the Eighteenth Century* (1989).

On tensions in the relationships between the élite and the non-élite, see J. Stevenson, *Popular Disturbances in England, 1700–1870* (1979; 2nd edn, 1992), which sets out the range of 'disorder' encountered; see also G. Rudé, *The Crowd in History* (1964). A. Charlesworth, *An Atlas of Rural Protest in Britain, 1548–1900* (1983) is wider than its title suggests, but gives a splendid overview of various kinds of disorder. For urban protests, see G. Rudé, *Paris and London in the Eighteenth Century* (1970), R. Shoemaker, 'The London "mob" in the early eighteenth century', *J.B.S.* (1987), reprinted in P. Borsay (ed.), *The Eighteenth-Century Town* (1990), and M. Harrison, *Crowds and History: Mass Phenomena in English Towns, 1790–1835* (1988). E.P. Thompson's 'The moral economy of the English crowd in the eighteenth century', *P.P.* (1971) posits a general interpretation of the significance of riots, especially food riots. Objections have been raised by J. Stevenson, 'The "moral economy" of the English crowd', in A. Fletcher and J. Stevenson (eds), *Order and Disorder in Early Modern England* (1985), E. Fox Genovese, 'The Many Faces of Moral Economy', *P.P.* (1973), D.E. Williams, 'Morals, markets and the English crowd in 1766', *P.P.* (1977) and J. Bohstedt, 'Gender, household, and community politics: women in English riots, 1790–1810', *P.P.* (1988). See also the response to Williams's article in *P.P.* 114 (1987). Political riots are discussed in the last chapter of G.S. De Krey, *A Fractured Society: The Politics of London in the First Age of Party, 1688–1715* (1985), G. Rudé's *Paris and London in the Eighteenth Century* (1970), G.S. Holmes, 'The Sacheverell riots: the crowd and the Church in early eighteenth-century London', *P.P.* (1976), N. Rogers, 'Popular protest in early Hanoverian London', *P.P.* (1978) and his *Whigs and Cities* (1990), last chapter, and G. Rudé, *Wilkes and Liberty* (1962). J. Bohstedt, *Riots and Community Politics, 1790–1810* (1983), early sections, suggests that riots were part of a 'community politics'. On popular politics generally, see H.T. Dickinson, *The Politics of the People in Eighteenth-Century Britain* (1995), J. Brewer, *Party Politics and Popular Politics at the Accession of George III* (1978), K. Wilson, 'Empire, trade and popular politics in mid-Hanoverian Britain: the case of Admiral Vernon', *P.P.* (1988), and the articles by K. Wilson, G. Jordan and N. Rogers in *J.B.S.* vol. 28 (1989). On popular participation in politics as voters, see N. Rogers, *Whigs and Cities* (1990), F. O'Gorman, *Voters, Patrons and Parties* (1989), J.H. Plumb, 'The growth of the electorate in England from 1600–1715', *P.P.* (1969), W.A. Speck, *Tory and Whig: The Struggle in the Constituencies* (1970), G.S. Holmes, *The Electorate and the National Will in the First Age of Party* (1976), J.E. Bradley, 'Nonconformity and the electorate in eighteenth-century England', *P.H.* (1987), and the articles by Speck and Landau listed under topic 2. For London, see De Krey's *A Fractured Society*.

7. War, seapower and empire

The older historiography of the first British empire has begun to be fleshed out with more penetrating studies of the resources of war and administration, and the political conditions which permitted Britain to become the dominant maritime and commercial power. For the first part of the century such an outcome seemed less than certain: the Seven Years War brought a major success only to be followed by a thumping disaster in America. The political and economic parameters of military mobilisation and the constraints or otherwise imposed on the use of the power of the State are also worth considering.

Sources and documents   Jonathan Swift, *The Conduct of the Allies* (1711), reprinted in A. Ross and D. Woolley, *Jonathan Swift* (Oxford Authors series, 1984) is a classic statement of 'Country opposition' to continental warfare. T. Hayter (ed.), *An Eighteenth-Century Secretary at War: The Papers of William, Viscount Barrington* (1988) gives an insight into military administration of mid-eighteenth-century England. J.S. Bromley, *The Manning of the Royal Navy: Selected Public Pamphlets, 1693–1873* (Navy Record Society, 1974) reprints pamphlets on the press gang system; T. Keppel, *The Life of Augustus Viscount Keppel* (1842) is a useful memoir.

Secondary works   Britain's foreign policy and world role is considered in P. Langford, *Modern British Foreign Policy: The Eighteenth Century, 1688–1815* (1976), J.R. Jones, *Britain and the World, 1649–1815* (1980), C. Bayly, *Imperial Meridian: The British Empire and the World, 1600–1830* (1989), P.N. Miller, *Defining the Common Good: Empire, Religion and Philosophy in Eighteenth-Century Britain* (1994), L. Stone (ed.), *An Imperial State at War: Britain from 1689–1815* (1994), and J. Black, *A System of Ambition? British Foreign Policy 1660–1793* (1991). For the earlier period, see J. Black, *British Foreign Policy in the Age of Walpole* (1985) and for the long-running Anglo-French conflict, his *Natural and Necessary Enemies* (1986). Spain is considered in J. McLachlan, *Trade and Peace with Old Spain, 1667–1739* (1940); see also R. Pares, *War and Trade in the West Indies* (1936). J.H. Parry, *Trade and Dominion: The European Overseas Empires in the Eighteenth Century* (1971), R. Davis, *The Rise of the Atlantic Economies* (1973), chs 12–18 and P.J. Marshall and G. Williams, *The British Atlantic Empire before the American Revolution* (1980) are good on imperial and commercial expansion, and Marshall and Williams, *The Great Map of Mankind: British Perceptions of the World in the Age of Enlightenment* (1982) is a stimulating study of an important topic. J. Brewer, *The Sinews of Power: War, Money and the English State, 1688–1783* (1989) is a powerful analysis of the growth of military potential. The naval side is considered in P.M. Kennedy, *The Rise and Fall of British Naval Mastery* (1976) chs 2–5,

M. Duffy, 'The foundations of British naval power', in M. Duffy (ed.), *The Military Revolution and the State, 1500–1800* (Exeter Studies in History, No. 1, 1980), J. Ehrman, *The Navy in the War of William III* (1953), D. Baugh, *British Naval Administration in the Age of Walpole* (1965) and J. Black and P. Woodfine (eds), *The British Navy and the Use of Naval Power in the Eighteenth Century* (1988), especially the introduction and the essays by Baugh and Woodfine. Also valuable is N.A.M. Rodger, *The Wooden World* (1986). S. Baugh, 'The conduct of the Seven Years War' in his edited collection *England's Rise to Greatness, 1660–1763* (1983) and P. Mackesy, *The War for America, 1775–1783* (1964) are good examples of high-level military history. M. Rediker, *Between the Devil and the Deep Blue Sea: Merchant Seamen, Pirates and the Anglo-American Maritime World* (1987) offers a wide perspective, see esp. ch. 1.

For the army see A.J. Guy, *Oeconomy and Discipline: Officership and Administration in the British Army, 1714–63* (1985), J.A. Houlding, *Fit for Service: The Training of the British Army, 1715–1795* (1981), while J. Childs, *Armies and Warfare in Europe, 1648–1789* (1982) and A. Corvisier, *Armies and Societies in Europe, 1494–1789* (1979) are European-wide surveys.

On finance, see G.M. Sperling, 'War finance, 1689–1714', in *The New Cambridge Modern History: vol. 6: The Rise of Great Britain and Russia, 1688–1715/25* (ed J. Bromley, 1971), W.R. Ward, *The English Land Tax in the Eighteenth Century* (1953), and D.M. Joslin, 'London bankers in wartime, 1739–1784', in L.S. Presnell (ed.), *Studies in the Industrial Revolution* (1960). The larger economic effects of war are brought out in T.S. Ashton, *Economic Fluctuations in England, 1700–1800* (1959); see also John and Hoppit articles (below).

For popular attitudes towards war, see the works on public opinion under topic 14. Direct effects of war and post-war problems on the population are discussed in W.J. Shelton, *English Hunger and Industrial Disorders* (1973), chs 4 and 6. The role of the City of London is examined in G.S. De Krey, *A Fractured Society: The Politics of London in the First Age of Party, 1688–1715* (1985), L. Sutherland, 'The City of London in eighteenth-century politics', in R. Pares and A.J.P. Taylor (eds), *Essays Presented to Sir Lewis Namier* (1956) and the older A.J. Henderson, *London and the National Government, 1721–1742* (1945).

Articles P. Mathias and P. O'Brien, 'Taxation in England and France, 1715–1810', *Journal of European Economic History* (1976), J. Beckett, 'Land Tax or excise: the levying of taxation in seventeenth- and eighteenth-century England', *E.H.R.* (1985), P.K. O'Brien, 'The political economy of British taxation, 1660–1815', *Econ.H.R.* (1988), J.W. Osborne, 'The politics of resentment: political, economic and social interaction in eighteenth-century England', *E.L.* (1983) and C. Brooks, 'Public finance and political stability: the administration of the Land Tax', *H.J.* (1974). On the early formation of anti-commercial lobbies, see J.A. Downie, 'The commission of public accounts and the formation of the Country Party', *E.H.R.* (1976). A.H. John, 'War and the English economy, 1700–1763', *Econ.H.R.* (1955) and J. Hoppit, 'Financial crises in 18th-century England', *Econ.H.R.* (1986) discuss the effects of war; see also D. Hay, 'War, death and theft in the eighteenth century', *P.P.* (1982). Public opinion is considered in P. Langford, 'William Pitt and public opinion in 1757', *E.H.R.* (1973) and K. Wilson, 'Admiral Vernon and popular politics', *P.P.* (1988).

8. Agricultural change

The 'Agricultural Revolution', like the 'Industrial Revolution', has been placed within the context of a more gradual and complex process of economic development. Explanations for the expansion of British agricultural output no longer concentrate upon the 'discovery' of a few techniques and inventions but upon the factors which stimulated a more enterprising approach to agriculture from the early years of the eighteenth century (if not before). The Agricultural Revolution, and the enclosure movement, in particular, was seen as a social disaster by contemporaries such as Cobbett and by later historians, such as the Hammonds, but modern work has increasingly modified this picture, athough a number of the most recent studies have endorsed the Hammonds' views. The story remains complex and often repays study from a regional or local perspective.

Sources and documents Daniel Defoe, *A Tour thro' the Whole Island of Great Britain* (1724–27) is invaluable for the earlier period. William Cobbett, *Rural Rides* (1830), immensely readable and prejudiced, is available in many modern editions. A. Young, *Tours in England and Wales* (reprinted 1932) is valuable for checking generalisations against contemporary views. A.E. Bland, P. Brown and R.H. Tawney, *English Economic History* (1914), pt III, section II, has some useful documents on enclosure, while W.E. Tate and M.E. Turner, *A Domesday of English Enclosure Acts and Awards* (1978) permits the study of enclosures county by county.

Secondary works The authoritative study for the first part of the period is J. Thirsk (ed.), *Agrarian History of England and Wales, vol. v: 1640–1750* (2 vols, 1984–85) and the story is taken up by G. Mingay (ed.) *Agrarian History of England and Wales, vol. vi: 1750–1850* (1989). The state of play at the end of the seventeenth century is summarised in C. Clay, *Economic Expansion and Social Change: England, 1500–1700* (2 vols, 1984), while A. Digby and C. Feinstein (eds), *New Directions in Economic and Social History* (1989) contains succinct overviews. The most recent general works on the subject are A. Kussmaul, *A General View of the Rural Economy of England, 1538–1840* (1990) and M. Overton, *Agricultural Revolution in England: The Transformation of the Agrarian Economy, 1500–1850* (1996). Many of the standard economic histories contain sections on agriculture: see especially the essays in R. Floud and D. McCloskey, *The Economic History of Britain since 1700*, vol. 1 (1981) by Jones and Hueckel; D.C. Colman, *The Economy of England, 1450–1750* (1977), ch. 7; C. Wilson, *England's Apprenticeship, 1603–1763* (1965), ch. 12; P. Mathias, *The First Industrial Nation: An Economic History of Britain, 1700–1914* (1969), ch. 3; and P. Deane and W.A. Cole, *British Economic Growth, 1688–1959* (1969), ch. 2.

J.D. Chambers and G.E. Mingay, *The Agricultural Revolution, 1750–1880* (1967) and J. Clapham, *An Economic History of Modern Britain* (33 vols, 1926–38), chs 4 and 11 are still useful. E.L. Jones, *The Development of English Agriculture, 1815–1873* (1968) deals with the later stages. A.H. John, 'The course of agricultural change, 1660–1760', in L.S. Pressnell (ed.), *Studies in the Industrial Revolution* (1960) is crucial on the timing of change; see also the essays by E.L. Jones and A.H. John in E.L. Jones and G.E. Mingay (eds), *Land Labour and Population in the Industrial Revolution* (1967). D.B. Grigg, *The Agricultural Revolution in South Lincolnshire* (1966) is a good regional study, and for Scotland see E. Richards, *The Leviathan of Wealth* (1976). J.L. and B. Hammond, *The Village Labourer, 1760–1832* (1911) remains the classic 'pessimistic' view of the effects of agricultural change, but is now rather dated. More balanced is P. Horn, *The Rural World, 1780–1850* (1980). More recent additions are K.D.M. Snell, *Annals of the Labouring Poor: Social Change and Agrarian England, 1660–1900* (1985), J.M. Neeson, *Commoners: Common Right, Enclosure and Social Change in England, 1700–1820* (1993) and R.C. Allen, *Enclosure and the Yeomen: The Agricultural Development of the South Midlands, 1450–1850* (1992). E.J. Hobsbawm and G. Rudé, *Captain Swing* (1969) deals with the agricultural protests of 1830–32 and in doing so sheds considerable light on early nineteenth-century conditions. R.A.C. Parker, *Coke of Norfolk* (1975) discusses one of the pioneers of agricultural improvement. See also G.E. Mingay, *Enclosure and the Small Farmer in the Age of the Industrial Revolution* (1968) and *The Gentry: The Rise and Fall of a Ruling Class* (1976). No Scot could forget that this was the era of the clearances, for which see E. Richards, 'The Highland Clearances', in R. Quinault and J. Stevenson (eds), *Popular Protest and Public Order* (1974) and his *The Highland Clearances* (1982), and for Wales see D.J.V. Jones, *Before Rebecca* (1973) and/or *Rebecca's Children: A Study of Rural Society, Crime, and Protest* (1989). See also G.E. Mingay (ed.), *The Unquiet Countryside* (1989).

Articles G.E. Mingay's views are summarised in 'The Agricultural Revolution – a reconsideration', *Ag.H.* (1963); see also his 'The size of farms in the eighteenth century', *Econ.H.R.* (1962). E.L. Jones, 'Agriculture and economic growth in England, 1600–1750', *J.Econ.H.* (1965) is stimulating, while J.D. Chambers, 'The Vale of Trent, 1670–1800: a regional study of economic change', *Econ.H.R.* Supplement No. 3 (1957) is a useful case study. G.E. Mingay, 'The agricultural depression, 1730–1750', *Econ.H.R.* (1956), R.A.C. Parker, 'Coke of Norfolk and the agrarian revolution', *Econ.H.R.* (1955), T.H. Marshall, 'Jethro Tull and the new husbandry of the eighteenth century'. *Econ.H.R.* (1929–30), J.D. Chambers, 'Enclosure and the small landowner', *Econ.H.R.* (1940) and 'Enclosure and labour supply in the Industrial Revolution', *Econ.H.R.* (1953) are also highly relevant. E.L. Jones, 'The agricultural labour market in England, 1793–1872', *Econ.H.R.* (1964–5) and F.M.L. Thompson, 'The second Agricultural Revolution, 1815–1880', *Econ.H.R.* (1968) deal with the later period.

9. The Industrial Revolution

This is a huge subject which can be dealt with on several different levels. It is important to recognise that there are varying interpretations among economic historians of how industrialisation happens. The once-fashionable 'take-off' theory is now being modified by one which stresses a much broader and more complex process of economic development. Much of the emphasis on industrialisation proper now lies in the nineteenth century, though the long lead-in of population growth, commercial development and urbanisation in the eighteenth century has given rise to the concept of 'proto-industrialisation'. Some aspects, such as population growth, have almost become separate topics, raising a host of fresh questions. Traditional concerns are reflected in the debate over the effects of industrialisation on living standards and the quality of life. In general, research on the Industrial Revolution has tended to create a growing awareness of the sheer complexity of the changes taking place. A regional or one-industry approach is often the best way of tackling the question.

Sources and documents A.E. Bland, P.A. Brown and R.H. Tawney (eds), *English Economic History: Select Documents* (1914), pt III, sections I, III, IV, V. The collection edited by C. Harvie, G. Martin and A. Scharf, *Industrialization and Culture, 1815–1880* (1970), is also useful.

Secondary works and articles P. Hudson, *The Industrial Revolution* (1992) sums up the highly complex debate. Modern scholarship is reviewed by J.J. Mason, 'The Industrial Revolution' in *Hist.* (1988), J. Hoppit, 'Counting the industrial revolution' *Econ.H.R.* (1990), J. Mokyr, 'Has the Industrial Revolution been crowded out?', *E.E.H.* (1987), J. Mokyr, 'The Industrial Revolution and the new economic history', in J. Mokyr (ed.),

The Economics of the Industrial Revolution (1985), and in his essay in F. Crouzet (ed.), *Britain Ascendant: Comparative Studies in Franco-British Economic History* (1990).

P. Mathias, *The First Industrial Nation: An Economic History of Britain, 1700–1914* (2nd edn, 1983) is the standard economic history. R.M. Hartwell, *The Industrial Revolution in England* (Historical Association pamphlet, 1965) is a short guide to the sort of questions economic historians ask. R. Floud and D. McCloskey (eds), *The Economic History of Britain since 1700* (1981) has several important interpretative essays. In the article literature, some general issues are raised by N.F.R. Crafts, 'Economic growth in the eighteenth century: a re-examination of Deane and Cole's estimates', *Econ.H.R.* (1976), N.F.R. Crafts, 'Industrial Revolution in England and France: some thoughts on the question, "why was England first?"', *Econ.H.R.* (1977), M. Fores, 'The myth of a British Industrial Revolution', *H.* (1981) and A.E. Musson, 'The British Industrial Revolution', *H.* (1982). See also the wide-ranging essay on 'continuity' and 'discontinuity' in R.M. Hartwell (ed.), *The Industrial Revolution and Economic Growth* (1971). E.A. Wrigley, *Continuity, Chance and Change: The Character of the Industrial Revolution in England* (1988) attempts to provide a model of the changes that comprised the Industrial Revolution.

Other significant works include A.E. Musson, *The Growth of British Industry* (1978), P. Mathias and J.A. Davis (eds), *The First Industrial Revolutions* (1989), N.F.R. Crafts, *British Economic Growth during the Industrial Revolution* (1985), W.E. Minchington (ed.), *The Growth of English Overseas Trade in the Seventeenth and Eighteenth Centuries* (1969), A.E. Musson (ed.), *Science, Technology and Economic Growth in the Eighteenth Century* (1972), T.C. Barker and C.F. Savage, *An Economic History of Transport* (1959), G.N. von Tunzelman, *Steam Power and British Industrialization to 1860* (1978), and P. Hudson, *The Genesis of Industrial Capital* (1986). For Scotland, see R.H. Campbell, *Scotland since 1707: The Rise of an Industrial Society* (1965).

For the origins of the Industrial Revolution, see R.M. Hartwell (ed.), *The Causes of the Industrial Revolution* (1967), C. Wilson, *England's Apprenticeship. 1603–1863* (1966) and A.H. John, 'Aspects of economic growth in the first half of the eighteenth century', *E.* (1961). The concept of proto-industrialisation has spawned a furious debate, for which see L.A. Clarkson, *Proto-Industrialization: The First Phase of Industrialization?* (1985), M. Berg, *The Age of Manufactures, 1700–1820* (1985), D.C. Coleman, 'Proto-industrialization: a concept too many', *Econ.H.R.* (1983). This subject is best treated at the regional level: see P. Hudson (ed.), *Regions and Industries: A Perspective on the Industrial Revolution in Britain* (1988) and the local and regional histories cited below. For proto-industrialisation, see D. Hey, *The Rural Metalworkers of the Sheffield Region* (1972), J.V. Beckett, *Coal and Tobacco: The Lowthers and the Economic Development of West*

Cumberland, 1660–1760 (1981) and D. Levine and K. Wrightson, *The Making of an Industrial Society: Whickham, 1560–1765* (1991).

The concept of a 'consumer revolution' is best stated in N. McKendrick, J. Brewer and J.H. Plumb, *The Birth of Consumer Society: The Commercialization of Eighteenth-Century England* (1982). The concept has since been refined and attacked in L. Weatherill, *Consumer Behaviour and Material Culture in Britain 1660–1760* (1988), C. Shammas, *The Preindustrial Consumer in England and America* (1990), P. Borsay, *The English Urban Renaissance: Culture and Society in the Provincial Town, 1660–1770* (1989), J. Brewer and R. Porter, *Consumption and the Worlds of Goods* (1993), J. Brewer and A. Bermingham (eds), *The Consumption of Culture* (1995), H.C. and L.H. Mui, *Shops and Shopkeepers in Eighteenth-Century England* (1989), B. Lemire, *Fashion's Favourite: The Cotton Trade and the Consumer in Britain, 1660–1800* (1991) and B. Fine and E. Leopold, 'Consumerism and the Industrial Revolution', *S.H.* (1990). Much of this literature is reviewed by J. Barry in *H.J.* (1991) and J. Ward in *J.B.S.* (1990).

For the connections between population growth and industrial growth, see M.W. Flinn, *British Population Growth 1700–1850* (1970), N. Tranter, *Population and Society, 1750–1940* (1985) and E.A. Wrigley and R. Schofield, *The Population History of England 1541–1841* (1981). This last book is reviewed by M.W. Flinn in *Econ.H.R.* (1982) and aspects of its argument are summarised in E.A. Wrigley, 'The growth of population in eighteenth-century England: a conundrum resolved', *P.P.* (1983).

The classic 'pessimistic' assessment of the social effects of industrialisation is J.L. and B. Hammond, *The Town Labourer, 1760–1832* (1917). The subsequent 'standard of living debate' took place mainly in articles: R.M. Hartwell, 'The rising standard of living in England, 1800–50', *Econ.H.R.* (1961), E.J. Hobsbawm, 'The British standard of living, 1790–1850', *Econ.H.R.* (1958), E.J. Hobsbawm and R.M. Hartwell, 'The standard of living during the Industrial Revolution – a discussion', *Econ. H.R.* (1963), R.S. Neale, 'The standard of living, 1780–1844: a regional and class study', *Econ.H.R.* (1966) and J. Williamson and P. Lindert, 'English workers' living standards during the Industrial Revolution: a new look', *Econ.H.R.* (1983). A.J.P. Taylor (ed.), *The Standard of Living in Britain in the Industrial Revolution* (1975) includes many of these articles. New evidence is presented in R. Floud, K. Wachter and A. Gregory, *Height, Health, and History: Nutritional Status in the United Kingdom, 1750–1980* (1990). Other works on the social effects of industrialisation include M.L. Thomis, *The Town Labourer and the Industrial Revolution* (1974), J. Rule, *The Labouring Classes in Early Industrial England, 1750–1850* (1986), J. Belchem, *Industrialization and the Working Class: The English Experience, 1750–1900* (1990) and two articles on the significance of factory discipline: S. Pollard, 'Factory discipline in the Industrial Revolution', *Econ.H.R.* (1963) and E.P. Thompson, 'Time, work-discipline, and industrial capitalism',

P.P. (1967). A. Randall, *Before the Luddites: Custom, Community and Machinery in the English Woollen Industry 1776–1809* (1991) assesses the impact of the new machinery and factories on the wollen workers. For the impact of industrialisation on the social structure and on relations between the social classes, see under topic 6.

The importance of a regional perspective is advanced in P. Hudson (ed.), *Regions and Industries: A Perspective on the Industrial Revolution in Britain* (1988). Local histories of industrial development include J.D. Chambers, *Nottinghamshire in the Eighteenth Century* (2nd edn, 1966), N.H. Chaloner, *The Social and Economic History of Scotland in the Eighteenth Century* (1963) and *The Industrial Revolution in Scotland* (1966), A.H. John, *The Industrial Development of South Wales, 1750–1850* (1959), A.H. Dodd, *The Industrial Revolution in North Wales* (3rd edn, 1971), C. Evans, *The Labyrinth of Flames: Work and Social Conflict in Early Industrial Merthyr Tydfil* (1993), J. Rowe, *Cornwall in the Age of the Industrial Revolution* (1953), B. Trinder, *The Industrial Revolution in Shropshire* (1973), J. Thomas, *The Rise of the Staffordshire Potteries* (1971), G. Malmgreen, *Silk Town: Industry and Culture in Macclesfield, 1750–1835* (1985), T.C. Barker and J.R. Harris, *A Merseyside Town in the Industrial Revolution: St Helens, 1750–1900* (1954), J.C. Beckett and R.E. Glassock (eds), *Belfast: Origin and Growth of an Industrial City* (1967), I. Adams, *The Making of Urban Scotland* (1978) and J.O. Chambers, 'The Vale of Trent, 1760–1800', *Econ.H.R.* supplement no. 3 (1957).

For individual industries, see P. Mathias, *The Brewing Industry in England, 1700–1830* (1959), T.S. Ashton, *Iron and Steel in the Industrial Revolution* (1951), A.P. Wadsworth and J. Mann, *The Cotton Industry and the Rise of Industrial Lancashire to 1780* (1965), M.M. Edwards, *The Growth of the British Cotton Trade, 1780–1815* (1967), D.J. Jenkins and K.G. Ponting, *The British Wool Industry, 1770–1914* (1982), T.S. Ashton and J. Sykes, *The Coal Industry in the Eighteenth Century* (2nd edn, 1964), M.W. Finn, *The History of the British Coal Industry, vol. 2: 1700–1830* (1984), S.D. Chapman, 'The transition to the factory system in the Midlands cotton-spinning industry', *Econ.H.R.* (1965).

Case studies of particular firms include J.R. Harris, *The Copper King: A Biography of Thomas Williams of Llanidan* (1964), T.S. Ashton, *An Eighteenth-Century Industrialist: Peter Stubs of Warrington, 1756–1806* (1939), G. Unwin, *Samuel Oldnow and the Arkwrights: The Industrial Revolution at Stockport and Marple* (1924), R.S. Fitton and A.P. Wadsworth, *The Strutts and the Arkwrights* (1964), A. Raistrick, *Dynasty of Ironfounders: The Darbys and Coalbrookdale* (1953), E. Roll, *An Early Experiment in Industrial Organisation, Being a History of the Firm of Boulton and Watt, 1775–1805* (1930), J.P. Addis, *The Crawshay Dynasty: A Study in Industrial Organisation and Development, 1765–1867* (1957) and T.C. Barker, *Pilkington Brothers and the Glass Industry* (1960). On entrepreneurs, see C.H. Wilson, 'The entrepreneur in the Industrial Revolution', *H.* (1957).

10. Religion and the Churches

The role of religion in the eighteenth century, and in particular the state of the Church of England, have received a great deal of attention over the last ten years. Several main topics emerge: What was the condition of the eighteenth-century Church of England, and was it worse than it had ever been? What were its relations with Protestant dissent and Catholicism? Why was it unable to harness Methodism as a revival movement? And what effects did Methodism have upon an industrialising England? It is worth considering if, and if so why, the Church found it difficult to adjust itself to meet the new challenges of population growth and social and economic change. Elie Halevy's claim that Methodism prevented revolution in England deserves some attention.

Sources and documents An excellent and wide-ranging source-book is W. Gibson (ed.), *Religion and Society in England and Wales, 1689–1800* (1998), and C.H. Sissons (ed.), *English Sermons, 1650–1750* (1968) gives something of the flavour of what were arguably still the dominant ways of communicating information in this period. For the Church's pastoral role, see *The Speculum of Archbishop Thomas Secker* (ed. J. Gregory, 1995), *Archbishop Herring's Visitation returns, 1743* (ed. S.L. Ollard and P.C. Waller, Yorkshire Archaeological Society Record Series, vols lxxi, lxxii, lxvii, lxix). E.N. Williams, *The Eighteenth-Century Constitution* (1960) and the relevant volumes of *English Historical Documents* have useful sections on the Church. There are several clerical diaries in print: James Woodforde, *The Diary of Parson Woodforde, 1758–1802* (ed. J. Beresford, 1949), John Skinner, *Journal of a Somerset Rector, 1803–1834* (ed. H. and P. Coombs, 1984 edn), and *Paupers and Pig Killers: The Diary of William Holland* (ed. J. Ayres, 1984) are available in paperback. See also *A Parson in the Vale of the White Horse. George Woodward's Letters from East Hendred, 1753–61* (ed. D. Gibson, 1983). John Wesley, *Journals*, are valuable for the flavour of Methodism in its 'heroic' phase.

Secondary works The starting points now are J. Walsh, C. Haydon and S. Taylor (eds), *The Church of England, c. 1689–1833* (1993), especially the introduction, K. Hylson-Smith, *The Churches in England from Elizabeth I to Elizabeth II; vol. 2: 1689–1833* (1997) and I. Green, 'Anglicanism in Stuart and Hanoverian England', in S. Gilley and W.J. Sheils (eds), *A History of Religion in Britain: Practice and Belief from Pre-Roman Times to the Present* (1994). J. Spurr, *The Restoration Church of England, 1646–1689* (1991) is an excellent survey of the state of the Church at the start of the period, and G.V. Bennett, 'Conflict in the Church', in G. Holmes (ed.), *Britain after the Glorious Revolution, 1689–1714* (1969) and *The Tory Crisis in Church and State* (1975) shed light on the Church's problems in the decades after 1688/89. O.P. Grell, J. Israel and N. Tyacke (eds), *From Persecution to Toleration: The Glorious Revolution in England* (1991) examines some of the factors leading up to, and the broad consequences of, the Toleration Act. Useful general treatments can be also found in G. Rupp, *Religion in England, 1688–1791* (1987), E.R. Norman, *Church and Society in England, 1770–1970* (1976) and W. Gibson, *The Achievement of the Anglican Church* (1995). Although old, the work of N. Sykes remains well worth reading, notably his *Church and State in England in the Eighteenth Century* (1934), *From Sheldon to Secker: Aspects of English Church History, 1660–1768* (1958) and *Edmund Gibson: Bishop of London* (1926).

The late eighteenth and early nineteenth centuries are well covered in R. Hole, *Pulpits, Politics and Public Order in England, 1760–1832* (1989), B. Hilton, *The Age of Atonement: The Influence of Evangelicalism on Social and Economic Thought, 1795–1865* (1988), E.R. Norman, *Church and Society in England, 1770–1970: A Historical Study* (1976), W.R. Ward, *Religion and Society in England, 1790–1850* (1972), P. Nockles, *The Oxford Movement in Context: Anglican High Churchmanship, 1760–1857* (1994), D.W. Lovegrove, *Established Church, Sectarian People: Itinerancy and the Transformation of English Dissent, 1780–1830* (1988) and F.C. Mather, *High Church Prophet: Bishop Samuel Horsley (1733–1806) and the Caroline Tradition in the Later Georgian Church* (1992). J.C.D. Clark, *English Society, 1688–1832* (1985) argues that England was a 'confessional' state prior to 1832 and examines its defenders and assailants. D. Hempton, *Religion and Political Culture in Britain and Ireland: From the Glorious Revolution to the Decline of Europe* (1996), his 'Religion in British society, 1740–90', in J. Black (ed.), *British Politics and Society from Walpole to Pitt* (1990) and P. Virgin, *The Church in an Age of Negligence: Ecclesiastical Structure and Problems of Church Reform, 1700–1840* (1989) consider Clark's views.

Useful local studies are J.H. Pruett, *The Parish Clergy under the Late Stuarts: The Leicestershire Experience* (1978), A. Warne, *Church and Society in Eighteenth-Century Devon* (1965), M. Smith, *Religion in Industrial Society: Oldham and Saddleworth, 1740–1865* (1994), J. Chamberlain, *Accommodating High Churchmen: The Clergy of Sussex, 1700–1745* (1997), J. Jago, *Aspects of the Georgian Church: Visitation Studies of the Diocese of York, 1761–1776* (1997), A.M. Urdank, *Religion and Society in a Cotswold Vale: Nailsworth, Gloucestershire, 1780–1865* (1990), D. McClatchey, *The Oxfordshire Clergy, 1777–1869* (1960) and V. Barrie-Curien, 'The clergy in the diocese of London', in J. Walsh, C. Haydon and S. Taylor (eds), *The Church of England, c. 1689–1833*. W.M. Jacob, *Lay Piety and Religion in the Early Eighteenth Century* (1996) is a significant survey of the laity's attitude to religion, and some light on popular religiosity is also shed in A. Smith, *The Established Church and Popular Religion* (1971), J.C.F. Harrison, *The Second Coming: Popular Millenarianism, 1780–1850* (1979) and B. Reay, *The Last Rising of the Agricultural Labourers: Rural Life and Protest in*

Nineteenth-Century England (1990). H. Schwartz, *The French Prophets: The History of a Millenarian Group in Eighteenth-Century England* (1980) is a lively study of an often neglected theme. For women and religion, see P. Crawford, *Women and Religion in England, 1500–1720* (1993), G. Malmgreen (ed.), *Religion in the Lives of English Women, 1760–1930* (1993), S. Gill, *Women and the Church of England from the Eighteenth Century to the Present* (1994), C. Campbell Orr (ed.), *Wollstonecraft's Daughters:. Womenhood in England and France, 1780–1920* (1995) and D.M. Valenze, *Prophetic Sons and Daughters: Female Preaching and Popular Religion in Industrial England* (1985). For the economic position of the Church, see G.F.A. Best, *Temporal Pillars* (1964) and E.J. Evans, *The Contentious Tithe: The Tithe Problem and English Agriculture, 1750–1850* (1976).

For Catholics, see J. Bossy, *The English Catholic Community, 1570–1850* (1975) and E. Duffy (ed.), *Challoner and his Church* (1981) (and for anti-Catholicism, see C. Haydon, *Anti-Catholicism in Eighteenth-Century England: A Political and Social History* [1993], and L. Colley, *Britons: Forging the Nation, 1707–1837* [1993]). For dissenters, see M.R. Watts, *The Dissenters, vol, I: From the Reformation to the French Revolution* (1978), his *The Dissenters, vol. II: The Expansion of Evangelical Nonconformity* (1995) and M. Spufford (ed.), *The World of Rural Dissenters, 1520–1725* (1995). For Methodism, see R. Davies and E.G. Rupp (eds), *A History of the Methodist Church of Great Britain* (1965) and B. Semmel, *The Methodist Revolution* (1973). The origins of Methodism are succinctly explored in J. Walsh, 'The origins of the evangelical revival', in G.V. Bennett and J.D. Walsh (eds), *Essays in Modern Church History in Memory of Norman Sykes* (1966). A. Armstrong, *The Church of England, the Methodists and Society, 1700–1850* (1973) is a useful guide to the relationship between Methodism and the Church of England, while A.D. Gilbert, *Religion and Society in Industrial England, 1740–1914* (1976) places Methodism within the context of religious adherence in general. On Wesley himself, see F. Baker, *John Wesley and the Church of England* (1970), V.H.H. Green, *John Wesley* (1964), H.D. Rack, *Reasonable Enthusiast: John Wesley and the Rise of Methodism* (1989) and H. Abelove, *Evangelist of Desire: John Wesley and the Methodists* (1991). Whitefield is given compelling treatment in H.S. Stout, *The Divine Dramatist: George Whitefield and the Rise of Modern Evangelicalism* (1991). On Methodism's impact, R.F. Wearmouth, *Methodism and the Common People of the Eighteenth Century* (1945) contains a great deal of information, but is rather uncritical. See also T. Laqueur, *Religion and Respectability: Sunday Schools and Working-Class Culture* (1976). W.R. Ward, *The Protestant Evangelical Awakening* (1992), places the British religious revivals in their continental and transatlantic setting. E.P. Thompson, *The Making of the English Working Class* (2nd edn, 1968), ch. 11 is polemical but interesting. J.D. Walsh, 'Methodism and the mob in the eighteenth century', in G.J. Cuming and D. Baker (eds), *Popular Belief and Practice: Studies in*

Church History, vol. VII (1972) throws light on the reception of Methodism. D. Hempton, *Methodism and Politics, 1750–1850* (1986) is an excellent modern study. See also his *Religion of the People: Methodism and Popular Religion, 1750–1900* (1996) and his *Religion and Political Culture in Britain and Ireland: From the Glorious Revolution to the Decline of Empire* (1996).

The Churches in Ireland are studied in S. Connolly, *Religion, Law and Power: The Making of Protestant Ireland, 1660–1760* (1992), G. O'Brien (ed.), *Catholic Ireland in the Eighteenth Century: Collected Essays of M. Wall* (1989), R. Gillespie, *Devoted People: Belief and Religion in Early Modern Ireland* (1997) and A. Ford, J. McGuire and K. Milne (eds), *As by Law Established. The Church of Ireland since the Reformation* (1995). For Scotland, see C. Brown, *The Social History of Religion in Scotland since 1730* (1987). Religion in Wales is well served by G.H. Jenkins, *Literature, Religion and Society in Wales, 1660–1730* (1978), his *The Foundations of Modern Wales, 1642–1780* (1987), chs 5 and 9, and by D.L. Morgan, *The Great Awakening in Wales* (1988).

On the intellectual context to eighteenth-century religious life, see J.A.I. Champion, *The Pillars of Priestcraft Shaken: The Church of England and its Enemies, 1660–1730* (1992), J. Gascoigne, *Cambridge in the Age of the Enlightenment: Science, Religion and Politics from the Restoration to the French Revolution* (1989), J. Redwood, *Reason, Ridicule and Religion: The Age of Enlightenment in England, 1660–1750* (1976), I. Rivers, *Reason, Grace and Sentiment: A Study of the Language of Religion and Ethics in England, 1660–1780* (1991) and A.M.C. Waterman, *Revolution, Economics and Religion: Christian Political Economy, 1798–1833* (1991). Other relevant studies include G.R. Cragg, *From Puritanism to the Age of Reason* (1966), R.N. Stromberg, *Religious Liberalism in Eighteenth-Century England* (1954) and R. Porter, 'The Enlightenment in England', in R. Porter and M. Teich (eds), *The Enlightenment in National Context* (1981).

Articles J.C.D. Clark, 'England's *Ancien Régime* as a confessional state', *A.* (1989); and the rest of the essays in the volume are crucial. See also P. Corfield, 'One state, many faiths', *H.T.* (1995), E. Duffy, 'Primitive Christianity revived: religious renewal in Augustan England', *S.C.H.* (1977), D. Hirshberg, 'The government and Church patronage in England, 1660–1760', *J.B.S.* (1980–81), J.J. Hurwich, 'Dissent and Catholicism in English society: a study of Warwickshire, 1660–1720', *J.B.S.* (1976), T. Isaacs, 'The Anglican hierarchy and the reformation of manners, 1688–1738', *J.B.S.* (1982), T. Curtis and W.A Speck, 'The societies for reformation of manners: a case study in the theory and practice of moral reform', *L.H.* (1976), S.J.C. Taylor, 'Sir Robert Walpole, the Church of England and the Quakers' Tithe Bill of 1736', *H.J.* (1985). F.C. Mather, 'Georgian churchmanship reconsidered: some variations in Anglican public worship' 1714–1830', *J.Eccl.H.* (1985) is an important overview of regional patterns. R. Currie, 'A micro-theory of Methodist growth', *Proc.Wesley Hist.Soc* (1967) is interesting. See also J.D. Walsh, 'Elie Halevy and the birth of Methodism', *T.R.H.S.* (1975), his 'Religious societies: Methodist and evangelical, 1738–1800', *S.C.H.* (1986) and E. Royle, 'The Church of England and Methodism in Yorkshire, c. 1750–1850: from monopoly to free market', *N.H.* (1997). C. Clay, 'The greed of the Whig bishops? Church landlords and their lessees, 1660–1760', *P.P.* (1980) examines the economic position of the Church, as do W.R. Ward, 'The tithe question in England in the early ninetenth century', *J.Eccl.H.* (1965) and E.J. Evans, 'Some reasons for the growth of English rural anti-clericalism, c. 1750–c. 1830', *P.P.* (1975).

11. Culture and the arts

Scholars working on the eighteenth century have been at the forefront of interdisciplinary studies, especially in their attempt to relate cultural artefacts to the wider political and social concerns of the age. The topic raises important theoretical questions of how historians can use source material such as poetry and painting to discuss the period under review. Moreover, should we distinguish between 'high' culture and popular culture? If so, how, and what criteria should we use? Recent work has also opened up the role of the cultural infrastructure in the production of a work of art and explored the role of patronage, the art market and cultural institutions.

Sources and documents   Sources for this topic are endless, but among the most accessible are Jonathan Swift, *Gulliver's Travels* (1726), John Gay, *The Beggar's Opera* (1728), William Hogarth, *Works*, Handel, *The Messiah* (1741), Pope, *Windsor Forest* (1713), Thomson, *Britannia* (1729), *The Seasons* (1730), William Wordsworth and Samuel Taylor Coleridge, *Lyrical Ballads* (1798). R. Lonsdale (ed.), *The New Oxford Book of Eighteenth-Century Verse* (1986) and his *Eighteenth-Century Women Poets: An Oxford Anthology* (1989) contain a good selection of poems. A wide range of literary material is quoted (with a running commentary) in J.A. Downie, *To Settle the Succession of the State. Literature and Politics, 1678–1750* (1994). For sources for art and design history, see B. Denvir, *The Eighteenth Century: Art, Design and Society, 1689–1789* (1983) and his *The Early Nineteenth Century: Art, Design and Society* (1983), which have useful collections of documents from the period.

Secondary works and articles   The most recent overview is J. Brewer, *The Pleasures of the Imagination: English Culture in the Eighteenth Century* (1997). B. Ford (ed.), *Seventeenth-Century Britain, Eighteenth-Century Britain* and *The Romantic Age in Britain* (1989) are useful introductions to cultural history, containing essays on individual art forms, while L. Lipking,

The Ordering of the Arts in Eighteenth-Century England (1970) tackles a theme which crosses the arts. G. Newman, *The Rise of Nationalism: A Cultural History, 1740–1830* (1987) raises some interesting issues, while J. Black and J. Gregory (eds), *Culture, Politics and Society in Britain, 1660–1800* (1991) and J. Black (ed.), *Culture and Society in Eighteenth-Century Britain* (1997) have essays pertinent to the theme.

For the political and social resonances of literature, see H. Erskine-Hill, *Poetry of Opposition and Revolution: Dryden to Wordsworth* (1996), J. Barrell, *English Literature in History, 1730–80: An Equal, Wide Survey* (1983), R. Sales, *English Literature in History, 1780–1830: Pastoral and Politics* (1983), his *Jane Austen and Representations of Regency England* (1994), J. Sambrook, *The Eighteenth Century: The Intellectual and Cultural Context of English Literature, 1700–1789* (1986), C.T. Probyn, *English Fiction of the Eighteenth Century* (1987), R.W. Bevis, *English Drama: Restoration and Eighteenth Century, 1660–1789* (1988), G. Kelly, *English Fiction of the Romantic Period, 1789–1830* (1989), J.R. Watson, *English Poetry of the Romantic Period, 1789–1830* (1992), C. Rawson, *Satire and Sentiment, 1660–1830* (1994), A. Ingram, *Intricate Laughter in the Satire of Swift and Pope* (1986), F. Nussbaum and L. Brown (eds), *The New Eighteenth Century: Theory, Politics, English Literature* (1987), J. Lucas, *England and Englishness: Ideas of Nationhood in English Poetry, 1688–1900* (1990), M. Butler, *Romantics, Rebels and Reactionaries: English Literature and its Background, 1760–1830* (1982), W.A. Speck, *Society and Literature, 1700–60* (1983) and his *Literature and Society in Eighteenth-Century England: Ideology, Politics and Culture, 1680–1820* (1998). J. Bate, *Shakespearean Constitutions: Politics, Theatre, Criticism, 1780–1830* (1989), M. Dobson, *The Making of the National Poet: Shakespeare, Adaptation and Authorship, 1660–1769* (1992) and G. Taylor, *Reinventing Shakespeare: A Cultural History from the Restoration to the Present* (1990) are interesting accounts of the political uses of Shakespeare during the long eighteenth century, while H. Weinbrot, *Britannia's Issue: The Rise of British Literature from Dryden to Ossian* (1993) uses literature to explore the growth of national identity. C. Gerrard, *The Patriot Opposition to Walpole: Politics, Poetry and National Myth, 1725–1742* (1994) and the rather older B. Goldgar, *Walpole and the Wits: The Relation of Politics to Literature, 1722–42* (1976) explore the literary responses to the Walpolean regime. J.C.D. Clark, *Samuel Johnson: Literature, Religion and Cultural Politics from the Restoration to Romanticism* (1994) is a stimulating attempt to apply his model of English society to a literary figure, and offers a different interpretation to that given by J. Cannon, *Samuel Johnson and the Politics of Hanoverian England* (1994). On some key eighteenth-century writers, see J.A Downie, *Jonathan Swift: Political Writer* (1984), F.P. Lock, *The Politics of Gulliver's Travels* (1980), I. Higgins, *Swift's Politics: A Study in Disaffection* (1994), H. Erskine-Hill, *The Social Milieu of Alexander Pope: Lives, Example and the Poetic Response* (1975), H. Glen, *Vision and Disenchantment: Blake's Songs and Wordsworth's Lyrical Ballads* (1983), S. Gill, *William Wordsworth: A Life* (1989) and R. Holmes, *Coleridge: Early Visions* (1989). See also S. Curran (ed.), *The Cambridge Companion to British Romanticism* (1993) and M. Butler, 'Romanticism in England', in R. Porter and M. Teich (eds), *Romanticism in National Context* (1988). M. Byrd, *London Transformed: Images of the City in the Eighteenth Century* (1978), G. Perry and M. Rossington (eds), *Femininity and Masculinity in Eighteenth-Century Art and Culture* (1994) and A. Ingram, *The Madhouse of Language: Writing and Reading Madness in the Eighteenth Century* (1991) offer interdisciplinary insights.

For art, see I. Pears, *The Discovery of Painting: The Growth of Interest in the Arts in England, 1680–1768* (1988), D. Solkin, *Painting for Money: The Visual Arts and the Public Sphere in Eighteenth-Century England* (1993), M. Pointon, *Hanging the Head: Portraiture and Social Formation in Eighteenth-Century England* (1993), D. Shawe-Taylor, *The Georgians: Eighteenth-Century Portraiture and Society* (Tate Gallery exhibition catalogue, 1990), *Manners and Morals: Hogarth and British Painting, 1700–1760* (1987), K. Cavers, *A Vision of Scotland: The Nation Observed by John Slezer, 1671–1717* (1993), J. Barrell, *Painting and the Politics of Culture: New Essays on British Art, 1700–1850* (1992), his *The Dark Side of the Landscape: The Rural Poor in English Painting, 1730–1840* (1980), D. Klingender, *Art and the Industrial Revolution* (1968) and R. Rosenblum, *Transformations in Late Eighteenth-Century Art* (1967). On Hogarth, arguably the first major 'English' artist, see R. Paulson, *Hogarth: His Life, Art and Times* (1971) and J. Uglow, *Hogarth: A Life and a World* (1998). M. Pointon, *Milton and English Art* (1970) is an interesting account, while T. Fawcett, *The Rise of Provincial Art: Artists, Patrons and Institutions Outside London, 1700–1830* (1974) explores artistic production in the regions; and L. Lippincott, *Selling Art in Georgian London: The Rise of Arthur Pond* (1983) is a pioneering study of the art market.

For architecture, see M. Foss, *The Age of Patronage: The Arts in Society, 1660–1750* (1971), J. Hook, *The Baroque Age in England* (1976), K. Downes, *Hawksmoor* (1980), *Vanbrugh* (1977), D. Cruickshank (ed.), *A Guide to the Georgian Buildings of Britain and Ireland* (1985), J. Summerson, *The Architecture of the Eighteenth Century* (1986), T.C. Barnard and J. Clark (eds), *Lord Burlington: Architecture, Art and Life* (1995), M. Girouard, *Life in the English Country House* (1978), G. Worsley, *Classical Architecture in Britain: The Heroic Age* (1994), K. Clark, *The Gothic Revival* (1974 edn), J.M. Crook, *The Greek Revival: Neo-Classical Attitudes in British Architecture, 1760–1870* (1972), T. Mowl and B. Earnshaw, *John Wood: Architect of Obsession* (1988) and T. Faulkner and A. Gregg, *John Dobson, Newcastle Architect, 1787–1865* (1987). For the rise of a distinctly 'English' garden design, see C. Hussey, *English Gardens and Landscapes, 1700–1750* (1967), J. Dixon Hunt and P. Willis, *The Genius of the Place: The English Landscape Garden, 1620–1820* (1988), J. Dixon Hunt, *Garden and Grove: The Italian Renaissance Garden in the English Imagination, 1600–1750* (1986), D. Jacques, *Georgian Gardens: The Reign of Nature* (1983) and T. Williamson, *Polite Landscapes: Gardens and Society in Eighteenth-Century England* (1995).

Using music as a source for historians has proved problematic, but see W. Webber, *The Rise of the Musical Classics in Eighteenth Century England: A Study in Canon, Ritual and Ideology* (1993), J. Keats, *Handel: The Man and his Music* (1985), R. Smith, 'Intellectual Contexts of Handel's English Oratorios', in C. Hogwood and R. Luckett (eds), *Music in Eighteenth-Century England: Essays in Memory of Charles Cudworth* (1983), R. Leppert, *Music and Image: Domesticity, Ideology and Socio-Cultural Formation in Eighteenth-Century England* (1993), and the relevant volumes in *The New Oxford History of Music*.

On print culture, see J.A. Downie and T.N. Corns, *Telling People What to Think: Early Eighteenth-Century Periodicals from the Review to The Rambler* Special Issue *Prose Studies* (1993), E.A. Bloom and L. Bloom (eds), *Educating the Audience: Addison, Steele, and Eighteenth-Century Culture* (1984), K. Shevelow, *Women and Print Culture: The Construction of Femininity in the Early Periodical* (1989), I. Rivers (ed.), *Books and their Readers in Eighteenth-Century England* (1982), J. Spencer, *The Rise of the Woman Novelist* (1986), J. Todd, *The Sign of Angelica: Women, Writing and Fiction, 1660–1800* (1989), J. Raven, *Judging New Wealth: Popular Publishing and Responses to Commerce in England, 1750–1800* (1992) and M. Wood, *Radical Satire and Print Culture* (1994). On public opinion, see J.A. Downie, *Robert Harley and the Press: Popularity and Public Opinion in the Age of Swift and Defoe* (1979), P. Langford, *The Excise Crisis* (1975), M. Peters, *Pitt and Popularity* (1981), D. Reed, *The English Provinces, c. 1760–1960* (1964), pt 1; P. Langford, 'William Pitt and public opinion', *E.H.R.* (1973), and H.T. Dickinson, 'Party, principle and public opinion in eighteenth-century politics', *H.* (1976). For the press, see G.A. Cranfield, *The Development of the Provincial Press, 1700–1760* (1962), his *The Press and Society from Caxton to Northcliffe* (1978), R.M. Wiles, *Freshest Advises: Early Provincial Newspapers in England* (1965), J. Black, *The English Press in the Eighteenth Century* (1987) and H. Barker, *Newspapers, Politics and Public Opinion in Late Eighteenth-Century England* (1998). For political prints and satires, see P. Langford, *Walpole and the Robinocracy* (1985) and the others in the series, D. Donald, *The Age of Caricature: Satirical Prints in the Reign of George III* (1996), H. Atherton, *Political Prints in the Age of Hogarth* (1974) and D.M. George, *Hogarth to Cruikshanks: Social Change in Graphic Satire* (1987).

It is also worth thinking about the founding of cultural institutions as a way of linking cultural and politcal and social history. See in particular E. Miller, *That Noble Cabinet: A History of the British Museum* (1973), D.G.C. Allan, *William Shipley, Founder of the RSA* (1968), I. Ousby, *The Englishman's England: Taste, Travel and the Rise of Tourism* (1990) and J. Black, *The British Abroad: The Grand Tour in the Eighteenth Century* (1992).

On popular culture, see T. Harris (ed.), *Popular Culture in England, c. 1500–1850* (1995), P. Anderson, *The Printed Image and the Transformation of Popular Culture* (1991), M. Baer, *The Theatre and Disorder in Late Georgian London* (1991), R. Porter and M. Roberts, *Pleasure in the Eighteenth Century* (1996) and P. Burke, *Popular Culture in Early Modern Europe* (1978). Books listed under the following topic will also be relevant. Cultural consumption is studied in J. Brewer and R. Porter (eds), *Consumption and the World of Goods* (1993) and A. Bermingham and J. Brewer (eds), *The Consumption of Culture, 1660–1800: Image, Object, Text* (1995).

12. Intellectual history and the history of education

Once seen as an area reserved for philosophers and theologians, the intellectual history of the eighteenth century has benefited from the recent stress on interdisciplinary studies, and modern scholarship has been at pains to link the leading thinkers of the era to the social and political developments of the period. Much intellectual history has moved away from concentrating on the 'great thinkers' of the period, and now encompasses the context in which those thinkers operated, the reception of their ideas, and an interest in some of the more general assumptions and attitudes of the age. In particular, historians have investigated the nature of the British Enlightenment, and asked how far some of the leading intellectuals of the day abandoned or worked within traditional religious priorities. Much of the most stimulating work has been on the history of science and medicine.

Sources and documents The works of many of the leading thinkers of the period have been published in modern editions. Useful collections of documents include D.C. Goodman (ed.), *Science and Religious Belief, 1600–1900. A Selection of Primary Sources* (1973) and S. Eliot and B. Stern (eds), *The Age of Enlightenment: An Anthology of Eighteenth-Century Texts:* (2 vols, 1979), which include extracts from Joseph Butler, David Hume and Adam Smith.

Secondary works and articles The most comprehensive treatment of eighteenth-century intellectual history remains L. Stephens, *A History of English Thought in the Eighteenth-Century* (1876; reprinted 1967). General developments can also be traced in B. Willey, *The Eighteenth-Century Background: Studies on the Idea of Nature in the Thought of the Period* (1940) and his *The English Moralists* (1964), which deals with Locke, Shaftesbury, Addison, Hume, Chesterfield and Burke. For a general interpretation of the intellectual life of the period, see D. Spadafora, *The Idea of Progress in Eighteenth-Century Britain* (1990), and for themes which affected various intellectual aspects of the period, see J. Sekora, *Luxury: The Concept in Western Thought, Eden to Smollett* (1971) and C. Vereker, *Eighteenth-Century Optimism* (1967). On different approaches to 'intellectual history' see B. Kuklick, 'What is Intellectual History?', *H.T.* 35 (1985) and A.O.J. Lovejoy, *The Great Chain of Being: A Study of the History of an Idea* (1936). For an interesting study of the medieval background to some aspects of eighteenth-century thought, see R.J. Smith, *The Gothic Bequest: Medieval Institutions in British Thought, 1688–1863* (1987). An accessible summary of some of the leading intellectual movements is J. Sambrook, *The Intellectual and Cultural Context of English Literature, 1700–1789* (1986).

For the history of political and economic ideas in the period, the major works are by J.G.A. Pocock. See, in particular, his *The Machiavellian Moment: Florentine Political Thought and the Atlantic Republican Tradition* (1975). Many of his most influential essays have been published in *Politics, Language and Time: Essays on Political Thought and History* (1971) and *Virtue, Commerce and History: Essays on Political Thought and History, Chiefly in the Eighteenth Century* (1985). For an important study of the radical tradition, see C. Robbins, *The Eighteenth-Century Commonwealthman: Studies in the Transmission, Development and Circumstance of English Liberal Thought from the Restoration until the War with the Thirteen Colonies* (1968). An important re-evaluation of Locke is R. Ashcraft, *Revolutionary Politicks and Locke's Two Treatises of Government* (1986), to be read in conjunction with J. Marshall, *John Locke: Resistance, Religion and Responsibility* (1994). J.P. Kenyon, *Revolution Principles: The Politics of Party, 1689–1720* (1977), H.T. Dickinson, *Liberty and Property: Political Ideology in Eighteenth-Century Britain* (1977), D. Forbes, *Hume's Philosophical Politics* (1975) and B. Bailyn, *The Ideological Origins of the American Revolution* (1967) place ideas in their political context. See also R. Browning, *The Political and Constitutional Ideas of the Court Whigs* (1982) and P. Brown, *The Chathamites: A Study in the Relationship between Personalities and Ideas in the Second Half of the Eighteenth Century* (1967). The leading economic theories of the late eighteenth and early nineteenth centuries are given fresh treatment in A.M.C. Waterman, *Revolution, Economics and Religion: Christian Political Economy, 1798–1833* (1991). Scottish developments are studied in I. Hont and M. Ignatieff (eds), *Wealth and Virtue: The Shaping of Political Economy in the Scottish Enlightenment* (1983) and J. Robertson, *The Scottish Enlightenment and the Militia Issue* (1985).

For the nature of the British Enlightenment, see the essays by Porter and Phillipson in R. Porter and N. Teich (eds), *The Enlightenment in National Context* (1981), J. Champion, *The Pillars of Priestcraft Shaken: The Church of England and its Enemies, 1660–1730* (1992), J. Redwood, *Reason, Ridicule and Religion: The Age of Enlightenment in England, 1660–1750* (1976), R. Sher, *Church and University in the Scottish Enlightenment: The Moderate Literati of Edinburgh* (1985), A.C. Chitnis, *The Scottish Enlightenment: A Social*

History (1976), M.C. Jacob, *The Radical Enlightenment: Pantheists, Freemasons, and Republicans* (1981), and J.G.A. Pocock, 'Clergy and commerce: the conservative Enlightenment in England', in R. Ajello, M. Firpo, L. Guerci and G. Ricuperati (eds), *L'Eta dei Lumi: Studi Storici sul Settecento Europea in Onore di Franco Venturi* (1985).

For various approaches to religious and philosophical ideas, see J. Passmore, *The Perfectibility of Man* (1970), F.E. Manuel, *The Eighteenth Century Confronts the Gods* (1959), C.L. Becker, *The Heavenly City of the Eighteenth-Century Philosophers* (1932), R. Stromberg, *Religious Liberalism in Eighteenth-Century England* (1954), D.D. Raphael, *The Moral Sense* (1947), I.C. Tipton, *Berkeley: The Philosophy of Immaterialism* (1974) and F.E. Manuel, *The Religion of Isaac Newton* (1974).

Interesting approaches to the history of science can be found in M. Jacob, *The Newtonians and the English Revolution, 1689–1720* (1976), which was an attempt to link Newtonian science to the political ideologies of the Whig Party, R.E. Schofield, *Mechanism and Materialism: British Natural Philosophy in an Age of Reason* (1970), J. Golinski, *Science as Public Culture. Chemistry and Enlightenment in Britain, 1760–1820* (1992), G.S. Rousseau and R. Porter (eds), *The Ferment of Knowledge: Studies in the Historiography of Eighteenth-Century Science* (1980), J. Gascoigne, *Joseph Banks and the English Enlightenment: Useful Knowledge and Polite Culture* (1994) and R. Porter, *The Making of Geology: Earth Science in Britain, 1660–1815* (1977). For criticism of Jacob's thesis, see A. Guerrini, 'The Tory Newtonians: Gregory, Pitcairne and their Circle', *J.B.S.* (1986), and the review of Jacob by G. Holmes in the *British Journal for the History of Science*, II (1978). For challenges to the dominant Newtonian world-view, see A.J. Kuhn, 'Glory or gravity? Hutchinson vs Newton', *J.H.I.* 22 (1961) and C.B. Wilde, 'Hutchinsonianism, natural philosophy and religious controversy in eighteenth-century Britain', *H.S.* 18 (1990).

Individual thinkers can be approached through the Past Masters series. In particular, the following can be recommended: J. Dunn, *Locke* (1983), M. Philip, *Paine* (1989), J.O. Urmson, *Berkeley* (1982) and D. Winch, *Malthus* (1987). For Locke, see also R. Ashcraft, *Revolutionary Politics and Locke's Two Treatises of Government* (1986). The thought of two of the most distinguished historians of the period can be traced in R. Porter, *Edward Gibbon: Making History* (1988) and N. Phillipson, *Hume* (1989).

Educational developments can be traced in M.G. Jones, *The Charity School Movement: A Study of Eighteenth-Century Puritanism in Action* (1938), H. MacLachlan, *English Education under the Test Acts: Being the History of the Nonconformist Academies, 1662–1820* (1931) and L. Stone, 'Literacy and Education in England, 1640–1900', *P.P.* (1969), R.S. Tompson, *Classics or Charity? The Dilemma of the Eighteenth-Century Grammar School* (1971), J. Gascoigne, *Cambridge in the Age of the Enlightenment. Science, Religion and*

Politics from the Restoration to the French Revolution (1989) and L.S. Sutherland and L.G. Mitchell (eds) *The History of the University of Oxford, vol. V: The Eighteenth Century* (1986).

13. Crime, the law and punishment in the eighteenth century

Eighteenth-century England had no professional police force, experienced widespread concern about crime, and possessed one of the most ferocious penal codes in Europe. Crime and the prosecution and punishment of crime have been the subject of considerable historical controversy over the last two decades. Much ink has been spilled on the question of whether we can know how much crime actually occurred, and how far the full extent of the law was implemented; more than most this is a topic on which historians must be aware of the limitations of the evidence. Interesting questions concern popular attitudes towards crime and the law (whether certain crimes were forms of social protest, and whether ordinary people believed in the legitimacy of the law), and the extent to which the judicial and penal systems operated as agents of social control. The study of crime, justice and punishment thus touches fundamental issues concerning the nature of the state and social relations in the eighteenth century.

Sources and documents   Much of the formal legislation regarding crime and punishment in the period can be found in the relevant volumes of *English Historical Documents*.

Secondary works and articles   Excellent starting points are J.A. Sharpe, *Crime in Early Modern England 1550–1750* (1984) and C. Emsley, *Crime and Society in England 1750–1900* (1987). The introduction to A. Fletcher and J. Stevenson (eds), *Order and Disorder in Early Modern England* (1985) discusses some of the issues raised by historians over the last fifteen years. For reviews of some of the issues, see J. Innes and J. Styles, 'The crime wave: recent writing on crime and criminal justice in eighteenth-century England', *J.B.S.* (1986), R. Shoemaker, 'The "crime wave" revisited: crime, law enforcement, and punishment in Britain 1650–1900', *H.J.* (1991) and his *Prosecution and Punishment: Petty Crime and the Law in London and Rural Middlesex, c. 1660–1725* (1991).

On crime, J. Beattie, *Crime and the Courts in England, 1660–1800* (1986) is essential reading. See also his articles, 'The pattern of crime in England, 1600–1800', *P.P.* (1974) and 'Crime and the courts in Surrey, 1736–1753', in J. Cockburn (ed.), *Crime in England 1500–1800* (1977). Economic influences on crime are considered in D. Hay, 'War, dearth and theft in the eighteenth century', *P.P.* (1982).

The classic definition of 'social crime' is provided by E.J. Hobsbawm in the *Bulletin of the Society for the Study of Labour History* vol. xxv (1972);

see also the essay by E.P. Thompson in the same issue, and J. Rule, 'Social crime in the rural south in the eighteenth and early nineteenth centuries', *Southern History* (1979). Studies of particular crimes can be found in J. Brewer and J. Styles (eds), *An Ungovernable People: The English and their Law in the Seventeenth and Eighteenth Centuries* (1980), and D.P. Hay, P. Linenbaugh and E.P. Thompson (eds), *Albion's Fatal Tree* (1975), E.P. Thompson, *Whigs and Hunters: The Origin of the Black Act* (1975), P. Munsche, *Gentlemen and Poachers* (1981) and P. King, 'Gleaners, farmers, and the failure of legal sanctions in England 1750–1850', *P.P.* (1989). See also the works about riots in topic 14. For attitudes towards the law, see the introduction to Brewer and Styles, *An Ungovernable People* and the conclusion to Thompson's *Whigs and Hunters*, the article just cited by P. King, and the articles by R. Paley and D. Hay in D. Hay and F. Snyder (eds), *Policing and Prosecution in Britain 1750–1850* (1989).

On the judicial treatment of criminals, see Beattie, *Crime and the Courts in England* (above) for felons, and R. Shoemaker, *Prosecution and Punishment: Petty Crime and the Law in London and Rural Middlesex, c. 1660–1725* (1991) for misdemeanours. Douglas Hay's article 'Property, authority and the criminal law', in *Albion's Fatal Tree* raises significant questions about the social significance of the judicial system; his interpretation is challenged by John Langbein, 'Albion's fatal flaws', *P.P.* (1983) and P. King, 'Decision-makers and decision-making in the English criminal law, 1750–1800, *H.J.* (1984). Hay replies to some of these criticisms in both the introduction and his article in *Policing and Prosecution* (above). Two large studies provide a wealth of detail: V.A.C. Gattrell, *The Hanging Tree: Execution and the English People, 1770–1868* (1994) and P. Linenbaugh, *The London Hanged: Crime and Civil Society in the Eighteenth Century* (1991).

On new attitudes towards criminals and new methods of punishment, see Beattie, *Crime and the Courts in England* (above), R. Ekirch, *Bound for America: The Transportation of British Convicts to the Colonies 1718–1775* (1987), M. Ignatieff, *A Just Measure of Pain: The Penitentiary in the Industrial Revolution, 1750–1850* (1978) and M. Foucault, *Discipline and Punish: The Birth of the Prison* (1977). Ignatieff and Foucault are criticised by M. DeLacy, *Prison Reform in Lancashire 1700–1850* (1986). Ignatieff revises his thesis in 'State, civil society, and total institutions: a critique of recent social histories of punishment', in S. Cohen and A. Skull (eds), *Social Control and the State* (1983).

14. Popular protest and popular politics

Eighteenth-century England had a formidable reputation for riot and disorder; crowd protests expressed a wide range of grievances. But what was the social and political meaning of popular protest? Did it represent the genuine views of the common people, or were riots organised 'from above'? If the former is true, what goals and values did such protests express? Popular participation in politics also occurred through 'public opinion', a concept which needs to be defined carefully. The main question here is how far down the social scale did popular interest and participation in politics extend, and how influential was it? The franchise was wider than you might expect, but historians differ on whether non-élite voters were allowed to exercise their vote independently without control by their social superiors. These issues are closely tied up with questions about the nature of Whig oligarchy.

Secondary works and articles J. Stevenson, *Popular Disturbances in England, 1700–1870* (1979) sets out the range of 'disorder' encountered; see also G. Rudé, *The Crowd in History* (1964). A. Charlesworth, *An Atlas of Rural Protest in Britain, 1548–1900* (1983) is wider than its title suggests, but gives a splendid overview of various kinds of disorder, as does A. Randall and A. Charlesworth (eds), *Markets, Market Culture and Popular Protest in Eighteenth-Century Britain and Ireland* (1996). I. Gilmour, *Riot, Risings and Revolution: Governance and Violence in Eighteenth-Century England* (1992) is a lively discussion. For urban protests, see G. Rudé, *Paris and London in the Eighteenth Century* (1970), R. Shoemaker, 'The London "mob" in the early eighteenth century', *J.B.S.* (1987), reprinted in P. Borsay (ed.), *The Eighteenth-Century Town* (1990), and M. Harrison, *Crowds and History: Mass Phenomena in English Towns, 1790–1835* (1988). E.P. Thompson's 'The moral economy of the English crowd in the eighteenth century', *P.P.* (1971) posits a general view of the significance of riots, especially food riots. Objections have been raised by J. Stevenson, 'The "moral economy" of the English crowd', in A. Fletcher and J. Stevenson (eds), *Order and Disorder in Early Modern England* (1985), E. Fox Genovese, 'The many faces of moral economy', *P.P.* (1973), D.E. Williams, 'Morals, markets and the English crowd in 1766', *P.P.* (1977) and J. Bohstedt, 'Gender, household, and community politics: women in English riots, 1790–1810', *P.P.* (1988). See also the response to Williams's article in *P.P.* 114 (1987).

Political riots are discussed in the last chapter of G.S. De Krey, *A Fractured Society: The Politics of London in the First Age of Party, 1688–1715* (1985), Rudé's *Paris and London in the Eighteenth Century*, G.S. Holmes, 'The Sacheverell riots: the crowd and the Church in early eighteenth-century London', *P.P.* (1976), N. Rogers, 'Popular protest in early Hanoverian London', *P.P.* (1978), his *Whigs and Cities* (1990), last chapter, and G. Rudé, *Wilkes and Liberty* (1962). J. Bohstedt, *Riots and Community Politics, 1790–1810* (1983), early sections, suggests riots were part of a 'community politics'.

On popular politics generally, see H.T. Dickinson, *The Politics of the People in Eighteenth Century Britain* (1995), J. Brewer, *Party Politics and*

Popular Politics at the Accession of George III (1978), K. Wilson, *The Sense of the People: Urban Political Culture in England, 1715–85* (1995), his 'Empire, trade and popular politics in mid-Hanoverian Britain: The case of Admiral Vernon', *P.P.* (1988), and the articles by K. Wilson, G. Jordan and N. Rogers in *J.B.S.* (1989).

On popular participation in politics as voters, see Rogers, *Whigs and Cities*, F. O'Gorman, *Voters, Patrons and Parties* (1989), J.H. Plumb, 'The growth of the electorate in England from 1600–1715', *P.P.* (1969), W.A. Speck, *Tory and Whig: The Struggle in the Constituencies* (1970), G.S. Holmes, *The Electorate and the National Will in the First Age of Party* (1976), J.E. Bradley, 'Nonconformity and the electorate in eighteenth-century England', *P.H.* (1987), and the articles by Speck and Landau listed under topic 2. For London, see De Krey's *A Fractured Society*.

On public opinion, see J.A. Downie, *Robert Harley and the Press: Popularity and Public Opinion in the Age of Swift and Defoe* (1979), P. Langford, *The Excise Crisis* (1975), M. Peters, *Pitt and Popularity* (1981), D. Reed, *The English Provinces, c. 1760–1960* (1964), pt 1, P. Langford, 'William Pitt and public opinion', *E.H.R.* (1973) and H.T. Dickinson, 'Party, principle and public opinion in eighteenth-century politics,' *H.* (1976). For the press, see G.A. Cranfield, *The Development of the Provincial Press, 1700–1760* (1962), his *The Press and Society from Caxton to Northcliffe* (1978), J. Black, *The English Press in the Eighteenth Century* (1987) and H. Barker, *Newspapers, Politics and Public Opinion in Late Eighteenth-Century England* (1998). For political prints, see P. Langford, *Walpole and the Robinocracy* (1985) and H. Atherton, *Political Prints in the Age of Hogarth* (1974).

15. Women's history and gender history

This is a topic which, needless to say, has only recently started to receive the attention it deserves. Women's experiences varied enormously, and the first issue to address is how their experiences varied according to the social environment in which they lived: their marital status; their social class; and their place of residence (especially urban vs rural areas). Traditionally, historians of women have focused on family life, but the related question of women's work (both within and outside the family) is now in the forefront. It is important to consider how women's work changed over the period in response to the dramatic changes which took place in agriculture and industry. Only at the end of the eighteenth century was the subordinate role of women in society first questioned; here it is important to consider what historians mean when they use the term 'feminist'. More recent studies have taken seriously the need to study men's experience as well as women's.

Sources and documents For contemporary views by and of women B. Hill (ed.), *Eighteenth-Century Women: An Anthology* (1990), V. Jones (ed.), *Women in the Eighteenth Century: Constructions of Femininity* (1990), *A Governess in the Age of Jane Austen: The Journals and Letters of Agnes Porter* (ed. J. Martin, 1998), Anne Hughes, *The Diary of a Farmer's Wife, 1796–97* (ed. M. Croucher, 1964), although some doubts have been cast on its authenticity, and *The Collected Letters of Mary Wollstonecraft* (ed. R.M. Wardle, 1979). For interesting insights into aspects of masculinity, see *Boswell's London Journal, 1762–1763* (ed. F.A. Pottle, 1990), *The Diary of Thomas Turner, 1754–65* (ed. D. Vaisey, 1984), and *The Grand Tour of William Beckford* (ed. E. Mavor, 1986).

Secondary works and articles General works on women include M. Prior (ed.), *Women in English Society, 1500–1800* (1985), B. Hill (ed.), *Eighteenth-Century Women: An Anthology* (1990), V. Jones (ed.), *Women in the Eighteenth Century* (1990), B. Hill, *Women, Work and Sexual Politics in Eighteenth-Century England* (1989) and O. Hufton, *The Prospect Before Her: A History of Women in Western Europe, vol. I: 1500–1800* (1995) For middle-class women at the end of the century, see L. Davidoff and C. Hall, *Family Fortunes: Men and Women of the English Middle Class 1780–1850* (1987). See also the important critique of their work by A. Vickery, 'From Golden Age to separate spheres: a review of the categories and chronology of English women's history', *H.J.* (1993). The classic studies of women's economic role are A. Clark, *The Working Life of Women in the Seventeenth Century* (1919), which covers the pre-industrial period more generally, and I. Pinchbeck, *Women Workers in the Industrial Revolution, 1750–1850* (1969). More recent studies include A. Clark, *The Struggle for the Breeches: Gender and the Making of the British Working Class* (1995), P. Earle, 'The female labour market in London in the late seventeenth and early eighteenth centuries', *Econ.H.R.* (1989), L. Charles and L. Duffin, *Women and Work in Preindustrial England* (1985), J. Rendall, *Women in an Industrializing Society: England 1750–1880* (1990), N. McKendrick, 'Home demand and economic growth: a new view of the role of women and children in the Industrial Revolution', in his *Historical Perspectives: Studies in English Thought and Society in Honour of J.H. Plumb* (1974), P. Hudson and W.R. Lee (eds), *Women's Work and the Family in Historical Perspective* (1990), D. Valenze, *The First Industrial Woman* (1995) and M. Berg, 'What difference did women's work make to the Industrial Revolution?', *H.W.J.* (1993). Important information on women's work is also included in the books and articles on proto-industrialisation, listed under topic 9. For women's work in rural areas, see D. Valenze, 'The art of women and the business of men: women's work and the dairy industry *c.* 1740–1840', *P.P.* (1991) and K.V. Snell, *Annals of the Labouring Poor* (1985).

On family life, L. Stone, *The Family, Sex and Marriage in England, 1500–1800* (1982) posits the rise of a new type of family relationship based on affection, but see the criticisms in R. Houlbrooke, *The English Family, 1450–1700* (1984), esp. chs 5 and 10. See also R. Trumbach, *The Rise of the Egalitarian Family: Aristocratic Kinship and Domestic Relations in Eighteenth-Century England* (1978). Bastardy and illegitimacy are considered in P. Laslett, *Family Life and Illicit Love in Earlier Generations* (1977). Two studies of marriage which have attracted attention are A. MacFarlane, *Marriage and Love in England, 1300–1840* (1986) (pt III is the most relevant) and J.R. Gillis, *For Better For Worse: British Marriages, 1600 to the Present* (1985). The trilogy by L. Stone, *The Road to Divorce, England, 1530–1987* (1990), *Uncertain Unions: Marriage in England, 1660–1753* (1992) and *Broken Lives: Separation and Divorce in England, 1660–1857* (1993), charts the breakdown of marriage, and especially the ways in which women were affected. See also V. Fildes (ed.), *Women as Mothers in Preindustrial England* (1990). For women without families, see O. Hufton, 'Women without men: widows and spinsters in Britain and France in the eighteenth century', *J.F.H.* (1984). In addition, useful material can be found in J. Beattie, *Crime and the Courts in England 1660–1800* (1986) and R. Shoemaker, *Prosecution and Punishment: Petty Crime and the Law in London and Rural Middlesex, c. 1660–1725* (1991), ch. 8. For women and popular protest, see the article by J. Bohstedt under topic 6.

Elite women have begun to get some serious attention. See F. Harris, *The Life of Sarah, Duchess of Marlborough* (1991), B. Hill, *That Republican Virago: The Life and Times of Catherine Macaulay, Historian* (1992), S. Tillyard, *Aristocrats: Caroline, Emily, Louisa and Sarah Lennox, 1740–1832* (1994), A. Foreman, *Georgiana, Duchess of Devonhire* (1998), A. Vickery, *The Gentleman's Daughter: Women's Lives in Georgian England* (1998), K. Chisholm, *Fanny Burney: Her Life* (1998) and S.H. Myers, *The Bluestocking Circle: Women, Friendship and the Life of the Mind in Eighteenth-Century England* (1990). See also P.J. Jupp, 'The roles of royal and aristocratic women in British politics, c. 1782–1832', in M. O'Dowd and S. Wichert (eds), *Chattel, Servant or Citizen Women's Status in Church, State and Society* (1995), E. Chalus, '"That epidemical madness": women and electoral politics in the late eighteenth century', in H. Barker and E. Chalus (eds), *Gender in Eighteenth-Century England* (1997), and T. Lummis and J. Marsh, *The Woman's Domain: Women and the English Country House* (1993). A. Clark, 'Queen Caroline and the sexual politics of popular culture in London, 1820', *Representations* 31 (1990), is suggestive of the interaction between élite and popular worlds.

For the rise of the first feminist ideas, see J. Rendall, *The Origins of Modern Feminism: Women in Britain, France and the United States, 1780–1860* (1985), A. Browne, *The Eighteenth-Century Feminist Mind* (1987), R. Perry, *The Celebrated Mary Astell: An Early English Feminist* (1986) and K.M.

Rogers, *Feminism in Eighteenth-Century England* (1989). Mary Wollstonecraft occupies a prominent place as a pioneering feminist: see C. Tomalin, *The Life and Death of Mary Wollstonecraft* (1974) and M. Tims, *Mary Wollstonecraft: A Social Pioneer* (1976).

Gender history has been studied in H. Barker and E. Chalus (eds), *Gender in Eighteenth-Century England: Roles, Representations and Responsibilities* (1997), L. Davidoff and C. Hall, *Family Fortunes: Men and Women of the English Middle Classs, 1780–1850* (1992), A. Fletcher, *Gender, Sex and Subordination in England, 1500–1800* (1995), B. Fowlkes-Tobin (ed.), *History and Gender and Eighteenth-Century Literature* (1994) and T. Hitchcock and M. Cohen (eds), *English Masculinities, 1660–1800* (1999). Much of the recent work on gender has focused on the issue of sexuality. For an excellent summary of the debates, see T. Hitchcock, *English Sexualities, 1700–1800* (1997) and his 'Redefining sex in eighteenth-century England', *H.W.J.* (1996). Other studies include P.G. Boucé (ed.), *Sexuality in Eighteenth-Century Britain* (1982), G.J. Barker-Benfield, *The Culture and Sensibility: Sex and Society in Eighteenth-Century Britain* (1992), G.S. Rousseau and R. Porter (eds), *Sexual Underworlds of the Enlightenment* (1988), T. Laqueur, *Making Sex: Bodies and Gender from the Greeks to Foucault* (1990), R. Norton, *Mother Clap's Molly House: The Gay Subculture in England, 1700–1830* (1992), E. Donaghue, *Passions between Women: British Lesbian Culture, 1668–1801* (1993) and R.P. Maccubbin (ed.), *'Tis Nature's Fault': Unauthorised Sexuality in the Enlightenment* (1987).

16. The Elder Pitt

The Elder Pitt, Earl of Chatham, has, with his son, traditionally been seen as one of the 'great men' of British history. In large part this fame rests upon his leadership in the Seven Years War and his role in the development of Britain's overseas empire. His achievements have been subject to examination, and recent work by Brewer on the 'fiscal-military state' examines Britain's rise to colonial pre-eminence in broad terms. Historians have also become increasingly interested in his domestic support, which in some respects prefigured the reform movement of George III's reign. Pitt's role in the early stages of the conflict with the American colonists also should not be ignored.

Sources and documents   *The Letters of Horace Walpole* (various editions available) are valuable for the mood of the country in 1756–57 and Pitt's role generally. See also *The Memoirs and Speeches of James, 2nd Earl Waldegrave, 1742–63* (ed. J.C.D. Clark, 1988) and Lord Hervey, *Some Materials towards the Memoirs of the Reign of George II* (3 vols, ed. R. Sedgwick, 1931). D. Horn and M. Ransome (eds), *English Historical Documents, vol. X: 1714–1783* (1957) also has relevant material.

Secondary works The chapters in H. van Thal (ed.), *The Prime Ministers*, vol. 1 (1974) and in P. Brown, *The Chathamites* (1967) are essential places to start. There are several biographies, of which M. Peters, *Pitt the Elder* (1997) and J. Black, *Pitt the Elder* (1993) are the most accessible and up to date. B. Williams, *Life of Chatham* is old (1913) and pro-Pitt. A. von Runville, *William Pitt, Earl of Chatham* is also elderly (1907), but massive, learned and anti-Pitt: a book to be quarried rather than read. J.H. Plumb, *Chatham* (1953) and B. Tunstall, *William Pitt, Earl of Chatham* (1938) are one-volume studies. Other biographies available include those by C. Grant Robertson (1946), O.A. Sherrard (3 vols, 1952–58). P.D. Brown (1978) and S. Ayling (1976), the last being well worthwhile. The best study of the conduct of the Seven Years War is now R. Middleton, *The Bells of Victory: The Pitt–Newcastle Ministry and the Conduct of the Seven Years War, 1757–1762* (1985), but see also S.B. Baxter, 'The conduct of the Seven Years War', in his *England's Rise to Greatness, 1660–1763* (1983) and Peters (below). Reed Browning, *The Duke of Newcastle* (1975) discusses the man who raised the money for the war, and the theme of money and military power forms the basis for J. Brewer, *The Sinews of Power: War, Money and the English State* (1989), see especially chs 1, 4–7. See also J. Black and P. Woodfine (eds), *The British Navy and the Use of Naval Power in the Eighteenth Century* (1988) and A.J. Guy, *Oeconomy and Discipline: Officership and Administration in the British Army, 1714–63* (1985).

A brief outline of foreign policy can be found in P. Langford, *Modern British Foreign Policy; The Eighteenth Century, 1688–1815* (1976) and J.R. Jones, *Britain and the World 1649–1815* (1980), but more detailed studies include D.B. Horn, *Great Britain and Europe in the Eighteenth Century* (1967), R. Pares, *War and Trade in the West Indies, 1739–1763* (1936) and K. Hotblack, *Chatham's Colonial Policy* (1917). Britain's role in the Seven Years War is covered in J. Corbett, *England in the Seven Years War* (1907) and R. Savory, *His Britannic Majesty's Army in Germany during the Seven Years War* (1966).

Pitt's domestic significance is reflected in Brown, *The Chathamites*, but especially in the Langford article below and in M. Peters, *Pitt and Popularity: The Patriot Minister and London Opinion during the Seven Years War* (1981). The important role of the City of London is considered in L. Sutherland, 'The City of London in eighteenth-century politics', in *Essays Presented to Sir Lewis Namier* (eds R. Pares and A.J.P. Taylor, 1956). B.W. Hill, *British Parliamentary Parties, 1742–1832* (1985) and J.B. Owen, *The Eighteenth Century* (1974) have straightforward accounts of the political background. More contentious is J.C.D. Clark, *The Dynamics of Change: The Crisis of the 1750s and the English Party Systems* (1983), arguing for the disappearance of the old Whig and Tory parties, but the articles (see below) contain the essence of the argument. R. Robson, *The Oxfordshire Election of 1754* (1949) reveals the interplay of national and local politics in the 1750s. Pitt's rivalry with Henry Fox is brought out in E. Eyck, *Pitt versus Fox* (1950) and his career in the 1760s is discussed in L. Namier, *England in the Age of the American Revolution* (2nd edn, 1961) and J. Brooke, *The Chatham Administration, 1766–1768* (1956).

Articles   P. Langford, 'William Pitt and public opinion in 1757', *E.H.R.* (1973) is helpful. Good on the background to his war policy are C.M. Andrews, 'Anglo-French commercial rivalry, 1700–50', *Am.H.R.* (1914–15) and R. Pares, 'American and continental warfare, 1739–63', *E.H.R.* (1936). See also J.C.D. Clark, 'The decline of party, 1740–1760', *E.H.R.* (1978) and his 'A general theory of party, opposition and government, 1688–1832', *H.J.* (1980).

17. British colonial policy and the American War of Independence

This is a complex subject embracing political conflicts on both sides of the Atlantic and the general conduct of British imperial policy in the latter half of the eighteenth century. The view of American secession as inevitable needs to be carefully scrutinised and the divisions within America given full weight. Why there was a progress from resistance to taxation to 'revolution' needs to be examined carefully and the rhetoric of the colonists put in perspective. The impact of the American crisis on attitudes to the Empire is an important aspect of the topic.

Sources and documents   J.R. Pole (ed.), *The Revolution in America, 1754–1788* (1970) has a very useful selection of documents; see also R.C. Birch, *1776: the American Challenge* (1977). Edmund Burke's speeches on American taxation can be read in B.W. Hill's collection of his works, *Edmund Burke on Government, Politics and Society* (1975). M. Beloff (ed.), *The Debate on the American Revolution* (1949) is also valuable. See also M. Jensen (ed.), *English Historical Documents: American Colonial Documents to 1776*.

Secondary works   A good historiographical essay is I.R. Christie, 'The historian's quest for the American Revolution', in A. Whiteman, J.S. Bromley and P.G.M. Dickson (eds), *Statesmen, Scholars and Merchants* (1973). See also I.R. Christie, *Crisis of Empire: Great Britain and the American Colonies, 1754–1783* (1966) and K. Perry, *British Politics and the American Revolution* (1990). B. Donoughue, *British Politics and the American Revolution: The Path to War, 1773–75* (1964) is a more detailed account of the immediate crisis. H.M. Scott, *British Foreign Policy in the Age of the American Revolution* (1990) is a narrative of British diplomacy set in the context of international relations. J.C. Miller, *The Origins of the American Revolution* (2nd edn, 1959) is an alternative outline. P. Langford, *Modern British Foreign Policy. The Eighteenth Century, 1688–1815* (1976), chs 11 and 12 deals with foreign policy in general, as does J.R. Jones, *Britain and the World, 1649–1815* (1980). Two studies which place the war in an imperial context are P.J. Marshall and G. Williams (eds), *The British Atlantic Empire before the American Revolution* (1980) and I.R. Christie and B.W. Labaree, *Empire or Independence* (1976). The Stamp Act is discussed in P. Langford, *The First Rockingham Administration, 1756–1766* (1973) and P.D.G. Thomas, *British Politics and the Stamp Act Crisis* (1975). The link between rebellion and taxation is brought out in R.A. Becker, *Revolution, Reform and the Politics of American Taxation* (1980). J.R. Pole, *Foundations of American Independence, 1763–1815* (1972) is important on the American background. Two useful collections are E. Wright (ed.), *Causes and Consequences of the American Revolution* (1966) and J.P. Greene (ed.), *The Reinterpretation of the American Revolution* (1968). P. Mackesy, *The War for America, 1775–1783* (1964) and J. Black (ed.), *The British Navy and the Use of Naval Power in the Eighteenth Century* (1988), introduction and essays by Baugh and Syrett, deal with military affairs. J. Brewer, *The Sinews of Power: War, Money and the English State* (1989) explains how the war was financed, see especially chs 4, 5 and 6.

On the political significance of the war in Britain, see J.G.A. Pocock, '1776: the revolution against Parliament', in J.G.A. Pocock (ed.), *Three British Revolutions: 1641, 1688, 1776* (1980). Lord North's conduct of the war is discussed in P.D.G. Thomas, *Lord North* (1976) and his fall in I.R. Christie, *The End of Lord North's Ministry, 1780–82* (1958). The impact on the reform movement is explored in I.R. Christie's *Wilkes, Wyvill and Reform* (1962) and E. Royle and J. Walvin, *Radicals and Reformers, 1776–1848* (1984). Opposition to the war in Britain is examined by P. Langford in J. Stevenson (ed.), *London in the Age of Reform* (1976), J. Sainsbury, *Disaffected Patriots: London Supporters of Revolutionary America, 1769–82* (1987), J. Bradley, *Popular Politics and the American Revolution in England: Petitions, the Crown and Public Opinion* (1986) and his *Religion, Revolution and English Radicalism: Non-conformity in Eighteenth-Century Politics and Society* (1990). The ideas generated by the war are discussed in B. Bailyn, *The Ideological Origins of the American Revolution* (1967) and E. Foner, *Tom Paine and Revolutionary America* (1976), and are placed in a broader context in J.C.D. Clark, *The Language of Liberty, 1660–1832: Political Discourse and Social Dynamics in the Anglo-American World* (1994).

Articles See P.D.G. Thomas, 'George III and the American Revolution', *H.* (1985) for a good survey. Also, R.W. van Alstyn, 'Europe, the Rockingham Whigs and the War for American Independence: some documents', *H.L.Q.* (1961), P. Marshall, 'Radicals, conservatives, and the American Revolution', *P.P.* (1962) and G.H. Guttridge, 'The Whig opposition in England during the American Revolution: revisions in need of revising', *W.M.Q.* (1957) are all useful.

18. George III, the constitution and the parliamentary reform movement, 1760–89

The latter years of the eighteenth century witnessed growing concern about the working of the constitution, and in particular the power of the Crown. George III's attempts to exercise his right to choose his own ministers, the Wilkes affair and the conflict with America brought fresh issues into politics and led to the first widespread demands for parliamentary reform. It is important to understand why fears grew up about Crown influence and whether they were justified. The broader factors providing support for reform need to be considered, as well as the different meanings given to 'reform'.

Sources and documents   Edmund Burke, *Thoughts on our Present Discontents* (1770 and later editions) is the classic statement of grievances against George III which provided the impetus for the 'economical reform' movement. E.N. Williams, *The Eighteenth Century Constitution, 1688–1815* (1960) has documents both on the role of the monarch and on parliamentary reform.

Secondary works   A balanced and lucid exposition of the constitutional developments after 1760 can be found in I.R. Christie, *Myth and Reality in later Eighteenth-Century British Politics, and Other Papers* (1970), especially the introduction and chs 1 and 2. See also R. Pares, *King George III and the Politicians* (1953). On the reform movement, J. Cannon, *Parliamentary Reform in England, 1640–1832* (1973), chs 3 and 4 is a good introduction. I.R. Christie, *Wilkes, Wyvill and Reform* (1962) has a full discussion of the various elements in reform; see also E. Royle and J. Walvin, *British Radicals and Reforms, 1760–1848* (1982). J. Brewer, *Party Ideology and Popular Politics at the Accession of George III* (1978) examines the political forces at work in the 1760s. A challenge to received orthodoxy is J.C.D. Clark, *English Society, 1688–1832* (1985), especially chs 1 and 4. See also his *The Dynamics of Change: The Crisis of the 1750s and English Party Systems* (1982). An old but still useful study is G.S. Veitch, *The Genesis of Parliamentary Reform* (2nd edn, 1964). G.Rudé, *Wilkes and Liberty: A Social Study of 1763–1774* (1962) is essential on the metropolitan background and Wilkes's support, but see also L.S. Sutherland, *The City of London and the Opposition, 1768–74* (The Creighton Lecture, 1958), reprinted in J. Stevenson (ed.), *London in the Age of Reform* (1976). For the ideology of the English reformers, see R.W. Harris, *Political Ideas in England, 1760–1792* (1963) and the latter sections of H.T. Dickinson, *Liberty and Property* (1978). C. Robbins, *The Eighteenth-Century Commonwealthman* (1959) and C. Hill, 'The Norman yoke', in his essays *Puritanism and Revolution* (1958) trace continuities with earlier ideas. On leading personalities, see P.D.G. Thomas, *John Wilkes: A Friend to Liberty* (1996), J.W. Osborne, *John Cartwright* (1972), E. Foner, *Tom Paine and Revolutionary America* (1976), J. Keane, *Tom Paine: A Political Life* (1995), F. O'Gorman, *Edmund Burke* (1973) and J. Brooke, *George III* (1972).

Articles I.R. Christie, 'Economical reform and the "influence of the Crown" in 1780', *C.H.J.* (1956) explains the crucial link between years of executive 'tyranny' and the demand for reform. His 'The Yorkshire Association, 1780–4', *H.J.* (1960) and H. Butterfield, 'The Yorkshire Association and the crisis of 1779–80', *T.R.H.S.* (1947) examine the 'County' movement. P.D.G. Thomas, 'The beginnings of parliamentary reporting in newspapers, 1768–74', *E.H.R.* (1959) discusses the growing influence of the press.

19. The impact of the French Revolution on Britain

Traditional interest focused upon the effects of the French Revolution on party politics, especially on the Whigs, the rise of popular radicalism and its suppression, and the longer-term effects of the French Revolution on British politics. Much attention has also been directed on the popular political societies, E.P. Thompson seeing this as a crucial stage in the development of 'class consciousness' among working people. Goodwin reworked much of the available evidence, and is especially strong on the provincial and dissenting origins of the early reform movement. The period after 1795 has recently received more serious attention than it has hitherto.

Sources and documents The ideological debate can be followed in the various editions of Tom Paine, *The Rights of Man* (1791–92) and Edmund Burke, *Reflections on the Revolution in France* (1790). A. Cobban (ed.), *The Debate on the French Revolution* (1950) contains selections from contemporary writers, as does M. Butler (ed.), *Burke, Paine and the Revolution Controversy* (1984); see also G.D.H. Cole and A.W. Filson (eds), *British Working-Class Movements: Select Documents, 1789–1875* (1951). *The Autobiography of Francis Place* (ed. M. Thale, 1972) gives an insider's account of one of the popular societies in the 1790s; see also 'A memoir of Thomas Hardy', reprinted in D. Vincent (ed.), *Testaments of Radicalism* (1977). J. Stevenson, *Artisans and Democrats: Sheffield and the French Revolution* (1989) has documents on the most important provincial radical society.

Secondary works H.T. Dickinson (ed.), *Britain and the French Revolution* (1989) and his *British Radicalism and the French Revolution, 1789–1815* (1985) offer a succinct introduction to recent debates; but the older P.A. Brown, *The French Revolution in English History* (1918) is still a useful treatment, while G.S. Veitch, *The Genesis of Parliamentary Reform* (2nd edn, 1965) retains its value. J. Cannon, *Parliamentary Reform in England, 1640–1832* (1973) has some lucid chapters on the period. E.P. Thompson, *The Making of the English Working Class* (2nd edn, 1968), especially pt 1, chs 1–5, is a stimulating, if often controversial, account of popular radicalism. On the London Corresponding Society see the introduction to M. Thale (ed.), *Selections from the Papers of the London Corresponding Society* (1986) and G.A. Williams, *Artisans and Sans-Culottes: Popular Movements in France and Britain during the French Revolution* (1968). A. Goodwin, *The Friends of Liberty* (1979) is a thorough discussion of reform and radical movements, and for one provincial centre, see J. Stevenson, *Artisans and Democrats: Sheffield and the French Revolution* (1989). C. Emsley, *British Society and the French Wars, 1793–1815* (1979) ranges widely into both the political and social repercussions of the French Wars. F. O'Gorman, *The Whig Party and the French Revolution* (1967) and L.G. Mitchell, *Charles James Fox and the Disintegration of the Whig Party, 1782–1794* (1971) examine party developments, while D.G. Barnes, *George III and William Pitt, 1783–1806* (1939) is useful on the administration. E.N.C. Black, *The Association* (1963) has a section on loyalist organisations. A.D. Harvey, *Britain in the Early Nineteenth Century* (1978) is particularly helpful on the period 1800–12, but see also R. Wells, *Insurrection: The British Experience, 1796–1803* (1984) for the survival of radicalism and the threat of revolution. I.R. Christie, *Stress and Stability in Late Eighteenth-Century England* (1984) explicitly examines the stabilising forces in the British polity, for which see also M. Thomis and P. Holt, *Threats of Revolution in Britain 1789–1848* (1977). The development of political ideology is admirably presented in H.T. Dickinson, *Liberty and Property* (1978). For the popular disturbances of the period, see J. Stevenson, *Popular Disturbances in England, 1700–1870* (1979; 2nd edn, 1992), R. Wells, *Dearth and Distress in Yorkshire, 1793–1801* (Borthwick Paper No. 52, 1977), his *Wretched Faces: Famine in War-Time England, 1793–1801* (1988), J. Bohstedt, *Riot and Community Politics, 1790–1801* (1985), D.J. Jones, *Before Rebecca: Popular Protests in Wales 1793–1835* (1973) and K.J. Logue, *Popular Disturbances in Scotland, 1789–1815* (1979).

Articles The fears of the government are discussed in C. Emsley, 'The London "insurrection" of December 1792: fact, fiction or fantasy', *J.B.S.* (1978). The reaction to the French Revolution is also dealt with in R.B. Rose, 'The Priestley riots of 1791', *P.P.* (1960), and A. Mitchell, 'The Association Movement of 1792–3', *H.J.* (1961), D.E. Ginter, 'The Loyalist Association Movement of 1792–93 and British public opinion', *H.J.* (1966), J.R. Western, 'The Volunteer movement as an anti-revolutionary force, 1793–1800', *E.H.R.* (1956) and P. Schofield, 'Conservative political thought in Britain in response to the French Revolution', *H.J.* (1986).

For popular distress, see W.M. Stern, 'The bread crisis in Britain, 1795–96', *E.* (1964) and A. Booth, 'Food riots in north-west England, 1790–1801', *P.P.* (1977). Local movements are discussed in F.K. Donnelly and J.L. Baxter, in S. Pollard and C. Holmes (eds), *Essays in the Economic and Social History of South Yorkshire* (1976) and W.A.L. Seaman, 'Reform politics at Sheffield, 1791–1797', *T.H.A.S.* (1957). For the continuity of radical activity after 1795, see J.R. Dinwiddy 'The "Black Lamp" in Yorkshire, 1801–1802' and J.L. Baxter and F.K. Donnelly, 'The revolutionary "underground" in the West Riding: myth or reality', *P.P.* (1974) and M. Elliott, 'The "Despard conspiracy" reconsidered', *P.P.* (1977).

20. Pitt and Fox

The two central characters of late eighteenth-century politics have received a great deal of scholarly attention. Pitt the Younger's career in the 1780s is now much clearer and it is important to assess the importance of the financial and administrative reforms he attempted. Discussions of his career often stop in the mid-1790s, and it is necessary to take in his conduct of the war and second administration for a full assessment. Fox remains a fascinating figure. It is equally important to see his *full* career in perspective (up to 1806) and in the context of the fortunes of his party as a whole. Some grasp of party developments and the continuing, but changing, role of the Crown is important to the careers of both men.

Sources and documents A. Aspinall and E.A. Smith (eds), *English Historical Documents, vol. XI: 1783–1832* (1959) has a selection of documents on the period. *The Later Correspondence of George III, December 1783–December 1810* (ed. A. Aspinall, 1962–70) also has relevant material. *The War Speeches of William Pitt* (ed. R. Coupland, 1915) and Pitt's *Orations on the French War* (1906) are useful for the war years. On Fox, see A. Bullock and M. Shock (eds), *The Liberal Tradition: From Fox to Keynes* (1956).

Secondary works A reliable guide and overview for this and the following period is J. Derry, *Politics in the Age of Fox, Pitt and Liverpool* (1990). For Pitt, the essential study is the trilogy by J. Ehrman, *The Younger Pitt: The Years of Acclaim* (1969), *The Reluctant Transition* (1984) and *The Consuming Struggle* (1996). J.W. Derry, *William Pitt* (1962) is succinct, while the older J. Holland Rose, *William Pitt and the National Revival* (1911) and *William Pitt and the Great War* (1911) are still valuable. Pitt's reaction to the French Revolution is considered in J. Mori, *William Pitt and the French Revolution, 1785–1795* (1998), P.A. Brown, *The French Revolution in English History* (1918) and F. O'Gorman, 'Pitt and the Tory Reaction', in H.T. Dickinson (ed.), *Britain and the French Revolution, 1789–1815* (1989).

P. Langford, *The Eighteenth Century, 1688–1815* (1976), chs 14 and 15 is useful on foreign affairs; for a more detailed study, see J. Black, *British Foreign Policy in an Age of Revolutions, 1783–93* (1994). See also C. Emsley, *British Society and the French Wars, 1793–1815* (1979). J. Binney, *British Public Finance and Administration, 1774–92* (1958) is relevant on Pitt's administrative reforms. On the role of the Irish crisis, see G.C. Bolton, *The Passing of the Act of Union* (1966).

On Fox, J.W. Derry, *Charles James Fox* (1973) and L. Mitchell, *Charles James Fox* (1992) are the best lives, but Loren Reid, *Charles James Fox: A Man for the People* (1969) is useful on Fox as an orator. An older alternative is E.C.P. Lascelles, *Charles James Fox* (1936). The early part of his career is considered in J. Cannon *The Fox–North Coalition: Crisis of the Constitution* (1970). The effects of the French Revolution are considered in F. O'Gorman, *The Whig Party and the French Revolution* (1967), while L.G. Mitchell, *Charles James Fox and the Disintegration of the Whig Party, 1782–94* (1970) deals more generally with Fox's relationship with the Whigs. The organisation of the Whig Party is discussed in the introduction to D.E. Ginter, *Whig Organisation in the General Election of 1790* (1967).

Of relevance to both careers are F. O'Gorman, *The Rise of Party in England* (1975), his shorter *The Emergence of the British Two-Party System, 1760–1832* (1982) and A.D. Harvey, *Britain in the Early Nineteenth Century* (1978). See, too, R. Pares, *George III and the Politicians* (1953).

Articles On Pitt, see R.J. White, 'The Younger Pitt', *H.T.* (1952) and A.S. Foord, 'The waning of the influence of the Crown, 1780–1832', *E.H.R.* (1947). For Fox, see I.R. Christie, 'C.J. Fox', *H.T.* (1958), H. Butterfield, 'Charles James Fox and the Whig opposition in 1792', *C.H.J.* 1947–49), A.S. Foord (above), J.R. Dinwiddy, 'Charles Fox and the people', *H.* (Oct. 1970), H. Butterfield, 'Sincerity and insincerity in C.J. Fox', *P.B.A.*, 57 (1971), M.D. George, 'Fox's Martyrs: the general election of 1784', *T.R.H.S.* (1939).

21. *Reform, radicalism and the Tory Party in Regency England*

The later years of the Napoleonic Wars and the period up to the early 1820s have frequently been viewed as ones in which the country faced agitations of almost revolutionary proportions. A combination of wartime and post-war distress, the effects of industrial development and a revival of reform activity led to a phase of widespread agitation and government repression. The nature and implications of the popular movements of these years need examining, especially the reasons for the failure of the reformers to achieve any legislative results in spite of periods of intense activity. The government of Lord Liverpool has often been criticised for its reactionary character, and some assessment of its strengths and weaknesses is necessary. Liverpool's reputation has been revised in recent years, some seeing the years 1820–22 as marking a turning point from which a new 'liberal Toryism' emerged.

Sources and documents   G.D.H. Cole and A.W. Filson (ed.), *British Working-Class Movements: Select Documents, 1789–1875* (1951) has documents on trade union and radical groups. S. Bamford, *Passages in the Life of a Radical* (1844, and later editions) is a famous account of radicalism in the post-war years; see especially the description of Peterloo. *The Autobiography of William Cobbett* (ed. W. Reitzel, 1967) is a compilation of Cobbett's writings on his life. See also A. Prentice, *Historical Sketches and Personal Recollections of Manchester: Intended to Illustrate the Progress of Public Opinion from 1792–1832* (1851, new edn with introduction by D. Read, 1970). For ministerial politics see *The Croker Papers* (3 vols, ed. L.J. Jennings, 1884), vol. 1.

Secondary works   The later sections of A.D. Harvey, *Britain in the Early Nineteenth Century* (1979) and C. Emsley, *British Society and the French Wars, 1793–1815* (1979) are starting points, with I.R. Christie, *Wars and Revolution* (1982) and N. Gash, *Aristocracy and People* (1980). Radicalism is well served by J.R. Dinwiddy, *From Luddism to the First Reform Bill* (1986), D.G. Wright, *Popular Radicalism* (1989) and E. Royle and J. Walvin, *British Radicals and Reformers, 1760–1848* (1982). E.P. Thompson, *The Making of the English Working Class* (2nd edn, 1968), chs 14–15 is also crucial. Popular disturbances of the period are discussed in F.O. Darvell, *Popular Disturbances and Public Order in Regency England* (1934), M.I. Thomis, *The Luddites* (1970), M.I. Thomis and P. Holt, *Threats of Revolution in Britain, 1789–1848* (1977) and J. Stevenson, *Popular Disturbances in England, 1700–1870* (1979, 2nd edn, 1992). D. Read, *Peterloo: The 'Massacre' and its Background* (1958) remains the best account of the famous event. G. Spater, *William Cobbett: The Poor Man's Friend* (1982) supersedes the older life by G.D.H. Cole, but see also I. Dyck, *William Cobbett and Rural Popular Culture* (1992) and J.W. Osborne, *William Cobbett: His Thought and his Times* (1966). For other reformers, see J. Belcham, *'Orator' Hunt* (1985), W. Thomas, *The Philosophic Radicals* (1979) and J. Dinwiddy, *Christopher Wyvill and Reform, 1790–1820* (Borthwick Paper No. 39, 1971). For the rise of public opinion, see D. Read, *The English Provinces, c. 1760–1960* (1964) and his *Press and People, 1790–1848* (1955).

Ministerial politics are best treated in N. Gash, 'The Earl of Liverpool (1812–27)', in H. van Thal (ed.), *The Prime Ministers, vol. 1* (1974), expanded into N. Gash, *Lord Liverpool* (1984), J.E. Cookson, *Lord Liverpool's Administration: The Crucial Years, 1815–1822* (1975), J.J. Sack, *The Grenvillites, 1801–29: Party Politics and Factionalism in the Age of Pitt and Liverpool* (1979) and W.R. Brock, *Lord Liverpool and Liberal Toryism, 1820 to 1827*

(2nd edn, 1967). J.C.D. Clark, *English Society, 1688–1832* (1986), ch. 6 is also useful. Debates about economic policy are considered in A.B. Hilton, *Corn, Cash and Commerce: The Economic Politics of the Tory Governments, 1815–1830* (1977), B. Gordon, *Political Economy in Parliament, 1819–1823* (1976) and *Economic Doctrine and Tory Liberalism, 1824–1830* (1979). Major political figures on the government side are also considered in D. Gray, *Spencer Perceval: The Evangelical Prime Minister, 1762–1812* (1963), N. Gash, *Mr Secretary Peel: The Life of Robert Peel to 1830* (1961), P. Ziegler, *Addington: A Life of Henry Addington, First Viscount Sidmouth* (1965), C.J. Bartlett, *Castlereagh* (1966), C.R. Fay, *Husskisson and his Age* (1951) and W. Hinde, *George Canning* (1973).

The Whigs are treated in M. Roberts, *The Whig Party, 1807–1812* (1939), A. Mitchell, *The Whigs in Opposition, 1815–1830* (1964) and L. Mitchell, *Holland House* (1980). The principal Whig personalities are discussed in E.A. Smith, *Lord Grey, 1764–1845* (1990), J. Derry, *Charles, Earl Grey: Aristocratic Reformer* (1922), R. Stewart, *Henry Brougham, 1778–1868* (1986), P. Jupp, *Lord Grenville, 1759–1834* (1985) E.A. Smith, *Whig Principles and Party Politics: Earl Fitzwilliam and the Whig Party, 1748–1833* (1975), and L. Mitchell, *Lord Melbourne, 1779–1848* (1997). R. Hole, *Pulpits, Politics and Public Order in England 1760–1832* (1989) addresses some of the interconnections between religion, politics and public order during this period, as does J. Sack, *From Jacobite to Conservative: Reaction and Orthodoxy in Britain, c. 1760–1832* (1993), while W. Stafford, *Socialism, Radicalism, and Nostalgia: Social Criticism in Britain, 1775–1830* (1987) sums up the various remedies for perceived social and political problems in the late eighteenth and early nineteenth centuries.

Articles A.S. Foord, 'The waning of the influence of the Crown, 1780–1832', *E.H.R.* (1947), D. Large, 'The decline of the party of the Crown and the rise of parties in the House of Lords, 1783–1837', *E.H.R.* (1963), A. Briggs, 'Middle-class consciousness in English politics, 1780–1846', *P.P.* (1956), A. Aspinall, 'English party organisation in the early 19th century', *E.H.R.* (1926) are useful on high political matters. J. Dinwiddy, 'Luddism and politics in the North', *S.H.* (1979) is a judicious survey of the upheaval of those years. T.M. Parsinnen, 'The revolutionary party in London 1816–20', *B.I.H.R.* (1972) shows the genuine revolutionaries at work. For the North, see F.K. Donnelly and J.L. Baxter, 'Sheffield and the English revolutionary tradition, 1791–1820', *I.R.S.H.* (1974). Significant radical personalities are discussed in J.R. Dinwiddy, 'Sir Francis Burdett and Burdettite Radicalism', *H.* (1980) and J.C. Belcham, 'Henry Hunt and the evolution of the mass platform', *E.H.R.* (1978); see also J.C. Belcham, 'Republicanism, popular constitutionalism and the radical platform in early 19th-century England', *S.H.* (1981).

SECTION FOURTEEN

Maps

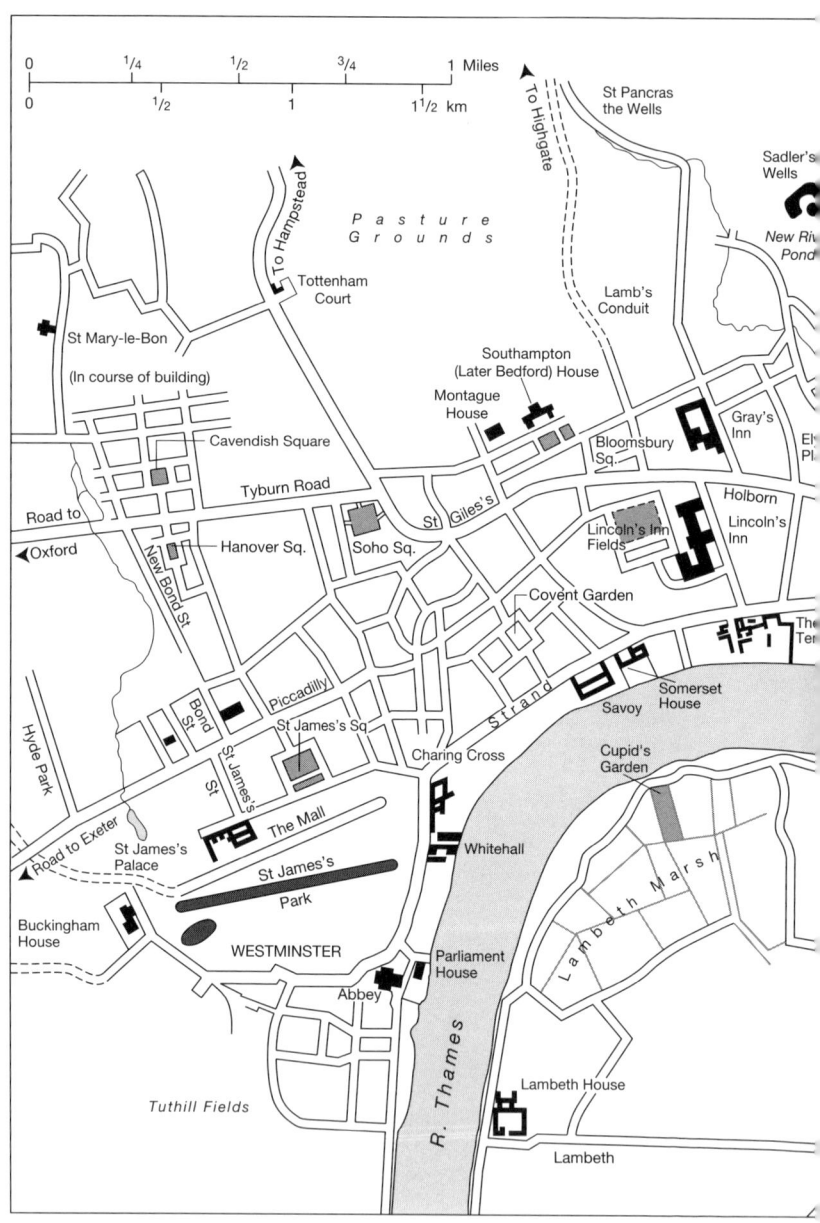

Source: John Stevenson, Popular Disturbances in England, 1700–1832 (Second Edn) (London, 1992), p. 70–1.

London c. 1714.

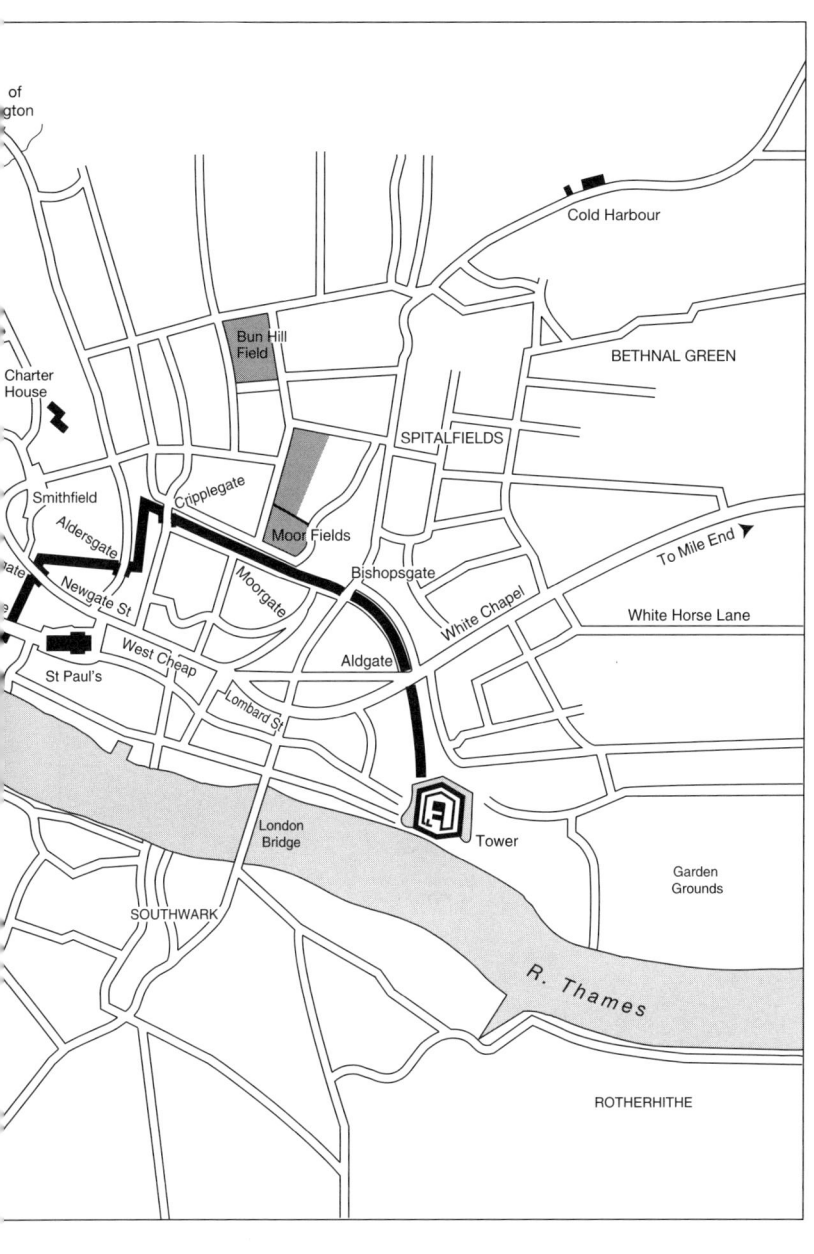

Counties of Ireland.

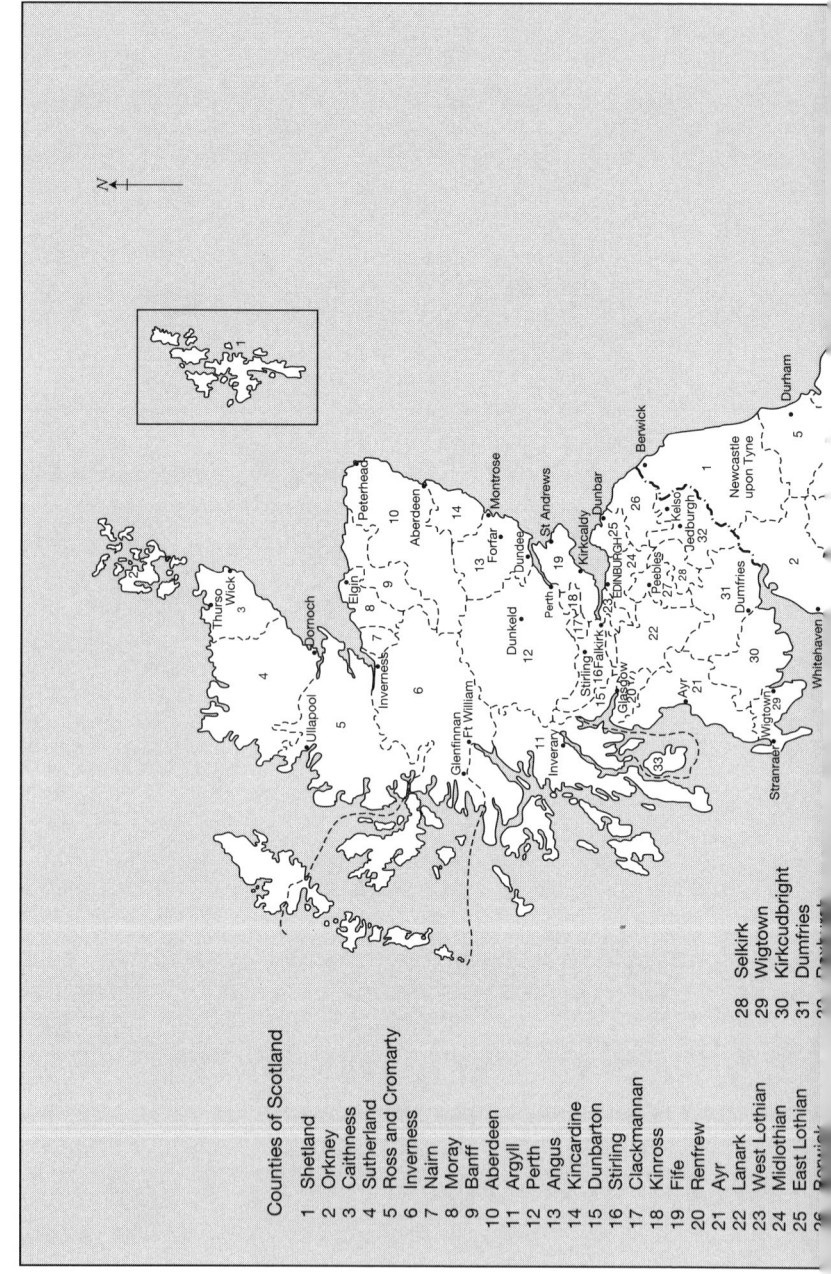

MAPS 543

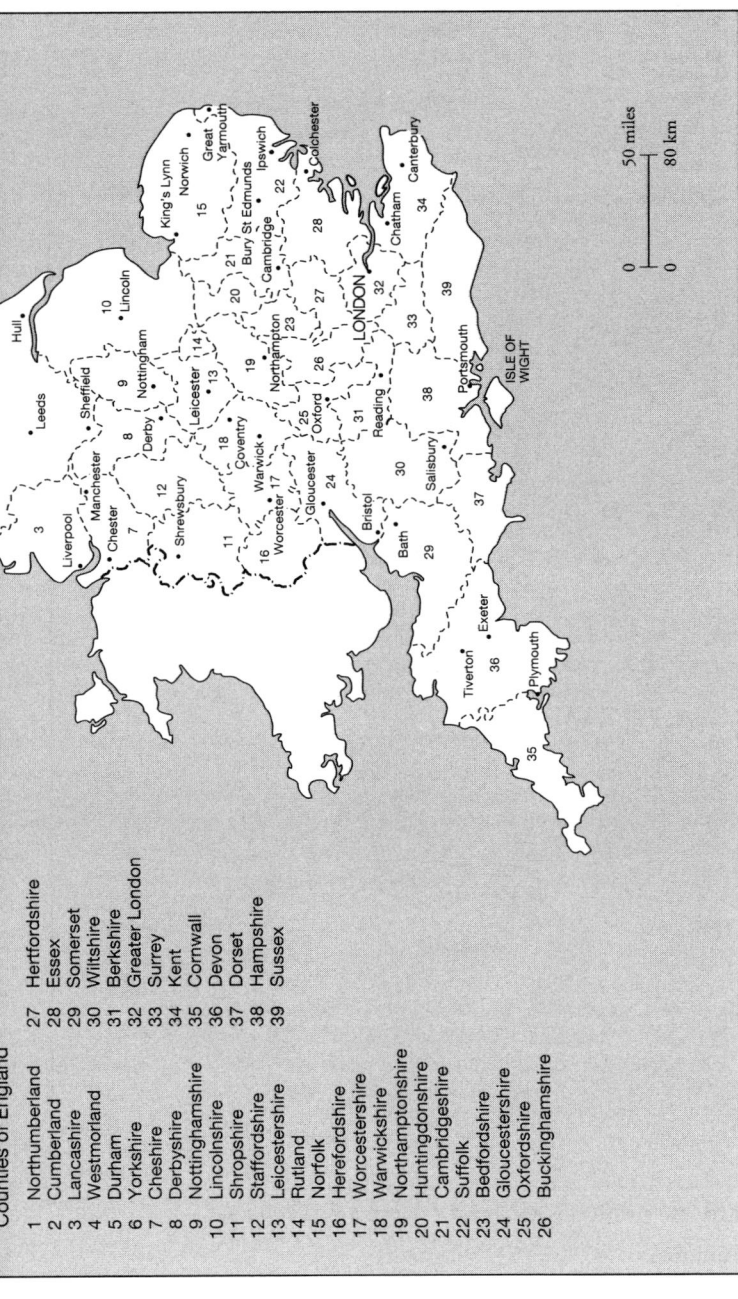

Counties of England and Scotland.

Source: Geoffrey Holmes and David Szechi, The Age of Oligarchy (London, 1993), p. 407.

North America.

Index

Abbot, Charles 81
Abingdon, Earl of 5
Adam, Robert 343, 345, 347, 349, 353, 355, 367
Adam, William 335
Addenbrooke's Hospital 346
Addington, Henry (Viscount Sidmouth) 27, 29, 42, 60–1, 62, 63, 64, 66, 68, 69, 72, 73, 81, 367
Addington, J.H. 78
Addison, Joseph 14, 47, 71, 330, 332, 367
Administration of Justice Act (1774) 170
advowson 459
Africa 162, 189
African Institution 434
Agriculture, Board of 354
Aikenhead 256
Aislabie, John 14, 15, 47, 72
Aix-la-Chapelle, Treaty of (1748) 19, 135, 164, 168, 182, 185, 340
Akenside, Mark 338
Alberoni, Giulio 180
Albuera 192
aldermen 322
Alexandria 191
Algiers 122, 123, 125, 129, 132, 136, 137, 141, 143, 145, 149
Aligarh, storming of 186
Alkmaar, Battle of (1799) 191
'All the Talents', ministry of 28, 42, 62, 109, 358, 473
Alleghenies 169
Allen, Ethan 187
Allen, Joseph 239
Almanza, Battle of (1707) 179
Almeida, fall of 192
America, North 21, 22, 24, 138–47 *passim*, 150, 151, 152, 162, 165–71
  Declaration of Independence (1776) 23, 170, 187, 348
  and the Seven Years War 20, 168, 183–4
  War of Independence 23, 107, 111, 169–70, 187–9, 348
  and War of 1812 193–4
  see also Canada
America, South 191
Amherst, Lord 60, 183
Amiens, Peace of (1802) 27, 108, 143, 356
Amity and Commerce, Treaty of (1778) 23
Ancien Régime 459
Andros, Sir Edmund 165
Anhalt-Zerbst 138
Annapolis 166
Anne, Queen of Great Britain and Ireland 6, 10, 11–13, 33, 36, 44, 74, 328, 332, 367–8
Anson, George 51, 52, 53, 54, 74, 163, 338, 368
anti-clearance riots 220, 222, 224
anticlericalism 459
anti-crimp house disturbances 220, 221
anti-enclosure riots 216, 217, 218, 220, 222, 223
Anti-Slavery Society 298
anti-turnpike riots 216, 217
Apsley, Lord 57
Arbuthnot, John 332, 368
Arcadia 168
archbishops and bishops 236–44, 257–8, 260–1
Archer, Thomas 331, 368
Arden, Lord 61
Argaum 186
Argyll, Earl of 3, 17
Arianism 459
Arkwright, Richard 346, 368
Arminianism 459
army, strength and cost of 195–8
Arne, Thomas 339, 369
art and architecture 327–61 *passim*
Asbury, Francis 251, 347

Ashburnham, William 238
Ashburton, Lord *see* Dunning, John
Assaye 186
Assiento with Spain 128, 129, 163
Association Movement for Parliamentary Reform 350
Association for the Relief of the Manufacturing and Labouring Poor 298
Astell, Mary 326, 328, 331, 369
Atkinson, William 357, 361
Atterbury, Francis 15, 234, 242, 254, 329, 334, 369
Auckland, Lord 62, 75
Aughrim, Battle of (1691) 8, 154, 176
Austen, Jane 358, 360, 369
Austerlitz, Battle of (1805) 358
Austria 18, 19, 27, 188, 189, 190, 193
  loans and subsidies to 148, 202, 203, 204
  and Seven Years War 183
  treaties and conventions 144-53 *passim*
  and Triple Alliance 180
Austria-Hungary 133, 134, 135
Austrian Netherlands 129, 140, 182
Avison, Charles 343, 369

Badajoz 192
Baden 148, 150, 151, 200
Bage, Robert 354
Bagot, Lewis 238, 241, 261
bailiffs 315, 322
Baird, General Sir David 191
Baker, William 241, 260
Bakewell, Robert 369-70
Baldwin, Thomas 353
Bangaloore, Treaty of (1748) 186
Bangorian Controversy 333
Bank of England 9, 26, 326, 353, 468
banks 273
Banks, Joseph 370
Baptist Missionary Society 249, 263, 355
Baptist Union 359
Baptists 248, 249, 347
Barbauld, Anna Laetitia 370
Barcelona, seige of 179
Barham, Lord 61, 74
Barlow, Thomas 240
Barré, I. 58, 78
Barrier Treaty (1715) 129

Barrington, William Wildman, Viscount 53, 54, 55, 56, 57, 58, 72, 77, 242, 243, 260
Barry, James 353
Bastille, storming of the 25, 210, 352
Batavian Republic 143
Bath, 1st Earl of (William Pulteney) 16, 18, 41, 46, 51, 77, 428-9
Bath, architectural development of 335, 337, 343, 347, 349, 353, 452
Bath and West of England Agricultural Society 350
Bathurst, C. 62, 64, 76
Bathurst, Henry Bathurst, 2nd Earl 57, 62, 63, 64, 67, 68, 73, 75, 241
Baum, Colonel 187
Bavaria 134, 135, 142, 143, 148, 149, 150, 151, 152, 175, 201
Beachy Head, Battle of (1690) 175
Beadon, Richard 238, 239
Beattie, James 346
Beauclerk, James 240
Beaw, William 260
Beckford, William 370
Beckford, William (the younger) 352, 370
Bedford, Duke of *see* Russell, John
Behn, Aphra 326, 370
Belgium 147
Bell, Andrew 370-1
Bell, Robert 303
Belle Ile 163, 184
Bellers, John 326, 371
Belvoir Castle 357
Bemis Heights 188
Benefit to Clergy Act (1823) 228
Benson, Martin 239
Benson, Robert 45, 71
Bentham, Jeremy 348, 350, 354, 367, 371
Bentinck, William 371
Bentley, Richard 327, 328, 371
Berbice 152
Beresford, Viscount 191
Bergen, Battle of (1759) 182
Bergen-op-Zoom, Battle of (1799) 191
Berkeley, George 330, 336, 338, 371-2
Berkeley, James 47, 48, 74
Berkeley, William 45, 46, 75
Berlin decrees 28
Bertie, Thomas 75
Bethell, Christopher 239, 240

Beveridge, William 261
Bewick, Thomas 353, 357, 361, 372
Bible Christians 251, 361
Bible Society 451
Bill of Comprehension (1689) 8
Bill of Rights (1689) 6, 8, 326, 460
Bingham, Joseph 331
Binns, John 211
Birmingham Music Festival 347
bishops and archbishops 236–44, 257–8, 260–1
Bisse, Philip 240, 261
'Black Act' (1723) 207, 208, 215, 334
Black, John 304
Blackall, Offspring 239
Blackburn, Lancelot 239, 243
Blackburne, Francis 235, 345
Blackmore, Sir Richard 372
Blackstone, Sir William 344, 372
Blackwood's Magazine 360
Bladensburg, Battle of (1814) 194
Blair, Hugh 344, 372
Blake, William 352, 354, 358, 362, 372
'Blanketeers' 29, 115, 223
Blathwayt, William 44, 77, 373
Blenheim, Battle of (1704) 11, 177, 330
Blenheim Palace 331, 405, 445
Bligh, William 373
Blomfield, Charles James 237, 244
'Bloody Assizes' (1685) 3
Bloody Code 460
Bloomfield, Robert 356
Blore, Edward 361
Blücher, Gebbard Leberecht von 193
'Blue-stocking' group 340, 420
blue-water strategy 460
Board of Agriculture 354
Board of Trade and Plantations 162
Böhler, Peter 250
Bolingbroke, Henry St John, 1st Viscount 11, 12, 13, 14, 15, 16, 44, 45, 70, 71, 77, 334, 340, 342, 373
Bolton, Duke of (Charles Powlett) 47, 48, 76
Bonaparte, Joseph 192
Bond, J. 359
bonded warehouses 15
Bonnie Prince Charlie *see* Stuart, Charles Edward
'Bonnymuir, Battle of' 224
Book of Common Prayer 460
Booth, Henry 71

Bosanquet, Mary 373
Boscawen, Admiral 19, 20, 184, 185
Boston 'massacre' 169
Boston Port Act 170
Boston Tea Party 22, 170, 348
Boswell, James 352, 354, 373
Botany Bay 352
Boulter, Hugh 238
Boulton, Matthew 374
Bourne, Hugh 251
Bow Street Police Office 208, 338
Bowers, Thomas 238
Boyce, William 345, 374
Boyle, Henry (Lord Carleton) 43, 44, 48, 67, 70, 156
Boyle, Richard 335, 374
Boyle, Robert 374, 408
Boyne, Battle of the (1690) 8, 154, 176, 326
Braddock, General Edward 164, 168, 183
Bradford, Samuel 242, 243
Bradshaw, William 238
Brady, Nicholas 329
Bragge, C. 61, 78
Brand, John 350
Brand, Thomas 114, 115
Brandenburg 175
Brandenburg, Elector of 121
Brandenburg-Anspach 138
Brandreth, Jeremiah 29, 212
Brandywine Creek 188
Bray, Thomas 472
'Bread or Blood' riots 360, 461
Bremen 132
Brest 176
bribery 111, 114
bridge building 357, 359, 362, 442
Bridgeman, Charles 333, 374
Bridgewater, Francis Egerton 375
Brighton Pavilion 361
Brihuega 179
Bristol Education Society 248
Bristol, George William Hervey, Earl of 56, 69
British Convention 25–6, 113, 115
British Critic 355
British and Foreign Bible Society 236, 263, 298, 359
British and Foreign School Society 298
British Museum 342
'broad-bottomed administration' 461

Broglie, Charles-François 182, 183
Bromley, William 45, 70, 81
Brooke, Henry 344
Brooks' Club 350
Brown, John 342, 375
Brown, Lancelot 'Capability' 341, 345, 375
Bruce, Andrew 258
Bruce, Sir William 327
Brummell, George Bryan 'Beau' 375
Brunswick 200, 201
Brunswick, Duke of 136, 137, 141
Brunswick, Elector of 125, 126, 127
Brunswick, Prince Ferdinand of 182, 183
Brunswick-Lüneburg 124, 126, 140
Bryanites 251
Brydges, James 44, 46
Buckingham, John Sheffield, Duke of 15, 44, 67, 68
Buckingham, Marquis of 77
Buckinghamshire, John Hobart, 2nd Earl of 62, 63, 64, 76, 77
Buckner, John 238
Buenos Aires 191
Bull, George 261
Buller, William 239
Bunker Hill, Battle of (1775) 23, 187
Burdett, Sir Francis 28, 114, 115, 212, 222
Burdon, Rowland 357
burgage boroughs 461
Burgess, Thomas 242, 261
Burgoyne, General John 187, 188, 375
Burke, Edmund 23, 342, 346, 348, 354, 356, 376, 463
  Civil Establishment reform 24, 112
  Pay-Master General 59, 78
  Reflections on the Revolution in France 25, 113, 116, 210, 249, 352, 376
  Thoughts on the Present Discontents 22, 111
Burnet, Gilbert 242, 333, 334, 376
Burney, Charles 349, 376
Burney, Fanny 350, 376
Burns, Robert 352, 376
Busaco Ridge 192
Bussy, Marquis de 164
Bute, John Stuart, 3rd Earl of 20, 21, 41, 53–4, 66, 70, 183, 376–7
Butler, James, 2nd Duke of Ormond 13, 14, 76, 178, 180, 377

Butler, John 240, 241
Butler, Joseph 238, 243, 335, 337, 377
Butts, Robert 239, 241
Buxar, Battle of (1764) 186
Byng, Admiral John 12, 19, 164, 180, 184, 342, 377
Byng, George 49, 74
Byrne, Nicholas 303
Byrom, John 377
Byron, Admiral 188
Byron, George Gordon, 6th Baron 358, 360, 378

Caesar, Charles 45
Cage, Governor 170
Calamay, Edmund 329
Calcutta 162, 185
  'Black Hole' of 164, 185
calendar reform 19, 168, 305, 342, 461
Calvinism/Calvinists 250, 251, 339, 347, 459, 461
Camden, Battle of (1780) 188
Camden, Earl 61, 63, 64, 65, 68, 73, 77
Camden, Lord 56, 58, 59, 67, 68
Cameron, Donald of Lochiel 378
Campbell, Alexander Hume 96
Campbell, Colen 333, 378
Campbell, James Colquhoun 260
Campbell, Lord Frederick 96
Camperdown 190, 356
Canada 20, 22, 164, 167, 169, 184, 187, 193
canal construction 281–5, 356
Canning, George 30, 62, 63, 64, 73, 78, 378
Cape Breton Island 163, 167, 169
Cape Finisterre 163, 182
Cape of Good Hope 143, 191
Cape Passaro 180
Cape St Vincent 190
capital offences, abolition of 228–9
capital punishment 227, 228–9
'Captain Swing' disturbances 225
Carey, Anthony 73
Carey, William 239, 261
Carleton, Lord (Henry Boyle) 43, 44, 48, 67, 70, 156
Carlile, Richard 304, 378
Carlisle, Charles Howard, 1st Earl of 46, 66
Carlisle, Frederick Howard, 5th Earl of 57, 59, 69, 75, 77

Carmarthen, Marquis of 24, 59, 73
Carolina 162, 163, 166, 167, 168, 169
Caroline of Brunswick, Queen 379, 398
Caroline, Queen 30, 224, 338, 362, 378
Carr, John 343, 347, 349
Carr, Robert James 238, 243
Cartagena 163, 167
Carte, Thomas 340
Carter, Elizabeth 379
Carteret, Lord John, Earl Granville 15, 16, 17, 18, 41, 49–50, 51, 52, 53, 54, 68, 70, 71, 76, 156, 181
Cartwright, Edmund 352
Cartwright, Major John 111, 115, 117, 348, 379, 465, 472
Cartwright, Thomas 244
Castle Howard 329, 405, 445
Castlecomer, Viscount 77
Castlereagh, Robert Stewart, Viscount 29, 30, 61, 63, 64, 73, 160, 379–80
Catalonia 125, 128
Catholic Association 161, 423
Catholic Board 161
Catholic Emancipation 27, 109, 161, 236, 254, 351, 367, 461
Catholic Relief Act (1778) 23
 (1793) 159, 254
Catholics/Catholicism 3–4, 8, 10, 233, 236, 247, 253–8, 460, 470
 anti-Catholic riots 5, 214, 217, 219
 Irish 154, 155, 156, 157, 159
 in North America 22, 165, 170
 refugees from continent 255
 in Scotland 4, 256, 257
Cato Street Conspiracy 30, 213, 224, 362
Cavendish, Henry 344
Cavendish, Lord J. 58, 59, 72
Cavendish, William *see* Devonshire, Duke of
Cecil, Charles 238, 260
censorship 9
Centlivre, Susanna 380
Ceylon 186
Challoner, Richard 339, 380
Chambers *Cyclopaedia* 334
Chambers, Sir William 343, 347, 380
Chanda Sahib 164, 185
Chandler, Edward 240, 243
Chapone, Hester Mulso 348, 380
charities and philanthropic societies 298
 see also individual societies

Charleroi 175, 193
Charles II, King of Spain 102, 176
Charles VI, Emperor 129, 130, 181
Charles, Thomas 259
Chatham, 1st Earl of *see* Pitt, William (the Elder)
Chatham, John Pitt, 2nd Earl of 59, 60, 61, 62, 63, 64, 66, 68, 69, 74, 191
Chatterton, Thomas 346, 350, 380–1
Chester Music Festival 347
Chesterfield, Philip Dormer Stanhope, 4th Earl of 50, 51, 70, 76, 156, 348, 440
Cheyne, George 336
Chippendale, Thomas 343, 381
Chippewa, Battle of (1814) 193
Chiswick House 335, 374
Cholmondeley, Earl of 49, 50, 69, 75
Church Building Acts 236
Church Building Society 236, 298, 361
Church of England 3, 4, 14, 233–46
 archbishops and bishops 236–44
 High Church 465
 Low Church 467
 plurality and non-residence 245–6
 revenues from bishoprics 246
'Church and King' riots 25, 220, 235, 249, 428
Church Missionary Society 236, 263, 298, 357, 451
Churchill, Charles 381
Churchill, John *see* Marlborough, John Churchill, Duke of
Churchill, Sarah, Duchess of Marlborough 382
churchwardens 318–19
Cibber, Colley 382
cider tax 21
Cintra, Convention of (1808) 28, 192, 358
City Elections Act (1725) 16
Ciudad Rodrigo 192
Civil Establishment Act (1782) 24, 112
Civil List 10, 16
Claggett, Nicholas 239, 261
Clancarty, Earl of 64, 65, 75
Clapham Sect 236, 359, 461
Clare, John 362, 382
Clare, Viscount 56, 75
Clarence, Duke of 74
Clarendon, Edward Hyde, 1st Earl of 328

Clarendon, Henry, 2nd Earl of 57, 60, 76, 410
Clark, J.C.D. 462
Clarke, Samuel 333, 382
classicism 462
Clavering, Robert 241, 260
Clayton, Robert 341
Cleaver, William 244, 260, 261
Cleland, John 340
Clerk, Sir James 347
Clerke's Act (1782) 24
Clerks of the Peace 315
Clinton, Governor 168
Clinton, Sir Henry 187, 188, 189
Clive, Robert Clive, Lord 164, 185, 340, 382
cloth industry 278
   disturbances among workers in 215, 216, 217, 218, 219, 221, 223, 224, 307, 308, 309
   see also cotton industry; linen industry; woollen industry
Clowes, William 251
coal trade 277
Cobbett, William 29, 114, 212, 303, 356, 360, 382, 470
Cochrane, Lord 114
Coke, Thomas 251, 346, 383
Coleridge, Samuel Taylor 303, 356, 360, 383
collective bargaining by riot 462
College of William and Mary 165
Collier, Jeremy 328, 383
Collier, Mary 383
colliers, disturbances among 220, 223, 224, 225, 307
Collingwood, Cuthbert, 1st Baron 383
Collins, Anthony 464
Collins, William 383–4
Cologne, Elector of 134
Colquhoun, Archibald 96
Colquhoun, Patrick 354, 360, 384
Combe, William 359, 384
Combination Acts 27, 211, 307, 309–12, 356, 462
Company of Scotland 162
Compton, Henry 237
Compton, Spencer (Earl of Wilmington) 18, 48, 49, 66, 68, 69, 78, 81
confessional state 462
Congregationalists 249

Congreve, William 326, 328, 384
Connecticut 166, 167, 168
Constable, John 361, 384
constables 319
constituencies
   England 85–90
   Scotland 92–3
   Wales 91
Constitutional Society 444
Convention Parliament 6, 8, 101
Conway, General 58, 59
Conway, Henry Seymour 21, 55, 56, 70, 71
Conybeare, John 238
Cook, Captain James 346, 348, 350, 384
Cooke, G. 56, 78
Copenhagen, Battle of (1801) 191
Copland 341
Copley, John S. 351
copper 279
Coram, Thomas 385
Corn Laws 29, 223, 275, 360, 462
Cornbury, Lord 5
Cornwall, Charles Wolfran 81
Cornwall, Folliot H.W. 238, 240, 243
Cornwallis, C.M. 60, 61
Cornwallis, Charles, 1st Marquis 23, 77, 188, 189, 190, 385
Cornwallis, Frederick 237, 240
Cornwallis, James 240
Cornwallis, Lord 73, 78
coroners 315
Corporation Act 235, 236, 248, 468
Corsica 141, 190
Corunna, Battle of (1809) 192
Cotman, John Sell 359, 385
Cotton Factory Act (1819) 306
cotton industry 278, 308, 368
   Ireland 155, 158
County movement 462
Court of Ecclesiastical Commission 4
Court of Quarter Sessions 316
Court and Treasury Party 463
Courtenay, Henry Reginald 238, 239
courts of the municipal corporations 323
Covrepauk 185
Cowpens, Battle of (1781) 189
Cowper, Lord 46, 47, 67
Cowper, William 351, 352, 385
Crabbe, George 352, 358, 385
Craggs, James 47, 71, 77

Cranfield, Lionel (Earl of Dorset) 49, 52
Cressett, Edward 260
Crew, Nathaniel 243
Crewe's Act (1782) 24
Crigan, Claudius 244
Criminal Justice Act (1827) 228
criminal statistics 226–7
Criminal Statutes (Repeal) Act (1827) 228
Croft, Herbert 240
Crompton, Samuel 350, 385
Crotch, William 359
Crowley, Sir Ambrose 385
Cruden, Alexander 337
Cuba 163, 167
Culloden, Battle of (1746) 18, 180, 340
Cumberland, Richard 241
Cumberland, William Augustus, 1st Duke of 386
Curwen, John Christian 114
Cust, Sir John 81
Custos Rotulorum 314

D'Adda 4
Daily Courant 302, 328
Dalton, John 356, 358, 386
Dampier, Thomas 239, 242
Dampier, William 162, 328, 386
Danby, Earl of (Thomas Osborne, Duke of Leeds) 3, 4, 9, 67
Danzig 126
Darby, Abraham 386
Darcy, Robert (Earl of Holdernesse) 19, 47, 48, 51, 52, 53, 70, 71, 75
Darien 162, 165
Darlington, Earl of 78
Dartmouth, William Legge, Lord 44, 45, 55, 57, 61, 68, 69, 71, 73, 75
Darwin, Erasmus 354, 386
Dashwood, Sir Francis 54, 72, 386
Daubeny, Charles 236, 357
Davy, Sir Humphrey 358, 360, 386
Davys, George 242
Dawes, William 243, 244
Deccan 164
Declaration of Indulgence 4, 233, 247, 253, 470
Declaration of Rights (1689) 6, 8
Declaratory Act (1766) 169
  Ireland (1719) 332
Defoe, Daniel 247, 328, 330, 332, 334, 387

Deism/Deist Movement 247, 463
Delany, Mary 387
Delaware 162
Demerara 152
Denain, French victory at 178
Den Helder 190–1
Denmark
  loans and subsidies to 204
  treaties and conventions with 121, 122, 123, 130, 131, 133, 138, 143, 146, 150, 151, 152, 188
Dennis, John 328, 330, 387
De Quincy, Thomas 387
Derby, Earl of 59, 62, 76
Derby, James Stanley, Earl of 44, 75
Derham, William 333, 387
Derwentwater, James Radcliffe, 3rd Earl of 14
Desaguliers, J.T. 334, 387–8
Despard, Col. Marcus 212, 474
Dettingen, Battle of (1743) 181, 338, 396
De Veil, Sir Thomas 208
Devis, Arthur 341
Devonshire, Duke of 4, 19, 41, 46, 48, 49, 50, 52, 66, 67, 68, 69, 76, 156
Devonshire, Georgiana, Duchess of 388
Dibdin, Charles 345
Disarming of the Highlands Act 19
dissenters 463
  Protestant 4, 234, 247–9, 337, 463, 473–4
Dodd, William 388
Doddridge, Philip 248, 343, 388
Dodington, George Bubb 17, 388
Dominica 164, 184, 188
Donauwörth 177
Dorchester Heights 187
Dorset, Lionel Cranfield Sackville, 1st Duke of 50, 51, 68, 76, 156
Douglas, John 242, 243
Douglas, Robert 258
Dowdeswell, W. 55, 72, 111
Downie, David 211
Dr Williams' Library 248
Drumlanrig Castle 327
Drummond, James 257
Drummond, Robert Hay 243, 261
Dryden, John 327, 328, 388–90
Dublin Agricultural Society 336

Duck, Stephen 336, 389
Dundas, Henry *see* Melville, Henry Dundas, 1st Viscount
Dundas, R. 63
Dundas, W. 62, 78
Dunning, John, 1st Baron Ashburton 23, 58, 59, 76, 112, 389
Dunton, John 330
Dupleix, Joseph 163, 164, 185
Dupplin, Viscount 78
duties, import 3, 21, 22, 169, 275
Dyer, John 334, 342

Eachard 330
East India Company 22, 24, 133, 162, 163, 170, 186, 463
East Indies 163
Eaton, Daniel Isaac 210
'economical reform' 23, 463
economy and finance 267–86
Edgcumbe, Lord 50, 51, 52, 53, 76
Edgeworth, Maria 356, 389
education 294
Edwards, Jonathan 343, 390
Egerton, Henry 240
Egerton, John 240, 243, 260
Egerton, John (Earl of Bridgwater) 73, 74
Egmont, Earl of 55, 74
Egremont, Earl of 21, 53, 54, 55, 71
Egypt 191
Eldon, Lord 60, 61, 63, 64, 67
election riots 214, 215, 216, 217, 219, 220, 221, 222, 224
elections and election results 100–10
Elizabeth, Empress of Russia 183
Ellenborough, Lord 62
Elliot, Sir G. 58
Ellis, Anthony 261
Ellis, Welbore 54, 57, 73, 77
Elstob, Elizabeth 332, 390
Emden 184
Emmet, Robert 161, 474
Empiricism 463
enclosure 463–4
 see also anti-enclosure riots
Enclosure Acts 274
Encyclopaedia Britannica 346
England 82
 franchise 83–4, 85–90
 patronage 94
 population 289

Enlightenment 464
Episcopal Church 12, 256, 257, 327
Erskine, Ebenezer 257, 337
Erskine, John, 11th Earl of Mar 13, 14, 179, 390
Erskine, Thomas 62, 67, 117, 390
Essequibo 152
Eugène, Prince 127, 177, 178, 179
Evangelical Movement 235, 464
 see also Clapham Sect
Evans, Evan 344
Evans, John 260
Ewer, John 260
excise 464
Excise Bill (1733) 16, 105, 336

Factory Act (1802) 356
Falkland Islands 137, 346
famine, Ireland 156
Fane, Thomas (Earl of Westmorland) 48, 49, 75
Farmer, Anthony 4
Farqhar, George 330
Fell, Margaret 391
Fenwick, Sir John 9, 391
Ferguson, Adam 346, 391
Ferrier, Susan 360
Fielding, Henry 208, 336, 338, 340, 391
Fielding, Sir John 208, 209, 391–2
Fielding, Sarah 338, 340, 392
Fiennes, Celia 392
'The Fifteen' 179–80
finance and economy 267–86
Financial Revolution 464
Finch, Anne 332, 451–2
Finch, Charles, Earl of Nottingham and Winchilsea 45, 75
Finch, Daniel, Earl of Nottingham and Winchilsea 5, 7, 8, 9, 11, 13, 14, 44, 46, 67, 69, 70, 71, 392
Finch, Heneage, Earl of Aylesford 75
fiscal-military state 464
Fisher, John 239, 242
Fitzgerald, Lord Edward 160
Fitzherbert, Maria 398
Fitzpatrick, R. 59, 77, 78
Fitzwalter, Earl 49, 75
Fitzwilliam, Earl 59, 62, 68, 77, 159
Flanders 176–8
Flaxman, John 355, 361, 392
Fleetwood, William 239, 261

Fleming, George 243
Fleurus, Battle of (1690) 175
Flood, Henry 112, 113, 156, 158
Florida 163, 167, 169, 189
flying shuttle 412
Foley, Paul 81
Fontenoy, Battle of (1745) 18, 181
food riots and disturbances 214–24 *passim*
Foot Bailiffs 315
Fordyce 345
Forgery Acts (1830 and 1832) 229
Fort Dusquesne 164, 168, 183
Fort Edward 164
Fort Frontenac 164, 183
Fort Necessity 183
Fort Niagara 183, 193
Fort Oswego 183
Fort Ticonderoga 164, 183, 187
Fort William 162
Fort William Henry 164, 165
'The Forty-Five' 180
Foundling Hospital, London 263, 338, 403
Fowler, Edward 239
Fox, Charles 44
Fox, Charles James 23, 24, 25, 26, 28, 41, 58, 59, 62, 73, 108, 392–3
Fox, George 247
Fox, Henry 19, 20, 53, 54, 55, 71, 77, 78, 393
Framebreaking Act (1812) 212
Frampton, Robert 239
France 8, 11, 18, 25, 122, 124, 126, 127, 138, 181
  and the American colonies 19–21, 163–4, 165, 166, 167, 168, 183–4
  and Catalonia 128
  commerce with 121, 125, 128
  Grand Alliance against 121, 175–6
  indemnity 153
  in India 185
  loans and subsidies to 204
  Napoleonic period 26, 27, 28, 29, 189–93
  and Partition Treaty 10
  and the Peninsular War 192–3
  postal convention with 143
  prisoners of war 138, 142
  and the Quadruple Alliance 129, 180
  revolution in 25, 210
  and the Seven Years War 19, 20, 21, 168, 182–5
  treaties and conventions 16, 19, 23, 24, 123, 130, 131, 132, 135, 137, 139, 146–53, 189, 352
  and Treaty of Hanover (1725) 16, 131
  and Treaty of Versailles 24, 189, 352
  and Triple Alliance (1717) 14
  and the War of the Austrian Succession 181–2
  and War of the Spanish Succession 176–9
franchise 83–93, 112, 114
Francis, Philip 393
Franklin, Benjamin 168, 393–4
Fraser, Simon 394
Frederick the Great 20, 181, 182
Frederick Lewis, Prince of Wales 17, 340, 394, 396–7
free-thinkers 464
Freeman's Farm 187
friendly societies 296–7
Friendly Societies Act (1793) 306, 307
Friends of the People 113, 117
Frost, John 210
Fry, Elizabeth 360, 394
Fuentes de Oñoro 192
Fuseli, Henry 351, 395

'Gag' Acts 29, 212
Gainsborough, Thomas 341, 343, 347, 349, 395
Gambia 189
game laws 207, 208
Gaol Act (1823) 213
Gardiner, James 240
Garnett, Jeremiah 304
Garrick, David 338, 341, 395
Gastrell, Francis 244
Gay, John 334, 395
General Baptist New Connexion 248, 249, 347
General Body of Protestant Dissenting Ministers 248
Genoa 135, 149
George Frederick of Waldeck, Prince 175
George I, King of Great Britain and Ireland 13, 14, 16, 33, 334, 395–6
George II, King of Great Britain and Ireland 16, 20, 33, 181, 334, 344, 396–7

George III, King of Great Britain and Ireland 20, 25, 28, 30, 34–5, 358, 362, 397
George IV, King of Great Britain and Hanover 30, 34, 362, 397–8
as Prince of Wales 25, 28, 358
George, Prince of Denmark 74, 367, 398
Georgia 163, 164, 167, 168, 169
German Confederation 151
Germantown 188
Germany 200, 201, 202
Germany, Emperor of 141
Ghent, Treaty of (1814) 194
Gibbon, Edward 348, 356, 398
Gibbons, Grinling 398
Gibbs, James 333, 335, 339, 398–9
Gibraltar 16, 23, 162, 163, 178, 179, 188, 350
Gibson, Edmund 234, 237, 240, 326, 333, 339, 399
Gilbert, John 242, 243, 260
Gilbert, Thomas 399
Gilbert's Act (1782) 306, 350
Gillray, James 351, 399
Gilpin, Sawrey 350, 352, 357
Gilpin, William 399–400
Gin Act, (1736) 17, 216, 305, 336 (1743) 338
Glasgow, Earl of 96
glass industry, Ireland 156, 157
Glasse, Hannah 340
Glassite Sect 256
Glatz 182
Glenbervie, Lord 78
Glencoe, Massacre of (1692) 9, 326
Glorious Revolution (1685–89) 3–7, 326
Gloucester, William, Duke of 10, 33, 368
Godden v. *Hales* (1686) 3
Godolphin, Lord 5, 9, 10, 11, 13, 17, 41, 43, 49, 69, 400
Godwin, William 354, 400
Gold Coast 164
Goldsmith, Oliver 344, 346, 348, 400
Gooch, Thomas 238, 239, 241
Goodenough, Samuel 244
Gordon, John 258
Gordon, Lord George 23, 235, 254, 401
Gordon Riots 23, 208, 219, 254, 350
Goree 189
Gothic revival 464–5
Gough, Strickland 337
Gower, Earl 52, 56, 57, 59, 68, 69

Gower, Lord 44, 50, 51, 52, 69, 75, 78
Grace, Act of (1690) 8
Grafton, Augustus Henry Fitzroy, 3rd Duke of 21, 22, 41, 55, 56–7, 58, 66, 69, 70, 107, 401
Grafton, Charles Fitzroy, 2nd Duke of 48, 49, 76, 155
Graham, Archibald 258
Graham of Claverhouse and Dundee, Viscount 176
Graham, Marquis of 78
Graham, Richard 69
Granby, John Manners, Marquis of 55, 56, 57, 401
Grand Alliance, against France 121, 175–6
Grand Juries (or Grand Inquests) 317
Grand Tour 465
Grange Moor conspiracy 362
Grantham, Lord 57, 58, 59, 60, 73, 75
Granville, Earl *see* Carteret, Lord John
Granville, George (Lord Lansdowne) 45, 52, 77
Grassineau 339
Grattan, Henry 158, 159, 160, 161, 350, 401
Gray, Robert 238
Gray, Thomas 340, 401
Great Seal 5
Great Storm 328
Greek Church 234
Greek revival 465
Green, John 240
Green, Thomas 241
Greenbriar Company 164
Greene, Thomas 239
Greenshields 256
Greenwich Hospital 327, 331, 453
Gregorian calendar 19, 168, 305, 342, 461
Grenada 184, 188
Grenville, George 19, 20, 21, 53, 54–5, 66, 70, 72, 74, 401–2
Grenville, Richard (Earl Temple) 52, 53, 54, 59, 69, 72, 73, 74
Grenville, T. 62, 74
Grenville, William Wyndham 28, 59, 60, 62, 66, 73, 78, 81, 402
Grey, Charles (Viscount Howick) 25, 62, 73, 74, 113, 114, 117, 402
Grey, Edward 240
Grey, Henry 48, 68

Grey, Thomas (Earl of Stamford) 44, 45, 74, 75
Grove, Robert 238
Grub Street 465
Guadaloupe 147, 152, 184, 342
Guastalla 182
Guildford, Lord 46, 75
Guildhall Declaration (1688) 5
Guilford, Battle of (1781) 189
Gurkhas 186
Guy's Hospital 334
Gwyn, Francis 77

Habeas Corpus 465
  suspension of 15, 26, 29, 159, 210, 212, 354, 367
Hackney Phalanx ('Clapton Sect') 236
Hales, Stephen 334
Haliburton, George 257
Halifax, Charles Montagu, 1st Earl of 5, 8, 9, 10, 13, 46, 66
Halifax, George Montagu, 2nd Earl of 21, 51, 52, 53, 54, 55, 57, 69, 70, 71, 74, 75, 76
Halifax, George Savile, 1st Marquis of 68
Halifax, Samuel 239, 261
Hall, John 238
Hall, Timothy 241
Halley, Edmond 330, 332, 342, 402
Hamburg 130
Hamilton, Emma 403
Hamilton, John 258
Hamilton, Sir William 403
Hampden Clubs 114, 117, 465
Handel, George Frederick 333, 335, 337, 339, 341, 353, 403
Hanmer, Sir Thomas 81
Hanover 140, 141, 148, 149, 175, 181, 200, 202, 204
Hanover, Elector of 122, 125, 126
Hanover, Treaty of (1725) 16, 131
Hanoverians 38
Hansard 348
Hanway, Jonas 403
Harcourt, Earl of 76
Harcourt, Edward V. Vernon 243
Harcourt, Lord 67
Hardwicke, Earl of 77
Hardwicke, Lord (Philip Yorke) 48, 49, 50, 51, 67, 235, 455, 467
Hardy, Thomas 26, 116, 117, 210, 211

Hare, Francis 238, 261
Harewood House 343
Hargreaves, James 344, 403
Harley, John 240
Harley, Robert, 1st Earl of Oxford 10, 11, 12, 13, 41, 44, 45–6, 70, 71, 81, 400, 404
Harrington, Lord (William Stanhope) 16, 18, 49, 50, 51, 68, 70, 76, 440
Harris, Howell 259, 337, 404
Harris, John 260
Harrowby, Dudley Ryder, 1st Earl of 61, 62, 63, 64, 68, 73, 76
Hartley, David 340, 404
Harwich, Lord 56, 57, 73
Hastenbeck, Battle of (1757) 182
Hastings, Selina, Countess of Huntingdon see Huntingdon, Countess of
Hastings, Warren 188, 346, 352, 404–5
Havana 184
Hawke, Sir Charles 74
Hawke, Sir E. 56, 57
Hawkesbury, Lord see Liverpool, Charles Jenkinson
Hawkesworth, John 348
Hawkins, Sir John 349
Hawksmoor, Nicholas 331, 333, 337, 405
Hay, Thomas (Earl of Kinnoull) 53, 54, 76
Hay, William 258
Haydn, Joseph 355
Haymarket Theatre 330
Hayter, Thomas 237, 241
Hazlitt, William 405
Health and Morals of Apprentices Act (1802) 306
Hedges, Sir Charles 44, 70, 71
Hedley, William 360
Heights of Abraham, Battle of (1759) 164
Henley, Robert see Northington, Robert Henley, 1st Earl of
Henley, Sir Richard 53, 55
Henry, Cardinal 358
Hepplewhite, George 353, 405
Herbert, Arthur (Earl of Torrington) 73
Herbert, Thomas (Earl of Pembroke) 44, 67, 73, 74
Heron, Sir Robert 115
Herring, Thomas 237, 243, 260, 405
Herschel, William 350, 406

Hertford, Earl of 76
Hervey, George William, Earl of Bristol 56, 69
Hervey, James 341, 406
Hervey, John, Lord Hervey of Ickworth 17, 49, 50, 69
Hesse-Cassel
  loans and subsidies to 19, 137, 200, 201, 202, 203
  treaties and conventions 124, 125, 126, 131, 133–40 *passim*, 150, 151, 152
Hesse-Darmstadt 140, 141, 148, 150, 151, 152, 200, 201
Hesse-Hanau 137, 138
Hickes, George 327, 406
High Church 465
High Constables 315
High Sheriffs 314
Highmore, Susanna 406
Hillsborough, Earl of 55, 56, 57, 71, 75
Hinchcliffe, John 242
Hoadly, Benjamin 234, 237, 240, 242, 260, 337, 407
Hobart, Lord 61, 73
Hobsbawm, E.J. 462
Hogarth, William 337, 339, 341, 342, 407
Hogg, James 356, 407
Holderness, Earl of *see* Darcy, Robert
Holkham Hall 337, 374
Holland 10, 14, 25, 139, 147, 180, 189, 190
  see also Netherlands
Holland House 465
Holland, Lord 62, 69
Holles, John 44, 45, 68
Holstein, Duke of 124
Home House 367
Home, John 342, 407
Hondschoote 189
Hone, W. 212
Hood, Admiral 189
Hooke, Robert 374, 408
Hooper, George 237, 261
Horne, George 235, 241, 349, 408
horse patrols 208–9
Horsfall, William 29
Horsley, Samuel 242, 261
Horticultural Society of London 359
hospital foundations 299–300

Hough, John 240, 241, 242
House of Commons 81–94
House of Lords 95–7
Howard, Charles, 1st Earl of Carlisle 46, 66
Howard, Frederick *see* Carlisle, Frederick Howard
Howard, Henry 46, 47, 75
Howard, John 350, 408
Howe, Earl 60, 74
Howe, John 44
Howe, Sir William 187, 188, 190
Howe, Viscount 55, 56, 57, 58, 74
Howick, Viscount *see* Grey, Charles
Howley, William 237
Hubertusburg, Treaty of (1763) 183
Hudson Bay territory 163, 178
Hudson's Bay Company 162
Humbert, General 27, 160, 190
Hume, David 235, 338, 340, 343, 351, 408
Hume, John 238, 241, 242
Hume, Joseph 310, 311, 408
Humphries, Humphrey 240, 260
Hundred Jury 317
Hungary 133, 134, 136
Hunt, Henry 212, 408–9, 470
Hunt, John and Leigh 303
Hunter, John and William 409
Huntingdon, Countess of 235, 250, 251, 259, 347, 351, 404, 462
Huntingford, George Isaac 239, 240
Huntsman, Benjamin 338
Hurd, Richard 240, 243, 344
Huskisson, W. 64, 75, 409
Hutcheson, Francis 334, 342, 409
Hutchinson, John 335, 409, 466
Hutchinson, William 348
Hutton, James 354, 410
Hutton, Matthew 237, 243, 260
Hyde, Anne 33, 36
Hyde, Henry, 2nd Earl of Clarendon 57, 60, 76, 410
Hyde, Laurence, 1st Earl of Rochester 3, 4, 11, 45, 67, 76, 410
Hyder Ali 186

Islay, Earl of 96
import duties 3, 21, 22, 169, 275
Inchbald, Elizabeth 410
Incitement to Mutiny Act (1797) 211
income tax 27, 29, 272

INDEX 557

Indemnity Act (1727) 234, 248
  (1827) 228
Independents 466
India 139, 164, 185, 186
India Act (1784) 352
Indian tribes 166, 167
Insurrection Act (1796) 159
Inverary Castle 339
Ionian Islands 149, 152
Ireland 8, 9, 23, 26, 27, 82–3, 112, 154–61, 176, 190
  Act of Union with (1801) 27, 108, 160, 474
  coinage 155, 156
  famine 156
  independence 158
  parliament 98–9, 155, 160
  population 289
  religion 262
  representative peers 96–7, 160
  trade 155, 156, 157–8
  Volunteer movement 157, 158
  Whiteboys 344, 475
Iriquois 166
Ironside, Gilbert 238, 240

Jackson, William 241
Jacobin Club 116
Jacobins 466
Jacobites 13, 14, 15, 18, 36–7, 176, 179–80, 217, 328, 332, 338, 466
James II 3–7, 8, 11, 36–7, 154, 176, 253, 410–11
Java 191
Jebb, John 115
Jeffreys, Judge 3
Jenkins, Captain 17
Jenkinson, John Banks 261
Jenner, Edward 356, 411
Jenyns, Soame 343, 349
Jervis, John, Earl of St Vincent 61, 74, 190
Jesuits 257
Jewish Naturalisation Act (1753) 19, 342
Johnson, James 239, 243
Johnson, John 333
Johnson, Samuel 338, 340, 342, 344, 348, 350, 353, 411
Jones, Edward 260
Jones, Griffiths 259
Jones, Inigo 468
Jones, John Paul 188

Jones, Sir William 412
Jones, William, 'of Nayland' 235, 343, 412
Judgement of Death Act (1823) 228
juries 317–18
Justices of the Peace 315–16, 466

Kames, Henry Home 340
Kauffman, Angelika 412
Kay, John 336, 338, 368, 412
Kaye, John 238
Kean, Edmund 412
Keats, John 362, 412
Kedleston Hall 343, 367
keelmen disputes 219, 220, 223, 224, 308, 330, 338
Keene, Edmund 239, 244
Keith, George 413
Kenmure, William Gordon, 6th Viscount 14
Ken(n), Thomas 237, 413
Kennett, White 241
Kent, William 335, 337, 374, 413
Kenwood House 345
Keppel, Augustus, 1st Viscount 58, 59, 74
Keppel, Frederick 239
Kidder, Richard 237
Kildesley, Mark 244
Killala Bay 160, 190
Killiecrankie, Battle of (1689) 176, 326
King, Gregory 328, 413
King, Lord 48, 67
King, Walter 242
King, William 329
King's Friends (Court and Treasury Party) 463
King's Mountain, Battle of (1780) 188
Kippis 340
Kit Cat Club 329, 413, 466
Kloster Kamp 182
Kloster-Seven, Convention of 182
Kneller, Sir Godfrey 327, 329, 413

labour force, distribution of 293
Lagos, Battle of (1693) 175
La Hogue, Battle of (1692) 175
Lake Erie, Battle of (1812) 193
Lake, John 238
Lally-Tollendal, Comte 185
Lamb, Charles 358, 413–14
Lambe, Robert 242

Lambton, George 117
Lamplugh, Thomas 243
Lancaster, Joseph 356, 414
Langley, Batty 335, 339, 414
Lansdowne, Lord (George Granville) 45, 52, 77
Larceny Act (1808) 228, 229
Latitudinarians 466
Lauffeld, Battle of (1747) 182
Lavington, George 235, 239, 341, 414
Law, Edmund 243
Law, George Henry 238, 244
Law, William 335, 341, 414
law and order 207–29
Lawrence, Thomas 353, 414–15
League of Augsburg 10
Leake, Sir John 45, 179
Lechmere, Lord 47, 49, 75
Le Despenser, Lord (Francis Dashwood) 54, 72, 386
Lee, Sir William 51, 72
Lee, William 212
Leeds, Duke of (Thomas Osborne, Earl of Danby) 3, 4, 9, 67
Legge, Edward 241
Legge, Henry Bilson 19, 51, 52, 53, 72
Legge, William *see* Dartmouth, William Legge, Lord
Leng, John 241
Lennox, Charlotte 342, 415
Leslie, Charles 327, 415
Leuze, Battle of (1691) 175
Leveson-Gower, Granville (Earl Gower) 52, 56, 57, 59, 68, 69
Leveson-Gower, John (Lord Gower) 44, 50, 51, 52, 69, 75, 78
Levinz, Baptist 244
Lewis, Matthew Gregory 356
Lexington, Battle of (1775) 23, 170, 187
Liberal Toryism 467
Licensing Act 9, 326
Ligny 193
Ligonier, Earl 54
Lillo, George 336
Limerick
 siege of 154
 Treaty of (1691) 9, 154, 155, 176
Lincoln, Earl of 46, 47, 48, 78
Lindsey, Theophilus 235, 474
linen industry, Ireland 155, 157
Lisle, Samuel 241, 261
literature 326–62 *passim*

Littleton, Sir Thomas 44, 81
Liverpool, Charles Jenkinson, 1st Earl of 58, 60, 61, 75, 76, 77, 415
Liverpool, Robert Banks Jenkinson, 2nd Earl of 27, 28, 29, 42, 61, 63, 64–5, 66, 72, 73, 109, 415–16
Liverpool Night Asylum for the Homeless 298
Liverpool School for the Indigent Blind 298
Lloyd, Charles 241
Lloyd, Humphrey 260
Lloyd, William 240, 241, 242, 260
Lloyd's List 302
loans and subsidies to foreign states 200–4
 see also subsidy treaties
local government 313–23
Locke, John 233, 326, 327, 416, 463
London Corresponding Society 25, 26, 27, 113, 114, 116–17, 211, 354, 444, 470
London Missionary Society 263
London Revolution Society 25, 113, 116
London Society for Promoting Christianity among the Jews 263
Londonderry, seige of 154, 176
Long eighteenth century 467
Long Island, Battle of (1776) 187
Lonsdale, Viscount 68
Lord Lieutenants 314
Lords of Articles, abolition of 8
Lothian, Marquess of 96
Loudon, John 359
Loudoun, Lord 183
Loughborough, Lord 59, 60, 67
Louis XIV, King of France 10, 175, 176
Louis XVI, King of France 25
Louisburg 164, 181, 182, 183
Louisiana 165, 169
Low Church 467
Lowth, Robert 237, 241, 261, 342
Lowther, Henry (Viscount Lonsdale) 49, 69
Loyal Company 164
loyalist associations 210
Lucas, Charles 156
Luddite disturbances 28–9, 222, 308, 358, 462, 467
Lumley, Richard 4, 46, 47, 75
Lunar Society 340
Luxembourg 150

Luxembourg, Duc de 175, 176
Luxmore, John 238, 240, 261
Lyndhurst, Lord 67
Lyttelton, George 51, 72, 416
Lyttleton, Charles 243

McAdam, John Loudon 416
Macaulay, Catherine 344, 416–17
Macaulay, Zachary 461
Macclesfield, Lord 47, 48, 67
Macdonald, Flora 417
machine-breaking 217, 218, 219, 220, 221, 222, 223, 224, 307, 308, 462, 467
see also Luddite disturbances
Mackenzie, Henry 346, 417
Mackintosh, Sir James 354
Macpherson, James 417
Madan, Spencer 238, 242
Maddox, Isaac 242, 261
Madras 163, 182, 185
Madrid, Treaty of (1715) 129, 179
Madrigal Society of London 339
Magdalen College, Oxford 4
Magdalen Hospital, London 263, 342, 403
Mahon, Lord 112, 113
Mainz, Elector of 134
Majendie, Henry William 244, 260
Malaga, Battle of (1702) 178
Mallett, David 338
Malone, Edmond 350
Malplaquet, Battle of (1709) 12, 178, 330
malt tax 16, 216
Malta 143, 190
Malthus, Thomas 356, 417–18
Manchester, Charles Montague, Earl of 71
Manchester Constitutional Society 116
Manchester Guardian 304
Manchester Patriotic Reformation Society 116
Mandeville, Bernard 332, 333, 418
Manila 184
Manley, [Mary] Delarivière 418
Manners, Charles *see* Rutland, Charles, 4th Duke of
Manners, John, Duke of Rutland 49, 75
Manners-Sutton, Charles 81
Manningham, Thomas 238
Mansel, William Lort 238

Mansfield, David Murray, 2nd Earl of 59, 60, 68
Mansfield, William Murray, 1st Earl of 52, 55, 72, 248, 418
Mar, Earl of 13, 14, 179, 390
Maratha 186
Marbella, Battle of (1705) 179
Marchmont, Earl of 96
Margarot, Maurice 210
Maria Theresa 181
Marine Society 298, 403
Markham, William 243, 244
Marlborough, George Spencer, 4th Duke of 55, 60, 69
Marlborough, John Churchill, Duke of 5, 9, 11, 13, 41, 44, 45, 46, 55, 127, 177, 178
Marriage Act (1753) 235, 305, 342, 455, 467
Marsh, Herbert 242, 260
Marshall, William 352, 418
Martin, John 361, 418
Martinique 149, 184
Mary of Modena 4, 5, 36, 419
Mary II, Queen of Britain and Ireland 6, 7, 8, 9, 33, 36, 162, 326, 419
Masham, Abigail 419
Mason, George 244
Mason, William 351, 419
Massachusetts 162, 165, 166, 168, 170
Masséna, André 192
Master and Servant Act (1747) 305
Mather, Cotton 335
Mauduit 344
Mauritius 191
Mawson, Matthias 238, 239, 260
Melville, Henry Dundas, 1st Viscount 24, 58, 59, 60, 61, 72, 73, 74, 389
Mendip, Lord 54, 55, 58, 77
Metcalf, John 419
Methodist Bible Christian Society 361
Methodist Missionary Society 361
Methodists 216, 234, 236, 250–2, 259, 339, 347, 355, 357, 359, 462
Methuen, Charles 46
Methuen, Paul 71
Metropolitan Police Act (1829) 213
Mew(s), Peter 237
Middlesex Justices Act (1792) 210
Middleton, Conyers 341
Mildert, William Van 243, 260
Mildmay, Benjamin 49, 75

Militia Act (1757) 20, 209, 217
Mill, James 360, 362, 420
Minden, Battle of (1759) 182, 342
Minorca 19, 162, 163, 164, 179, 184, 189, 190, 342
Minto, Lord 62
missionary and benevolent societies 263
  see also individual societies
Mitford, Sir John 81
Modena 135, 136
Modena, Mary of 4, 5, 36, 419
Mohammed Ali 164
Moira, Earl of 62
Molyneux, William 328, 420
monarchy 33–8
Monk, James Henry 240
Monmouth, Duke of 3
Monongahela River 183
Monro, Alexander 257
Mons 175, 178
Monson, Lord 49, 50, 51, 75
Montagu, Charles *see* Halifax, Charles Montagu, 1st Earl of
Montagu, Elizabeth 420
Montagu, George *see* Halifax, George Montagu, 2nd Earl of
Montagu, John *see* Sandwich, John Montagu
Montagu, Lady Mary Wortley 420
Montague, Charles, Earl of Manchester 71
Montcalm, Field Marshal 164, 183, 184
Montevideo 191
Montgomery, Earl of 68
Montreal 164, 184, 187, 344
Montrose, Duke of 46, 61, 75, 96
Moore, John 237, 239, 241, 260
Moore, Sir John 192
Moore, Thomas 46, 78
moral economy 467
Moravian mission 248, 335
More, Hannah 353, 354, 357, 358, 421, 454, 461
Morland, George 355, 421
Morning Post 303, 346
Morocco 128, 131, 132, 133, 135, 136, 138, 140, 143, 203
Morris, Roger 339
Moss, Charles 237, 241, 261
'Mug-house' riots 215
Muir, James 210

Mulgrave, Lord 61, 62, 63, 64, 73, 74, 76, 78
municipal corporations 320–3
Munster, Bishop of 123, 124
Murray, George 242, 244, 261, 421
Murray, Sir James 96
Murray, William (Earl of Mansfield) 52, 59, 248, 418
Musgrave, Thomas 243
music 327, 333–49 *passim*, 353, 355, 359, 361
mutinies 26, 221, 352, 356
Mutiny Act (1780) 158
Mysore 186

Namierites 467
Namur, seige of 9, 176
Naples 146, 148
Napoleon I, Napolean Bonaparte 27, 28, 29, 152, 192, 193
Nash, John 359, 361, 421, 465
Nash, Richard (Beau Nash) 421
national debt 271–2, 326, 468
National Society for Educating the Poor in the Principles of the Established Church 359, 371
National Society for Promoting Education 298
navy, strength and cost of 199
Needham 340
Neerwinden 175
Negapatam 188, 189
Nelson, Horatio 27, 190, 191, 422
Nelson, Robert 331, 422
Nepal 186
Netherlands
  Austrian 129, 140, 182
  treaties and conventions with 121–41 *passim*, 147–52 *passim*, 175, 177, 188
  United Provinces of the 129
  see also Holland
New East India Company 162
New England 162, 166
New Orleans 194
New York 166, 167
Newcastle, Duke of *see* Pelham, Thomas Pelham Holles
Newcome, Richard 260, 261
Newcomen, Thomas 332, 422
Newfoundland 163, 166, 178, 189
newspapers and the press 9, 301–4
Newton, Isaac 330, 334, 337, 422

INDEX 561

Newton, Thomas 238, 351
Newtonians 468
Ney, Michel 193
Nicholas, Edward 46, 78
Nicolson, William 243
Nile, Battle of the (1798) 27, 190, 356
Nine Years War 326
Noblemen's and Gentlemen's catch club 345
Nollekens, Joseph 351, 355
non-jurors 234, 468
nonconformists *see* dissenters
Nore naval mutiny 26, 221, 356
Norris, Henry Handley 236, 328
North, Brownlow 237, 240, 243
North, Francis 46, 75
North, Lord 108, 170, 423
   Chancellor of Exchequer 21, 22, 55, 56, 57–8
   First Lord of the Treasury 22, 41, 57–8, 66, 107
   Home Secretary 24, 59, 72
   Paymster-General 78
Northington, Robert Henley, 1st Earl of 53, 54, 55, 56, 67, 68, 77
The North Briton 20, 21, 111, 302, 344, 451
Northumberland, Earl of 76
Norton, Sir Fletcher 81
Norwich Society of Artists 357
Nottingham, Earl of *see* Finch, Daniel
Nottingham Peace Act 212
Nova Scotia 163, 164, 178

Oath of Association (1696) 9
The Observer 303, 354
occasional conformity 11, 13, 14, 233, 234, 247, 248, 331, 332, 468
O'Coigley, Rev. James 211
O'Connell, Daniel 161, 423
O'Connor, Arthur 211
Offences against the Person Act (1828) 228
Oglethorpe, General James 163, 167, 423
Ohio 164
Ohio Company 164, 168
Old Corruption 468
Old Pretender *see* Stuart, James Francis Edward
Onslow, Arthur 81
Onslow, Sir Richard 46, 71, 81

Orange, Prince of 142, 201, 203
Orange, William of *see* William of Orange
Orange Society 159
Ordnance Survey of England 352
Orford, Earl of *see* Russell, Edward; Walpole, Robert
Ormond, Duke of *see* Butler, James
Orthez 193
Osbaldeston, Richard 237, 243
Osborne, Thomas (Earl of Danby and Duke of Leeds) 3, 4, 9, 67
Ossian 344
Ostend East India Company 16
Osterley Park 345, 367
Ottley, Adam 261
Oudenarde, Battle of (1708) 12, 177, 330
Owen, Robert 308, 309, 356, 360, 362, 423–4
Oxford, Earl of *see* Harley, Robert

Paine, James 424
Paine, Thomas 25, 113, 115, 210, 348, 354, 424
Paley, William 235, 236, 352, 355, 357, 424
Palladio, Andrea 468
Palmer, John 353
Palmer, Thomas Fyshe 210
Palmerston, Viscount 64, 78
Pardo, Convention of (1739) 17, 338
Paris, First Treaty of (1763) 21, 169, 344
parish vestry 320
parishes 313, 318–20
Parker, Richard 211
Parker, Sir Hyde 191
Parker, Thomas 67
parliamentary reform 111–17, 159, 160
   Pitt's proposals 24, 112
Parma 150, 151, 152, 180, 182
Parry, John 303
Parsons, John 242
Partition Treaties 10, 123, 328
Paterson, John 258
Patrick, Simon 238, 239
patronage 93–4
Payne Knight, Richard 424–5
Peacock, Thomas Love 360
Pearce, Zachary 242, 260
Peel, Sir Robert 29, 30, 64
Peerage Bill (1719) 15, 468–9

Pelham, George 238, 239, 241
Pelham, Henry 16, 18, 19, 41, 49, 50, 51, 66, 72, 76, 77, 78, 106, 425
Pelham, Thomas Pelham Holles, 1st Duke of Newcastle 16, 17, 18, 19, 20, 41, 49, 50, 51–2, 53, 55, 66, 69, 70, 71, 106, 425
Pembroke, Earl of 44, 67, 73, 76
Peninsular War 192–3
Penn, William 165, 166, 425
Pennant, Thomas 344
Pennsylvania 165, 166
Pentrich 'rising' 29, 115, 212, 223
Peploe, Samuel 244
Pepperell, William 163, 167
Perceval, Spencer 28, 29, 42, 63–4, 66, 76, 222, 356, 425–6
Percy, Hugh 242, 244
Percy, Thomas 426
Persia 143, 145, 147
Peterloo 'Massacre' 29, 212, 224, 362, 469
Petty, Lord H. 62, 72
Petty Sessions 316
Petty, William *see* Shelburne, Earl of
Phelipps, Robert 75
Philanthropic Society (for Children) 298
Philharmonic Society 361
Philip V, King of Spain 176
philosophy and science 326–62 *passim*
Phipps, Sir William 165
Piacenza 180, 182
Piedmont 189
Pierrepoint, Evelyn (Duke of Kingston-Upon-Hull) 46, 47, 48, 67, 68, 69
pig iron production 279
Piozzi, Hester Thrale 426
Pitt, William (the Elder, Earl of Chatham) 17, 18, 19, 20, 21, 22, 41, 52–3, 55–6, 71, 78, 170, 183, 426
Pitt, William (the Younger) 24–5, 26, 27, 108, 236, 303, 356, 427
   Chancellor of the Exchequer 58, 59–60, 61–2, 72
   First Lord of the Treasury 41, 42, 59–60, 61–2, 66
   parliamentary reform proposals 24, 112
   'Sinking Fund' 24–5
   resignation of 27, 356
   death of 28

Place, Francis 310, 311
Plains of Abraham, Battle of (1759) 20
Plassey, Battle of (1757) 164, 185, 342
Plattsburg 194
pluralism 469
Poland 127, 134, 136
Police Bill (1785) 209
policing 208, 213
The Political Register (Cobbett) 29, 114, 303, 356, 360, 382
Polwarth, Lord 96
Pondicherry 163, 185
Poor Laws 469
poor relief 295, 305, 472
   see also Speenhamland system
Pope, Alexander 330, 332, 333, 334, 336, 427
Popham, Captain 186
'Popish Plot' 411
populations 289–92
porcelain production 339, 341, 343
Porden, William 359
Port Mahan 189
Port Royal 166
Porteous Riots 17, 216, 336
Porteus, Beilby 237, 244, 427
Portland, Duke of 24, 26, 27, 28, 42, 59, 60, 61, 63, 64, 66, 68, 72, 77
Porto Bello 163, 181
Porto Novo 186
Portugal 192
   loans and subsidies to 201, 202, 203
   treaties and conventions 125, 137, 140, 144, 145, 148, 150, 151, 162, 178, 179, 188
Potter, John 237, 241, 427
Potwalloper 469
Poulett, Earl 45
Powle, Henry 81
Powlett, Charles (Duke of Bolton) 47, 48, 76
Poynings' Law 158
Pragmatic Army 181
Pragmatic Sanction 18
Pratt, Sir John 72
Presbyterians 12, 248, 256, 262, 333
press 9, 301–4
press-gangs 221
Prestopans, Battle of (1745) 180
Price, Richard 113, 116, 248–9, 342, 346, 348, 352, 427–8
Price, Uvedale 355, 428

Priestley, Joseph 220, 235, 249, 346, 348, 350, 351, 354, 428
Princeton, Battle of (1777) 187
Princeton College 167
Pringle, Robert 77
Printers' Case (1771) 22, 111, 303
Prior, Matthew 428
prison riots 222
Proclamation Society 451
production 278–80
Property Qualification Act (1711) 13
Protestant Association 23, 254
Protestant dissenters 4, 234, 247–9, 337, 463, 473–4
Protestant Union against Catholic Emanicipation 434
Protestant Yeomanry 159
Prussia 189, 193
  loans and subsidies to 124, 141, 144, 146, 148, 182, 200, 202, 203, 204
  treaties and conventions 16, 19, 20, 123–6 *passim*, 130–6 *passim*, 139, 140, 141, 145–53 *passim*, 182, 183, 188
public petitions 83
'pudding-time' 470
Pulteney, J.M. 63, 78
Pulteney, William, 1st Earl of Bath 16, 18, 41, 46, 51, 77, 428–9
Purcell, Henry 327

Quadruple Alliance (1718–19) 14, 15, 129, 332
Quakers 4, 233, 247, 248, 263
Quakers' Retreat 263
Quartering Act (1774) 170
Quarterly Review 358
Quatre Bras 193
Quebec 20, 164, 165, 184, 187, 342
Quebec Act (1774) 22, 170
Queen Anne's Bounty 11, 233, 331, 368, 470
Queensbury, Duke of 3
Quiberon Bay, Battle of (1759) 184

Radcliffe, Ann 352, 354, 429
Radcliffe, John 429
Radcliffe Camera, Oxford 339
Radcliffe Observatory 349
radicals 470
Raeburn, Henry 361, 429
'rage of party' 470

Raikes, Robert 351
Ramillies, Battle of (1706) 12, 177, 330
Ramsay, Allan 334, 345, 429
Ramsay, James 258
Randolph, John 237, 241, 260
Ray, John 327, 429
Recognition, Act of (1690) 8
Recorders 322
recruiting riots 221
rectors 470
recusants 470
reform societies and clubs 115–17
  see also individual societies and clubs
'Regency Crisis' 25, 108, 471
Reid, Thomas 344
Relief of the Infant Poor 298
religion 3, 12, 233–63, 327–39 *passim*, 343–61 *passim*
  see also Catholics/Catholicism; Church of England
Religious Tract Society 236, 263, 357
Renunciation Act (1783) 158
Repton, Humphry 355, 359, 430
Réunion 191
Revenue Act (1767) 21, 169
reversionary interest 471
'Revolution Societies' 113, 116, 352
Reynolds, Sir Joshua 347, 349, 353, 430
Reynolds, Richard 240, 260
Ricardo, David 360, 430
Richardson, Jonathan 430
Richardson, Samuel 338, 340, 342, 430
Richmond, Duke of 55, 58, 59, 60, 71, 77, 112
Richmond, Richard 244
Rickman, Thomas 361
Rigby, R. 78
Riot Act (1715) 14, 207–8, 209, 332, 471
riots and disturbances 214–25, 307, 308, 360
Rivers, Earl 45
Robertson, William 342, 430
'Robinocracy' 471
Robinson, F.J. 64, 72, 75
Robinson, John 45, 68, 237, 238
Robinson, Sir Thomas 52, 71
Rochambeau, Comte de 189
Rochefort expedition 20, 184
Rochester, Earl of *see* Hyde, Laurence
Rochford, Earl of 56, 57, 70, 71

Rockingham, Charles Watson Wentworth, 2nd Marquis of 21, 24, 41, 55, 58, 66, 107, 431
Rodney, George Brydges 188
Rolica 192
Romanticism 471
Romilly, Samuel 431
Romney, George 431
Ronkesley, William 212
Rooke, Admiral 178
Rose, Alexander 258
Rose, Arthur 258
Rose, G. 63, 64, 78, 303
Ross, John 239
'rotten' boroughs 471
Roubilliac, Louis-François 431
Roucoux, Battle of (1746) 181
Rowe, Elizabeth 431
Rowe, Nicholas 328, 330, 431–2
Rowlandson, Thomas 351, 432
Roxburghe, Duke of 46, 47, 48
Royal Academy 347
Royal Artillery band 345
Royal Dublin Society 337
Royal Mail 352
Royal Marriages Act (1772) 346
Royal National Life-Boat Institution 298
Royal Society of Musicians of Great Britain 339
Royal Society for the Prevention of Cruelty to Animals 298
Russell, Edward, Earl of Orford 4, 9, 44, 45, 46, 73, 74
Russell, John, 4th Duke of Bedford 18, 50, 51, 52, 53, 54, 55, 68, 69, 74, 76, 218
Russell, Richard 340
Russia
  loans and subsidies to 148, 201, 202, 203, 204
  treaties and conventions 19, 27, 133, 135, 137, 140–53 *passim*, 183, 188, 193
Rutland, Charles Manners, 4th Duke of 59, 60, 69, 77
Rutland, John, Duke of 49, 75
Ryder, D. 60, 61, 63, 78
Ryder, Henry 240
Ryder, R. 72
Rymer, Thomas 330
Rysbrack, John Michael 337, 432

Ryswick, Peace of (1697) 10, 122, 162, 165, 176, 328

Sacheverell, Dr Henry 12–13, 215, 233, 234, 247, 330, 331, 432
Sackville, Lionel Cranfield, Duke of Dorset 50, 51, 68, 76, 156
Sackville-Germain, Lord 57, 73, 75
sailors, disturbances among 26, 217, 218, 221, 307, 356
St Eustatius 189
St George's Fields, 'massacre' of 21, 22, 218
St John, Henry *see* Bolingbroke, Henry St John
St John's Smith Square 331
St Kitts 162, 163, 178, 189
St Leger, Barry 187
St Lucia 164, 184, 188, 189
St Martin 189
St Martin-in-the-Fields 335
St Mary Le Strand 333
St Paul's Cathedral 329, 331, 453
St Petersburg, Treaty of (1762) 183
St Vincent 164, 184, 188
St Vincent, John Jervis, Earl of 61, 74, 190
The Saints, Battle of (1782) 189, 350
Salamanca 192
Salbai, Treaty of 186
Salem 165, 326
San Domingo 190
Sancroft, William, Archbishop of Canterbury 4, 233, 236, 432–3
Sandwich, John Montagu, 4th Earl of 51, 55, 57, 70, 74, 433
Sandys, Lord 49, 53, 54, 72, 75
Saratoga 23, 188, 350
Sardinia 179, 180
  loans and subsidies to 148, 200, 201
  treaties and conventions 130–5 *passim*, 140, 146, 148–52 *passim*
Saunders, Sir Charles 74
Savannah 163, 167, 188
Savoy 125, 175
Sawbridge, John 111
Saxe, Marshal de 181, 182
Saxe-Gotha, Duke of 125
Saxony 148, 150, 151, 152, 175, 182, 183
Saxony, Elector of 122, 126, 128
Scheemakers, Pieter 339

Schism Act (1714) 13, 14, 155, 234, 247, 248, 332, 333, 471
Schomberg, Marshal 154
schools 294
science and philosophy 326–62 *passim*
Scone Palace 357
Scot and Lot 471
Scotland 82, 105, 106, 176
   Act of Union with (1707) 12, 103, 330, 474
   Disarming of Highlands 19
   franchise 84, 92, 93, 112
   patronage 94
   population 289
   religion 4, 256–8, 327
   representation in parliament 95–6, 112, 113
Scott, Sarah 433
Scott, Sir Walter 356, 358, 360, 362, 433–4
Scottish Convention (1689) 7, 8
Scottish Parliament 3, 4, 11, 12
Scriblerus Club 368
Seabury, Samuel 257, 353
seaman's strikes 218, 219, 220, 223, 224, 307, 308
Seaton Delaval 333, 445
Secker, Thomas 235, 237, 238, 241, 434
Secrecy, Committees of 210, 211, 212
secret service money, disbursement of 94
Security, Act of (1703) 11
Sedgemoor, Battle of (1685) 3
sedition 210, 211, 212
Seditious Meetings Act (1795) 211, (1817) 212
Selkirk, Earl of 96
Senegal 189
Sensibility movement 472
Septennial Act (1716) 14, 16, 332
Seringapatam 186
Settlement Act (1697) 305
Settlement, Act of (1701) 10, 328, 472
Settlements and Removals Act (1662) 472
'Seven Bishops', arrest and trial of 4, 327
Seven Years War 19, 20, 21, 164, 168, 182–5, 342
Seville, Treaty of (1729) 16, 334
Seward, Anna 434
Seymour, Charles (Duke of Somerset) 67, 438

Shaftesbury, Anthony Ashley Cooper, 3rd Earl of 330, 434
Sharp, Granville 236, 434
Sharp, John 243
Sheffield, John Sheffield, Duke of Buckingham 15, 44, 67, 68
Sheffield Park 349
Sheffield Society for Constitutional Information 116
Shelburne, Earl of 24, 56, 58–9, 66, 71, 72, 426
Shelley, Mary 360, 435
Shelley, Percy Bysshe 360, 362, 435
Shenstone, William 341, 435
Sheraton, Thomas 355, 435
Sheridan, Richard Brinsley 62, 115, 117, 310, 348, 350, 435
Sheriffmuir, Battle of (1715) 179
sheriffs 314–15
Sherlock, Thomas 237, 242, 260, 337, 435–6
Shipley, Jonathan 260, 261, 436
Shippen, William 436
shipping 286, 362
ships taken or destroyed (1793–1814) 194
Shirley, William 163
Shovell, Sir Cloudesley 179
Shrewsbury, Earl of *see* Talbot, Charles, Earl of Shrewsbury
Shuckford 335
Sicily 129, 140, 142, 144, 145, 149, 151, 180, 188, 202, 203
Siddons, Sarah 436
Sidmouth, Viscount *see* Addington, Henry
Silesia 181, 182
Simeon, Charles 235, 436
Sindhia of Gwalior 186
'Sinking Fund' 24–5
'Six Acts' (1819) 212, 362, 367, 472
'Six Nations' Indian Confederacy 168
Skirving, William 210
slave trade 28, 148, 149, 150, 163, 236, 263, 358
Sloane, Sir Hans 436
Smallbrooke, Richard 240, 261
Smallwell, Edward 241, 261
Smalridge, George 238
Smart, Christopher 342, 344, 437
Smirke, Sir Robert 465
Smith, Adam 342, 348, 437

566　INDEX

Smith, John 43, 71, 81
Smith, Sidney 437
Smith, Thomas 243
Smithfield Club 356
Smollett, Tobias 340, 342, 344, 346, 437–8
Smyth, J. 61
Soane, Sir John 353, 438, 465
social structure of populations 291–2
Society for the Abolition of the Slave Trade 263
Society of Antiquaries 331
Society of Arts 342
Society for Bettering the Condition of the Poor 298, 451
Society for Constitutional Information 112, 115–16, 444, 472
Society for the Conversion of the Jews 434
Society of Dilettanti 337
Society of the Friends of the People 113, 117
Society for Promotion of Christian Knowledge (SPCK) 233, 235, 263, 298, 329, 442, 472
Society for the Propogation of the Gospel in Foreign Parts (SPG) 233, 263, 298, 329, 442, 472
Society for the Reformation of Manners 233, 327
Society of the Supporters of the Bill of Rights 111, 115, 169, 443
Society for the Suppression of Vice 263, 357
Society of United Irishmen 159, 354
Socinianism 472
Somers, Lord 9, 10, 44, 67
Somerset, Charles Seymour, 6th Duke of 67, 438
Somerset, Lord 78
Somerset House 349
Somersett case 346
Sophia, Electress of Hanover 10, 12, 472
Soult, Marshal 192
South America 191
'South Sea Bubble' 15, 332, 396, 472
South Sea Company 15, 16, 104, 163, 472
Southcott, Joanna 357, 361, 438
Southey, Robert 438–9
Spa Fields conspirators 212, 360

Spain
　and American War of Independence 188, 189
　Assiento with 128, 129, 163
　and Convention of Pardo 17
　loans and subsidies to 202, 203
　and Peninsular War 192
　and the Quadruple Alliance 15, 180
　succession of 123
　treaties and conventions 17, 24, 122, 124, 126, 129–52 *passim*, 175, 179
　and Treaty of Versailles 24
　war with 11, 14, 16, 17, 23, 26, 166, 167, 181, 184, 188, 189
　see also 'War of Jenkins' Ear'; War of the Spanish Succession
Sparke, Bowyer Edward 239, 244
The Spectator 302
Speenhamland system 306, 354, 469, 472
Spence, Thomas 348, 354, 439
Spencer, Charles, 3rd Earl of Sunderland 12, 13, 14, 15, 41, 44, 46, 47–8, 66, 67, 68, 71, 76, 103, 439
Spencer, Earl 60, 62, 72, 74
Spencer, Robert, 2nd Earl of Sunderland 3, 10
spinning machines
　Crompton's mule 350, 385
　spinning jenny 344, 403
Spitalfields weavers 215, 217, 218, 305, 307
Spithead naval mutiny 26, 221, 356
Sprat, Thomas 242
Squire, Samuel 261
Stage Licensing Act (1737) 338
Stamford, Earl of (Thomas Grey) 44, 45, 74, 75
Stamp Act (1712) 302, (1765) 21, 169, 344
Stanhope, George 327, 331
Stanhope, James Stanhope, 1st Earl 13, 14, 15, 41, 46–8, 66, 71, 179, 439–40
Stanhope, Philip Dormer, 4th Earl of Chesterfield 50, 51, 70, 76, 156, 348, 440
Stanhope, William, 1st Earl of Harrington 16, 18, 49, 50, 51, 68, 70, 76, 440
Stanley, Edward 241

Stanley, James (Earl of Derby) 44, 75
Stealing from Bleaching Grounds Act (1811) 228
Stealing in Shops Act (1820) 228
steam engines 348, 360, 422
steel 338
Steelboy disturbances 346
Steele, Sir Richard 329, 330
Steele, T. 78
Steenkerke, Battle of (1692) 175
Stephen, James 236, 461
Stephenson, George 360
Sterne, Laurence 346, 440
Stevens, William 236
Stewart, William 261
Stillingfleet, Edward 242
Stoddart, Dr John 303
'storming the closet' 473
Stormont, Viscount 57, 59, 68, 70
Stourhead 333
Strange, Lord 54, 55, 56, 57, 76
Stratford, Nicholas 244
Strawberry Hill 341
Strickland, Sir William 77
Strype, John 331
Stuart, Charles Edward (Young Pretender) 18, 19, 36, 180, 344, 441, 469–70
Stuart, James Francis Edward (Old Pretender) 11, 12, 14, 36, 180, 344, 411, 469
Stuart, John *see* Bute, John Stuart
Stuart, Peter and Daniel 303
Stuart, William 261
Stuarts 38, 358
Stubbs, George 345, 347, 353, 441
subscription controversy 473
subsidy treaties 122, 124, 137, 141, 142, 143, 144, 145, 146, 148, 149
Suffolk and Berkshire, Earl 57, 69, 70
'Suffolk Resolves' 170
Sumner, Charles Richard 237, 260
Sumner, John Bird 244
Sunday School Society 298
Sunday School Union 263
Sunday schools 351
Sunderland, Earl of *see* Spencer, Charles; Spencer, Robert
Surajah Dowlah 185
Surveyor of the Highways 319–20
Sutton, Chas. Manners 237
Sutton, George Manners 241

Sweden
 loans and subsidies to 144, 145, 202, 203, 204
 treaties and conventions 122–5 *passim*, 130, 131, 133, 134 *passim*, 151, 188
Swift, Jonathan 155, 156, 330, 334, 441
Swiss Confederation 148, 150
Switzer, Stephen 333
Switzerland 149, 151, 153
Sydall, Elias 239, 261
Sydney, Henry 69
Sydney, Lord (Thomas Townshend) 24, 56, 58, 59, 60, 72, 75, 77, 78
Syon House 367

Talavera, Battle of (1809) 192
Talbot, Catherine 441
Talbot, Charles, Earl of Shrewsbury 4, 8, 9, 13, 45, 69, 70, 76, 155
Talbot, Charles, Lord Talbot 48, 67
Talbot, Earl 77
Talbot, William 241, 242, 243
Talents, Ministry of all the 28, 42, 62, 109, 358, 473
Talman 331
Tanner, Thomas 261
Tate, Nahum 329, 441
Taylor, Anne and Jane 359
Taylor, John Edward 304
tea 21, 22, 169, 170
Tea Act (1773) 22, 170
Teignmouth, Lord 236
Telford, Thomas 359, 362, 442
'Temple Bar, Battle of' 218
Temple, Richard Grenville, Earl 52, 53, 54, 59, 69, 72, 73, 74
Temple, William 326, 459
Tenison, Thomas 236, 240, 442
Terrick, Richard 237, 241
Test Acts 3, 4, 17, 116, 155, 234, 235, 236, 248, 468, 473
Thatched House Society 298
theatre riots 222
Thelwall, John 210, 211, 354, 442
Thirty-Nine Articles 473
Thistlewood, Arthur 213, 442
Thomas, John 237, 240, 241, 242, 261
Thomas, William 242
Thomson, George 337
Thomson, James 334, 336, 338, 340, 442
Thornhill, Sir James 331, 333, 442

Thornton, Henry 236, 461
Thurlow, Lord 57, 58, 59, 67
Thurlow, Thomas 240
Tierney, George 62, 114, 117
Tijou, J. 327
Tillotson, John 236, 443
The Times 303, 352
tin 279
Tindal, Matthew 234, 337, 443
Tippoo Sahib 186
tithes 473
Tobago 164, 189
Toland, John 247, 329, 443
Toleration Act (1689) 7, 8, 233, 247, 253, 326, 470, 473–4
Toleration Act for Scotland (1712) 256
Tomline, George Pretyman 237
Tone, Theobold Wolfe 27, 159, 160, 354, 355, 443, 474
Tooke, Rev. John Horne 115, 210, 443–4
Toplady, Augustus 349
Tories 474
Toulon 189
Toulouse 193
Tournai 181
Tourville, Admiral de 175
town clerks 322
Townshend, Charles, 2nd Viscount 13–14, 15, 46, 47, 48, 49, 67, 70, 444
Townshend, Charles (1725–67) 21, 53, 54, 55, 56, 72, 75, 77, 78, 169, 444
Townshend, George, 4th Viscount 76
Townshend, Thomas (Lord Sydney) 24, 56, 58, 59, 60, 72, 75, 77, 78
trade 277
trade unions 307–12
Trafalgar, Battle of (1805) 27, 191, 358
transport 281–6
Transportation Act (1718) 208
Traverse or felons' Juries 318
Treasonable Practices and Seditious Meetings Act (1795) 211, 354
treaties 121–53
  see also particular treaties
Treby, George 77
Trelawney, Jonathan 237, 238
Trenchard, Sir John 69, 70, 332, 444
Trenton 187
Treves, Elector of 124, 127
Trevor, Lord 48, 68, 69

Trevor, Richard 243, 261
Trevor, Sir John 81
Trewlawney, Jonathan 239
Trichinopoly, seige of 164, 185
Triennial Act (1694) 9, 326
Trimmer, Sarah 444–5
Trimnell, Charles 237, 241
Trincomalee 186, 188
Trinidad 190
Triple Alliance (1717) 14, 129, 180
Tripoli 122, 129, 132, 136, 142, 145, 149
Trotter, Catherine 445
Trumbull, Sir William 70
Tull, Jethro 328, 336, 445
Tunis 123, 129, 136, 145, 146, 149, 150
Turkey 142, 144, 150
Turner, Francis 239
Turner, J.M.W. 359, 361, 445
Turnpike Acts 285
  see also anti-turnpike riots
Turpin, Dick 338
Tuscany 132, 150, 151, 152, 180
Tuscaroras 166
The Two Sicilies 142, 144, 145, 149, 151, 188
Tyler, John 260
Tyrconnel, Earl of 176

Ulster rising 160
Union, Act of (Ireland) (1801) 27, 108, 160, 356, 474
Union, Act of (Scotland) (1707) 12, 103, 330, 474
Union Jack 12
Union for Parliamentary Reform 114, 117
Unitarian Relief Act (1813) 249
Unitarians 233, 235, 247, 248, 349, 359, 474
United Britons 211
United Company of Merchants of England 163
United Englishmen 211
United Irishmen 159, 160, 211, 474
United Provinces 129
United Scotsmen 211
United States of America *see* America, North
universities 91
Unlawful Oaths Act (1797) 211, 307
Ushant 190

INDEX 569

utilitarianism 474–5
Utrecht, Treaty of (1713) 13, 163, 166, 178, 332
Utrecht, Treaty of (1717) 14

Vanbrugh, Sir John 328, 329, 331, 333, 335, 405, 445
Vansittart, N. (Lord Bexley) 64, 72
Vaudreuil, Marquis de 184
Vellinghausen 183
Vendôme, Duc de 177, 178
Venn, Henry 345
Venn, John 236
Vernon, Admiral Edward 163, 181, 445–6
Vernon, Edward Venables 243
Vernon, James 70, 71
Versailles, Treaty of (1783) 24, 138, 189, 352
vicars 475
Vienna, Congress of (1820) 151
Vienna, Peace of (1815) 29, 360
Vienna, Treaty of (1731) 16, 132
Villeroi, Duc de 176
Villiers, Edward 70
Vimeiro 192
Vinegar Hill 160, 190
Virginia 167, 168
Vitoria 193
Voltaire 336

Waddington, Edward 238
Wade, George 446
Wade, John 446
Wager, Charles 49, 74
wages and wage disputes 218, 222, 223, 224, 307, 308, 309–11
Wake, William 237, 240, 329, 446
Walcheren expedition 28, 191
Walcourt, Battle of (1689) 175
Waldeck, Prince of 137
Wales 82
  franchise 83–4, 91
  religion 259–61, 339
Wales, Frederick Lewis, Prince of 17, 340, 394, 396–7
Wales, George, Prince of (Prince Regent) 25, 28, 358
  see also George IV
Walker, John 333
Walker, Thomas 116
Wallace, T. 65

Walpole, Horace 341, 344, 345, 347, 349, 446, 465
Walpole, Robert 16–18, 45, 104, 105, 106, 248, 396, 446–7
  Chancellor of Exchequer 48, 71, 72
  First Lord of Treasury 14, 41, 46, 48–9, 66
  imprisonment of 13
  Paymaster-General 15, 78
  resignation of 18, 338
  Secretary at War 12, 44, 77
Wandiwash, Battle of (1760) 164, 185
War of the Austrian Succession 19, 181–2, 338
'War of Jenkins' Ear' 17, 163, 181, 338
War of Polish Succession 336
War of Spanish Succession 162, 166, 176–9, 328, 468
Warburg, battle of (1760) 182
Warburton, William 234, 239, 337, 447
Ward, Edward 328
Ward, James 361
Ward, Seth 242
Ward, William 244
Warren, John 260, 261
Warton, Joseph 338
Warton, Thomas 348
Washington, George 168, 183, 187, 189
Waterland, Daniel 337, 447
Waterloo Bridge 359
Waterloo campaign 29, 193, 360
Watson, Joshua 236
Watson, Richard 260, 448
Watson, Thomas 261
Watson, William 350
Watt, James 348, 448
Watt, Robert 211
Watts, Isaac 331, 333, 448
Waugh, John 243
Wayne, John 237
Wedgwood, Josiah 345, 347, 349, 448
Wellesley, Arthur, 1st Duke of Wellington 29, 63, 64, 73, 186, 192, 193, 448
Wellesley, Lord 63, 73
Wellesley Pole, W. 65
Wesley, Charles 250, 449
Wesley, John 156, 234, 235, 250, 251, 337, 339, 341, 347, 348, 355, 449, 459
Wesley, Samuel (1662–1735) 449
Wesley, Samuel (1766–1837) 449

Wesley, Susannah 449–50
Wesleyan Missionary Society 263
West, Benjamin 345, 347, 450
West Indies 190
  see also individual countries
West, Thomas 350
Westminster Abbey 337
Westminster Watch Act (1735) 208, 336
Westmorland, Earl of 60, 61, 62, 63, 64, 69, 77
Westmorland, Thomas Fane, Earl of 48, 49, 75
Weston, Stephen 239
Weymouth, Viscount 44, 56, 57, 70, 71, 75, 76
Wharton, Thomas 9, 46, 68, 76
wheat prices 276
Wheatley, Francis 355
Whig Club 159
Whig 'Junto' 9, 101
Whigs 475
Whiston, William 331
Whitaker, John 348
Whitbread, Charles 117
White, Gilbert 352
White, Thomas 241
Whiteboys 344, 475
Whitefield, George 234, 235, 250, 339, 341, 404, 450, 459, 462
Whitelocke, General 191
White's Club 326
Whitworth, Earl 77
Wilberforce, Samuel 237
Wilberforce, William 236, 357, 450–1, 461
Wilcocks, Joseph 239, 242
Wilkes, John 20, 21, 22, 107, 111, 115, 218, 302, 344, 451
Wilkins, David 339
Wilkins, William 465
Willes, Edward 237, 261
William of Orange (William III) 4–7, 8, 10–11, 33, 154, 162, 175, 176, 326, 328, 451
  invasion by 4–6
  proclaimed King 6, 8
  death of 11, 177, 328
Williams, Dr 248
Williams, John 238
Williams, Peter 259
Williams, Richard 259
Williams Wynn, C.W. 64

Willis, Richard 237, 239, 242
Wilmington, Earl of (Spencer Compton) 18, 48, 49, 66, 68, 69, 78, 81
Wilson, Christopher 238
Wilson, Thomas 244
Winchilsea, Ann Finch, Countess of 332, 451–2
Winchilsea, Earl of see Finch, Daniel
Winckelmann, J.J. 465
Windham, W. 60, 62, 73, 77, 452
window tax 24
Windsor Castle 357, 453
Winnington, Sir Thomas 78
witches 165, 217, 326, 336
Wolaston, William 335
Wolfe, General James 20, 164, 184, 452
Wolfenbuttel 123
Wolfenbuttel, Duke of 131, 135
Wollstonecraft, Mary 354, 452
Wood, Andrew 258
Wood, John (the Elder) 335, 337, 452
Wood, John (the Younger) 343, 452
Wood Rogers, Captain 166
Wood, Thomas 240
Wood, William 155, 156
Wooler, T.J. 212
woollen industry 157, 308
Woolston, Thomas 335
Wordsworth, William 356, 358, 453
Wotton 326
Wren, Christopher 327, 453
Wright, Joseph (Wright of Derby) 347, 351, 453
Wright, Sir Nathan 67
Wright, Thomas 453
Wright, Thwaites 304
Württemburg 149, 150, 151, 152
Württemburg, Duke of 142
Wyatt, James 349, 353, 355, 357, 359, 454
Wycombe, Lord 55, 75
Wyndham, Sir William 17, 45, 71, 77, 454
Wynne, John 261
Wyvill, Christopher 23, 454, 462

Yale College 166
Yamassees 166, 167
Yearsley, Ann 454
Yelverton, Barry 158
Yonge, Philip 238, 241
Yonge, Sir G. 58, 77

Yonge, Sir William 77
York, Frederick Augustus, Duke of 28, 189, 190–1, 454
York, Henry Benedict 36–7, 254, 455
York, James 239
Yorke, C. 56, 61, 67, 78
Yorke, C.P. 61, 72, 74
Yorke, James 239, 261
Yorke, Philip (Lord Hardwicke) 48, 49, 50, 51, 67, 235, 455, 467

Yorkshire Association 112, 115
Yorkshire reformers 23, 112
Yorktown 23, 189, 350
Young, Arthur 346, 352, 354, 455
Young, Edward 455
Young Pretender *see* Stuart, Charles Edward

Zell, Duke of 125
Zoffany, John 347, 455